Renewing Italian Socialism

Renewing Italian Socialism

Nenni to Craxi

Spencer M. Di Scala

New York   Oxford
Oxford University Press
1988

Oxford University Press

Oxford   New York   Toronto
Delhi   Bombay   Calcutta   Madras   Karachi
Petaling Jaya   Singapore   Hong Kong   Tokyo
Nairobi   Dar es Salaam   Cape Town
Melbourne   Auckland

and associated companies in
Berlin   Ibadan

Published by Oxford University Press, Inc.,
200 Madison Avenue, New York, New York 10016

Oxford is a registered trademark of Oxford University Press

Library of Congress Cataloging-in-Publication Data
Di Scala, Spencer.
Renewing Italian socialism.
Bibliography: p.   Includes index.
1. Partito socialista italiano—History.
2. Socialism—Italy—History. I. Title.
JN5657.S6D534 1988   324.245′074   87-31545
ISBN 0-19-505235-8

1 3 5 7 9 8 6 4 2
Printed in the United States of America
on acid-free paper

To Laura, with love

Foreword

Among the many intrinsic merits of Spencer Di Scala's book on sixty years of Italian socialism—and of its vicissitudes through dictatorship and defeat, exile and war, resurgence and dramatic political struggles, often bitter and without victories, in the new era of restored precarious peace and delicate democracy—there is one feature that is practically extrinsic in a purely fortuitous way. A brief word about it offers an occasion to suggest the general lines of the historiographical context in which this book appears.

The obvious point is that this volume is neither on Italian fascism nor Italian communism, subjects that have been the predominant favorites of Anglo-American historical writing for the past thirty years and more. A whole generation of scholars, publicists, historians, political scientists, sociologists, students of intellectual history, and journalists, both good and bad, have played a significant part in the bipolar but related hegemony of fascism as movement and practice and communism or Italian neo-Marxism as theory and praxis. Leaving the historiographical situation in Italy aside, it is a fact deserving a vast analysis and evaluation onto itself that this generation has chosen to ignore other important aspects of Italian political history. Regardless of what the academic masters were teaching in the graduate seminars of American and British universities—and a mere glance at selected course catalogues reveals a great variety of major themes (outside of the Middle Ages and the Renaissance), whether circumscribed for single intensive attention or studied within European comparative contexts—their pupils or disciples quickly leaped over even the Risorgimento, the liberal period, and the Giolittian era to swim in the "more exciting" pools of the Italian fascist "consensus" or the Gramscian neo-Marxist chimera of "hegemony."

I can attest that from his graduate student days to his present scholarly mastery Di Scala has never been tempted by the siren calls of popular topical history. He has tested and worked with other subjects on other grounds as well. As the attentive reader of this book will not fail to note, Di Scala's interviews with a number of major and minor protagonists of his "story" testify to his possession of the talents of a fine political journalist. But I feel, beyond any doubt, he will remain faithful to his calling as a genuine historian.

In this work, the author has also avoided another apparent alternative to ideological history: the vogue of typological approaches prevalent, but not exclusively so, in Anglo-American intellectual milieus. In our day, the impact of a very popular book on the "character" of "the Italians" has been strong and nearly inescapable. The adoption as a hermeneutic method, mode, and model for the collective characteriological interpretation of Italians in history has played havoc with the very nature and spirit of historical thought and procedure. According to this type of approach, an "Italian character" was supposedly stamped on generation after generation of men and women born on a Mediterranean peninsula and some surrounding islands. These "Italians" have apparently had no choice but to act out their set roles in life as personages in successive spectacles of a historical *commedia dell'arte* condemned to reinvent and repeat the same vicissitudes, be they as "morality plays," "social drama," or other imaginative theatrical pieces. For the classic Spanish dramatist, "life is a dream"; for the modern typologists, Italian historic life is a series of moving but unchanging tableaux and "spectacles." Just as there are eternally unique brands of "Italian" pasta, so too are there perenially distinctive styles of Italian divorce, of Italian nongovernments, and Italian politics. The "stylized" view of historic life is obviously almost as flawed as a metaphysical, transcendent, or fatalistic view of human eschatology. One cannot but rejoice that Di Scala has not in the least fallen prey to the temptation of typological or analogous interpretations of modern Italian socialism.

There are very few subjects as selectively appealing, yet unquestionably challenging and worthy of periodic self-renovating historical inquiry, as modern socialism. There are many reasons for this. First of all, semantic degeneration has annihilated every last trace of substantive and historical meaning from the concept and reality of "socialism." Such has tended to be the fate suffered by "liberalism" and "conservativism," "fascism" and "communism," "imperialism" and "nationalism." I found it very revealing that in Italy during the late 1970s, while a famous philosopher, Norberto Bobbio, was asking in the title of his provocative essay "Quale Socialismo?" ("which," or was it "what," social-ism?), an answer was forthcoming, as if preventively, in the socialist program manifesto entitled *L'alternativa dei socialisti: Il progetto di programma del PSI presentato da Bettino Craxi 1978*. The group of specially selected socialist intellectuals, ideologues, and publicists who under the guidance of Bettino Craxi shaped the "alternative" contained in *Il progetto* aimed not only to redefine the concept of socialism but to give it a powerful, novel meaning and through their "new" socialist vision and program to reinvigorate and therefore renovate the whole of Italian social consciousness and life.

This book deals with the long, hard journey of Italian socialism from the terror of its Babylonian captivity under fascism in the mid-1920s and 1930s to the Second World War, the hard-won Liberation, and the struggles of the post-war period. The ascent to the highest offices of the Italian republic by an "old" socialist, Sandro Pertini, who in July 1978 became president of the republic, and later by a "new" socialist, Bettino Craxi, who became president of the Council of Ministers in the first socialist government in Italian history in August 1983—a fascinating meeting of the best idealism of the "old" socialism and the most promising realism of the "new" socialism—is illuminatingly reconstructed in Mr. Di Scala's work.

The steps along the Italian socialist road were fraught with grave uncertainties in both the national and international contexts. Spencer Di Scala details, sometimes with gener-ous profusion, the complicated aspects, motivations, and personalities in the chronicle of Italian political involvements. He dispenses with elaborate comment on the particulars of a number of situations that he has brought under his almost microscopic scrutiny. Nev-ertheless, a further word may be useful concerning some of the more important motivating forces apparently behind socialist political thought and action before and after the ascent to official power by leaders of the PSI.

The more than thirty years from the end of the war to 1978 receive generous attention in Di Scala's reconstruction. In particular he emphasizes the general elections of April 1948, the coming of the Cold War, the impact of the anti-Russian-Soviet revolts in

Hungary and Czechoslovakia, the slow evolution of internal Italian politics toward the formation of a center-left government, the outbreak of the student youth revolts in the universities and outside, the wave of corruptions and scandals in high-placed quarters of official institutions and corporations, and the frightening series of terrorist actions culminating in the assassination of Aldo Moro. These and other similar vicissitudes constitute the inescapable elements demanding a reappraisal of the role of socialism and the PSI in the immediate and long-range future of Italy. The last three chapters of the book analyze clearly and with exceptional acumen the general thrust as well as the details of the socialist reassessment. As I have already suggested, *Il progetto* is the most important of the documents resulting from this self-examination of the social consciousness and the socialist conscience in Italy. Its thematic sweep and programmatic particulars (ranging from statements of principles to detailed views on the relationship between substantive socialist initiatives in Italian national problems) testify to its self-awareness that not only had a moment of truth arrived for it in Italy but also that a truly nonrecurrent, unique moment of necessity and opportunity was at hand.

When in the preface to *Il progetto* Bettino Craxi writes, "We must focus our attention upon the fundamental problem of our time which has been and remains that of [realizing] justice in freedom and peace," we cannot but agree that he is right. In the body of *Il progetto,* under the rubric of "Democracy and Socialism," occurs the statement: "Socialism is not the suppression of the social dialectic based on diversity and conflict— it is rather the foundation of a higher level of social dialectic; it is not the end of history but rather the foundation of a new history." Again, we must assent, but further comment may be helpful here.

The reference to a possible dawn of a new, "higher" level in the unfolding of the social dialectic is a genuinely fascinating idea. But it is neither completely new nor indigenous to democratic socialism as a vision of the ultimate historic palingenesis. Perhaps the true novelty lies in the fact that it was deemed necessary to assert and insert this idea as part of the fundamental philosophic rationale of the "Socialist Alternative." The chiliastic projection in the phrase *nuova storia* is indeed very old, as old as the poetic and philosophic visions of historic fulfillment and social perfection.

In light of the rich, long, and contradictory history of utopian thought and millenarian visions, the phrase "new history" may seem merely to compound the complexities of the concept of renewal and innovation. And yet, one hopes that the dawn of the third millennium of the Christian era may usher in not a nightmarish doomsday but an epoch of genuine redemptive renewal.

With his expansive and solid work on modern Italian socialism, Spencer Di Scala joins the select ranks of American (and Italian) social and political historians who have made an extraordinarily attractive and original contribution to contemporary historical writing. As is evident, he has chosen a particular way, his own, to tell the complicated "story" of two generations of Italian socialism. It is not essentially a pleasant or simple "story." But it is, I believe, as close to the reality of what occurred in Italian socialism as a contemporary historian can give us. Di Scala depicts the would-be renovators of Italian socialism in their moments of maximum activity and influence, and we have the almost cinematic succession of "old," "intermediate," and "new" spokesmen and leaders of the party. But among these, the portrait of Bettino Craxi in Chapter 13 is undoubtedly the most striking and suggestive. It cannot be denied that Craxi is himself truly for good or ill, a *homo novus,* the quasi-Machiavellian prince who seems to possess the quintessential *virtù* of the born leader of a vigorous "new" group of socialist intellectuals, empiricists, and activists. He and they have in common not only a special kind of political energy and sense of mission but also a view of politics and socialism that is both unique and innovative. Perhaps neither the "old" masters of the Italian socialist movement like Filippo Turati (whom Di Scala has studied exceedingly well) nor Pietro Nenni, who in a way "sponsored" Craxi, nor even Sandro Pertini, whose humanism was both socialist and universal, nor the "intermediate" leaders of the PSI (Morandi, Lombardi, Lelio Basso, and others) would easily recognize their image of socialism in the "new" socialism reflected in *Il progetto*. As he clearly demonstrated during his relatively long tenure as prime minister, Bettino Craxi aimed to realize some of the most important points of his programmatic statements. In due time he dedicated much of his energy to fulfilling his visions of a systematic reform of the administration of justice in Italy and to bringing about an economic austerity program.

I believe that Spencer Di Scala's book will serve as a superb work of history as well as a valuable guide, and perhaps model, for the protagonists of the Italian political struggle. It is, I feel, a truly admirable exemplar of a new Italian historiographical alternative.

Ardmore, Pa.   A. William Salomone
November 1987

Acknowledgments

In writing this book, I have had the good fortune to deal with many friends, old and new, in the United States and Italy, who have extended their aid willingly and generously. I would like to thank, above all, those persons who allowed themselves to be interviewed and whose opinions form such an important part of this work. Among these, I would especially like to thank President Sandro Pertini, the magnificent and warm human being and socialist hero who opened the doors of the Quirinale and who shared his long memories with me so generously. I also thank the head of the president's press service, Minister Michelangelo Jacobucci, for his efficiency and enthusiasm in facilitating my access to President Pertini.

One of the more pleasant aspects of writing this book was contact with new persons who not only aided in the research but did so in such a gracious manner that they became friends. In this category, I would like to thank two superb scholars, Luciano Pellicani and Antonio Landolfi.

In 1984 a Fulbright Senior Research Fellowship enabled me to conduct many of the conversations reported in the book and to complete my research in Italian archives. Exchange Commission head Cipriana Scelba and Luigi Filadoro shared their ideas with me, smoothed my access to a number of the persons I interviewed, and made my stay in Italy particularly pleasant.

In researching the book, I received the cooperation of several libraries, but I wish to single out the CGIL library in Rome and the John F. Kennedy Library in Boston for special thanks. At the latter institution, I wish to express my appreciation particularly to Sheldon Stern and William Johnson. I also thank Robert D'Attilio, Emilio Gentile, and Giovanni Sabbatucci for making important materials available to me. I also wish to thank the staff of Oxford University Press, especially Marion Osmun, for the professional manner in which they produced this book.

Besides the help already acknowledged, I received encouragement of a wider kind for which I have a special gratitude.

Guy Halverson, Richard Cattani, and the staff of the opinion page of *The Christian Science Monitor* immediately recognized the important recent developments occurring in Italy and allowed me to express my opinions on them in numerous articles, giving them wide currency.

One late autumn night in 1982, I told A. William Salomone about my ideas for this book. He may recall the stimulating conversation about the themes and influence of Italian socialism which followed. Anyone who has known him understands how he is a continual source of sophisticated and subtle ideas and gives his aid generously, tirelessly, and willingly. Professor Salomone is the dean of Italian historians in the United States, and probably no one has had as much influence on the recent historiography of Italy in this country. Legions of scholars in the United States and Italy owe him a special intellectual debt, as do I.

Finally, the most pleasant debt I acknowledge is to my wife, Laura Clerici Di Scala, to whom I dedicate this book. She had to cope not only with the rigorous demands of a new baby but also with her husband's obsession with a book on Italian socialism. Nonetheless, she created a pleasant environment in which to write, served as my most demanding and best critic, and greatly influenced the book's methodology. I thank her, above all, for her wise counsel and constant support.

Sharon, Mass.   S. M. Di S.
June 1987

Contents

Abbreviations

ACS	Italian State Archives (Rome)
CGIL	Italian General Labor Confederation (Communist-Socialist)
CIA	Central Intelligence Agency
CIS	Internal Socialist Center
CISL	Italian Confederation of Workers' Syndicates (Catholic)
CLN	Committee of National Liberation
CLNAI	Committee of National Liberation for North Italy
COMISCO	Committee of International Socialist Conferences
CONFINDUSTRIA	Italian Industrialists' Confederation
CPSU	Communist Party of the Soviet Union
DC	Christian Democratic Party
DCM	Deputy Chief of Mission
ENEL	Italian State Electrical Agency
ENI	Italian State Hydrocarbon Agency
EUR	State Department Operations Branch
GL	Justice and Liberty Movement
INR	State Department Bureau of Intelligence and Research
IRI	Institute for Industrial Reconstruction
ISS	Institute of Socialist Studies
JFK Library	John F. Kennedy Library (Boston)
MLF	Multilateral Nuclear Force
MSI	Italian Social Movement (Neo-Fascist)
MUP	Movement of Proletarian Unity
NAS	Socialist Factory Nuclei
NATO	North Atlantic Treaty Organization
PCI	Italian Communist Party
PLI	Italian Liberal Party
PRI	Italian Republican Party
PSDI	Italian Social Democratic Party
PSI	Italian Socialist Party
PSIUP	Italian Socialist Party of Proletarian Unity (same as PSI before 1947, left-wing Socialist party after 1964)
PSLI	Italian Socialist Workers' Party (Social Democrats before 1951)
PSU	Unified Socialist Party (1966–69)
PSULI	Unified Socialist Party of the Italian Workers
SDI	Strategic Defense Initiative ("Star Wars")
SIFAR	Armed Forces Intelligence Service
UIL	Italian Union of Labor (Socialist–Social Democratic)

Introduction

In August 1892, delegates taking advantage of state railway discounts celebrating the four hundredth anniversary of Columbus's discovery of the New World gathered in Genoa and founded the Italian Socialist Party. Despite the many divisions that would afflict the new organization in the future, the delegates had established Italy's first modern political party. The PSI became the vehicle by which the Italian masses participated in the nation's politics and greatly contributed to the country's social and economic modernization and development in a social democratic direction. The party rescued Italy's democratic institutions between 1898 and 1900, animated a liberal government in 1901, established a nationwide union in 1906, and acted as a powerful stimulus for reform. Perhaps reflecting the backwardness of Italian society, however, frequent demands for revolutionary tactics and violence also characterized the party's discussions. In 1912, the revolutionaries seized control of the party but probably would have been defeated without the radicalization of Italian politics after World War I.

During that crisis, the Socialists threw over their original program advocating a gradual reformist road to socialism and adopted the bolshevik model of seeking power through violence. Ignoring their old leaders' predictions of a backlash, they preached a revolution which they proved incapable of implementing. As a result, in 1921, the left wing split off and formed the Italian Communist Party. Anxious to establish itself and appealing to the same groups as the PSI, the new organization competed with its parent body by mercilessly criticizing its contradictions. At the same time, reformist predictions of a backlash came true as the PSI lost the support of important segments of Italian society and as alarmed industrialists and large landowners financed a new and ruthless repressive machine guided by former Socialist Benito Mussolini: fascism.

Pounded by Fascists and Communists, half the PSI attempted a reversal of the socialist revolutionary stance, but they were too late. In October 1922, the PSI split in two, leaving the road clear for a Mussolini government.

Between 1922 and 1926, Socialists in both parties valiantly opposed fascism's steady destruction of Italian democracy. In 1923, the Acerbo law established a mechanism by which a plurality could be transformed into a two-thirds majority. In 1924, following massive government interference in national elections, fascist thugs murdered Giacomo Matteotti, PSULI secretary. Mussolini survived the ensuing crisis by installing a totalitarian dictatorship and a one-party state.

Having failed in directing the opposition to fascism as the country's once largest party, the Socialists suffered the greatest damage to their prestige. Dispirited, lacking the Communists' international support, ignored by European Socialists who refused to take seriously fascism's threat to other countries, the Italian Socialists seemed finished as a significant force.

And yet, as partly founder Filippo Turati wrote at the end of a previous dark age, "*Heri dicebamus.*" This book is the story of Italian socialism's revival from its defeat by fascism to its newfound capacity to dominate Italian politics and set the national agenda.

Building upon their tradition in bitter exile, the Socialists reestablished their organizations, reunified, and brought their message of fascist insidiousness to a previously deaf Europe. In 1943, they returned to Italy to discover that their ideals still commanded a vast following in a country suspicious of communist goals.

Looking backward at their 1920s defeat, however, socialist leaders concluded that the working class must be united in order to come to power, and they placed unity with the Communists above every other consideration. This mistaken policy caused the socialist leadership to renounce the PSI's tradition against the rank and file's resistance and to graft Leninism onto their party structure. The result was disaster. The PSI lost much of its following and in the 1950s became an auxiliary organization of the PCI. Once he realized his error, it took Secretary Pietro Nenni more than a decade to pull the Socialists out of the communist embrace, and he could do so only at the cost of a formal split and great division in the party.

Nenni's "opening to the left" alliance with the Catholics in the 1960s, however, not only rescued the Socialists from their subordination to the PCI but also aided the nation at a crucial juncture in its history and set the stage for the country's modernization.

For his efforts, Nenni discovered the fate of unsung prophets. Under communist hammering, Italian political observers judged the center-left a failure. Although this time with greater independence, the PSI swung back toward the Communists. In the meantime, by the 1970s, the Communists were apparently well advanced in their appropriation of the socialist tradition they had so roundly denounced and through it had escaped the dismal fate of communist parties in the West. The socialist rapprochement with the Communists had the usual result: political disaster for the PSI.

In the wake of these developments, the party made a comeback with Bettino Craxi, who fought to bring Italian socialism into the European socialist mainstream. Through a series of brilliant maneuvers, Craxi unabashedly dragged the PSI back to its origins, proudly adopting the dreaded label of reformist. Making use of a widely respected socialist tradition, Craxi also claimed power, despite the small percentage of votes held by the PSI. Confronting more than a decade of double-digit inflation, its economy in shreds, torn by political terrorism unseen elsewhere in the Western world, shaken by unmatched labor agitation, with rumors of rightist coups following one upon the other, the country could hardly conceive of salvation in a bipolar world in which for thirty-five years Catholics had dominated the government and Communists the opposition.

Both comfortable in their respective hegemonies, Christian Democrats and Communists had wasted three decades; the first had let Italy's potential go unrealized, and the second succeeded primarily in frightening the bourgeoisie and the United States.

The early 1980s witnessed the decline of Christian Democrats and Communists and a spectacularly successful record stay in power by the socialist leader. Building on his success as prime minister, Craxi must now fulfill his vow to reverse the anomaly, when compared to other Western democracies, of a small socialist party and a large communist organization. Only success will allow the Socialists to implement their program; failure threatens the party's existence.

But what program? Because of his taste for power and emphasis on pragmatism, Craxi has been criticized for being a blend of subtle pragmatist and Machiavellian politico for whom old socialist ideas and ideals have become instruments of power. Has he abandoned socialism, or is he the instrument through which Italian socialism struggles to adapt its cherished ideals to the modern world?

Persons Interviewed

Giuliano Amato, advisor to Bettino Craxi, later under secretary to the presidency of the Council of Ministers; interviewed 2 February 1983.

Valdo Spini, vice secretary of the Italian Socialist party; interviewed 13 October 1983.

Renato Ravasio, Christian democratic deputy and former secretary of the DC for Bergamo province; interviewed 4 October 1983 and 7 October 1984.

Sandro Pertini, president of the Italian Republic, military commander of the socialist Resistance, and longtime official of the Italian Socialist Party; interviewed 11 October 1983 and 9 October 1984.

Michelangelo Jacobucci, chief of Press Services, presidency of the republic; interviewed 9 October 1984.

Leo Wollemborg, Rome correspondent for the *Washington Post* and confidant of major Italian and American political figures during the 1960s and 1970s; interviewed 6 October 1984.

Charles Stout and *Pat Garland,* political analysts, Rome Embassy of the United States; interviewed 16 October 1984.

Giovanni Pieraccini, collaborator of Pietro Nenni and minister of Budget and Planning during the center-left period; interviewed 14 November 1984.

Enzo Marzo, correspondent for the *Corriere della Sera;* interviewed 12 December 1984.

Giuseppe Sacco, professor at the Free University of Rome, political analyst, and Socialist party observer; interviewed 30 October and 17 December 1984.

Guglielmo Negri, vice secretary general of the Chamber of Deputies and Republican party official; interviewed 26 October 1984.

Antonio Landolfi, Socialist party senator, scholar, and former political advisor to Giacomo Mancini; interviewed 18 December 1984 and 8 January 1985.

Giuseppe Tamburrano, Socialist historian and political counselor to Pietro Nenni; interviewed 18 December 1984.

Paolo Flores d'Arcais, former head of Cultural Affairs for *Mondoperaio;* interviewed 20 December 1984.

Giorgio Ruffolo, chairman of the Finance Committee, Chamber of Deputies, and Socialist party economic expert; interviewed 22 December 1984.

Antonio Giolitti, former minister for the Budget and Planning, ally of Riccardo Lombardi; interviewed 27 December 1984.

Luciano Pellicani, editor of *Mondoperaio* (Socialist party ideological review) and advisor to Bettino Craxi; interviewed 8 January 1985.

Mauro Ferri, collaborator of Pietro Nenni, secretary of the Unified Socialist Party, confidant of Giuseppe Saragat, and post-1969 leader of the Social Democratic Party; interviewed 9 January 1985.

John Di Sciullo, former analyst for Southern European Affairs, Bureau of Intelligence and Research, U.S. Department of State; interviewed 15 May 1985.

James Miller, Historical Office, U.S. Department of State; interviewed 16 May 1985.

Harvey Fergusson, political analyst, Bureau of Intelligence and Research, West European Affairs, U.S. Department of State; interviewed 17 May 1985.

John Volpe, former U.S. ambassador to Italy; interviewed 11 June 1985.

Arthur M. Schlesinger, Jr., presidential advisor to John F. Kennedy; interviewed 24 June 1985.

Robert Komer, former analyst for European Affairs, Central Intelligence Agency, and member of National Security Council staff, currently analyst for the RAND Corporation, telephone interview 7 October 1985.

Renewing Italian Socialism

CHAPTER 1

Exile

On 24 November 1926, Filippo Turati, patriarch of Italian socialism, slipped out of his apartment above Milan's Galleria and eluded the policemen who had been keeping him under surveillance. Despite Mussolini's desperate mobilization of police and carabinieri, Turati arrived in Savona, a small city near Genoa, on 8 December. There a young socialist militant and fugitive from fascist "justice," Sandro Pertini, joined him, assigned by the underground to accompany the veteran political leader into exile.

After three sleepless nights during which they reminisced about the past, the pair boarded a motorboat at Vado Ligure with a group of men which included legendary antifascists Ferruccio Parri and Carlo Rosselli. The angry sea buffeted the boat, and the crossing became dramatic. Pertini recalled, "We were lying down under the prow. Turati was heavy while I was thin. I remember how powerful gusts of wind hit us and Turati rolled over onto me; I anxiously awaited another gust to liberate me from his weight."

At Calvi, Corsica, French officials gave their illustrious guest a cordial reception, and Turati informed friends in the French government that he had arrived in exile. The next day, 13 December, Turati led Pertini to the top of a tower where the old man could better view the departing motorboat carrying his comrades back to Italy. He became wistful and said to Pertini, "You are young and will return to a free Italy. I am old; I will return, but in a hearse."[1]

In 1947, Turati's friends brought back his ashes and solemnly reinterred them in Milan's Cimitero Monumentale. Pertini had become a military leader of the Resistance, participating prominently in Italy's political life, and in 1978 he became president of the Italian republic.

Continuing Struggle: The Concentrazione Antifascista

Beaten and dispirited by the fascist triumph in Italy but part of a stirring "new Risorgimento,"[2] the socialist exiles slowly organized themselves in France and elsewhere. Overcoming the difficulties of exile, the aging socialist leaders who had respected international reputations gave direction to the mushrooming antifascist groups. Because of its history and its attraction for Italian political exiles who had frequently sought refuge there from the reactionary waves that periodically overwhelmed their country, and because of the large number of Italians who had emigrated there for economic reasons, France became the center of antifascism. About a million Italians residing in France provided the material for reconstitution of Italian parties broken by the fascist dictatorship. The two socialist parties, the Communist party, the General Confederation of Labor, the Italian

League for the Defense of Human Rights, and, later, Giustizia e Libertà implanted their nerve centers, established their press organs, coordinated their international activities, and diffused their ideas from the French capital.

The divisions that characterized the Italian left carried over into exile, but recognition that its divisiveness had damaged its ability to block fascism took the edge off traditional debates, except for the Communists. The polemics continued, but with the realization that only by achieving some measure of unity could the antifascists challenge Mussolini.

In 1927, this understanding resulted in the "Concentrazione Antifascista," which coordinated the ideological and political action of member groups. The Concentrazione integrated all major Italian exile organizations except the Communists, who denounced the "social Fascists," as they labled their former socialist comrades.[3]

Composed of disparate individuals with conflicting ideas about combating fascism, lacking sufficient physical means, badly prepared for an underground struggle, the Concentrazione nevertheless made significant contributions to the Italian antifascist fight. The prestigious prewar Socialists Filippo Turati and Claudio Treves[4] headed the Concentrazione; the active Pietro Nenni served as secretary. Through their efforts, the Italian antifascist movement intensified its international character and alerted the world to the dangerous supranational nature of Italian fascism, still considered a local quirk by non-Italians.

The generous, taciturn, red-haired Turinese Socialist and former parliamentary leader Claudio Treves edited the Concentrazione's weekly newspaper, La Libertà. A skilled newspaperman and former Avanti! editor, Treves meticulously documented fascism's crimes and advocated democracy, liberalism, and European solidarity to fight international fascism. La Libertà denounced the Savoy monarchy, condemned Victor Emmanuel III for his role in fascism's establishment, and speculated on the working-class role in the future restoration of Italian freedom and the coming of socialism. According to a scholar of the antifascist press, La Libertà "established a precedent for interparty cooperation against fascism that was to prove valuable to the organizers of the underground press during the Resistance of the years 1943–1945."[5]

The Concentrazione's spiritual head was Italian Socialist Party founder Filippo Turati. He conducted a battle against fascism which animated the younger generation, even though he had witnessed the seeming collapse of his life's work, the murder of his "spiritual son," Giacomo Matteotti, and the loss of his lifelong companion, Anna Kuliscioff.[6]

Turati's dramatic flight from fascist Italy had electrified Europe, challenged Mussolini, and galvanized the antifascists.[7] Having abandoned a cheerful apartment in Piazza del Duomo in Milan for a small, cold hotel room in Paris, the sixty-nine-year-old leader suffered depression until he took a room with Bruno Buozzi—the exiled leader of the General Confederation of Labor—and Buozzi's family. In this apartment, Turati reestablished his old habits. In the morning, he woke early; made himself a potent cup of espresso; methodically washed and dried the cup, saucer, and pot; and settled to work at his cluttered desk. There he wrote numerous articles for European and American dissemination and kept up a vast correspondence. Immediately after writing his letters, he went out to mail them, taking time to play with children in a park on his way to the mailbox. In the evening, once more seated at his desk, he received his friends, as he had done for so many years in Milan, and engaged in animated conversation with them.[8]

An Early Socialist Analysis of Fascism

Whereas in the past Turati's most important role had been organizational, he now analyzed the reasons for fascism's success. Turati's crucial reflection on the past provided the disoriented Socialists with their first ideological bearings in exile and refuted the mistaken and humiliating European leftist interpretation of fascism as a uniquely Italian phenomenon. A harsh critic of Turati's past leadership, Carlo Rosselli, admiringly admitted that Turati "confronted the problem of interpreting fascism . . . with a breadth of vision and a modern outlook which were astounding in a man as old as he and which make us lament the fact that Turati did not dedicate more time to the study of theoretical problems."[9]

Turati dismissed the current European opinion that Italy's backwardness and alleged political immaturity accounted for fascism, to which "advanced" nations were immune. He readily admitted that the Italians had committed errors, but only because they faced the new phenomenon first. "Are you certain, hypercritical sirs," he addressed the delegates to the 3rd Congress of the Socialist Workers' International (Brussels, 7 August 1928), "that you have never made mistakes and that you will not make any in the future?" By a cold and compelling logic, Turati focused discussion on the fascist problem, considered by the delegates a boring Italian fixation.[10]

By his spirited intervention at this and other international meetings; a lively newsletter published in French, English, and German; and his organization of traveling exhibits documenting fascist atrocities, Turati admonished other nations to learn from the Italian experience in time to save themselves. This lonely battle and a stimulating analysis of fascism earned Turati the title of "first protagonist of the European struggle against fascism"[11]

Far from being limited to Italy, Turati argued in 1928, fascism lurked beneath the capitalist surface in all countries and would emerge under certain circumstances. First, Turati believed, a great war must occur. Such conflicts suspend normal democratic processes and encourage dictatorships, murder, torture, contempt for human life, and other ordinarily condemned "heroic" gestures. Moreover, they coalesce agitated individuals incapable of readapting to normal society and wishing continuation of the conflict. Because the great industrialists and large landowners—the "plutocracy"—are unwilling to pay for wars, they link up with the violent groups produced by great conflagrations and transform the original conflict into a civil war in order to shift the enormous economic burden onto the workers. In short, the plutocracy denies its own heritage, destroys its own institutions, even negates its own economic interests by reestablishing an "economic and political middle age" and a facsimile of unproductive slave labor. Seeking to create a servant, the bourgeoisie produces a monster which turns into its master: fascism.

Thus, according to Turati, fascism presented an "international and worldwide danger." Italy taught Europe; in response, Europe must drop its "noninterventionist" attitude and impose an immediate economic and moral boycott of fascism. Fascism required conflict to divert the attention of its own oppressed people, and Turati predicted that Mussolini would provoke a war if democratic nations did not isolate him immediately. In a flash of insight, Turati defined fascism as permanent war, a society "no longer of classes but of races of masters and slaves."

Because fascism had proven that violence could still play a preeminent role in history, Turati warned that Europe's "pacifist illusion" must end. On the other hand, the working class must refrain from empty threats, because the intemperate language of socialist maximalists and Bolsheviks drove large segments of the population to support reactionaries. The proletariat must enter alliances with non-Marxists to fight Mussolini, and the Socialist International must coordinate the struggle against fascism.[12]

Fully elaborated by 1928, Turati's early analysis of fascism has endured in social democratic interpretations, which enriched but never supplanted his views.[13]

Propaganda or Direct Action?

Concentrazione Antifascista ideology bolstered exile morale, but the organization itself foundered on the question of practical action. Within the Concentrazione, dominated by older reformists who had had their last serious brush with the law at the turn of the century, disputes raged over the issue of direct action against fascism within Italy. The elder statesmen agreed with Turati that the regime would collapse under the moral condemnation of democratic nations and its own contradictions. This attitude bred resentment among young antifascists, especially those who remained in Italy.[14]

Socialist direct action often proved dramatic but ill fated. Fernando De Rosa and Sandro Pertini slipped into Italy to link up with surviving clandestine socialist groups, but the police nabbed Pertini and chased out De Rosa.[15] Other antifascists dropped leaflets and plotted Il Duce's assassination. In Brussels, a De Rosa assassination attempt against Crown Prince Humbert drew attention to the monarchy's complicity with fascism.[16]

Clamorous action of this kind frequently bore the mark of Giustizia e Libertà (GL), founded by Gaetano Salvemini's former student Carlo Rosselli. Although inspired by socialist principles and endorsing a "liberalsocialist" revision of socialist ideology, GL advocated spectacular deeds to demonstrate fascism's fragility and concentrated on organizing a conspiratorial network in Italy.

Giellisti and Socialists maintained an uneasy alliance. The Socialists had reservations about direct action and resented blanket condemnation of their past political policies by GL ideologues. Rosselli, for example, conceived of GL as radical, revolutionary, and intransigent and pinned fascism's success on the Socialist party's supposed lack of aggressiveness, past and present. Furthermore, Rosselli aimed to usurp the party's role. Conversely, for the historic socialist leaders, GL bore the irrationalist taint of the new century. As the polemics heated up, Claudio Treves suggested that GL smelled of fascism. These kinds of charges exacerbated the divisions between the two groups and produced a rancorous dispute which dissolved the Concentrazione.[17]

The debate over propaganda or direct action, the deaths of Turati in 1932 and Treves in 1933, and the changing international situation in the 1930s ended the Concentrazione in 1934. This remarkable organization informed Europe of fascism's true nature, served as the relatively united voice of the Italian exiles, prevented the automatic identification of Italians and fascism, laid the basis for socialist reunification, and "added dignity to our exile."[18]

The PSULI and the PSI

During its existence, the Concentrazione Antifascista linked the two major socialist exile parties, the reformist PSULI and the maximalist PSI.

Because the most prestigious socialist leaders—Turati, Treves, Modigliani—headed the PSULI, this organization had greater visibility than the maximalist party. Turati and Treves ran the Concentrazione, and Modigliani organized party sections in the major Italian population centers in France and founded *Rinascita Socialista*. the PSULI newspaper. The PSULI had a smaller membership than the PSI but greater influence and financial resources, thanks to its leaders' reputations and the Socialist Workers' International's subsidies.

The PSI also reconstituted itself on the prefascist model, electing a directorate and establishing French, Swiss, Belgian, English, Austrian, U.S., and Argentinian affiliates. The PSI's membership has been estimated at twenty-five hundred to three thousand, including the one hundred fifty militants who ran the party. The combative party newspaper *Avanti!* reappeared as a weekly with a circulation of five thousand. In exile, the PSI continued to be faction-ridden, with one faction advocating fusion with the Communists, another wanting to join with the reformists, and a third desiring autonomy.

The PSI faced a perpetual financial crisis. Because it criticized both the Communist Third International and the reformist Socialist Workers' International, it received subsidies from neither and survived on dues and voluntary contributions, barely enough to publish the newspaper. Its membership in the International Bureau of Revolutionary Socialist Parties brought it no financial aid.[19]

United in their common misfortune, the two Socialist parties slowly recognized reunification as the essential precondition for fighting fascism efficiently. In the PSULI, Turati had long championed reunification, and the PSI's Pietro Nenni worked with him.

The Emergence of Pietro Nenni

The son of a peasant family of the Romagna, Pietro Nenni suffered the death of his father at an early age. Put in an orphanage by his family's employers, Nenni voraciously devoured every book he could find. After attending technical school, Nenni took his first job at a ceramic factory in Faenza, making direct contact with the working class and its milieu. In 1908, he joined the Republican party, becoming secretary of a day laborers' league and participating in the social and economic struggles which agitated the Romagnol countryside. Because of his active role in a strike, in May 1908 Nenni tasted prison for the first time. The experience made him a confirmed revolutionary, hostile to the prevalent socialist reformism. Nenni linked up with Benito Mussolini, then an active socialist agitator, and published articles for Mussolini's extremist *Lotta di Classe*.

Nenni was attracted by Mussolini's decisive character, political savvy, anti-reformism, and predilection for Georges Sorel, and the friendship endured until Mussolini became Il Duce. Although their political discussions frequently ended in fistfights, Nenni and Mussolini demonstrated together against the establishment. In 1911, the police arrested both men for actively resisting the Libyan war and sentenced them to jail terms, which they served in the same cell. During the men's imprisonment, Rachele Mussolini befriended the pregnant Carmen Nenni, often bringing a bottle of Marsala to keep up her friend's spirits.

Untamed by prison, Nenni rejected Giolitti's liberal system, participated in the "Red Week" riots of June 1914, and advocated Italian intervention in World War I. Agreeing with Mussolini on the revolutionary potential of the Great War, Nenni volunteered for active duty at the front with his mercurial friend.[20]

At war's end, Nenni remained close to Mussolini, writing for the *Popolo d'Italia*. In 1919, when Mussolini's politics changed, the relationship cooled. At a meeting in Cannes, described by Nenni in touching terms in his *Sei anni di guerra civile*, the two parted company. Nenni denounced Mussolini's politics but retained a doleful affection for an old friend who had gone wrong.

By this time, Nenni had left the republican camp, having converted to maximalist socialism. Nenni distinguished himself as the combative de facto editor of *Avanti!*. Nenni's continual condemnation of fascist atrocities provoked an assault on *Avanti!* offices while Nenni, revolver in hand, mounted a vain defense. When the Fascists devastated his home and shot full of holes a picture of his dead mother, Nenni left the country.

In France, the former editor worked as a proofreader, and his wife was employed as a tailor. The family lived in two rooms where, during rainstorms, they held an umbrella over the food as it cooked. Remaining active in the exile movement, Nenni served as political secretary of the Concentrazione Antifascista and dedicated himself to socialist reunification. Nenni would be arrested during Vichy, and one of his daughters would die in a nazi concentration camp.[21]

Factional Strife in the PSI

Reunification could not occur without significant changes in the PSI, dominated by Angelica Balabanoff, Mussolini's maximalist ally of 1912. Her followers claimed direct descent from the last Italian Directorate, controlled PSI executive organs, and campaigned against fusion with the PSULI. Balabanoff argued that the dissolved Italian Directorate had ordered the exile Directorate to maintain the party's political integrity. Any merger decision could be authorized only by a national congress held in Italy.[22]

This logic truncated debate. By unimaginatively stifling discussion when the young socialist generation needed to make its own decisive contribution, the Directorate embalmed the party. Moreover, by inflexibly implementing its regressive policy, the Directorate reduced itself to an ineffective and petulant splinter.

At a convention in Marseilles in January 1928, the Directorate tried but proved unable to limit debate to technical issues. Two clear-cut positions emerged, one advocating maintenance of maximalist positions and the other favoring unification with the PSULI.

Nenni represented this latter movement, remaining true to his preexile principles. In 1925, in fact, he had opposed "fusing" with the Communists, advocating instead a merger with Turati's party.[23]

In 1928, Nenni urgently advocated socialist ideological renovation and exhaustive discussion of socialist plans to combat fascism. He labeled absurd the Directorate's contention that the exiles could not consider substantive matters without the participation of Socialists in Italy.

With regard to the fascist question, Nenni focused on the socialist view of liberty. Contrary to maximalist contentions, Nenni boldly declared liberty not a class issue. Approximating the classical reformist interpretation, Nenni argued that liberty is to socialism as air is to life—one could not exist without the other. Socialists, therefore, must be present on all fronts where liberty struggled for survival. To avoid equivocation, Nenni boldly asserted that freedom manifested itself in Europe's democratic liberal institutions, including the conservative English and French political systems, which no maximalist ideological gymnastics could equate to fascism. Courageously courting his comrades' displeasure, Nenni praised the maligned Aventine secession—the defeat of which had consolidated Mussolini's government—interpreting it as a heroic struggle for liberty sabotaged by maximalists and Communists.

Complementing the fight for liberty, Nenni called for PSI revision of its strategy for achieving socialism. Given the obsolescence of both maximalist intransigence and parliamentary reformism, debilitating debate about past errors should cease, and the Socialists should recognize the ideological reflowering occurring in the new socialist generation. Tempered by exile, armed struggle, and reality, this new generation replaced old ideas with a pragmatic, bold socialism "based on action, not definitions." These aggressive young Socialists demanded a realistic antifascist campaign, rebuilding the organizational network inside Italy, reestablishing contact with the Italian masses, and creating an Italian milieu in which to wage a decisive struggle for socialism.

Nenni left no doubts: the PSI repudiated its Directorate and demanded action inspired by these "new tasks" of socialism.[24] Unfortunately, Nenni wrote, "a small group of maximalists" hindered reunification even after most Socialists considered divisions in the PSI "futile or grotesque."[25]

The January 1928 Marseilles PSI convention deceptively appeared more notable for its color than for its decisions. Claudio Treves carried fraternal reformist greetings, but the secretary noted that he was really a PSULI "Trojan horse." The delegates treated the Italian Temperance League leader to a drink, while the "anglicized" exile delegation from England watched, "impassive and immoble." On the other hand, the communist sympathizers conspired in the dead of night.

But that convention clearly signaled disfavor with the Directorate. The delegates authorized discussion of reunification and delicately reshuffled the Directorate as best they could.

Under Balabanoff's forceful urging, however, the Directorate "interpreted" the convention's motion by rejecting fusion with any party and by ridiculously requesting both the PSULI and the PCI to dissolve themselves and join the PSI. As a consequence, criticism of the Directorate escalated beyond the capacity of the executive body to blunt it. Nenni demanded a congress to resolve the unification issue.

On 16 March 1930, the congress Nenni had requested met at Grenoble, and the two currents immediately split.[26] The PSI majority followed Nenni; the maximalists lingered for another decade before disappearing.[27] Even taking Nenni to court over his "usurpation" of the glorious title of *Avanti!* failed to revive maximalist fortunes.[28]

As editor of the Socialist party newspaper, Pietro Nenni acquitted himself brilliantly and sponsored PSULI unification on the basis of a pragmatic program. The Socialist International, Turati, Rosselli, and the young theoretician Giuseppe Saragat ably supported Nenni's efforts. Nenni wooed PSI members who had initially remained loyal to Balabanoff by emphasizing socialist problems. By April 1930, a reunification congress with the PSULI had already been scheduled. "At Grenoble you separated because you already were divided," Turati wrote to Nenni. "At Paris we will reunite because we are already one."[29]

Evolution of the PSULI

The PSULI evolved in an analagous manner, greatly facilitating reunification. As PSULI leaders realized that internal fascist contradictions would not end Mussolini's rule, they modified their thinking and eyed fusion along Nenni's lines. The PSULI imposed two conditions which Nenni readily accepted: political differentiation from the Communists and membership of the newly merged organization in the Socialist International. In the meantime, Giuseppe Saragat reworked reformist ideology, achieving virtual identification with Nenni.

Saragat criticized traditional reformism, which, he contended, had overemphasized the emergence of socialism from within prefascist bourgeois liberal democratic regimes. Simplistic application of this principle, Saragat believed, had led reformists to accept subordinate positions, to limit the scope of their proposed reforms, and to impose a totally electoral role on the party. For Saragat, Socialists must aim at the "revolutionary conquest of democracy." This concept meant political democracy in which concrete conditions existed for the elaboration of a revolutionary class consciousness and for the further development of the class struggle.[30]

Saragat's reformist reelaboration emphasized pragmatic action over abstract ideas and creation of an advanced democratic society in which the struggle for socialism could be successfully waged. Saragat thus admitted past mistakes and brought PSULI theory close to Nenni's revisions of maximalist ideology, setting the stage for reunification.

The Unity Congress

On 19 and 20 July 1930, in the Paris meeting hall of the French Socialist party, the 21st Italian Socialist Party Congress took place. It was a joyous occasion which, forty-seven years later, Nenni recalled as the greatest European antifascist demonstration up till that time.[31] The major European socialist leaders attended Italian socialism's rebirth: French Socialists Leon Blum and Paul Fauvre; Emile Vandervelde, Socialist International president; Fritz Adler and Wilhelm Ellembogen from Austria; and representatives from England, the United States, Hungary, and China. Filippo Turati, attending his last congress, served as president. He commented, "I feel the breath of the Sala Sivori" (the PSI's founding congress in 1892).

The congress reunited the two groups which had split in Italy in October 1922. Pietro Nenni and Claudio Treves presented a joint unification document which the delegates uncharacteristically voted without discussion.

Consisting of five major themes, this "Unity Charter" repudiated the party's maximalist heritage but reiterated the Socialist party's class, Marxist, and anticapitalist nature and advocated transformation of existing institutions into "instruments of liberation of the exploited class." In contradistinction to the Communists, the party emphasized the democratic nature of both its goals and its means. The charter endorsed alliances with bourgeois parties and repudiated violence, except if the ruling classes violently suppressed democracy.[32] Treves hailed the Unity Charter as synthesizing democracy, liberty, social justice, and the class struggle.

Treves also renounced international war as a means of defeating Mussolini. Socialists would accomplish their aims from within Italy.[33] Reinforcing Treves, Nenni specified that antifascist revolution would return the exiles to their homeland, not foreign bayonets.[34]

Excluding war as a means of returning to Italy opened the Socialists to the charge of vagueness in elaborating their action program against fascism, reunification's basis.[35] But, spurred by Saragat, their activity in Italy increased.

Giuseppe Saragat and Future Socialist Action

Born in Turin in 1898, trained in economics, and a member of the PSULI's Directorate, Giuseppe Saragat had fled Italy for Austria, finding his way to France after several years. Later imprisoned by the Germans, he risked execution. Italian President Sandro Pertini, military leader of the Socialist Resistance, remarked to me in October 1983 that Saragat impressed him because of his extraordinary dignity. Himself destined to be elected president of the Italian republic during the Center-Left period, in exile the elegant Saragat served as the chief reformist philosopher and in the immediate postwar period as Nenni's chief antagonist.

At the "Unity Congress," Saragat laid the foundation for practical socialist action. According to the stenographic report, Saragat expressed "what was in everyone's soul." Saragat argued that there could be no contradiction between the class struggle and liberty, his constant theme. While recognizing fascism as a class phenomenon and a potential danger in all countries, Saragat believed that in Italy fascism had resulted from a failed liberal bourgeois revolution during the Risorgimento and from socialist neglect of popular political aspirations. The Socialists should now utilize all their resources to champion these demands: democratic revolution and a republic.

Tragically contradictory, Saragat continued, the bourgeoisie favored democracy to increase production and dictatorship to repress socialism, the end result of a free economy; the bourgeoisie thus destroyed itself. Saragat's conclusion: democratic struggle must be revolutionary, even if socialism could only come gradually.

Unraveling this apparent contradiction, Saragat attacked the "gross and anti-Marxist equivocation of those who confused a political revolution with an economic one." In other words, Saragat retained the classic reformist concept of gradualism but combined it with immediate practical action. The Socialists must act decisively to restore the primary condition for socialism in Italy: freedom. Having attained this goal, however, socialism could only develop from a capitalist economy within a free atmosphere and could not be imposed from above. The Socialists must act now to achieve democracy, then nourish and protect it.[36]

The delegates pledged to implement Saragat's ideas by rebuilding a socialist network in Italy and by concentrating the party's efforts there. As usual, serious differences lurked beneath the surface, but as the party resumed its historic title—PSI—it felt great confidence issuing from its renewed movement and determination.

After the assembly, about five hundred comrades retired to a hall on the boulevard du Temple and held a banquet. At the head table sat the historic leaders and representatives of the Concentrazione Antifascista and of the Socialist International. The banquet reflected simpler times. Soon the old leaders would die, the Concentrazione Antifascista would dissolve, fascism would expand, and war would engulf the world. But reunification enabled Italian socialism to survive the chaotic decade of the 1930s.

Beginnings of Socialist Action in Italy

The Unity Congress acknowledged the absolute necessity of direct socialist action in Italy just in time. As discussed above, the Concentrazione Antifascista focused its action outside the country on the theory that little could be done in the homeland. This attitude alienated antifascists in Italy and induced many of them to join the Communists, who, unlike the Socialists, supported an active clandestine network. Future communist leader Giorgio Amendola has described his decision to join the PCI.

Attracted to socialism, Amendola wrote to Claudio Treves, urging socialist elder statemen to establish an underground movement in Italy. Amendola put his case directly to Treves in Paris in April 1928. The old man tearfully embraced him and said:

> My dear George, I respect your feelings very much, and I note with pleasure that in Italy there are young antifascists who wish to go their own way and who wish to continue the struggle. But I must tell you frankly: don't count on us. We are beaten. We are failures. Don't look to us for help. Find your own way.[37]

This attitude made it imperative to initiate socialist action or lose all support in Italy to the Communists.

Immediately following the Unity Congress, in July 1930, the Socialist party temporarily delegated its Italian activities to Giustizia e Libertà. In the meantime, the depression hit Italy, and declining economic conditions favored antifascist activities. The clandestine press grew bolder, strikes occurred in factories and on the land, and the level of discontent increased.

Spurred by these developments, socialist clandestine activity began. In 1931, a socialist nucleus under Rodolfo Morandi broke away from GL and established its own organization.[38] Within two years, Pietro Nenni gave a very encouraging report on socialist activities in Italy to the delegates assembled at the Congress of Marseilles (17–18 April 1933).[39]

Rodolfo Morandi, PSI fulcrum in Italy, illustrates perfectly a new-generation Italian Socialist's odyssey. Born on 30 July 1902, Morandi attended the universities of Padua and Milan, writing his thesis on Kant's and Mazzini's concepts of universal peace. Founder of an antifascist student group at the University of Milan, Morandi became attracted to socialism after the Matteotti murder. Morandi contributed articles to Piero Gobetti's La Rivoluzione Liberale; a brilliant young publisher and a major cultural force of the period, Gobetti died after a fascist beating. Morandi also wrote for the Quarto Stato, an antifascist review published by Rosselli and Nenni. During two research trips to Germany, Morandi studied Marxist dialectics and the writings of Karl Kautsky and Rosa Luxemburg. Morandi also maintained contact with Socialists and Giellisti and in June 1928 conferred with Nenni and Rosselli in Paris. As a result of his discussions with Nenni, Morandi researched his enormously influential Storia della grande industria in Italia in 1929 and 1930. Published in 1931, this work analyzed heavy industry and its role in the coming of fascism and greatly impressed antifascists.

In November 1931, Morandi and the young Milanese Socialists Lelio Basso and Lucio Luzzatto met secretly with Giorgio Amendola, communist delegate exploring a possible alliance with socialist and republican resisters. The meeting culminated in collaboration with the Communists two years before a formal unity pact signed by the exile PSI and PCI and clandestine publication of a newspaper, *Fronte Rosso*. During the next year, Morandi worked for a small Milanese publisher, converting the publishing house into a hotbed of intellectual antifascism. By 1933, Morandi had pieced together a secret socialist network in Milan, with branches in the major northern and some smaller southern cities.

After negotiations with exile PSI leaders, Morandi announced at a secret Milanese meeting the formal constitution of an "Internal Socialist Center," the Centro Interno Socialista (CIS). He invited the participants, including *Giellisti* and Republicans, to join him and the Socialist party in founding an extensive Italian socialist resistance organization.

"Following my advice," Giuseppe Faravelli ("Joseph") wrote to Angelo Tasca, his contact on the PSI Directorate, "they have decided to work in a politically organic and consistent manner, i.e., as a socialist party."[40] Faravelli, Morandi's friend from their student days and a former *Giellista,* directed Italian socialist clandestine activities from Lugano, Switzerland, and linked the CIS and PSI Directorate in Paris. Morandi maintained communications with Lugano, while Faravelli defended clandestine Italian socialist policy by close collaboration with Directorate member Tasca.[41]

International Developments and Their Impact

Coinciding with establishment of a socialist clandestine network, international developments triggered a revolution in socialist-communist relationships.

Adolf Hitler's rise to power in January 1933 fundamentally altered the balance of power among the different European Marxist parties. Hitler destroyed the German Social Democratic party and its collateral organizations, mortally wounding the Socialist International. Austrian Chancellor Dollfuss delivered another blow by finishing off the Austrian social democratic movement in 1934. The Socialist International appealed to other international Marxist organizations for aid, including the Third (Communist) International. Itself reeling from dissolution of the German Communist party and the new nazi threat, the USSR revised its implacable hostility toward the socialist parties. The Comintern responded to the Socialist International's appeal, but very slowly, requesting that local parties negotiate individual alliances.

Initially hindered by mutual suspicions, these talks assumed great urgency as Hitler consolidated his power between April and July 1933. From a diplomatic viewpoint, the Russians anxiously desired a French agreement, and they imposed a moderate policy on the French Communist party to secure it. In addition, pressure from below also spurred agreements between Marxist parties. Between May and June 1934, Stalin and the Third International assigned top priority to alliances. On 27 July, French Communists and Socialists signed a formal pact pledging cooperation.

Nenni and the Unity of Action Pact

Talks between the PSI and PCI paralleled these developments.[42] The major proponent within the PSI was Pietro Nenni. In March 1933, the PCI forwarded a unity-of-action proposal to the PSI, which rejected it because of the Communists' failure to alter their hostile attitude toward the Socialists. Nenni nevertheless persisted in his negotiations.

Convinced that the German social democratic collaboration with the bourgeoisie had been responsible for Hitler's rise, Nenni believed that the Italians should benefit from the German experience and seek unity on the left instead of the right.[43] When GL leader Emilio Lussu charged that the Italian Socialists had made the identical mistake in 1922 as the Germans had made during the Weimar period, the resulting uproar caused the Concentrazione Antifascista's dissolution. The Socialists thus urgently needed to replace the defunct organization.[44]

Nenni assumed the point position in favoring a communist alliance by revising socialist history. The Socialists had grievously erred by concentrating on economic reforms and by neglecting the crucial question of power, Nenni wrote in August 1933. Mistakenly assuming that changes in the economic structure of bourgeois society alone would produce revolution, the Italian Socialists concluded that any revolution before the economic conditions for socialism had been satisfied would be premature.

Nenni demanded revision of this dogma. Wherever the proletariat had a powerful social, political, and labor base and wherever it had soldily organized itself, there the political conditions for power existed. Nenni criticized the past socialist penchant for concentrating on economic organizations while renouncing the political power necessary to protect them.

Italian socialist and German social democratic experience had confirmed the foolishness of this policy, Nenni argued. At a certain point in the evolution of the class struggle, proletariat and bourgeoisie would always reach an impasse. Then either the proletariat would seize the means of production and exchange or the capitalists would break the Socialists, ending their own liberal system and imposing dictatorships. Socialist relegation of the revolution to the distant future ensured that the bourgeoisie would always win the battle.

This state of affairs raised the old question, What is to be done? Nenni carefully distinghished his position from a "Leninist" one, rejecting PSI transformation into an organization of professional revolutionaries. At the same time, he objected to continued reliance on elections as the sole means to power. To avoid repeating past errors, Nenni focused primarily on power, not building fragile socialist economic organizations. He specifically cited the Russian example, where Marxists had achieved power despite the immaturity of Russian society in 1917, had made serious errors, but had created a new economy—not yet socialist but not capitalist either.

Since power had become predominant, Nenni concluded, the first step in achieving it for the Socialists must be a communist pact. This alliance would cement the Socialists' commitment not merely to liberal restoration but also to the *revolutionary* overthrow of fascism and nazism.[45]

Nenni's advocacy of communist collaboration overwhelmed remaining reformist resistance. In July 1934, the PSI's National Council authorized continued talks with the Communists. By month's end, Nenni and communist negotiator Luigi Longo produced a manifesto previewing the agreement's major points.

This first socialist-communist pact reflected existing divisions between the working-class parties, in addition to delineating areas of cooperation. Openly admitting the major ideological and tactical differences between them, the parties discouraged speculation favoring very broad political cooperation and/or fusion. Instead, the document limited the entente to opposing big-power intervention in the Austrian crisis, amnesty for political prisoners, improvement of living standards, restoration of civil liberties, and establishment of free unions in Italy.

In an accompanying declaration, the Socialists noted that the Communists had suspended their libelous "social fascist" campaign not out of conviction but only on a temporary basis. Responding to this distrust, the Socialists themselves had adopted a wait-and-see attitude despite the new pact.[46]

In this early phase, it appears, the PSI did not enthusiastically support the communist connection.[47] Nenni probably could not have carried out his policy without Saragat's strong support. Saragat, whose ideological positions led directly to a condemnation of communism, had been shaken by the German social democratic collapse.[48]

Saragat feared a similar fate for the Italians. As the author of a report meticulously detailing the alarming hemorrhage of PSI members toward the PCI because of the PSI's supposedly excessive collaboration with bourgeois forces, Saragat understood the need to halt communist inroads.[49] In response to this concern, the pact included an important provision banning harmful raids on each other's members by both parties.

In sum, for Saragat, the alliance's political gains outweighed ideological considerations. Saragat reaffirmed his philophical anticommunism, deploring the Communists' failure to revise their ideas or renounce their malicious antisocialist behavior; but he acknowledged a positive development in a pact implicitly committing the PCI to behave democratically. Saragat's support proved so effective that within a short time suggestions for "fusion" with the Communists became commonplace in the PSI.

Even though the unity pact remained a major socialist reference point throughout the 1930s, the Communists treated the PSI as "just another bourgeois party" and campaigned for superiority over it. Criticism, polemics, debates, and protests against the Italian and other communist parties and the USSR litter the socialist press of the period. Socialist objections ranged from communist exploitation of the Brussels antifascist exile congress of 1935 to the absurd communist appeal to the Italian people on the basis of the 1919 fascist program.

Political necessity, however, relegated these disputes to a secondary role, because the Communists could count on the USSR's full support while Western diplomacy pursued a philo-fascist course. The more international conditions worsened, the more essential the unity pact appeared for Nenni and Saragat. Only after the Soviet-Nazi Non-Aggression Pact of 1939 did the Socialists denounce the unity agreement, to reaffirm it when the USSR resumed its antifascist function during World War II.[50]

Italian Unhappiness with the Unity Pact

If the unity pact caused problems among the socialist exiles, it functioned even less well in Italy, the crucible of antifascism. Living under a harsh dictatorship, the Italians anxiously shunned the potential dictatorship which they discerned in Soviet Russia.[51] Already at the end of 1934, Nenni expressed displeasure at the resistance to the unity pact within the socialist underground in Italy.[52]

In fact, in December 1935, Morandi's CIS complained to the Directorate about the Communists' "grave disorganization" and their disregard for or unawareness of the agreement with the Socialists. The Italian organization accused the Communists of bad faith and recommended a "prudent reserve" toward them.[53] In 1936, the CIS vigorously protested an alleged communist slander campaign against it. The Communists charged the CIS with inaction and excessive collaboration with bourgeois groups, which Morandi hotly denied. According to Morandi, communist behavior came close to finishing the pact in Italy.[54]

These events outraged Giuseppe Faravelli and Angelo Tasca, the CIS's major supporters outside Italy. Their correspondence spews resentment against the Nenni-Saragat "entente" which allowed the unity pact to evolve into an overly friendly arrangement with the Communists. Both men suspected the Communists, Faravelli having been a close follower of Turati, and Tasca having been expelled from the PCI because of his "rightist" convictions. As a consequence, these men insulated the Italian network from the Directorate's interference, successfully maintaining a high degree of independence.[55]

In fact, CIS publications frequently incorporated anticommunist themes. The Italian organization, for example, emphasized both the class struggle and internationalism but rejected either's identification with the Soviet Union.[56]

In 1936, the CIS forcefully introduced itself into the discussions on the unity pact's renewal with a harsh critique of the communist draft. According to the CIS, the Communists combined contradictory slogans and ideas, misconceived the role of propaganda, and suggested collaboration with bourgeois groups of a sort harmful to the proletariat—while denouncing the Socialists for allegedly doing the same thing. At the same time, the CIS sent its own draft pact to Paris.[57] This unhappiness with communist behavior subsisted in Italy even after the 7th Congress of the Third International had supposedly made peace with the Socialists. Nenni proclaimed that the pact had "assumed the character of a true and proper political alliance" and lamented its "slow" implementation in Italy.[58]

After the Munich Agreement isolated the USSR in 1938, Angelo Tasca called for an analogous isolation of the Communists in the Western countries by ending the unity pacts. Nenni and Saragat blocked him through a press campaign and at the PSI's National Council meeting in October 1938.[59] The CIS's role in Tasca's ill-fated maneuver remains unclear, but Faravelli reports a meeting with Nenni in which Nenni argued that the "sectarian" mentality of the Faravelli group had forced him and Saragat to accentuate their "pro-Stalin" position.[60]

Thus, for the Italian clandestine organization, the communist alliance worked poorly and provided few benefits, and the resulting unhappiness increased tensions within the exile PSI.

The Italian Socialist Clandestine Network

Thanks to Faravelli's skill in smoothing over inherent differences and in coordinating organizations operating in radically different circumstances, only the communist question strained relations between the underground resisters and the exiles. In their daily activities, the two groups interrelated symbiotically. The exiles could ill afford to lose contact with socialist militants in Italy, and the Italians drew sustenance from the international contact, political experience, and stimulating ideological debates which only outside communication could provide. The CIS continually bombarded its comrades with requests for reading material, while the exiles took heart at the spontaneous growth of a new generation of comrades in Italy, despite the severe censorship denying Italians access to the socialist tradition.[61] Together, the exile and domestic PSI nuclei prepared the spectacular postwar socialist resurgence in Italy.

This interaction took shape in the daily operations and aspirations of the CIS and Giuseppe Faravelli, its Lugano liaison. A short, soft-spoken man whose mild demeanor never betrayed his conspiratorial genius, "Joseph" survived later Nazi capture to play a crucial role in postwar socialist politics, to assume editorship of his beloved Turati's *Critica Sociale,* and to scour Milanese bookshops for works on his favorite subject, American Indians. During the exile and postwar periods, he never allowed any doubts to obscure his clarity or determination in implementing his views on socialist revival.

Driven by desire to resurrect the PSI in Italy, Faravelli focused on creation of new socialist cadres there. So decisively did Faravelli hammer at this point that the PSI officially sanctioned it in July 1934.[62]

Fascism, Faravelli insisted, had achieved its greatest success by "organizing" the proletariat against itself in the capitalist interest. Moral depression and loss of political consciousness had followed the proletariat's defeat. To reverse this situation, the Socialists must restore the workers' sense of political action and launch them against the regime.

This tremendous task would occur neither spontaneously nor rapidly; therefore, socialist action must begin as if the glorious socialist political and social tradition had never existed. Reality dictated that socialist organizers begin their work from within fascist labor institutions and advocate only legal means to increase the workers' living standard. This slow and patient work would create a crescendo of demands which would inevitably find their outlet in mass action.

Logic demanded this procedure because fascism would not be overthrown easily, nor fall of its own weight, nor evolve into something pleasant, Faravelli maintained. For too long the exiles had deluded themselves by believing in a fascism subject to sudden destruction of the type advocated by GL. Socialists must understand that fascism could be overthrown only with the consensus of all major groups in Italian society. Thus, contemporaneously with stimulating mass action in the factories, Socialists should appeal to peasants, small artisans, white-collar and technical workers, intellectuals—all groups the Fascists had deceived. Socialist nuclei operating in Italy must eliminate ideological confusion, exploit differences between them and the Fascists, and create the basis for common action with the masses.[63]

Given the impossibility of direct socialist implementation of these policies, socialist "advance guard" cadres must assume the task. These cadres had to be constructed, Faravelli argued, rebutting communist claims that powerful Italian Marxist cadres waited only to be unleashed. The Fascists had pulverized these groups. Not only did they hardly exist, but, worse still, a barrier separated the functioning nuclei from the masses.[64] This consideration accounted for Faravelli's insistence on both the building of cadres and the coordination of potentially antifascist groupings within Italian society.

Angelo Tasca echoed Faravelli's themes. Noted for his incisive study of Italian fascist origins, Tasca cited Italy as the major arena of antifascist struggle, vowed creation of socialist cadres in all major Italian cities, and advocated anchoring socialist activities to real conditions rather than abstract ideology. Upon taking power in Italy, Tasca promised, a revolutionary socialist government would immediately construct a socialist society while eschewing dictatorship by promoting a continual interchange of ideas among all groups of existing society.[65]

Thus, in Faravelli's words, socialist activities in Italy aimed to fulfill the "dual objective of creating a socialist general staff and a mass movement in a situation affording a minimum of liberty, and without compromises of any sort with the regime." Ironically, the first concrete stimulus in this direction in Italy resulted from a strange episode.

Mussolini had encouraged a former socialist mayor of Milan, Emilio Caldara, to establish a theoretical socialist review. A similar fascist maneuver had earlier resulted in publication of a journal edited by former socialist labor leader Rinaldo Rigola, allowing the regime to deny that it persecuted its political opponents.[66] Vowing to prevent another fascist propaganda coup, Morandi, the CIS, and Faravelli blocked Caldara and proposed a review to be written entirely by the Italian clandestine network and published in Paris.

This journal would studiously avoid the usual revolutionary flourishes which alienated intelligent Italian and foreign observers of contemporary Italian affairs, Faravelli explained to Directorate member Pallante Rugginenti, while at the same time rejecting compromises with Fascists, concentrating on Italian issues, and amplifying proposed socialist solutions to Italian problems.[67]

In truth, the review aimed at stimulating the growth of party cadres in Italy by engaging young socialist sympathizers in a cultural effort to strengthen their faith. After a trial run in September 1933, the review, *Politica Socialista,* appeared on a regular basis beginning in August 1934. *Politica Socialista* collaborators faced extreme conditions imposed not only by fascist repression but also by Nenni, who resisted the anticommunist flavor which Tasca, the editor, and Morandi's CIS imparted to the journal.[68]

The technique of gathering a cadre group around a review successfully advanced the primary socialist goal of recreating a basis for the Socialist party in Italy. A different kind of network had to be established. In smuggling the articles to France, for example, the CIS organized a secret courier service. In this way, the CIS viewpoint on Italian developments had an important impact abroad.[69]

By December 1935, the CIS claimed success in creating a high-quality socialist advance guard, establishing socialist nuclei in the major northern cites, and forging tenuous but real links with workers. Morandi guided this embryo party, coordinating communications between center and periphery and with other organized antifascist groups. Small meetings took place very frequently, resulting in fertile exchanges of ideas. Financially the CIS remained solvent through voluntary monthly contributions by members. The CIS also gathered hard data about Italian conditions for elaboration and interpretation by the Paris-based executive bodies. The Milan organization quickly claimed official recognition of its leadership by requesting that all other Italian socialist clandestine groups contact it for instructions.[70]

The Socialists did create cadres which allowed them to reenter the Italian scene in grand style after 1943, but they failed in their other important objective during the 1930s: "reawakening" the masses. As Faravelli had foreseen, this task proved extremely difficult despite dramatic international events which the Socialists attempted to turn to their advantage. For example, the Ethiopian War greatly agitated Italian antifascist circles abroad, culminating in massive demonstrations in Brussels on 12 October 1935.[71] This passionate response, however, could not be transferred to Italy, despite the CIS's initial assessment that unrest within the country might transform the conflict into an antifascist revolution.[72]

A joke making the rounds in Italy illustrates the mentality which fed this early optimism: A schoolgirl informed her teacher that her cat had given birth to three kittens. "And they're all Fascists," she said, "because all three are black." Two days later, a school inspector came to class, and the teacher proudly asked her pupil to repeat the story. "My cat had three kittens," the girl said this time. "And what else?" asked the teacher. The schoolgirl thought a while and answered pertly, "Oh, yes, they're all black, but since they have opened their eyes, they're no longer Fascists!"[73]

Far from damaging fascism, however, the Ethiopian War proved popular. The CIS attributed this fact to Mussolini's skillful anti-British propaganda.[74] The other major event of the decade, the Spanish Civil War, also had scarce effect within Italy. High unemployment spurred men to volunteer for Spanish service, reasoning that they would be drafted anyway and would receive less pay.

Finally, the Italian police limited the clandestine network's effectiveness.[75] In April 1937, the police decimated the CIS, arresting two hundred fifty persons in Milan alone, including Morandi. The conspirators wound up before the Special Tribunal and sentenced to internal exile or prison. Morandi received a ten-year jail sentence for his activities.[76]

The Socialists, however, urgently reorganized their underground network, profiting from their mistakes. "Joseph" wrote: "The existence of a sufficiently widespread cadre network is the absolute premise for all effective socialist antifascist efforts."[77]

The arrests had revealed a serious defect in socialist organization. The CIS in Milan controlled all socialist activity in Italy, both political and organizational. Once infiltrated, this structure had allowed the police to destroy the entire network. From now on, political and organizational tasks should be separated, organization should take place at the local level, and there should be no contact between different divisions of the underground movement. Local organizations should report not to an Italian center but to the closest socialist office abroad. The resulting "watertight compartments" would prevent the police from smashing the entire network should they succeed in cracking a particular organization.[78]

In 1938, the PSI Directorate reported that the Italian clandestine movement had been successfully reestablished, but the previous limitations remained. The underground could generate secret cadres ready to take their place in a renovated socialist party when fascism eventually fell, but it could not link up with and inspire the masses to overthrow the totalitarian regime.[79]

Only international developments capable of toppling fascism could accomplish that goal, and these events had already been set in motion.

CHAPTER 2

Returning Home

Perhaps the most traumatic international event of the 1930s, the Spanish Civil War, produced greater agitation in Italian exile circles than had the Ethiopian conflict.

The Spanish republic had openly demonstrated sympathy for Mussolini's Italian enemies, a fact that contributed to Rome's intervention.[1] When Francisco Franco received Italian fascist help, it proved "that the Italian political exiles were certainly not mistaken in warning foreign democrats about the process of expansion" of fascism. Carlo Rosselli raised the cry "Today in Spain, tomorrow in Italy," and Italian antifascist fighters appeared on the Spanish battlefield.[2]

In the context of their unity pact, the Socialists consulted with their communist allies and joined the "Garibaldi Legion" defending the Spanish republic. Italian antifascists had a primary role in the Battle of Guadalajara, a shattering propaganda defeat for Mussolini which produced an exaggerated interpretation of its military significance.[3] For the first time since the 1920s, Italian antifascists had engaged the enemy on the battlefield and won.

The PSI and the Spanish Civil War

The Spanish Civil War period represented a low point in Italian socialist fortunes, despite Nenni's prominent role in Spain. The socialists' subordination to the Communists explains this fact. After initially favoring only medical aid to the Spanish republic, the Italian Communists suddenly organized a volunteer Italian fighting unit, seized control of it, and relegated the Socialists to a subordinate role. The Communists founded a newspaper and initiated contacts with other Italian exile groups without informing their socialist comrades. Additionally, they created the Unione Popolare, a front organization, appointed socialist officers to it without consulting the PSI, and demanded PSI adhesion.

This drive for hegemony provoked a bitter reaction at the next Socialist Paris Congress (26 to 28 June 1938). Nenni, however, defined the socialist-communist alliance as the "sine qua non of the working class's offensive victory against fascism." He and Saragat controlled the Directorate, which blocked a move to denounce the unity pact. As a result, the PSI meekly joined the Unione Popolare and renewed the unity-of-action pact on an unfavorable basis. This new agreement pledged the PSI to a communist-dominated program of antifascist struggle and to continued collaboration with the PCI after fascism's demise. Furthermore, the pact's language awakened in many Socialists fears of a future totalitarian communist dictatorship.[4]

Denunciation of the Unity Pact

Nenni's communist connection allowed him to dominate the PSI until the 1939 Hitler-Stalin Non-Aggression Pact. This event shocked the party, which revolted en masse against the communist alliance. A stunned Nenni saw his position suddenly crumble.

Nenni initially expressed disbelief and outrage at the Soviet "betrayal" and employed all the moral arguments in his vast rhetorical arsenal against the Non-Aggression Pact in a 31 August 1939 *Nuovo Avanti* article. Noting the Italian communist dismay at the news from Moscow, he demanded PCI rejection of Stalin's new policy and maintenance of its allegiance to the unity pact.

By December, however, he had reversed himself. In a subtly argued report to the socialist Directorate, Nenni criticized Britain and France for their past philo-fascist policies, imperialism, and "propaganda" seeking to transform the newly initiated war into a conflict defending liberty and democracy. At the same time, Nenni summarized the Soviet Union's past policies, interpreting them in a favorable light, with the exception of the Non-Aggression Pact. This time, however, Nenni did not denounce the USSR's new course as betrayal but as an "error" which Stalin would eventually rectify. In the meantime, the PSI should reconstruct "our shattered unity."[5]

Nenni's sophisticated argument outraged his comrades, who were further irritated by his determination to save the communist coalition. On 7 September 1939, Nenni had already announced his resignation as party secretary and editor of *Nuovo Avanti,* but feeling ran so high against him that he escaped expulsion only through Modigliani's intercession. The PSI denounced the unity pact and withdrew from the Unione Popolare.[6] Stalin's diplomacy had made a shambles of Nenni's policy.

World War II

Thus shorn of Nenni's influence, Tasca and Saragat (who had distinguished himself sharply from Nenni) took the party's helm. When the war began, the Italian socialist exiles proposed an armed legion to defend France, but the French government feared such action would provoke Italian intervention. The French, in fact, prohibited all exile activities directed against Italy in order to deny Il Duce any pretext to move from "non-belligerance" to war.[7] On 10 June 1940, however, on the tail end of the German offensive and making a monumental miscalculation, Mussolini entered World War II.[8]

France's defeat in June 1940 scattered the antifascist exiles abroad or to the unoccupied areas, while in occupied Paris the elderly socialist leader Oddino Morgari vainly tried to hold the PSI together. In England, the United States, and Switzerland, small but active clubs greeted the Socialists. In South France, the Socialists faced house arrest and eventual consignment to Italian authorities, as had happened to Nenni and Faravelli.[9]

The fascist triumph in 1940 and 1941 thus decimated the prewar antifascist groups, but resistance organizations replaced them. Building on the exile groups' twenty-year experience and the expertise gained from clandestine operations, the Italian Socialists contributed enormously to this movement. In the time of deepest desperation, the Resistance began.

Il Duce had plunged Italy into World War II with criminal lightheartedness, gambling that the war would quickly end in a German victory and anticipating enormous gains at the peace table. Instead, fascism's battlefield performance, the criterion on which it craved judgment, belied its rhetoric. The armed forces foundered in Africa, lost the battle of the Mediterranean, and committed suicide in Russia. On the home front, vital shortages sapped what little will to fight had existed, and the people turned on the regime. War, "the logical conclusion of fascism,"[10] brought Mussolini to his knees.

Anticipating a conflict, Socialists and Communists had announced their intention to sabotage the fascist war effort. This socialist plank survived denunciation of the communist pact, but, as in the communist case, the pledge meant little during the war's first two years.[11]

The New Unity Pact: Origins of the Resistance

Important events, however, did occur during the early war period. After France's fall, Nenni's major PSI opponent also fell from grace.

Angelo Tasca had become a French citizen and a member of the *Section Française de l'Internationale Ouvrière,* figuring prominently in a movement which believed that the Vichy regime could be influenced to undertake socialist reforms. Tasca soon abandoned this ill-conceived position and joined the French underground in 1941, but his momentary lapse permitted Nenni to reimpose the communist alliance.

In October 1940, Nenni wrote to the communist magazine *Stato Operaio* brutally attacking Tasca and reaffirming the communist alliance. According to Nenni, the dispute between Socialists and Communists centered not around the nature of the imperialist conflict in course nor "the task which history has assigned to the conscious and revolutionary proletarian advance guard," but around the necessary tactics to attain common socialist-communist ends. Nazi-fascism imperiled both the working class and the USSR, but the Western imperialists threatened them almost equally. Nenni comprehended the reasons of state which dictated momentary Soviet agreements with Hitler but insisted that the unity pact would have survived except for the provocations of "bourgeois agents in working-class ranks," Tasca, "and the neo-reformist band."[12] Nenni's practical identification of nazism and Anglo-French imperialism coincided with the thinking of important Italian communist leaders, even though Moscow officially condemned the theory at the time.[13]

Hitler's Russian invasion prepared the way for a new socialist-communist alliance, signed in Toulouse in October 1941. Nenni's procommunist position has induced one observer to label this renewed alliance a vehicle for a return to the "acritical" socialist stance before the Non-Aggression Pact.[14]

Given the conditions, such a judgment seems harsh. Besides Socialists and Communists, the agreement included GL and appealed to groups of all kinds—political, social, religious, cultural—to unite against the Fascists; the agreement also installed a policy-implementation committee. The document demanded expulsion of German forces from Italy, Mussolini's removal from power, and restoration of civil liberties. In short, the new agreement did not merely reestablish the previous socialist-communist pact but also anticipated the tight antifascist cooperation which produced the Resistance and the republic. In this sense, Nenni's policy, at first glance subservient to the communist line, not only appears farsighted but set the premise for his return as leader of the Socialist party.[15]

As the war turned bad for the Axis, Italian authorities released many political prisoners arrested during the late 1930s, a development which intensified after Mussolini's fall on 25 July 1943. Socialist leaders such as Morandi and Pertini regained their liberty, exiles who had been turned over to the Italian authorities went free, and thousands of socialist militants who had refrained from politics resumed their activity. Along with the return of the exiles, this accelerating movement resulted in the PSI's reconstitution.[16]

The MUP and the PSIUP

Upon their return to Italy, the seasoned exiles found a new socialist rival, the Movimento di Unità Proletaria (MUP), established by Lelio Basso in Milan on 10 January 1943 after considerable clandestine preparation.

A dynamic, peppery young man from a well-off family, Basso had joined Morandi's CIS and represented the new generation of Italian socialist "leftists," angry at both traditional Socialists and Stalinist Communists. Basso's MUP incarnated the contrasts between two segments of a movement divided by space and time. The MUP "youngsters" shared the ideals of classic Socialists, but they had grievances against past policies and resisted simple reestablishment of the old party with its old divisions and its old leaders, "who looked more to the past than to the present and inevitably dragged with them the traditional ideas and rancors."

The MUP advocated a profoundly "new" party which would reorganize the socialist movement and present the nation with clear ideas and realistic policies. Should Socialists fail to produce programs capable of transforming the Italian political and social structure, MUP leaders insisted, the traditional power relationships of the old Italy would reestablish themselves.

Theoretical and practical difficulties between the MUP and the PSI appeared immediately. At first, these revolved around interpretations of fascism as a guide to future action. Socialist elements reentering the party after having been inactive during the regime considered fascism a historical "parenthesis," a fluke. Given this view, they favored reinstituting the parliamentary system Mussolini had destroyed. MUP members instead interpreted fascism as the political manifestation of basic economic and social tendencies in Italian society which must be eradicated through drastic structural reforms. Immediately implemented, these radical reforms would establish democracy and clear the road to socialism.

The MUP pushed for the twin radical renovations of the PSI and Italy with a sense of urgency which it failed to communicate to the party or the country. Attractive to intellectuals secretly discussing its ideas before Mussolini's overthrow on 25 July 1943, the MUP found itself overwhelmed when the relative freedom after fascism's fall produced a groundswell of support for the traditional PSI. As a consequence, Basso signed an agreement with PSI leaders on 8 August 1943 merging the two groups and changing the party's name to the Italian Socialist Party of Proletarian Unity (PSIUP).[17]

A very tense atmosphere prevailed at the August meetings, Nenni reported, with MUP members highly distrustful of the older exiles. The participants nevertheless agreed upon several fundamental policies: ending the monarchy, a "government of public safe-ty" with socialist participation, and strengthening socialist cooperation with the Commu-nists.

Few objected to the first two goals, but, ironically, the reformists favored closer communist ties against leftist objections because of the prevailing view that the Commu-nists had become more reformist than the reformists. Nenni dismissed this interpretation, considering communist conservatism a tactical ploy. He greatly feared polarization of the Italian political struggle, for and against the Communists, in which the bourgeoisie would defeat Communists and Socialists separately. As a result, Nenni still supported unity of action.[18]

The high-level meetings also physically reconstituted the Socialist party, with Nenni as secretary, Pertini and Saragat as vice secretaries, and a fresh program. In addition to three immediate demands—an armistice, liquidation of fascism, and restoration of civil liberties—the PSIUP advocated destruction of the bourgeois state, pledging nationaliza-tion of the means of production and exchange. Influenced by the MUP, the party declared its intention to create large national, regional, and municipal institutions to administer a "socialized" Italian economy. Side by side with these state firms, new institutions would coordinate small agricultural and artisan cooperatives, and bureaus would implement national planning. This new structure would favor foundation of a Socialist Workers' Republic, democracy, liberty, and true equality.

Pushed by Nenni and MUP leaders, the party also declared its strong desire for fusion with the Communists. According to the party, Socialists and Communists now shared essentially common doctrines and goals, so the reasons for the 1921 split no longer existed.[19] Within a month of the party's reconstitution, Socialists and Communists signed a new unity pact, but the "organic unity" issue would agitate the PSIUP throughout the immediate postwar period.[20]

The Armistice and the Resistance

During these discussions, the Italian situation took incredibly complex turns. With Mussolini's overthrow, the king established a military government under Marshal Pietro Badoglio, not a Fascist but strongly tained by corruption and fascist collaboration. Fas-cism simply collapsed, but the Badoglio government continued the war, refused to restore civil liberties, and brutally repressed the relatively mild popular demonstrations following fascism's fall.

Already on 26 July 1943, the antifascist parties had set up committees representing Socialists, Communists, Liberals, Christian Democrats, "Demoliberali" (mostly the old Radicals), and Actionists (the GL political party). In a manifesto to the nation, these parties demanded the total eradication of fascism, restoration of civil liberties, abolition of the racial laws, and an armistice. Rejecting temptations to demand immediate constitution of a coalition government representing all antifascist groups, the parties gave Badoglio an opportunity to take Italy out of the war in which the country still participated on the German side. The Badoglio government reacted by strictly prohibiting any new parties, promising elections only within four months, ruling out a constituent assembly, and setting the stage for a return to the prefascist order.[21]

On the international scene, Badoglio opened negotiations with the allies for an armistice, bungled them, and fled ignominiously with the king in tow when the Nazis attacked Rome. Leaving the army without orders and abandoning the capital without defense ruined what remained of the royal house's prestige.[22]

As the Nazis founded a puppet state under Mussolini in German-occupied North Italy, local Committees of National Liberation (CLNs) took charge of the Resistance, soon centralizing themselves under committees in Rome and Milan. The Rome committee delegated the armed struggle to a military junta composed of Communist Luigi Longo, Socialist Sandro Pertini, and Actionist Riccardo Bauer. Led by Pertini and Morandi, socialist fighting units contributed impressively to the final nazi-fascist defeat in North Italy, despite later communist denigration of socialist efforts. Socialist political leaders in Rome operated in very dangerous circumstances, and the socialist leadership in particular suffered great losses during this period.[23]

During the Resistance, the Socialists patiently rebuilt their labor and political organizations. In March 1943, Socialists and Communists cooperated in organizing an effective industrial strike in Turin which damaged Italian war production.[24] Despite organizational weakness, the Socialist party garnered impressive support from workers who remembered the PSI's championship of their cause before fascism and who particularly feared communist methods. While this action was primarily motivated by economics, the experience gained in organizing it prepared the ground for later political strikes. For example, the Socialists had a major role in the massive general strike of March 1944, which paralyzed war production throughout northern Italy for eight days—the only strike of its kind to take place in German-occupied Europe. Organized by a single secret committee of workers, this strike proclaimed "the proud resumption of the antifascist movement among the masses."[25]

The Socialist party's achievements during the Resistance appear all the more remarkable because the Socialists lacked international backing, unlike their political rivals.

The Badoglio government monopolized communications with allied forces pushing north. The Anglo-Americans, furthermore, had a strongly anticommunist bias which extended to the Socialists. In London, Churchill pursued a promonarchy policy. In Rome, Ivanoe Bonomi, a moderate former Socialist committed to restoring the prefascist political system, headed the six-party CLN. In Milan, an efficient and more radical National Liberation Committee for North Italy (CLNAI) directed the antinazi struggle, but this body could hardly contest allied decisions. The Communists could count on Russian support against the allies but not the Socialists. Indeed, communist subservience to Soviet policy and contrasting political perceptions thwarted socialist objectives.

The "Svolta di Salerno" and Socialist Acquiescence

In January 1944, the Socialists, along with Communists and Actionists, proposed the monarchy's abolition but encountered predictable resistance from the Christian Democrats and other conservative CLN parties. Unable to secure endorsement of their policy, the left parties compromised; they requested King Victor Emmanuel III's abdication and establishment of an antifascist government. Backed by the British, however, Victor Emmanuel refused, prompting the PSIUP to threaten a pullout from the antifascist alliance.

Responding to insistent demands by workers and northern partisans, the PSIUP initiated a vigorous campaign to end collaboration with the monarchy and install an antifascist coalition government.[26] In February, former Prime Minister Enrico De Nicola obtained the king's promise to turn over his powers to his son Humbert upon the liberation of Rome. Then the bombshell hit.

On 14 March 1944, the Soviet Union officially recognized the Badoglio government. Ten days later, Palmiro Togliatti returned from Russian exile and astonished his leftist allies by reversing Communist party strategy. Togliatti announced "postponement" of the "institutional problem" and advocated a Badoglio-led national unity cabinet to drive the Germans out of Italy. Togliatti also downplayed the PCI's revolutionary image and set the stage for the so-called new party willing to compromise and to come to power gradually within a democratic context.[27]

This strategy contributed to Togliatti's image as a cynical politician. As an example of Togliatti's calculating character, in October 1983, President Sandro Pertini recounted to me an episode between Togliatti and Umberto Terracini, a PCI founder:

> I met Terracini in *confino* [internal exile] at Ponza. He was always with [Camilla] Ravera, the one I nominated a life senator. . . . They were ignored, considered out of the party by Scoccimarro, who was a factious person. . . . Togliatti, a cunning person, feared the following: "Terracini could do this to me: pass over to the Socialists. If he passes to the Socialists he could drag many, very many, Communists with him. . . ."
>
> [Togliatti] called Terracini, and I remember that Terracini recounted the episode to me, so there already was the Botteghe Oscure building, which was given as a gift to the Communists by the builder, who was a Communist:
>
> "I entered Togliatti's office, and he was writing—but he was only pretending to write. He raised his eyes and said, 'You're here.'" This was the meeting between Togliatti and Terracini.
>
> At that time they had not seen each other for twenty years. They had fought together in Turin [when the party was founded], they had been side by side. Two comrades, one in Russia and the other in jail, by God! "And he says to me, 'Ah, you're here.'" Terracini himself told me this. "He didn't tell me anything else. He received me with this 'Ah, you're here.'"
>
> Togliatti, perhaps, having lived in Russia, ended by acquiring some of the toughness which I encountered in the Bolsheviks. . . . They were hard, really hard. They didn't listen to sentiment. It was a dogma of the Communist party not to be sentimentalists, not to listen to their hearts but to listen to their minds.

The "Svolta di Salerno" represented a shrewd reading of the world situation by Togliatti. He believed that the international situation had reached equilibrium between the United States and Russia, leaving the gradualist approach as the only practical hope for power in the West.[28]

Togliatti's new policy ignited a debate among the Socialists, who divided into three groups: for, against, and in the middle. Headed by Nenni, the middle group disapproved of the communist action but gingerly avoided damaging communist relations. Fully recognizing the exasperation caused by the sudden reversal of communist policy but convinced of Socialist party isolation should it oppose the Communists, Nenni persuaded the party Directorate to follow the communist lead. Nenni felt that the PSIUP could do nothing to alter the situation because international forces determined Italian policies. Stalin and the Western allies acted, Togliatti reacted, and the Socialists had to go along. The PSIUP national executive criticized the USSR's recognition of Badoglio, intimated that Togliatti had blindly followed Soviet orders, and evinced a newfound coolness at the idea of a communist merger—but acquiesced in the new PCI policy.

Forced to go along, Socialists' feelings toward the Communists on this issue remained intensely hostile, especially among the left-wing leaders. At the time, Basso accused the Communists of trampling on the teachings of Marx and Lenin just to follow Moscow's orders and excoriated the PSIUP for failing to break with the PCI.[29] In 1965, a still-impassioned Basso reiterated that the communist *volteface* blocked important reforms and favored a series of compromises by conservative political forces. In 1977, Nenni maintained that if the Socialists had not persuaded the Communists to modify their overly accommodating attitude, Italy would have had fascism without Mussolini, a policy which nervous Italian exiles in the United States had already attributed to the American government.[30]

On 1 May 1944, the Directorate reaffirmed the communist alliance and its desire to convert resistance into revolution but admitted that events had now rendered this goal impossible. The party remained firmly committed to a socialist republic, however, and reinforced its military apparatus. By this time, however, the old right-left socialist divisions had returned with a vengeance.[31]

Politics and the Failed Revolution

As more of Italy became liberated, debate focused on whether the nation should return to the prefascist order or give itself a new political structure as the CLNAI demanded: the "wind from the North." This titanic struggle traversed a number of tortuous phases and ended with the substantial victory of Italian conservatives backed by the British and Americans, reinforced by the USSR's recognition of Badoglio and Togliatti's collaborative policies.

With the svolta came a reshuffling of the Badoglio cabinet in April 1944 and major leftist concessions to the conservative parties and the allies. The leftist parties agreed not to upset the "lieutenancy"—the regime Prince Humbert would establish upon Rome's liberation—and to delay until war's end demands for social reform. In addition to military reasons, the allies imposed these conditions to preserve the existing social order.[32] Nenni now feared that Togliatti's svolta had seriously damaged the chances for a republic.[33]

With Rome's liberation in June 1944 came a socialist decision to reverse the conservative tide by eliminating Badoglio and setting up a cabinet responsible to the CLN. The socialist campaign culminated in a meeting between the old marshal and the six antifascist parties on 8 June.

Nenni vigorously pressed his points, informing Badoglio that the Socialists refused to participate in other cabinets which he might head because no government that included him could sincerely define itself as antifascist. The Socialists demanded a complete break with the past. Ministers must swear allegiance not to Humbert, by now "lieutenant general" of the realm, but to the CLN; a law convening the Constituent Assembly must be passed immediately; and an antifascist civilian must take over the War Ministry. The old marshal felt so hurt at Nenni's demands that the socialist leader gently brought the conversation around to the time he had served as Badoglio's sergeant in World War I.

The other antifascist ministers agreed with Nenni, but less forcefully. Togliatti tried to save Badoglio but could not, after which he appealed to his fellow Piedmontese to render a last service to his country by resigning.[34] Visibly moved by Togliatti's sympathetic demeanor, Badoglio and the PCI secretary warmly clasped hands and sealed the deal. This meeting, however, had mixed results. The moderate Ivanoe Bonomi, Rome CLN president, received Humbert's charge to form a cabinet representing the six antifascist parties. This move set the lieutenant general of the realm above the CLN. Nenni refused to join the new cabinet in response to this action.[35]

Bonomi confirmed Nenni's distrust by favoring the conservatives. In fact, the new government resisted the "purge" designed to clean out fascist influence from the state administration and to punish war profiteers. The Liberals objected to a serious purge because they feared its debilitating effects on the ruling class, considered it an attack on people who had done their duty, and resented its antiprofit implications. They also resisted turning over former government administrative powers to the local CLNs in the newly liberated areas.[36]

Bonomi gave in to liberal pressure, provoking a socialist withdrawal of confidence in his government. Over socialist objections, Bonomi presented his resignation to the lieutenant general, again acknowledging Humbert's supremacy over the CLN. In order to resolve the crisis, Humbert consulted with Badoglio and members of the defunct Senate and Chamber, casting further doubt on the CLN's legitimacy.

The question of sovereignty overshadowed all other issues. The Socialists refused to join a cabinet which did not emanate from the central CLN. Their communist allies deserted them at this crucial juncture by suggesting a new Bonomi government excluding the Socialists. Togliatti argued that his socialist comrades lacked "realism" and carefully refrained from frightening the political system into which he so fervently hoped to insert himself.[37]

Before the astonished Socialists recovered, the Communists suggested De Gasperi as prime minister and then supported him as foreign minister when the DC leader failed to become premier. Firmly convinced that "the axis of Italian democracy passes through the DC" and believing that the Communists could choose only between the Anglo-Americans and the Vatican, Togliatti chose the Vatican, which, he said, at least qualified as an Italian state.[38] In this manner, the new Bonomi cabinet took shape with the Socialists in the cold.[39]

The crisis thus concluded with a substantial conservative victory seriously damaging the CLN. This blow hit the Socialists particularly hard, because they considered the CLNs revolutionary emanations of the Italian people and possible instruments of a socialist revolution. At the same time, the allies adopted effective measures to whittle down the CLNs' military influence.[40] Despite socialist and partisan resistance and despite the second wind the CLNs received with Italy's final liberation in April 1945, these maneuvers succeeded.

Insurrection against the Nazis and Fascists in the North accompanied the war's end. In the euphoria, the CLNAI revived demands for a fascist purge and demanded the end of the Bonomi cabinet. This renewed vigor finished Bonomi, although allied opposition thwarted the CLNAI's more extreme demands. The "northern wind" brought great pressure for reform and a leftist government, translated by the Socialists into Nenni's candidacy to lead the cabinet. Nenni's warm reception in a number of major cities convinced the PSIUP secretary that he enjoyed great grass-roots support. "Nenni to power, De Gasperi to the rectory" was a popular slogan of the day. The Communists also appeared favorably inclined.

Nenni, however, encountered determined Christian democratic and liberal opposition. During negotiations, De Gasperi appeared willing to make concessions. Left-wing DC leader Giovanni Gronchi also appeared friendly, but in the end De Gasperi blocked the socialist bid. Neither the allies nor any of the DC's constituencies would accept Nenni, De Gasperi argued, because the unity pact would make the nation's highst office "common" to Socialists and Communists if Nenni succeeded. De Gasperi then claimed the office for himself. In the end, Nenni compromised. Partisan commander Ferruccio Parri—"Maurizio"—became prime minister and minister of the interior; Nenni received the posts of vice premier and minister for the Constituent Assembly. Togliatti became minister of justice and De Gasperi foreign minister.[41]

Parri was a member of the weak Action Party, and his good intentions ran afoul of Italian conservatives and the allies, who occupied Italy and controlled its economic lifelines. The Parri program raised havoc in the country. This program included a serious purge run by Nenni and socialist-influenced economic proposals for punishing fascist supporters, reconstructing the Italian economy, and redistributing the wealth: an exchange of the currency, a graduated income tax, a capital levy, and allocation of raw materials in a manner favoring small firms over large ones.

Elaborated in November 1945, Parri's plan encountered heavy opposition from Liberals and Allied occupiers. On a visit to Italy, Italian-American banker A. P. Giannini criticized Parri and warned that no American loans would be forthcoming while partisans remained in the factories. Partisans and workers had occupied the factories to save them from German reprisals rather than to expropriate them, but their continued presence struck fear in the industrialists' hearts. As a result, the Liberals brought down the cabinet. The Liberals aimed at stalling elections for a Constiuent Assembly and at achieving control of economic policy.

At the end of October 1945, Nenni had compelled the cabinet to set a date for national elections, but the question of a referendum on the monarchy remained unresolved. Socialist policy opposed a referendum, wishing to entrust the institutional issue to the Constituent Assembly. Liberals and other monarchists, however, judged that they had a better chance by holding a separate referendum and by calling local elections before those for the Constituent Assembly. In October, Nenni had given way on the local elections and personally doubted that the Socialists had made a wise choice in opposing a referendum, because the Catholics could barter their votes for favorable church legislation by "selling themselves to the clerical monarchy."[42] In the end, the Liberals achieved both local elections and a referendum but lost the monarchy.

The Liberals, however, obtained a stranglehold over economic policy in the De Gasperi cabinets which succeeded Parri. Both Socialists and Communists participated in these governments, but their capacity to resist liberal and DC initiatives strangely slackened as they focused on the upcoming referendum and elections for the Constituent Assembly, which would have full governing powers.

Parri's fall "marked the comeback of all the old conservative forces in Italian society." Indirect allied support allowed the conservatives to postpone indefinitely the currency change, end the purge of former Fascists and regular administrative officals tainted by fascism, and replace CLN-nominated local authorities.[43] "It was the end of the period of the burning bush," recalled historian Arturo Carlo Jemolo, "of the hope in a correct and clean Italian reconstruction . . . of an Italy with a stern visage, generous and just, making demands on its citizens, especially the rich, the cultured, and the intelligent."[44]

Socialist Rebirth

During the euphoric period following Mussolini's fall, the Socialist party developed into the largest leftist party, its membership surpassing the PCI.

In 1944, the PSIUP had issued a "Provisional Constitution," on the basis of which it rapidly reorganized. In lieu of a permanent document which had to await war's end and a national congress, the party temporarily organized itself according to its prefascist territorial model, with the sections and provincial federations as its basic units and including flanking organizations for youth and women. The legal socialist press reflowered, with the flagship *Avanti!* becoming the country's largest-circulation newspaper under Nenni's brilliant editorship.[45]

The party's long-clandestine hibernation and its spectacular growth raised several novel questions, especially the swelling of its ranks by less committed members and the urgency of modernizing its antiquated structure. A statistical glance at this enormous expansion provides an insight into the problem.

At the end of 1945, Rodolfo Morandi estimated PSIUP membership at seven hundred thousand; according to figures compiled for the 24th Congress, this number grew to eight hundred sixty thousand by April 1946. The North and Center contributed the bulk of the party's strength, with 2.7 percent of the Lombard, 2.3 percent of the Umbrian, 2.26 percent of the Emilian, and 2 percent of the Tuscan populations belonging to the PSIUP. The equivalent percentages for Sardinia, Sicily, Puglie, and Marche were, respectively, .62, .68, .87, and .96, revealing the need for work in the South and the Islands, in which the Socialists later made considerable headway.

Morandi's admittedly incomplete data revealed two important novelties: the great number of factory workers and young people joining the party, currently composed of 62 percent workers, 13.5 percent peasants, 5 percent white-collar workers, and 1 percent professionals. Morandi estimated the young people at between eighty and ninety thousand; with the women, who at forty thousand were relatively few, they made up 19 percent of the total. The PSIUP had become one of the largest organizations in the Italian political spectrum, with its appeal to workers and young people auguring particularly well for the future.[46]

Nenni, Romita, and the Birth of the Republic

Socialist success in the referendum, the elections, and the struggle to make the Constituent Assembly sovereign confirmed the lasting socialist influence on the nation.

The participation of two Socialists in De Gasperi's cabinet in major positions proved decisive for the republic's fortunes: Pietro Nenni as vice premier and minister for the Constituent Assembly, and PSIUP right-wing leader Giuseppe Romita as interior minister. The impulsive Sandro Pertini, initially mentioned as interior minister, took himself out of the running by ignoring Nenni's injunction to "be good, keep quiet" and publicly stating that should Humbert come to Milan there would be a "piazzale Loreto also for him." When Humbert did show up, Pertini took a squad of partisans to the lieutenant general's residence and machine-gunned the windows during dinner, provoking Humbert's hasty exit from the city. Humbert's absence from Milan during the campaign greatly damaged the monarchists in the referendum.[47]

As mentioned above, Nenni had secured the cabinet's agreement for a specific referendum date, later postponed to 2 June 1946. On a visit to London, Nenni extracted a cautious noninterference pledge from Ernest Bevin, Labor's foreign minister. In Italy, the struggle continued, with the Liberals Manlio Brosio and Leone Cattani producing a number of plans to aid the monarchists in the referendum and to blunt the Constituent Assembly's powers by making its decisions subject to yet another referendum. The Americans suggested making the Constituent Assembly into a study group, which made Nenni smile.

De Gasperi, pulled one way by his vague republican sympathies and another by the monarchical preferences of the Vatican and large segments of the DC, steered a neutral course. Togliatti played a relatively passive role as minister of justice, damaging the republican cause by making extreme statements about Victor Emmanuel's attempt to influence the elections by abdicating and threatening communist "freedom of action" should the monarchy win the referendum.[48] Togliatti had to beat hasty retreats from both positions and made Nenni appear a statesman in contrast.

Finally, on 28 February 1946, a lively cabinet session resolved all the outstanding issues holding up the elections. "Tonight the battle for the Constituent Assembly has been won!" a jubilant Nenni confided to his diary. A decree embodying the agreements and reluctantly signed by Humbert reached Nenni by plane in Milan on 20 March, where this peasant son of Italy proudly affixed his signature below that of the prince of the House of Savoy. Nenni felt certain that his signature had sealed the dynasty's fate.[49]

Ably seconding Nenni, socialist Interior Minister Romita devoted himself to eliminating the banditry and political violence that plagued postwar Italy and rebuilt the nation's police forces on a democratic basis. Acting as neutral as possible in a situation in which he faced constant temptation to influence a republican outcome to the referendum, Romita pacified the country in time for the scheduled elections and referendum; his success prevented conservatives from exploiting unrest as a basis for postponing or voiding the elections.[50] For the same reason, the Socialist and Communist parties kept their followers on their best behavior.

When the cabinet settled the last problems delaying the referendum, it also called immediate local elections, viewed by the Socialists as dress rehearsals for the more crucial Constituent Assembly and referendum balloting. Romita enhanced republican chances by choosing cities with large republican and leftist voting blocs to be the first to hold elections. The spectacular results earned Romita a rebuke from conservative cabinet members. Parties and groups favoring the republic won 44,614 seats in 2,336 cities and towns; those supporting the monarchy took only 6,472 seats in 318 localities. Furthermore, the socialist total compared favorably with the communist vote, with the PSIUP coming in first in pivotal Milan. "I have the republic in my desk drawer," said a confident Romita when he received the results.[51]

On 1 June 1946, Nenni asked De Gasperi how he would vote the next day. "The ballot is secret," De Gasperi answered, "but I'm willing to bet that my 'black' Trentino will give the republic more votes than your 'red' Romagna,'' a wager the wily De Gasperi won.

The calm elections made 2 June a boring day for Nenni, although Romita, counting the votes, had a more exciting time as the results seesawed. In the end, the republic won by a suprisingly close but decisive 12,717,928 to 10,769,284, with 1,498,138 ballots declared void.

King Humbert took his defeat badly, sounding out the British on Allied reaction to a possible monarchist coup and delaying his departure into exile. When the Allies gave him a negative answer and the Court of Cassation ratified the referendum's results, the king published a petulant proclamation and left Ciampino Airport for Portuguese exile at four o'clock P.M. on 13 June 1946.[52]

The campaign for the Constituent Assembly also boosted socialist morale. The PSIUP had promised to provide the future republic ''a profound social and economic content.'' On the land, the Socialists advocated expropriation of the latifundia and other large holdings, promised land to the peasants, and advocated modern forms of land tenure. In industry, they pledged to ''dismantle the plutocracy,'' reform the banking system, implement state-supervised planning, convert the economy to peaceful purposes, increase efficiency, and stimulate exports.[53] Almost 21 percent of the electorate endorsed this program, giving the PSIUP 115 seats in the Constituent Assembly, second only to the Christian Democrats.

The Socialists thus successfully participated in the struggle against fascism, contributed significantly to the coming of the republic, reintegrated themselves into the country's mainstream, and became the nation's largest leftist party.

In a free regime, however, the old disputes reappeared. The communist alliance remained the major complaint of powerful PSIUP segments. If the communist pact had functioned only tolerably well as a defensive instrument, in a peacetime situation it revealed its deleterious side for the PSIUP. The problems of organization in a rapidly changing domestic situation and the policies the party had to elaborate in a polarized international context remained. These issues caused dissension and splits, condemning the Socialists to repeat past mistakes.

As Nenni took his seat in the Constituent Assembly, he exclaimed, ''How beautiful the republic appeared when observed from the vantage point of the empire!''

CHAPTER 3

Rodolfo Morandi's "Class Politics"

The grayness that often follows heroic exploits did not affect the PSI's postwar history. In danger of being crushed between opposing domestic and international forces, PSI leaders acted decisively to ensure the party's future.

Their hopes for a clean break with both the fascist and prefascist past frustrated by Christian democratic moderation and communist "realism," the Socialists debated reorganization and new policies to achieve power. Crucial aspects of this struggle included the socialist endorsement of a referendum on the republic and a Constituent Assembly (discussed above), participation in the government, and, following the communist lead, a conciliatory policy toward the DC. Most importantly, however, the communist question lacerated the socialist party and determined its destiny for the next twenty years.

The Debate Resumes

Linked by common ideological roots and strong financial ties to the Communists, Nenni faced stubborn socialist resistance to the PCI connection incarnated in the unity pact. This ever-present opposition gained momentum after the war when Giuseppe Saragat openly disociated himself from the communist coalition.

As we have seen, Saragat had accepted communist cooperation for tactical reasons. After Togliatti's announcement transforming the PCI from a revolutionary organization into a "new party" aiming to seize control of the system from within, the Communists advocated the "fusionism" they had rejected in the 1930s—their goals: to absorb the PSI and create a one-class party ("partito unico").[1]

Police documents indicate that Nenni agreed with fusion but that violent reaction from northern partisans and Saragat forced him to backtrack. A police report dated 23 April 1945 states: "Only the intervention of moderate elements has avoided a true and proper schism between Nenni and the faction headed by Saragat. Nenni had agreed to the Communist party invitation proposing fusion between the two parties; if this union did not come about, it is owing for the most part to the party executive, which came out against it." According to this report, the majority of party members believed that PSI adherence to the Socialist International had superseded the communist alliance.[2]

Events confirmed this opinion. Writing in the first issue of the party review *Socialismo,* which he edited, Saragat emphasized the human and democratic values of socialism. In a clear criticism of the Communists, he stated that the "universalization" of socialist ideals manifested itself in the democratic struggle. Before fascism, Saragat elaborated, it had been possible for Marxists not to understand the antidemocratic and contradictory nature of the "dictatorship of the proletariat," but now they denounced the concept.[3] Much to Nenni's consternation, Saragat thundered for an hour against "my political line" at the Socialist National Council meeting in August 1945. Furthermore, the delegates' enthusiastic reception stunned Nenni.[4]

Even though the left won at this assembly, the dispute ruined relationships among key Socialists. Leftist PSIUP leaders could not understand why Saragat did not acknowledge the necessity of a communist alliance to retain mass support. According to Basso, Saragat would transform the Socialists into servants of the Western bourgeoisie, on the offensive after Winston Churchill's famous Fulton speech heralding the cold war. Although defeated, Basso believed, Saragat had "registered a tactical success: poisoning the party's atmosphere . . . paralyzing its action. . . . reducing its drive, and above all distracting it from its organizational activity and from the concrete elaboration of ideas and programs."[5]

Indeed, Nenni rushed to reassure his colleagues who distrusted his committment to socialist autonomy, softening his procommunist position with characteristic journalistic brilliance. Reviewing the history of the two postwar eras, Nenni cited proletarian advances toward radicalism and the consequent splitting of working and middle classes as the fundamental errors of the Marxist left after World War I. World War II, however, had produced a unified antifascist front, bringing the proletariat out of its isolation and opening before it the road to power. The proletariat would not divide the working and middle classes, a policy which had doomed the left after the first world war.

Communist as well as Socialists fully comprehended this point, Nenni insisted, discouraged any breaks, deemphasized the Soviets and the dictatorship of the proletariat, and sought common ground with other parties. These tendencies compelled not fusion, Nenni admitted, but only close socialist-communist collaboration. Nenni thus shifted the ground to *class,* not party, unity and grudgingly conceded Saragat's stress on democracy's primary importance, even citing Stalin. In short, Nenni placated Saragat by dangling before him the prospect of an Italian communist evolution in a less rigid and dictatorial direction, class unity rather then party fusion, tactics rather than ideology.[6]

In the end, however, Nenni failed to lay the communist beast to rest; it reappeared in the plans of powerful party leaders to restructure the PSIUP along PCI lines and in the abandonment of specifically socialist reforms for communist leadership of the left.

These reforms included Nenni's "Council of Chambers"—which would have replaced the Senate with a Chamber representing powerful worker councils—and, more crucially, national planning.[7]

A Constant Theme: National Planning

Economic planning in other European countries influenced Italian Socialists, especially Labour-controlled Great Britain. In this area, PSIUP leaders hoped to implement national planning by appropriating fascist-bequeathed economic intervention tools, specifically IRI and the public banking system. The major exponent of Socialist planning, Rodolfo Morandi, became minister of industry, thus strengthening socialist capacity to influence policy in this field. In principle, the Allies did not oppose planning; indeed, they encouraged initiatives promising efficient distribution of Marshall Plan aid and defusion of social tensions.

Ironically, Christian Democrats and Communists resisted socialist planning ideas. Although divided, the Christian Democrats adopted Liberal Luigi Einaudi's laissez-faire policy; the Communists simply dismissed planning in a capitalist economy. Guided by these ideological premises, catholic and communist policy coincided in practice, while internal socialist weakness doomed national planning during the Reconstruction era.[8] Surviving below the surface, however, national planning reappeared as an important issue in the center-left Italy of the 1960s and during socialist Prime Minister Bettino Craxi's tenure in the 1980s.

National planning and the other major issues affecting Socialist party developments in the immediate postwar period—the communist relationship, party reorganization, democracy—became crystallized in the ideologies of Rodolfo Morandi and Giuseppe Saragat, respectively representing left and right. A separate examination of their ideas sheds light on the key socialist dilemmas from the late 1940s to the 1960s.

Morandi's "Politica di Classe"

Probably the most influential postwar socialist thinker, Rodolfo Morandi shaped the Socialist party's course into the 1960s. Effective as a clandestine leader and organizer, capable of spellbinding his most esteemed party colleagues, Morandi had scarce direct effect on the masses.

In my October 1983 conversation with Sandro Pertini, I asked the president to recall Morandi for me. He answered:

> I had many contacts with Morandi. . . . I was his very good friend. He had fled to Switzerland [after the Nazi occupation]. It was I who, bombarding him with letters, compelled him to leave Switzerland and come back to Milan: "Your duty is not to stay in Switzerland to command, but to come to Milan to fight." And, in fact, he came to Milan.
>
> Morandi had a handicap: he did not know how to speak in public. He didn't succeed in speaking, not even at Montecitorio [Parliament], where . . . he spoke badly. He did write, but very, very slowly. . . . He was no tribune, he could not galvanize crowds. . . . But he was very well liked by the party, a very upright man, very honest, and of good intelligence.[9]

Jailed in 1937 for his antifascist activities as CIS leader, Morandi settled into the Castelfranco Emilia prison, making the best of a bad situation by intensifying his philosophical and historical studies. Morandi has chronicled this forced meditation in his letters to his brother.[10] Released in 1943 because of poor health, Morandi subsequently fled to Switzerland and, recalled by Pertini, became a major participant in the Resistance.

Besides his Resistance activities, Morandi contributed significantly to the socialist history of this period by editing the short-lived but extraordinarily influential review *Politica di Classe*. This clandestine journal anticipated the young socialist generation's positions on crucial issues confronting the PSIUP in the immediate postwar era.

Replicating his previous strategy as head of the CIS, Morandi created a socialist research group around this review in order to formulate policy. Appearing in September 1944, *Politica di Classe's* first number invited "our comrades to consider issues which affect the future . . . [and] to multiply our efforts to understand the reasons for our struggle."[11]

How the working class must achieve and exercise power rapidly became the journal's fundamental theme. Thus, "class politics" manifested itself in all the important issues of the day. For example, Morandi's elevation of the CLNs and the other Resistance-spawned committees into revolutionary government organs, although dated, is still highly significant for his future ideas.

Considering these committees the spontaneous nuclei of a new democracy, Morandi declared them nothing less than the sole instruments of a new state receptive to the establishment of socialism. For Morandi and a PSIUP which initially endorsed his argument, the masses' desire for self-government expressed itself concretely as committees of national liberation. Morandi admitted the imperfections of these committees but believed them capable of evolution into new and highly sophisticated democratic institutions.[12]

Morandi's eloquent defense of the CLNs long after allied administrators and Italian conservatives had emptied them of their revolutionary content illustrates his abiding faith in them. Although Morandi had to accept their dissolution in the autumn of 1945, the idea of worker self-government through committees embodied in the CLNs remained the core of his "class politics" concept.[13]

The Communist Connection: Morandi's Early Views

Morandi's interpretation of the CLNs as future organs of popular government has been viewed as an echo of his previous distrust of traditional parties,[14] an attitude that carried over into his early analysis of the different relationships of Communists and Socialists to the class they defended.

Locked in ideological debate after Togliatti's "svolta di Salerno," which subordinated all leftist ideals to the antinazi struggle, Morandi refuted communist allegations that the Socialists failed to devote their full strength to the armed resistance and delivered a devastating critique of PCI relations with the masses. "The truth is that the Socialists even in the heat of action take account of certain necessities which the Communists do not feel," Morandi charged. Socialists assigned clear goals to their action, policy changes, and ultimate aims, and they fully explained everything.

Both the means by which the masses expressed themselves and the instrument through which they took direct action, the Socialist party communicated constantly with its adherents. Instead, the Communists conceived of their party as the instrument by which the cadres maneuvered the masses to perform previously determined tasks. If the Communist party decided to fight for democracy and the country's liberation, the rank and file, used to follow orders, did so without further questioning but also without any understanding. When the Socialists explained to the masses the struggle's significance, how to prepare for socialist conquests, how to confront events, the necessity of bourgeois alliances, the Communists did not understand and accused the Socialists of wasting time and effort on useless disquisitions.

But, Morandi answered, while the Communists suppressed ideological debate to cement their alliance with the bourgeois parties, and as a result renounced revolution, the Socialists discussed freely how alliances might achieve socialism. Socialists stimulate debate; they do not suffocate it.

In sum, for Morandi, the PSIUP encouraged democratic "class politics" ("politica di classe"), a completely different concept from communist "politics on behalf of the class" ("una politica per la classe"). The same difference distinguished a regimented army and a democratic organization continually consulting and interacting with its base.

For this fundamental reason, Morandi disagreed with socialist leaders such as Basso, who had reservations regarding Socialist party reconstitution and who initially suggested confluence with the Communists. The Socialist party, Morandi insisted, had a proven survival capability and, above all, a democratic tradition which anyone who hoped to construct a new revolutionary society could ignore only at his peril.[15]

Morandi's early criticism of the Communist party and the USSR must not be confused with ideological incompatibility with communism, as in Saragat's case. Morandi could furiously disagree with the Communists on tactics, but he tenaciously defended the unity-of-action pact. Indeed, he became the principal architect and defender of an even closer communist alliance from 1948 until his death in 1955. For him, the Communists could be misguided but never enemies. Morandi's writings on the nature of bureaucracy, for example, confirm this contention.

Even convinced Socialists and communist sympathizers lamented the apparently inevitable association of bureaucratic rigidity with the collectivist state, as illustrated by the USSR. Morandi, however, stubbornly objected to the automatic identification of bureaucracy with collectivism. Explaining this defect in the USSR as the result of the socialist experiment's youth, Morandi believed that the Soviet bureaucratic experience merely warned the Italians about the pitfalls of collectivism.

While interpreting Soviet bureaucracy as an understandable mistake common to transition periods, Morandi turned the tables and identified bureaucracy with the bourgeois state. The bourgeoisie had created bureaucracy to conquer the state and to ensure capitalist expansion. Having achieved these aims, bureaucracy assumed a dual aspect: the centralization of administrative functions and, more importantly, strict limitation of state intervention in the productive process. On the one hand, this structure explained the rigid inefficiency of public management; on the other, the growth of monopolies. Far from being synonymous with bureaucracy, Morandi believed, only a democratic collectivist society could break capitalist-spawned monopolies and eliminate bureaucratic ineptness.[16]

From Idealism to Realism

Spurred by Morandi, the PSIUP adopted strong positions favoring the working class rather than joining the Communists in reneging on demands which might irritate the conservatives and jeopardize their chances for government participation.

Having confirmed its revolutionary and class nature, Morandi wrote in 1944, the Socialist party must pursue policies for the expropriation of great landowners and for nationalization of monopolistic industries, banks, and life insurance companies. In the future, democratically run government bureaus and cooperative institutions must manage activities in these areas. Totally rejecting the reformist label, Morandi conceived of these destabilizing measures as delivering a mortal blow to agrarian and industrial monopolies, capitalism's main defenses, and as prerequisites for building socialism while avoiding bureaucratic suffocation. Finally, national planning would ensure development of the new socialized economy, equitably distribute national resources, and coordinate the various productive phases of socialist society.[17]

Suggested in 1944, these ideas appeared in the 1946 socialist electoral program, influenced Nenni's "Chamber of Councils" proposal, and resurfaced during the debate on planning in the center-left period on the 1960s. Despite their continuous attraction for the socialist left, however, Morandi's ideas rapidly became diluted when they encountered political realities.

Failing first to grasp the momentous political changes occurring at the highest government levels immediately after the war, Morandi judged De Gasperi's nomination as prime minister to be a positive development because it supposedly forced the Christian Democratic party to operate under the scrutiny of public opinion, prompting it to break with its conservative supporters. Then Morandi adopted an accommodating position toward the Liberals, chiefly responsible for defusing the explosive postwar economic situation. In practice, Morandi himself deemphasized his own nationalization policies, concentrating instead on the institutional question and bringing the entire PSIUP with him.

This change absorbed all the party's energies and implied socialist acceptance of a liberal democratic state open to the rise of the masses rather than an immediate struggle for power by the working class as Morandi had theorized. By postponing national planning objectives, by justifying compromise and collaboration because the Socialists had joined the government, and by placing reconstructive production requirements before socialist equality and rapid structural change, Morandi signaled de facto abandonment of socialist ideals by the party and the entire left.[18]

These changes occurred after Morandi's first tenure as party secretary for organizational activities and reflect a highly complex Italian postwar situation in which no political force had freedom of action.

During his debut as head of organizational activities in December 1945, Morandi defended the PSIUP Directorate against charges that the executive organ had followed a moderate course, collaborating with Christian Democrats instead of stimulating divisions between workers and conservative/Vatican interests within the Catholic party. Socialist promotion of a tighter "left bloc" against the moderates would merely have provoked a similar alliance on the right, Morandi argued, on not only the national plane but the international plane as well. Instead, the Socialists knew what they wanted, collaborated with all democratic forces, and successfully countered DC pressures for a communist break. According to Morandi, this vigorous and consistent policy had made the Socialist party the shining hope of all Italians who supported strong democratic principles, progressive social policies, and radical structural reform. Morandi praised the Directorate for halting the nation's slide backward into tyranny.[19]

These rationalizations illustrate how Morandi emphasized political "realism" to an unprecedented degree, stressing cultivation of nonsocialist democratic forces. Obsessed after World War II with practical political action, Morandi exhorted the Socialists to accept their limited capabilities in the economic field, to postpone the great structural reforms he had so urgently advocated, and to stimulate production, employment, and reconstruction at any cost.[20]

Toward a New Split: The First Steps

Falling into a pattern all too typical for leftist Italian Socialists, Morandi combined his soft political policy at the national level with a "hard" analysis of party issues. Seemingly willing at first to compromise with the socialist right, Morandi adopted a tough line which eventually split the party and subjected it to the Communists.

As noted, in 1945, Morandi found little fault with recent party policy but insisted that the PSIUP must not renounce its future ideals. Although advocating "practical" action, Morandi argued that the party would burst through limitations which the political situation imposed on it, at which point its mass action must become more "agile"; the party would demand radical social reform from within the government.

In order to prepare for this future action, the party must reorganize itself and concentrate its burgeoning membership's full power in the political system so as to determine the course of national policy. In 1946, this structural reorganization meant for Morandi strengthening the party federations with respect to the sections, deemphasizing "personalities," and stimulating collegiality.

The period's most volatile issue, socialist relationship with the Communists, fundamentally affected Morandi's view of party policy. Despite his previous criticism of the Communists, the Milanese socialist leader became the most adamant advocate of communist cooperation. President Pertini's recollections on this score are particularly illuminating:

> When Morandi was in jail [during the fascist period] . . . he said to the Communists, "You keep to yourselves and leave me alone." . . . Yes, at first Morandi felt that a bond could not be formed with the Communists. Later, instead, no. . . . Morandi supported a single slate with the Communists, a gross blunder. . . .
>
> When he became party vice secretary, with the youngsters, Panzieri and the others, he worked for unity with the Communists. And I remember that I had a dispute with him because I had gone along to a meeting at the Botteghe Oscure [communist headquarters] with Longo, Scoccimarro, and Togliatti, of course, the [Communist party] secretary, and I was there, Morandi was there, and [inaudibile] was there, I believe.
>
> Morandi gave a report to Togliatti in which he let the following slip out. . . . He said, "It might take ten years, perhaps eight, but we must become the sole working-class party. . . ."
>
> Upon leaving I said to him, "You made a mistake. You should have let me read [that report]. . . . I don't approve; you have made a statement of which I don't approve. I do not know what will happen in ten years. In politics prophets have always been wrong. We are not prophets in politics. We must be careful. If you say this, it means that you are preparing the party to enter into the Communist party. . . .
>
> "I did not contradict you because we were with them, but I contradict you now that we have left the Botteghe Oscure. I disagree with you because, if you are thinking about this [fusion], it is necessary to begin preparing the party now for fusion with the Communist party. But I, as long as the Communist party is tied to the Third International, and dominated by the Third International, and feels itself tied to Stalin, . . . I would never enter the Communist party.
>
> "The Communist party must revise the position it took in '21 in Italy, when it broke off from us. It must revise that position, and it must admit that it was wrong and we were right! There's no doubt about it!"[21]

Several times during our conversation, President Pertini animatedly stated to me that the Communists must still revise the condescending and critical attitude they took toward the Socialists in 1921 and thereafter, illustrating very well both the depth of the distrust which many Socialists demonstrated toward the Communists in the late 1940s and how his own interpretation of this highly charged issue has not changed since then.

Morandi initially attempted to smooth over socialist objections to the communist connection by assigning each working-class party different tasks within the ambit of the class struggle. From the PCI's origins, Morandi wrote, it had had the same task as its sister parties in other countries: to defend the Soviet Union and promote its expansion as a revolutionary power. Faithful to this international aspect of the class struggle, all communist parties subordinated national working-class interests to an international revolutionary plan; individual communist parties could permit their national workers' movements neither internal democracy nor independent action, since the good of the party might conflict with the international revolutionary movement's grand design. Instead, untrammeled by an international plan, the Socialists devoted their energies to national workers' movements and pursued independent policies.

These purely tactical considerations, Morandi believed, did not result from differences of principle but from the class struggle's evolution over the past twenty years. According to Morandi, individual communist organizations loyally supported democratic goals and national independence. Transformation of national communist parties from elite into mass organizations and the future evolution of international politics would render the need for subordinate communist parties unnecessary, because all European workers would support socialist goals. At that point, the democratic objectives of national communist parties would reassert themselves and reestablish the original socialist aims which still existed within communist organizations. Since historically conditioned divergences between Socialists and Communists would disappear, Morandi confidently predicted, the two working-class parties must undertake the crucial task of defining their relationship in the present historical moment.

This concern meant revision of the unity pact at the upcoming socialist congress in April 1946 so as to refine the different aspects of the class struggle with which each party would deal. And because of the diverse historical functions of the socialist and communist parties during the current historical moment, there could be no question of "fusion," which Morandi officially declared a dead issue.[22] Thus, Morandi hoped to stave off attacks by the PSIUP's anticommunists while preserving a strong communist tie.

Besides Morandi's anticipation of a future "democratization" of the Italian Communist party, actually initiated only in the 1970s, the most significant point to note is Morandi's shift from his 1944 condemnation of the Communists as military instruments of Moscow to a subtle justification of their policies. In his speech to the 1946 socialist congress, Morandi objected vehemently to anyone who intepreted his remarks in an anticommunist vein, called for an end to destructive discussion of the communist link, and pleaded for peaceful revision of the unity pact.[23]

Morandi's passionate remarks illustrated how, far from being a closed issue, the communist relationship would split the party. In fact, the rhetoric escalated in 1946.

Forced to deal with the communist issue and its effects on the party, Morandi took the gloves off. Correctly interpreting the results of the 1946 congress, he argued that the large number of votes garnered by groups unhappy with the party leadership could not be forged into a true coalition and that the left wing would grow rapidly.

He also discerned an ideological polarization within the PSIUP. The left wing remained faithful to a class political conception, whereas the right wing, Morandi charged, had adopted political liberalism, expressed itself in humanistic terms, and divided the party from its proletarian base. Adopting a revolutionary viewpoint, leftists interpreted all gains as class conquests; party rightists visualized improvements as part of a general movement toward liberty, equality, and progress. Morandi condemned this interpretation as antihistorical and based on the old-fashioned and mistaken conviction that capitalists could be talked into adopting socialism. Coming out into the open, Morandi insisted on the primary importance of the communist link while the right "persisted in judging militant communism a degeneration of socialism, abnormal."[24] Morandi suggested the incompatibility of these right-wing views with membership in the PSIUP.

After June 1946, Morandi made this suggestion more explicit. Arguing that the PSIUP's victory in the referendum and elections of that month had reconferred freedom of action upon the party, Morandi demanded that the PSIUP mobilize the "conscious" rank and file so as to increase revolutionary effectiveness and spur radical measures in the government and the newly elected Constituent Assembly. This resurgent class struggle would prevent the "reformists" from bogging the party down in parliamentary squabbles.

At this point, Morandi hurled the dreaded epithet "Social Democrat" at the PSIUP right wing, defined it as socialism's dead branch inspired by pre-1914 ideology, and accused its adherents of playing the bourgeoisie's game while craftily exploiting old-style democracy to cover its tracks. For good measure, Morandi discarded his previous caveats with regard to the Communists, strongly coming out for unity.[25] By taking this major step toward driving out an important segment of the PSIUP, Morandi conjured up the ghosts of socialism past which had once paralyzed the party and would do so again.

In the Government

Counterbalancing his tough stance toward his comrades, Morandi adopted an accommodating attitude during his tenure as minister of industry and commerce in the two De Gasperi cabinets between July 1946 and May 1947. An examination of cabinet meeting discussions reveals his de facto classical economic bent.

On the whole, Morandi and his communist cabinet colleagues supported gradual elimination of subsidies for food staples, sharply raising prices to achieve deficit reductions, credit restrictions, shrinking consumer demand, resisting wage increases, and reducing the state bureaucracy. Both Socialists and Communists understood and accepted the price of this deflationary policy in the form of higher unemployment, more so than some of their Christian democratic colleagues.

Morandi discouraged investment in luxury items, opposed devaluation of the lira, and advocated a general tax on wealth, but a perusal of cabinet meeting minutes reveals little debate between Morandi and conservative ministers on the necessary financial measures to refurbish Italy's war-torn economy. The so-called Fourteen Points, the government's public program of 3 April 1947 to correct Italy's deteriorating economic situation—interpreted by socialist commentators as initiation of Morandian economic planning—concealed the true nature of the discussion among the ministers and cannot be considered a form of socialist planning.[26] At any rate, they had no practical effect, nor did the PSIUP or its collateral organs seriously elaborate on them. In sum, Morandi "did not do well as a minister,"[27] his tenure illustrating the dilemmas of professed revolutionaries participating in cabinets.

Despite the difficulties of practical application, Morandi's ideas exercised great influence on Italian socialist thought. Most suggestive are his ideas regarding direct participation of the working class in its own affairs and his concept of implementing structural changes within the capitalist system which, acting as "time bombs," would stimulate the socialist evolution of society. After De Gasperi expelled the left parties from the government in May 1947, Morandi assigned this function to national planning, but it already existed in a hotly debated issue of the period, the "consigli di gestione," or management councils.

The councils had distant origins in the post–World War I internal commissions— loosely analagous to Russian soviets—which still existed but had been defanged by the industrialists. In the chaos following Italy's World War II defeat, workers formed management councils to save the factories from nazi destruction and to continue production after the owners fled.

When peace returned, discussion raged regarding the councils' fate. The workers wished to preserve and expand their powers, and the owners pressed for their dissolution.

In October 1946, Morandi drafted legislation for regulation and juridical recognition of the councils. He emphasized the bill's limits, affirming that it neither altered property relationships nor achieved great working-class conquests.[28] Intimately linked to his ideas of direct democracy, however, the proposal would have allowed the workers a powerful voice in industrial planning.

By providing for direct participation of the masses in the determination of general production policy, Morandi aimed at putting capitalist institutions on a collision course with one another and impeding bureaucratic degeneration of planning by infusing it with a permanent political charge.[29] Logically enough, the legislation encountered the determined opposition of industrialists, whose association bitterly fought it.[30] As a result, Morandi's proposal failed, surviving, however, in the ideological sphere and influencing 1960s center-left proponents.

The Road to Socialism: Economic Planning

Central to Morandi's concept of working-class participation in activities deciding its future, the management councils also had the major task of humbling capitalism and constructing socialism through economic planning. Although most Western European countries undertook some form of planning after World War II, Morandi's version aimed at more than utilizing scarce resources rationally; his planning would establish socialism within a capitalist society not susceptible to forceful overthrow while avoiding discredited reformist gradualism. *Avanti!* noted that the Italian socialist concept of planning differed from the French, which supposedly conciliated Marxists and conservatives.[31]

Subtle, incisive, suggestive, capable of inspiring ideological loyalty, Morandi's economic planning ideas nonetheless suffered from two defects: a split personality and lack of faith on the part of their author.

The most important of three "strands" debating economic planning during the early postwar period, Morandi's group, which included Raniero Panzieri, Angelo Saraceno, and Guilio Pietranera, founded the Istituto di Studi Socialisti (ISS) in November 1945, shortly after Morandi became head of the PSIUP's research office. The ISS published a journal and organized conventions on the theme of economic planning, culminating in the First Socialist Economic Conference (Rome, 8 and 9 November 1947). Furthermore, Morandi's close relationship with leading catholic economist Pasquale Saraceno (Angelo's brother), whom he met in early 1945, led to the foundation of an association to promote southern industrialization, SVIMEZ, of which Morandi held the presidency until 1950. Morandi considered industrializing the South a key element of his plan.

Despite his radical view of planning, as minister of industry and commerce, Morandi depicted economic programming as a moderate measure for the rational distribution of resources which would not subvert the economic system. Indeed, he chastised the bourgeoisie for rejecting measures universally perceived as logical.[32]

After the socialist exclusion from power after May 1947, however, Morandi's view of planning became more openly radical, although it always preserved a common-sense aspect. In June 1947, Morandi assigned to planning the major purpose of coordinating production and the market in order to satisfy human wants, but, he added, planning must not simply confine production within the limits of current demand but stimulate it if demand dropped below productive capacity. In other words, planning must "free production from slavery to the market."[33]

Economic planning thus acquired the identical function, on a global scale, which Morandi had ascribed to the management councils, that is, to set working class and bourgeoisie on a collision course which would smash the capitalist system and launch society toward socialism.

Unlike capitalist plans, Morandi argued in November 1947, socialist programming surpassed mere economic rationalization, targeting the social system itself for progressive change: "Socialist planning is based on action which, developing within the capitalist order, dislocates the system's equilibrium to the point of completely overthrowing existing class relationships." By means of structural reforms, socialist planning corroded the capitalist economy's resistance capabilities. An integral part of planning, structural reforms guided socialist shock tactics, producing a chain reaction of change and propelling society toward socialism. This dynamic nature distinguished structural reforms from "reformist" reforms, Morandi argued, making his socialist planning conception "revolutionary and based on the principles of class struggle." "Reformist" reforms smooth out the capitalist economic systems; "revolutionary" reforms strike out against it.[34]

Faced at this point with the antique socialist dilemma of what is a reform, Morandi smoothly resolved the question by proposing a series of concrete measures, which he grouped under four fundamental themes: general aims, defined as specific political objectives, not a generic wish for progress; specific national goals, indispensable conditions for constructing a new society, most importantly elimination of the North-South dichotomy; institutions ensuring implementation of the plan and "democratizing" production; and a precise linking of structural reforms to "shock" capitalism and build socialism.

Illustrating these themes in a specific manner, Morandi called for the redistribution of national income through government action transferring the burden of reconstruction from the poorer to the richer classes, defending the real wages of the working classes by raising the workers' standard of living, and increasing production. Furthermore, the government must go beyond fiscal measures and redistribute income by modifying the relative capacity for consumption of rich and poor.

To achieve this goal, Morandi advocated extending preferential treatment for the working classes beyond foodstuffs to the other necessities of life—from housing to other public services, from health to education—in short, positive, radical, and decisive government social intervention on behalf of the workers.

With regard to the second theme, more than any other socialist thinker, and against vigorous communist objections, Morandi advocated systematic and drastic government intervention to industrialize the South. According to Morandi, the South's inability to realize all its economic potential provoked "the economic backwardness of the nation," undermining the entire Italian economy and ensuring the country's permanent state of imbalance.

For the South, the socialist plan recommended preferential financing of the area's infrastructure (roads, housing, irrigation, ports), expropriation of large landowners, obligatory institution of consortia to rationalize agriculture, and agricultural mechanization. Most importantly, the plan called for southern industrialization by channeling industrial activities from other areas to the region and creating great centers of production to stimulate Italian commercial expansion in the Mediterranean basin.

What about implementation? Morandi's third fundamental theme addressed this question. True to his underlying belief in the working class's "direct democracy," Morandi shunned administrative controls, preferring implementation of planning through "fundamental democratization of productive life and direct worker participation in the plan's management and regulation." Prime instruments of worker participation in economic planning for Morandi were the management councils, which would extend from industry to all other areas of economic life and would form the basis of other democratic workers' organizations participating in planning at the highest levels. These worker-run management councils would determine investment and distribution policies, resource allocation, management of state economic activities, administrative activities of joint stock companies—in sum, the whole gamut of modern economic life.

The great structural reforms, Morandi's fourth and last theme, had two aspects, economic and political. The economic aspect concerned primarily the rationalization of economic life. The political reforms would break the back of any groups opposing the plan's economic changes in the industrial, agricultural, and banking sectors.[35]

Morandi's design ran into criticism from his leftist colleagues. His friend Giulio Pietranera wondered if the plan could ever become operational, labeling it mostly a pious hope. Pietranera discerned positive aspects in the fixing of socialist objectives and the focusing of the party's technical capabilities on those goals.[36]

The major criticism came from Riccardo Lombardi, a recent convert from the defunct Action Party and intensely concerned with economic planning. Rather than an economic plan, Lombardi argued, Morandi had developed political objectives for the socialist movement. On these everyone agreed, Lombardi noted, but how to achieve the goals remained unclear. According to Lombardi, too many missing elements thwarted the enunciation of any economic plan, so he suggested discussing general socialist policy instead.[37] During the 1960s, however, Lombardi advocated a "plan" strikingly similar to Morandi's.

Ironically, the debate over socialist planning abruptly ended in early 1948. In an astoundingly weak reply to his critics, Morandi simply advocated further discussion of planning rather than undertaking a stout defense of his work.[38]

Ironically, Morandi's ideas on planning represented a coherent and sufficiently concrete answer to the question of how a party that wished to implement socialism without violence in a capitalistic system might begin the task. Morandi's concept of economic planning was capable of transformation into a powerful independent political platform in 1948 had the Socialists debated it, modified it, and presented it to the electors; Morandi instead abandoned his own potentially fruitful conception and placed his faith in the Communist party.

Morandi himself participated in killing his own fertile ideas. He dropped socialist planning primarily because of communist suspiciousness. As previously noted, the Communists frowned on any notion of planning as an instrument in building socialism within a capitalist society.

With the left's exclusion from cabinets after May 1947, international considerations became paramount for Morandi. Obsessed by the "inevitability" of a world struggle between U.S. imperialism, represented internally by the DC, and the socialist fatherland, led domestically by the PCI, Morandi believed that the Socialists should set aside their own projects and follow the communist lead. Morandi agreed with Stalin that in the American sphere of influence Marxists could not build socialism but only prevent reaction. Defending democracy thus meant uniting with the Communists against the DC, not devoting major energies to attaining socialist reforms.[39]

In homage to the communist alliance, Morandi abandoned his planning ideas, became the champion of the Popular Front, and suppressed socialist differences with the Communists. This policy alienated some of Morandi's closest followers and set the stage for the explosion that occurred in the PSI over the communist issue after 1956, immediately following his death. After that time, Morandi's faction resisted breaking the communist tie, split from the Socialist party in the 1960s, and joined the PCI.[40]

Morandi and the Popular Front

Morandi's conviction that the class struggle had been transmuted into an international contest between American and Soviet blocs marks his last, least interesting, but most important phase for the PSI.

Convinced that the United States menaced Italian democracy, Morandi called for an intimate alliance with the Communists. This position implied socialist acceptance of USSR and PCI guidance, fully accepted by Morandi despite a possible subconscious resistance to Stalinism. Interested at first in developing an original justification for closer communist collaboration, embodied in the Popular Democratic Front, Morandi quickly dropped his attempt because of possible exploitation by right-wing Socialists. Morandi's defense of the front rapidly became unilateral, referring always to the international situation and accepting the Leninist label for his party.[41]

Indeed, Morandi would interpret the dramatic Popular Front reversal in the 1948 general elections as a "cold war incident" and maintained that any socialist opposition to communism signified abandonment of the class struggle.[42] Even more important in the context of the times, he dismissed the risk the Socialists ran of being overwhelmed by their more militaristically organized allies.[43]

With Nenni's support, Morandi's strict alliance policy won out in the PSIUP, presenting Socialists wary of the communist connection with the dreary choices of silence or secession.

An incident symptomatic of this dilemma occurred in January 1949. Editor of

Avanti! Riccardo Lombardi published an article blaming the class struggle's degeneration on the cold war. Lombardi lamented the loss of socialist independence and subordination to the USSR's dictates. This being the case, Lombardi wrote, what justification existed for the continued presence of an Italian socialist party alongside the communist organization?

Raging furiously, Morandi viciously attacked Lombardi personally because he had supposedly questioned the international struggle's primacy. Reprimanded by a number of party leaders, Morandi limply explained that political parties had many reasons for existing and that the Socialist party survived because of its capacity to wage the class struggle.[44] This incident confirms not only Morandi's desire to suffocate any questioning of the communist alliance but also an awareness of his own weakness on the issue.

Although signs appeared that Morandi entertained loosening the communist connection in 1952 and 1953, when relations between Americans and Russians improved, he loyally supported the Communists and eyed Nenni's growing discomfiture with disapproval.

This final twist of Morandi's "class politics" had incalculable results for the Socialists, from splitting the party to the electoral defeat of 1948, from communist determination of socialist policy to a permanent American distrust of the Socialist party. In the long run, Morandi's legacy imposed a heavy burden on postwar socialist and Italian history.

CHAPTER 4

Liberty and Giuseppe Saragat

Rodolfo Morandi's ideology encountered its antithesis in Giuseppe Saragat, the other pole of Italian socialism. Saragat was severed from the Socialist party in 1947 after a bitter struggle, and his exit proved in the long run perhaps the greatest tragedy of post-World War II Italian socialist history. Contrary to innuendos rife at the time which suggested that Saragat split the party at the Americans' behest, an exposition of Saragat's ideology quickly reveals its incompatibility with Morandi and the Socialists' communist infatuation.

Saragat's Ideology: Liberty Above All

Particularly linked to Filippo Turati and Claudio Treves, Saragat inherited the original Italian (and European) mainstream socialist tradition. An instinctive ideologue and philospher, Saragat refurbished and adapted pre-1914 socialism to the modern world. A critical person by nature, Saragat did not spare his reformist predecessors, but while he corrected their errors, he demolished the left wing's entire thought system.

For Saragat, Marx aimed at a perfect form of human liberty whereas communist and leftist socialist Marxism inevitably produced dictatorship. The overriding concern of Saragat's socialism was liberty, "the indispensable premise for all civilized political struggle. Liberty determines the atmosphere in which all ideas live and, depending upon their vitality, become sterile or develop; it is the atmosphere within which the modern spirit wins its battles: 'In hoc signo vinces.' "[1]

Saragat developed into a major thinker in exile, studying with the Austrian social democratic theoretician Otto Bauer before settling in France. Out of his criticism of both reformism and maximalism emerged a sophisticated new noncommunist synthesis.

Contesting the usual reformist representation of themselves as struggling for reforms, Saragat charged that reformists adapted socialism to existing political systems. Neglecting the revolutionary implications of a struggle for socialist democracy against autocracy, reformists simply identified democracy and nonviolence.

As a result of this confusion, reformists ignored the proletariat's fundamental political requirement—true democracy—and compromised with capitalist autocracies to achieve reforms. This reformist evasion of Marxism's fundamental problems provoked a reaction within the socialist movement, which produced graver errors.

Replicating reformist blunders, maximalists also viewed democracy in purely formalistic terms, but they grievously compounded the mistake by negating democracy's value for the proletariat. Worse still, maximalists refused to carry their logic through to its natural end—a proletarian dictatorship—which would have made them Communists.

Instead, maximalists eternally oscillated between communism and reformism, depending on the particular issue.[2]

According to Saragat, resolution of the reformist-maximalist dichotomy meant not communism, "socialism's infantile malady," but "democratic Marxism." Citing Marx, Saragat believed that the proletariat had a "categoric imperative" to achieve democracy "understood as political autonomy, as a revolutionary conquest." In other words, Marxism—the fulfillment of the world's "profound essence"—existed only in potential form which must be transformed into reality by being brought to human consciousness.

For Saragat, liberty is history's "profound essence" and Marxism its concrete explication. History is nothing more than the consciousness of liberty-in-progress. If liberty is the real essence of human nature, reality is the current social organization in which humans operate. This social organization is oppressive and abets the economic exploitation of one class by another. The exploited class becomes conscious of its own oppression only gradually by comprehending the contrast between reality and humanity's free nature. As the exploited majority's consciousness increases, the masses destroy the oppressive conditions in which they exist and achieve historical progress.

Saragat thus did not interpret the class struggle as a collision of different interests but as "a means of historical development, i.e., of the development of liberty, of which class consciousness is the moving force."

This philosophical premise underpinned Saragat's entire Marxist system. The proletariat's consciousness of its own exploitation represented for Saragat the beginning of its redemption, rather than the oppressive conditions themselves. Historical examples of oppressed classes which failed to rebel abound, Saragat argued, but only Marxists explained reality and thus overthrew it.

Class consciousness and class struggle therefore went together, but, more importantly, class consciousness had as its essential prerequisite freedom of thought. For this reason, the proletariat must win the first and most important round, against its own fanaticism and dogmatism, the tyranny "we carry within our own hearts." Only after having conquered their own "internal tyranny" could the workers confront the "external tyranny" of existing social relationships.

Saragat distinguished between freedom of thought as the class struggle's prerequisite on the individual plane and political autonomy, the proletariat's collective prerequisite reflecting freedom on the class level.

By "political autonomy," Saragat stressed, he intended democracy. The working class transfers its individual interests to the factory, where it lives collectively, and orients its collective consciousness toward a specific end: socialism. Beyond productivity, the proletariat has a special revolutionary task, expressed by its party and union. Internally free and capable of organization, the workers can hone their understanding of reality and initiate the class struggle. "But what is this condition if not the spiritual autonomy of the proletariat and the political society in which it lives?"

Since the proletariat has inherited the idea of liberty and carries it to new heights through the modern class struggle, Saragat argued, the working class resolves all the problems of human liberty. The class struggle presupposes the political and spiritual autonomy necessary for liberty and achieves a synthesis of class struggle and democracy. Democracy, Saragat hastened to explain, did not mean the fragile paraphernalia and formal mechanisms which immediately leaped to the minds of its critics, but the spirit of people ready to defend it. This animating force emerged from the combination of spiritual and political autonomy. Only in the presence of both could democracy and the class struggle survive.[3]

Because for Saragat democracy guaranteed the proletariat's free development, the dictatorship of the proletariat became simply a contradiction in terms. Workers required a democratic society to achieve socialism, even if they did not possess a political majority, because the objective conditions for socialism would rapidly follow.[4]

Saragat's democratic conception of the class struggle made him the true heir of the pre-1914 reformists, as did his attempt to put "humanistic Marxism" on a philosophical plane. For Marx, Saragat wrote, the class struggle made sense only if it restored people to their full humanity. Primarily concerned with creating a humane society, workers must not lower human reality to the level of their class interests. This "integral humanism," of which liberty remained for Saragat the conscious expression, was the essential ingredient of class consciousness.[5]

Saragat thus labeled the dictatorship of the proletariat as an unauthorized and destructive reaction to a perfectly comprehensible bourgeois renegation of democracy. Socialist antidemocratic theories originated in the confusion of political autonomy with formalistic democracy and from the illusion that the proletariat could respond to undemocratic attacks by installing a dictatorship while remaining faithful to socialist democratic ideals. The Russian example, Saragat contended, proved different.[6]

As might be expected, Saragat's ideology put him on a collision course with Marxists who believed in the dictatorship of the proletariat, especially the Communists.

The Impossible Alliance

At the cost of denying his entire philosophy, Saragat could not agree to anything other than a tactical alliance with the Communists, as, in fact, his contacts with them before, during, and after World War II make explicit. Rejecting both of Saragat's fundamental prerequisites for the class struggle—political and spiritual autonomy—the Communists considered democracy merely a mechanism and believed that the proletariat should resort to violence against its enemies.[7]

Saragat did not exclude force, but he believed that the Communists reduced the subtle complexities of Marx's theory to matters of police behavior, five-year plans, and expropriation of individual bourgeois property. Although Saragat acknowledged the antiquated nature of some aspects of Marx's thought, he believed in its fundamental soundness. Marx's teaching that socialism would evolve from advanced capitalism, instead of being the intellectualistic and forcible imposition of a plan, remained Saragat's sacred principle.

For Marx, economics dominated politics, and the substructure determined the superstructure. Returning to utopian socialism of yore, the Communists reversed everything, Saragat charged, lowering economics to a "docile object of the bizarre experience of politburos" and becoming self-proclaimed ultra-realists in politics.

This truth explained communist preoccupation with the dictatorship of the proletariat. Saragat labeled this concept a tragic expression of a false dilemma which obliged the proletariat either to submit to bourgeois violence or to terrorize the bourgeoisie. In effect, the Communists had reversed the reactionary illusion that dictatorship would stop socialist progress in its tracks. But if the degenerate bourgeoisie could renounce liberty, the workers could not. Far from being congruent with proletarian necessities, Saragat believed, the dictatorship of the proletariat distorted economic development and damaged socialist regimes in the same manner as reactionary political policies hurt capitalistic systems.

Real strength issued not from arms but from harmony with the laws of historical development, which tended toward social liberty, not dictatorship. Dictatorship could never produce liberty, just as Lenin's implacable state tyranny would never achieve anarchy.[8]

Communist confusion over the dictatorship of the proletariat, Saragat wrote, originated in a misunderstanding of Marx, especially by Lenin. Marx never intended seizing control of the state for the purpose of suppressing the bourgeoisie but to obtain true liberty. Since, according to Marx, the state is always an expression of class relationships, the proletariat destroys the state and itself at the same time as it suppresses the bourgeoisie, thus attaining freedom.[9] Lenin's interpretation of Marx, in Saragat's view, had transformed communism into a totalitarian movement.

Saragat thus discovered in totalitarianism the common meeting ground between fascism and communism. Allowed free expression after World War II, his practical identification of communism and fascism put Saragat on a collision course with Nenni and Morandi.

According to Saragat, experience modified classic socialist theory. The will to power of human groups outside the liberal economic system was the most important of these factors and figured prominently in both fascist and communist regimes. These regimes, Saragat believed, had slowly lost the "class character of the capitalist economic forms which had generated them."

Manifested in liberal economy as class oppression, the will to power in fascist and communist regimes characterized those groups wielding control. Classic Marxism viewed the state apparatus as a committee managing the dominating class's business interests. But when this apparatus appropriates society's economic functions as well, as in the dictatorship of the proletariat, it becomes totalitarian, exhibits the old ruling class's oppressive power, and behaves toward its own people "exactly as the bourgeoisie acts toward the proletariat." By monopolizing all of society's productive forces, the state ceases being a superstructure and becomes "the instrument of total oppression." In other words, the new bureaucracy replaces the old ruling class and intensifies its tyranny.

This "bureaucratization" occurred in both fascist and communist regimes, Saragat contended, the major difference being that since fascism conserved the old ruling class, the bureaucracy acted as the middleman of oppression. The bolshevik system instead eliminated the old rulers, so the state utilized the bureaucracy directly to tyrannize its people.

Given the fundamental resemblance between fascist and communist totalitarianism, Saragat called on the Socialists to preserve and defend the democracies with all their strength. Despite the well-known liberal democratic imperfections, the democracies defended society's general interests even while struggling for their lives against Hitler and Mussolini. Because both fascism and communism trampled freedom, the indispensable conditions for socialist evolution existed only within the democratic social systems of the West. Socialist parties necessarily fought "against the totalitarian states to preserve civilized conditions and the premises for a socialist resurrection."[10]

Given Saragat's well-developed anticommunist ideology, it becomes difficult to understand how Nenni and Morandi could have so seriously misjudged the depth of Saragat's anticommunist feelings after World War II. They could only taunt him with having supported the communist unity pact; Saragat indeed did so during the war's darkest moments,[11] but only as a tactical measure.[12]

Saragat always chafed at the communist connection. For example, in the closing months of the war, he defended the unity pact as essential to the antinazi struggle but suggested this reason as its sole justification. In attacking the pact, he warned that national reconstruction must utilize "democratic means for democratic ends."[13]

In short, Saragat remained suspicious of the Communists and viewed with alarm their growing influence over the Socialist party. Saragat fought them not only in the ideological sphere but on the organizational plane as well.

Restructuring the Party

As discussed above, fusion of socialist exile and internal groups in August 1943 created the PSIUP, which constituted itself on the basis of a transitory "Political Declaration." The same document stated the socialist intention to fuse with the Communists.

At a National Council meeting of July 1945, a Morandi cosponsored motion prevailed against an "autonomist" proposal bearing Saragat's signature. The victorious "fusionists" called for a single working-class party and delegated to the upcoming national congress the task of unifying socialist and communist parties. The National Council brushed aside autonomist objections and even accepted Socialist party reconstitution only on a temporary basis, pending "fusion" with the PCI.

An analysis of the party's base during the same period, however, reveals the impossibility of implementing this decision. Exactly the reverse situation from that existing at the summit characterized the party membership. The PSIUP had rapidly expanded to seven hundred thousand, much larger than the PCI, in great measure because workers rushed to strengthen the Socialists in opposition to the undemocratic Communists. This development created an illusion of strength among socialist leaders, especially Nenni, convinced either that the Socialists need not fear communist competition or, even more unrealistically, that the PSIUP would absorb the PCI. Believing fusion on their terms to be imminent, an overconfident socialist ruling group badly neglected crucial party organizational and propaganda work in the immediate postwar period.

Backed by the Soviet Union's resources and brilliantly guided by Palmiro Togliatti, however, the PCI imaginatively combined mass-party and Leninist techniques to construct a modern political organization. This effort rapidly made the PCI the second most powerful party in Italy and the largest Communist party outside the Soviet bloc. Aided by the lowered socialist guard and by the common party institutions created as a consequence of the unity agreement, the well-oiled, financially powerful, and unscrupulous communist apparatus achieved control of many local socialist organizations and quickly reversed the power relationship between the two parties.

Reacting in self-defense, the PSIUP Central Committee in October 1945 suddenly declared communist fusion premature. Despite Nenni's hope that the Communists would understand and that Saragat would be placated, this abrupt policy inversion antagonized both. Saragat interpreted the hasty change as vindication of his views, and the Communists claimed that the PSIUP had unfairly blocked unification.[14]

If the surge in Communist party strength resulted from Italian social conditions and the ruthless application of Leninist principles, the inadequate socialist sense of urgency in restructuring the PSIUP reflected the debilitating divisiveness among its leaders.

With certain important exceptions, the Socialist party after 1944 replicated its pre-1914 territorially based organization.

Composed of neighborhood clubs, the party section remained the basic policymaking unit, only one being allowed in a particular city. The section's members gathered at a general assembly meeting to elect the executive committee, which administered the section. The sections federated at the provincial level, forming the provincial federation (minimum three sections). A committee elected by the provincial congress administered the provincial federation. The sections had important powers, voting their own motions, electing delegates to the national congress, and instructing them.

Based on decisions made at the local level, the national congress set national party policy and elected fourteen persons who, when joined by a youth representative, constituted the Directorate. During its term, the Directorate administered the party's affairs according to the national congress's stated policies and named the editor of the party newspaper, *Avanti!* The socialist youth movement had a parallel structure. The Central Committee, and an extraordinary deliberative body, the National Council, capped the party organization.

This picture strongly resembled the party's traditional prefascist structure, but time had imposed important changes. Operating underground during fascism and the Resistance, the national and provincial directing organs had become much more powerful, while the leadership had become less representative and more restrictive.

Against these developments at the top clashed those at the party's base. Immediately after the Liberation, party membership burgeoned, but alongside positive aspects appeared negative ones, especially the overly lax manner in which the PSIUP had welcomed new members. Too many new adherents had erroneous doctrinal conceptions, scarce socialist commitment, and active fascist pasts. This sloppy policy created a heterogeneous and at times unruly membership.[15]

The contradiction between an expanding base and a shrinking summit created organizational and policy implementation problems and occasioned ideological debates which greatly contributed to the 1947 split.

Another major problem was the South. Historically weak in the region, the party mushroomed spectacularly as the war wound down. In 1944, the PSIUP counted sixty thousand members organized in six hundred sections in the area.[16]

Finally, while socialist influence declined dramatically in the labor movement compared to the near monopoly the party had enjoyed in the prefascist period, the PSIUP had a solid presence in the factory through the Socialist Factory Nuclei (NAS). Facing fierce communist competition in the labor movement, some leftist socialist leaders viewed the NAS as the answer to communist rivalry, but they faced determined opposition from the socialist right wing, which had a more traditional conception of labor politics.

By 1945, the antiquated party structure had become the focus of contention because it inadequately translated socialist policy into action and because of its entanglement with the fusion question. Having agreed about the untimeliness of merging PSIUP and PCI, socialist leaders debated the question of when. Nenni would have liked to relegate the problem to a faraway future, but Lelio Basso kept the issue burning.

Basso reasoned that while conditions for fusion did not presently exist, Socialists should actively pursue class unity by emphasizing their common traits with the Communists and emulating their Leninist organization. A parallel party structure would make fusion with the PCI inevitable, Basso believed. Indeed, he aimed at outperforming the Communists at their own game, hoping to merge the parties with the PSIUP organizationally superior to the PCI.

As a result, Basso published a comprehensive plan to restructure the party. Completely alien to Saragat's ideas, this program highlighted the incompatibility of Saragat's ideology with the direction the PSIUP appeared to be taking.

Lelio Basso and the "Bolshevization" of the PSIUP

Basso's analysis of the PSIUP's situation and its relationship with the PCI revealed the Socialist party's full-blown crisis.

Basso attacked, stating that "reformism," that is, Saragat's ideology, mortally threatened the party because it spelled middle-class domination and complete loss of the PSIUP's working-class nature. Saragat distrusted the working class and advocated middle-class political domination of the workers. According to Basso, the middle classes maintained the dominant position they had achieved within the Socialist party before 1914 by arguing that to achieve power the party must appeal to society's middle elements, thus conditioning the PSIUP's action.

For Basso, instead, "there is no revolutionary class outside the working class." Since all workers must direct the socialist struggle, they must be unified, regardless of party. Working-class unity thus became for Basso the prerequisite for proletarian victory. This unity could include Catholics but had as its fundamental aspect the "organic union" of Socialists and Communists. Basso grudgingly admitted that conditions for unity did not currently exist, but he argued that participation in common struggles would produce gradual conciliation of Socialists and Communists. Thus Basso particularly resented what he interpreted as the residual reformist mentality of the Saragat-inspired socialist base and party press, which sabotaged communist unity.[17]

As a consequence, Basso issued a mortal challenge to Saragat by urgently organizing a faction to thwart the Italian bourgeoisie's supposed scheme to isolate and separately defeat the two workers' parties through the Piedmontese leader.[18] According to Basso, Saragat hoped to press the Socialist party into service for "the reconstruction of the old prefascist order."[19]

Basso drew the logical consequences of his ideological position by proposing a radically altered party structure. Saragat "reformists" hoped to transform the PSIUP once again into an old-fashioned electoral and parliamentary body and to sabotage the Resistance goal of Italy as a popular, self-governing worker state by retaining the old party organization.[20]

Basso's plan for "bolshevizing" the PSIUP illustrates his true ideological affinity with the Communists.

Two Plans

In October 1945, the PSIUP Central Committee accepted a series of "organizational norms," recently attributed to Basso. These regulations fostered a "cellular" organization of the communist type rooted in the factories, the above-mentioned NAS. This development aroused the ire of Saragat sympathizers, most notably the "Critica Sociale" group. This faction also objected to proposed establishment of a "political office," which, it noted, would supplant both Directorate and Central Committee.[21]

Adoption of the "norms" foreshadowed future developments. In the summer of 1945, the Directorate had named a commission to draft for the upcoming national congress a plan modernizing the party's structure. The commission promptly split, producing two reports, one signed by Basso and the other by Faravelli, Critica Sociale's point man.

Although later withdrawn, both drafts have ideological and practical importance. The Directorate appointed a new commission, which substantially accepted the Basso version. A national congress formally adopted this proposal after Saragat bolted the PSIUP; the Faravelli draft became the constitution of Saragat's new party.

Aiming primarily at an efficient organization along PCI lines, Basso's "Statuto" created a "capillary" structure, subdued the unruly sections, and vastly strengthened the party's executive organs. Imitating communist "democratic centralism," Basso outlawed organized factions and committed the entire organization loyally and without question to carry out the national organs' decisions.

Basso's plan envisioned "cells" incapable of challenging party executive organs, as the sections did with impunity. "Zones," intermediate bodies between sections and federations, supposedly ensured the periphery's collaboration in the center's decisions but served as window dressing. Most important, however, would be the NAS, socialist equivalent of communist cells.

Instituted on an experimental basis by Basso during his previous tenure as Lombard regional secretary, the NAS became the fulcrum of Basso's "new" Socialist party. Because the NAS democratically welded together the working class with its advance guard in the factory, Basso argued, they should replace the outmoded and middle-class-dominated section as the party's basic unit.[22]

Not surprisingly, Basso's project encountered hostility for imposing a totalitarian Leninist structure on the Socialist party and for favoring "operaismo," the pursuit of workers' narrow economic interests. In response, Basso claimed greater efficiency for "cellular" organizations and denounced "middle-class" exploitation of the sections to infiltrate the Socialist party.[23] Violent relationships currently characterized the party's internal life, he charged, while efficiency would produce more democracy.[24]

As mentioned above, Basso's ideas served as a blueprint for the Socialist party, especially after Morandi took charge of organization in 1949. Despite his disputes with Morandi and the different goal Morandi made the structure serve, Basso's organization characterized the Socialist party throughout the long Popular Front alliance with the Communists and may legitimately be considered the application of Morandi's ideology to party organization.[25] Ironically, Lelio Basso became the most illustrious victim of the newly "bolshevized" party structure.

Just as Morandi's ideology provided the basic conception for Basso's structural modifications, Faravelli drew inspiration from Saragat and the reformist tradition. Consequently, not efficient modernism but liberty animated Faravelli's proposed constitution for the Socialist party.

Conceiving of the Socialist party as a spontaneous association of free citizens, Faravelli's outline favored decentralization over centralization, weak executive organs over powerful ones, the section over the cell, autonomy of party groups over strict coordination, the legislative function over the executive, traditional over innovative labor organization, careful deliberation over rapid action, and strong guarantees for dissidents over obedience to party dictates.

Most significantly, Faravelli retained the PSIUP's territorial structure. Indeed, he lauded the section as the supreme expression of the free socialist spirit and the indispensable forum for discussion of general interests and policy deliberation. Even though Faravelli projected a number of other units (neighborhood and factory clubs, unions of city sections), the section remained the party's fulcrum. Suspicious of the NAS, Faravelli treated them cavalierly. Strong independent bodies protected dissidents against the party bureaucracy. Deliberations taken by the sections and formalized by regional and national congresses bound the national organs and prohibited the executive bodies from initiating independent action.

Furthermore, Faravelli specifically granted autonomy to all party organs: sections, federations, socialist parliamentary group, youth organizations. Faravelli's plan also substantially reduced the Directorate's power, transforming it into a representative organ including delegates named by the socialist deputies, labor groups, and the cooperative and youth movements. Contrary to Basso's powerful apparatus, Faravelli strictly limited the executive bodies to coordinating the party's different components and refining the strategy decided on by its deliberative organs.[26]

Based on nostalgia for pre-1914 socialism, Faravelli's draft had major flaws. The project provided a structure for a party that no longer existed. It seems doubtful that such an uncoordinated organism as Faravelli envisioned could have functioned efficiently. The overly strong guarantees for minority opinions, a backlash against "democratic centralism," would have encouraged insubordination. Faravelli's toothless executive organs could not have provided any clear direction. The excessive autonomy of the different party organs would have resulted in the practical leadership of the elected socialist deputies, already too independent. Ironically, Faravelli's extreme latitude for powerful individuals likely courted the authoritarianism Critica Sociale condemned in Basso. Finally, Faravelli erred in dismissing the NAS, in which the right wing had strong support but which Saragat's followers abandoned to contest the left wing's primacy alone.[27]

In sum, Faravelli's constitutional draft would have established the supremacy of deliberative assemblies over the party apparatus; Basso's would have done the opposite. Neither plan resolved the party's yearning for modernity combined with its traditional individualism.

The 24th Congress

The debate on restructuring the party dominated the months leading up to the 24th Congress, scheduled for Florence in April 1946, but failed to resolve the problem. As the assembly in which all the serious socialist divisions became public, however, the Florence congress has fundamental importance. Although the first postwar socialist split occured in 1947, the schism already existed at this meeting.

Even before the congress, Vice Secretary Basso dissolved the "League of Socialist Communes," a right-wing-dominated revival of a pre-1914 organization. Basso's action provoked the resignation of Party Secretary Sandro Pertini, eventually replaced by Morandi. Upset at the impending crisis, Pertini deserted the left, hoping to form a center coalition to salvage party unity. At a January 1946 Central Committee meeting, Nenni excoriated Saragat's representatives in their leader's absence as ambassador to France. Nenni confided his reason to his diary: "They all tell me that their triumph would mean the party's demise."[28]

In addition to opposing fusion, Nenni suspected, his rightist opponents planned to sabotage the unity-of-action pact. In fact, the right hoped to link up with Pertini and gain a majority at the party's next congress. At the Central Committee, three mutually exclusive proposals reached the floor, but their sponsors withdrew the motions in favor of one simply approving the Directorate's policies. Unable to resolve their disputes or to achieve a clear-cut victory, the party leaders covered them up. Following this meeting, Basso advocated a split at the upcoming Florence congress.[29]

Morandi, however, favored compromise, while Nenni flatly rejected a split. Eventually, these two leaders established a coalition which ran the party until 1955 and froze out the recalcitrant Basso.[30]

"A colorful spectacle" dominated by a classic Nenni-Saragat oratorical duel, the 1946 Florence congress failed to reconcile the widely divergent socialist positions and brought the party to the brink of division.

General Secretary Nenni took the podium first, defending the Directorate's policies since 1943, declaring fusion a nonissue, and praising unity of action with the PCI.

Nenni devoted a large part of his speech to criticizing Saragat. Since socialist experience with "revisionist" factions had been universally grim, Nenni confessed his suspicious and alarmed reaction to Saragat's theories. Nenni compared Saragat to a French revisionist Socialist who had theorized "middle-class socialism" and wound up supporting Hitler. Drawing a general lesson from this incident, Nenni declared Saragat's middle-class socialism nonexistent and claimed that ideas such as Saragat's always produced "Bonapartism, fascism, Hitlerism."

Nenni also took issue with Saragat's thesis of an ongoing struggle between totalitarian and democratic socialism. The secretary absolved the Soviet Union from the charge of imperialism and the PCI of subversion to Moscow. In fact, Nenni believed the PSIUP had a sacred duty to defend the USSR as the socialist fatherland, despite occasional differences with it. In this context, Nenni denounced Saragat's desire to establish a new Socialist International, branding it a Western tool in the emerging cold war. In sum, Nenni's speech foreshadowed the Socialist party's entangling Popular Front alliance with the PCI.[31]

Saragat replied with an incredibly vast summary of his ideology which merits close attention because of the misinterpretations of this statesman's activities in the immediate postwar period.

Saragat contradicted Nenni's report, thus publicly challenging the general secretary's leadership. During the long antifascist struggle, Saragat recalled, the Socialist party epitomized justice, liberty, and human values, which translated into a great swelling of party ranks after the war. But party leaders drew mistaken conclusions from this act of faith, stiffened, turned inward, and suspected nonworkers who joined the party.

Given the postwar chaos, some undesirable elements had unfortunately joined the Socialist party, Saragat admitted, but this development hardly explained the leaders' strange behavior. Lack of faith in the Socialist party's historical function and in the value of political democracy did.

This extremely serious state of mind clearly emerged from the Directorate's report and Nenni's address, Saragat continued. They considered Western European social democracy to be dominated by the rich and denigrated Italian socialism's reformist tradition, but, Saragat protested, both movements confirmed the evolution of humanistic socialism from within the most industrially advanced nations. These statements hinted at Saragat's intention to build a large Italian social democratic party on the lines of those in other Western European countries.

Saragat openly labeled the leftist-dominated PSIUP Directorate's policies as a dishonest parroting of fifteen-year-old Communist party themes. Worse still, Saragat said, Nenni represented a "profound commitment to the very substance of totalitarian thought." Nenni and the Directorate subtlely justified dictatorship, criticized capitalist but not communist bureaucracy, and liquidated in a few words the origins of the socialist-communist split. Nenni downplayed fusion with the Communists because he realized that Socialists rejected merging PSIUP and PCl, but his logic led straight to communist fusion and socialist liquidation. According to Saragat, the left's "mature conditions for fusion" were identical to those "which have imposed liquidation of their party upon our socialist comrades in Eastern Europe and East Germany."

Saragat warned Nenni that totalitarian values undermined Socialist party unity and accused him of harboring these totalitarian aspirations. Nenni had destroyed the synthesis between maximalism and reformism which the Socialists had achieved in 1930, sustituting for it a maximalist-communist amalgam which threatened socialist independence.

In Saragat's view, Nenni denied evidence confirming a war for supremacy between democratic and totalitarian socialism and reaffirmed the left wing's traditional insensitivity toward the Socialist party's humanistic Marxism. The PSIUP must reject the totalitarian socialist model as developed in the USSR: militarization of society and imposition of socialism.[32]

The rhetoric of the two major socialist leaders indicated that a split already existed. Only the PSIUP's emergence from successful local elections and its need to gear up for the referendum and Constituent Assembly balloting in June 1946 delayed a formal schism.

If Saragat had achieved victory at Florence, he would have established a PSIUP-DC national coalition. In Saragat's opinion, Italy sorely needed a large social democratic party of the Western type, fighting for liberty and reforms, while relegating the Communists to a permanent opposition.[33]

In order to realize this dream, Saragat had to carry as many sectors of the party with him as possible in case of a split, while Nenni must contain the damage. In this struggle, both lost. Saragat ended up with a splinter party deprived of its traditions while the main socialist body became a communist satellite.

On the surface, the 1946 congress's official results belied the grave socialist crisis. Nenni reports several failed attempts to reconcile Saragat,[34] although last-minute shuffling distilled the large number of motions into two major ones.[35] Neither motion received a majority, but, added together, the right and center outpolled the unified left groups by 7 percent.[36] The center, however, did not coalesce with the right and would never have followed Saragat out of the party.

As a result of the stalemate, the socialist leaders achieved an uneasy compromise, giving the major factions equal representation on the Directorate, creating the post of party president for Nenni, and naming the neutral Ivan Matteo Lombardo as political secretary. And the Communist *Unità* offered cautious thanks for Saragat's failure to capture control of the Socialist party.[37]

The Schism Matures

Communist fears of a Saragat takeover proved unfounded as the PSIUP lurched toward a schism. Believing a divorce to be salutary, Basso extended his influence at the local level.[38] Basso exhorted socialist militants to fight "bourgeois" infiltration and prepare for a new congress.[39]

On 25 October 1946, Socialists and Communists signed a new unity pact. Unanimously ratified by the PSIUP Directorate, the agreement bore Saragat's signature, as his opponents took pleasure in emphasizing.[40] In reality, however, Saragat and his friends found it politically impossible to oppose cooperation on an apparently equal basis with the PCI. Moreover, the new pact omitted all references to "organic unity" between the two parties and limited collaboration to certain clearly specified occasions. These points irritated the party left, which, however, received compensation through creation of permanently constituted bodies for the pact's implementation. Furthermore, PSIUP and PCI both enjoyed veto power allowing either to reject concerted action.[41] In short, although both right and left later complained, at the time both declared themselves satisfied.[42]

In fact, the different socialist factions interpreted the agreement from mutually exclusive perspectives. For the left, the alliance advanced the cause of working-class unity; for the right, it retarded fusion. These varying judgments explain why the pact became such a burning issue after the local elections of 10 November 1946.

As discussed above, the general elections of 2 June 1946 produced a clamorous PSIUP success, giving it 20.7 percent of the vote. The November local elections provided an opportunity to test the electorate's latest mood and presumably reveal a clear trend, because Socialists and Communists presented united slates in some regions and separate ones in others.

The elections went badly for the Socialist party. Its support dropped by a quarter, and electoral analysis demonstrated that its voters either abstained in large numbers or voted communist. Indeed, communist gains more than made up for socialist losses, moving Italy as a whole leftward. To complicate matters, the DC also declined, losing votes to the Uomo Qualunque ("Common Man") and other rightist groupings, prompting catholic leaders to revise the DC policy of collaboration with the two proletarian parties. Political observers widely predicted a government crisis by Christmas 1946.[43]

These elections lacerated the PSIUP because Nenni seized on the general leftist advance and interpreted it as a victory. Irritated by Nenni's statements, Saragat blasted the party leadership in a newspaper interview. Denouncing the party's "maximal fusionism," Saragat charged that PSIUP leaders paralyzed socialist action and plotted the party's liquidation. Saragat then attributed socialist losses to the recently signed unity pact, which had induced many PSIUP voters to abstain.

The interview had the effect of an "atomic bomb," Faravelli reported, Nenni especially smarting at what he considered a personal attack. Following Saragat, Mario Zagari, "Iniziativa Socialista" faction leader, released his own interview denouncing the party leadership. Critica Sociale chieftain Ugo Guido Mondolfo agreed with Saragat, stating that voters interpreted the new unity pact as de facto fusion. Although frequently at odds, the constellation of rightist groups concurred that the left's lack of confidence in the party had caused the debacle. The November 1946 elections thus galvanized the right and made it aggressive.[44] Perfectly aware of their minority status, the direct challenge by the groups on the right illustrated their readiness to bolt from the party if conditions worsened for them.

The left's less than tender response to these developments exacerbated the situation. As noted earlier, Nenni's positive interpretation of the November 1946 elections had provoked the rightist storm.[45] Nenni reacted to rightist criticism by championing an extraordinary conclave, even though he had previously opposed one. Nenni narrowly won his point as the Directorate voted five to four (one abstention) to hold a congress in January 1947.[46] Nenni defended his action by claiming that recent events had ended the equilibrium established at the Florence congress.[47]

Unfortunately, Nenni had misjudged the situation. He apparently supported an early congress in the hope of a clear mandate for the Directorate and with the conviction that Saragat would not bolt. Behind the scenes, however, Lelio Basso demanded the meeting to crush the right wing while the left controlled the party apparatus and local organizations. The practical conjunction of Nenni and Basso infuriated the right and astronomically increased the likelihood of a split.

The precipitating national political situation also exerted pressure on the party leadership to tame the unruly right. The impending end of the tripartite national governing coalition (DC-PCI-PSIUP) made it imperative for socialist leaders to put their house in order and prepare a bid for power with the Communists. Indeed, Nenni attributed to "the spectacle of our internal polemics" the socialist failure in the November 1946 elections and the consequent inability to name a socialist prime minister.[48]

In fact, however, the recent elections had inverted the power relationship between Socialists and Communists; should the dual proletarian alliance have come to power, the PCI would likely have dominated the cabinet. This possibility confirmed Saragat's fears, made worse by the polarized international situation.

Thunder on the Right

The groups organized as "Critica Sociale" and "Iniziativa Socialista" did the major fighting for the right wing.

Taking its name from Filippo Turati's review, Critica Sociale, the smallest, but most coherent and influential group, aimed at modernizing Turati's ideas. The Faravelli draft constitution represented Critica's blueprint for reconciling liberty, democracy, and efficient mass politics. Imbued with Turati's suspiciousness of Soviet-style communism,[49] Critica vigorously fought fusion but cautiously accepted unity of action, reserving full equality and autonomy for the PSIUP. It strenuously denounced Basso and Nenni for promoting de facto socialist subservience to the Communists.

Rejecting the dictatorship of the proletariat, Critica Sociale emphasized "a revolutionary party which is democratic in both means and ends." As a corollary of this thinking, Critica's adherents advocated a party that "interpreted the country's general interests," appealing to the middle class in addition to workers, a policy which drew Basso's fulminations. Also contrary to the left, Critica preserved Turati's distaste for joining cabinets, chiding the left wing for its collaborationist penchant. Critica also favored a new Socialist International as a means of affirming socialist independence from the Communists and of initiating a fresh bid for power in Europe.[50]

Although the rambunctious Critica Sociale leader Giuseppe Faravelli foresaw a split perhaps as early as December 1945, his group resisted formally dividing the PSIUP. Mostly experienced older politicians and theoreticians who had spent years in exile, highly skilled in intraparty warfare, Critica members had the patience to await their turn for power. Commonly identified with Saragat, with whom their ideas largely coincided, the extremely egalitarian adherents of Critica Sociale distrusted all leaders and fiercely defended their independence. For his part, Saragat rejected total identification with this group's contentious members, although he clearly exercised spiritual leadership over them. Finally, Critica Sociale frequently squabbled with the other major rightist faction, Iniziativa Socialista, about whose members Faravelli commented, "Those dear Iniziativa Socialista boys . . . are a group of crazies with whom it is difficult to agree."[51]

In contrast to Critica Sociale, youth, exuberence, and a touch of inconsistency characterized Iniziativa Socialista. Founded in January 1946, this group had its roots in the large socialist youth movement and consisted of young Socialists lacking the traditions and doctrinal sophistication of their Critica Sociale elders. Members of this faction, however, instinctively resisted growing PSIUP authoritarianism and stronger PCI political links. Defined by its aspirations rather than its consistency, Iniziativa Socialista called itself leftist before the Florence congress, became center during the deliberations, and supplied many of the soldiers for Saragat's split. While personal difficulties with Critica Sociale abounded, the Iniziativa program revealed a strong kinship to Saragat and Critica.

Led by Mario Zagari and Matteo Matteotti, Iniziativa Socialista rejected union with the Communists, denouncing their allegedly totalitarian nature. Like those of Critica, this group's exponents loudly protested the socialist inferiority complex toward the Communists and demanded independent PSIUP policies.

Accordingly, Iniziativa championed autonomy on the national and international levels, spurning both Soviet and American leadership, working for a new Socialist International, and advocating a "United Socialist States of Europe." With Saragat, Iniziativa rejected the dictatorship of the proletariat, welcoming middle-class participation in socialist politics, and committed to gradualism. As for internal party affairs, the faction considered democracy paramount and consequently favored the Faravelli plan to restructure the PSIUP. Surpassing Critica's political intransigence in national politics, Iniziativa called for a socialist pullout from the tripartite governing coalition and criticized the socialist left and the Communists for their excessive governmental collaboration.

Finally, Iniziativa shared with Critica the cult of absolute freedom, welcoming colorful individuals with widely diverse ideological orientations. Truly emulating the free socialist spirit which had once existed in Italy, libertarians, revolutionaries, gradualists, collaborationists, and anticollaborationists joined the group. Unfettered by Critica's ideological rigor, this exhilarating atmosphere also characterized the first years of Saragat's new party but would contribute to the faction's eventual demise.[52]

Consistent with his libertarian ideals, Giuseppe Saragat presided over this constellation in a shadowy, indirect, but ever-present manner. Relying on the power of his ideas and the force of his personality rather than on bureaucratic structures, Saragat's leadership methods embodied both the fascination and weaknesses of the right and of the reformist tradition which had molded him. Skilled in compromise, with a philosopher's aura and at the height of his prestige, this born leader, "tall, elegant, courteous . . . measured," and his winning personality enchanted the Italian public, especially the newly enfranchised ladies of Rome's most chic neighborhoods. His clear and powerful defense of democracy and his courageous repudiation of the dictatorship of the proletariat commanded the attention of middle-class groups suspicious of growing communist prestige and swelled the ranks of PSIUP supporters.

Alleging that the PSIUP had been "colonized" by the PCI, Saragat viewed with alarm the real prospect of a socialist-communist cabinet, brought within reach by Nenni's plan for a tight Popular Front alliance for the next general elections. In power, such a coalition spelled the end of Italian democracy, Saragat believed, vowing to reenter exile if such an eventuality occurred. While Nenni toured the South capturing votes which apparently promised the leftist coalition a majority, Saragat planned to restore socialist "freedom of action."[53]

Obviously, any weakening of the socialist-communist unity pact as the result of a socialist split would have important international implications by clearly favoring the Americans. Not surprisingly, the left wing accused Saragat of taking American and Vatican money to split the Socialist party and branded him a traitor.[54] No convincing evidence, however, has surfaced demonstrating that the American government or the Vatican financed the split, although the Italian-American Labor Council, led by unionists Luigi Antonini and Vanni Montana, did send funds.

In delving into the question of possible American interference, I asked President Sandro Pertini's opinion. The president responded:

What is certain is that Saragat went to America, and when he came back he positioned himself for a split. I can't say what happened in America; I wasn't there. Rumors are rumors, and we didn't verify them. Nenni was convinced that he [Saragat] was influenced by the Americans for the schism, that our unionists in America pushed him. You know that they were there.

Here I interjected, "Antonini and Vanni Montana."

Yes, and that [Nenni believed] they convinced him [Saragat] by saying, "You will receive the means to constitute a party from us, but break away from Nenni because he is procommunist." . . .

No, he received funds to constitute the party. He [Saragat] did not deny it. Afterwards [Saragat said]: "They are comrades, and I received funds from these unionists." They pushed him, and he let himself [be pushed].[55]

The public record sheds some light on this issue. Antonini wrote that the Italian-American labor movement helped finance the Italian Socialists during the exile and war periods. After World War II, Nenni supposedly asked Antonini to help finance the party rather than the labor movement or the party newspaper because Togliatti had returned "with millions from Russia," and *Avanti!* "pulled its own weight."

Antonini continued sending tens of thousands of dollars to Nenni, the union leader claimed, despite unhappiness with Nenni's "marriage" to the Communists and the conviction among Italian-American workers that Nenni had become an enemy of "socialism and democracy." During a 1946 trip to Rome, Antonini testified, Nenni's representatives informed him that Italian-American funds would be denied to the "autonomists," despite Italian-American earmarking of their resources for an independent Italian socialist movement "not subordinated to the Communist party."

Since that time, Antonini protested, the left wing had outrageously charged Italian-American labor "potentates" and "Wall Street" with financing the split, an insult to all Italian-American workers. Antonini calculated that thirty-eight thousand dollars contributed by Italian-Americans remained unspent in Socialist party coffers and demanded that it either be returned or turned over to Saragat.[56]

The Antonini group in New York had contributed money to the Italian Socialist party for years, making no secret of their deeply rooted reformist socialist preferences or of their anticommunism. The figures cited, however, illustrate the small sums which that movement could generate and which left-wing Socialists looked down on once they could count on more generous aid from their communist allies. The American government did not significantly aid anticommunist groups until the 1948 elections, and it seems unlikely that contributions ever matched the CIA-estimated fifty million dollars that the USSR sent to the PCI, part of which went to its PSIUP allies.[57]

Thus, the evidence hardly justifies the charges of betrayal which the socialist left wing so freely circulated against Saragat, further exacerbating relations with the right wing. The ideological genesis of the schism and the events leading to it confirm its Italian roots and development.

The 25th Congress and Palazzo Barberini

Caught unaware by the Directorate's call for an early congress, the right found itself quickly steamrollered by Basso's machine during the precongress deliberations. According to Saragat's supporters, the left, "supported by external forces," ruthlessly imposed their ideas and personnel at the preparatory meetings for the Rome congress scheduled for January 1947. Irregular application of rules and regulations, arbitrary behavior, intervention of nonsocialist elements in the deliberations, and moral and physical pressure amounting to "terror" reversed the majority of the Florence congress despite the crushing November 1946 electoral defeat into which the left had led the party. So charged Matteo Matteotti in his request for invalidation of the Rome congress.[58]

By December 1946, the climate within the party had become so oppressive for the right-wing groups that they decided to form their own party. If the right remained in the party after the congress, Faravelli explained to Vanni Montana, it would do so as "helots subjected to Nenni's planned 'iron discipline.'" If it won at Rome, the "fusionist" left planned to dismantle individually the groups composing the right wing, Faravelli reported, destroying forever the possibility of constructing a real socialist party in Italy. By now, all major right-wing exponents agreed that only by leaving together could they found a viable party committed to their ideals. Consequently, the right accentuated its differences with the left and energetically refused all compromise in late 1946.[59]

In the meantime, Saragat began consultations necessary for the organization of a new party.[60]

Last-minute conciliation attempts occurred but encountered resistance on the right and Basso's sullen hostility on the left.[61] Unaccountably, Nenni remained unconvinced to the last that the schism would actually occur. Sandro Pertini made the most determined reconciliation attempt, hoping to repeat his success of the previous congress. Saragat should follow his hero Turati's example, Pertini pleaded; morally justified in splitting the party on a number of occasions and assured of a large following, Turati had never taken that step.[62]

Pertini told me sadly in October 1983: "They [the party leaders] said that there wouldn't be a split, but I was convinced that there would be one. So I worked to prevent it. I always believed that splits within the Socialist party damaged us . . . and ended by helping the reactionary classes, which hurt the workers' movement. This principle has always been important for me, and I still believe today that splits damage the workers' movement."

Pertini at least induced the right's token participation in the 25th Congress. Later, he attended the Palazzo Barberini assembly which created the new Social Democratic party, attempting to bring the secessionists back home. Saragat appealed to him, "Sandro, stay with us, your heart is here," but a dejected Pertini returned to the PSIUP congress.

Even at this point, Nenni did not take the rapidly unfolding events seriously. Incredibly, Pertini informed me: "Nenni took my visit to Palazzo Barberini lightly. He did not think that the schism would actually take place. He considered it a rebellion stemming from Saragat's temperament, given to attitudes of nervous irritation. [Nenni said,] 'The split won't happen.' "[63]

Instead, the delegates to the Rome congress (9–13 January 1947) proved uncompromising and unruly. They shouted down socialist heroine Angelica Balabanoff, who complained that the Socialists had succeeded where the police of the world had failed: they had prevented her from speaking.

The delegates then voted a motion embodying the left's desires—full communist collaboration, a "modern" party structure along Basso's lines, and prohibition of permanently organized factions. Capping their adoption of the Leninist model, the delegates named Basso political secretary to implement the new policy.[64] Finally, fearing that Saragat would appropriate the party's traditional title with all its prestige, they formally renamed their organization the Partito Socialista Italiano (PSI).

At Palazzo Barberini, the Partito Socialista dei Lavoratori Italiani took shape (PSLI, Italian Socialist Workers' Party, from a title the Socialist party had taken in 1893; in 1951 modified to PSDI, Italian Social Democratic Party).

Saragat's keynote speech blamed the "fusionist" party for stalling Italian socialism and renewed his devotion to liberty. Confident that the workers would flock to the new organization, Saragat stressed the PSLI's attractiveness for "middle-class" workers as well. He declared that Italians would not gamble their freedom for the Soviet experiment's false hopes.

In delineating the PSLI's physiognomy, Saragat explained his concept of party discipline as sacrifice and devotion to a common cause, not conformity. Conscience surpassed party loyalty. The same went for worker unity, which resulted from harmony and democracy, not coercion. Saragat distinguished between socialist and "social communist" conceptions of democracy. For Socialists, democracy meant participation by all party members in policy elaboration, not imposition of leader-determined policy by the apparatus. Anticipating important criticisms of his new party, Saragat argued that "middle-class workers" would never be in a majority, but even if this occurred, at least the PSLI would have prevented their capture by the right, as had happened in 1922. Answering another criticism, he said that if the PSLI became prevalently southern, it would claim the merit of forcefully bringing the neglected southern problem to the nation's conscience. Finally, Saragat did not close the door to the Communists but proposed a dialogue with them.[65]

Notable for its restatement of Saragat's major themes, the speech also reveals what would become the PSLI's fatal weaknesses. Saragat always welcomed middle-class elements, but he superficially dismissed the problem of middle-class domination. Whatever his ideological justification, workers seemed to interpret the split as sabotage of their accession to power, and the PSLI never achieved a working-class base. In March 1947 came a veiled admission of failure, and by 1949 Saragat advocated cooperation between the "worker aristocracy" and the middle class to achieve socialist democracy.[66]

At the Italian Labor Confederation's first congress (CGIL), scarcely five months after Palazzo Barberini, PSLI supporters combined with Republicans and independents received only 5 percent of the votes, compared with 52 percent for the PCI and 30 percent for the PSI. One year after the split, the PSLI's own figures showed workers composing only 37.8 percent of its membership, while white-collar workers, artisans, merchants, professionals, students, teachers, and industrialists accounted for 41.5 percent.[67] The practical absence of a working-class link condemned the PSLI to the political sterility which Leonida Bissolati's Reformist Socialist Party had already encountered after the 1912 split.

Reconciling effective democracy, individual liberty, economic security, Marxism, and efficiency proved impossible. If the socialist left-wing authoritarian attraction had proved fatal, the PSLI overreacted in the opposite direction. On the one hand, the PSLI adopted Faravelli's model for its basic structure, making coercion difficult; on the other hand, the party exhorted Italians to emulate English laborism, which the Italian masses had consistently rejected.[68]

It has been estimated that representatives of two hundred thousand PSIUP members participated in the Palazzo Berberini deliberations and that forty-seven deputies from the one-hundred-fifteen-member PSIUP delegation adhered to the PSLI, but the new party remained small, given a measure of power only by the delicately balanced Italian political system.[69]

As usual in socialist politics, in the clash between left and right, both lost. Unable to take off, Saragat's party remained a permanent splinter, incapable of independent action and uncomfortably attached to the DC. Furthermore, Saragat's exit had extremely deleterious effects on Italian socialism, as President Pertini confirmed to me during my long conversation with him in October 1983, stating:

> In my opinion, Saragat committed an error. Still today I insist that Saragat committed a grave error in the Palazzo Barberini split, one from which we still suffer. It was a grave error. . . . Afterward Nenni modified his attitude toward the PCI; in fact he enters the government. He enters a center-left government.

"But that happened after 1957," I said. Pertini responded:

> Yes, all right, but Saragat should have given it more time. His thesis *had* support in the Socialist party. It was in his own interest to remain in the party and uphold his thesis. He would have made converts, and he would not have remained in the minority; rather, Nenni would have maintained a majority, but Saragat would have had a following in the future. In fact, the center-left happened. *There* is the proof that Saragat should have had the patience to wait. Even today, I maintain that the split was a mistake.

I asked the president if he believed that the Socialist party would have remained the strongest party on the left if it had not split in 1947. He became suddenly animated and exclaimed:

> Ah, there isn't any doubt about it. . . . [Without these polemics] we would have had . . . a solid Italian Socialist party. A strong Socialist party which would not have renounced the October Revolution. Try to follow my reasoning. . . . [A party] which would not have been dominated by Soviet bolshevism, which would not have become the *servant* of bolshevism—no. We would have supported [the principles of], we would have been happy about, the October Revolution, agreed with the Soviet Communists when they merited agreement, criticized them when they deserved criticism, but . . . excuse me.

Our conversation had been interrupted by a call from Carla Pertini. The eighty-seven-year-old president tenderly responded to her but jocularly remarked that she did not approve of his having accepted the presidency of the Italian republic. He hung up the telephone and said to me, "You know that my wife has declared war on the Quirinale." Then he continued just as excited as he had been before:

> We would have kept the workers' movement united under the Socialist party's flag. We would have supported the October Revolution, which was a great historical event, but we would also have opposed the behavior of the Bolsheviks, when in the Soviet Union they conducted their persecutions and filled the jails. *Then* we would have supported civil rights.[70]

Reactions to the split among PSIUP leaders in 1947 ranged from Basso's exultance to Morandi's resignation,[71] but Pertini is correct in insisting that the division greatly damaged the main party, even down to the present.

Unlike the 1912 schism, with Saragat's exit and later desertions, the Socialist party lost its entire reformist contingent and with it the progressive nonworker electorate and personnel which the right wing had kept anchored to the party for more than fifty years. This loss proved a key factor in the party's decisive 1948 electoral defeat.[72]

Furthermore, the schism weakened the PSIUP and speeded the process by which the Socialist party became a communist satellite. Reflecting on this issue in 1977, Nenni singled out autonomy as "the immediate and principal victim of the schism" and identified the Communist and Christian Democratic parties as the major beneficiaries.[73]

Indeed, PSI recovery from the 1947 split began only ten years later, when Nenni went to Canossa and adopted Saragat's principles.

CHAPTER 5

The Popular Front

Contrary to Lelio Basso's intentions, the Palazzo Barberini split ushered in a long subservience to the Communists. As political secretary, Basso proved unable to implement fully his own program or to resist a communist campaign transforming the PSI into a de facto satellite. Without reformist restraining influence, the Socialist party pursued a suicidal policy which gravely damaged its own political stature and adversely affected the Italian republic's political system.

Trauma's Fruits

Basso minimized the schism's effects in an interview released immediately after the split. The secretary claimed that the right's defection had left the PSI's base practically intact and that the PSLI posed only a minimal threat to the organized socialist workers. Later Basso insisted that the PSI had made good its losses in several weeks.[1]

Reality contradicted this rosy interpretation. PSLI did not threaten its former comrades' position in the labor movement, but the Communists did. They exploited the bitter struggle between leaders who had remained loyal to the PSI and those who had joined Saragat's party.

The Socialists had mistakenly not pressed for congresses of the CGIL and the League of Cooperatives and Mutual Aid Societies at the beginning of 1946 when they had enjoyed superiority over the Communists. As the Socialists suffered a series of electoral defeats and waged fratricidal warfare later in the year, the Communists attacked. They mercilessly stoked up the fires of the socialist dispute while at the same time portraying Socialists as contentious dilettantes who neglected the workers and the cooperatives.

The communist campaign scored particularly among nonpoliticized workers anxious to raise their standard of living and cooperative managers preoccupied with increasing production. As a result of the sophisticated communist propaganda campaign, a dramatic reversal in the relative strengths of Socialists and Communists in the elected factory committees and other workers organizations occurred between June 1946 and 1948. The Communists then solicited congresses to legitimize their superiority. In June 1947, congresses of the CGIL and the League of Cooperatives and Mutual Aid Societies awarded the Communists an overwhelming 57 percent and 58 percent of the votes, respectively, while PSI representatives picked up only 22 percent and 25 percent.[2] The Socialists had become subordinate in the area they had pioneered.

Concentrating on limiting the damage done by the social democratic split, Lelio Basso could do little to contest these developments. Saragat had taken with him a third of the socialist parliamentary delegation, the party's grand old men, and the socialist youth movement. The party had also lost a significant proportion of its local leaders, leaving many federations leaderless and their members adrift.

The PSI had given Basso a mandate to restructure the party, and in May 1947, he created new party sections by combining previous territorial organizations with the NAS, instituted nuclei at the neighborhood and the apartment-complex level, and built an organization in the South. He also established regional offices to coordinate local party organizations and assigned two hundred young managers to the provinces to replace those who had defected.

Basso also hoped to strengthen the party's theoretical foundations by instituting a party school, rationalizing the PSI's cultural resources, and injecting new life into the Socialist Studies Institute in Milan. He also fostered discussion of socialist planning by encouraging a Socialist Economic Conference (Rome, November 1947). Finally, Basso strengthened *Avanti!* and the socialist press by a series of actions improving its financing and circulation.[3]

These efforts brought in eighty thousand new members by the end of 1947, allowing Basso to claim that the losses to the PSLI had been made good. Two other positive developments occurred during Basso's administration. The Socialist International Liaison Office recognized the PSI rather than the PSLI as official representative of the Italian proletariat, and the Action Party's most prestigious leaders joined the PSI rather than the PSLI upon the breakup of their organization. Since both Basso and Saragat had wooed them, this decision gave Saragat a black eye.[4]

These developments, however, proved marginal. Even if Socialists occasionally differed from Communists on important issues, the PSI tagged along after the PCI rather than forge its own policy. In short, the PSI no longer contributed to setting the national agenda, nor did it have a role on the cutting edge of Italian politics.

Furthermore, Basso and Nenni seriously misjudged the Italian and international political situations. These leaders loudly proclaimed socialist unavailability for participation in cabinets without the Communists, downplayed communist victories in the labor movement, and publicly congratulated the Czech Socialists for helping the Communists come to power. These policies stimulated serious opposition and persistent speculation that Pertini would replace Basso as secretary.[5]

In the Cold

Within the cold war context, socialist aping of communist policy produced disastrous results. In January 1947, De Gasperi visited the United States. Uninvited by the Americans was Foreign Minister Pietro Nenni, a spectacular but not surprising rebuff.

In fact, Nenni's and the PSI's hostility to the West increased as PSI-PCI relations tightened. Nenni advocated neutrality for Italy, but, he warned, he did not mean this policy as equidistance between the United States and Russia. Nenni blamed the Americans for current world tensions and asserted that the United States had entered an imperialistic phase comparable to Britain in the nineteenth century.

Attributing this phenomenon to industrial America's search for world markets to satisfy its production, Nenni claimed that imperialism could not even exist in a country ruled by the working class, such as the USSR. Nenni rebutted the common belief that the Red Army had imposed communism on Eastern Europe, argued that the "preconditions" for revolution there had existed before the Russian occupation, and denied that Lenin and Stalin had advocated revolutionary wars. For Nenni, therefore, socialist neutralism signified "Not equidistance but denunciation of the warmongers. State neutrality, not neutrality for our consciences."[6]

When in October 1947 the Russians established the Cominform, their polemical tone toward some Western socialist parties surprised the PSI, causing it initially to dissent from communist criticism of the British and French socialist parties. Nenni, however, quickly "corrected" this judgment, writing that whatever the merits of the British and the French, the Italians admired Russia in the same manner as nineteenth-century liberals looked up to France as the revolutionary fatherland.[7]

In February 1948 came the communist takeover of Czechoslovakia, which Nenni hailed as the victory of the working class and which elicited congratulatory telegrams to the Czech Socialists from Party Secretary Basso and Tullio Vecchietti, head of the PSI's International Office.

The Italian socialist behavior provoked an extremely negative reaction from British labor, which warned that parties condoning communist action in the central European country betrayed democratic socialist principles. In a meeting with Basso, Morandi, and Vecchietti, British Socialists were "brutally frank." According to the American ambassador to Rome, James Dunn, the Italians asserted that they allied with the Communists to oppose De Gasperi, not the Americans, that they considered the communist connection merely a tactic to rebuild socialist strength, and that they considered themselves "completely free" to enter cabinets without the Communists. The British scoffed at these claims, declaring their dissatisfaction with PSI answers to their objections.[8]

As a result, in March 1948, the Committee of International Socialist Conferences (COMISCO) approved a British motion requiring affirmative action from Italian and Polish Socialists reaffirming their commitment to democratic socialism. PSI refusal resulted in ostracism from the International Socialist movement and recognition of the PSLI as official COMISCO representative of the Italian proletariat.

Waning international socialist recognition symbolized the PSI's long journey into the cold. Requesting aid for Italian reconstruction from his American hosts during his January 1947 Washington trip, De Gasperi found the Export-Import Bank extremely reluctant to grant a one-hundred-million-dollar loan "because of our internal political situation, considered precarious." The Americans expressed unhappiness at the presence of the Communists and their socialist allies in the government.[9]

Returning to Rome, De Gasperi found a tangled political situation. The Socialists had split, and Saragat had resigned as president of the Constiuent Assembly. Saragat's followers in the cabinet appeared ready to emulate him. More importantly, Nenni had declared his own intention to resign.

In his memoirs, Nenni appears convinced of American pressure on De Gasperi to exploit the socialist split and expel Socialists and Communists from the government. By resigning, Nenni hoped to prevent De Gasperi from causing the cabinet's fall on his own terms and utilizing the PSLI to shift the governmental axis to the right.[10] In his public judgment of the crisis, Nenni wrote that reactionary forces aimed at driving the Socialists into taking illegal action but had succeeded only in strengthening the tripartite governmental formula.[11]

Nenni had only postponed the inevitable. The leftist parties obtained fewer important posts in the new, short-lived De Gasperi cabinet. As the economic situation deteriorated, the Christian Democrats blamed escalating leftist attacks on the Americans, who supplied the food and raw materials ensuring Italy's survival.[12]

The weakening socialist position in the country damaged the PSI at the cabinet level and in the Constituent Assembly. Here, for example, the Socialists exercised less influence in the drafting of the new Italian constitution than their representation warranted. By November 1946, they made petulant objections to DC use of "small" majorities to pass their proposals.[13] On the other hand, the Socialists followed the communist lead too closely. Their loyalty, however, hardly prevented their allies from ignoring their wishes. Despite strong PSI condemnation of "a grave offense to the principle of liberty," the PCI successfully combined with the DC to include the Lateran Pacts in the new constitution.[14]

For all the socialist talk of the new constitution as a "revolution," the Constituent Assembly merely did not exclude the possible evolution of Italy into a socialist state. This evolution, however, required substantial majorities in elections, which the left-wing parties mistakenly foresaw in 1947. As a result of the poor leftist performances during and after the Constituent Assembly, enabling legislation did not follow the progressive pronouncements of the Italian constitution, which lay dormant over the next thirty-five years, except where the courts haphazardly intervened.[15] For this outcome, socialist abdication to the Communists in the immediate postwar years bears a significant responsibility.

Birth of the Popular Front

Pushed by Nenni, Morandi, and Basso, ignoring reconciliation attempts by Saragat, the PSI sealed the communist alliance despite considerable rank-and-file opposition.[16] The resulting political instability contributed to the demise of the tripartite governing formula which had uneasily united Christian Democrats, Communists, and Socialists.

Although the PSI and PCI subsequently discovered the reason for their "expulsion" from the governing coalition in De Gasperi's January 1946 trip to the United States, in May 1947 this exclusion did not appear significant. Heading toward general elections in which Communists and Socialists assumed they would win, both parties believed that they had already benefited from governmental participation and hoped to gain further political advantage for the general elections originally scheduled for 1947 by attacking the United States for interference in Italian internal affairs.

Without this conviction of certain victory, it is difficult to explain leftist behavior, especially in the sensitive foreign policy area. Palmiro Togliatti, for example, continually attacked the United States, reaching the height of bad taste in a famous article entitled "Ma come sono cretini!" ("How cretin they are!") rebutting American charges that the Communists planned a *putsch*. "Do you know why Togliatti, always in control of his nerves, loses his head on the subject of foreign affairs?" De Gasperi asked Nenni. Privately, the socialist leader agreed with the Christian Democratic leader.[17] The Socialists, however, did nothing to moderate communist behavior on this crucial issue but joined in.

In addition to foreign affairs, the rapidly escalating inflation exacerbated the inability of leftist parties and DC to work together and caused the cabinet's fall in April 1947. De Gasperi alleged a desire to enlarge the government's base.

Once more, Nenni misjudged the situation. He insisted first that De Gasperi's support in the country and the Constituent Assembly had evaporated and then summarily dismissed as impossible De Gasperi's intention to exclude both Communists and Social-ists from his next government. Finally, he mistakenly assessed De Gasperi's chances of obtaining a majority in the Constituent Assembly as very poor.[18] In a 31 May 1947 editorial, Nenni blamed the crisis on the absurd desire to exclude the Communists from power and accused De Gasperi of serving "internal and foreign reactionary forces." Assuming a failure of the new cabinet to win the Constituent Assembly's confidence, Nenni refused to join a government if the Communists did not participate.[19]

This attitude subordinating PSI governmental collaboration to PCI participation per-vaded the entire socialist left and caused it to draw mistaken conclusions from the crisis. A strangely complacent Basso, for example, predicted a clear electoral win for the leftist parties in the upcoming national elections.[20] Echoing the Nenni and Basso theses, the Morandi wing made similar optimistic assertions.[21]

More accurate in its assessment, the PSLI Directorate stated that the internal contra-dictions of the tripartite formula had finally consumed it. Blaming the erosion of popular unity on the lack of an independent and autonomous socialist policy, the PSLI warned that Italy faced a shift to the right. When the turn came, Saragat correctly attributed it to communist and "fusionist" socialist policies.[22]

In fact, the PSI's self-identification with the PCI conveniently allowed De Gasperi to exclude Socialists as well as Communists from his new governement. The new De Gasperi cabinet (May 1947) consisted of Christian Democrats, Liberals, and indepen-dents. The prime minister turned over economic policy to the prominent prewar economist Luigi Einaudi and the Liberals. By immediately implementing stringent deflationary measures, Einaudi weakened the working class and vetoed the left's financial program. The currency exchange, a progressive wealth tax, a special tax on war profits, and other leftist-supported measures went by the boards. Furthermore, Einaudi instituted a laissez-faire policy welcome to the industrialists. In short, Einaudi successfully restored to the middle classes their role as pillars of the democratic liberal state, receiving their strong support in return.[23]

This economic program drove Nenni and Morandi deeper into the communist embrace as the only salvation from the fresh "reactionary" campaign.[24] As a conse-quence, the Socialists initiated a drive for a Popular Front. Only this alliance could ensure structural and economic reforms, Nenni wrote, recalling that working-class unity had expelled the Nazis and had achieved a republic.[25] In July 1947, the PSI Directorate officially condemned the De Gasperi government and sanctioned a new popular unity with the Communists.[26]

Different socialist leaders had varying views of the communist alliance's new role. For example, Basso did not believe in communist leadership of the front, unrealistically conceived of the Socialist party as the "axis of a vast democratic deployment," and proclaimed in June 1947 that the PSI could meld all the nation's democratic forces and achieve a socialist government.[27]

Opposing him was Nenni. Nenni counted on Togliatti's and the powerful PCI's support, his Popular Front version's elegant simplicity, and his ability to represent the average party member's thinking, and he won out.

Nenni envisioned the Popular Front as an electoral cartel presenting an advanced social program to voters anxious to sweep it into power to implement structural reforms. Quite clearly derived from Nenni's experience with the French Popular Front of the 1930s, the most serious problem with this strategy resulted from the PSI's organizational weakness in relation to the PCI. Nenni hoped to neutralize this basic defect by making full use of his charismatic relationship with the crowd. Even admitting his oratorical prowess, this time Nenni overreached himself.

On this point, in October 1983, President Pertini commented to me, "Nenni used to pull slogans out of the hat and then go to bed at night happy because he had pulled slogans out of the hat." It has been suggested that Nenni advocated a unified voting list with the PCI in the upcoming national elections to prevent socialist votes from being counted, a move which allowed the Communists to concentrate their votes on their own candidates in the preferential balloting. Given their superior organization, they swamped the Socialists.

In the Directorate, Basso argued that Nenni's Popular Front issued from summit politics and agreements among the parties, while only a mass movement capable of rekindling the Resistance spirit could defeat the government. The "electoral cartel" Nenni wanted must result from a campaign liberating new energies, not precede it. In short, the party could cooperate with the Communists and assume a leadership position without creating a common electoral front, a thesis the PSI Directorate rejected. Unwilling to become "the leader of the anticommunist right," Basso forced a call for a new congress, scheduled for January 1948, but eventually acquiesced with Nenni.[28]

Also committed to mass action, Rodolfo Morandi objected to Basso's insistence on a premier socialist role in the communist alliance. Morandi accepted PSI organizational inferiority but evaded its implications by arguing that a vast popular movement would at once dilute the communist "militarist" structure and sweep the united left to power. Morandi based his conclusions on a number of popular rallies favoring the front and on the support of the communist leaders Pietro Secchia and Luigi Longo. Morandi, however, underestimated the iron discipline which rapidly brought his communist allies into line with PCI policy and overlooked the communist infiltrators into the PSI who strongly supported Nenni because Togliatti agreed with him. Morandi hoped to give the Popular Front a global and mass focus but failed. In the end, he contributed to the ultimate result of the front as a pact between unequal partners.[29]

Surprisingly enough, hostility to a close communist connection remained entrenched within the Socialist party after Saragat's defection. Influential leaders including Sandro Pertini, Giuseppe Romita, Riccardo Lombardi, and Ivan Matteo Lombardo and a significant portion of the rank and file had strong reservations about the front as conceived by Nenni and Morandi, especially their advocacy of a single electoral list.

This opposition did not find full expression in precongress discussion, however, because the right wing had been decimated and because of the war which the "ultra-fusionist" Oreste Lizzadri faction and the communist infiltrators waged on Basso. Basso reacted energetically to this challenge, but Nenni and Morandi intervened against him.[30]

Of the four leaders mentioned above, only Ivan Matteo Lombardo adamantly contested the whole idea of the front; the others recognized the futility of total opposition and emphasized the perils of implementation. They especially feared curtailment of socialist autonomy and the greater number of communist deputies which the PCI's efficient organization, proportional representation, and preferential voting would produce. As a result, the front's socialist doubters did not analyze the alliance but debated whether to present a single electoral slate with the Communists or separate ones.

In fact, on 28 December 1947, Communists and Socialists officially constituted the "Popular Front for Work, Peace, and Liberty," thus presenting the delegates preparing to meet at the Astoria Theater in Rome in January with a fait accompli. The decision the delegates had to take endorsing a single list with the Communists, Nenni wrote in his diary, "is hard for many comrades."[31]

At the January congress, opponents of separate lists made such a strong case that the two sides tied, and Basso emerged as the balance of power. Basso remained vague until the outspoken Pertini forcefully drew him out. He then weakly accepted a single slate with the Communists as the front's "logical consequence." Later he claimed that the Directorate had made acceptance of a unified list a question of confidence.

Nenni forcefully argued for the front but privately admitted that he could have been less adamant about demanding a unified slate if he had not been convinced that the opposition masked a residual rightist position within the PSI.[32]

Although most delegates agreed on the general principle of a Popular Front, about one-third cast ballots against a single list with the PCI.[33] This result is all the more significant considering that the Communists actively intervened in this congress, using "well-organized agitprop groups" to sabotage speakers opposing their viewpoint and threatening to renege on their promise to pay for the meeting's expenses if the socialist representatives failed to adopt a motion satisfactory to them.[34] Soon after the meeting, Lombardo and Romita would leave the party, rendering the PSI helpless to resist the PCI.

The congress left the chief moderate leader unhappy. In my interview with him amid the calm and softly ringing chimes of his eighteenth-century study in the Quirinale Palace, Sandro Pertini judged his old comrade Nenni and the decision the congress had taken very harshly:

> I spoke very firmly, making this point: "You support the unity-of-action pact with the Communists. By presenting a single slate with the Communist party you are renouncing socialist tradition and the Socialist party's function, and we will suffer defeat. No, not the Communist party, because the Communists are so well disciplined and well organized that they will gain at our expense." And it's true, they did gain at our expense.
>
> "You say you want unity, but in this manner you are saying that Saragat was right. Saragat split from us . . . saying, 'Nenni wants fusion with the Communist party. . . .' You justify the Palazzo Barberini schism because the Social Democrats will have a perfect opening and will say, 'Today a single slate, tomorrow a single group in the chamber, because you will have to form a single group with the Communists, the day after tomorrow, one party. That's why we were right when we split . . . from the Socialist party.'
>
> "You are providing grist for Saragat's mill, and then this will happen: You know that I have always been for unity of the working *movement,* which is different from unity of the two parties, . . . in order not to strengthen the bourgeoisie and Italian capitalism and not to provide grist for the Christian democratic mill. But beware, the Socialist party will be defeated. Once defeated, you will blame the Communists. By blaming the Communists, you will break the unity of the working class."
>
> And in fact that's what happened.

Responding to my question asking why he campaigned for the Popular Front, Pertini answered, "It's clear that when one is in the middle of a fight one must forget disagreements. Either I withdraw from the struggle, or if I fight, I fight."

Pertini told me with conviction several times that while Nenni was a great journalist he made a poor politician. He also insisted to me that the Communists fooled Nenni, giving me his view of Nenni's behavior during this period:

Nenni deluded himself because of our rallies, . . . I was pretty good at them and listened to. The piazzas filled to overflowing when we spoke. *I know why they overflowed.* It was the Communists who filled the piazzas. They had all the interest in the world to provide an audience for the Socialists.

Nenni used to come back from the rallies deluding himself. That's why he was a bad politician: "We won't have enough comrades to fill all the government positions." He was convinced that he would be president of the Council of Ministers and would form [inaudible] a socialistic government. Also his rallies overflowed, for example, in Milan, organized by the Communists, who went en masse to listen to Nenni, Pertini, and the others.[35]

Pertini's assessment of Nenni during this period appears substantially correct. Full of arrogant references to his own success as an orator, Nenni's diary reveals even more serious political faults. He quotes the results of a number of local elections as being victories of the "popular bloc" without noting that the socialist share of the vote declined continually and unproportionally in comparison to that of the Communists.[36]

Now Nenni and Morandi had persuaded the PSI to adopt the same losing tactics on the national level for the crucial 1948 general elections and provoked a disaster from which the party would not soon recover.

The 1948 Elections

The PSI's adoption of a common slate confirmed communist domination of the Popular Democratic Front. Lacking financial and other resources, their own electorate confusing PSI and PCI candidates, the Socialists abdicated to the Communists.[37] This situation gave the Communists a free hand and created domestic and international difficulties prompting the front's defeat and a socialist collapse.

Despite socialist claims to lead the front,[38] the PSI adopted PCI attitudes. Nenni himself rationalized this policy by writing that the Communists represented the working-class advance guard as the maximalists had done in 1919.[39] Nenni also reinforced this unconscious inferiority by interpreting past and current Italian socioeconomic conditions in a Leninist vein. The failure of workers, peasants, and revolutionary intellectuals to unite had sabotaged the post–World War I revolutionary situation, but their cooperation now made victory inevitable. This new "class alliance" implied that the front transcended electoral politics and had become a permanent feature of the Italian left.[40]

Similar attitudes on foreign policy confirmed socialist subjection to communist views. Nenni reiterated socialist neutrality, conceived as hostility to the United States and fawning approval of the Soviet Union. Citing the keen interest which the upcoming Italian general elections aroused in worldwide "conservative" circles, Nenni defiantly denounced Italian inclusion in a Western bloc. In a nationwide radio broadcast, he warned that Italy faced a new war if it joined a Western military alliance. He objected to Italian participation in bloc politics, which would "lower our people to the rank of a foreign legion." In conclusion, he strenuously objected to American manipulation of economic aid to slant internal politics.[41]

Flanking Nenni, the socialist press conducted a venomous propaganda campaign against the United States. Italians no longer regarded Americans with goodwill, asserted one writer, because Americans staunchly supported Italian reactionary groups.[42] Particularly stung by Italian-Americans writing to their relatives urging them not to vote for the "Reds," the Socialists branded Generoso Pope, editor of New York's *Il Progresso Italo-Americano,* as Mussolini's "greatest friend."[43] An increasingly strident *Avanti!* portrayed the United States as "racist, monopolist, [and] imperialist" and stated that "Marshall is like Mussolini."[44]

Alarmed by these attitudes, the American ambassador in Rome viewed "with great concern the strong position of the Communists created by their victory over the anti-Nenni PSI forces." Estimating the front's share of the votes in the upcoming general elections at 40 percent, the embassy judged the Italian situation "extremely dangerous."

According to the embassy, "unlimited funds" available to the Communists, control of the labor movement, uncontested assertions that American aid would not be cut off even if the front won, and constant leftist harping on the inevitability of Italian involvement in a fresh war because of De Gasperi's pro-West foreign policy all favored the front.

Revulsion against communist totalitarianism worked against the front, but the ambassador believed that communist manipulation of the socialist "Trojan horse" might neutralize that fear. Luckily, most Italians appreciated American aid and preferred the West to the East, but this feeling alone hardly sufficed to guarantee the front's defeat and would have to be supplemented by more vigorous action. To counteract leftist propaganda discrediting De Gasperi's conduct of foreign affairs, the ambassador recommended coupling continued civilian and military aid with a strong statement expressing doubt that "a communist-controlled Italy subserviently assimilated into the Soviet orbit would in any way be willing to participate in ERP or be eligible for U.S. aid which is predicated upon the maintenance of true democracy and cooperation with other democracies toward general European recovery."[45]

Italy's pivotal strategic location provoked even more drastic American action. Stung by intelligence reports indicating the possibility of a communist takeover in Italy, the National Security Council (NSC) in November 1947 had recommended interruption in the rate of American troop withdrawals if the Communists took power anywhere in Italy before December 15. Aware of massive Russian aid to the PCI—Ambassador Dunn reported a communist electoral budget of three billion lire in the three northern industrial provinces alone—and convinced that the Communists harbored insurrectionary designs, Secretary of Defense James Forrestal, supported by President Truman, decided on clandestine action.

Fitting within the Truman Doctrine's general framework, Italy became the major theater of American intervention. The NSC authorized CIA operations in Italy and delegated to the director of Central Intelligence responsibility for enforcing compatibility of antileftist psychological warfare with American foreign policy.

An interim Special Procedures Group initiated operations in Italy until the Office of Policy Coordination could create a permanent structure. Ten million dollars secretly found its way from the Economic Stabilization Fund into a fund for Italian local campaigns, bribes, and anticommunist activities. At the same time, the government stimulated the letter-writing campaign by Italian-Americans, and Truman threatened to reduce aid if the front won.

These initiatives produced immediate results, the CIA reporting that the "political trend in Italy has been reversed by effective Western support of the anticommunist parties."[46] Former CIA Director William Colby called the Italian operation the agency's biggest until then or since and stated that it became a model for other countries, including Chile in 1973.[47]

Perfunctorily using American interference as an electoral issue, the front had little idea of its true effectiveness. Only a week before the balloting, Nenni claimed to have neutralized both the Americans and the Christian democratic campaign, based on scare tactics. Blinded by his new Leninist rose-colored glasses, Nenni triumphantly announced the continuing viability of the worker-peasant-revolutionary-intellectual alliance. Nenni believed that the front's prospects for winning the elections ranged "from the certainty of a plurality to the possibility of an absolute majority."[48] It is difficult to understand how Nenni could have been so mistaken, even though Pertini had warned him.

In my interview with Pertini, the president described his first contacts with Nenni after the election: "I came home after the defeat, and Carla says to me—Carla's my wife—'Look, Nenni has already called you five or six times, he wants to talk to you.'"

Leaning toward me, his eyes alive as if the incident had occurred yesterday, he exclaimed: "'Ah,' I say, 'I'm not going to that man who has brought ruin upon the Socialist party!' *Stia nella sua acqua, nuoti nella sua acqua e lasci che io nuoti nella mia!*"

After this explosion, he went on in a more subdued tone:

"No," she rightly says, "you will cease being a politician. Eh, until proven otherwise, he is the secretary of the Socialist party. You must hear him. Go there, argue with him, but go." So, listening to my wife, I went.

I found him *sbragato* in an armchair. "OOH," he says, "you were right, you were right. There's nothing to be done with the Communists."

"*See!* I told you at the Astoria [the last congress], and now it's come true! I told you: 'We will suffer defeat, and, after the defeat, you will take an anticommunist position.'" I said exactly that, addressing Nenni, who was behind me at the Astoria. And in fact I found him *sbragato,* all like this [and here, carried away by the part, Pertini imitated Nenni sticking out his stomach] with his belly sticking out. "You were right. There's nothing to be done with the Communists."

"See that I was right when I told you at the Astoria that you would have reached this conclusion. It's not true that there is nothing to be done with the Communists. There is *this* to be done with the Communists: that we must not suffer from an inferiority complex. *They* wanted the schism in '21, and we must remind them that they were the ones who split the working class, breaking away at Leghorn in '21, not us, *them!*

"We must remember this, but we must keep communications open. We must try to get the Communists to revise their position. Let them try to leave the Soviet bolshevik beehive and insert themselves into the beehive of the Italian working and socialist class. We must try to help the Communists"—I was hung up with this—"and maintain Italian working-class unity despite our differences with the Communist party; otherwise we will bring grist to the Christian democratic mill. Don't you understand that De Gasperi is following a politically conservative Italo-American and Atlantic policy?"[49]

Nenni had ample reason for lamentation. Not only had the front gone down to defeat, but within it the Socialists had collapsed. The Popular Democratic Front received only 31 percent of the vote to the Christian Democrats' 48.4 percent, which the Italian electoral system transmuted into an absolute majority in the Chamber of Deputies.

Within the front, communist organization and preference voting for their own candidates had made the Socialists the big losers, giving the PCI its long-sought hegemony over the Italian left. The PCI obtained 141 seats in the Chamber of Deputies compared to 104 in the Constituent Assembly, while PSI representation dropped from 115 to 42. As nearly as could be calculated, total PSI share of the vote declined to 10 percent, less than half that of the PSIUP in 1946. The elections had transformed the PSI into a second-class party.

Which factors explain this outcome? Most importantly, Nenni's policy of socialist participation in a communist-dominated Popular Front doomed the PSI. By renouncing the still-robust autonomous socialist political ideas and space, Nenni and Morandi suffocated socialist initiative and *brio* to follow Moscow-dictated PCI domestic and foreign policy initiatives. While the front claimed to champion democracy, Italians identified communism and Russia with the totalitarianism under which they had recently suffered. The supposed lack of voter maturity and Christian democratic propaganda on which the Socialists blamed their defeat are hardly convincing. Instead of dissociating themselves from Russian policy—for example, Czechoslovakia—PSI leaders supported it, confirming voter fears and further debasing the party's image.

Socialist policy thus backfired. It provoked the U.S. government to use its full power against the PSI on the grounds that the party had become a communist satellite. Italians also considered Marshall Plan aid necessary to their survival and understood that it would be lost if the front won, not only because of American threats but because the communist states had rejected it.

The Nenni-Morandi policy also produced a serious backlash within the socialist movement. Large numbers of party workers and voters disapproved of the single slate with the Communists. These persons did not bolt from the party, but neither did they work hard for it.

Furthermore, many voters cast ballots for splinter socialist groups fighting for autonomy from the Communists. ''Unità dei Socialisti'' (US), a coalition of these groups headed by Ivan Matteo Lombardo, joined with the PSLI and benefited from this trend. In an amazing showing, US won 7.1 percent of the votes (33 seats) in 1948, equal to one-third of the PSIUP ballots in the 2 June 1946 elections. US did especially well among northern workers.

This result highlighted the front's poor showing in the North and its relativly good performance in the South, the reverse of predicted. Appropriately enough, the front's socialist opponents interpreted this development as proof that the sophisticated and progressive northern voters had rejected front politics, which instead had appealed to the more politically backward South.

Finally, close socialist-communist collaboration had concentrated anticommunist votes on the DC, the major bulwark against a communist takeover, instead of being fractured among the smaller right-wing parties. This development decimated the Uomo Qualunque, the Monarchists, and the Neo-Fascists. In addition to picking up frightened conservative and reactionary voters, a considerable number of disgruntled socialist voters also flocked to the DC. Although these votes did not remain with the DC when the communist specter receded, they contributed significantly to a victory which ushered in five years of undisputed catholic superiority during the critical postwar recovery period; and they ensured the failure of Nenni's policy.[50]

Despite his despair following the election and an understanding that the PCI had settled for hegemony over the Italian left rather than make a credible bid for power by loosening their Moscow ties,[51] Nenni, Morandi and Basso defended and preserved the communist connection. They publicly attributed the front's defeat to American intervention, DC religious charlatanism, and electoral fraud.

The 1948 elections had heightened the need to defend democracy and thus to maintain the front, stated Nenni's *Avanti!* When he got his wind back, Nenni wrote that the front had been primarily designed to break the left's isolation, and he claimed to have achieved this aim despite electoral failure. The Morandi wing dismissed the electoral results, proclaiming, "We did not make a mistake," because only a strengthened front could combat the privileged classes.[52]

Predictably enough, however, the dismal electoral results stimulated demands for a new congress.[53] In preparation for the 27th Congress in Genoa on 27 June 1948, a "center" group led by Sandro Pertini, Riccardo Lombardi, Alberto Jacometti, and Giovanni Pieraccini obtained a plurality.

Calling itself "Riscossa Socialista" ("Socialist Comeback"), this coalition urged socialist autonomy within the communist alliance. Somewhat equivocally, Riscossa criticized the Cominform's policies but expressed confidence in the USSR, rejected all collaboration with the DC a priori, and protested the PSI's ostracism from Western social democratic international organizations. Riscossa, however, strongly rejected a "Leninist" conception of the PSI.

Most significantly, Riscossa refused to ally with the Giuseppe Romita faction within the PSI because it would have terminated PCI collaboration. Had Riscossa and Romita allied, a powerful new group commanding two-thirds of the vote and creating the premise for a reunification with Saragat would have come into being.

Unfortunately, Riscossa's lack of clear ideas and its inability to attract any of the party's major leaders (Lombardi had been in the party for only a year) account for Riscossa's inability to lead firmly at this crucial time. Winning only a weak plurality at the 27th Congress, Riscossa lost control soon thereafter to Nenni and Morandi, who reaffirmed their policies.

By their inadequate reaction to the 1948 political disaster, the Socialists missed their grand opportunity to liberate the PSI from the communist burden and prepared the ground for its further subjugation.[54]

The "Stalinist" Phase

Although Riscossa Socialista resembled the PSI left, its uneasiness with PCI tutelage, its moderate view of international politics, and its rejection of internal Leninism made it anathema to Nenni and Morandi.

Morandi had been especially shocked by the 1948 developments. Interpreting the 1948 elections and American interference as skirmishes within the larger cold war context, the Milanese leader dropped all differences and mutual recriminations between Socialists and Communists, including his own past criticisms of communist behavior. Because of the American threat, everything must be sacrificed to unity and maintenance of the Soviet myth.

Morandi imposed this view on the party by suffocating traditional socialist debate, enforcing a strict centralized authority, and transforming the PSI into a militaristic organization on the communist model.

Although he ultimately proved less dogmatic and more flexible than Morandi, Nenni during this period argued that an international capitalist "war party" incited by the United States had adopted Hitler's designs against the Soviet Union.[55] Nenni accordingly reinterpreted the PSI's role, viewing it as the leader in the creation of a powerful peace movement struggling alongside the PCI for the purpose of laying low this "war party." Accordingly, Nenni and Morandi renewed their coalition to overthrow the Riscossa faction.

Thus, when Riscossa attempted to translate its ideas into action, it encountered a stone wall of leftist opposition buttressed by the Communists.

Lombardi rejected Morandi's drastic international vision because he believed it mistaken and served to make the PSI an appendage of the PCI and the Cominform. As a result, in August 1948, the Riscossa-dominated Directorate formally dissolved the Popular Front but retained the unity pact. It also reaffirmed traditional socialist principles and promised a more independent socialist policy in the future.[56] In addition, the Directorate promised internal democracy and pledged to recuperate Socialists alienated by recent PSI policies.

Events, however, conspired against the Lombardi group. In March 1949, Italy joined NATO against fierce socialist opposition in the country and Parliament. During the same month, the COMISCO made good on a previous ultimatum to the PSI to cut the communist connection or be expelled. The PSLI proclaimed itself a "third force" between Communists and Catholics. On July 14, 1948, a right-wing student gravely wounded Togliatti, provoking a general strike and raising fears of a communist insurrection.[57]

The strike capped a period of communist-inspired labor agitation and split the CGIL. Catholics and Social Democrats formed their own labor unions, condemning the CGIL Socialists to a permanent minority position. Minister of the Interior Mario Scelba initiated harsh police repression which exacerbated social tensions.

Morandi and the left wing utilized these events and their influence over the PSI apparatus to make a comeback. By making use of resentment over the right wing's attraction to the "third force" and Ricossa's ideological confusion, the leftists successfully pressured the Directorate to call a new congress for May 1949.[58]

The inability of right and center to coalesce guaranteed the left's survival, but its communist allies' moral and financial aid allowed it to mount a winning offensive, Rome police officials reported. The Riscossa Directorate had not paid its workers for three months, and *Avanti!* would already have closed down if it had not been for contributions from *L'Unità*. The anticommunist Romita had been backed into a corner, police informants reported, and had organized a last stand at the congress.[59]

These events and the outcome of precongressional meetings favored a leftist victory. Morandi and Nenni captured 51 percent of the vote, the center received 39 percent, and the right 9.4 percent. This result caused Romita's exit and eventual merger with Saragat.

Having regained supremacy, the left now added a Stalinist internal structure to the PSI's pro-Moscow foreign policy.[60]

Morandi lieutenant Venerio Cattani readily accepted the label "orthodox Leninist" for his group and added, "For at least three or four years we were not Communists only for reasons of temperament and of organizational survival."

During this period, Socialists ignored reports of Stalinist brutalities emerging from the Soviet Union or provided a "revolutionary justification" for them. Speaking of this time, a former Action Party leader, Morandi exponent, and future PSI secretary—

Francesco De Martino—discerned in the PSI's failure to condemn Stalinism as the party's greatest failing of the 1948–53 years. In foreign policy, De Martino added, "we acritically accepted Soviet positions without realizing that the struggle for socialism did not necessarily coincide with loyalty to Soviet politics."[61]

In fact, Stalinism signified the primacy of Soviet international politics over internal issues. The new leftist Directorate adopted a pro-Soviet policy at its first meeting, vowing to campaign against the government, the church, and NATO. Noting this result, the Rome police chief commented that the party had "lost all possibility of conducting an autonomous policy . . . and that it will . . . transform the party into an appendage of the PCI."[62]

The point man in the socialist campaign against NATO and the government's pro-American policies, Pietro Nenni, wrote articles, organized mass demonstrations, promoted dialogues, demanded increased Eastern trade, and proposed nonaggression pacts. For him, the peace struggle superseded all others. Party members understood the peace struggle's true significance. Said socialist labor leader Vittorio Foa, "When Nenni adopted . . . the 'Struggle for Peace' policy, discussion ended. 'Struggle for Peace' signified alignment with Russian foreign policy . . . belief in the Red Army as a democratic instrument."[63] For Nenni during this period, "neutrality" signified working-class identification with the USSR as world socialist leader against world capitalism captained by the United States.[64] As a significant part of his activities, Nenni visited the East and published ecstatic articles about Soviet technical and social achievements.[65] His vast efforts earned him the Stalin Peace Prize in 1951.

Despite the one-sided nature of his activities during this period, Nenni retained his integrity. His position derived from pure sources: nostalgia and analogy with interwar antifascist coaliton politics, not rigid ideology.[66] Furthermore, Nenni carefully nurtured a dialogue with his political opponents. His political realism and the smoothness with which he could alter his course constituted his great strength. Completely opposite to Morandi in this regard, Nenni's flexibility permitted him to disengage from the Communists when he understood the front's detrimental effect on the PSI and the country.

Nenni's politics during the Popular Front period, however, had devastating and permanent effects on the socialist movement and cannot be condoned by heightening cold war tensions. The Americans and international aid agencies recognized the Italian privileged classes' opposition to reform and publicly criticized it. Had the PSI pursued an independent reform program instead of abdicating to communist leadership, it might have secured international Western support. By subordinating the Socialist party to the Communist, Nenni and Morandi not only disregarded one of Europe's most glorious socialist traditions but also justified thirty-five years of Christian democratic hegemony by depriving Italy of a viable political alternative to Catholics or Communists.

Unable to attain its own goals, the left contributed to the defeat of other reform efforts. Socialists and Communists stimulated labor unrest whenever they could not achieve their aims, thus stiffening conservative resistance. Socialist and communist misuse of the labor movement justified conservative interpretation of any government reform effort as a capitulation to the extreme left. At the same time, Socialists and Communists denounced any reform as too little because they aimed at a complete alteration of the existing economic structure.[67] These tactics hampered rather than enhanced the chances of positive changes in Italy in the 1950s and beyond.

The republic would come, Socialist party founder Filippo Turati had predicted in

1893, but it would be the republic "of the monarchists, the reactionaries, the spec- ulators." Little did he suspect how much his heirs would contribute to that result.

The Dictatorship of the Apparatus

To the Stalinist face which the PSI presented to the world corresponded an internal Stalinism imposed by the new vice secretary for organizational affairs, Rodolfo Morandi. Intertwined international, domestic, doctrinal, and party considerations explain Morandi's policies between 1949 and his death in 1955.

Convinced of the inevitable decadence of capitalism, Morandi believed that the bourgeoisie planned to save itself by projecting the class struggle onto the international plane, producing dangerous crises such as the Korean War. According to Morandi, this international struggle had drastic domestic repercussions in all countries subject to Ameri- can influence.

In Morandi's judgment, police repression, censorship, civil liberty violations, layoffs and factory closings, shootings of workers and peasants, increasing church influence in education, threatened church excommunication of communist and socialist voters, and the proposed formation of an anticommunist bloc by the DC made a solid alliance of Italian working-class parties imperative. Given what he considered an emergency situation, Morandi deferred to the leadership of the USSR and its Italian representative, the PCI.

This objective required taming the unruly PSI. To achieve this end, Morandi pro- posed absolute leftist control of the party by means of an internal apparatus which would smoothly, efficiently, and unquestioningly carry out the Directorate's orders. This goal challenged the PSI's sixty-year tradition which in the end proved more robust than Morandi had bargained for.

The left had received only a bare majority of 51 percent at the 1949 Florence Congress but had attained it with Basso's grudging support. Now Basso objected to the subservience Morandi planned for the PSI. Basso had planned to assume an independent position at the congress, but "Probably on that occasion I proved to be a terrible tactician. I planned to present my own motion, leftist, but not favorable to the front, but then I let myself by convinced by Nenni to join the unified left."[68] Without Basso's half-hearted support, the left would not have won at Florence.

To the Nenni-Morandi coalition's uncertain showing at the congress corresponded a feebleness at the lower levels. Influential socialist rank-and-file elements passively but stubbornly resisted the communist alliance. This resistance movement lost its leaders with Saragat's exit in 1947, I. M. Lombardo's in 1948, and Romita's in 1949, but it survived in the local party organs and the unions, maintaining through the traditional party structure the capacity to sabotage Morandi's policies. According to one estimate, fully half of the local federations remained under autonomist control even after their leaders' expulsion or defection; even the left's own candidates for the party succession, the highly vaunted NAS, opposed close communist collaboration.[69]

By exploiting his position as vice secretary for organizational affairs and calling on communist support, however, Morandi crushed this resistance by creating a new apparat- us, adopting "democratic centralism," and modifying party structure. For his personnel, Morandi built on the base Basso had constructed during his tenure as party secretary.

Aiming at creating a party not equal to the PCI but subordinate to it, Morandi utilized

Basso's technical principles only to achieve effective control, not the new spirit of which Basso had dreamed. A host of politically reliable young managers of petit bourgeois extraction descended on local party affiliates, ostensibly to stimulate reorganization after the 1948 debacle but really to replace older leaders opposed to the PSI's new line. Financed by the Directorate, these managers traveled from place to place doing their work at the pleasure of PSI executive organs.

Morandi did not substantially alter the party's territorial organization or introduce a "cellular" structure on the communist model. Judging the PSI too ideologically "backward" for a cellular organization, Morandi contented himself with retaining the federations and sections while removing their initiative and autonomy. Beyond these methods, Morandi applied "functional articulation" and "capillarization."

Considering the PSI's electoral origins a grave defect, a determined Morandi wished to eliminate local socialist preoccupation with politics and abstract discussion, a prerequisite to the PSI's transformation into a modern "classist" mass organiation. In the future, deliberations and action had to have concrete, "practical" purposes and stress "efficiency."

No longer intended to coordinate local initiatives, the party regional organization had one overwhelming purpose: to transmit orders from the center to the periphery. The socialist founders' conception of the PSI as a free association of citizens deliberating among themselves and communicating their opinions to their executive organs now disappeared. If this "socialism in embryo" had exacted a price in the form of a gap between intentions and actions, Morandi spurred the PSI to the other extreme by mechanizing the chain of command.

Which structural alterations did the Morandi group implement to achieve their purpose, and to what extent did they succeed? At the top, the Organization Office and the Central Commission for Organization studied organizational problems, made suggestions, and monitored implementation.

Morandi's lieutenant Giusto Tolloy dismantled traditional socialist ideology, which identified federations and sections as the primary defenders of the rank and file. Both organizations suffered as the Morandi group expanded the rival NAS, assigned identical functions to both federation and section, restricted their role to implementing orders, shifted personnel, and created a well-defined hierarchy.

The federation now grouped sections according to *zone* or areas and named officials responsible for them. These area officials subdivided section members into street or farmhouse "nuclei," each with a leader. These leaders in turn subdivided their groups, controlled by yet another party official, the *collettore*. The NAS, "factory nuclei," entered into this scheme as factory subdivisions of the section. This "capillarization" of the party structure made the local organs unable to resist the center.

Neither expansion of the NAS role nor Basso's earlier theorization of their superiority saved the factory nuclei from a fate analagous to that of the federations and sections. As centers of autonomist resistance, they too lost their independence. In Morandi's conception, they merely facilitated the party's control of militant workers in the workplace itself. Politically subordinated to the section or the federation's labor office, they were manipulated by Morandi against the staunchly autonomist socialist labor leaders.

In 1950, both the PSI's Labor Office head, Elio Capodaglio, and CGIL Secretary Oreste Lizzadri complained about the socialist labor leaders' recalcitrance to PSI "Stalinization" and subordination to the Communists. Lizzadri estimated that fully 80 percent of the disputes which arose between Socialists and Communists originated in the labor movement and involved important matters of principle. Extremely angered by the hostility of the CGIL's socialist contingent to the Directorate's policies, Lizzadri proposed its liquidation. The PSI imposed "unified" slates with the Communists in elections for CGIL and Chamber of Labor offices and for factory internal commissions. Willingly lending their support, the Communists helped PSI leaders gradually replace autonomist cadres with new administrators sympathetic to the PCI.[70]

Besides these structural changes, the party simplified expulsion procedures for party members who disagreed with the Directorate's front policy. At the First National Organizational Conference, November 1950, Morandi defined this policy as "identity" with PCI policies.

The most prominent victim of this policy was Lelio Basso, unquestioningly devoted to "unity of action" but whose gadfly status irritated Morandi. Morandi inspired a campaign of personal abuse against Basso, forced his resignation from the Directorate and Central Committee, ostracized him from socialist politics, purged his followers, and initiated expulsion proceedings. Basso's office was broken into and his desk rifled. With few exceptions, his fellow socialist deputies stopped greeting him, and Morandi broke off relations until shortly before his death. Only Nenni's intervention prevented Basso's expulsion.

Having made this concession, Morandi, Lizzadri, and Tolloy won the Directorate's assent to the delegation to federation officers of the right to initiate expulsion proceedings against party members guilty of public acts or declarations "prejudicing" party policies.[71] This procedure gave the apparatus de facto power to expel its opponents and capped off the climate of ideological terrorism.

These developments reflected the polarized Italian political system of the cold war period. The Christian Democrats headed a constellation of smaller governmental parties which included the Liberals, Republicans, and Social Democrats, whose "Third Force" conception of a political organization capable of challenging Communists and Catholics had failed. Paralleling this dominant "centrist" governmental coalition, the PCI ruled over a powerful leftist opposition enormously strengthened by Communist hegemony over the PSI.

The Communist party exercised control over the PSI through infiltrators, financial contributions, and technical assistance. Most important, however, was the allegiance of Morandi, who deferred to communist cold war leadership, and Nenni, who distrusted the PSI's ability to survive without powerful allies. In addition, a number of influential leaders secretly held dual PSI-PCI membership; Carmine Mancinelli, Lizzadri's close collaborator, and Francesco De Martino, future PSI secretary, are two influential leaders allegedly in this category.[72]

Morandi's new apparatus amply repaid the investment of communist resources in the PSI. By transforming its former rival into an auxiliary party, the PCI neutralized opposition within the PSI and reduced socialist competition in the leftist labor movement to a minimum. By means of the PSI, the PCI also extended a de facto influence over those militant noncommunist labor forces and electorate attracted to socialism but opposed to communism. An apparently monolithic PSI anchored this support to the communist-dominated left, preventing further leakage of votes to the social democratic groupings, which had proven their appeal to workers in the 1948 elections. In short, during this period, the PSI served communist, not socialist, ends.[73]

What other effects did the "Morandian revolution" produce? Not many from the standpoint of new members. Cutting through the exaggerated claims of PSI leaders, membership increased only by about fifty thousand from 1949 to 1953, rising to three hundred fifty thousand.

Furthermore, the data demonstrate that the *apparatchiks* increased at a far more rapid clip than either the membership or local organizations. For example, while the NAS hardly doubled in four years, the Collettori tripled in two years, reflecting the party's intensive bureaucratization.

Socialist subordination to the Communists prevented the NAS and PSI unionists from making significant inroads in the factories. As a result, workers joined either communist, social democratic or catholic labor organizations. Reflecting this serious situation, the increase in socialist activity and membership occurred in the Center, South, and the Islands, while the more traditional socialist strongholds in the northern industrial areas languished.

In all the Italian regions, the Communists increased their support at socialist expense. Even in the South, where the Socialists strengthened themselves while Saragat and other Social Democrats lost ground, socialist gains hardly compared with the impressive communist advances.[74] By impeding autonomous socialist expression and advocating communist leadership of the left, Morandi consolidated the PSI's new second-class status. But Morandi acknowledged just before his death that he had failed in creating an iron-willed "front" party.[75]

Grafting "democratic centralism" onto the traditional PSI structure proved futile and crucially damaged the PSI's image and psychology. In the opinion of foreigners ignorant of PSI history, the Socialists became "fellow travelers," a continuing stigma very useful for Italian conservatives, as Nenni discovered when he began disengaging from the Communists. During the Popular Front, socialist leaders squandered the reservoir of goodwill earned by the PSI over a sixty-year period.

The Popular Front also implanted a permanent inferiority complex within socialist militants, accomplished by continuous denigration of socialist tradition, participation in communist-led mass organizations, and the PSI's second-class auxiliary status. The PSI would finally reacquire its independence after a long struggle, but the Popular Front's scars remained visible long afterward. The Popular Front phase of the PSI's history thus spelled disaster for the party. "Surely. Ten lost years, as many as necessary to get out of it."[76]

CHAPTER 6

Pietro Nenni's Realignment

Given socialist tradition, the PSI's transformation into an auxiliary PCI organization could be neither complete nor permanent so long as democracy survived in Italy. Resistance to communist domination continued underground despite the exit of autonomist leaders, blocking Morandi's attempt to transform the PSI into a completely reliable front organization.

The cold war had subordinated the PSI to the PCI, and in the 1950s international trends reversed this development. International tensions eased following Dwight Eisenhower's election as President of the United States in 1952. And the increased confidence of the Soviet Union after its development of the hydrogen bomb in 1953 undermined unquestioning socialist fidelity to the Communists; the proletarian fatherland seemed safe from an imminent assault by the West.

Aided by the lessening of world tensions and cracks in the Soviet system made obvious by riots in East Germany and Poland, and the Hungarian Revolution, Nenni cautiously modified the PSI's Popular Front commitment. By substituting the communist connection with a catholic one, by reunifying Socialists and Social Democrats, and by constructing a great Socialist party to rival both PCI and DC, Nenni reasoned, the Socialists could set the national reform agenda and move Italy leftward.

Nenni alone could head such a bold operation because, as his leftist opponent Oreste Lizzadri correctly stated, "The fact is that no leader, perhaps not even De Gasperi or Togliatti, personified their party as Nenni personified the PSI from the Saragat schism to the 1956 turn after Pralognan . . . and the Hungarian events."

Now Nenni aimed at the great social democratic dream which had been Saragat's but which Nenni himself had destroyed in 1948.

Italy in the 1950s

Economics set the tone for Nenni's realignment of the PSI. Although the 1950s are considered as establishing the basis for the Italian "economic miracle," gravely unbalanced progress characterized that and later decades.

Italy was still overwhelmingly agricultural, with 40 percent of the population living off the countryside, and rational land reform should have been the country's first priority. In fact, the Communist and Socialist parties agitated the countryside in a determined push for land reform, and the government struck back. In an interview with me, socialist leader Mauro Ferri recalled the struggles of his youth on the land: "In that period, the prefects and the carabinieri were openly at the landowners' service, arresting union leaders. At that time, militancy in the Socialist party was really a very difficult choice."[1]

Opposition by the landowners' association (Confagricoltura) stalled land reform until American Marshall Plan administrators pressured the government to act and peasants began seizing land in parts of the South. Unable to pass a coherent law because of effective landowner resistance, the cabinet pushed through part of the legislation (*stralcio* law) in October 1950 and quietly abandoned the remainder of the bill.

Many weaknesses outweighed the positive effects of government-mandated land redistribution. The legislation affected limited areas of the country: the Sila (Calabria), the Tuscan Maremma, Sardinia, and certain areas of the Po delta and the southern mainland. Landowners retained their best holdings and received excellent compensation for marginal land. Officials distributed "expropriated" land by lot, ineffective land reform agencies provoked hostility because of their ties to the Christian democratic patronage network, and division of the land into small plots ensured inefficient farming.

Furthermore, the government had assumed permanent rural overpopulation and created tiny farms. After 1959, this assumption proved fallacious as the industrializing North drew peasants off the land. Finally, while the unhappy peasants continued to vote for the extreme left, resentful landowners reinforced the right-wing Monarchists and MSI (Neo-Fascists). Nenni viewed these results as the fruits of half-measures.

Mixed success also characterized other government measures during this period. The Cassa per il Mezzogiorno (Fund for Southern Italy) aimed at creating a southern industrial and commercial infrastructure by spending twelve hundred billion lire over ten years and by providing low-interest loans and tax benefits. Despite undoubted successes, political considerations and corruption diminished the fund's effectiveness. Using the fund as an excuse, traditional cabinet departments reduced their spending in the South. Most important, however, the fund favored the North by stimulating demand for heavy machinery and other equipment needed to modernize the economy, while failing to create a skilled labor force in the South. Furthermore, the government did not provide sufficient incentives to pull new industries southward.

To its credit, however, the government did shake up the traditionally narrow Italian industrialist mentality by utilizing the large proportion of the Italian economy under state control, particularly IRI (Istituto per la Ricostruzione Industriale) and by joining international agencies such as the ECSC (European Coal and Steel Community), which spurred competition. Aided by low wages depressed further by high unemployment and a curb on unions, Italian industry responded by increasing efficiency and production. From 1950 to 1955, the Italian gross national product increased at an annual rate of between 5 and 6 percent.

Workers in the most advanced industries enjoyed increases in real wages, but unemployment remained high and salaries low in the artisan, retail, and agricultural sectors. The unemployment rate during the early 1950s has been estimated at 10 percent, braked only by a vigorous and partially successful emigration policy, and underemployment could not be measured. The hard-money policies of liberal and right-wing Christian democratic economic ministers worsened matters. According to an American scholar, "The result was that during the 1950's the gap between the two Italys was enlarged, rather than diminished."[2]

Political unrest resulted from this economic imbalance. Linked with Interior Minister Mario Scelba's name, the early 1950s have remained synonymous with repression. Special police squads ruthlessly crushed the slightest antigovernment manifestation. Scelba ordered political parties out of the factories, prohibiting meetings and the affixing of posters. In Milan, the protests culminated in a general strike during which socialist leader Riccardo Lombardi led demonstrators against army units occupying Piazza del Duomo. In December 1954, this time as prime minister, Scelba instituted stringent measures to block "security risks" from penetrating central and local administrations. Requiring no special legislation and bureaucratically enforced, this action outraged not only Marxists but also moderate civil rights advocates such as Gaetano Salvemini and Piero Calamandrei.[3]

On the positive side, this repression kept alive the spirits of Socialists who justified the PSI's existence by its participation in "impetuous, and at times heroic, struggles."[4]

"We Are the Third Party"

Even during the bleak period of communist domination, the PSI's independent spirit survived, stimulated by government repression and the electoral contests which the Socialists periodically faced.

Between 1951 and June 1953, a series of local and general elections confirmed Christian democratic inability to repeat the 1948 victory. Alarmed by leftist gains in the 1951 local elections, Alcide De Gasperi proposed measures which alienated large sectors of the Italian electorate and provided the Socialists with an emotional issue allowing the PSI to bring itself forcefully to the nation's attention, recapture its dignity, and embark on the long road to independence.

In the hope of containing expected losses in the next general elections, Christian democratic leaders presented the "electoral bonus" plan. This scheme would have teamed up "related," or allied, parties on the same electoral list. The alliance achieving 50.01 percent of the votes for the Chamber of Deputies would receive two-thirds of the seats. In this manner, the DC would have retained its majority in the Chamber while losing it in the country. Supported by the minor parties hoping to increase their parliamentary representation, the DC defended its proposal as the only way to ensure political stability.

The electoral bonus touched off a major political crisis. Marxists and moderate leftists denounced the proposals, but the PSI appealed to its tradition and assumed a leading role in the opposition. According to the Socialists, history demonstrated that only universal suffrage combined with proportional representation could guarantee the right of different interest groups to express their opinions according to their effective support in the nation. PSI leaders compared their struggle against the electoral bonus to their heroic fight against the infamous "Acerbo law" which had emasculated the Italian electoral system in 1924 and guaranteed fascism's final victory. The PSI branded as "criminal gangs" any association which sought alteration of proportional representation in order to distort universal suffrage.[5] Under Nenni's leadership, in February 1952, the PSI Central Committee officially adopted this theme, stating that Italian reactionary movements moved against democracy by first destroying proportional representation.[6]

While placing his party in the forefront of this principled national struggle, Nenni also remained politically flexibile. Meeting with De Gasperi at the Viminale Palace in March 1952, Nenni forcefully stressed the importance the PSI attached to proportional representation. Blaming DC conservatives for the drive to mutilate the electoral system, Nenni warned the prime minister that he flirted with civil war and dictatorship. Convinced that De Gasperi in his heart supported proportional representation but had doubts about its democratic value, Nenni pitched his argument to its continuing positive influence on the Italian state.

Then Nenni made a startling offer to prove socialist good faith. If De Gasperi would commit himself not to tamper with the representational system, the Socialists would present their own electoral slate independent of the Communists for the 1953 general elections. According to Nenni, if the DC persisted in its hostile attitude toward the left, the Catholic party would become a prisoner of an ever more rabid right. The left did not threaten democracy, Nenni maintained; in fact, in recognition of this truth, the smaller rightist groupings had pulled out of the electoral coalition they had formed with the DC in 1948.

De Gasperi failed to grasp the significance of the socialist leader's offer. For the first time since the PSI's subordination to the PCI, Nenni acted to reestablish socialist autonomy. Instead of acknowledging this qualitative shift and encouraging it, De Gasperi simply answered, "Agreement with you is possible and desirable; with Togliatti it is impossible." Convinced of Togliatti's dictatorial aspirations, De Gasperi would not hear of anyone associated with the communist secretary coming close to the center of power.

Nenni vainly objected that his new policy superseded personalities. De Gasperi believed that Togliatti would always remain "two hand-lengths" ahead of the Socialists on any road they should choose if the communist leader believed the policy would bring him to power.[7]

Nenni's desire for an independent PSI slate demonstrated more than his devotion to proportional representation. Primarily responsible for the PSI's predicament as a communist satellite, he had initiated a long and complicated process which would lead to socialist autonomy from the PCI.

Reduced to minor-party status by the 1948 elections, only proportional representation could ensure the PSI's survival when the party declared its independence from the PCI. In order to recoup socialist fortunes and restore movement to the Italian political system, Nenni offered the DC an opportunity to reverse its traditional policy and reach an understanding with the PSI instead of extending its ties with the right. Nenni based his calculations on the strong DC left wing unhappy with current catholic politics. Unfortunately for the PSI, Nenni's past policies made influential groups suspicious of him as a communist "Trojan horse"; this fear made it possible for the DC right wing to combat his new line, while the Marxist left accused him of betrayal.

Always sensitive to changes in the political situation, Nenni gambled on the decline of De Gasperi's "centrism." In fact, increasingly bitter divisions within the DC, President Harry Truman's firing of General Douglas MacArthur, interpreted by Italians as a lessening of cold war tensions, insistent Vatican demands to block the left at any cost, the last-ditch electoral bonus itself—all produced tensions which would soon destroy the "centrist" coalition which had emerged from the 1948 elections.

At the same time, the PSI edged toward its own political space without immediately severing the communist connection. The 1951 local elections produced gratifying results despite PSI subordination to PCI goals. Contemporaneously, Nenni sought and received encouragement for his new course from leading industrialists, including Fiat's influential Vittorio Valletta and publisher Angelo Rizzoli, both with important international connections. Even the dean of Italian journalism, Mario Missiroli, assumed a friendly attitude toward Nenni.[8]

The First Steps

Within the PSI, Nenni had been patiently preparing the groundwork for his new policy for a year. The 29th PSI Congress initiated a dialogue with the government majority

(Bologna, 17–20 January 1951). If the government would raise the nation's standard of living through investments and economic development, undertake important industrial and agrarian reforms, nationalize industrial monopolies, and present enabling legislation to implement the constitution's guarantee of civil rights, the PSI would pledge its full support.

At the same time, however, the delegates scuttled all possibility of agreement by insisting on Italian denunciation of NATO. Under Nenni's goading, the Central Committee periodically renewed the offer throughout 1951, becoming more flexible as the year progressed on everything but NATO, which remained a serious obstacle into the 1960s. On domestic issues, the PSI sought government recognition of common problems and the opportunity to demonstrate its reasonableness.

Nenni tied this internal "detente" to objective conditions rooted in Italian and international reality. Given the existing international equilibrium and excluding a suicidal appeal to violence, he recognized that the 1948 constitution represented the limits of Marxist influence on Italian society. Italian political forces had attained the same balance as had the superpowers. This stalemate had elevated tensions, making it imperative to defuse an exasperated situation "which risks a crisis of the entire society and its institutions." The PSI's new distensive policy thus corresponded to a new phase of the class struggle, no longer of "movement" but of "position."[9]

In May 1952, Nenni advocated an independent socialist slate allied but not subordinated to the Communists in the Rome city elections. He viewed this policy as the practical initiation of socialist disengagement from the Communists and as an opportunity for the voters to judge the PSI's new course and provide feedback.

Led by procommunist Oreste Lizzadri, the Rome Socialist Federation denounced Nenni's plan and demanded a united slate with the Communists. PCI Secretary Togliatti informed Nenni that local communist organizations insisted on a single slate. Nenni rejected Togliatti's arguments and proposed sounding out independent politicians for a slate including Socialists, Communists, and prominent moderate leaders. A reluctant Togliatti initially agreed, but PCI and communist-supported socialist federations continually presented obstacles. The Socialists found it necessary to fire off a note to Togliatti protesting communist behavior.

Nenni's determined efforts produced a slate headed by prefascist Prime Minister Francesco Saverio Nitti and including forty independent candidates, twenty Socialists, and twenty Communists. While not the solution Nenni had hoped for, this compromise slate attained a respectable showing and represented a small but important victory for Nenni's new policy.[10]

Nenni's Roman initiative had immediate effects in the opposing camp. Panicked by the prospect of the Holy City in leftist hands, Pope Pius XII encouraged Catholic Action leader Luigi Gedda's negotiations for a list embracing all conservative parties, including Neo-Fascists (MSI). Also ventilated publicly by Don Luigi Sturzo, elderly founder of the Popular Party, this idea encountered De Gasperi's disdain and touched off a crisis within the DC.[11] The DC's contradictory reaction illustrated what would become Nenni's major problem in the future. The PSI could regain its own freedom of action, but the DC could not decide whether to further the dialogue.

This issue faced the Socialists squarely during the May 1952 local elections. DC support receded from its 1948 levels as voter perception of the "communist threat" declined. Pushed by Gedda, the DC right wing clamored for an agreement with the

Monarchists, and perhaps the Neo-Fascists, in order to maintain the catholic edge. The DC's small center coalition allies, especially the PSDI and the Republican party (PRI), resisted.

Thus, the real question mark of the 1952 elections concerned monarchist and neo-fascist performance. Would they emerge strengthened, especially in their southern strong-holds? De Gasperi himself lamented that the recent incomplete agrarian reforms had alienated the landowners and strengthened the Monarchists without achieving increased peasant support for the DC; in the meantime, the Trieste issue bolstered the Neo-Fascists. An increase in monarchist and MSI votes would influence the DC's future attitude by strengthening its right wing. Nenni understood the DC dilemma very well. The right wing aimed at a "clerical-agrarian-fascist" conjunction, while the "center-left" current was "not prejudicially closed toward a more radical democratic experience."

The 1952 elections furthered socialist independence from the Communists. PSI strategy centered on electoral alliances with "popular" forces in towns with populations under ten thousand, while the party presented independent slates in cities of over ten thousand. Claiming that the electoral law discriminated against smaller parties in the latter category, the PSI carefully balanced its action by sanctioning alliances with the PCI. But the Socialists delicately diluted communist influence by endorsing alliances with Social Democrats, Republicans, and Liberals and by joining unified slates headed by prominent lay and democratic leaders.

Despite a numerical socialist increase in the 1952 elections, Nenni radiated pessi-mism after the contest. The results confirmed the DC fall from majority status, but most of the left's gains went to the Communists. In some cities, the PSI percentage approached that of 1946, but in others PSI performance lagged. Worse still, the monarchist and fascist right dominated the elections by attracting large crowds to hear fascist war heroes Rodolfo Graziani and Valerio Junio Borghese and by making significant gains in the South. Scissored by an upswing of right and left forces in the country, the burden on PSI and DC moderates increased. Furthermore, the DC embarrassed Nenni by downplaying economic reforms and demanding a clamorous socialist break with the Communists and a PSI pledge to support NATO as conditions for an alliance.[12]

At the same time, Nenni discovered that he was too far ahead of his own party. In talks with Milanese Socialist party leaders, the Central Committee, and the Directorate, Nenni failed to spark a political debate. "Nothing doing," he wrote in his diary. Dead-ened by the prevailing conformism, the party's executive organs routinely approved Nenni's statements without discussion but without understanding their import. The party's automatic attachment to maximalist Marxist formulas cut the PSI off from Italian realities. Only a dramatic electoral victory or a serious Christian democratic overture could gal-vanize the party, Nenni mused, but neither was forthcoming. More importantly, the Socialists had no interlocutor within the DC with whom to initiate a dialogue.[13]

In his own memoirs, leftist socialist leader Oreste Lizzadri provides a startingly different version of these events. At the June 1952 Central Committee cited by Nenni above, Lizzadri recalls, Nenni presented his new political course as merely a continuation of the old one—"The elaboration of workers' unity and of the unity-of-action pact." Morandi immediately grasped Nenni's meaning and warned him against exploiting any policy as a lever against "working-class unity." This lever, Morandi believed, would immediately "bend in his [Nenni's] hand like tin."

This incident illustrates a major problem within the PSI. As Mauro Ferri emphasized in my interview with him, Morandi, not Nenni, had real control of the party through his domination of the apparatus.[14]

Contrary to Nenni's recollections, the left clearly understood his plan to open a dialogue with the Christian Democrats but decided to avoid a crisis of the PSI leadership by not dissenting openly. Weakened by the recent death of one of their most esteemed members, Luigi Cacciatore, and by the transfer of Lizzadri to head the CGIL, the leftists chose prudence. They resisted Nenni from their entrenched base in the apparatus. Lizzadri, who favored an open battle against Nenni, viewed the June 1952 Central Committee meeting as the beginning of a war between the "Nenniani and Morandiani."[15] The dispute never leaked into official party documents, because, loyal to "democratic centralism," the Central Committee unanimously continued to agree on official PSI positions as if nothing had happened. Ironically, leftist discipline favored Nenni's new course.

Besides continuously approving Nenni's initiative, this cover allowed the secretary's followers to carry the struggle into the leftist-dominated party apparatus.

The observant Italian police registered signals heralding autonomist revival as early as 1950. In June of that year, for example, a police official monitoring the CGIL reported a PSI attempt at "disengagement from the PCI's political positions." At year's end, the Bologna Prefect detailed a struggle between Nenni and Basso over substitution of the PSI provincial secretary because Nenni "apparently intends to adopt a PSI policy tending . . . toward a certain autonomy from the PCI."

In 1952, the undercover battle heated up. Several Venetian Federation members circulated a memo arguing that PSI dependence on the PCI accounted for lack of socialist electoral success and ventilating establishment of a new socialist party. In Lucca, a confidential source sent the prefect a copy of a motion which opponents of the unity pact intended to introduce at the upcoming PSI congress. In December 1952, Bologna autonomists demanded publication in *Avanti!* of their motion obligating the PSI to present voting slates independently of the PCI in the next general elections. Riccardo Lombardi discreetly supported this rebellion until Morandi crushed the revolt.[16]

While the struggle raged at the local level, Nenni concentrated on the grand strategy he loved. The PSI offer of detente to the DC remained valid because it had already won significant support among the people, Nenni asserted in June 1952. If not, the DC would have quickly buried it. Noting the DC's decision to press for the electoral bonus, Nenni shifted his focus from an understanding among party leaders to creation of a mass movement in favor of his new course. Counting on his charisma, Nenni hoped to rally his own party and prevent the DC from turning to the right for support.[17]

Nenni's emphasis on a mass alliance rather than an entente between political parties appealed to Morandi, who long ago had theorized collaboration between socialist and catholic masses. Given Morandi's concern with the cold war, Nenni sought a compromise between Italy's rigid "atlanticism" and Morandi's pro-Soviet orientation. Nenni redefined his previous concept of "neutrality" to mean not moral approbation of the USSR but Italian equidistance between Eastern and Western blocs, to be endorsed by the United States and the Soviet Union. During his trip to Moscow in July 1952 to accept the Stalin Peace Prize, Nenni personally illustrated his plan to Stalin, but the Russian leader rejected the idea and proposed instead a nonaggression pact between Rome and Moscow.[18] This attitude illustrated Stalin's unchanged hope to detach Italy from NATO.

The Italian and international press denounced Nenni's attempts to revise Italian foreign policy and confirmed this issue as a serious obstacle to Nenni's new course.[19] As late as the 1960s, Nenni's sympathy for the Russians prompted distrustful American diplomats to sabotage a socialist-DC alliance, while the socialist leader's progressively more flexible attitude toward the Atlantic alliance earned him the enmity of the PSI left wing.

The 30th Congress

On 22 October 1952, Nenni informed Togliatti of his intention to seek the PSI's 30th Congress's approval of separate socialist slates in all the country's electoral districts in the June 1953 general elections. The press reported stiff opposition from Morandi, which Nenni denied.[20]

Furious debate over the electoral bonus—effectively baptized by the left as the "swindle law"—dominated Italian political life at the end of 1952. Attempting to block the law's passage, the left obstructed parliamentary proceedings and stimulated general strikes in the country. These efforts proved futile, and the bill squeaked by.[21]

Held in Milan from 8 to 11 January 1953 in the midst of this fury, the 30th Congress attracted little press attention, despite its importance. At this assembly, Nenni launched one of his more effective slogans, spelled out in a huge banner dominating the entire stage: "ALTERNATIVA SOCIALISTA."

"Socialist Alternative" signified socialist political cooperation with the DC as an alternative to the present centrist majority, which Nenni denounced as clerical and conservative. He identified Saragat's Social Democrats as the pivotal mediators in this process of dialogue with the Christian Democrats.

Concretely, Nenni explained, Alternativa Socialista must be based on immediate implementation of the Italian constitution's political and economic provisions, that is, adoption of enabling legislation guaranteeing civil rights, liquidation of large landholdings, and nationalization of industrial monopolies. In foreign policy, the Socialist Alternative meant disengagement from alliances and neutrality. With regard to communist relationships, the Socialist Alternative dictated separate PSI slates in all electoral districts in the upcoming general elections.

In short, Nenni aimed at an alliance of all democrats who believed in social progress and peace and cautiously excluded the PCI from this category.[22] Within the party organization, Nenni's "autonomists" reinforced their presence on the Directorate.

The press's failure to react enthusiastically to Nenni's initiative bitterly disappointed the socialist leader. "If Morandi had contested it [Socialist Alternative], or if I had torn the vote from the congress with my teeth, . . . the bourgeois press would have made me a hero," Nenni wrote in his diary. But how could the country trust the endorsement of party workers who did not discuss issues but who automatically voted for their leaders' proposals? On the other hand, once debate within the PSI began, Nenni's conservative opponents in other parties would argue that the PSI would not follow him.[23]

Controlled by these opponents, the press organs of Nenni's intended allies reacted suspiciously. For the catholic *Il Popolo* and the governmental *Il Messaggero,* the PSI's promise of electoral slates independent from the PCI did not outweigh the negative aspects of Nenni's alternative.[24]

Nenni's desire to give away as little as possible at the beginning of negotiations is comprehensible, but it is nonetheless difficult to understand how he could seriously expect the DC to accept as a negotiating position the denunciation of NATO, neutralism, the expropriation of large landholdings, and the nationalization of large industries, even if left-wing catholic currents sympathized with these measures. A combination of factors probably explain Nenni's position during this period. Nenni knew that he must move with extreme caution if he hoped to disengage from the Communists while maintaining socialist unity. If the Socialists entered a new alliance with the DC, they must do so on the strongest possible terms.

This necessary caution aroused suspicion among Nenni's intended allies. For example, in a report to the Ministry of the Interior, the Milan Prefect interpreted the socialist congress's endorsement of separate voting slates as a pure and simple tactical expedient to increase socialist votes and not as a change in political orientation. The prefect cynically attributed to Nenni's demagogic skill a statement by the general secretary that he would denounce the unity pact if the Communists initiated any antidemocratic adventures. In an amazingly illogical tour de force, the prefect informed the minister that Nenni really aimed at weakening autonomists within the PSI, wooing dissident Social Democrats, and increasing PSI votes at PSDI expense.[25] This mentality pervaded not only the bureaucracy but also the country's highest political levels, at which similar arguments would be heard into the 1960s.

Nenni's inability to move quickly without causing distress within the PSI lent credence to the "Trojan horse for communism" argument. For instance, in an address to the Central Committee after the 30th Congress, Nenni had to counterbalance his friendly overtures to the DC and the PSDI by strongly reaffirming his demands for Italian neutrality and by lauding the Socialists' special relationship with the Communists, "which nothing in this electoral campaign will damage."[26]

Even at this early date, however, Nenni privately indicated his goal of breaking with the Communists. An American journalist instrumental in the coming of the center-left in the early 1960s, Leo J. Wollemborg, confirmed Nenni's conviction. Just before the elections, in a May 1953 conversation, Nenni gave Wollemborg the "distinct feeling" that he was moving away from the Communists. Tremendous difficulties faced the socialist leader, Wollemborg told me. Wollemborg believes that while Nenni alone could not have made the break, "without Nenni it could not be done."

In response to my inquiry about Nenni's reasons for distancing himself from the Communists, Wollemborg revealed the complexity of Nenni's political thinking.

According to Wollemborg, in the late 1940s, Nenni considered the Soviet Union the paramount power in Europe. Nenni's devotion to working-class unity and his certainty that in Italy the Communists would take power even before the Soviets arrived spurred him to ally with the Communists. In the early 1950s, however, Nenni noted that the end of the wartime alliance had resulted in permanent communist and socialist expulsion from Western European governments. In Italy, Wollemborg recalled, not only had the Popular Front lost, but the Communists had "screwed" the Socialists, assigning them fewer deputies than their vote total warranted. "That is the kind of lesson that is not lost on a smart politician like Nenni," Wollemborg pointed out.

By the early 1950s, Nenni understood that important objectives of the PSI and large segments of the government parties converged. The Social Democrats could not long oppose the PSI's transformation into a more reasonable organization, despite the loss of status they would suffer as the only "leftist" representatives in the government. Furthermore, seduced by socialist advances, the DC would paralyze its own conservatives and "unload" the governmental coalition's right wing, the Liberal party, moving leftward to broaden its national consensus. "As things worked out," Wollemborg commented wryly, "Nenni worked under some delusions."[27]

Sympathetic to Nenni's objective, Wollemborg followed up his interview with the socialist leader by explaining the rapidly evolving Italian political situation to American Embassy representatives in Rome, State Department officials, and the American public.

In the *Washington Post* and the *Boston Post*, Wollemborg wrote that although Nenni had been a loyal communist ally, Italians still considered him an authentic "Italian" party head—unlike Togliatti—because he personified the vigorous prewar anticommunist Italian socialist tradition. Freely admitting Nenni's past negative aspects, Wollemborg concluded that the socialist leader harbored no revolutionary designs and, at any rate, suggested reasonable safeguards in working with him. Convinced of the genuine nature of Nenni's policy reversal, the journalist argued that even De Gasperi appreciated the damage the PCI would suffer if Nenni successfully inserted the socialist-inspired working class into the governmental coalition.

Such an operation undoubtedly would have had incalculable beneficial results for the entire Italian political system. Given the rapidly dwindling governmental majority, a socialist alliance would strengthen the government, allow De Gasperi to keep his unruly DC at bay, and broaden the base of Italian democracy. At the same time, the alliance would greatly increase Nenni's prestige and independence from the Communists. Most important for Wollemborg, the Italian political context would become dynamic and reformist and would overcome the exasperating "immobilism" of the past years, thus avoiding an inevitable explosion.[28]

For future American champions, this would be the most powerful argument in favor of the center-left. "Operation Nenni" had begun.

The 1953 Elections

In his articles, Wollemborg strongly objected to Nenni's corollary to his Socialist Alternative, a resounding centrist defeat in the upcoming elections as the prerequisite for a socialist alliance. The journalist mused: would not such a loss spur the DC to seek out the Monarchists and Neo-Fascists as allies?

Events proved Wollemborg correct: the DC preferred to open to the right if it could, progressive catholic currents notwithstanding. If the centrist coalition held up well in the elections, there would be no incentive for a leftist coalition, but if it did not, would DC elements advocating an understanding with the Monarchists, and perhaps the Neo-Fascists, win out? Behind the scenes, Clare Boothe Luce, the new American ambassador, strongly favored a monarchist rather than a socialist entente.

Alcide De Gasperi became the first major casualty of this situation. An honest and sincere politician, he allowed himself to be dragged into championing the "swindle law." This position opened him to leftist charges of plotting clerical totalitarianism—"Demochristian totalitarianism which, while formally different, in substance is the successor of fascist totalitarianism," wrote Lelio Basso in the typical rhetoric of the time.[29] In addition to Marxists, prominent Democrats denounced the "swindle law," and their opposition determined the measure's defeat.

The 1953 elections initiated a long spell of political instability by causing the crisis of centrism. The electoral bonus formula failed as the center parties missed their goal by about fifty-seven thousand votes (achieving 49.8 percent of the vote instead of the required 50.01 percent). Confirming the nation's suspicion, all governmental parties lost heavily, while all opposition parties, right and left, made significant gains.

On the right, the monarchist (PNM) vote increased from 2.8 percent to 6.9 percent; PCI and PSI percentages climbed to 22.6 percent and 12.8 percent, respectively. The DC had expected a drop, but the failure of catholic allies to pick up any of the lost votes caused great consternation. Unfortunately for Nenni, although the 1953 elections made the centrist coalition unstable, the results made both the "opening to the left" and the "opening to the right" viable alternatives and did not make a compelling case for the Socialist Alternative.

Beyond statistics, the 1953 general elections proved among the most significant in Italian history. DC mismanagement of the electoral bonus convinced many electors that the left had correctly characterized the measure. This same issue had produced serious splits in minor parties, most importantly on the PSDI left wing. Furthermore, the balmier international situation following Stalin's death and the separate PSI and PCI electoral slates liberated voters from the communist incubus and encouraged them to vote their consciences.

The small centrist parties underestimated these factors and campaigned on the threat of a communist takeover which had waned. The DC, however, shrewdly pitched its appeal to the right and there made up part of the support it lost on the noncommunist left. In the 1951–52 local elections, the catholic vote had declined by four million ballots with respect to 1948. In the 1953 general elections, the DC recuperated two million votes compared to the previous local elections. Compared to 1948, the DC contained its losses to about 17 percent; its small allies lost about one-third of their support.

Saragat's PSDI took the brunt of the centrist coalition's loss of votes to the left. Joined by Unità dei Socialisti (US) in 1948 and by Romita in 1951, this party could count on two million votes at that date. Immediately afterward, however, Saragat imposed close PSDI collaboration with the DC.

In a conversation with me, former PSI official Mauro Ferri argued that the PSDI leader adopted this position as the consequence of an "iron logic." Deprived of a plausible leftist policy by a powerful Communist party and its satellite Socialists, Saragat understood the danger Italian democracy faced and considered it his duty to ally with the Catholic party for stability's sake. Under those conditions, the PSDI could only be a subordinate ally of the DC. During the 1953 elections, held under the sign of the "swindle law," Ferri told me, "the Social Democrats were for us a favorite target because we attributed to them the coresponsibility for this law."[30] Hammered by this campaign, a third of the PSDI electorate took off in Nenni's direction.

Not all of these voters made it. Many were attracted to the intermediate UP and USI, the new groups formed by prestigious PSDI dissidents Tristano Codignola and Antonio Greppi, which, however, eventually found their way into the PSI.

Indeed, these intermediate socialist groups provided a way station for large numbers of potentially socialist voters still suspicious of the PSI's continuing communist connection. In all, Nenni's Socialist Alternative attracted four hundred thousand votes to the PSI, well below the number it might have gained if it had successfully convinced the voters that the PSI had become independent and willing to serve as the nucleus of a third force between PCI and DC.[31]

The 1953 elections thus ended the centrist stranglehold and, while disappointing socialist leaders, placed the PSI in a position to assume the political initiative. Italian politics had become fluid again.

The Door Ajar?

Given the novel situation produced by the 1953 elections, Giuseppe Saragat reacted immediately. The social democratic head met with Nenni, and, as Mauro Ferri told me the story, "already then the possibility of a rapprochement was sketched out." Saragat approached De Gasperi to sound Nenni out himself about the possibility of the PSI secretary's breaking with the Communists, but De Gasperi refused. De Gasperi's dauphin, Giulio Andreotti, wrote that this disagreement heralded the breakdown of PSDI-DC collaboration. Ferri confirmed: "In fact, Saragat contributed to bringing down De Gasperi's last cabinet, refusing to remain part of the government or of the majority."[32]

Nenni in the meantime mistakenly concluded that the electoral setback had transformed Saragat into the "paladin" of the opening to the left and that the Socialists had become "the arbiters of the new legislature." A talk with Togliatti at Nenni's country home also convinced the socialist leader that he had full communist support. "The Communists will push us to commit ourselves, rather than brake us," a happy Nenni noted.[33]

Under Saragat's continual urging, De Gasperi agreed to consult with PSI leaders, but only to shut the door. In a meeting with Nenni and Morandi on 6 July 1953, De Gasperi alleged foreign policy differences and continued communist links as the major obstacles to socialist participation in a cabinet. According to participant Andreotti, the socialist leaders clearly asserted that they would denounce NATO if they ever achieved a majority. On the communist issue, De Gasperi acknowledged recent socialist moves toward autonomy but alleged that the Sociaists lacked true independence, conceived as "internal disengagement from the totalitarian conceptions of the extreme left." In a calm rebuttal, Nenni argued that Italian conditions differed from those in Eastern Europe, where the Red Army had installed the Communists, and that the Italian Communists had evolved in a more democratic direction.

Nenni told De Gasperi that he considered the unity pact a "piece of paper," recognizing its importance only as a symbol of working-class unity. For De Gasperi, however, precisely this working-class unity made the PSI dangerous in the government, even if it denounced the pact. For De Gasperi, Socialists would always represent workers and Communists. Leaving the meeting convinced that De Gasperi's past made it impossible for the DC leader to head a new leftist-oriented coalition which the PSI general secretary considered imminent, Nenni left him to his fate.[34] *Avanti!* initiated an anti–De Gasperi campaign declaring the prime minister unfit to lead the opening to the left which alone could resolve the governmental crisis.[35]

Having once been prepared to abstain, the PSI thus joined Communists, Monarchists, and Neo-Fascists in voting against De Gasperi in the famous confidence vote of 28 July 1953, which ended the DC leader's long tenure in office.

Not surprisingly, Nenni interpreted this dramatic development positively, believing that he had dispensed with a DC flirt with the right. The Socialists joyously discerned in

De Gasperi's fall the counterpart of the left's exclusion from power in May 1947.[36] During the remaining months of 1953, however, the PSI discovered that De Gasperi's fall failed to bring a center-left coalition any closer. After De Gasperi's fall, President Luigi Einaudi encharged DC exponent Attilio Piccioni with forming a new cabinet.

During talks with Nenni, Piccioni begged for the opportunity to belie his right-wing reputation, completely undeserved, protested the DC leader. Nenni offered PSI abstention, which would ensure a Piccioni parliamentary majority if Piccioni met certain conditions. These included a general amnesty for persons arrested for political infractions during the past five years, formal abrogation of the "swindle law" and civil rights restrictions, the elemination of formal distinctions in the workplace, a pay increase for state workers, swift government intervention to stimulate national employment, and a campaign to decrease international tensions.[37] At the same time, the PCI announced abstention in the confidence vote if the PSI did, news which Nenni leaked to Piccioni.

Piccioni, however, stunned Nenni's spokesman by informing him that he planned a cabinet based on monarchist abstention. Asked whether he had considered the resistance this course would provoke both among leftist DC currents and the smaller DC allies, Piccioni snapped, "I thought about it, but that's nothing compared to the trouble I would have had in my party if I had presented my cabinet with the indirect support of Nenni, and even of Togliatti!"

What had happened? When Piccioni informed President Einaudi that agreement on a new cabinet had been reached on the basis of socialist abstention, a revolt of De Gasperi's followers and a general furor on the DC right had occurred. This uprising sabotaged the agreement. The communist connection continued to haunt the Socialists.[38]

Nenni reacted to these developments with impotent frustration. The communist connection had become a heavy liability. The Socialists wished to strengthen Italian democracy by bringing to it the consent and aid of the working classes and therefore had made requests for "simple" adjustments in Italian foreign and domestic policy. In fact, they no longer asked for denunciation of NATO but only attenuation of Italy's "atlanticist extremism" and a softening of the cold war. Indeed, the Italian Socialists anticipated a general European discussion on these issues, and debate had proceeded normally until it had degenerated because the Communists publicly announced their agreement.

The same course could be noted on domestic issues. No one objected to the PSI's conditions for supporting Piccioni until Togliatti assented. Such actions conferred control of Italian politics on the Communists, concluded an irritated Nenni—but he remained unwilling to dump the Communists to satisfy his detractors.[39]

Given their slight majority and the inability to agree on a dynamic government, the parties of the old center coalition formed a caretaker cabinet composed of technicians and headed by an exponent of the DC right wing, Giuseppe Pella. Interesting enough, Nenni and Pella got along, meeting frequently and engaging in frank discussions, which, however, did little to further socialist participation in ruling the country.[40]

Nenni attributed continued PSI exclusion from the governing coalition not to suspicion of the Socialists' communist ties but to the DC's stubborn refusal to accept the recent general election's verdict. The DC could choose to open either to the right or to the left, Nenni reasoned. By selecting the right, it would achieve only a slight parliamentary majority and court disaster in the country. If it wished stability, the DC must change its attitude toward the PSI and "the entire popular and working-class movement."

As a result, the Socialists emphasized their desire to collaborate with the Christian Democrats in a great common effort to solve Italy's social plagues. By stressing the "social content of the meeting between Socialists and Catholics, i.e., the concretization of 'the fundamental evangelical precept: feed the hungry, clothe the naked, offer employment and a house to those who do not possess them, etc,' " Nenni hoped to strike a responsive chord among the powerful Christian democratic purists who contested powerfully the economic interests for control of their party.[41]

In addition to the DC, Nenni lashed out at Saragat and the PSDI for hindering the center-left, despite their apparent support. Saragat's party had lost its original character and lent only lip service to PSI participation in the governing coalition, Nenni charged. Nenni also denounced Saragat's "vulgar" anticommunism.

In a meeting in Rome, I asked socialist historian and Nenni's former political counselor Giuseppe Tamburrano to explain Nenni's obstinate attachment to the Communists and his continued defense of them. Nenni's hope of "opening" to the Catholics while maintaining strong ties with the Communists, I stated, had a certain simplistic air. Tamburrano answered that in Nenni's experience, the Socialists and Communists always encountered defeat when divided but scored crucial political victories when united. According to Tamburrano, Nenni did not understand the different post–World War II world.[42]

Recalling his talks with Nenni during the period, Leo Wollemborg cited the conventional interpretation of why Saragat had continued doubts about PSI collaboration: his own influence in the government would be "cut down to size" with the entrance of a larger socialist party into the governing coalition.[43]

Mauro Ferri, however, denies this contention, insisting instead that, as always, Saragat made his choices according to higher principles: "Even then, even then, . . . his governmental choice was conditioned by his general political vision because it was still a very difficult period internationally. There was the problem of the EDC [European Defense Community], against which the left—Socialists included—conducted a very violent campaign, while the Social Democrats believed, along with the lay parties and the DC, that the EDC must be accepted."

According to Ferri, this overriding concern explains why Saragat entered a cabinet formed during this period by arch-conservative Mario Scelba, the violence of Nenni's attack, and why this early attempt at a center-left understanding came to nothing.[44]

In fact, Nenni vehemently objected to Saragat's "atlanticism," an issue which exploded, ironically, when Nenni had seriously altered PSI foreign policy. Despite unanimous opposition to the Western military alliance, Socialists no longer demanded denunciation of NATO but a different "articulation" of Italian foreign affairs. Nenni cited English Labourites and German and Scandinavian Social Democrats to bolster his point. Concretely, he opposed German rearmament, favored Chinese communist entry into the United Nations, and rejected new American military bases on Italian soil. In domestic affairs, Nenni deemphasized nationalizations.

This increased socialist flexibility failed to overcome entrenched moderate distrust of the PSI as a communist "tool." The Socialists maintained myriad organizational and emotional links with the PCI, Nenni continued praising the Communists, and Togliatti endorsed Nenni's new policies.[45]

"Neo-Centrism"

The continued strong communist connection helped sabotage this first attempt at an opening to the left but had not yet yielded its most bitter fruits.

Encharged to replace Pella as prime minister, new leftist DC leader Amintore Fanfani consulted with Nenni and Morandi, who both judged him unimpressive.[46] The dispirited Socialists again offered their abstention if Fanfani would break with the DC's conservative economic forces and open to the masses.[47] Fanfani refused, courting the right wing instead. In the end, he failed to secure a parliamentary majority.

Unable to resolve the unclear political situation produced by the 1953 elections, the DC resurrected the old centrist coalition in a cabinet headed by Mario Scelba, the left's bête noir. Saragat shocked the Socialists by joining the government as vice premier.

Interpreting this result as a slap in the face of the entire left, the Socialists bitterly campaigned against this "SS" (Scelba-Saragat) government. With several key posts reserved for Social Democrats, this cabinet distinguished itself by its attention to social reforms. On the political plane, however, Scelba equated PSI and PCI and slammed the door against any "opening" in favor of the "totalitarian" Socialists.[48]

Cultural Reorientations

If the opening to left encountered insuperable political obstacles at this stage, the opposite occurred in the cultural arena. Here Nenni's new course caused debate, despair, or hope, but especially ferment. The PSI's outstretched hand determined the parameters of political discussion and the national agenda. For a decade, the media argued the "socialist question" and the effects PSI participation in the ruling coalition would have on the nation.

Curiously enough, within the PSI, Nenni's opening raised fewer hackles in 1953 than it did later. In his diary, Nenni constantly cites Morandi's encouragement. "Unity with the catholic workers," Morandi supposedly gasped on his deathbed before turning to the future leaders of the anti-Nenni left wing, Tullio Vecchietti and Aldo Valori, and ordering, "Rally 'round Comrade Nenni." More consistent with the Milanese leader's Hamlet-like fears about the opening to the left, however, were his final words: "Beware, Comrade Nenni, of the dangers."[49]

The defects in his world vision had become clear to Morandi by 1953, and questions had crept in. As we have seen, Morandi had suppressed his own trenchant criticisms of communism because of the supposed imminence of a new world war between "imperialism" and "socialism." Because of this view, Morandi had abdicated to the Communists, but then international events developed in a different direction. World tensions relaxed as the Korean War ended, as the big powers confabulated at summit conferences, and as the specter of war retreated. Furthermore, following a long line of distinguished Marxists, Morandi watched the supposedly imminent capitalist economic collapse flower into a broad-based boom in the West and an "economic miracle" in Italy.

In short, given his own doubts and Nenni's growing appeal, Morandi could not simply veto the new course. Furthermore, his own creation of a professional party bureaucracy had produced considerable "party patriotism" and resentment against communist domination. Given his interest in uniting with the catholic masses, theorized years before, the opening to the left seized Morandi's attention, although, according to Mauro Ferri, he remained constitutionally unable to break with the Communists,[50] and this firm position conditioned Nenni's actions. In sum, despite the late Morandi's guardedly flexibile view toward PSI political compromise with the DC, the communist alliance remained his idée fixe. Indeed, when the PCI moved to the center after his death, his faction elaborated a radical criticism of the Communists, making an essential contribution to the "new left" ideology of the 1960s.[51]

Not unexpectedly, Nenni's struggle for PSI autonomy brought the greatest response from the PSDI left wing, which had deserted the PSI because of the communist link but resented Saragat's transformation of Italian social democracy into a DC satellite. In November 1953, *Critica Sociale* editor Ugo Guido Mondolfo demanded concrete steps for gradual reunification. As a token of good faith, Mondolfo fostered PSDI action for formal abrogation of the "swindle law." Then the party should actively encourage PSI "Social Democrats" gradually to empty the PSI-PCI connection of its content, since the PSI would veto denunciation of the pact. Because great numbers of secret PSI "Social Democrats" passively resisted the communist yoke, and hordes of others who had dropped out of politics after 1947 would again become active, the optimistic Mondolfo counted on reunification to alter Italian socialist fortunes.[52]

Irritated by Saragat's lack of support for this position, influential leftist PSDI leaders withdrew from the party, forming the previously mentioned UP and USI and contesting the electoral bonus law. Convinced of Nenni's sincere desire to break with the Communists, these groups entered the PSI in November 1954. They had not escaped PCI control in 1947, they declared, only to submit to catholic domination in the PSDI.[53]

Nenni shrewdly exploited this view, denouncing Saragat in May 1954 as the opening's most dangerous adversary. Since the opening to the left had found "vigorous expression among the catholic masses and their exponents," Nenni argued, the PSDI left wing should reverse Saragat's policies.[54]

At the 1954 congress, left-wing PSDI leaders Mondolfo, Faravelli, Zagari, and Grimaldi reasoned that the PSI would never be in a position to break with the Communists until it had replaced the PCI alliance with a solid new political entente. Although Saragat maintained control of the PSDI at this assembly, the left wing successfully imposed on him the obligation to initiate a dialogue with the PSI.[55]

Socialist developments also stimulated debate within the DC. Writing in the papal *Civiltâ Cattolica* in June 1953, Vatican spokesman Father Antonio Messineo reiterated Christian Democratic party exclusion of the communist-dominated Nenni Socialists as potential allies. In order to resolve the political crisis of centrism, Messineo favored a monarchist alliance based on a conservative legislative platform.[56]

Instead of allowing this traditional position to go unchallenged as usual, liberal Catholics contradicted it. Carlo Colombo, professor at the prestigious Catholic University of Milan, warned the church against just such a conservative alliance. Given the Italian political situation, any catholic move to the right would inevitably boomerang, increase communist popularity, and raise the spector of a democratically elected leftist majority which might impose an Eastern European–style police state. Colombo argued that it was much better to encourage the PSI's new course, an expression of the legitimate, noncommunist aspirations of a significant segment of Italian society.[57] Other catholic writers adopted intermediate positions.

Summarizing the catholic dilemma, Nenni wrote: "If the left's votes are accepted, a social policy is possible; if the right's votes are accepted, a social policy is not possible."[58]

The Catholic Crisis

Counterpointing this ideological ferment, socialist developments encouraged significant changes within DC institutions which had direct contact with important social groups.

The formerly mild catholic union, CISL, linked up with the communist-socialist

CGIL and UIL and acquired a certain aggressivity. Thanks primarily to new cadres heavily influenced by the school of leftist catholic thinker Guido Dossetti, CISL participated in several important labor disputes in 1953 and 1954. One successful strike supported by Fanfani's intimate friend and mystical mayor of Florence, Giorgio La Pira, and by several hundred priests greatly impressed the nation. At the same time, Civic Committee leader Luigi Gedda's hold on Catholic Action slipped, and the movement strengthened its social commitment. Finally, Catholic University students renewed their pledge to social action.

These events portended a reorientation of power within the Christian Democratic party. The generation in control had founded the Popular party in 1919 and had dominated the DC since its constitution but would lose its grip at the Naples congress in June 1954 to a new generation which had come of age after World War I.

Led by Amintore Fanfani, these leaders rebelled against the hierarchical conception of society typical of the older leaders and advocated direct mass participation in the setting of national objectives. The younger leaders envisioned catholic unions and party permanently linking ''the sovereign people with the legislative and executive powers, receiving its desires, critically weighing its demands, conscientiously transmitting them, and overseeing their satisfactory implementation.'' In this manner, the left wing hoped to defuse the unrest which characterized the spring of 1954—caused by the social imbalances of the ''economic miracle,'' the crisis of centrism, and erosion of the DC's base in the country. Concretely, Fanfani urged adoption of the long-range social and economic reforms elaborated by DC Budget Minister Ezio Vanoni.[59]

A blueprint for modernizing Italian society, the ''Vanoni Plan'' also appealed to Socialists and therefore represented the common ground on which PSI and DC could meet and end the debilitating political stalement.[60]

Seizing the opportunity offered by the weakened hold of the old DC generation, Nenni marshaled history to his cause. The socialist and catholic masses, which had been excluded from the Risorgimento, were now ready for an ''encounter.'' If Fanfani favored the opening to the left after the Naples congress, the PSI would make three important concessions: reject communist totalitarianism, champion social reforms, and accept the same alterations in the Atlantic relationship requested by the British and French governments.[61]

Following the Fanfani victory at the Naples congress, Nenni claimed that the PSI's offer of collaboration had helped ''revolutionize'' the DC. According to him, the catholic masses had ''terminated'' right-wing domination and had ''created very vast areas of encounter between Socialists and Catholics on the plane of reform.'' DC champion of the opening to the left Giovanni Gronchi had brilliantly demonstrated that only in alliance with the Socialists could the reforms the new DC leaders desired be achieved.[62]

Unfortunately, Nenni painted an overly optimistic picture of the Naples congress. Undoubtedly, the catholic masses sympathized with the Socialists, the new leaders controlled the important party positions, and the congress had rejected the opening to the right; but the delegates had not endorsed the opening to the left.[63]

In fact, Gronchi lacked the strength to impose the opening to the left on his party. Instead, the Naples congress ushered in a crisis among the numerous catholic power centers that the DC never adequately resolved.

Future president of the republic and leader of the opening-to-the-left proponents within the DC, Giovanni Gronchi moved maladroitly among the centers of catholic power. Gronchi's manner aroused hostility among DC leaders, and his independent approach to Italian foreign policy irritated American Ambassador Clare Boothe Luce. When in late 1953 Gronchi objected to the ambassador's inspiration of an antisocialist press campaign in the United States, he won Nenni's sympathy but Luce's undying enmity. Elected president largely through Nenni's maneuvering, Gronchi appeared a powerful ally, convinced that only a center-left coalition could implement a reform program.[64]

Gronchi, however, conceived of the opening to the left as an instrument for DC supremacy, and this ideal ironically caused him to support Fernando Tambroni's opening to the right in 1960, bringing Italy to the brink of civil war and discrediting himself.

In addition to influential DC elements, the opening to the left made friends among industrialists interested in labor peace and in increased exports to the communist world which would result from improved Italian relations with the Eastern bloc. These industrialists would exercise a powerful influence in favor of the center-left.

Besides influential private entrepreneurs, the booming state industrial sector strongly supported the opening to the left, particularly the dynamic president of ENI, Enrico Mattei.

A Christian Democrat with solid anticommunist credentials, Mattei challenged the oil cartel by allying with the Third World oil-producing countries on the international plane. In Italy, he opposed cartel policies and American policy by favoring the importation of Soviet oil to contrast the "Seven Sisters." Sensitive to the problems of emerging countries, Mattei also supported the social objectives of the opening to the left and favored the increased Italian independence from the United States likely to result from socialist participation in a governing coalition. Mattei hoped that a center-left cabinet would reduce foreign control of Italian hydrocarbon resources, ensure greater Italian access to world energy reserves, and stimulate the nation's economic development. Actively pursuing this policy, in 1956, Mattei established the only major daily to support the center-left, Milan's *Il Giorno,* and partially compensated for communist withdrawals of subsidies from the PSI by his financial contributions.[65]

This financial support allowed Mattei to manipulate events to a certain extent, as did a host of other forces in this fascinating political game. Opposing Mattei, the giant Italian electric industry led private industry, conservative politicians, and the nation's press in a crusade against the opening to the left.

The resistance of private industry had important effects on the DC. Ideologically inspired by Guiseppe Dossetti's social philosophy and organized politically by Amintore Fanfani, the catholic left wing championed public industry as a countervailing force against private industry. In a conversation with me, Antonio Landolfi, the scholar and lieutenant of Giacomo Mancini, attributed this view to the economist Fanfani's "answer" to Max Weber, who had theorized a link between protestantism and capitalism; Fanfani conceived of catholicism as being rooted in public enterprise.[66] The DC left wing thus hoped to strengthen and dominate the public sector as a powerful force for social reforms favoring workers and the poor.

Consequently, socialist and left-wing DC policies forcefully coincided on a pragmatic plane. The Socialists campaigned strongly and successfully for a powerful Ministry for State Industry (Ministero delle Participazioni Statali), an effective state hydrocarbon agency capable of challenging the oil cartel for development of Italian resources, and nationalization of the electric industry, the economic citadel of Italian conservatism.[67]

These aims cost Socialists and leftist Catholics years of titanic struggle, a possible coup attempt, and perhaps "a couple of strange deaths," including Mattei's.[68]

The opening to the left thus revealed itself as an extraordinarily complicated domestic and international political operation which a lengthy conflict only partially resolved. Instead of masterminding a quick reversal of alliances, Nenni found himself caught in a crossfire between an "economic right wing" struggling to preserve its prerogatives by manipulating conservative DC elements and a PCI anxiously avoiding isolation by employing its considerable influence over PSI institutions to sabotage the general secretary's new course.

CHAPTER 7

The Pralognan Road

Nenni had brilliantly prepared the terrain for an alliance reversal which he believed would alter Italy's future. His new policy benefited neither major party. Both DC and PCI fought to retain their hegemony, the Catholics over the country and the Communists over the left. His opening to the left anathema to both DC and PCI, Nenni would struggle for years until he could implement the center-left.

The Turin Congress

Although the DC left wing had won a spectacular victory at the Naples National Congress, the still-powerful DC right wing advocated opening to the right, the Monarchists and Neo-Fascists.[1] Realization of this accounted for Nenni's attempt to reach an immediate entente between the PSI and the DC left wing.

Speaking in Naples before the March 1955 opening of the PSI Turin congress, Nenni pledged bold action to achieve an "encounter" between socialist and catholic masses on the basis of social and economic reforms. These included revision of land contracts to benefit peasants, reorganization of IRI, the state holding company, detachment of IRI firms from the private Manufacturers' Association (Confindustria), allowing them to bargain separately, development of ENI into a powerful force for Italian energy independence, and implementation of the Vanoni Plan.

Nenni envisioned workers, peasants, and middle classes working together to resolve the "historic problem" of Italian democracy by liberating the national executive from the grasp of the "economic right"—the Confindustria, the landowners' association, and the international oil cartel. Nenni compared reformists to organ grinders. "Crank the reform handle," Nenni told the DC, to the crowd's great delight.[2]

Approriately enough, therefore, the Turin congress (31 March–3 April 1955) launched the new line "Dialogue with the Catholics." Keynote speaker at this assembly, Nenni criticized economic maldistribution of national income, which produced a shameful gap between rich and poor and regional imbalances unworthy of a modern nation. Scarcely represented in Parliament, controlling the press and government, and using political repression, industrial concerns such as Edison, SME (the Southern Electric Company), Fiat, Montecatini, Pirelli, Snia, Falck, and Italcementi, and large financial groups including Centrale, Bastogi, and Assicurazioni Generali, utilized monopolistic powers to strangle the nation's economic development and sponsor reactionary political movements.

Nenni proposed that socialist and catholic masses together rescue Italian democracy and modernize their country's economic and social system. For now they could agree on national land reform, industrialization of the South, priorities for IRI and ENI, rational

economic planning as suggested by DC leader Ezio Vanoni, softening of cold war conflicts as outlined by European Social Democrats, and a commitment "to adhere to a
genuinely defensive and geographically well-delineated interpretation of the Atlantic Pact
and of the WEU [West European Union]." In return, the PSI would deemphasize the
unity pact with the Communists.

Once again, Nenni got stuck on the communist issue. Unitary politics, he said, need
not be spelled out in the articles of a formal pact but existed in the daily life of both
parties. Coupling this statement with an emphasis on PSI autonomy publicly set the stage
for a formal denunciation of the pact, but the press misinterpreted his remarks to mean that
the alliance would continue even if a formal agreement did not exist.[3]

Already a year earlier, Nenni had privately proposed to Togliatti the formal end of
the pact between their two parties on grounds of its superfluity; Nenni had claimed
Morandi's support, and Togliatti had promised to give the matter his thought. Nenni's
Turin remarks, however, allowed the Italian press to stick to its usual story of Communists and Socialists secretly in league to seize power.[4]

Generally interpreted as the "first step" toward a socialist-communist divorce and
the center-left, the Turin congress may be viewed in different ways. The key is Morandi,
whose solid control of the apparatus determined the PSI's course. Undoubtedly, Morandi
modified his strongly procommunist attitude at this assembly, arguing that the PSI had
chosen the Leninist model solely to restore the party's initiative, function, and cohesive-
ness which the splits of 1947 and 1948 had seriously debilitated. Significantly, he admitted that Leninism was extraneous to socialist tradition. In his speech and communications
with the party bureaucracy, Morandi indicated his willingness to work for an agreement
with the catholic world and to pay a price for this understanding.[5]

Further evidence for Morandi's supposed cooling toward the Communists exists in
the testimony of important autonomist leaders. One of these leaders, actually closer to
Nenni, Giovanni Pieraccini, argued not only for the "major turning point" claim for the
Turin congress but also for Morandi's leadership in the process.

In his response to my question of whether Morandi supported the change which the
PSI supposedly initiated at Turin, Pieraccini reacted strongly:

> Morandi became convinced of the necessity of opening a dialogue with the catholic
> world, and consequently with the DC, and it was he who elaborated this policy which
> manifested itself at the Turin congress. The proof of this is that we youngsters who
> were brushed aside after the left's victory were called back. . . . During preparations
> for the congress of Turin, Morandi reestablished contacts with us—with me—and
> reinserted us into the party's active life.

"Then it was Morandi who intervened in this sense," I said. Pieraccini responded,
"Certainly!"[6]

Morandi had called for an alliance between socialist and catholic masses in the past,
as had the Communists, and, despite Pieraccini's conviction, the Turin "turning point"
may appear so only given the hindsight of later developments.

Another protagonist of the times, Mauro Ferri, categorically denied that Morandi
even "imagined that he could break with the Communists" and that, even though he
favored a catholic understanding, the Turin svolta took place with communist consent.

When I sounded him out on Pieraccini's observations, Ferri fervently insisted:

Don't forget that the Turin approach [to the Catholics] was made with Togliatti's permission, that Togliatti himself had made the same approach. At the PCI's congress of 1952, I believe . . . there is a Togliatti speech, in which he said without much ado that the Communist party would cease its opposition against the Italian government run by the DC if it met only one condition. He didn't ask for social reforms: he requested a change in international policy, namely Italian exit from NATO.

Therefore, approaches and attempts to link up with the catholic world and with the DC have always existed; furthermore, there have always existed among the Catholics currents fascinated by neutralist and pacifist ideas. You know that the decision to join NATO was initially a much discussed and painful decision among the Catholics—there was a strong current which favored pacifism and neutralism. The Communists have always exploited this feeling, and I would say that Nenni's—Morandi's—approach to the Catholics fit into the same context.

In my opinion, to interpret the Turin congress as an anticipation of the center-left would be a grievous error—it was very different. The center-left became possible as a result of the 1956 crisis of the communist world.

And then Gronchi's election [as president, shortly after the congress]. Gronchi represented this neutralist and anti-American soul within the DC. Gronchi's election was accomplished by Nenni. . . . The Turin congress, the appeal to the Catholics, anticipated Gronchi's election . . . because it was the line that the Socialists, and also the Communists, favored. The line, that is, of a Christian democracy which would weaken its ties with the Western world, with America, because of a very light accentuation of its social policies.[7]

These contrasting interpretations of the Turin congress indicate the continuing fluidity within the PSI of the period. In fact, the socialist attitude toward the Communists had not been defined, and it is unlikely that Morandi, had he lived, would have allowed Nenni to bring the PSI as far from the Communists as quickly as the secretary actually did.

Ferri is correct in identifying this movement in subsequent developments. In his own comments on the Turin congress, Nenni noted that the opening to the left had to mature in the country before it could do so in Parliament and called on the Directorate to concentrate on a number of upcoming political issues.[8]

Thus, the Turin assembly confirmed the PSI as the force to be reckoned with in Italian politics, as a rapid-fire series of developments demonstrated. Combined with the communist crisis of 1956, these developments allowed Nenni to utilize the PSI's momentum to challenge Togliatti.

The "Propulsive Force"

Pietro Nenni's brilliant "Grand Elector" role in Giovanni Gronchi's election as president of the republic in April 1955 represents the spectacular coronation of the work undertaken at Turin.

Nenni's skillful management of Gronchi's campaign against Fanfani's official candidate—Senate President Cesare Merzagora—is less important than the manner in which he permeated the entire operation with a distinct center-left flavor. "Tonight they will all be here . . . , hats in hand," Nenni informed an initially discouraged Gronchi. Even leftist socialist leader Tullio Vecchietti saluted Gronchi's election as a highly significant heralding of the opening to the left. In Nenni's first talks with the new president, Gronchi agreed to press for a center-left government with direct socialist participation before the end of the current legislature.[9]

The first step on this road involved ending the detested Scelba cabinet, a commitment Gronchi fulfilled by accepting Scelba's routine resignation following the presidential election.

After complicated consultations and maneuverings, Antonio Segni, a Sardinian land-owner identified with previous land-reform laws, put a government together. Segni hoped for socialist abstention and on 7 July held a lengthy secret meeting with Nenni to convince him. Segni's program contained many important points favored by the PSI, but Nenni objected to Segni's selection of Fernando Tambroni as interior minister and Liberal party inclusion in the coalition, so he informed Segni that the PSI would vote against him.[10]

The Christian democratic crisis, caused by socialist pressure on the DC to open to the left, explains the continuing inability to reach agreement. The DC left wing approved the opening philosophically and considered it essential for the stability of Italian society, but the right wing and the Vatican vigorously contested it.

This opposition obliged leftist Catholic Fanfani to move cautiously. His efforts to build robust party institutions independent of the traditional catholic flanking organizations aroused rightist resistance, and his faction's sympathy for public over private enterprise caused the Confindustria to shift financial and moral support to the Liberals.[11]

As rumors of an impending DC split into "Christian Socialist" and "Clerico-Moderate" parties flew, Fanfani and Segni consulted Nenni "clandestinely," Segni begging the socialist secretary not to call because Scelba had probably bugged the prime minister designate's telephone! This intense infighting caused Fanfani to shift his position continuously, sometimes startling the socialist leader. On the other hand, socialist interests favored keeping the DC intact, so Nenni had to pull his punches.[12]

Despite the DC question mark, PSI influence grew tremendously between the spring of 1955 and that of 1956. Running independently of the Communists, the party increased its percentage in the regional Sicilian elections from 7.5 percent to 9.7 percent, leapfrogging to third place in Sicily and making a center-left government there arithmetically possible.[13]

Despite the PSI's negative vote against Segni, the government could not ignore increasing socialist influence in the country. The prime minister consulted Nenni regularly, concurring that a reformist program must be implemented by daily action and could not be based on abstract ideological considerations. To describe this policy, Nenni often used the phrase "the politics of things," originally coined by Turati.

This era thus records a string of significant victories on issues pushed by the Socialists. The Constitutional Court finally functioned. ENI received exclusive exploration and production rights in the Po Valley, and in January 1956 the Ministry of State Participations finally came into being to oversee public industry. Parliament also detached IRI-controlled industry from the Confindustria, a move which eliminated public industry contributions to the private industrialists' association, which had used the funds to influence government support of the private economic sector. Public industry also established its own bargaining group, Intersind, permitting it to negotiate fairer contracts with its workers without Confindustria's determining influence.

In an effort to spur southern industrialization, Parliament also required public industry to place 60 percent of its new investments in the South (a step toward having 40 percent of its total investments there); once again, the government rebuffed private industry, which hoped to restrict state activity to the infrastructure, thus leaving the more lucrative direct industrialization to the privates.[14] While the new state-influenced industrialized system would present its own future problems, Italian society assumed a shape desired by the Socialists.

Counterpointing important international developments such as the 1955 Geneva Summit Conference, the PSI also actively engaged in foreign policy. President Gronchi's conviction of Italian subservience to U.S. policy bolstered Nenni. Between 17 September and 19 October, Nenni traveled to Russia and China for discussions with the leaders of both countries on two issues of deep concern: Italian admission to the United Nations and the opening of trade relations between Italy and China.

In Russia, Nenni had long conversations with a dour Georgi Malenkov, a Marxist textbook-quoting Mikhail Suslov, and a wise-cracking Nikita Khrushchev, "who needs a good tailor." With Khrushchev, Nenni praised the recent reduction of world tensions, arguing that the opening to the left "was the national aspect of detente in the international field." Because of socialist policy, Italy had greater prospects for leftward movement than that any other European country, Nenni explained. The Soviet Union could help in three ways: demonstrating its desire for peace, persuading the Italian Communists to give up the unity-of-action pact, and withdrawing its veto against Italian entry to the UN. The Soviet leaders objected to Nenni's position on the unity pact, but they did agree to remove their veto to Italian admission to the UN if other unrelated issues could be ironed out. In December 1955, Italy entered the UN, at least partially a result of what one observer called Nenni's "decisive" contribution.[15]

In China, Nenni had a lengthy meeting with Chou En-lai and a conversation with Mao Tse-tung, who expressed his admiration for Italian films. The talks dealt with opening commercial relations between the two countries, which would have a major impact. Nenni's activities helped put Italy at the forefront of the Western nations pressing for recognition of communist China, although regard for the United States prevented Italy from taking this step until 1969, under Foreign Minister Nenni.

These developments mark the beginning of a more independent foreign policy within the Atlantic Alliance favored by the Socialists and left-wing Christian Democrats in the Mediterranean, Middle East, and Africa. In a controversial 1957 move, for example, Mattei overturned the 50-50 formula used by the Western oil companies and granted Iran 75 percent of the profits generated from its petroleum. Based on trade considerations, however, these policies attracted the support of important Italian business interests.[16]

Pralognan

The PSI's "propulsive" activity had major effects on the party's relations with the Communists. Sandro Pertini replaced Morandi after his death in July 1955. Pertini, however, lacked Morandi's authority, so Nenni now had a clear field to implement his "revisionist" views.

Fully cognizant of right-wing exploitation of the unity pact to block the center-left, Nenni substituted socialist tradition for the communist connection. As part of this operation, he intensified pressure for socialist reunification. Major cracks in the communist world's monolithic structure in 1956 permitted Nenni to challenge PCI supremacy and make a bid for renewed socialist leadership of the Italian left. These developments included Khrushchev's denunication of Stalin's crimes at the 20th Congress of the Communist Party of the Soviet Union (CPSU) in February, and the Hungarian Revolution and Soviet invasion in October and November 1956.

In December 1955, even before Khrushchev's attack on Stalin, Nenni moved to free the PSI organization from subordination to the Communists. PSI directing organs secretly ordered their local affiliates to stall establishment of the mixed socialist-communist committees called for by the unity pact. Bent on scuttling the agreement, they instructed the federations to revise and reorganize socialist cadres and to focus on penetration and propaganda work among PSI members, "in such a manner as to form an independent political conscience within every member so as to determine the precise conviction that the Socialist party is not subject to the Communist, and that it has a powerful tradition and sufficient means to determine its own politics free from the sufferance or aid of other parties." As a result of this policy, the Pisa Prefect reported, relations between socialist and communist managers cooled considerably.[17]

Once the Khrushchev Report became known, Nenni seized on it to conduct a full-fledged offensive against the Communists. Nenni praised Khrushchev's revelation of Stalin's crimes but criticized the Russian leader's attribution of them to Stalin's circumvention of collegial government. Not a "personality cult," Nenni argued, but the Soviet system had spawned Stalin's criminal behavior.

Nenni developed his arguments in a series of *Mondo Operaio* articles between March and July 1956. Astounding the Communists, Nenni wrote that fundamental Marxist principles such as the dictatorship of the proletariat had progressively shorn the primitive Soviets of their powers and had emptied them of their "democratic content." As a result of democracy's destruction, the Soviet system had produced the dictatorship of the party over the proletariat and of the apparatus over the party.

What lessons had Soviet experience taught the Socialists? The importance of democracy and the validity of the "parliamentary road" to socialism. Nenni emphasized this technique in terms not of numbers but of "respect for democratric legality . . . whether one is in the opposition or has the majority." While reserving the right to react violently if capitalists threatened democratic institutions, Nenni cited the recent socialist congresses of Milan and Turin as proof of the PSI's sincere commitment to democracy.

In sum, Nenni publicly rejected the Soviet model, emphasizing democratic socialist traditions instead. He had courageously rehabilitated Saragat and Turati. Mauro Ferri remembers this period as the one in which the scales fell from his eyes and those of other young PSI members. In fact, they criticized Nenni for waiting so long to demolish the communist myth.[18]

Even now, however, Nenni's ideological attacks and subterranean maneuvers stopped short of a clamorous break with the PCI. The Communists not only represented the majority of the Italian working class and controlled the labor and social institutions in which communist and socialist workers inextricably mixed, but Togliatti skillfully adapted the new Soviet course to Italy by affirming an "Italian road to socialism" through enactment of structural reforms. Unlike Togliatti, however, Nenni clearly intended to win reforms from within the Italian political system.

In May 1956, the voters judged the PSI's activity during the past year in local elections. Domestic and international considerations interwove tightly during the balloting. Shaken by an internal feud between left- and right-wing elements, the Segni cabinet teetered and awaited the electorate's verdict. Nenni hoped the elections would sanction the opening to the left; Togliatti desperately calmed communist confusion after the 20th CPSU Congress's dramatic revelations.

The local elections unquestionably demonstrated voter approval for the opening to the left. The PSI advanced throughout the country, increasing to 15.25 percent, 2.27 percent over 1953. In Milan the Socialists outdistanced the Communists, and they made impressive showings in other crucial areas. Most significantly, the electorate rewarded the Socialists where they presented slates independently from the Communists, such as in the cities; in the provincial elections, where Socialists and Communists presented unified slates because of the nonproportional voting system, the Social Democrats advanced. Where voters could not vote either for PSI or PSDI alone, the number of blank ballots increased.

The elections produced other positive signs. Even though the Communists contained their losses, they suffered a general decline for the first time in the postwar period. An interesting development favoring the opening also occurred among the Christian Democrats; they maintained their percentage but witnessed a redistribution of votes which strengthened their left wing. Finally, with certain local exceptions, the right-wing parties lost heavily.

Despite these results, the Italian political system failed to respond to the 1956 election's clear verdict favoring the center-left.[19] Following the elections, Nenni advocated formation of center-left local administrations based on a four-party coalition (DC, PSI, PSDI, and PRI) as a prelude to agreement on the national level. However, negotiations for these *giunte* dragged on among myriad difficulties. Some cities presented ominous signs, as Christian democratic politicians made up their deficiency of votes by opening to the right.[20]

This stalled situation exacerbated the political situation. Not only did the Socialists fail to gain entrance into the governing coalition in the next few months, but the Communists maneuvered furiously to avoid isolation. A confidential source provided the police with a secret communist circular mobilizing PCI provincial federations to block all attempts at PSI organizational independence by unmasking "socialist traitors of their communist comrades. . . . At the first hint of Socialists attempting to become independent from the Communists, go up to them immediately, without waiting, try everything to bring them once again to the true path. . . . Given the proper circumstances, . . . [you may] use threats and reprisals."[21]

At the highest levels, Saragat responded to the election results by threatening his resignation from the Segni cabinet in July 1956.

While observers such as British political scientist Roy Pryce expressed doubts about Nenni's intention to break with the PCI after the 20th CPSU Congress, his new relationship with the PSDI proves the secretary's resolve. Without admitting it, Nenni articles demonstrate a commitment to Saragat's social democratic reformism, nullifying the cause of the 1947 split. Nenni planned to replace the communist alliance with socialist reunification. This action would attract masses of new voters, challenge PCI and DC, return the PSI to the mainstream of socialist internationalism, restore its membership in COMISCO, and crown Nenni's long career. But could PSI and PSDI leaders reconcile their organizations' ten years of divergent development?

On 6 June 1956, Nenni officially initiated the reunification process by conferring with PSDI heads Matteo Matteotti and Mario Tanassi in his Parliament building office.

Nenni suggested a year or two of common action, confronting the next elections with a common program, PSI-PSDI cooperation in a cabinet, and, finally, reunification. When the PSDI leaders expressed uncertainty about Saragat's attitude, Nenni cited the support of French and British Socialists in requesting a meeting with his former adversary. "Not a bad beginning," Nenni commented in his diary.[22]

On 25 August 1956, Nenni and Saragat met in a historic colloquy at the French Alpine resort of Pralognan. Saragat's excellent humor contradicted the gloomy weather, Nenni remarked. Convinced that Nenni's attitude following the 20th Congress had indeed invalidated the 1947 schism, Saragat enthusiastically endorsed a reunified Socialist party as a powerful alternative to Christian Democrats and Communists. Saragat made very specific proposals. Delegates to a reunification congress must end the unity-of-action pact, Saragat said, not rejecting a PCI alliance in principle but judging the PCI's democratic development by its actions. Finally, regarding foreign policy, Saragat endorsed Italian neutrality "of the Swedish type," provided Italy remained an integral part of the western ambit. In response to Saragat's optimism, Nenni commented, "It was my lot to act as a fireman, reminding him that we had not arrived but were at the beginning of a long and controversial process."

Highlighting the two men's different styles, Nenni counterposed practical political considerations to Saragat's grand design. First there should take place a series of common cultural and political initiatives. Cooperation in setting up city administrations would be an excellent beginning and a prelude to a center-left national coalition. These developments should culminate in a common platform for the 1958 general elections. Despite Saragat's usual impatience with politics' petty details, Nenni hopefully concluded, he had won over the PSDI leader.[23]

According to Saragat, he had convinced Nenni. At a PSDI conclave in September 1956, Saragat reported that at Pralognan he and Nenni had agreed on foreign policy, an ideology—democracy, "not as a means, but as a system"—and communist exclusion from all governmental coalitions.[24]

The publicity following Pralognan annoyed Nenni, who had inexplicably expected the encounter to be kept "reserved," if not secret. Hoping to calm the agitated PSI left wing, Nenni implied that nothing new had happened and promised to keep PSI directing organs fully informed. As far as repudiating the PSI's past communist connections, he stated, "we have nothing to repudiate." Astoundingly, he wrote, closer PSDI connections would not compromise relationships "with our communist comrades."[25]

The Debate

The PSI left wing reacted uneasily to Nenni's initiatives. Its major spokesman, *Avanti!* editor Tullio Vecchietti, rejected Nenni's interpretation of the 20th CPSU Congress. Vecchietti attributed Soviet errors not to fundamental flaws of Marxism-Leninism but to Western imperialism and the defensive "war communism." Echoing Togliatti's position after the 20th CPSU Congress, Vecchietti believed that "polycentrism" and the roads of individual countries to socialism had replaced democratic centralism and the Soviet Union's guiding function. Socialists and Communists could still cooperate in the struggle for world peace.[26]

Initially taken aback by the Pralognan meeting, the PSI left wing wavered, hoping to salvage "unitary politics" but not rebuffing Nenni.[27] Imprisoned by its own bureaucratic mentality, the left initially objected only that no party organ had sanctioned Nenni's activities. Democratic centralism still imposed unanimity in official proceedings and covered up serious disputes, as the left wing utilized the party apparatus to block Nenni.

Thus, on 2 September 1956, the Central Committee shocked the secretary by its sharply negative response to his report on Pralognan. The members criticized his assent to unification with the PSDI on an equal basis because the Social Democrats had only 20 percent of the PSI's parliamentary strength, only 10 percent of its membership, and much weaker economic, labor, and international support. In short, the Central Committee conceived of unification as absorption of the PSDI by the PSI. True to democratic centralism, however, the Central Committee unanimously approved a bland statement favoring unification and reflecting none of the disagreements expressed.[28]

At the end of September 1956, the Central Committee blocked early reunification by lauding the unity pact and demanding a PSDI endorsement of a single union for all workers, the end of discriminatory differentiation among civil service employees, and a neutralist foreign policy. The Central Committee required the PSDI to acknowledge publicy the failure of centrism and to secure official DC recognition of the inevitability of the opening to the left. The left wing also viciously attacked French socialist senator Pierre Commin, in Italy to mediate the reunification process. These "disloyal attitudes of a group of apparatus comrades" made Nenni consider resigning.[29]

Instead, however, Nenni's support in the PSI helped him win several victories in October 1956. He replaced the communist unity pact with a bland "consultation pact" and instituted a joint commission with the Social Democrats to discuss reunification. Neither of these victories came cheaply, however, and they antagonized different groups within the PSI and outside it.[30]

Saragat had joined the commission to implement unification, but since PSI opposition forced Nenni to take a harder stance against the PSDI leader, Nenni accused Saragat of dwelling too much on the socialist connection with the Communists instead of concentrating on a brand new PSDI relationship with the DC and the center parties. Nenni admitted, "It was a slightly arduous argument while Soviet tanks vomited fire in Budapest." Saragat feared an indecisive socialist alternative tinged with "frontismo," which Fanfani would exploit to recover the DC's absolute majority.

In fact, Saragat proved correct. As the Hungarian Revolution escalated, provoking Soviet army intervention and universal revulsion, the DC pressured President Gronchi to hold early elections in the hope of riding the anti-Soviet tide and electorally decimating the Italian left. Under these conditions, Saragat cited unfair socialist attitudes toward him and resigned from the unity commission.[31]

From Budapest to Venice

The Hungarian Revolution and the Soviet invasion dealt internal PSI unity a death blow. Shocked by these events, Nenni struggled with his conscience and swiftly denounced the Soviet Union. The PSI left wing, however, did not condemn the socialist fatherland or break with the PCI.

On 28 October 1956, *Avanti!* printed a vehement Nenni article condemning Soviet intervention in Hungary and Poland. Italian Socialists, the secretary wrote, demanded

Soviet withdrawal from both countries and the national independence of Eastern Europe. In doing so, the Socialists did not question the right of revolutionaries to defend themselves, a false issue. Nenni resented Soviet condemnation of the Hungarian students as dupes of foreign powers and contested the Soviet contention that foreign agents had fomented the revolution. Nenni bluntly attributed the uprising to the crimes and errors of the old Marxist ruling groups. By calling for evacuation of all Eastern Europe, Italian Socialists simply reaffirmed their traditional policy of nonintervention in the internal affairs of other countries by West or East.[32]

Despite the PCI conviction that the PSI secretary exploited communist difficulties for political reasons, Nenni believed that the Hungarian invasion had "excavated an abyss between us and the Communists." In November 1956, the Nenni-influenced PSI Directorate attributed the Hungarian revolt to "a degeneration of popular power into bureaucratic and police forms." Nenni addressed the Central Committee, announcing that the new consultation pact would not go into effect and that henceforth the PSI-PCI relationship would be one of "reciprocal liberty within the limits of class solidarity." Finally, Nenni returned the Stalin Peace Prize and donated the money that went with it to the victims of the Hungarian Revolution and of the Anglo-French war against Egypt.[33]

The PSI left wing defied the PSI secretary. Vecchietti's *Avanti!* dispassionately denied that the Hungarian uprising revealed contradictions between liberty and socialism and vehemently objected to substituting a PSDI alliance for the PCI connection. Vecchietti denounced Saragat for equating the Soviet Union to Hitler's Germany and denounced PSDI approval of a DC-sponsored measure seemingly protecting private electric company interests. There could be no unification with this "bourgeois-protected socialism," Vecchietti warned. Finally, Vecchietti undercut a Nenni statement that the PSI had "reacquired its liberty" by agreeing with Togliatti that reciprocal liberty had always characterized PSI-PCI relationships.[34]

In short, the left-wing "carristi" (i.e., favoring Soviet tanks) observed with dismay Nenni's dumping of the communist alliance and its substitution with a social democratic pact.

Ironically, the 20th CPSU Congress had set in motion events which would gradually reduce PCI subordination to the Soviet Union, but as usual the PCI moved very cautiously. Togliatti shrewdly elaborated upon Khrushchev's major themes, such as "peaceful coexistence" and the end of the "historical necessity" of the Soviet model. Togliatti realized instantly that greater flexibility and political freedom would benefit the PCI. He theorized many communist centers ("polycentrism") and an "Italian road to socialism."[35]

Furthermore, in December 1956, the 8th PCI Congress endorsed a democratic and constitutional road to socialism. Although Togliatti disagreed with Nenni's thesis of Stalinism as a fundamental attribute of communism, he did believe that the phenomenon had wider implications than Soviet leaders admitted. Moreover, Togliatti initially interpreted the Hungarian Revolution as a popular uprising and contested the Soviet line which branded it a counterrevolution, although Soviet pressure later elicited his approval of the Russian invasion. In short, the 1956 crisis signals the beginning of a "qualitative shift" in PCI policy with respect to the Soviet Union.[36] This change strengthened the PSI left wing in its struggle against Nenni.

The 32nd PSI National Congress (Venice, February 1957) discussed these issues and reached decisions in the confused manner of a party still embroiled in the problems of "democratic centralism."

In one of his most compelling speeches, Nenni boldly traced the history of the past decade, the imbalance characterizing Italy's impressive economic statistics, the task of transforming the nation into a modern social democracy, and the difficult political choices facing the Socialist party.

Nenni dutifully paid homage to the unity pact but skillfully and courageously gave it a decent burial by drawing on socialist tradition and citing Soviet repression. From a fount of inspiration the pact had become an impediment to socialist action. Although Nenni set as a condition Saragat's withdrawal from the "centrist" coalition as the PSI had withdrawn from the "frontist" one, he insisted that PSDI unification would replace the PCI pact. This policy issued "from the present phase of the class struggle and the struggle for democracy." Finally, the secretary summarized organizational, tactical, and strategic goals in line with his philosophy and asked for the delegates' approval.[37]

The delegates unanimously voted for Nenni's motion but in a spectacular demonstration of the left wing's grip on the apparatus elected a clear majority of Nenni's opponents to the Central Committee. Laborious negotiations ensued to draw up a list for the Directorate. The congress finally elected a Directorate unfriendly to the secretary: ten Nenni "autonomists," ten "Morandians," and three Basso leftists.[38]

Nenni had officially changed the PSI's policy, but the left wing had boxed the victor of Venice in a leftist majority which would constantly harass implementation of the new policy.

Nenni's Via Crucis

In his preface to the second volume of Nenni's diaries, Giuseppe Tamburrano has written:

> In 1956, Nenni opened his eyes. . . . The USSR is not a pacific nation which has annexed Eastern Europe to defend itself; it is a colonialist power which employs tanks to crush the aspiration of a people for independence and liberty. . . . The delusion, the bitterness burn: it is a political and psychic trauma. Afterward, Nenni is no longer the same.[39]

In an astounding turnabout, Nenni had rediscovered his reformist roots. Previously erased from PSI history, either not mentioned or only in embarrassed tones, approving citations of pre–World War I socialism now sprinkled Nenni's speeches and writings.

"My situation today is a little like that of Turati's in 1922," Nenni wrote on 17 November 1956. "He preached the truth in a desert of incomprehension and resentment." In a diary entry for 1 May 1959, Nenni admitted:

> Turati and his collaborators brought socialism to a height of organizational and political development at least equal to today's. Over time, the savage communist and maximalist criticism appears infantile. . . . There is no doubt that many hasty judgments . . . including mine, should be revised.[40]

Having reoriented his thinking between 1953 and 1956, Nenni arrived at the updating of pre–World War I socialism which Saragat had achieved between the wars. Seeking to explain how the Russian Revolution could produce Stalinism and evolve into an imperialist force by 1956, Nenni came to Saragat's conclusion of liberty as the highest good: "Without democracy, everything is degraded, everything is corrupted, even institutions created by proletarian revolutions, even the transformation of the means of production and exchange which is the fundamental condition of a socialist economy." Practically adopting Saragat's language, Nenni now considered liberty "not . . . a finality but . . . a method."[41]

Nenni's acceptance of Saragat's ideology and of prewar reformist tradition explains his reasons for assuming that the major obstacles to reunification had been removed. Unfortunately for Italian socialism, ten years of participation in the political process had changed Saragat. Nenni had kept an appointment with a ghost. In fact, in April 1957, Saragat forced the resignation of Matteo Matteotti, PSDI secretary sympathetic to Nenni.[42]

In the meantime, Fanfani exploited anti-Soviet revulsion to plot early elections and restore the DC's absolute majority. Nenni's inability to lead his party to a clean break with the Communists encouraged the DC secretary, while Fanfani's tactic in turn aided Vecchietti in his struggle against the opening to the left. Nenni denounced Fanfani's policy and successfully intervened with President Gronchi to end the early election threat.[43]

Despite his frustration at being checkmated in Venice, Nenni traveled to Milan immediately after the congress. On 27 March 1957, he met with major bankers, industrialists, and international traders (including one interested primarily in Chinese trade) in Lelio Basso's house on the elegant Corso Venezia. The main purpose of the meeting—as stated in a secret report marked "Seen by the Minister"—was to arrange new subsidies for the PSI and *Avanti!* and to guarantee the PSI's autonomy.

At these talks and others held at Via Appiani, Nenni stated that a new war had become impossibile; this being the case, he declared any Italian rearmament policy unjustified. Furthermore, convinced that Russia had a great thirst for capital in order to increase consumer-goods production, he believed that the Russians were prepared to pay a heavy price for detente.

In the domestic area, Nenni blamed the snags in the socialist reunification process squarely on Saragat, who stalled unification at the behest of the Americans. "[Saragat] operates to retard [unity] because of pressure from the American embassy in Rome," Nenni stated explicitly. "The interest of the United States . . . is the maintenance of a state of political tension in Italy, at least until the Americans have favorably resolved the knotty Middle Eastern question."

As a result, Nenni concluded, socialist unification could not occur before the next general elections, which, he hoped, would produce good results for both PSI and PSDI. Total achievement of his goals, however, would have to wait until after the 1963 elections. By then, both detente and continuing deterioration in the DC's position would have done their job.[44] Nenni's *via crucis* had just begun.

CHAPTER 8

Neo-Socialists and New Frontiersmen

On the table for five years by 1958, Nenni's center-left proposal would linger for a similar period before the Socialists could join the Italian government. By 1963, however, the enemies of the opening to the left had practically worn out the formula before it could be put into effect.

Furthermore, given the Italian political situation's extreme rigidity and sensitivity to international developments, it appears improbable that the center-left coalition would have come to fruition without John F. Kennedy's election as president of the United States and without Presidental Advisor Arthur M. Schlesinger's activities. The evidence leads to this conclusion, despite the contentions of State Department experts arguing the purely Italian nature of the center-left and of Nenni's lieutenant Giovanni Pieraccini, who in my 14 November 1984 conversation with him disagreed with this thesis.

As political conditions for the center-left matured, its Italian opponents delayed endlessly. In a 7 October 1985 telephone conversation with the person who focused Kennedy administration attention on the opening to the left, Robert W. Komer, the former CIA official told me that many Italians believed the United States opposed the opening, allowing its opponents to stall the center-left. For this reason, Komer and other administration officials communicated to the Italians that Kennedy did not oppose the center-left—then the struggle between New Frontiersmen and the entrenched American bureaucracy began.

These themes emerged in my 25 June 1985 conversation with Arthur Schlesinger. I began: "I get the distinct impression that if the Kennedy administration hadn't been there, if there hadn't been some kind of 'positive reinforcement,' the Italians would not have worked it out. . . ." Schlesinger replied: "Certainly it would have taken much longer. Because the people opposed to it on other grounds, as you say, would have invoked the Americans as a reason why they shouldn't have a center-left."

During the late 1950s and early 1960s, the Italian political system twisted and turned and thwarted the opening to the left before implementing more questionable tactics against it.

The Miracle Continues

As a result of the unstable governmental situation, the Italian economic system continued its haphazard boom. Behind the comforting economic statistics which chronicle Italy's development into a world industrial leader, trouble lurked. Fueled by EEC membership, low wages, and cheap energy but lacking a logical plan, rapid economic progress produced a lopsided distribution of wealth, overcrowded cities, an exodus from the countryside, pollution, real estate booms and busts, housing shortages, and permanent environmental damage.[1]

Economic anarchy had political consequences. The demand for cheap labor stimulated a massive influx of southern emigrants into the cities of the North and Center, willy-nilly "southernizing" and urbanizing the country.[2] Among these emigrants were a large proportion of young people eager to claim a share of the new prosperity. They swelled the ranks of the communist-socialist CGIL, spurring the labor agitiation which characterizes the 1959–63 period. This unrest, in turn, split the entrepreneurs and the DC. Should they resist or at least accept labor's socialist contingent into the government? Pietro Nenni discovered in this division an incentive for negotiation within the DC which contributed to the opening to the left.[3]

Civil Wars: The Christian Democrats

Within the DC, dialogue went forward with leftist General Secretary Amintore Fanfani, who hoped to transform the DC and reorganize it into a modern mass party. But DC conservatives fought to maintain the party's traditional policies and structure, based on financial contributions from private industrialists and an organization rooted in the parishes and flanking institutions such as Catholic Action. Counting on powerful Vatican support and industrialist animosity to Fanfani's championship of public industry, these opponents blocked the new secretary. In a partial success, however, Fanfani altered the DC's social composition by increasing the percentage of working-class members, which escalated pressure for a socialist accommodation.[4]

Caught between a possible DC split if he moved leftward too rapidly and a heterogeneous coalition against his party should he reinstitute centrism, Fanfani sought a new DC majority in the 25 May 1958 general elections. If he failed, Fanfani informed the DC National Council on 12 July 1957, the Catholics would have to consider seriously a socialist alliance. In response, the DC right wing revolted by casting twelve blank ballots against the secretary.

In the influential American review *Foreign Affairs,* Fanfani went further: "In case we do obtain an absolute majority, we shall seek a broad basis of collaboration with all democratic groups; and, of course, if our majority is less than absolute, it is even more obvious that such collaboration will be our aim."[5]

The 1958 elections disappointed Fanfani. While the DC percentage increased by 2.3 percent, to 42.4 percent, the new votes came primarily from Monarchists and Neo-Fascists. In addition, the elections also produced a PSI increase and finished off Adone Zoli's monarchist and MSI-supported cabinet, in power since May 1957.

As a result, Fanfani received a mandate to form a "clean" center-left government—a cabinet with PSDI and PRI which lacked but looked forward to PSI support. Guarding his back from his own party, however, Fanfani emphasized his nonacceptance of socialist votes, provoking the ire of respected republican leader Ugo La Malfa. Convinced of Nenni's communist break, La Malfa strongly favored the center-left and announced the PRI's "critical abstention" toward the new cabinet.[6]

Despite Fanfani's reform-mindedness, this feeble majority and a scandal produced political disaster. Hoping to strengthen his government, Fanfani flirted with Nenni, which irritated Catholic Action leader Luigi Gedda, right-wing DC notables Mario Scelba and Giuseppe Pella, and Confindustria mouthpiece, the *Corriere della Sera*. As a consequence, DC "snipers" voted against important legislation in parliamentary secret ballots. At the same time, Fanfani failed to gain unqualified support from PSI sympathizers within his coalition, and he resigned on 26 January 1959. Angry at his own party's behavior, Fanfani also quit as secretary.[7]

On 14 March 1959, the DC National Council ratified Fanfani's defeat by accepting his resignation after a heated debate. Fanfani's faction, "Iniziativa Democratica," dissolved, and a loose coalition, the "Dorotei," replaced it as the majority current and elected as secretary Aldo Moro, DC leader from Bari.[8]

Incarnating the DC's doubts and hesitations, Moro renounced Fanfani's plan to make the DC into a modern party but accepted the center-left as the DC's only choice to stay in power. But he could convince his party only by agonizingly slow action.

Reflecting party developments at the governmental level, Antonio Segni had replaced Fanfani as prime minister on 24 February 1959. Unlike his previous reform government, however, this time Segni relied on a center-right coalition sustained by liberal and monarchist votes and neo-fascist sympathy. On 10 March, the Christian Democrats officially sanctioned Segni's solution to the government crisis.

Running contrary to the country's mood, DC conservatives had dealt the opening to the left a severe defeat by the beginning of 1959.

Civil Wars: The Socialists

Paralleling Fanfani's troubles, Nenni encountered determined resistance to a catholic agreement in the PSI.[9] Bolstered by Fanfani's commitment to an alliance if the DC did not achieve a majority, Nenni claimed victory when the socialist percentage increased from 12.7 to 14.2 in 1958. As we have seen, these results produced the "clean" center-left foreshadowing socialist support, but Fanfani's failure and the surprise emergence of an antiunification majority at the October 1957 PSDI congress emboldened the socialist left wing.

At a 16 October 1958 Central Committee meeting, seven leftist leaders rejected a Nenni report drafted for presentation at the upcoming National Congress. As a result, the socialist leadership presented three separate reports to the next party conclave. The socialist left thus demolished its cherished "democratic centralism" which had turned to Nenni's benefit.[10]

Interestingly enough, the increasingly free PSI atmosphere divided the left wing, allowing three factions to emerge.

Gadfly Lelio Basso rejected alliances with both Communists and Catholics, advocating instead a peaceful, democratic, and reformist road to socialism—the "Democratic Alternative." Basso now favored party alliances in theory but not with the DC.[11] This posture allowed Nenni to take tactical advantage of Basso's position.

Another faction led by Morandi heir Raniero Panzieri hoped to establish a fresh ideological basis for leftist socialism. Panzieri resurrected Morandi's concept of "exploding" capitalism through structural reforms.[12] More interesting ideologically than

Vecchietti's "apparatus" Morandians but too abstract and independent, Panzieri withdrew from active politics in 1959 to protest Vecchietti's subservience to the Communists.

Claiming the Morandi mantle for themselves, the Vecchietti group paid little attention to ideology but fought Nenni because he had severed the communist link. Instead of the DC deal advocated by the general secretary, Vecchietti refurbished the Morandi concept of a grand alliance of Marxist and catholic *masses*, "class autonomy" in contradistinction to Nenni's "false" autonomy. In truth, however, this tactic restated socialist inferiority to the Communists because the PCI would direct masses using the USSR as a model.[13]

On 29–30 October 1958, the Central Committee adopted Vecchietti's report over Nenni's for the January 1959 National Congress by a 38 to 26 vote, with 19 cast for Basso. In a dramatic gesture, Nenni and the Directorate resigned, but the overconfident leftists rejected the resignations.[14]

On the surface, Nenni seemed to have suffered Fanfani's fate, but this interpretation is misleading. While the DC leader had support in the party but encountered defeat at the top, the opposite occurred in the PSI. Despite a communist campaign to condition the upcoming PSI assembly by a massive outpouring of manpower and money in Vecchietti's favor,[15] Nenni swept the provincial assemblies electing delegates to the National Congress.

At the PSI Naples congress (15–18 January 1959), Nenni shrewdly shifted from hard to conciliatory positions on national issues, from apparent acceptance of Basso's Democratic Alternative to soothing pro-DC statements. "Italy loves these matches of eloquence," he wrote in his diary on 18 January. The delegates gave Nenni a comfortable majority of 58.3 percent; Vecchietti received 32.7 percent, and Basso 8.7 percent.[16]

The next day, the new Nenni-controlled Central Committee selected the Directorate. A victorious Nenni instructed his Central Committee supporters to exclude the leftists from the party's directing body. Nenni turned aside an emotional Vecchietti appeal not to do so. In his diary, Nenni wrote: "Under other conditions, I would have accepted, but not today, because it would have been a means of keeping the left intact."[17] In addition to the Directorate, Nenni also shut off leftist access to *Avanti!* and other important party publications.

Unhampered by opposition in the Directorate, Nenni freely wooed sympathetic Christian Democrats, but by early 1959, those sympathizers no longer had charge of the catholic party.[18] In order to continue the catholic dialogue, Nenni supported friendly Christian democratic currents and promised an easy socialist agreement upon reestablishment of their influence. The Nenni camp believed that the nation's domestic problems favored a leftist comeback in the DC.[19]

By the eve of the DC's Florence congress in October 1959, a confident Nenni claimed that the right-wing Andreotti and Scelba-Pella factions had been "pulverized," while Fanfani's fortunes had revived. Fanfani's modernizing influence would inevitably burst ecclesiastical and reactionary economic constrictions on the Catholic party, Nenni predicted. This development would usher in a new era in PSI-DC relations and in Italian history.[20]

One of the DC arguments against the center-left had been that Nenni did not have enough control of his own party to implement his policies. Ironically, when Nenni in command of the PSI sought to negotiate with the Catholics, no one in the DC had the power to do so.

Civil Wars: Italy

Nenni's prognostications for the DC's Florence congress proved optimistic, although Fanfani did brush victory. Not only did the Dorotei need rightist votes to win, but, more important, Aldo Moro, leader of the leftist "undercurrent" within the Dorotei, emerged strengthened as secretary. In his characteristically obscure manner, Moro favored substituting the PSI for the Liberal party within the ruling coalition, but only if the Socialists actively combated the Communists. In this attitude, Moro resembled Fanfani, but unlike him advocated continued alliances with the right-center while socialist negotiations proceeded.

The quirks of the DC voting system produced a Dorotei-dominated National Council and Directorate. At the same time, the victorious faction pursued a center-right policy while contending with a powerful center-left minority which could reverse the balance of power at a moment's notice.[21] Despite his hopes, Nenni proclaimed the DC right wing as the real victors of the Florence assembly.[22]

Having temporarily blocked the center-left, Andreotti and Scelba conspired with liberal leader Giovanni Malagodi to scuttle socialist hopes of joining the governing coalition. Since his Liberals would be cut out of the government should the center-left succeed, Malagodi forced the DC's hand by pulling out of the ruling coalition. The aim was to force the DC to choose between a reinvigorated centrist coalition and a premature center-left.[23]

Malagodi gambled that the DC would stick with the Liberals. On the other hand, should the Catholics agree with the PSI, they would be unprepared to face local elections scheduled for the fall of 1960, and their losses would quickly induce them to pull back.

The political situation became extremely confused when the Liberals secured Segni's resignation in February 1960. President Gronchi and the DC Directorate squabbled over a candidate for prime minister, but Segni received the mandate with authorization to open discussions with the Socialists.

According to historians of the DC and the center-left, Segni had Moro's approval to negotiate PSI voting support or abstention in Parliament. As proof, they cite the massive campaign mounted by Confindustria and the Vatican to block agreement, reflecting Pope John XXIII's initially unfriendly attitude toward the center-left.[24]

Nenni, however, testified that the Socialists never considered Segni a viable candidate: "It's the old transformist habit of entrusting implementation of a leftist policy to men of the right, which, naturally, they can't do." On 12 March 1960, Nenni and his advisors conferred with Segni. Even though the Socialists had only three basic demands—implentation of the constitution-mandated regions, nationalization of energy resources, especially electric power, and school reform—Segni rejected them, confirming Nenni's opinion.[25]

Earlier, the suspicious Socialists had denounced a deal between the DC right wing and the Neo-Fascists for MSI support of a cabinet against Moro's intentions. The proof: the "fascistic DC right" had threatened to split the DC if it did not have its way in the lengthy negotiations for a Sicilian administration, a prelude of the technique it would employ against Fanfani later in the crisis.[26]

Unable to reach a positive conclusion, Segni renounced his mandate. President Gronchi then appointed Fernando Tambroni to break the impasse. Gronchi told Nenni that he aimed at a center-left, leaving the secretary very perplexed.[27]

Tambroni had distinguished himself at the last DC congress by his defense of Fanfani, and he apparently planned to make political concessions to the Socialists in an effort to obtain PSI abstention in a confidence vote. To please the Socialists, his cabinet included distinguished DC leftists—but he rejected the three basic PSI conditions for support.[28]

Furthermore, while he negotiated with the Socialists, Tambroni secretly wooed the MSI. Astoundingly, in requesting the chamber's confidence on 3 April 1960, Tambroni accepted neo-fascist votes but stated his determination to continue searching for socialist support. Within a few days, his three left-wing DC representatives resigned, followed shortly by seven other ministers. The DC Directorate had already asked Tambroni to withdraw but on 11 April did so more forcefully. This time the prime minister designate obeyed. Gronchi thereupon asked Fanfani to form a government.

"The crisis is back on its natural track," Avanti! happily commented. Following satisfactory talks between Fanfani and Nenni, PSI autonomists mistakenly concluded that the pro-center-left faction had regained control of the Catholic party.[29]

Unhappily for the Socialists, Cardinals Alfredo Ottaviani and Giuseppe Siri brought the Vatican's veto, and the DC Directorate rejected socialist support. With the votes of several independents, in the chamber, Fanfani would have had a majority of one if the DC remained compact. Immediately, however, two conservative catholic deputies announced that they would not vote for him. On 22 April 1960, Fanfani withdrew.[30]

Incredibly, President Gronchi then rejected Tambroni's resignation and invited him to complete his investiture by seeking a vote of confidence in the Senate. He had no other choice, Gronchi informed Nenni. Nenni suggested that Gronchi dissolve Parliament and call early elections, but the president refused.[31] The DC Directorate reversed itself by approving Gronchi's plan, and Tambroni received his Senate confirmation, again with MSI support, after stating that his cabinet would handle only routine administrative matters and would resign on 31 October 1960.

Quite clearly, the DC right wing had again blocked socialist entrance into the governing coalition by opening to the right instead of to the left. Furthermore, Tambroni violated his promise to the Senate by not behaving as a "caretaker" prime minister and by initiating important political measures.

To powerful business leaders, Tambroni pledged strong government; to increase his popularity among the middle classes, he lowered the price of gasoline, sugar, and other commodities and raised wages. Furthermore, Tambroni addressed important speeches directly to the nation instead of to Parliament. During the delicate international period following the downing of a United States U2 spy plane and the resulting clamorous breakup of the Geneva Summit, Tambroni projected the image of a strong leader. Rumors flew that Tambroni had established a secret police and awaited radicalization of the political situation in order to "save" the country. He had supposedly laid the groundwork for this police by utilizing the Italian intelligence service, SIFAR, in 1955 during an earlier tenure as interior minister in conjunction with Rome CIA chief Robert Driscoll.[32]

Furthermore, Tambroni's dependence on neo-fascist votes conditioned his action toward the MSI. In June 1960, the Neo-Fascists scheduled their congress for Genoa, a major resistance center against the Fascists. Some MSI leaders have argued that the party chose that city to distance itself from prewar fascism, which would have allowed it to extend its voter appeal and provide a more solid foundation for Tambroni, but the Genoese considered the congress an intolerable provocation.

Spontaneous strikes and riots protesting the MSI congress began in the port city on 30 June and spread across the country, including the capital. The massive police forces which Tambroni mobilized clashed with the rioters. After a vain attempt to change the locale of the congress, the government announced its postponement. Having lost face, Tambroni rejected all compromise and ordered the carabinieri to attack antifascist demonstrators with greater ferocity.

The people's intervention, however, ended the Tambroni experiment. The Communists had initially exploited the disorders, but Togliatti appealed for calm when the situation escalated. Nenni feared repetition of the events which had doomed Italian democracy in 1922, but no one had predicted the depth of antifascist feeling that permeated the nation. The riots allowed Moro to press the DC for immediate truncation of Tambroni's tenure and his substitution by Fanfani. Given the emergency, Moro secured support for such a cabinet from the PSDI, PRI, and PLI and the abstention of the PSI and the Monarchists. The DC Directorate thereupon requested Tambroni's resignation, which arrived on 19 July 1960.

The people had saved Italian democracy, but the Tambroni affair put the Socialists on notice that Italian conservatives would employ extreme measures to block what they considered radical leftward lurches of the political system.[33]

The "Parallel Convergences"

Modifying a famous phrase of prewar statesman Giovanni Giolitti, who defined church and state in Italy as two parallels which would never meet, Aldo Moro dubbed the Fanfani cabinet as that of the "parallel convergences."

Heralding the cabinet as an emergency solution, Nenni advocated PSI abstention in the parliamentary vote.[34] Nenni interpreted Fanfani's mission as liquidation of the "Clerico-Fascists" and recreation of the "conditions of democratic cohabitation and the free confrontation of ideas and programs."[35] Nenni considered the Fanfani cabinet one of "transition and transaction" which would stabilize Italy and prepare the center-left.

In requesting approval for his policy from the PSI Central Committee, however, Nenni met stiff opposition from the leftist minority, which dismissed the Fanfani cabinet as an expedient to salvage the DC. The leftists lost, and on 4 August 1960, the Socialists abstained in a Senate confidence vote.[36]

Fanfani's "parallel convergences" produced a number of reforms, especially socialist-inspired legislation establishing proportional representation in elections for provincial governments. The previous single-member voting system had forced PSI alliances with the PCI. Alteration of the provincial electoral system thus severed the last electoral connection between the former Popular Front parties and provoked Togliatti's ire.[37]

Unfortunately for the Socialists, the first local elections held under this system, 6 November 1960, produced poor results, with the PSI declining at the provincial level and the PCI increasing. The probable defection of leftist PSI voters to the Communists and disappointment of antifascist electors with the PSI's moderate policy after the Tambroni episode explain this outcome.

Lack of an electoral breakthrough complicated the next step toward a center-left coalition: establishment of local four-party center-left administrations foreshadowing a national center-left government. The Christian Democrats demanded an immediate end to local socialist coalitions with the Communists, while political realities in the provinces dictated gradual socialist disengagement. Only in January 1961 did a full-fledged center-left administration appear in an important center—Milan. The Milanese development served as a model, and by the end of Fanfani's tenure, thirty-three such administrations existed.

Within the DC, the difficulties in establishing local center-left *giunte* in late 1960 provided more ammunition for opponents of the opening to the left. Aldo Moro favored gradually reaching accommodations with the Socialists on specific issues. The Dorotei majority, however, advocated a ''great dialogue,'' an impossible theoretical and practical agreement on all questions. Furthermore, during this period, the catholic hierarchy fired its last shots against the center-left before Pope John XXIII altered his hostile attitude. Cardinal Siri brutally informed Moro that the bishops could not condone DC collaboration with the Socialists until they had guaranteed their independence from the Communists, and Cardinal Ruffini condemned the local center-left administration in Sicily.[38]

Lengthy negotiations for the *giunte* also rekindled PSI leftist opposition to Nenni. The longer the opening to the left dragged, the more the formula became worn out. At this point, however, international developments became decisive.

The American "Veto"

As has been observed, American policy in Italy opposed PSI governmental participation because of the communist connection and because the Americans feared repercussions on Italian foreign policy, particularly Italy's NATO commitment.

The Eisenhower administration's two ambassadors, Clare Boothe Luce and James D. Zellerbach, strictly enforced the American ''veto'' and ignored Nenni's gradual revision of PSI foreign policy attitudes. Luce openly interfered in Italian politics, advocating an opening to the right by inserting the Monarchists into the governing coalition. In a telephone conversation, Robert Komer recalled a Rome luncheon during which Luce defined Mario Scelba as a ''far leftist.'' Even as late as 1961, she insisted that ''for all practical purposes the P.S.I. and Communists must be considered as one grouping—the extreme Left.''[39] Rome CIA chief and future director William Colby recounts how the embassy influenced the 1956 local elections by authorizing him ''to fill the back seat of my Fiat with millions of lire and pass them on through my outside agent, an ostensible student, in one rather tense evening's work.''[40]

Zellerbach muted the embassy's style during his tenure (1957–1960), but the veto remained intact. The embassy refused all contact with socialist representatives while maintaining cozy relations with liberal leader Malagodi, a rarity among Italian politicians because of his excellent English.

Even during this period, however, American views toward the opening to the left differed, foreshadowing serious splits during the Kennedy administration. Colby favored the opening because it would isolate the Communists politically and, he estimated, bring an additional fifteen percentage points to the government's majority. Since lack of funds inhibited a quick PSI break with the Communists, he also favored American financial support for the Socialists. Liberal leaders of the CIA's International Division also sympathized with the progressive social and political changes sought by many Italian voters through an opening to the left. In Komer's recollection, CIA Director Allen Dulles favored the center-left. In the ensuing struggle over the direction of U.S. policy, however, Ambassador Luce scored a clear victory.[41]

In the State Department's Intelligence and Research Bureau (INR), John Di Sciullo, a man of uncommon energy and impeccable academic credentials, emphasized the importance of splitting Socialists from Communists and gaining PSI support for a stable democratic governing coalition after the 1953 elections. Convinced that the Americans should reach an accommodation with the Socialists, he inserted this thesis in the 1958 National Intelligence Estimate for Italy.[42]

The New Frontiersmen

These ideas remained rumblings until after John F. Kennedy's election in 1960. In the early days of the Kennedy administration, March 1961, National Security Council (NSC) Mediterranean Affairs expert Rober Komer sent a memorandum to McGeorge Bundy, special assistant for national security affairs, raising the possibility of altering American attitudes toward the opening to the left. Subsequently forwarded to the president, nothing came of this memorandum because of more pressing business.[43]

Komer, however, spoke to Presidential Advisor Arthur Schlesinger, Jr., who became interested in the problem and took the lead in changing American policy toward the center-left. Komer aimed primarily at ensuring that U.S. policy should not be construed by the Italians as opposing the opening to the left, he informed me during our telephone conversation of 9 October 1985. "Only two people ever listened to me [on this issue]," Komer said, "Arthur Schlesinger and Jack Kennedy." In his memos, Komer would refer to himself and Schlesinger as "Romulus and Remus."

In Schlesinger, Komer tapped the New Frontiersman best qualified to deal with Italian affairs. Having closely followed Italian politics since World War II as a member of the OSS, Schlesinger became, in his own words, "a fellow traveler of the Partito d'Azione" and knew La Malfa, Nenni, and Saragat. In describing his involvement in Italian affairs after Kennedy's election, Schlesinger told me: "I'd had a long-standing interest in it [Italian politics], and I thought that the veto imposed by the Eisenhower administration was nonsense. I talked to Kennedy about it, and he agreed."

In attempting to modify American policy, however, the New Frontiersmen ran into strong objections from entrenched State Department opponents. About this opposition, Schlesinger said:

> When [Ambassador-at-Large Averell] Harriman made a visit to Rome [in March 1961], he came back very irritated by Outerbridge Horsey [Rome deputy chief of mission], who was very rigid in his opposition. So there was just a general feeling, with which Mac Bundy agreed, in the White House, that this veto should be withdrawn and that we should look for an appropriate moment. And one of the oddities is the way in which our action was regarded as intervention in Italian politics. In fact, our point was to terminate the intervention of the Eisenhower administration and to allow Italian politics to take its natural course. And it seemed to us that the center-left was the solution to which the autonomous forces of Italian politics were moving and that, moreover, the resulting government would be a government which the Kennedy

administration would find more sympathetic. So for all these reasons, I got involved, and Kennedy sort of gave me the green light to be a gadfly on this issue.[44]

It might also be noted that Kennedy admired the British Labourites, with whom Nenni had close connections.

Schlesinger made a strong case for supporting the center-left in a memorandum to the president. Although Americans had voiced support of social reform in Italy, he wrote, their actions during the Luce period had "convinced most Italians that we really favor the big business interests." With Nenni's increased independence from the Communists and his closeness to the left wing of the DC came a more apparent need for social reform and an increasing belief among Italians that the opening provided the best hope for a stable democracy. Schlesinger urged Kennedy to make it clear to Fanfani during the prime minister's June 1961 trip to Washington that "if there is any real prospect of reclaiming a large segment of the Italian working class for democracy, the U.S. would welcome such a development."[45]

Besides similar ideological outlooks, several other motivations favored Kennedy administration support for the center-left. The administration sought Italian aid for resolution of the balance-of-payments problem. Efforts to have the Italians place new orders for arms proceeded apace, but Schlesinger emphasized increased Italian aid for lesser developed countries (LDCs), especially in Latin America, the Middle East, and Africa. Citing their own problems in the South, Italian contributions to LDCs had lagged. In his draft of remarks to be made by Vice President Lyndon Johnson at a dinner for Fanfani, Schlesinger cited Italian economic progress within a free society as "a valuable addition to the ideological arsenal of democracy." Taking particular note of Italy's classic southern problem, Schlesinger stated: "Italy's underdeveloped areas give her a common bond with most of the new, uncommitted nations of the world. If her own 'Operation Bootstrap' in Southern Italy . . . can show lasting results, Italy will loom large as a model and mentor for these nations."[46]

This view of Italy as a model for lesser developed countries remained an important administration theme. In talks with Italian President Antonio Segni in July 1963, Kennedy not only urged Segni's support for the center-left but also expressed hope that the DC would take a livelier interest in Latin America and encourage democratic development there. Harriman had previously raised the problem with President Gronchi on 9 March 1961, and Schlesinger had intervened against questionable American business practices toward Italian companies in Argentina.[47]

Along similar lines, talks took place between high administration officials and an important Italian consulting company for a Mediterranean regional approach to social and economic development. Fiat's Gianni Agnelli enthusiastically endorsed the project and awaited an appointment to speak directly with Kennedy about the matter, in which UN bodies had already expressed interest.[48]

In my conversation with him on 25 June 1985, Schlesinger confirmed his own formulation of the idea of center-left Italy as a model for other countries, and Kennedy's sympathy, especially in Latin America. Equally interesting, Schlesinger advocated the center-left formula for post-De Gaulle France and post-Adenauer Germany. In more immediate terms, as the diplomatic traffic between the Rome embassy and the State Department bears witness, the Americans fretted over the Gaullist model for Europe and viewed a stable center-left government as a barrier to a potential Italian De Gaulle.

In addition to working out a conceptual framework, the New Frontiersmen also took practical action. Averell Harriman visited Rome in March 1961, where he extended an invitation to Prime Minister Fanfani to visit Washington.

The interplay of Italian affairs and New Frontier thinking clearly emerges through the heavily censored ("sanitized") memoranda of conversations of Harriman's contacts with Italian leaders. In speaking with Saragat, for example, Harriman inquired why the Italian communist vote had not declined, despite Italy's impressive economic progress. Saragat's response has been struck out, but the revamped American anticommunist strategy is clear from Harriman's reply:

> Mr. Harriman replied that the Kennedy administration held this view as well. He added that the United States had learned from its experience in trying to help under-developed countries that it was not enough just to give financial assistance and that a social reform, even social revolution, was also necessary. The ambassador added that the new Democratic administration desired to advance the social and economic interests of the common people and that this was included in the concept of the 'New Frontier,' whereas the Republicans were more concerned with business interests.[49]

At the same time, Harriman demonstrated concern about the impact on foreign affairs of a possible PSI entry into the government.[49]

Schlesinger and I discussed Harriman's reservations, which Schlesinger cited as the official line toward Italian officials. Schlesinger spoke to Harriman after the ambassador's return from Rome, "and he was always, as I recall, in favor of it [the center-left]."[50]

Shortly after Harriman's trip, in April 1961, Schlesinger traveled to Italy to attend a conference on American foreign policy, sponsored by the Bolognese leftist DC review *Il Mulino*. Schlesinger considered contact with European intellectuals an important asset for the new administration, as he explained in a memorandum to the president. Although the meeting itself had scarce significance because the Bay of Pigs crisis erupted at the same time, the trip had important consequences.

The American delegation included a long-time Schlesinger friend, Institute for Defense Analysis senior analyst James E. King, Jr., who himself favored the opening to the left. Participation in the conference stimulated further interest in the center-left and created an influential group advocating its implementation. Besides Schlesinger and King, this group included *Washington Post* writer Leo Wollemborg, whose articles pepper the Schlesinger files at the John F. Kennedy Library; Victor Sullam, Washington representative of the Italian Federation of Farmer's Cooperatives; Victor Anfuso, an Italian-American member of Congress; Richard Gardner, future Carter ambassador to Italy; labor leaders Victor and Walter Reuther; and Fabio Cavazza, an influential member of the *Mulino* group. Along with Robert Amory, Jr., and Dana Durand of the CIA, Labor Secretary Arthur Goldberg, USIA Director Edward Murrow, and other highly placed Schlesinger allies, these people constituted a powerful lobby for the center-left.

Through Cavazza, King obtained appointments with Gronchi, Fanfani, Moro, and Nenni immediately following the Mulino conference. According to King, "I used the talks as a reason to encourage his [Moro's] conviction that it was in the interest of the United States to encourage, instead of continuing to oppose, collaboration between Socialists and Christian Democrats."[51]

Upon his return to the United States, King reported on his talks with Italian leaders and embassy officials in a memorandum circulated to influential Kennedy administration members. King provided an intelligent and sympathetic analysis of the opportunities and the risks of the center-left.

King argued that Rome embassy Deputy Chief of Mission Outerbridge Horsey exaggerated the risks of an opening to the left. All the leaders to whom King spoke agreed on the genuineness of Nenni's split from the Communists, although they did raise the question of what percentage of his own party Nenni actually controlled. Even right-wing DC leader Codacci Pisannelli dismissed the alleged danger of a DC split if the opening occurred, as did Aldo Moro—a specter agitated by the embassy.

As frequently happened in Italian politics, each party involved wished the other to take major action first, weakening itself internally and therefore vis-à-vis its opponent. Consequently, Moro complained that Nenni asked the DC to break off with the right and form a government which would depend on the Socialists but refused to provide "guarantees" that he would truncate relations with the Communists in the labor unions and the local administrations. Nenni in turn objected that a sudden break with the Communists in these areas would shatter the unity of the workers' movement, throwing many of them into communist and catholic unions, and would turn over control of fifteen hundred communes to the center and right—out of the two thousand under leftist administration.

On the other hand, Moro said he considered the center-left "inevitable" because a PSI alliance provided the only vehicle for progressive control of Italy's communes in all regions. Nenni stated his willingness and ability to bring his party with him but wearily informed King that he had already offered to do so three times—in 1956, in 1959, and "recently." The discussion over guarantees "has a distinctly chicken-and-egg flavor," King commented.[52]

In addition to circulating his memorandum to a privileged audience, King arranged for Nenni to write an article for *Foreign Affairs* in order to clarify his views for an American audience. In that article, Nenni argued that "The P.S.I. is not, and never was, a copy of the Communist Party" and attributed their former collaboration to the need for common action against fascism.[53]

This activity had a positive influence on Kennedy. In preparation for Fanfani's visit in June 1961, Schlesinger talked with State Department officials William Knight, who headed the Italian desk, and William Blue, director of the Office for Western European Affairs. Convinced by the embassy's arguments that the Socialists might take Italy out of NATO and promote nationalizations harmful to American business interests in Italy, these officials remained unmoved by Schlesinger's arguments. Accordingly, they advised Kennedy not to raise the issue with Fanfani and to respond blandly if the prime minister alluded to it.

Irritated by this rigid position, Schlesinger did not approach the State Department again on this question but called on his allies in the administration and communicated directly with the president. As a result, Kennedy told Fanfani that if he "thought it [the opening to the left] was a good idea, we would watch developments with sympathy."[54]

Ironically, Fanfani concealed this "sympathy" upon his return to Rome, probably to allow himself more room to maneuver, until a group of New Frontiersmen informed Italian observers during dinner in a Washington restaurant. Fanfani's "strange silence" irritated both Moro and Nenni.[55]

The "Bureaucracy" vs. "White House Characters"

Kennedy did not immediately implement his stated policy toward the opening to the left, and this failure encouraged American opponents of socialist participation to continue their opposition.

DCM Horsey defined the opening as "a fantasy—worse, a dangerous trap." He argued that fellow travelers still dominated the PSI, that a center-left coalition would split the DC in half, and that such a coalition would depend on communist votes. The center-left would mean neutralization of Italy and, as quoted by King, "a tremendous boost to Communism in Western Europe."[56]

Within the embassy, Horsey crushed all opposition by acting against First Secretary George Lister, whose career Harriman saved in extremis. According to Leo Wollemborg, Nenni did not expect such resistance from U.S. diplomats in Italy because they should have considered the center-left a "plus." Wollemborg, who encountered embassy hostility because of his *Washington Post* articles favorable to the center-left, explained the embassy conduct by citing the "cold war atmosphere" of the 1940s and 1950s, in which embassy officials had matured. They said to their critics, in effect, "We might have lost China, but look at the stability we have in Italy."[57]

After the president's expressed sympathy for the opening to the left, the embassy's arguments against it changed. After so many years of interfering in Italian affairs, American diplomats in Rome now championed "neutrality." According to Horsey:

> The central question was whether the influence of the United States government, overt or private, should be used to favor or oppose a development in internal Italian politics. It was my view . . . that the United States government should not intervene in this process. The process involved considerable risks, and the United States government was not in a position to repair damage or the consequences which might be caused by its action.[58]

As Horsey knew, however, in this case "noninterference" meant preserving the status quo to which the embassy had mightily contributed.

More open-minded but weak, President Kennedy's ambassador to Italy, G. Frederick Reinhardt, did not alter the embassy's policies. In substance, he agreed with Horsey and became angry with Schlesinger's actions attempting to circumvent the embassy's resistance. Reinhardt complained directly to Kennedy about Schlesinger's "interference" during a March 1962 meeting. According to Reinhardt, the president "quickly got the point and reassured me that my interpretation of his attitude and the Government's policy was a correct one, and that I was not to be misled or pushed one way or the other by these people, who, I've forgotten to say, were also working on me as well as they were working on Italians." However, in a memorandum of conversation concerning this meeting, drafted by the ambassador himself, Reinhardt made no mention of this statement or anything resembling it.[59]

In fighting the embassy and its allies in State Department operations (EUR), notably William E. Knight of the Italian desk, Schlesinger traveled to Rome to convey Kennedy's attitude on the center-left directly to Italian leaders, including Nenni. He wrote to Italian contacts on White House stationery and solicited the support of a host of New Frontiersmen. In late 1961, he obtained the collaboration of Senator Hubert Humphrey, noted for his sympathy with social democratic ideas. During a trip to Rome, Humphrey lobbied to change the embassy's attitude and met with Nenni and other PSI leaders to convey the administration's new thinking to them.

Far from convincing Reinhardt and Horsey, these efforts irritated them. In Washington for a four-month period at the end of 1961, an angry Horsey stormed INR demanding alterations in the 1962 National Intelligence Estimate, sympathetic to the opening to the left. He failed miserably and then tried to discredit it. Through its director, Roger Hilsman, INR lined up with Schlesinger against EUR on the center-left. A 19 January 1962 INR research memorandum flatly contradicted numerous embassy reports by detailing the socialist shift away from pro-Soviet positions and by concluding that "no stable or viable alternative to a 'left-of-center' government appears to exist."[60]

Schlesinger and the embassy also differed on covert American financial support for the PSI and an invitation for Nenni to visit the United States. A fragment of a larger document in the Schlesinger Papers, written on paper marked in bold red characters "Cabinet Paper—Privileged. Property of the White House—For Authorized Persons Only," makes the case for aid against Reinhardt's advice. (Obviously a draft, the more revealing original title, "The Arguments for Assistance to the PSI," is crossed out and replaced with "Pro and Con on Assistance to the PSI.")

According to the document, Reinhardt's reasons against assistance included that the PSI autonomists did not need assistance; future PSI gains would be at the expense of the DC and PSDI; as the PSI grew stronger, its contest with the Communists for working-class support would force it to pressure the Italian government to assume more radical positions; the center-left would not isolate the PCI but give it greater respectability and produce a Popular Front mentality; and American support should be conditioned on "a fairly clean break" with the PCI or a PSI split. The author refers to the authority of Moro, Fanfani, and Saragat on the points of internal Italian politics, summarily stating that those leaders "are presumably the best [judges of those issues, but the next page is missing]."

Noting that the PSI already "receives covert assistance from the Italian Government through state economic organizations," the argument for support, typical of Schlesinger's position, "would be that it is to the US interest to seek out the PSI rather than wait for them to come to us—that the more we can implicate them, the more we bind them to the west. Moreover, the PSI provides us what we have not had up to this point—a means of broad contact with the Italian working class through which we can reach the Italian masses and intensify the polemics between the PCI and the PSI." Handwritten notes in the margin added: "It is a serious question, for example, whether a split in the PSI would be to our advantage—whether it might not turn Nenni into another Saragat and deliver the *carristi* to the PCI." The reference to Saragat is to the drastic decline in PSDI support in the years following the 1947 split, cited, amazingly, by embassy officials to "prove" that Nenni's influence would decline if he broke with the Communists.

If American covert aid is extended to the PSI, the document continues, "we will face a problem within the American labor movement." American labor, in the persons of Walter and Victor Reuther, had long extended financial aid to PSDI labor organizations, and probably to the party. The Reuthers "are strongly in favor" of aid, the document states, but the George Meany group, influenced by Vanni Montana's Italian-American Labor Council, opposed assistance. It might be noted here that Knight cited Montana's doubts as evidence that the Italian-American community opposed the center-left. On the aid issue, the document concludes, "I don't think that we know enough for a final decision," but actually makes a powerful case for covert help to the PSI.

The document ends with arguments against Horsey's opposition to a Nenni visit to the United States and skillfully uses a phrase in a Horsey Airgram to favor a Saragat visit to President Kennedy as a prelude to a Nenni visit. Other documents demonstrate that Schlesinger closely coordinated his activities with higher State Department echelons through McGeorge Bundy.[61] Within a few months, Saragat had visited the president, and Nenni had been invited.

Although Schlesinger still maintains that their personal relations remained good, in 1963 he advised Kennedy to replace Ambassador Reinhardt with Liberal Barry Bingham. The new ambassador, Schlesinger wrote in his memo, should be capable of conducting "*creative* diplomacy in Rome. It is not enough to 'watch events closely' and report on them. We must have an active policy . . . if we are to help Italy to move toward a stable and democratic regime."[62] At the time, Reinhardt had been exploiting the MLF issue to block the center-left.

Obviously, Kennedy's unwillingness to intervene directly gave State Department opponents of the opening ample room to maneuver. One State Department source told me that Kennedy said in his presence, "Don't put this monkey on my back. If it goes well, we won't get the credit; if it goes badly, we'll get the blame."[63] Italian desk officer Knight made a similar observation.[64]

In response to my question on Kennedy's "nonintervention," Schlesinger answered:

> That's true. Kennedy permitted *me* to agitate . . . but he had too many other battles with the State Department, and this was not one of the pressing issues. So he gave me a hunting license . . . but he didn't overrule. As I say, there were other issues which he thought were more consequential about which he was fighting with the State Department. You can't fight on every front.[65]

In fact, the Cuba and Berlin crises put Italy on hold, but the administration's Italian goals demonstrate its long-term policy aims very well.

Despite Kennedy's other pressing problems and his reluctance to overrule the State Department on the center-left, Arthur Schlesinger emphasises that the president clearly conveyed his sympathy for socialist participation in the governing coalition to Italian leaders.

Not only did Kennedy express to Fanfani in June 1961 that the previous American "veto" no longer existed, but he did so again during his trip to Italy in July 1963. William Fraleigh, embassy counselor who accompanied Kennedy in Rome, recalls hearing Kennedy say "how much he hoped that the new coalition government in Italy would be a success and how much opportunity it seemed to offer for useful achievement."

At a Quirinale garden reception for party secretaries of the "democratic" area, including Nenni, Kennedy took pains to demonstrate his esteem for the socialist secretary while the other leaders fumed, especially Malagodi. According to Fraleigh, Kennedy spoke to Nenni privately, in the presence of an interpreter:

> And they stood in the middle of this platform and talked and talked and talked. The crowd began to buzz with interest in this. And some of the other democratic leaders, I think, began to get a little restless—they were out in the wings—from

wondering whether they'd ever get to speak to the President, and especially whether they'd ever get to speak to the President for anything like as long as Nenni was.

As we shall see later, the negotiations for the center-left passed through a particularly delicate phase during this time, and Kennedy's attention bolstered the secretary's image.

According to Fraleigh, Nenni was "absolutely enraptured and happy as he could be," while Schlesinger informed me that Kennedy considered Nenni a "legendary figure," deliberately intended to signify his acceptance of the Socialists, and did so again in his talks with Segni. Nenni claimed that Kennedy told him that while he, Kennedy, represented the present, Nenni represented the future, and Schlesinger believed such a Kennedy statement likely.[66]

The next day, at a luncheon Kennedy gave for President Segni at the Villa Taverna, a telephone call cited by Fraleigh announced that the Socialists would abstain in a vote of confidence for Giovanni Leone's stopgap government, allowing more time to complete center-left negotiations.

In addition, the Kennedy administration finally broke formal State Department and embassy resistance to its policy because opposition in these quarters had gotten out of hand.

In late November 1961, an incredible meeting took place at the Rome embassy during which some participants advocated American military intervention to block the center-left. Alan Platt, author of a dissertation on the center-left and American policy, interviewed most of the protagonists and cites a confidential interview as his source for this statement. Italian sources have consistently identified Vernon Walters, then Army charge d'affaires in Rome and present American ambassador to the United Nations, as the proponent of armed intervention. Walters has denied this allegation, but his hostility to the center-left, his close association with SIFAR director, General Giovanni De Lorenzo, against whom strong evidence of plotting a coup d'etat in 1964 exists, and the unreliability of Walters's memoirs when discussing American attitudes toward the opening to the left all indicate that he might indeed have made such a suggestion.[67]

Ironically, Walters's opponent from this period defends him from the charge. Arthur Schlesinger manifested surprise when I raised this issue with him on 25 June 1985. Schlesinger said:

> Dick Walters is not one of the smartest people in the world, but even *he* must—I mean, he might conceivably have mused about it, God knows—but his recommendations—he was regarded as an interpreter, a military liaison with the Italian government; he had no role in the policy process. And if he made such a recommendation, which is possible, though not in my opinion probable, certainly no one dreamed of paying any attention—why the whole-out notion is crazy.

Schlesinger added that Walters "is a man of *extreme* right-wing views," had "very close relations with the Italian military," and mentioned his closeness to Clare Boothe Luce (he met her in Italy during World War II). Although Walters may have had no policymaking role, he definitely conveyed to Italian military men hostile to Socialists a very different idea on where the Americans stood than the one the administration held. Given his own and the ambassador's position, their attitude could very well have encouraged Italian opponents of the center-left to take illegitimate measures against it once they lost the political battle and once Kennedy and the New Frontiersmen had left the scene.

At the end of 1961 and the beginning of 1962, therefore, the New Frontier removed the last major obstacles to American support for the center-left. In November 1960, Enrico Mattei had concluded a giant oil deal with the Soviet Union. As noted, Mattei supported the center-left, even though his ultimate goals are difficult to pin down. Nenni sympathized with Mattei's oil activities, and he met with Mattei shortly after the Soviet agreement. "Mattei says that he wants to issue a warning to America," Nenni recorded in his diary, "so that it will understand that it cannot continue to exploit us by making us pay exorbitant prices for Middle Eastern oil." Nenni noted that the Socialists backed him "in the interests of the nation."[68]

Mattei's activities perplexed even New Frontiersmen. A secret memorandum of conversation which I obtained under Executive Order 12065 details a meeting on the subject on 17 March 1962 among presidential advisors and the highest levels of the State Department. Alarmed at Mattei's apparently growing power, Under Secretary of State George Ball cited his "alleged responsibility for the establishment of the new Fanfani government dependent on the PSI and the possibility that he was becoming a front for the Chinese Communists and an agent for the Soviets in the sale of oil."

After an "exhaustive reassessment" of Mattei, however, Under Secretary of State George McGhee, from oil-rich Texas, proposed an accommodation with ENI, and the participants agreed that McGhee should ask Walter Levy of Standard Oil of New Jersey to come to Washington to discuss the details of a possible deal. Ball "said the net result of such an arrangement, if it could be accomplished, would be to remove Italy from the category of oil-short countries" and that this would change Italian actions in this "entire field for the better." On 19 April 1962, McGhee spent several hours with Standard Oil of New Jersey's director and executive vice president, W. R. Stott, hammering out the details of an agreement with Mattei, and both Stott and Ball prepared to meet the ENI director.[69]

The Kennedy administration therefore mediated between American oil companies and Mattei for resolution of their differences, eliminating a major obstacle to favorable American policy on the center-left and helping Italy obtain the cheap energy necessary for its economic development.

Finally, the administration dismantled the internal opposition. The appointment of Averell Harriman as under secretary of state for political affairs in 1963, natural turn-overs, transfers—Horsey's nomination as ambassador to Czechoslovakia, Knight's pro-motion, Walters's transfer to Brazil—produced a bureaucracy which lined up with the president's policy in late 1962 and 1963.

Influential American resisters who feared a communist takeover through the PSI, however, remained active behind the scenes. Former Ambassador Luce wrote a long, rambling letter to the president, predicting a communist takeover of Europe. Her Italian analysis follows:

> Italy's pro-West government has had one foot on the Moscow banana peel for seventeen years. The Italian government, which two years ago included the pro-Moscow Nenni Socialists, cannot survive a debacle of the French center, and Italy will probably anticipate it, by bringing the pro-Communist Socialists into power.

In effect, the Italians had hoodwinked Kennedy, Luce intimated:

> The Italians have *no* problem: they are shutting up, while putting up—as usual, next to nothing. They have for a long time had a solution against the day U.S. troops are withdrawn. . . . They keep a large Communist party in readiness to act as receivers in

bankruptcy for the nuclear realities. The Italian Communist Party will negotiate Italy's future with the U.S.S.R.[70]

Two responses from Kennedy and McGeorge Bundy in the Kennedy Library's President's Office Files demonstrate how gingerly the administration had to treat Luce because of her powerful press connections.

By 1963, the New Frontier had eliminated overt American opposition to socialist participation in the Italian governing coalition and had made its support clear, thus providing a powerful impetus to the center-left's formation.

CHAPTER 9

Birth of the Center-Left

Despite strong support from the New Frontiersmen, the Italian political system still caused Nenni significant difficulty in his campaign to bring the center-left into being.

The "Executory Phase"

While the New Frontier slowly implemented its policy favoring the center-left, cracks appeared in the PSI, making it more difficult for Nenni to retain control just as the center-left became operative. In January 1961, the different PSI factions filed three reports at the Central Committee meeting preparing the 34th Congress; Basso's distinguished itself for its impracticality, Vecchietti's for its procommunism, and Nenni's for its pragmatism.[1]

At the 34th National Congress (Milan, 15–20 March 1962), Nenni lectured the delegates on what he viewed as the continuing plot of Italian conservatives to destroy democracy and argued that socialist abstention on the vote for the "parallel convergences" cabinet had rescued Italy from a situation similar to that which had preceded fascism. His constant fear of a rightist takeover, strangely denied by the left, conditioned Nenni's future policies.

Nenni cited the "parallel convergences" agreement to demonstrate that the dialogue with the Catholics had entered an "executory phase." He praised the DC left wing for implementing its policy against the powerful catholic right wing and criticized Basso and Vecchietti for dangerously undervaluing the continuing reactionary peril and the progress made toward the opening to the left. Categorically stating that the PSI would never again enter a Popular Front, Nenni presented the center-left as the greatest guarantee of democracy and the only realistic combination capable of implementing reforms.[2]

The Congress gave Nenni's "Autonomy" faction 56.8 percent of the votes, a slight gain for the left, which regained representation on the Directorate. The executive body included seven leftists and thirteen autonomists; on the Central Committee, the Nenni camp counted forty-five representatives to the left's thirty-five (plus Pertini in a maverick position). "This creates a new situation," Nenni wrote in his diary, preoccupied that an influential member of his group, Lombardi, would cause him trouble.[3]

Immediately after the Milan meeting, Nenni tackled the static political situation: the "parallel convergences" cabinet had outlived its usefulness. From an "emergency solution," an impatient Nenni admitted, the cabinet had become an obstacle to a full-fledged center-left. Too many right-wing DC notables graced that cabinet, which also did little to ensure a more equitable distribution of Italy's growing wealth. As a result, all categories of workers took to the streets. Man-hours lost to strikes increased from forty-six million in 1960 to more than seventy-nine million in 1961.

In May 1961, therefore, Nenni attacked the government, and on 6 July the PSI sponsored a no-confidence motion. Rather than the government's fall, Nenni aimed at forcing Italian political factions to take public positions on the Socialists because the left's increase at Milan congress had provoked criticism of the PSI's foreign policy. In fact, Moro and Fanfani defended Nenni's actions within the PSI and the general socialist line.[4]

Given Fanfani's Washington talks with Kennedy in June 1961 and Pope John XXIII's definitive swing to the left in mid-July with *Mater et magistra*, the DC left wing appeared finally to have gained the upper hand in the party.

The church's leftward shift had important ideological and political consequences. In September 1961, DC leaders and intellectuals met at the small northern town of San Pellegrino to draw the new encyclical's implications. Left-wing catholic economists Pasquale Saraceno and Achille Ardigò dominated the meeting. Their position was that the church recognized the growing importance of social problems and pressed political authorities to resolve them. Concretely, they argued, the church sanctioned state intervention in the market in order to correct social, geographic, and productive imbalances which a totally free market accentuates. This new mission. in turn, authorized state implementation of "planning" to alter the production levels and income distribution necessary to eliminate imbalances.

Both DC and PSI accepted these premises and helped produce a political agreement, but according to historian Giuseppe Tamburrano, catholic and socialist understanding of "planning" differed fundamentally. Whereas San Pellegrino exalted the state's role and emphasized political choices over economics, Tamburrano argues, the conference ignored the question of whether the state would be given the coercive means to enforce its decisions on which investments to make, and where, when indirect means did not work. In other words, catholic "planning" guided the existing economic system, eliminated its harshest realities, and thus salvaged it.

On the other hand, socialist planners Riccardo Lombardi and Antonio Giolitti viewed planning as the transition to socialism. According to them, the Socialists aimed at the extension of the economy's public sector, primarily through nationalizations, in order to achieve state control over production and investments. According to Lombardi, this policy must characterize the center-left. Of course. the DC would go along only until a certain point, but by then, Lombardi argued, the DC would probably split, the Communists would acknowledge the policy's effectiveness, and the workers would support the PSI. In other words, the center-left would polarize the struggle between capitalism and the partisans of socialism.[5]

Lombardi's "revolutionary reformism" thus doomed the center-left because the Catholics would hardly accept such developments. Furthermore, Lombardi's ideas clashed with Nenni's pragmatism, causing an explosion in the Nenni camp.

Reflecting the leftward DC drift and expecting the Catholics to sanction socialist entrance into the governing coalition at their upcoming congress, the PSI Central Committee accepted a report by its Economic Commission in January 1962. Headed by Lombardi, this commission backed economic planning and listed a number of "structural" reforms, among which nationalization of the electric industry figured most prominently. Autonomists and leftists argued over its significance, but both finally accepted it. Nenni saw it as the basis for an agreement with the Catholics, and Vecchietti expected the DC to turn it down.[6]

In fact, however, at the Naples congress (27–31 January 1962), Fanfani, Moro, and the Dorotei also accepted the San Pellegrino conclusions and the ideas expressed at the PSI Central Committee meetings. Characterized by a six-hour Moro speech, this congress authorized a socialist alliance but not socialist participation in the government.[7]

On 2 February, Fanfani resigned in order to set up a new cabinet reflecting these developments. Fanfani won PSI abstention for his government in a vote of confidence in March 1962. Nenni characterized his party's abstention no longer as an "emergency" but as support to guarantee Fanfani a majority. The Central Committee judged Fanfani's program positively. "A miracle in Via del Corso [PSI headquarters]," was Nenni's comment on the left's favorable vote and agreement that the government program coin-' cided the PSI's previously accepted Economic Commission's report.[8]

The Fanfani program contained "nothing very radical as compared with programs and accomplishments of other recent governments," American Ambassador Reinhardt reported home.[9] Fanfani emphasized the need for economic planning and agricultural, social, and fiscal reforms, and hedged on nationalization of the electric industry.

According to Nenni's diary, Fanfani and Moro had technical or tactical reservations to socialist demands for nationalization of the electric industry, school reform, institution of regions, and exclusion of rightist leader Andreotti from the cabinet, not objections of principle. In his declaration of benevolent socialist parliamentary abstention, Nenni rebelled against aid to private schools but strongly intimated that he had a Fanfani agreement to nationalize electric power within three months and a commitment to create the regions and hold regional elections before the current legislature's end.[10]

On the eve of the PSI abstention on Fanfani, Neo-Socialist Nenni met with New Frontiersman Schlesinger at the home of a journalist whom the American regularly visited on his Rome trips. They discussed foreign policy, both men agreeing on PSI support of detente and hoping for serious discussions of disarmament and peace. On domestic policy, Schlesinger compared the evolution of Italian policy to "forcing open a door which kept the masses distant from the state." The two men agreed that, despite remaining difficulties, "the hope of a new policy has been born."[11] St. Gregory, however, complicated that hope.

St. Gregory's Night

Despite Fanfani's apparent ambiguity, the first center-left government got off to an excellent start. With decisive socialist backing, it nationalized electric power, imposed a new withholding tax on stock dividends, implemented obligatory school attendance till age fourteen, and passed a host of other potentially significant reforms. Far from satisfying the contending political forces, however, this intense activity irritated practically all of them.

Hungered after by Socialists, nationalization of the electric industry yielded unsatisfactory short- and long-term results. Besides frightening conservatives, who pressured the DC to repudiate the government, nationalization did not achieve the socialist goal of eliminating the "economic right" and its political influence. The government paid electric companies directly for their assets, not individual stockholders. This enabled the "economic right" to take over the chemicals industry, where it established a new power base—the giant Montedison. Furthermore, Lombardi's insistence on a socialist vice president for the new state electric agency (ENEL) conveyed the impression of socialist participation in a new spoils division and negated the PSI image favoring "moralization" of the political climate. Finally, while nationalization did aid planning and investment, it hardly lowered rates or dispelled the arrogant image of state agencies. Nor did this reform become a "time bomb" set to explode the capitalistic system, as Lombardi had predicted. Indeed, if anything, it strengthened capitalism by rationalizing its energy needs.[12]

The other dramatic reform of this period had similar mixed results. The withholding tax on stock dividends addressed a hoary means of tax evasion in Italy, but the law did more than frighten investors. Legislation in December 1962 established a *cedolare secca,* a maximum 15 percent rate on foreign holders of Italian stock. To the fear of nationalization, this provision added a powerful economic incentive for sending Italian currency abroad and further stimulated a massive exodus of Italian capital. Although an undetermined proportion of this capital returned to Italy as "foreign" capital enjoying the lower tax rate, the exodus probably accounted for more than half of a huge balance-of-payments deficit which suddenly reversed a three-years surplus in Italian accounts.

The unions worsened the economic situation. Despite the friendliness of the CISL, the UIL, and the Nenni CGIL component, CGIL policy coincided with the communist line of sabotaging the center-left. The CGIL rejected Budget Minister La Malfa's "incomes policy" tying higher wages to production increases and struck for higher pay. As a result, 1962 witnessed a record one hundred five million man-hours lost to strikes. Despite very real immediate gains for workers, this strike policy wounded the government and damaged the workers' long-range interests. Wages rose, sometimes by 35 percent creating greater internal demand, increasing imports, and aggravating the balance-of-payments deficit. The resulting inflation may be measured by the consumer price index, which jumped from 117.8 in 1962 to 123.3 in 1962 and 132.5 in 1963.[13]

Socialist economists headed by Paolo Sylos Labini proposed immediate and long-term measures to ward off the economic crisis. These steps included price and rent controls, defense of the lira, selective support of the stock market, reorganization of the public administration, urban reform, credit expansion, and agricultural reform. In effect, these proposals seconded La Malfa's famous "Nota Aggiuntiva" advocating government intervention to guide free-market forces.[14] The center-left coalition's inability to implement this program, however, passed the initiative to the Bank of Italy, which applied credit restrictions and choked off industrial expansion.

In addition to these difficulties, the PSI lost a contest with the Communists. Fully comprehending the isolation to which a successful center-left would have condemned them, Togliatti adopted a middle line between PCI leaders Pietro Ingrao and Giorgio Amendola. Ingrao agreed with PSI left-wing rejection of the center-left; Amendola recognized that the government's program contained reforms the PCI had advocated. These positions risked either isolation or inversion of communist-socialist roles by subordinating the PCI to PSI initiatives. In a brilliant maneuver, Togliatti publicly acknowledged the renovating potential of the center-left but also the resistance to reform action which existed within the coalition. On 5 March 1962, he therefore committed the PCI to "constructive opposition" in Parliament while promising continued struggle in the country as a stimulus to reform.[15] The CGIL-inspired strike wave began the same month.

In an interview with Amendola, Giuseppe Tamburrano pointed out that this policy hit the government twice, by lending credence to arguments branding the center-left a communist "Trojan horse" and by sabotaging the government's economic policy. Amendola replied that the Communists could not do otherwise.[16]

In fact, the PCI faced a difficult dilemma. De-Stalinization and the Sino-Soviet rift caused the Italian Communists to apply " 'Polycentrism' in fact if not in name," according to an INR memorandum, and they cautiously challenged Moscow by acting more independently in domestic affairs.[17] In reorienting themselves into a more purely Italian political force, the Communists fought for their survival in opposing the political isolation to which the center-left would have consigned them.

It is questionable, however, whether the center left ever really threatened the Communists. Put together by Moro's alchemy, the coalition slowly began to unravel as early as May 1962. In return for right-wing acquiescence for the center-left experiment, Moro pledged Segni's election as president to oversee the center-left's development. When Gronchi's term expired, Moro dodged Nenni's proposal for an official center-left candidate and pushed for Segni's election. The result was an extremely complicated presidential election marathon. Fanfani's friends refused to follow Moro, and the PSI left wing bolted discipline by not voting for Saragat, the "official" PSI candidate. The coalition barely survived the complex balloting. "A black day for the center-left. A very black day for our party," Nenni commented.[18] Segni's election proved a powerful obstacle to the center-left. After nationalization of the electric industry, the withholding tax on stocks, the strikes, and the economic consequences of the Fanfani government's program, the majority Dorotei had had enough.

In the autumn of 1962, the focus shifted to creation of the regions, to which Fanfani had by now publicly committed himself. On 27 December, however, the DC Directorate asked the PSI for guarantees that it would not form Popular Front governments in the regions. Confronting heavy left-wing opposition at an October Central Committee meeting, Nenni accepted on "practical" grounds but requested an agreement on reform implementation which would last for the entire upcoming legislature.[19]

The DC refused and pressured Secretary Moro to slow down the political process, making it impossible for Fanfani to meet his target date of 31 October 1962 for institution of the regions. Moro exploited fear of communism to block decentralization and called for a clean break at all levels between Socialists and Communists. Fear of voter reaction against the DC in the upcoming national elections contributed to this policy and sabotaged Fanfani, who unsuccessfully resisted his party's new course. The DC's reversal also embarrassed Nenni, who, however, successfully dissociated his party from the DC's position on the regions while resisting left-wing socialist exhortations to join the PCI in a no-confidence vote.[20]

In addition to nationalization, withholding taxes, and decentralization, Moro feared widespread losses to the Liberal party in the upcoming elections because of a proposal for urban reform. Presented by the DC left wing ("Base") minister of public works, Fiorentino Sullo, this legislation aroused widespread opposition. Directed against large companies speculating in the cities, driving up the cost of housing and ruining the environment, attention focused instead on a minor provision which critics maintained would drastically limit property rights. The most effective slogan compared this limit to "a temporary use of the soil similar to the one currently in use for crypts in cemeteries." As opposition escalated, Moro hurriedly dissociated his party from its own public works minister. In the short term, the DC lost the support of small property owners to the PLI. In the long run, Sullo's urban reform attracted Socialists and occasioned a possible coup attempt; urban reform became too hot for governments to touch, thus provoking massive housing shortages beginning in the 1970s.[21]

The center-left paid for these developments in the national elections of 28 April 1963. The DC lost its more conservative supporters, dropping from 42.3 percent to 38.2 percent. The votes it lost went to the PLI, which also picked up votes from the dissolving Monarchists and doubled to 6.9 percent.

While the DC lost votes to its right, the PSI lost them to its left. The slight socialist fall from 14.2 percent to 13.8 percent becomes significant in light of the unexpected PCI increase from 22.7 percent to 25.3 percent. Many left-wing voters accepted the communist argument that the Socialists had "sold out," and PCI gains came primarily from the socialist left wing. In his diary, Nenni reports socialist resentment at a hard communist campaign against the PSI; the CIA quoted Fanfani as saying that the PCI "instructed" the four hundred thousand left-wing Socialists it controlled to vote communist.

The CIA strove to find positive aspects. According to the same report, Fanfani said it was

> fortunate that the center-left government was formed before, and not after, the election. The PSI was thus compromised with the DC, PSDI and PRI, and therefore incurred the ire of the PCI. . . . As a result of the elections the PCI and PSI together and for the first time have more votes than the DC party. Had the government not been formed before the elections, and the PSI therefore not been compromised, a "Popular Front" could have resulted. Today, a Popular Front is almost impossible because of the mutual hatred which exists between the PSI and the PCI.[22]

These results had important consequences. They confirmed the Dorotei belief that Fanfani had gone too far to the left and made party leaders more determined to remove him. As a whole, Italy had moved leftward, Nenni noted bitterly, but the political system would move to the right.

The elections had negative results for the Socialists but some positive ones for Nenni. If reduced socialist influence on the left cut the party's bargaining power, the elections altered the PSI's internal makeup. The party's percentage had remained stable despite the hemorrhage of leftist votes because of gains among new voters. In the Chamber, twenty-one of twenty-seven newly elected socialist deputies favored Nenni; fifteen out of eighteen new senators did so. Previously, the influential socialist parliamentary delegation had been more evenly divided between the factions. This result, however, hardly compensated the PSI for its electoral failure, which lay in its apparent inability to attract large numbers of voters to its center-left policy. As Nenni put it to a visiting American professor, the "DC lost votes, but we lost a battle."[23]

In Washington, the New Frontier put as good a face as possible on the election results. Edward R. Murrow, U.S. Information Agency director, informed the president that Fanfani would be able to form a government with support from Nenni and Saragat and encouraged him not to call off plans for his Italian trip. One State Department memorandum emphasized PSI "purification" from philo-communists; another argued that the elections made the center-left more valid. Center-left parties still commanded a 62 percent majority in Parliament, making it the most stable and homogenous coalition possible.[24]

In fact, Moro confirmed this interpretation while turning down an ill-considered Togliatti bid for entrance into the governing coalition on the basis of the electoral results. Mindful of the pressures within his own party, however, Moro emphasized the anticommunist function of the center-left. This argument, in turn, created serious problems for Nenni where it did the most damage: within his own autonomist coalition.

The elections occasioned a serious rethinking of the PSI's course by the influential Riccardo Lombardi and Antonio Giolitti. Because the electorate had demonstrated its displeasure at the slow pace of reform, the PSI could support only a more advanced government with a program guaranteed against DC interference. Socialists should reject a new cabinet which offered less than Fanfani, Lombardi thought. In addition, given the communist performance in the recent balloting, the PSI could hardly sanction an anticommunist characterization of the center-left. Giolitti believed that the center-left must defeat the PCI in the struggle for reforms, not truncate the dialogue with them.[25]

In short, whereas Moro sought to overcome the center-left crisis by slowing down the pace of reforms and by shutting out the Communists ("delimitation of the majority"), Lombardi insisted on a guarantee of structural reforms and dialogue with the PCI.[26] These opposing positions caught Nenni in the Middle.

In May 1963, DC Secretary Moro received a mandate to put together a cabinet. He aimed at socialist participation. In his talks with Moro, Nenni found the catholic leader sympathetic but unable to withstand conservative pressure, especially after Pope John XXIII's death in June. On 14 and 15 June, however, socialist and catholic leaders finally hammered out the basis of a new government program in the "Camilluccia Accords."[27]

On 16 and 17 June 1963, St. Gregory's Night, the explosion occurred. Lombardi had demanded a leftist solution to the crisis but would have accepted a program which at least matched that of the previous government. In this light, Lombardi judged the Camilluccia agreement unsatisfactory and, at a Central Committee meeting which lasted until six A.M. on 17 June, joined with the left in voting against the agreement. This switch put Nenni in the minority and caused the ignominious collapse of the proposed center-left government.

Nenni viewed Lombardi's action as a "stab in the back," and the socialist press seconded this interpretation. In fact, Lombardi had been present in the talks with DC leaders, and Nenni maintained that he gave no hint of his future desertion. Lombardi, however, objected that he had stated explicitly that he deemed renunciation of certain provisions of the Sullo urban reform proposal as "unacceptable." Unfortunately, the two men did not discuss their differences frankly; otherwise they might have reached agreement.[28]

Symptoms of trouble came through to the Americans in a report on conversations with Lombardi and Pieraccini which an American university professor submitted to the embassy before St. Gregory's Night but which, curiously, reached Schlesinger much later. According to Professor Robert G. Neumann of UCLA, Lombardi denied reports of major differences between himself and Nenni but strongly objected to DC renegation of its promises and its call for a PSI declaration of a clean break with the Communists. According to Lombardi, this latter request unreasonably asked the PSI to remove itself from its "natural habitat." Because the PSI had a higher proportion of industrial workers than the PCI, this "stupid" demand meant abandoning the unions to the Communists. Lombardi advocated competition and contact with the Communists at the same time. He distinguished between "matters of state" and "matters not of state." The first referred to national governmental concerns such as police and foreign affairs, on which the PSI should break off contact; the second, however, concerned local matters and imposed dialogue with Communists. Even on this subject, a working relationship between DC and PSI could only be achieved gradually, not by issuing declarations.

On formation of a new center-left coalition, Lombardi accused the DC of delay by magnifying the security risks of decentralization. As a prerequisite for his agreement on a new government, Lombardi requested DC commitment on implementation of six essential reforms: "agrarian reform; urban reform; fiscal responsibility and reform of taxation; controls on corporations (no additional nationalizations for the time being) to correspond with public needs, such as over the location of new industries; school reforms; establishment of regions."

On foreign policy, Lombardi accepted "without reservation the Atlantic Pact" but expressed reservations on the Multilateral Nuclear Force (MLF) currently being exploited by DC conservatives to discredit the Socialists in American eyes. Lombardi categorically excluded a Popular Front if negotiations for a new cabinet were to break down.

Adopting a completely different tone, *Avanti!* editor Pieraccini downplayed the difficulties among the autonomists, attributing them to "tactical" considerations. Pieraccini's own stated priorities would not have presented any serious impediment to formation of a new cabinet. Curiously, however, of Lombardi's six reforms Pieraccini emphasized only the agrarian area because of the low level of farmer income. Furthermore, Pieraccini endorsed the MLF, a highly volatile issue in the PSI, and opposed Lombardi's "neutralism." Finally, he characterized Lombardi as "neurotic, changeable, mercurial."[29]

Clearly, the differences between the Lombardi and Nenni groups involved fundamental issues, even though they eventually patched things up enough to agree on socialist participation in a government.

The "Organic" Center-Left

St. Gregory's Night (16–17 June 1963) precipitated a crisis in the PSI and the country on the eve of President Kennedy's 1 July visit.

The PSI Directorate tendered its resignation, which the Central Committee rejected. The Central Committee's criticism of the Camilluccia Accords and reaffirmation of the center-left as the only possible political solution signaled Lombardi's unwillingness to draw extreme consequences from his arguments or to conclude a permanent alliance with the left wing. At the same time, President Segni authorized Giovanni Leone, president of the Chamber of Deputies, to form a stopgap *monocolore* government until Socialists and Christian Democrats could iron out their internal differences and resume negotiations for a full-fledged center-left. The Socialists hesitated on Leone, but Segni threatened to dissolve Parliament and hold early elections.[30]

As previously mentioned, the news of socialist abstention on the Leone government reached Segni during a luncheon with Kennedy. Indeed, the difficult gestation of the center-left probably induced the American president to make his sympathies for Nenni and PSI participation clear in the manner already noted. Closely observing these events, Schlesinger consulted with Averell Harriman and recommended replacement of the American ambassador.[31]

Lombardi had thrust Nenni into a difficult spot. Nenni's tactical concessions to Lombardi and the left wing following St. Gregory's Night weakened the secretary inside and outside the PSI. Doubts about their majority, declining funds, and poor showings in several by-elections depressed Nenni's men. Appeasement also furnished the DC right wing with a pretext to sabotage negotiations with the PSI. According to the catholic organ *Il Popolo,* for example, the Socialists could not establish a cabinet without PCI "consent." The only bright spot, according to a State Department observer: "if Nenni is really willing and able (politically and financially) to move forward, Lombardi will have to follow suit, also because he has nowhere else to go."[32]

Unwilling to reverse the majority in the PSI by combining with the left wing, Lombardi compromised with Nenni in the "July Orientations" agreement. Variously interpreted as both a Lombardi and a Nenni victory, both men's mental visions of the center-left coexisted in this document: Lombardi's center-left as a transformation of the existing system and Nenni's as a political encounter of secular and catholic forces for the strengthening of Italian democracy.[33]

Quite clearly, the July Orientations papered over fundamental differences between the two leaders, and Lombardi's subsequent behavior has been interpreted as an attempt to capture the more moderate left-wingers in order to form his own faction.[34] If true, Lombardi failed.

At the 35th Congress (Rome, 25–29 October 1963), Nenni once again emphasized the danger from Italian reactionaries and the urgency of defending democracy, but Lombardi declared that he conceived of the center-left as a means for the proletariat to achieve power, not a few improvements. As Lombardi passed by Nenni after he had finished his speech, Nenni whispered to him, "You have put yourself out of the majority." Nenni had written before this assembly: "The dilemma is: either we participate in the government, or else there will be a chronic instability of power, with new elections . . . and a general shift of center forces to the right, with the DC first and the Social Democrats following."[35] Although these different conceptions of the center-left would haunt Italy in the future, a break at this point suited no one. By a 57.42 percent vote, the delegates accepted the Nenni-Lombardi compromise motion, sanctioning further talks with Moro.

Amid myriad difficulties, Nenni and Moro had already begun discussions before the congress. Major issues remained: the posts which Socialists would obtain; the "delimitation of the majority," which meant that the new government would resign if it ever became dependent on communist votes to stay in power; and the MLF.

Nenni's anxiety to reach agreement induced him to give in as much as possible on domestic issues. Future Budget Minister Antonio Giolitti recalled for me a telephone call he received from Nenni asking if he would accept the Foreign Trade Ministry instead of one of the important economic posts. Giolitti refused, arguing that Socialists should get at least one of the three key cabinet economic positions. After accusing Giolitti of endangering the negotiations, Nenni made the request, stood his ground, and called back to inform Giolitti of Moro's acceptance.[36]

The MLF proved a more difficult case because of its importance in American politics. Fearing German rearmament through the MLF, many Socialists strongly opposed the concept. Leo Wollemborg vividly recalls socialist inquiries about exactly how important the Americans considered it, the passions it aroused in the United States, and the deals its die-hard supporters—the "Theologians"—allegedly made with the Italian ambassador to secure his support. According to Wollemborg, Giovanni Malagodi, in contact with the embassy, exploited socialist reluctance to accept the MLF in a last-ditch effort to block the center-left. John Di Sciullo's letters from Rome also testify to the intense debate over this question. Nenni's view coincided with the English Labour party's critical position, and he hoped for a Labourite victory to kill the proposal.[37]

An eleventh-hour alliance arose to block the center-left. Die-hard American opponents of the center-left combined with President Segni, who worked for the failure of negotiations between Nenni and Moro. Again the New Frontier swung into action. The CIA's Office of Current Intelligence made a compelling case for the center-left in late May 1963.[38] McGeorge Bundy kept close tabs on the embassy and blunted negative State Department input into the Italian situation. Schlesinger applauded Bundy. "I do think that, while Reinhardt says that we are not insisting on a definite Italian commitment to MLF," Schlesinger wrote to Bundy on 22 November 1963, "he then goes on to explain how vital we regard the MLF to be, therefore blurring the point and making it possible for the Segni crowd to use the MLF issue as a means of blocking the center-left."[39]

On the same day, negotiations for socialist entrance into the government continued in an unpromising atmosphere. Socialist and Christian democratic negotiators had agreed on the MLF, but domestic problems resurfaced.

Then news of Kennedy's tragic assassination came. Riccardo Lombardi recalled:

> We were arguing. . . . Cattani [PSI] was talking with Rumor [DC] and every so often came to tell us that the Christian Democrats appeared to be irremovable, when all of a sudden news of Kennedy arrived. Without a doubt, it was this element which precipitated the agreement. On the other hand, I did not have it in me to try another St. Gregory's Night. I thought that we should try the experiment, that the DC should be tested.[40]

By this tragic irony, the New Frontier made its last contribution to the center-left's birth.

CHAPTER 10

The Center-Left and Its Enemies

By December 1963, a center-left cabinet which included PSI representatives came into being, but the opening's internal enemies remained adamant, and its most powerful foreign sympathizer had been assassinated. On 17 April 1964, Arthur Schlesinger visited Rome and had a long conversation with Nenni. Nenni asked to what extent "Kennedyism" continued with President Lyndon Johnson. "The answer (chilling, even if true): 'In the same way Truman continued Roosevelt.' I.e., in its routine, not in its initiatives."[1] The center-left could no longer count on active American support.

Among the center-left's enemies, the PSI left wing proved the most immediately insidious.

Losing the Left

The original PSI left-wing factions drew nearer the more Nenni marked the party with his brand and the closer he came to his objective. For a while, Basso and Vecchietti voted with Nenni for tactical reasons, hoping that leftist input into party policy statements would sabotage negotiations with the DC and encourage Lombardi to link up with them. These aims having failed by late 1963, the left wing split away from the party.

As discussed above, Nenni had been pulling away from the Communists since 1953 but inextricably linked Stalinism and communism in 1956. The divisions among the Italian Socialists which followed issued from this reasoning, the Pralognan rapprochement with Saragat, and Nenni's alteration of PSI policies. Alarmed by these developments, the leftists jumped to the defense. Chief ideological spokesman Basso refuted Nenni's identification of Stalinism with the dictatorship of the proletariat.

In his rebuttal, Basso accepted the Second Internationalist argument that socialism developed within the structure of capitalism and "emerged" when sufficiently mature conditions warranted. He also admitted the corollary of this thesis: the more industrially developed and advanced a society, the smoother and less violent the transition to socialism. Therefore, primitive economic conditions in Russia had forced Lenin to employ revolutionary means to achieve socialism. In other words, Lenin had applied Marxist analysis, developed for the West, to a country for which it had not been designed. For Basso, Lenin had simply erred by underestimating the difficulties of establishing socialism in an area which had a weaker proletariat and a more tenacious, less progressive bourgeoisie than the West. The contradiction which arose from the backwardness of the masses compared to the enormous tasks of the revolution—the "objective conditions"—resulted in the sacrificing of democracy, the progressive alienation of the masses from their leaders, and "the iron Stalinist dictatorship."

Drawing on his studies of the German Marxist thinker Rosa Luxemburg, Basso concluded that Stalinism originated in Russian and world conditions in 1917, the difficulties of establishing socialism in a precapitalist society, the need for defense, and Stalin's personality. In short, Basso limited Stalinism to a particular historical context and carefully differentiated it from revolutionary Marxism. He insisted: "Let us not confuse the infinite richness of Marxism with this unique and exceptional experience [Stalinism], which will probably never occur again."[2]

Having secured its ideological rear, the left wing accused Nenni of distorting Stalinism's significance and exploiting it for propaganda purposes. As a consequence, it rejected his "neo-reformism" and fought his attempt to "social democratize" the PSI in concert with Saragat and the Americans.[3]

If Basso led the ideological charge against Nenni, chief leftist strategist Tullio Vecchietti aimed at reinvigorating the unity pact which Nenni had reduced to shreds. Vecchietti's thinking was that in democratic nations, the working class does not provide itself with a revolutionary organization to overthrow governments. In Italy, the existence of two parties guiding the proletariat dictated alliances to attract unorganized masses "tricked" by the nation's religious political orientation. Without unity among Socialists and Communists, therefore, the class struggle would become a waiting game for a parliamentary majority, not "the index of a general advancement of the working class in terms of effective power, of structural conquests within the society."

Furthermore, for Vecchietti, foreign policy paralleled internal "unity" politics. He admitted the end of the USSR's role as "guide" (*Stato-guida*) but did not draw any substantial conclusions for policy changes because

> In the struggle against imperialism and for peace, until such time as the world shall be governed by force, the Soviet Union represents not only a guarantee for the peoples' democracies and the Afro-Asian people against the recurrent adventures of the imperialist powers, but gives pause to those countries which wish to resolve by war the duel between imperialism and socialism.

As a result, Vecchietti denounced Nenni's distancing of the PSI from the Soviet Union.[4]

This mentality also provoked leftist condemnation of Nenni's relationship with the American New Frontier. While the Nenni group viewed the Kennedy administration as encouraging the democratic evolution of Italian society, favoring detente, and advocating the Italian political model against De Gaulle's reactionary nationalism, leftist leaders interpreted U.S. support of Italian liberalizing trends as gross interference in internal Italian affairs and proof of Italian submission to the Americans. For the left wing, Kennedy hoped only to solidify American predominance in Western Europe, and De Gaulle paradoxically became the champion of European political and economic independence.[5]

In addition to different worldviews, the left also rejected Nenni's belief in the continuing menace of a rightist reaction, by which he justified joining the ruling coalition and avoiding the socialist error which in 1919–1922 had furthered fascism's takeover.[6]

Basso simply interpreted Nenni's policies as a hodgepodge of snap decisions without basis in a well-defined strategic whole. This tendency led Nenni to cave in to DC demands and would transform the PSI into an appendage of the catholic organization. Even though the left sympathized with progressive catholic forces, right-wing catholic utilization of "the massive pressure of bishops and cardinals, in public or private, directly or indirectly," doomed DC autonomy, dialogue with the catholic masses, and a real PSI entente. Like Metternich, the PSI left wing did not consider the possibility of a liberal pope or of the church hierarchy revising its policies.[7]

This reasoning occasioned leftist socialist deprecation of any Christian democratic movement in a progressive direction. During the complicated discussions which produced local center-left administrations, for example, the left declared impossible the formulation and application of a progressive program in concert with the DC. The leftists stuck to this ideological stance even when confronted by a center-left cabinet promising substantial reforms and simply demanded that the PSI truncate its dialogue with the DC.[8]

Even leftist sanction for PSI abstention in the parliamentary vote for the March 1962 "parallel convergences" government did not signal a change in left-wing thinking.

Basso adopted a wait-and-see attitude toward the new cabinet, because by 1962 Pope John XXIII exercised a liberal influence on the DC. Basso now admitted the possibility of a temporary understanding with the DC and agreed that by compromising with its adversary the PSI had behaved correctly from a Marxist viewpoint. Basso, however, castigated Nenni for risking the PSI's subordination to the DC. In short, despite substantial changes in the church, DC, and the entire Italian political context, Basso persisted in interpreting Nenni as "a nineteenth-century democrat" obsessed by a possible fascist resurgence, while maintaining that "there exist in Western Europe today the objective conditions for a struggle that is not merely democratic but socialist."[9]

Basso and Vecchietti complemented each other. While justifying the left wing's 1962 vote favoring PSI abstention for Fanfani because of its partial "convergence with our program," Vecchietti's domestic and international objections to Nenni's position revealed fundamental incompatibilites with the PSI secretary. Vecchietti concurred in Nenni's alleged inability to integrate single reforms into a strategic conception for the attainment of socialism. For him, Nenni's cautious case-by-case approach to DC agreement ("the politics of things") inevitably led to PSI "social democratization." The socialist left wing thus paralleled the DC Dorotei, which had hoped to sabotage the center-left by demanding a "Great Dialogue" and global agreement before an alliance between the two parties.

The left's concept of electric industry nationalization served as the most glaring example of this tactic. Leftists did not endorse simple nationalization and creation of a state agency to rationalize Italy's energy requirements, as actually occurred. Echoing the early Morandi, they demanded "democratic worker control" of the agency from below. This type of nationalization would fire the imagination of the most advanced workers and serve as a model to be extended to the rest of the Italian economy. In short, leftists sought a state capitalism open to rapid evolution toward forms of socialism.

The left's idealistic conception of nationalization explains its dismissal of what Nenni called the first great achievement of the center-left. The left's approach to electric industry nationalization also justifies Nenni's criticism of leftists as completely unrealistic; Lombardi's conception of nationalization closely resembled theirs, and he discovered its limitations while managing negotiations on the socialist side. As a result, Nenni continued on the center-left path, and Vecchietti exploited the impossibility of attaining reforms tailored to the left's ideology as a reason to return to the PSI's traditional alliance policy with the Communists.

The final incompatibility between the left and the PSI majority concerned the leftist demand that a domestic accord among Italian political forces be subordinated to an agreement on foreign policy. In a clear move to sabotage the center-left, the PSI left wing increased its hostility toward the United States and retained its servile attitude toward the USSR. Furthermore, leftists interpreted the EEC and other Western economic organizations necessary for the country's economic survival as tools of "Atlantic extremism" through which Italy participated in the exploitation of the underdeveloped world. Vecchietti viewed the EEC as "a customs union of the economic realities of Western Europe, a Europe dominated by the monopolies and the oligopolies" which favored economic planning for the rationalization and modernization of capitalism.[10]

Contrasting these views, Nenni headed off overt PSI condemnation of Italy's entrance into the EEC and commissioned his lieutenant Giovanni Pieraccini to take the lead in future economic planning discussions.

When the DC hierarchy sabotaged the Fanfani cabinet in early 1963, the internal PSI contest escalated. The left wing decreed that the "parallel convergences" marked the limits of the DC's progressive program. Misled by Nenni's exaggerated fear of a rightist reaction, Basso argued, the majority current had missed the center-left's true significance as a "momentary tactical compromise with the class adversary" within the context of a long-range power shift to the workers. By caving in to every DC demand, weakening the DC left wing, "social democratizing" the PSI, and integrating the Socialists within the DC's power orbit, Nenni had performed an enormous disservice for the worker's movement. Only the immediate termination of the center-left and left-wing supremacy within the PSI could save the party.[11]

The disappointing PSI performance in the April 1963 general elections encouraged the left's drive for supremacy. Despite the PSI merger with the MUIS, a PSDI splinter group, leftist leaders contended that the PSI had declined drastically in relative terms compared to the PCI and the PSDI. While in 1958 the PSI vote represented two-thirds of the communist and more than triple the social democratic, Basso argued, in 1963 it had dropped to 55 percent of the PCI total and to only double the PSDI. Clearly, the voters had rejected Nenni's center-left and understood its Kennedy-inspired aims: communist isolation and closer ties with the Atlantic alliance through PSI domestication. As a result, Basso demanded that PSI should condition its support for a new cabinet upon ironclad DC guarantees of reform implementation.[12] Basso hoped to detach Lombardi from Nenni and reverse the prevailing majority within the PSI, and he came perilously close to doing so.

The left wing sharpened its battle themes for the PSI's 35th Congress (Rome, October 1963), realizing that it would either achieve a last-minute win against Nenni or leave the party.

According to leftist orators, the prevailing international policy of "peaceful coexistence" combined with developments in the communist world after the 20th CPSU Congress had opened new vistas for Socialists in advanced capitalist countries. The threat of an immediate nuclear war having dissipated, the class struggle within individual countries could develop without being conditioned by the rigid division of the world into two camps. At the same time, the reduction of Soviet influence on national communist parties encouraged individual roads to socialism.

This being the case, no justification remained for "social democratization," bringing the PSI into the DC orbit. The PSI left wing rejected the center-left because it reversed the class alliance with the Communists and made the PSI subservient to the DC. The left's primary condition for avoiding a PSI split was unity of action with the Communists.

Besides violating traditional political tenets, the left condemned Nenni for diluting beyond recognition the socialist conception of economic planning. Absolutely essential for the left was a "plan" controlled from below and furnished with coercive instruments for the demolition of all resistance, "none excluded, including nationalization and prohibition of certain types of production." Planning's economic and social goals would take precedence over the profit motive and impose expropriation and state determination of investments. Another condition of the left to forestall secession was endorsement of leftist programming concepts over those of the EEC—"Europe of the trusts and the cartels."

Finally, for the left wing, accepting Nenni's foreign policy was "a price we cannot pay" for socialist entrance into the governing coalition. According to the left, the Nenni majority had sacrificed "equidistance" between the two superpowers by accepting NATO and its fascist fringes, Spain and Portugal, and German nuclear rearmament through the MLF. Thus, the final condition for unity was active PSI neutralism.[13]

The left admitted that at the Rome congress it had proposed conditions for remaining in the party "which today no longer existed within the PSI: ideological unity, a common strategic view, agreement on the fundamentals of socialist policy."[14]

Having made its public declaration of faith, the left did not follow Nenni and the majority in voting confidence for the Moro "organic" center-left cabinet in December 1963. Leftists did everything possible to obstruct negotiations and then violated party discipline by voting against the Moro cabinet in the Chamber and by walking out in the Senate.[15] To an international audience, Basso explained, "The break did not take place over the principle of participation but on the political significance that this participation has had in reality."[16]

Forced to act decisively against leftist indiscipline, Nenni set PSI machinery into motion against the rebels, suspended them from party life for a year, and blocked their demand for an extraordinary congress. Despite contentions that the left could have avoided expulsion had it behaved differently, both minority and majority currents considered a schism inevitable by 1963. "There was only one way of avoiding the split," Nenni correctly wrote: "turn the party over to the minority."[17]

Following the traditional course of left-wing Socialists breaking away from the PSI since 1906, the leftists gave birth to a new party in January 1964. Calling itself the PSIUP, the new party proved unsuccessful in establishing its own political space between the PSI and the PCI. Although it had received almost 40 percent of the votes at the Rome congress, the rebels claimed that one-quarter of the PSI rank and file had followed them into the PSIUP. About the same percentage of the PSI parliamentary delegation went over to the new party.[18]

In fact, however, PSI cadres, the leftovers of Morandi's bureaucracy, accounted for a large proportion of the new party's membership. Far from being born free of the "mortgages" which weighed on the Italian working-class movement, as PSIUP leaders claimed, the veteran Morandians rapidly assumed the PSIUP leadership, excluding Basso and other imaginative leaders from effective power and imposing subservience to the Communist party.[19]

Without this oppressive apparatus, the PSI became a freer and more open organization. On the one hand, this development produced a less disciplined party, but on the other, it allowed for the infusion of new members from different classes, which changed the PSI's nature over the next several years.

Besides these organizational considerations, the left wing's secession had incalculable political results. By weakening the PSI's contractual strength, the split severely damaged socialist ability to negotiate with the DC and to achieve dramatic reforms. Combined with PCI hostility and conservative resistance, this factor contributed to the center-left's image of failure—which Italian leftists then exploited to cut down support for the PSI.

The obvious Christian democratic preference for a weakened PSI as a coalition partner had produced strong suspicions of DC stimulation of the leftist break. In a confidential discussion with me on this issue in Rome, a prominent PSI leader of the period assured me that the Italian state oil combine close to the DC—ENI—did indeed finance the socialist split in order to debilitate the PSI.[20] The official did not go into details but gave the information as certain.

At the same time, criticism has been leveled at Nenni (and Lombardi) for not understanding the split's significance or doing enough to prevent it.[21] According to the same official quoted above, the left wing might have actually won a majority in the Rome congress if he and a colleague on the Credentials Committee had not managed to disqualify Sardinian delegates who favored the left. This official stated that when Nenni discovered this development, he became convinced of the necessity of a split because the left would have threatened his majority during the difficult period he knew would ensue upon socialist entrance into the government. Convinced, furthermore, that the left wing did not have as much appeal in the country as it did in the party, Nenni favored a schism. Nenni indirectly confirms this thesis in his diary. The left could have achieved the majority within three or six months, he states, if events had proven him wrong. "They lacked patience, which is a revolutionary virtue."[22]

Finally, in the unlikely setting of a Campo dei Fiori coffee shop, the PSI official and scholar Senator Antonio Landolfi expressed his conviction to me that the PSI had erred in allowing the 1964 schism. According to Landolfi, Basso could have been "saved" for the PSI. Landolfi also stated that the PSIUP turned out to have a greater appeal for the voters than Nenni and his autonomists suspected, about 2 to 3 percent. He dates the electoral growth of the PCI to this development, even though the Communists initially opposed the split.

In the 1963 elections, the PSI received around 14 percent of the vote, but it later settled on 9 to 10 percent. In 1963, the PCI received about 25 percent of the vote. With the 1964 split, a PSIUP-PCI coalition emerged, culminating in the entrance of the *psiuppini* into the PCI in 1972. The Communists thus achieved a monopoly over the Italian left, and their vote rose even more rapidly because the PSI, now embroiled in coalition politics, could not make good its case to be a significant leftist force.[23]

Given the radically different political orientation of the PSI left and right wings which had evolved since 1956, however, how could the Socialist party's laceration have been prevented? Italian socialist history is littered with splits on the eve of momentous events. Sectarian and idealistic as always, the left preferred suicide to compromise; as usual, the pragmatic right wing took liberties with socialist ideology to prevent the general crisis of imperfect Italian democracy.[24]

Lombardi Bound

The left's desertion of the PSI had an effect beyond those discussed above: it isolated the major socialist thinker Riccardo Lombardi within the party. At the beginning of the 1960s, Lombardi formed a small but intensely active group which viewed the impending center-left experience as one which would "test not only the Socialist party's governmental capacities but those of the entire Italian left."[25] Unlike Nenni, who harbored a primarily defensive conception of the center-left, Lombardi took a wider view and considered socialist governmental participation a means by which the entire Italian left would achieve power, Communists included. In a 1960 analysis of evolving capitalism, Lombardi noted that the Italian state had moved into areas of production, from which it had previously been excluded, and had given itself institutions which intervened directly in the economy on behalf of the bourgeoisie. This development had a profound significance for the proletariat, which must no longer consider the state simply an instrument of oppression controlled by the exploiting classes. Since the state had now acquired powerful means of social and economic intervention, Lombardi argued, the masses must reverse the outdated Marxist conception of destroying the state, taking it over instead and employing its new machinery to achieve their aims. Lombardi wrote:

> The Italian working classes struggle not for the destruction of the bourgeois state and its substitution by the socialist state, but to conquer and exercise power within the existing state, according to the goals and within the forms of the democratic constitution. The Italian working classes must consider that the instruments which the Italian state possesses for directing and controlling the economy are such that they may be utilized for the socialist direction and control of the economy.

In this context, Lombardi emphasized the "potentially socialist" nature of the existing instruments of economic intervention. If by participating in governments the proletariat had access to these instruments, which were currently exploited by the bourgeoisie, it could achieve socialism peacefully and democratically through structural reforms and economic planning. Obviously, Lombardi's conception of planning retained coercive elements regarding investments and profit limitation which drew opposition from conservatives.[26]

Later Lombardi appropriated Morandi's concept of important structural reforms acting as "detonators" sabotaging capitalism, producing his "revolutionary reformism." This ideology had its major test in nationalization of the electric industry. Thus, Lombardi visualized socialist participation in the government of a capitalist state not as helping resolve capitalism's ills or correcting its imbalances but effecting real change by redirecting investments.[27] Lombardi's answer to the socialist dilemma "Revolution or management of the system?" was "Revolutionary management of the system."[28]

Although these opinions seemed close to the PSI left's conception of planning, they differed in one important respect. Believing that socialism should be the "guarantor of democracy," Lombardi eschewed the totalitarian bent of left-wing programming concepts. While Lombardi continued a lively dialogue with the leftists, their antithetical views kept them apart.

Lombardi's ideology also alienated him from the Nenni group, but in a more subtle manner. I asked the minister for programming during the center-left period, Giovanni Pieraccini, to define the major differences between Nenni and Lombardi on the planning issue. After a moment of thought, Pieraccini responded:

> Lombardi believed that programming must be more incisive and coercive, but not in the totalitarian sense. More incisive, in terms of breaking the decision centers of capitalism. He believed that our programming was instead a kind of system adjust-

ment, not transformation. I think that our type of planning would have been equally valid because an economy governed by reason would be an enormous revolution.

Pieraccini explained further:

I believe that a *hard*, authoritarian, form of programming cannot be initiated without being brought to its extreme consequences. . . . I mean that the logic of a certain type of programming which is coercive cannot stop halfway but leads to an experience of the Soviet type. This development is not a result of madness or the evil intentions of men, but a logic which arises from economic factors. If one must govern the economy in an authoritarian manner, he cannot leave gaps which will cause the entire system to collapse. On the other hand, it seems to me that an authoritarian type of programming has not given such great results, as we have seen.

The other type of programming is the kind we tried, democratic planning. But this requires . . . a more closely united country in which the social forces become the protagonists of a great dialogue which searches for solutions which are logical and civilized. This unity is extremely difficult to find in any country in the world, and in Italy even more so, especially in a situation of political fracture, as was the case during the center-left period.[29]

If anything, Pieraccini's recollection of a political "fracture" during this period understates the case. By July 1964, Nenni's obsession with the possible destruction of Italian democracy had become overwhelming. As a result, Nenni subordinated planning and reforms—everything—to saving Italian society as it had emerged from World War II.

After the left wing's secession, Lombardi lost his negotiating position. He could only protest to the PSI's new secretary, Francesco De Martino, that Nenni had limited socialist policy to stabilizing the system. Commenting on an October 1964 Nenni statement, Lombardi wrote to De Martino: "The glorious role assigned to the Socialist party is that of the guardian of order, equilibrium, stability. The thrust to transform society has been replaced by a preoccupation to maintain the status quo. Order, therefore; perhaps even 'order and progress'; but above all, order."[30]

From then on, Lombardi remained a voice in the wilderness, a respected thinker whose practical influence failed to match the homage Socialists rendered to his ideas. On 27 September 1984, shortly after the Sicilian Socialist's death, his friend Antonio Giolitti wrote Lombardi's political epitaph: "Ubiquity and isolation are two apparently contradictory but coexistent characteristics in the political personality of Riccardo Lombardi."[31]

Did SIFAR Slay the Center-Left?

Lombardi's fate had not been apparent in December 1963. Fear of another Lombardi revolt induced Nenni to hold out for concessions from Moro which he ordinarily would not have insisted on. As we have seen, negotiations produced a four-party "organic" cabinet (DC, PSI, PSDI, PRI) and a respectable platform.

Including Pietro Nenni as deputy prime minister, Antonio Giolitti as minister of the budget and programming (Lombardi refused the post), and several other socialist ministers, the new cabinet pledged enactment of a five-year plan by June 1964, establishment of regions, and urban, agricultural, and educational reforms; in foreign policy, the agreement emphasized NATO's defensive role. The program's progressive nature touched off a conservative DC revolt led by Scelba and Pella, but the Vatican subdued it.[32]

Lombardi seemed pleased with the program, arguing that proposed legislation on urban planning would have greater social impact than nationalization of the electric industry. But he recommended vigilance to ensure enactment.[33]

To their surprise, the Socialists soon discovered that membership in the governing coalition did not ensure reforms.

Constitution of the Moro cabinet coincided with the difficult economic situation described above in chapter 9. Electric company nationalization, flight of Italian capital abroad, strikes, and rapid inflation threatened Italian economic life. As a result, industrialists demanded postponement of the reforms on which the Moro coalition had been constituted. To back their case, they instituted massive layoffs and work-week reductions and urgently requested government support for a wage freeze, strike prohibitions, and other austerity measures. After a round of talks with the employers' associations, Deputy Premier Nenni concluded that they had declared open warfare on the center-left.[34]

The media backed the employers, particularly targeting the urban-planning legislation drafted by Giovanni Pieraccini, which closely followed Sullo's previous bill.

Alarmed by the situation, Prime Minister Moro solicited union support and in February and March 1964 formally requested that the labor organizations moderate their demands. Influenced by the Communists, labor leaders rejected the prime minister's plea. Citing government inability to institute profit and income tax reforms, the unions denounced the government for shifting the price of economic stabilization onto the workers. In April, negotiations between government and unions collapsed, and a strike paralyzed the public sector. "A slap in the face" for the Socialists, Nenni commented in his diary.[35]

Political turmoil and economic crisis produced persistent rumors of an impending emergency government. Old wounds and the desire for revenge seized the DC. Fanfani, whose previous cabinet Moro had supported only lukewarmly, pronounced the center-left "not irreversible." According to Fanfani, the Moro experiment had failed, and the nation should seek alternative political solutions, perhaps through early elections.[36] Unheard of at the time, this suggestion greatly impressed public opinion and underlined the seriousness of the political impasse.

At the same time, disagreements escalated within the cabinet, but the PSI resisted pressure to moderate its program. In May 1964, by-elections in the Friuli-Venezia Giulia area produced ominous losses for the PSI and gains for the PCI and the PSIUP. Convinced that socialist association with a do-nothing cabinet had produced the defeat, the PSI Central Committee asked for a June "verification" of the government's activity.

Francesco De Martino had replaced Nenni as secretary when the Romagnol Socialist entered the cabinet. De Martino indicated that continued socialist participation in the governing coalition depended on immediate implementation of agricultural reforms and establishment of regions, cabinet approval of urban planning—including the right of expropriation at 1958 prices—and rapid imposition of national planning measures. De Martino had presented Moro with what appeared to be an ultimatum at the wrong time. Nenni softened the secretary's tone and later attributed the cabinet's fall to De Martino's errors.[37]

On 27 May 1964, the political crisis took a dramatic turn with publication by the Rome daily *Il Messaggero* of a letter which Christian democratic Treasury Minister

Emilio Colombo had previously delivered to Aldo Moro and which the imperturbable prime minister had ignored in the hope of avoiding further complications.

According to Colombo, the Italian economy faced collapse if the government did not drop expensive reforms pushed by the PSI—particularly urban planning, decentralization, and national economic planning—and immediately implement instead austerity measures demanded by the business community. These included a wage and public spending freeze. Colombo's initiative corresponded with those of governor of the Bank of Italy Guido Carli, French vice president of the EEC's Executive Board Robert Marjolin, and the French and German press, all of whom echoed Colombo.[38] Beyond a legitimate concern for the economy, the treasury minister's maneuver has been variously interpreted as Dorotei pressure on Moro to revoke his concessions to the Socialists and as a prelude to a possible coup d'etat.[39]

Needing time to renegotiate the agreement which had led to socialist participation, the cabinet resigned on a minor issue. Because of the intransigence of the new Dorotei secretary, Mariano Rumor, Moro pleaded with Nenni to moderate his party's program, but the PSI Directorate refused on 13 July. The next day, PSI, PSDI, and PRI negotiators presented a united front to Rumor, but the DC secretary rejected their overture. The breaking point had been reached, Nenni commented.[40]

During these tension-filled talks, President Segni consulted with Senate President Cesare Merzagora, most vocal advocate of an emergency government, and, more suspiciously, with General Aldo Rossi, Army Chief of Staff, and General Giovanni De Lorenzo, Carabinieri Commander and former head of SIFAR, the country's intelligence service.

On 17 July, the Socialists suddenly ended their resistance, consented to exclusion of the Lombardi group from the cabinet, and agreed to a new government. What accounted for this sudden shift?

A conservative fascistic government of large landowners and industrialists waited in the wings if the Socialists held out, Nenni wrote at the time. Had the Socialists not blocked such a government, the 1960 events would have "paled in comparison."[41]

It is not the purpose of this book to examine the details of the alleged plot by President Segni and Carabinieri Commander Giovanni De Lorenzo to impose an authoritarian government. Known as the SIFAR scandal, these events have been examined and reexamined in a number of books and by a parliamentary investigating commission which produced a majority report of fourteen hundred pages and several minority reports. The evidence, however, demonstrates that De Lorenzo had prepared a military plan which would have allowed the carabinieri to gain control of the country acting substantially alone ("piano solo"). According to this plan, De Lorenzo would have needed some cooperation from the army, navy, and air force, but, in addition to the carabinieri, the plan would have utilized SIFAR, the armed forces intelligence service he had headed for six years and which his closest collaborators continued to run. Under the guise of keeping tabs on potential security risks, De Lorenzo's SIFAR had compiled dossiers on parliamentarians, party leaders, and other prominent politicians. Continually updated, these records included not only information necessary for the implementation of a mass-arrest order but accurate and manufactured material on "irregular" sexual and other habits potentially useful as blackmail against important personalities.

Did this plan indicate a plot to take over the country? On balance, the majority of the SIFAR investigation commission interpreted the preparations as falling within the armed forces' mission to defend the existing constitutional order. Given the tense political situation in June–July 1964, it appeared only natural to the majority that the president of the republic should consult with the head of the carabinieri and other military forces to ensure public order, especially considering the novel possibility of early elections. The frenetic consultations De Lorenzo had with other military commanders, "piano solo," and the gathering of information on "suspect" persons appear in this light as normal activities of security forces in a modern state, even though the commission recommended reorganizing SIFAR as a result.

This version of events, however, leaves open some serious questions. De Lorenzo purposefully kept the Pubblica Sicurezza, Italy's centralized police coresponsible with the carabinieri for maintaining public order, in the dark. Moreover, the nation's highest officials all agreed that the minor disturbances which occurred hardly threatened public order. Despite this fact, lists of persons to be arrested were issued. Persons who examined these lists before their secret destruction testified that they included Communists, Socialists, and persons in the government. Furthermore, provision had been made for the air force to transport prisoners to camps in Sardinia. The plan also called for occupation of the state television network, RAI-TV, and the training of outside television technicians capable of operating the system. If a plot did exist, this capability would have given the conspirators a monopoly over direct communication with the nation. Finally, unknown to the responsible civilian authorities, arrangements had been made for creation of a mechanized brigade and for the callup of former carabinieri to augment the existing force. The evidence also suggests that a SIFAR colonel had enrolled neo-fascist and other right-wing elements for the purpose of manufacturing disturbances which could justify declaration of a national emergency. This officer, Renzo Rocca, headed SIFAR's sensitive Research and Industries Section and died by apparent suicide under suspicious circumstances on the eve of the parliamentary commission's investigation into the affair.[42]

According to some observers, this alleged plot had the backing of the CIA. Roberto Faenza, the scholar who has done the most work on this subject, has argued that former Ambassador Clare Boothe Luce sponsored De Lorenzo as head of the Italian intelligence service in 1956; in return, De Lorenzo supposedly subordinated SIFAR to the CIA by pledging his support of a secret American plan for anticommunist intervention— "Demagnetize"—without his superiors' knowledge. "Since that time, SIFAR will be bound hand and foot to the interests of the United States government," Faenza writes.

Faenza's allegations of formal SIFAR subservience to the CIA, subsequently picked up in Giuseppe De Lutiis's 1984 book on the Italian intelligence services, created a flap in the Italian press which required Defense Minister Giovanni Spadolini's direct intervention to quiet.

Faenza alleges that at the meeting in the Rome embassy during which Vernon Walters allegedly advocated employing American troops to undo the center-left, cited earlier, the participants accepted instead a more subtle plan advocated by CIA Station Chief Thomas Karamessines. Karamessines suggested covert action to weaken center-left proponents while strengthening its opponents. Faenza believes that Walters and De Lorenzo jointly worked out the details of this plan and left responsibility for its implementation to Karamessines and Rocca in late 1962, when Walters was transferred to Brazil and De Lorenzo became head of the carabinieri.[43]

By 1963, Karamessines had been replaced as Rome station chief by William Harvey, nicknamed "the Cowboy" by his SIFAR counterparts because of a drunken penchant for waving his pistol. Faenza portrays Harvey as sabotaging Kennedy's policy of supporting the center-left, even after August 1963, when the president had made his wishes clear during his Rome trip. In Faenza's version of events, Harvey enlisted the aid of CIA Director John McCone and counterespionage chief James Angleton against Pope Paul VI's support of the center-left and conspired with De Lorenzo and Rocca in all of the maneuvers which ended Moro's first cabinet, threatened Italian democracy, and precipitated socialist acceptance of a watered-down center-left. Once stirred up, Faenza believes that these occult forces contributed to the terrorism and attempted coups of the late 1960s and 1970s.[44]

Faenza's work is marred by a strong anti-American bias, a sometimes strained interpretation of the documents, and a general thesis which inserts these developments into a worldwide plot by American capitalists. But does his argument have merit?

On 7 October 1985, I telephoned Robert Komer and asked him to react to Faenza's conclusions on CIA involvement with SIFAR. Now employed by the Rand Corporation, Komer spent thirty years in CIA Intelligence and initiated discussion about the center-left in the Kennedy administration. While stressing that he no longer dealt with Italian affairs in July 1964, Komer angrily told me that any allegation of U.S. involvement in an attempt to overthrow the Italian government during the period under discussion struck him as "weird on the face of it." He asserted that during all his years in the CIA, he had never heard of "Demagnetize." Komer considered the CIA much more progressive on the center-left than the State Department and emphatically stated that in his opinion Faenza's charges had no foundation. Komer did not rule out the possibility that Italian opponents of the center-left exploited supposed American support for SIFAR to tame the Socialists.

Arthur Schlesinger also denied knowledge of SIFAR *putsch* preparations when I questioned him, but he did recall rumors of a possible coup d'etat and of an "Italian De Gaulle." As he recalled, these rumblings came from Italy and did not indicate any American involvement. I did ask Schlesinger about whether a "split" existed between CIA Intelligence and Operations on the opening to the left, and whether Operations might have actively opposed the center-left. This issue appears not to have left a strong impression on him; he responded that he had no precise memory, although "there may very well have been; probably the covert action people, the people who had been funding the Christian Democrats, were . . . opposed."[45]

Because the SIFAR events became public in 1967 in the prestigious left-leaning Italian weekly *L'Espresso,* immediately after the colonels seized power in Greece by implementing a NATO contingency plan, skeptics of the "SIFAR plot" have accused the Italian press of reacting to normal security precautions in an exaggerated manner.

Giuseppe Tamburrano, the most respected historian of the center-left, takes a more subtle approach. In his 1971 work, *Storia e cronaca del centro-sinistra,* Tamburrano argued that, in addition to the real political problems, the threat of a military takeover induced the Socialists to scuttle their own reform program, thus dooming the center-left, blocking real progress, and setting the stage for the Italian turmoil of the 1970s and 1980s.[46] During our conversations on this issue, I asked Tamburrano if he still held to his argument and tested his thesis on a number of protagonists of the period.

The person who replaced Antonio Giolitti as minister for the budget and economic planning as a result of the July 1964 events, Giovanni Pieraccini, affirmed that "We—at least I, but I think also Nenni—did not have this feeling of being threatened by a coup d'etat." Pieraccini attributed the difficulties of the center-left to the fear of the Confindustria that economic planning might lead to a totalitarian regime of the "Eastern" type and to lack of support from the unions. To my inquiry about the possibility that conservative political forces *used* rumors of a coup to threaten the Socialists, even if no real possibility of a military takeover existed, Pieraccini responded, "No, honestly. I was in the government all those years, and I never heard [anything]. I never feared that I might have to make decisions which went against my conscience because a coup would otherwise have resulted."[47]

When I reported this conversation to Tamburrano, he manifested great surprise. Political counselor to Nenni at the time, editor of Nenni's memoirs, and then writing a biography of the socialist leader which has recently appeared, Tamburrano asserted that he remembered very well the pressure of a possible coup on Nenni. Although Nenni did not examine this issue in detail publicly or in his diaries, Tamburrano maintains, the "warning" of a possible coup and the consequent defeat of the left reached the deputy premier directly from the Quirinale. Beyond the politics of the situation, Tamburrano cited the compelling "logic" of events. President Segni had announced his determination not to sign legislation implementing urban planning, even if Parliament passed it. Had Segni kept his word, early dissolution of Parliament would have resulted, considered revolutionary at the time. What would have happened then? Would PSI support for a cabinet still have been necessary to form a government? Would the Communists have increased their vote? Would the political impasse have produced riots? Since the 1960 disorders which toppled Tambroni had caught the state unprepared, Tamburrano believes it only natural that an already ill Segni (he suffered a paralyzing stroke shortly after the July 1964 events) called in De Lorenzo and ordered him to prepare for any eventuality. Tamburrano believes that De Lorenzo used this cover to conduct illegitimate preparations.[48]

Another participant in the center-left story, Leo Wollemborg, disagrees with Tamburrano. Wollemborg believes that De Lorenzo had no specific political views and pursued his own personal interest, which consisted in gaining more influential jobs. When I asked his opinion on the real possibility of a coup in the summer of 1964, he surmised, "I don't really think so."

I asked, "A real attempt?" Wollemborg responded:

> Things are complicated. How many people in the Christian Democratic party, possibly including Moro himself, did not believe that there was a real danger of a coup but felt that it suited their party's interests to have Nenni and the Socialists, and other people too, *believe* that a coup may be coming, and therefore put more pressure on Nenni?

I then asked, "Do you think that they actually played this game?

> I don't know again who specifically played this game, and how they played it, how clearly they told Nenni, "Look, we better work out another compromise, and you better give up Lombardi and some ideas which are too leftist, otherwise we are all going to be in trouble."

I mentioned that Nenni in his diaries and in *Avanti!* of the period always said that this was a real threat, but he didn't go into details. Wollemborg responded:

> My feeling is that *perhaps* he believed that there was a real threat, and in any case, there is also this. Can we rule out—again, I'm thinking aloud—that Nenni, who had

certainly not forgiven Lombardi for the *Notte di San Gregorio* . . . who can rule out that Nenni said, "Well, look, this is a good opportunity to get rid of Lombardi, politically speaking." Let's not forget that Lombardi was the editor of *Avanti!* during that period between the formation of the first Moro government and July of the following year, 1964, and it's a fact that after that, Lombardi was completely out of power as far as the party was concerned.

I certainly cannot rule out that *this* kind of consideration among many others, played a role in Nenni's decision: "OK, let's cut our losses, let's try to get the best deal we can, let's in any case avoid this *golpe* [coup], whether it's a real threat or not. Let's take at face value what some Christian Democrats who apparently are favorable to the continuation of our relationship with them tell me about this—and this son-of-a-bitch of Segni is certainly out to get the center-left."

In short, according to Wollemborg, Nenni accepted the reconstituted center-left in July 1964 because he disagreed with Lombardi's vision, because he could eliminate Lombardi as a PSI force, and because the agreement with Moro represented the best he could achieve at the time.[49]

Antonio Giolitti, who personified the Lombardi faction excluded from the center-left by the June–July 1964 events, believes that Tamburrano's thesis is only partially correct. When I asked Giolitti if SIFAR had drained the reformist content from the center-left, he answered that the fear that Italian democracy would be overthrown obsessed Nenni and that this fear determined events in July 1964. Giolitti summarized Nenni's thinking:

We have received warnings that there can be some grave dangers; therefore, assuring democratic stability must have priority. Therefore, we must be moderate. Let's not raise the price of our participation in the government too much, let's not create too much tension with the DC, because if this experiment with the center-left enters a crisis, what will happen? It will be dangerous.

As an old anti-fascist, Nenni was always obsessed by fear of the . . . fascist right. This turns to his honor, this priority of defending democracy. But the crisis of June–July 1964 was due to the tension which had been created inside the government by socialist pressure for reform and Christian democratic resistance. . . . The symbol of this contrast was the project for economic programming that I presented at the end of June. I remember the talks I had during the crisis with Treasury Minister Colombo and Prime Minister Moro. They asked me to renounce, to modify that heading. I refused. The Socialist party's answer instead, of Nenni and the majority, [was positive]. In fact, I stayed out of the government because I maintained that excessive concessions had been made to the Christian Democrats.

Thus, Tamburrano's thesis is correct only in part. It is correct with regard to Nenni's morale . . . his fear that dangers existed for democracy, that the center-left government must be saved at all costs, even if something must be renounced. So, too, many things were renounced. It was an aspect of the Socialist party's dual inferiority complex toward the DC and PCI, which it was [Prime Minister Bettino] Craxi's great merit to overcome.[50]

Giolitti thus reconfirms the Lombardian and leftist view that a real danger of a military coup did not exist but that Nenni's understandable obsession with a repeat of the fascist takeover in 1922 induced him to cave in to Christian democratic demands.

Mauro Ferri, intimately involved in the 1964 events and close to Nenni at the time as leader of the socialist delegation in the Chamber of Deputies, responded thoughtfully to my question on SIFAR. Ferri confirmed Segni's "heavy intervention" in the July 1964 crisis, Segni's involvement with the military, and his determination never to allow passage of significant socialist reforms. Considering the DC right wing's wish to block socialist demands as normal, Ferri views events from a different angle:

> Unfortunately, we must admit that we, Socialists and Social Democrats, were weak, also because the Communists did not cooperate with us. If the Communists had given a boost to the reform effort, even from the opposition, they would have increased our force.
>
> On the other hand, we knew very well that in collaborating with the Christian Democrats, we had to deal with an organization which had different faces and souls. Moro . . . at the time represented a moderating force within the DC. But even there, everything has its explanation. Just as I maintain that the Communist party must change very slowly, we must understand that even for the Christian Democrats, the switch to an alliance with the Nenni Socialists represented at the time a traumatic shift. . . .
>
> Therefore, *now* I understand that a party like the Christian Democratic had to move gradually and prudently. If it had accepted something which was too advanced, it would have risked an . . . electoral hemorrhage and a split.[51]

Ferri thus shifts the focus to a weakness of left-wing forces, accentuated by communist pique at being left out of the governing coalition and their interest in power rather than reforms which even they supported. Given the right-wing DC interpretation of Nenni as a "Trojan horse" for the Communists, however, there arises the question of whether PCI support would not have confirmed this thesis and strengthened opposition, perhaps even led to a coup. Whether or not direct evidence will eventually confirm or deny a serious military threat to the nation's democratic institutions, the machinery existed and had come close to being put into motion.

SIFAR signified the end of PSI innocence. Ever since its foundation in 1892, the party had been debating whether representative democracy accepted only reforms which strengthened capitalism or also others which altered its nature and paved the way for socialism.[52]

Other European socialist parties, such as the German, had discovered that when socialism loomed, capitalism turned to repression. As a result, they renounced their more radical proposals and propagated reforms which did not threaten the existing economic and political system. Facing the same dilemma in 1964, an all too common one in Italian history, the Italian Socialists reacted as their European counterparts had done years before.[53]

Nenni confirmed this thesis. Asked why the Socialists did not break with the Catholics in July 1964, when they realized that their presence in the government would not affect the ability of conservative forces in Italy to block modernizing reforms, Nenni answered: "Because we had no solution to propose beyond the center-left and because a constitutional crisis, in that particular moment, and under those circumstances, would only have favored the right, both within and outside the DC, in its attempt to secure control of the the levers of power."[54]

The PSI and the Center-Left

Leftist Italian scholars and publicists have emphasised the above-described threats by rightist forces and supposed socialist collapse to condemn the center-left period as a dismal failure. The influential communist press skillfully translated this alleged socialist "sellout" into political gain. After 1964, the PCI dramatically increased its electoral percentage, and the socialist share continually declined. Undoubtedly, socialist participation in the center-left boomeranged against the PSI, but can the experiment be considered a total failure?

Nenni argued for the center-left in order to preserve Italian democracy. In contrast, the socialist left wing and the Communists downgraded this threat, characterizing Nenni as "obsessed by the fear of a return of fascism."[55] In subsequent analyses, however, leftist writers allowed no room for doubt about the existence of a plot but ignored Nenni's role in averting it.[56]

If Italian society is as continually prone to coup attempts as these writers asserted in the two decades since 1964, it appears partisan not to give Nenni and the Socialists their fair due for saving Italian democracy. This position is especially ironic, because in the 1970s and the 1980s, the PCI adopted strikingly similar policies to those of the Socialists in the 1960s.

Clearly, the center-left did not achieve socialism, which is hardly surprising. The major goal of the left wing and Lombardi—economic planning—encountered the immediate and successful resistance of powerful, nonsocialist forces. These opponents first utilized the recession to oust Antonio Giolitti from the Moro cabinet and, subsequently, to postpone agreed-upon planning measures indefinitely—despite Budget and Planning Minister Pieraccini's drafting of a five year plan and despite institution of planning machinery.[57] This outcome is understandable given the socialist minority position within the four-party coalition, PCI hostility, and the opposition of the powerful communist-dominated labor union to Pieraccini's efforts to garner labor support for structural reforms. Pieraccini informed me that when he was minister, labor leaders even refused to confer with him.[58] Considering these circumstances, the center-left cannot be characterized as a failure.

On the positive side of the ledger are a number of important reforms in which Socialists had a major hand. Besides rationalizing the nation's energy requirements by nationalizing the electric industry and creating a state monopoly over nuclear energy, the center-left in 1964 provided for the gradual elimination of sharecropping. As existing contracts ended, sharecroppers received first option to buy the land, and the government provided low-interest loans for land, necessary equipment, and supplies. Within the next ten years, that age-old form of land tenure disappeared. At the same time, school reform progressed, with increased building, greater accessibility, and the establishment of nursery schools. In addition, socialist-inspired reforms benefited the working class. Most importantly, a bill of rights for workers was drafted under the supervision of socialist Labor Minister Giacomo Brodolini. This legislation prohibited firings except for cause and instituted other changes which revolutionized the workplace.[59] In foreign policy, Nenni took the lead in Italy's recognition of Communist China and in furthering trade relations with the Chinese.

The product of compromise, center-left legislation had its share of flaws, did not resolve all of Italy's problems, and created new ones linked to the expansion of state industry. A legislative balance sheet, however, is a poor yardstick by which to judge the center-left. Observers have interpreted the center-left as a socialist "duty," recalling that only an authoritarian alternative existed on both right and left.

Besides the rightist threat already discussed, the PCI had only recently begun its democratic socialist evolution, and the "Italian road to socialism" had hardly progressed as far as communist commentators later claimed. Caught between twin oppositions, one socialist scholar has written, the center-left constituted a historic turning point because "it was the first serious attempt to press the working class's candidacy for participation in (and I stress participation in, not assumption of) the process of guiding the state."[60]

Thus, the center-left should not be judged primarily by its legislative accomplishments or its concrete formulation as a squabbling four-party coalition. Debate will continue on these aspects, but not about the spirit which it infused into Italian society—modernizing it. The center-left succeeded as a policy, even though it might have failed as a political formulation.

Nenni judged the center-left in the following terms:

> It is said about rightist political systems and authoritarian regimes that everything functions and nothing lives. Of the political system which has taken its name and dates from the center-left, we may say the opposite, i.e., that nothing functions and everything lives. . . . Power always breeds abuses, but liberty permanently corrects arbitrariness.[61]

Asked by me to judge the center-left experience, Antonio Giolitti, Giovanni Pieraccini, and Mauro Ferri all agreed that the center-left had changed the country for the better and had fostered a modern spirit, even if its "grand design" of economic planning remained unfulfilled. Ferri emphasized the center-left's championship of civil rights, while Pieraccini said:

> The center-left operated as a force for renovation. You can say to me, I don't know if Italy has improved much, because the problems which the nation has today are very grave and many. But I think it [the center-left] has [so operated] because it seems to me that this country, with *all* its probelms, with *all its crises,* is a country which is much more modern, much more dynamic . . . and has an extraordinary vitality. . . . All of this means that the center-left has been an important element for renovation.[62]

This positive view of the center-left has become more acceptable to the Communists the farther the PCI has evolved in a democratic and autonomous direction. Nenni recalled Togliatti's lament that domestic and international pressures prevented the PSI from negotiating for communist support and the PCI from acting in a completely autonomous manner. But Togliatti exclaimed, "Lucky you, that you can engage in real politics [*fare politica*]!" In 1976, Communist Party Secretary Enrico Berlinguer acknowledged the center-left's positive achievements, and the PCI ideological review *Rinascita* recognized in the center-left a fresh analysis of, and a new beginning in, Italian politics.[63]

As the PCI has become more mature, responsible, and independent, it has discovered that within the Italian and Western context it could do no better than follow in the PSI's footsteps. Ironically, the PCI also discovered that while its electoral increases depended in large measure on its successful campaign denigrating the Socialists and the center-left, the greater range of support it garnered led to modification of communist aims.

As a result, the PCI has adopted a program similar to that of the PSI in the 1960s, and in the 1980s it lost its focus as a protest party. The PCI's 1985 defeats in the local elections and in the referendum on cost-of-living adjustments seem to confirm the controversial opinions of a socialist writer, Franco Gaeta, who attributed the PCI's social democratic evolution to the opening to the left—which may also take its place on the positive side of the center-left's ledger.[64]

CHAPTER 11

Drift and Decline

Buffeted by its enemies, the benefits of the center-left unclear, the PSI bore the political brunt of the experiment's apparent lack of success. At first, logic dictated reunification of the Nenni and Saragat Socialists to create a new socialist pole. When this attempt failed, the Socialists swung violently in the opposite direction, practically committing suicide.

The Failure of Reunification

In August 1964, President Segni suffered a stroke. Senate President Merzagora asssumed Segni's duties in the four months before the president of the republic resigned.

In order to strengthen the center-left, the PSI and PSDI forcefully presented Giuseppe Saragat's candidacy to succeed Segni. Hoping to strengthen himself with the ruling group in the DC, Fanfani criticized the center-left and announced his candidacy, but an unforgiving DC nominated the colorless Neapolitan lawyer Giovanni Leone. The result was another marathon campaign for the Italian presidency. Nenni resisted declaring his own candidacy and successfully advocated Saragat's election.[1] This cooperation provided renewed impetus for PSI-PSDI reunification, on the table since 1956.

Within the PSI, a suspicious Lombardi opposed reunification, believing that fusion would slam the socialist door in the Communists' face. PSI Secretary Francesco De Martino agreed and advocated a lengthy transition to reunification. At the PSI's 36th National Congress (Rome, 10–14 November 1965), the delegates accepted De Martino's position.[2]

At this point, however, several factors produced rapid movement toward reunification. Nenni had gone along with De Martino only because he wished to prepare the merger as thoroughly as possible, but his fear of communist and PSIUP electoral competition got the better of him. In November 1964, local elections had produced a PSI decline of about 3 percent, with some PSDI gains. Since neither capitalism nor communism had ensured the democratic exercise of power, Nenni dreamed Saragat's old dream: a great Socialist party capable of presenting Italian society with an alternative to the DC and the PCI, the "Third Pole." Despite the National Congress, Nenni believed that the time had come for the Socialists to acquire, by unification, "greater weight, in the government or in the opposition, and to open the way to an alternative."[3]

Lombardi's isolation limited hard-core PSI opposition to unification to 20 percent, while De Martino lacked the prestige to contrast Nenni. Having previously suffered serious splits on the reunification issue (e.g., the MUIS), the PSDI accepted Nenni's renewed invitation at the end of 1965, and discussion proceeded on the issue in the socialist and social democratic press.

In January 1966, PSI and PSDI parliamentary groups began concerted action. In March, the two parties created a joint committee to plan the technical aspects of unification, and by 24 July they had agreed on the principles which would guide the new party and the procedure for fusion. PSI Vice Secretary Brodolini aimed at combined lists for the upcoming local elections in June 1966, but this step proved impossible to implement.[4]

The June 1966 elections again produced slight decreases for the PSI and gains for the PSDI, but in general the center-left coalition held its own. Socialists and Social Democrats interpreted this result as a message favoring quick PSI-PSDI fusion. Faravelli's *Critica Sociale* commented that the elections "confirmed the hope and enthusiasm with which an ever-growing public-opinion sector views socialist unification."[5] Fusion had become irresistible.

The 37th PSI Congress gathered in Rome from 27 to 29 October 1966; the 14th PSDI Congress met in the same city on 29 October. The delegates to both meetings unanimously accepted an identical motion favoring unity.

In his speech, Nenni appealed to formerly active Socialists, progressive middle-class groups, and workers unhappy with communist policies. Together they would achieve "a free democratic and socialist Italy," Nenni said. The delegates to both congresses reaffirmed their commitment to Italian socialist tradition, Italy's foreign policy commitments, European unity, and a single socialist labor union. Finally, the new organization sought recognition from the Socialist International.[6]

The new "PSI-PSDI Unificati," or PSU, disappointed all these hopes. Instead of becoming a "third force" by cutting into DC and PCI constituencies, the Socialists got caught between communist and catholic onslaughts. The PCI accused the Socialists of having no confidence in the masses, of resigning themselves to becoming integrated into "the system," and of accepting outdated PSDI positions. On Vietnam, an emotional issue which engendered strong criticism against the United States, communist official Giancarlo Pajetta branded as betrayal the socialist abandonment of common leftist ideals of justice and shrewdly remarked, "Certainly, in the past Nenni would not have remained silent on Vietnam, nor would the Socialists have expressed confidence in a declared policy of understanding for Pentagon massacres and White House diplomacy." The more subtle Catholics blunted the PSI drive for change by combining stonewalling of reform with increased patronage opportunities for Socialists.[7]

More important than external factors, internal disputes account for the dismal outcome of reunification. While Nenni attributed the failure of unification to an incomplete fusion of party structures, former PSU Secretary Mauro Ferri goes beyond this explanation. Although he admitted to me the "superficiality" of a reunification which left two separate and duplicate party structures intact, Ferri blames pressure from both Saragat and Nenni for the failure. Even though powerful political differences divided the PSI and the PSDI, Ferri maintained, Saragat pressed for unification because it vindicated his 1947 split, whereas Nenni viewed unification as crowning his political career. According to Ferri, a majority of both parties merely suffered reunion. While Ferri admitted that no major ideological impediments to unification existed, he insisted;

> On the political plane, everything was unclear. Everything was conditioned to a great degree on being together in the government. The center-left government seemed to have resolved everything: as long as we are in the government, everything goes well,

everything is easy. In fact, as soon as the center-left went into crisis, so did unification.

In the Social Democratic party, there was still an attitude of complete rejection toward the Communists; in the Socialist party, there was the conviction that the Social Democrats had not liberated themselves from their subservient attitude toward the Christian Democrats. . . . In the unions, the great majority of socialist workers belonged to the CGIL, while the UIL was the social democratic union. In the local administrations, even if the center-left had greatly modified the situation, there were still many administrations in which the Socialists remained allied with the Communists, while for the Social Democrats communist alliances were still taboo.

In sum, Ferri believes, reunification within the center-left context doomed the entire operation because the goals of socialist reunification exceeded the narrow political context to which it had become tied—the four-party coalition—which could function just as well with two socialist organizations.[8]

The fundamental problem which had existed for the PSI before unification, Ferri emphasizes, remained afterward: inability to pressure an unwilling DC to implement needed reforms. Between 1964 and 1968, the impression of socialist ineffectuality in changing the policy of their Christian democratic allies had become widespread. In 1965, socialist deputy Loris Fortuna presented a divorce bill, which the DC blocked for a number of years. A major scandal involving a former Christian democratic finance minister, Giuseppe Trabucchi, also found Socialists and Catholics on opposite sides. In 1967, the SIFAR scandal broke, and the Moro government stonewalled a parliamentary investigation. Great irritation also greeted Treasury Minister Emilio Colombo's concession of insignificant pension increases in 1968. Moreover, the center-left's inability to agree on reform of university education and the Italian student revolution protesting the inability of the society to reform disappointed constituencies which had believed in socialist capacity to influence the government in a more progressive direction and thus avoid such disturbances. Finally, the U.S. role in Vietnam and the "Prague Spring," which suggested the democratic evolution of Eastern bloc communism, also hurt the Socialists.[9]

These events help account for the shocking socialist defeat in the 19 May 1968 general elections. The PSU received 14.5 percent of the votes, compared to 20 percent combined for the PSI and PSDI in the 1963 elections, a 25 percent drop. The big winner, the PCI, increased its percentage from 25.3 to 26.9, profiting from protest votes; its PSIUP allies received 4.5 percent. The DC gained slightly.[10]

Bitterness followed the 1968 elections, with Socialists blaming DC do-nothingness for their defeat. Nenni shared this feeling but could find no alternative to the center-left, which still commanded a parliamentary majority. The precipitating Czechoslovak situation, ending in the August 1968 Soviet invasion, strengthened the convictions of Nenni and his major supporters, Mauro Ferri and Giacomo Mancini, a highly successful and flamboyant Calabrian leader.

The De Martino faction, however, advocated withdrawal from the government until the DC yielded to socialist demands for reform. Surprisingly, De Martino's cosecretary Mario Tanassi, a social democratic notable, temporarily allied with De Martino in recommending socialist "disengagement" from the governing coalition. This constellation carried the field in Directorate and Central Committee meetings in the summer of 1968.[11]

These events doomed the Moro cabinet. The coalition partners agreed to let Giovanni

Leone head a caretaker cabinet while the Socialists debated their future policy at the 38th Rome Congress (23–27 October 1968). The party proved helplessly split at this assembly. Five factions entered motions, and none received a majority. Before the congress's close, however, the Nenni-inspired and Ferri-led "Autonomia" current recombined with Tanassi's "Rinnovamento Socialista" on a platform reaffirming reunification principles. This shaky alliance had a 52.6 percent majority. As a result, the majority entente had only twelve out of twenty-two votes on the highly fractured Directorate, ensuring the party's paralysis. Considering his center-left policy a shambles, Nenni refused the secretary's post but blocked De Martino as both secretary and then president. The congress's moral balance sheet was "zero minus zero."[12]

The new secretary, Mauro Ferri, wrote in an unpublished manuscript: "I found myself in extreme difficulty, with almost half the party and a majority of my comrades of PSI origin in the opposition." Ferri and De Martino fought over the Directorate's composition; the local party federations feuded publicly, and fifty-seven federation secretaries out of eighty-five signed a document against the majority current.

The Ferri-Tanassi faction rapidly split asunder, as Ferri writes, "in a manner which I still do not understand." Nenni, however, records Ferri's progressive identification with social democratic positions, while Mancini objected to automatic socialist support for center-left governments. As social conflicts boiled over and the police fired on demonstrators, the two leaders clashed. Mancini favored disarming the police and advocated PSI leadership of the new leftist course the nation seemed to have embarked upon. (The PSU had adopted the old name again.) Mancini's former lieutenant, Antonio Landolfi, told me that Mancini aimed at party reorganization and direct PSI linkage with the masses. Considering the party a federation of separate groups handicapped by rigidly run factions, Mancini hoped to implement a middle-road policy between centralism and autonomy.[13]

Mancini had risen to prominence as minister of public works in the Moro cabinet. In 1966, he became famous by fiercely denouncing the urban speculation which had destroyed overbuilt areas of Agrigento (Sicily) and threatened the region's famous Greek temples in July 1966. On 4 November 1966, a disastrous Florence flood damaged important art objects and holdings of the National Library, again provoking Mancini's criticism of the nation's shameful failure to prepare for preventable natural disasters. Unable to translate this momentum into concrete legislation because of Christian democratic resistance, Mancini argued that PSI participation in the government did not "exhaust" socialist action. Consequently, he opposed freezing out the Communists from local government by extending the center-left coalition, a major DC demand. Since the nation had moved leftward, Mancini favored aggressive socialist responses to the major themes of the 1970s. These included the youth protest, growing worker and peasant militancy, civil rights, and international solidarity among peoples.[14] All these considerations implied an understanding with De Martino.

In May 1969, Ferri learned from the press that a new PSI majority had been formed. Consisting of De Martino, Mancini, and Giolitti, with external support from Lombardi, the new alliance announced the center-left's supersession and the search for more advanced "equilibria," in practice a rapprochement with the Communists.

This new policy isolated the former Social Democrats, who now threatened to secede. Ferri himself claims that he had always resisted a deal with De Martino precisely because it would have violated agreements with the Social Democrats. Ferri's extreme effort to salvage unity by persuading the aging and dispirited Nenni to sponsor a compromise at a 4 July 1969 Central Committee meeting failed as Nenni's motion went down to defeat by a 67 to 51 vote.

This humiliation produced a walkout by Ferri and the Social Democrats, reestablishment of the PSDI (which temporarily adopted the PSU label), Nenni's resignation as PSI president and foreign minister, and the fall of the shaky Mariano Rumor center-left government.[15]

The classic phase of the center-left had come to an ignominious end.

Left, Right, Left: Touching Bottom

Socialist redivision resulted in two parties of approximately the same size as before unification, although the followers of Italo Viglianesi, social democratic labor union (UIL) secretary, remained in the PSI.

Despite the social democratic schism, the PSI that entered the 1970s differed considerably from the PSI of the 1950s or early 1960s. It has been noted how the attempts of Morandi and Basso to recast the party had failed as the PSI maintained its traditional territorial organization. By its 1966 merger with the PSDI, the PSI had quietly renounced its commitment to orthodox Marxism and, in the opinion of a prominent scholar, had become "a-ideological." The Unity Charter negotiated between the two parties confirms this statement.

Socialist party membership reflects the development. In the 1960s, membership did not expand significantly, became more southern, and attracted fewer workers. Between 1961 and 1970, for example, Socialist party members in the "industrial triangle" declined from 22.4 percent to 19 percent, while "Red Belt" membership dropped from 29.4 percent to 15.8 percent. At the same time, the proportion of members from southern Italy increased from 39.8 percent to 57.2 percent. In addition, the social composition of members changed, with the traditional high representation of workers and peasants giving way to white-collar service-industry workers, small shopkeepers, and public employees. In short, the PSI lost its character as a working-class organization. Italian scholars are unclear or disagree about the immediate impact of these phenomena, but they help account for the confusion of PSI policy in the early 1970s and suggest an increasing "embourgeoisment."[16]

Convinced that the 1968 elections had revealed the nation's leftward trend, PSI leaders concluded that the electorate had rebelled against socialist inability to attain reforms. As a result, socialist leaders raised the price of their participation in the governing coalition. The DC, however, refused PSI conditions, forcing Rumor to establish a stopgap single-party DC government on 5 August 1969.

When political cooperation broke down, Italy had entered upon the intense turmoil which characterized the 1970s. In April 1969, riots at Battipaglia, south of Naples, had left several people dead. In October, the "Hot Autumn" began. The three major labor unions—CGIL, CISL, and UIL—initiated a long series of strikes for higher wages, better working conditions, and reforms. Not only did the labor federations collaborate closely, but they also acted as a political party by making demands for a series of reforms.

On 12 December 1969, reaction to Italy's leftward direction came in the form of the "strategy of tension." Terrorists planted four bombs in Milan and Rome, killing thirteen people at Milan's Banca dell'Agricoltura. The police quickly arrested several anarchists, but over the years neo-fascist and Italian intelligence service complicity became clear. Fifteen years of terrorism of the right and the left followed.

Within the PSI, the specter of pre-1922 Italy again haunted party leaders, and they agreed to enter a new Rumor cabinet in March 1970. Hoping to defuse the volatile situation, the Rumor coalition hurriedly implemented important measures which the Socialists had been advocating for years.

Most importantly, Parliament vastly reorganized relationships in the workplace according to the plans of the late Giacomo Brodolini, socialist labor minister in a previous Rumor government. In the future, employers had to justify firings, could no longer send doctors to a worker's home to check up on illness-related absences, had to recognize labor unions, and must allow meetings at the workplace. In addition, the government finally presented enabling legislation for the regions and a divorce law. Because of DC and Vatican objections, the lay parties agreed to submit the latter measure to a nationwide referendum.

The electorate rewarded the PSI for sponsoring these reforms in the first regional elections, 7 June 1970, by increasing the PSI percentage to 10.4 percent. The PSI's leftist rivals did poorly; recent PCI gains eroded, and the PSIUP dropped from 4.4 percent to 3.2 percent, beginning its slide to extinction. The rightist Liberals also faltered, as did the DC.[17]

Attributing this success to a leftward shift in the country, the Socialists entered regional coalitions with Communists in Tuscany and Umbria. In a pact drafted by DC Secretary Arnaldo Forlani, the coalition partners had agreed to exclude the Communists, but in justifying their action the Socialists cited the nonexistence of center-left majorities in these regions. Simultaneously, the PSI supported the labor federations, which called a general strike to reinforce their demands for housing, health, and transportation reforms. This move heralded intimate cooperation between the labor federations and the PSI.

The increasingly unsettled national situation had once more produced right-wing DC calls for an emergency government to restore order. In a replay of the center-left debate, the DC was divided between advocates of a strong government and sympathizers of stabilization through extending the dialogue with the left to the Communists. The press speculated that the intelligence services manipulated the violence in order to block the Communists and provide DC leaders with an excuse to declare a national emergency. In the shifting sands of the DC, Fanfani represented the strong government position, while Giulio Andreotti favored liberalization. The struggle toppled Rumor in July 1970.[18]

During this period, PSI Secretary Mancini had a special relationship with Andreotti, and both apparently planned to introduce the PCI into the ruling coalition by cutting out the nettlesome PSDI. Mancini unilaterally informed PSI federations of the center-left's "death" and authorized exclusion of the PSDI from local governing coalitions and its replacement by the PCI. The DC quickly dashed these plans by torpedoing Andreotti. Within the PSI, De Martino pressured Mancini to give up his plans, and in August 1970 the PSI joined another four-party government led by Emilio Colombo. De Martino sympathized with the Communists but feared PSI isolation. Even the PCI preferred gradual change and probably instigated De Martino's intervention.[19]

During the next several months, PCI moderation in parliamentary debates on pressing economic issues indicated further communist evolution in a social democratic direction. De Martino theorized closer ties with the PCI, known as the "more advanced equilibria." De Martino's activity signaled his impending return to PSI leadership from his post as deputy prime minister.

Feeling the heat of competition, Secretary Mancini accentuated the PSI's leftist course by citing Salvdor Allende's Chile as a model for Italy and by demanding the election of a Socialist in the upcoming Italian presidential balloting.[20] Only the semi-retired Nenni and his heir, Bettino Craxi, objected to the PSI's determined leftism during a November 1970 Central Committee meeting. "They all competed in spitting at the center-left," the embittered eighty-year-old leader commented.[21]

When De Martino returned to active party politics in 1971, several factors had weakened Mancini. In July 1970, Reggio Calabria had revolted because it would not be made capital of the new region of Calabria. Christian democratic, social democratic, and neo-fascist elements made Mancini, a Cosenza Calabrian, the primary target of their year-long protests, and their campaign severely damaged him.[22] A March meeting of the Central Committee elected De Martino president of the Socialist party, a largely honorary post which De Martino used to strengthen himself. The PSI quickly divided between him and the general secretary. The two leftists competed on how to move the PSI farther left, a novel way to paralyze the party.

De Martino's "more advanced equilibria" aroused interest among the Communists. PSI and PCI collaborated in passing legislation keeping agricultural rents below market value and giving tenants wide-ranging rights against landlords, striking fear into Italian conservative hearts. In May 1971, PCI Secretary Luigi Longo formally endorsed PSI cooperation in the building of a new majority which would rule the country.[23]

Unfortunately for both DeMartino and Longo, the political pendulum in the country had begun a new rightward swing. Besides the Reggio Calabria violence, there occurred in 1970 a strange and still unexplained coup attempt headed by Fascist Prince Junio Valerio Borghese. In 1971, the catholic-MSI referendum campaign for abrogation of the new divorce law gained steam. MSI-influenced conservatives adopted President Richard Nixon's "Silent Majority" label and marched all over Italy protesting the nation's leftist course.

As a result, in the June 1971 local election, MSI votes doubled or tripled in some cities, while PCI, PSIUP, and DC percentages dropped. The PSI, however, gained slightly, conveying the false impression of voter endorsement for a continued leftward push. During the next few months, the PSI advocated a PCI-DC coalition, presenting itself as essential mediator.

The attempt culminated in a series of complicated maneuvers during the presidential elections of December 1971. The left opposed Fanfani as president because it accused him of planning to imitate De Gaulle. Its slogan was "Fanfani, maiale—niente Quirinale! (Pig Fanfani—no Quirinale for you!). The Socialists secretly aimed at Moro's election with PCI and dissident DC votes. The epic battle ended with the nondescript Giovanni Leone's election with MSI support. The socialist intention of serving as a "bridge" between DC and PCI had provoked a dangerous DC–neo-fascist conjunction. The 1971 presidential election left both the center-left and the new PSI policy a shambles.

In the ensuing debate, De Martino retreated from the "advanced equilibria" and reconstructed the four-party coalition. Mancini stubbornly resisted the rapprochement, even when publicly criticized by the new PCI secretary, Enrico Berlinguer. Mancini won an apparent success when President Leone called early elections and commissioned Mancini ally Andreotti to guide them at the head of a single party cabinet. Refusing all advice to back away from his pro-PCI attitude, Mancini conducted the electoral campaign on that platform.[24]

The 7 May 1972 elections greatly shocked Mancini and the PSI, which dropped to its low point of 9.6 percent. Both DC and PCI totals changed little, while the MSI practically doubled its consensus.

PSI Secretary Mancini could not escape responsibility for the electoral disaster. In addition, his ally Andreotti turned about face, forming a center-right cabinet with the Liberals and initiating a conservative economic policy.

The reaction came quickly. At an 18 May 1972 Directorate meeting, Bettino Craxi resurrected the issue of PSI autonomy from the PCI, criticized past errors, and demanded renewal of the center-left. Nenni followed suit the following month at a Central Committee meeting. In July, an "autonomist" convention debated Craxi's plans to alter the PSI's course during the National Congress scheduled for October 1972. The autonomists feared the new neo-fascist threat to Italian democracy, Christian democratic involution, and Andreotti's center-right brought about by Mancini's mistakes.[25]

Influential socialist leaders denounced recent PSI policies, suggesting a two-pronged course to repair the damage: (1) PSI emphasis on inexpensive reforms capable of immediate implementation—justice administration, civil rights, public order, reduction of criminality, and women's rights; (2) long-range party policies—attracting the growing white-collar class produced by the developing Italian economy, government planning to stimulate economic growth, and increased investment in the South.[26]

Mancini unrealistically rejected these criticisms and moved farther left. He proclaimed the 1972 elections a victory, declaring the combined left's 40 percent vote tally an insuperable barrier to any authoritarian government. Hoping to profit from the Italian people's opposition to the Vietnam War, he praised the opening of negotiations and strengthened the PSI's links with the international left. According to Mancini, the world had come around to the PSI's twenty-year-old position against rigid East-West divisions. This argument appeared as a fresh attack on NATO.

As a corollary to these positions, the secretary steadfastly continued championing communist entrance into the ruling coalition and dialogue between PSI and PCI, "parties which are distinct but not opposed." In support, he cited the PCI's "evolution" away from strict Marxism, its condemnation of Russia's Czechoslovak invasion, and its "positive contribution" to Italian democracy. Finally, in an amazing turnabout, Mancini agreed with union opposition to the "incomes policy" which socialist economists had been advocating for years (wage increases based on production increases).[27]

By refusing to admit the PSI's grave crisis, Mancini sealed his own fate. The original "advanced equilibria" proponent, De Martino, skillfully led the assult. While maintaining the theoretical value of his formulation, De Martino admitted that the PSI's opponents had skillfully exploited his ideas against the party. He therefore called for a "new" center-left coalition which would lead to fresh proletarian conquests.[28]

These events and a major scandal involving his past tenure as minister of public works finished Mancini as PSI secretary.

From Crisis to Crisis

Italian democracy passed through an incredible series of trials from the middle to late 1970s. In January 1973, police intervention against student agitation in Milan led to one death and a dramatic manhunt for student leader Mario Capanna. In the same city, on 12 April, armed youths objecting to a neo-fascist march threw a bomb, killing a police officer. On 15 April, in the Roman quarter of Primavalle, the extremist "Potere Operaio" group burned the house of a MSI official, provoking several deaths.

The next year produced several political murders, uncovered a plot of Italian colonels to overthrow the government (the "Rosa dei venti"), witnessed the arrest of intelligence service head Vito Miceli on charges of a similar plot, and saw the bombing of a Bologna-bound train, which killed twelve and wounded forty-eight. The press speculated about intelligence service plots to modify the constitutional order. At the same time, the Red Brigades made their dramatic entrance on the scene, kidnapping and "trying" the Genoese judge, Mario Sossi. This action intitiated a long period of leftist terrorism.[29]

These events occurred in the midst of a hot political battle over divorce and nonstop scandals ranging from public roads construction to oil import bribes, to charges of payoffs by the Lockheed Corporation to the prime minister, the defense minister, and President Leone.

During 1973, two foreign occurrences profoundly influenced Italy: the Yom Kippur War with its resulting oil embargo, and Allende's overthrow in Chile. The oil embargo occasioned draconian conservation measures which shut down recreation facilities at night, restricted automobile circulation, and set off fifteen years of drastic inflation jeopardizing the energy-short country's economy.[30] Chilean events provoked an important rethinking of leftist strategy.

The PSI leadership gave an inadequate response to this novel situation. In November 1972, the PSI's 39th National Congress ended Mancini's tenure as secretary. The new majority counted on the De Martino and Nenni currents, 45 percent and 13 percent, respectively, to Mancini's 42 percent. The majority got control of the Directorate and Central Committee and elected De Martino secretary in December 1972.

In addition, organizational changes established a Political Office, including all faction leaders, and a Secretarial Office, which grouped all their lieutenants. Insignificant from the organizational viewpoint, these changes favored the 1976 "revolt of the forty-year-olds," allowing the party's "Number Twos" to seize power at the low ebb of the party's fortunes.

Francesco De Martino's "new" center-left policy aimed at restoring the four-party coalition on the basis of dynamic reforms. The support of leftist DC currents and PSI gains in partial elections in November 1972 and June 1973 allowed De Martino to scuttle Andreotti's center-right cabinet.

De Martino had hoped for support from the DC congress of June 1973, but this assembly turned out to be "one of the strangest in the party's history, concluded before it began, without the delegates' knowledge." The congress produced a deal which returned Fanfani as secretary with Moro's support.[31]

Following this congress, lackluster Mariano Rumor put together his fourth cabinet with socialist support. Sparks flew over the cabinet's composition, but no new reform-mindedness marked this "new" center-left, only habit and personality clashes.

For all its rhetoric, the new socialist administration had no solutions to offer. Flaccidness, unaggressive leadership, and allowing the Communist party to set the tone for the Socialists and the left marked De Martino's tenure as PSI secretary.

PCI Secretary Enrico Berlinguer took up the slack brilliantly. He focused political debate in the fall of 1973 with a series of articles on the lessons of Chile.

Chilean developments had proven that the democratic renovation of society could be achieved only through the support of the great majority of the population, Berlinguer argued, not by achieving 51 percent of the votes. This basic truth necessitated wide social alliances and collaboration among *all* democratic and popular forces, culminating in a solid political alliance not only of Communists and Socialists but of progressive Catholics as well. Consequently, Berlinguer emphasized not a "left alternative" but a "democratic alternative" linking all these forces. In order to defeat the reactionary forces threatening Italian democracy, to cure Italy's ancient ills, and to ensure Italian economic and social development, Berlinger offered a "historic compromise" among the progressive forces which represented the majority of Italy's population.[32]

The most imaginative socialist reaction to Berlinguer's initiative came from Riccardo Lombardi, who cited François Mitterand's regeneration of the French Socialist party and advocated refounding the PSI in the opposition to prepare itself for a true governing role; as in France, once strengthened, the Socialists could cooperate with the Communists, but not simply tag along with Berlinguer.[33] De Martino could neither bear this suggestion to surrender the PSI's post in government nor play a decisive flanking role with the Communists.[34] As a result, he allowed Berlinguer to dominate Italian socialist debate.

In the meantime, center-left cabinets continued falling one after the other. In early 1974, the PSI Directorate debated the sense of remaining in a governing coalition with a party which diametrically opposed them on economic policy, the looming divorce referendum, and reforms. Contradicting itself, the Directorate stuck with the governing coalition but vowed no quarter for its DC allies during the referendum.

Italian political forces had skillfully avoided the referendum for several years, with the PCI most anxious to find a compromise with the DC which would settle the divorce issue without recourse to the voters. By 1974, however, fresh factors had revolutionized the divorce issue.

Since his return as DC secretary, Fanfani had seized on the referendum as a means of gaining popular support, even though the DC had a legislative majority sympathetic to conservative changes in the divorce law. Supposedly, Fanfani counted on southern support to give him a plebiscitary triumph, which he could exploit to become the Italian De Gaulle.

Allegedly backing Fanfani's plan with crucial financial support were Montedison President Eugenio Cefis and the multinational oil companies. The Italian left sensed that a big referendum win would stimulate Fanfani's establishment of a presidential system in Italy. According to leftists, the oil crisis demonstrated the fragility of the Italian economy, making it imperative for the economic magnates to bolster the instrument of their political power, the DC, before the Italian crisis progressed further.[35]

On 12 May 1974, the country voted. The divorce law had been in existence several years, and the nation had become convinced that it did not threaten the family. As a consequence, the antidivorce DC and MSI went down to a surprisingly large defeat, with 59.1 percent of the electorate upholding the law.

This result raised the possibility of a wide alliance of the secular parties against the Catholics, but De Martino rejected such hopes as "neither realistic nor useful." The Socialists listlessly perpetuated the old center-left.

Undaunted by his referendum defeat, the tireless Fanfani pressed for early elections. In September 1974, a PCI request to become part of the ruling coalition had received PSI backing—and condemnation from Confindustria President Gianni Agnelli and American Secretary of State Henry Kissinger. With PSDI backing, Fanfani tried to exclude the PSI from the ruling coalition and create a center-right majority. For a year, amid terrorist bombings and massacres, political scandals, and arrests for alleged *putsch* preparations, Socialists and Christian Democrats squabbled.

Nenni and other socialist leaders pressed De Martino to leave the coalition. At the end of 1974, the PSI withdrew from the cabinet, but its external support remained necessary for any government. De Martino announced that in future the PSI would collaborate with the DC only to prepare a government that counted on the active support of PCI and the unions. In the meantime, the Socialists pursued an aggressive anti-DC policy which glaringly contrasted with communist moderation. The PSI publicly denounced the DC for its rightist shift and carefully cultivated the non-PCI left: Marco Pannella's Radicals, proabortionists, students, extraparliamentary left, "Lotta Continua" extremists, and the Manifesto movement, expelled by the PCI for radicalism and indiscipline.[36]

Steadily spreading disaffection characterized the PSI in 1975. In February, a Florence meeting discussed PSI reorganization. As usual, this conference had little impact on the party's structure, but it provided important publicity for younger leaders who would combine to achieve power in 1976: Bettino Craxi, Enrico Manca, Antonio Landolfi, and Claudio Signorile. These younger Socialists fretted about the effects on the PSI's image of socialist participation in a spoils system instituted within the state television organization (RAI) and the party's positive vote for the Reale Law.

Restricting civil rights and providing wide police powers to combat growing political and common criminality, this legislation alienated the young leaders from PSI decision makers because it violated socialist tradition. Furthermore, the PSI suffered in accepting the legislation in a deal for extension of the franchise to eighteen-year-olds, while the PCI bolstered its pro-civil rights image by voting against it. In the June 1975 local elections, the new voters cast their ballots for the Communists, giving them a large 6 percent increase compared with the small socialist gain of 2.4 percent. The PCI's 33.4 percent now approached the DC's 35.5 percent.

The unexpectedly large and dramatic PCI increase jarred the Socialists, many of whom believed that they had plowed the field for the Communists. Still, they took no new course of political independence or autonomy, which might have reversed PSI fortunes. PSI leaders cited the left's combined percentage totals, ignored the socialist-communist imbalance, announced once more the center-left's oft-proclaimed end, and pursued a "left alternative" with the PCI in the latter half of 1975.[37]

In early July, the Socialists issued a joint statement with the PCI criticizing the rigid Marxist positions adopted by the Portugese Communists after the revolution ending fifty years of dictatorship in that Iberian country. Socialist adhesion to what appeared to be a self-serving PCI document reinforced the impression of PSI subservience to the Communists. Socialists also joined Communists in leftist local governing coalitions supposedly foreshadowing similar developments at the national level. Socialist subordination appeared so complete that in the fall of 1975, PCI official Paolo Bufalini recommended "unification" of the two parties amounting to absorption of the PSI by its big brother.

Unlike the past, however, a spontaneous general protest greeted the proposal. PSI intellectuals cited their socialist heritage and resented their party's dismissal and ill use by PCI leaders.[38]

Developments within the DC also threatened the PSI. The June 1975 electoral defeat ended Fanfani's reign as DC secretary. After negotiations for a successor stalled, Aldo Moro proposed leftist Benigno Zaccagnini for the position. Universally respected for his honesty, "Zac" was interpreted by the Catholics as the ideal lackluster candidate to take temporary charge of the DC while its more famous leaders worked a deal. Moro's strategy, however, surpassed stopgap considerations. With his customary prudence, Moro announced the opening of a "third phase" in the DC's history. After centrism and the center-left, Moro suggested, the DC seriously considered allowing Communists entrance into the governing coalition.[39]

Direct negotiations between the two giants of the Italian political system officially sealed the PSI's demotion. The "communist problem" in Italy captured the world's attention, and in its eyes Socialists had significance only insofar as they contributed to its solution. The new situation placed the PSI in exactly the PSDI's position of twenty years earlier—when Nenni had launched the opening to the left.

Furthermore, emergence from this unenviable situation appeared impossible because of the PCI's seeming invulnerability to criticism. Having been excluded from power so long, the PCI could disclaim responsibility for the ills of Italian society, while socialist initiatives appeared as crass attempts to reinsert the party into the governing coalition.

Secretary De Martino responded to the PSI's dilemma in a confused and contradictory manner. He solidified relations with the PCI, increasing resentment in his own party. He opposed demands for withdrawal of PSI external support for the Moro government until the end of 1975 but then suddenly forced its resignation against communist advice and without informing his own party. In an interview on Danish television, De Martino demanded early elections if his party and the DC failed to achieve rapid agreement. He got his wish, but those elections would eliminate him as secretary.[40]

The PSI held its 40th Congress from 3 to 7 March 1976 in Rome, at the height of scandals over the Lockheed bribes and revelations of CIA payments to the center-left parties. These developments eliminated PSDI Secretary Mario Tanassi, a dangerous opponent, and shook the DC. In the PSI, the preelection climate muted differences and criticism of De Martino's disastrous policies. Indeed, the factions compromised on a single motion before the delegates gathered, and this proposal carried the congress. In his speech, the secretary persisted in his contradictions, attacking the DC, accepting the "alternative," but holding open the possibility of renewed understandings with the Catholics.

The "alternative" swept the delegates, who greeted Riccardo Lombardi with chants of "Alternativa." By now, of course, interpretations of the new policy had proliferated, with Lombardi being most consistent and least realistic.[41]

In contrast to De Martino's contradictory speech, Bettino Craxi emphasized PSI autonomy, leadership, and realism: "The party must aim at creation of a *socialist pole* of movement and organization, which must become the point of attraction and the link for all the forces of the noncommunist left."[42] Craxi represented the "lieutenants" of the myriad socialist factions who now controlled the party bureaucracy and who would emerge from the shadows after the 1976 elections.

De Martino's slogan for the 1976 elections synthesized his errors: "Never again in the government without the PCI." This theme aroused old Popular Front fears and portrayed the PSI as listless and incapable of formulating an independent policy. In addition, uncoordinated statements of socialist leaders created confusion.

This image contrasted with that of an uncorrupted and vigorous PCI, Italy's only hope of implementing reforms, whose leaders consulted with Spanish and French Communists, initiated Eurocommunism, and courageously distanced themselves from Moscow. Berlinguer thanked NATO for protecting the PCI's independence from the USSR.

Socialist floundering also contrasted with the catholic revival. A DC congress in late March 1976 adopted Moro's policy of dialogue with the Communists and reconfirmed Zaccagnini as secretary.

The general elections of 20 June 1976 produced results consistent with this situation. The DC received 38.8 percent, making good its losses of the year before. The PCI reached its highest support, 34.4 percent. The PSI remained at its historic low of 9.6 percent. This outcome produced an earthquake within the Socialist party. Telegrams deluged party headquarters in Rome's Via del Corso. A number of socialist officials resigned their. posts. Former Secretary Alberto Jacometti and Loris Fortuna called for the Directorate's resignation, a special congress, and election of a new secretary. De Martino defended himself at a 24 June meeting of the Directorate, but the pressure proved intolerable.

At a Central Committee meeting at the Hotel Midas in Rome, a coalition of Lombardi, Mancini, and former De Martino supporters removed De Martino as secretary and elected a new Directorate. The Lombardians had hoped to replace De Martino with Antonio Giolitti, but Giolitti had scant support from the apparatus, and Mancini opposed him. On 16 July 1976, the Directorate agreed on a compromise candidate and elected him secretary: Bettino Craxi.[43]

Despite his own close links with the Communists, President Sandro Pertini expressed the PSI's consensus on De Martino's tenure as secretary when, seventeen years later, he told me, "Just think, this man used to leave on Thursdays and came back on Tuesdays. He used to spend his time in Naples. He used to fish. His hobby was hunting and fishing."[44]

With Craxi, the son of Sicilian immigrants to Milan, the PSI in its despair gave itself a leader with enormous drive and energy—and the capability of reversing the socialist slide.

CHAPTER 12

Bettino Craxi's "Socialist Alternative"

It had happened many times before. At low points in the PSI's history, when opponents and friends counted the party out, it revived. Demonstrating once more this surprising resilience, the Socialists rebounded, reversed De Martino's heritage of subordination, and adopted an aggressive ideological and political posture which placed the PSI in the national forefront.

In 1978, the eighty-two-year-old Sandro Pertini became the republic's first socialist president after Giovanni Leone's disgrace following the Lockheed scandal. Credited with a major role in keeping the country together during his seven-year term, this colorful and effective president became a national hero. Five years later, for the first time in history, the nation also had a cabinet headed by a Socialist. The longest period of governmental stability in fifteen years followed.

Presiding over the party's spectacular turnaround, PSI Secretary Bettino Craxi has received both credit for this development and blame for the new problems it has produced.

A New Breed of Leader

Bettino Craxi leaves no one neutral. He has received high praise for his accomplishments and harsh criticism for his methods. Italian cartoonists have portrayed him as Mussolini, claiming to find a physical resemblance to the dictator, and commentators play on the similarity of "Bettino" to "Benito." Correspondents have pictured him as being arrogant, carrying a grudge, and prone to revenge. Riccardo Lombardi accused him of running the PSI "according to Fuhrerprinzip principles."[1]

On the positive side, Craxi is a cool and politically consistent orator who speaks his mind clearly and simply. This style has not made him popular in an Italian intellectual milieu still influenced by German Hegelianism, and which discovers in this clarity another resemblance to Mussolini.

After analyzing Craxi's speaking method in 1981, however, Mario Medici, a noted specialist in this field, concluded:

> From the manner in which he speaks, there emerges the image of a very practical man who has psychological savvy. He is a doer who immediately concentrates on the essential issues, not ideology. He uses brief and clean paragraphs, and he trusts nouns more than adjectives. Like Nenni, Craxi seems attentive to "the politics of things," but he has imagination and hardly ever repeats himself. Craxi does not use slogans like

the Romagnol leader, but, perhaps because of family tradition, he specializes in proverbs, which he adapts well to the political moment.

. . . Mussolini's language was much more arrogant and fanatical. In Craxi, there is no linguistical or ideological mysticism; there is much good sense and a high degree of sincerity.[2]

It is enough to see one of his news conferences to note how his speaking style resembles that of American rather than Italian politicians.

Part of his image of arrogant efficiency is owing to Craxi's upbringing in fast-paced Milan. His father, Vittorio, a socialist sympathizer, left Sicily for Milan in 1929, shortly after receiving a law degree and refusing to join the Fascist party. In 1933, Vittorio married a woman from the outskirts of the city, Maria Ferrari. On 24 February 1934, they had their first child, Benedetto, called Bettino. With the beginning of World War II, Vittorio participated in the Resistance, and his law office became a reference point for the regime's opponents such as Basso and Pertini. In 1945, Vittorio Craxi became vice prefect of Milan, and, at Nenni's instigation, prefect of Como.

In the meantime, Bettino learned to read at age four, could write by age five, and decided to become a priest at ten. He lacked the pacific qualities needed for this vocation. At eleven, he got his father into trouble with the authorities by heading a band of children attacking local fascist headquarters, defacing a picture of Mussolini, and breaking several windows. He had always liked to fight and regretted not being born in the Middle Ages, Craxi said, when he could have become a knight.

Bettino Craxi participated in his first political campaign in 1948, when Vittorio Craxi ran for office on the Popular Front ticket. The 1948 elections convinced the young Craxi that Communists would always cheat Socialists if given half a chance and gave him an abiding interest in Garibaldi, whose protrait symbolized the front. He told a biographer:

You go into party offices and headquarters, into intellectual clubs, and you see portraits of Mao, of Ho Chi Minh, of Ché Guevara, of Marx and Lenin. I instead have Garibaldi. Why disdain everything we [Italians] have? . . . Frankly, my love for Garibaldi is the result of being pissed off [*incazzatura*], of a spurt of national pride.[3]

Craxi's 1953 trip to Prague with an Italian student organization strengthened his anticommunism. There the future leader read Arthur Koestler's *The God That Failed* and witnessed firsthand the failures of Soviet-style communism. According to Carlo Ripa di Meana, a Communist who would soon leave the party and become Craxi's close supporter, "For the first time, I met someone of my age . . . who tore the scales from his eyes . . . who listened, asked direct questions, and received direct answers; who repudiated dialectical explanations about what happened in the East and who refused to smuggle in horrors as errors."[4]

Craxi joined the PSI at age seventeen, where he distinguished himself by opposition to communist domination of the party's youth movement and apparatus. He published reviews critical of the Soviet Union, established a socialist club inspired by Turati's ideas, and worked with *Critica Sociale*. He soon attracted the attention of Pietro Nenni and of his Milanese representative, Guido Mazzali. Nenni's support secured Craxi's election to the PSI Central Committee at age twenty-three, but his open hostility to the Communists caused his exclusion in 1959. At the same time, Craxi entered the university intending to get a law degree, but he never finished.

His political career, however, proceeded differently. After Craxi's Central Committee reelection failure, Mazzali and Milanese party official Giovanni Mosca assigned him to organizational work in Sesto San Giovanni, the most heavily communist and working-class district in the province, paying him a salary of forty thousand lire a month (about sixty dollars). According to Mosca, Craxi damaged the party because he "broke with everybody and pissed off the Communists, who considered Sesto an untouchable sanctuary." Craxi's retort: "They forced me to go to Sesto. Some people tried to screw me, but I gave it to them." In fact, Craxi engaged in fistfights with his communist comrades.

Following the Sesto stint, Craxi hurled himself into the politics of center-left Milan. Heading a group of young rebels, he objected to procommunist local PSI politics, tweaking the noses of the party elders. He displayed a gift for organization and became PSI provincial secretary in 1964. Although he quarreled with PSDI notables, he ardently supported PSI-PSDI unification. Elected to the Chamber of Deputies in 1968, he left the secretary's post to his close supporter and friend, Antonio Natali.

Over the next fifteen years, Craxi gained absolute control of the unruly Milanese party. Like his hero Turati, Craxi considered local control crucial to his national image, constructed a powerful local base, and retained strategic control of his Milanese faction even after he went to the national capital.[5]

Craxi learned important political techniques from the internecine Milanese quarrels and applied them to Roman politics: conquer the party; create a new, loyal, and cohesive ruling group; exploit the new image in elections.

In Milan, Craxi established a "bunker" at Piazza Duomo 19. Decorated by an architect friend with portraits of Garibaldi and Turati, perfectly outfitted with modern means of communication, these headquarters became the focal point of the Craxian brain trust: Paolo Pillitteri, brother-in-law and "Murat to Craxi-Napoleon"; Carlo Tognoli, future Milanese mayor; Natali; and Claudio Martelli, the dauphin. In Rome, Craxi duplicated this setup, beefing up his brain trust, calling in architects to modernize the drab PSI headquarters at Via del Corso 476, demoting the hammer and sickle and adopting the flaming red carnation of the early socialist leagues as party symbol. Craxi consciously established an Italian version of John Kennedy's "Irish Mafia," efficiency, and style in politics.

Having early diagnosed Nenni's weakness as managerial inability, Craxi pioneered a new electoral efficiency in Milan by combining a number of techniques. More typical of American than Italian campaigns, Craxi saturated his electoral district with "millions" of campaign flyers picturing him with Nenni, sent dozens of workers door to door with his literature, and taped speeches, which cruising microphone-equipped cars disseminated throughout the city. In the 1968 elections, he came in second only to Nenni.

Craxi introduced extensive use of the telephone as well, a novelty in Italian politics. By contacting influential community leaders directly, he aimed not only at winning votes but at making converts. Even as he became more famous, his telephone number remained in the directory, and he did not install an answering machine. Craxi also emphasized television's predominant role before other Italian politicians, maintaining that ten seconds on the air had more impact than a long interview in print. In fact, he paid special attention to all the mass media, charging his lieutenant Martelli with responsibility in this field.[6]

When Craxi became PSI secretary in 1976, *La Repubblica* called him "the German" because of his links with the SPD and his skill in managing the apparatus. Demonstrating greater political acumen, the dissident communist *Manifesto* group labeled him "Bettino the American."[7] In fact, the new secretary also excelled at poker.

In Rome, Craxi's career proceeded slowly and steadily rather than brilliantly. Utilizing two rooms at the Hotel Raphael as his headquarters, Craxi made contacts crucial for his career with other autonomist leaders such as former Bari Mayor Rino Formica and Lelio Lagorio, Tuscan regional president and future defense minister who would theorize the "Bulgarian connection" in the Pope John Paul II assassination attempt.

In July 1969, Craxi suffered a major defeat with the breakup of the PSI-PSDI merger. A crisis of conscience followed; he contemplated leaving the PSI for the PSDI, as his brother-in-law Pillitteri initially did. Instead of making a hasty decision, however, Craxi suddenly asked a friend if he could use his rented house south of Rome for a two-day vacation. He remained there for the next two weeks, reading, playing the guitar, and conversing about every subject except politics. Finally, before leaving for Rome, he told an associate, "One has to know how to wait."[8]

In the beginning of 1970, De Martino became deputy premier in the Rumor cabinet, leaving the PSI secretaryship to Mancini. Hoping to offset the effects of the recent socialist split, these leaders reorganized the hierarchy by installing three vice secretaries representing different party currents. Asked to nominate one of these officials, the semiretired Nenni chose Bettino Craxi as the most reliable representative of autonomist values.[9]

Having reached this exalted position, the plucky Craxi discovered himself a pariah in the ever more leftward-leaning PSI of Mancini and De Martino. His dogged opposition to Lombardi's "left alternative" and Berlinguer's "historic compromise" isolated him from his socialist comrades.

Craxi blocked the "historic compromise" in Milan's city government. If successful, DC and PCI strategies had planned to follow up this local development with a similar solution at the national level. Countering the communist "historic compromise," Craxi theorized a "socialist pole"—returning to formal partnership with the Christian Democrats but seizing the political initiative for the Socialists.[10]

Perhaps to distract him, De Martino put Craxi in charge of PSI foreign relations. Craxi became PSI representative to and vice president of the Socialist International and served on the Chamber of Deputies' Foreign Affairs Committee. Anticipating his active interest in this as prime minister, Craxi threw himself into foreign affairs, which Italian socialist leaders had consistently neglected. Besides providing him with invaluable contacts, Craxi's foreign policy experiences aided his rise to secretary and gave him the idea of countering Berlinguer's "Eurocommunism" with his own "Eurosocialism."

In fact, Craxi's early pronouncements provide clues to his policies as prime minister. Having reached maturity during the center-left period, Craxi not surprisingly admired John Kennedy and America. In the early 1980s, for example, Craxi influenced his friend, Defense Minister Lagorio, to authorize placement of American cruise missiles in Sicily. In addition, after Craxi became prime minister in 1983, he surrounded himself with pro-American advisors and made successful trips to the United States.

Typically, however, Craxi's admiration for the United States left his independence unhampered. In the 1970s, Craxi criticized American policies in Vietnam and openly protested against them in a 1967 letter to Vice President Hubert Humphrey.[11] These actions foreshadowed his pro-Arab policies after he became prime minister, despite early Israeli sympathies, and his lively protest against what he considered American heavy-handedness in the *Achille Lauro* affair in late 1985.[12]

If this latter event cooled Craxi's ardor for America and may have occasioned a rethinking of his relations with the Communists, he has remained critical of the Soviet Union and its allies. Craxi considered his generation marked by the Soviet repression of

Hungary. Friendship with Jiri Pelikan, a "Prague Spring" leader he met in Czechoslovakia and befriended in Italian exile, and Spartaco Vannoni solidified his impressions. Long conversations with Vannoni—Raphael Hotel owner, former PCI financier who bolted from the party after Hungary, former assistant to the Italian ambassador to Warsaw, businessman with close Eastern European connections—convinced Craxi that the PCI would never break with Moscow. At a conference of Czech exiles in Paris, Craxi accused the Soviet Union of following only its national interests and called on Western Communists to demonstrate any dissension from Russia in deed rather than word.

Following through on these feelings, the Italian leader adopted a critical attitude toward French Socialist François Mitterand's union with the Communists, unlike Lombardi. Craxi greeted the French socialist agreement with the Communists coldly, objecting as well to the French economic program: "There is a contradiction between the proposals of public control of the economy and the renunciation of coercive means." Instead of the French, Craxi preferred Willy Brandt's SPD as a model, and he established a special relationship with the German leader and with Spanish Socialist Felipe Gonzalez, future Spanish prime minister.[13]

Thus, by the time of the PSI's June 1976 electoral defeat, Craxi had a reputation as a solid, consistent, and reliable leader with ties to the international community and the apparatus, but not brilliant. These qualities, however, did not secure him the secretary's position. The PSI's sorry state, the lack of other credible candidates, and the underestimation of him by other party leaders worked in Craxi's favor.

At the Midas Hotel Central Committee meeting in July 1976, the "colonels" agreed that the "old men" had to be set aside for the party's good—De Martino, Mancini, Nenni, and Lombardi. Given the bad situation, these leaders allowed their seconds-in-command to go forward.[14]

Because of the uproar produced by the PSI's defeat in the 1976 elections, socialist leaders proceeded delicately in naming a new secretary. Manca's open "betrayal" of De Martino eliminated him temporarily. Another possibility, Claudio Signorile, was excluded for the opposite reason: he was too closely identified with Lombardi's "left alternative" obsession. The aloof and intellectual Antonio Giolitti had support which cut across the factions, but he had alienated Manca and Mancini, who vetoed his candidacy.[15]

The ideal choice under the circumstances was Bettino Craxi. The Milanese leader lacked charisma, knew his way among the party workers, had labor connections, and could count on only a 10 percent autonomist vote in the party. Craxi would thus make the weakest secretary, easily dislodged when the feuding factions could agree and the notables had settled on a suitable candidate.

In the hot July weather, Mancini approached *demartiniano* leader Giovanni Mosca and proposed Craxi for secretary: "He doesn't count shit and can put everybody together," Mancini explained.[16] The expected length of Craxi's tenure was six months.

On this note, Bettino Craxi became PSI secretary.

The Blueprint

Unexpectedly catapulted into the secretary's position, Craxi refused to play according to script. In a mid-November 1976 Central Committee meeting, Craxi unveiled an ambitious program to renovate the party and to thrust it once more into the forefront of Italian life. In an amazingly clear and practical document, Craxi declared the PSI's independence by wrenching the party back to its tradition and to its basic tasks as a political organization.

Craxi considered ideological clarification, and clarity, as essential to PSI survival. He expressed pride in Italian and European socialist tradition as the real source of PSI strength. As such, he embraced revisionism, making it official party policy. He identified revisionism with reformism—the continual quest for a method capable of gradually transforming capitalism into socialism. Only by constantly adapting socialist theory to reality could the Socialists maintain their commitment to economic and political pluralism, unlike the Communists, who favored forceful implementation of their preconceived ideology.[17]

Theory would be useless without a powerful organization to implement it. The shambles the PSI had become called for immediate and drastic action on several fronts, Craxi stressed.

In order to keep the PSI's image clean and curb cases of corruption, Craxi endorsed extension of the recently created Central Control Commission's investigative powers. In line with this theme, he promised to overhaul the party's financial administration, which had produced a catastrophic economic situation and had "gravely weakened our internal democratic life." Ignoring good management of the PSI's financial resources, limiting participation of party members in this area, and relying exclusively on the public funding law encouraged a proprietary attitude of party professionals toward the PSI which must be eliminated.

Craxi next tackled the factional divisions, primary cause of the party's paralysis. A perennial problem: leaving party members free to speak and to act resulted in the proliferation of powerful dueling currents; emulating the PCI's "democratic centralism" imposed totalitarian restrictions.

Craxi chose a middle course. He pledged freedom of expression in the party but vowed elimination of PSI mechanisms ensuring the survival of socialist factions and promised to make it harder for them to appeal to the general public.

Intimately linked to the currents was the problem of a continually degenerating organization. The factions had parceled out the local organizations among themselves and thus had become rooted within the PSI's structure itself. In addition to paralyzing the party's action, this procedure had isolated the PSI from Italian society and had conferred an abstract quality to the issues socialist leaders believed important. Craxi called for closing the gap between the theory and practice of the party's organizational life. He favored neither democratic centralism nor a party based on local clienteles but one "linked to society and to the vital movements that express themselves in it." In practice, this goal required revitalization of the federations, the sections, and the NAS and close coordination with socialist union leaders.

At the same time, he urged the party to concentrate on external activities. Thus, the PSI could overcome its major weaknesses—inability to retain moderate votes which had once accrued to the party, the differential between the high percentage of votes it received in local balloting as compared to general elections, and the "inflation" in party membership—by making certain that only committed persons joined the organization.[18]

In February 1975, a Craxi-inspired national conference on PSI structure and organization had been held in Florence. After a thorough analysis of the party's state, the participants suggested a series of sweeping changes to strengthen PSI efficiency while ensuring freedom, orderly procedures, and the widest possible participation. Craxi called for implementation of the revisions suggested by the Florence conference.[19]

In 1976, Craxi supporters discovered in the PSI's incapacity to implement socialist principles widely accepted by large strata of Italian society the primary explanation of a

nagging contradiction: the difference between the PSI's consistently poor voting performance and widespread approval of its ideology. In the June 1976 elections, for example,
the Socialists had blundered by insisting on communist participation in the government as
the only means of resolving the nation's political crisis. Voters who agreed with the
socialist analysis voted PCI; those who disagreed voted DC. The remedy was reorganization, increased efficiency which would convert the vast "socialist area" of Italian society
into votes for the PSI.

Furthermore, at least until the PSI gained strength, the party had to distinguish itself
sharply from the PCI. *Mondo Operaio* noted that the Socialists had always progressed
while following a reformist policy, whereas maximalism had always spelled disaster.
Other European Socialists had come to power by demonstrating that they knew how to
govern, even when, as in Germany, they had originally been part of a coalition. Moreover, the Communists had made spectacular electoral advances by appropriating the
reformist heritage.[20]

Craxi hoped to implement these policies as secretary by outlining a vast program of
social reforms which the PSI would pursue during his tenure. He committed the PSI to
tax, education, health, and justice reform, revision of the Concordat, protection of the
environment, demilitarization of the national police, and civil rights. In this manner, the
PSI would make a lasting contribution to the modernization of Italian society.[21]

Turning to political strategy, Craxi envisioned the PSI as heading a new grouping of
existing socialistic forces. This design implied destroying the communist hegemony of the
left, which Craxi vowed to do. Because of powerful Italian communist ties to Moscow—
Craxi believed that communist actions belied their rhetoric on this subject—the PCI could
never offer a valid alternative to Christian democratic rule.

In short, communist hegemony of the Italian left blocked the evolution of the Italian
political system. DC dominance depended on this "imperfect bipolarism" of the Italian
political world, that is, two giant parties incapable of alternating power. The journalist
Indro Montanelli expressed this situation best when he wrote, "Hold your nose and vote
DC."

Only a combination of small leftist parties headed by the PSI—the "socialist
pole"—could break this vicious circle. This concept explains Craxi's constant emphasis
on the percentage of votes received by the small lay parties as contrasted to the total DC
and PCI vote. The greater the percentage received by the smaller parties, the healthier the
policial system. Craxi believed that the small secular parties could work with the PSI,
despite existing problems. Furthermore, Craxi aimed at rectifying the Italian anomaly of a
large Communist party occupying socialist political space and would consider a PCI
alliance only under such conditions.[22]

Completing this design, Craxi made PSI cooperation with other European socialist
parties a main theme of his administration. Seizing the opportunity of the upcoming
European Parliament elections, he proposed close collaboration with other European
socialist parties, and he assumed a very active role in the Socialist International as its vice
president.

Craxi thus counterposed "Eurosocialism" to "Eurocommunism." Craxi lauded
Eurocommunism as the attempt of Western communist parties to differentiate themselves
from the authoritarian Marxism-Leninism of the East but considered it proof of communist backwardness. On the other hand, Eurosocialism counted on a democratic tradition to
confront Europe's premier problem, that of "a socialist alternative to the conservative and
reactionary forces of Europe."[23]

In his blueprint, Craxi aso called for a series of conferences on the major issues facing the party. The next few years witnessed an amazing intellectual revival of socialist theory while the new secretary skillfully eliminated his opponents within the party.

Primum Vivere: Taming the Party

In 1976, a series of political initiatives steadied Craxi's tenure along with the new secretary's ideological underpinning of his administration.

Italy faced a grave economic and political crisis. Rapid inflation, devaluation of the lira, and spiraling unemployment followed dramatic oil price increases. Political debate over an abortion law escalated, with Christian Democrats and Neo-Fascists voting together. The Lockheed bribery scandal broke, and terrorism increased dramatically. The end of 1976 and 1977 witnessed several fascist bombs explode in Brescia, sharp violence between "Workers' Autonomy" demonstrators and police in Rome and Bologna, and Red Brigade attacks on journalists and other prominent members of Italian society.

Unable to put together a national emergency government, the parties agreed on a new Christian democratic cabinet headed by Guilio Andreotti and kept alive by abstention of all "constitutional" parties supporting the political system.

Craxi did not endorse this government of "non no-confidence" [*non sfiducia*] but went along for the time being. At the same time, he announced a program to renovate the PSI apparatus by favoring younger faces, and he took a trip to the capitals of European countries run by Socialists.

Within the PSI, Craxi moved decisively first against Mancini, wrongly and embarrassingly perceived as his mentor by the press. Mancini had helped Craxi become secretary because of his conviction that he would be the power behind a weak throne. As a consequence, Mancini pressed his followers' candidacies to important positions in the Italian judiciary and television. Instead of giving in, Craxi publicly rebuffed him.

Craxi coordinated this action with coparticipants in the "Midas Revolution," Claudio Signorile and Gianni De Michelis, Lombardi wing "colonels" charged with revamping the PSI organization. These leaders engineered a series of public defections from Mancini, further weakening his party position. In January 1977, Mancini scurried to Naples, proposing an anti-Craxi alliance with his former archrival De Martino. Having just emerged from a period of internecine warfare, party leaders denounced Mancini's challenge, and hundreds of protesting telegrams flooded *Avanti!* in what appears to have been an orchestrated campaign. De Martino backed off, leaving Mancini discredited.[24]

As one acute observer noted, in this case Craxi perfected the method he would use against future PSI opponents. Unlike his predecessors, who conducted a series of wars punctuated by truces against the same enemies, Craxi enmeshed his opponents in agreements, patiently awaiting a favorable political moment; he would then initiate hostilities, allow no time for regrouping, and utterly destroy his foes.[25]

Craxi faced a more formidable threat in Enrico Manca, who was favorable to a communist agreement and who had inherited De Martino's large faction.

The struggle erupted in early 1977 on the question of whether to agree to the trial of former Premier Mariano Rumor on the Lockheed corruption scandal. Convinced that the evidence did not warrant such a step, Craxi and the socialist deputies withheld their assent, causing the attempt to fail. This policy provoked a revolt in the PSI and strong press condemnation. Craxi revealed that negotiations had taken place with the Communists, who shared his position. Since they feared the consequences of supporting Rumor, they proposed that the Socialists announce their intentions first, after which they would have followed suit. According to Craxi, when the Socialists refused to condemn Rumor, the Communists reversed themselves, coming out against Rumor and leaving the Socialists to take the consequences.[26]

The other issue emerged in April 1977, when kidnappers took Francesco De Martino's son, Guido, and demanded a high ransom from the Socialist party. Reacting to signs that the party might pay, the Communists denounced the PSI. Known for its hard line against terrorism, the PCI accused the Socialists of potentially weakening the state and furthering criminal activity.[27]

As a result of these events, Craxi became convinced that the Communists and Manca's faction had decided to overthrow him and made a closer alliance with Signorile. While disagreement existed between these leaders, both of them considered Manca too subservient to the Communists.

Manca hinted at calling a special congress and announced his availability to succeed Craxi. At a Central Committee meeting in late May 1977, Manca made his move, threatening to reject the secretary's report. His current scarcely represented, Craxi sought and achieved a compromise with the help of the party elders, who ordered Manca to back off, added a soothing sentence to Craxi's report, and ensured that it did not come to a vote.

Having suffered this defeat, Manca claimed that he did not aim to replace Craxi. Manca told an interviewer, "Just as Mussolini, Hitler, and many other dictators did in the past, [Craxi] follows the technique of *discovering* plots against his person in order to unloose witch hunts."[28]

In November 1977, the two contenders joined battle once again over the question of PCI entrance into the ruling majority. Manca opened to the Communists certain local coalitions from which they had been excluded. In response, Craxi removed a local party official tied to Manca. Manca criticized Craxi and conspired to overthrow him in the Directorate, where he reportedly had twenty-one votes to Craxi's eleven. At the last moment, however, Manca desisted. Probably, he feared that any Directorate decision would be reversed by the Central Committee, where he had been stopped the previous May.[29]

Manca's two unlucky sorties caused consternation in his ranks, and his followers lost confidence. During the balloting in preparation for the Turin congress, scheduled for April 1978, Craxi's brilliant organization chief Gianni De Michelis decimated Manca's following. Having been charged by the secretary to shake up the cadres and to replace entrenched party functionaries with younger men, De Michelis eliminated Craxi's opposition, achieving a 90 percent majority in the precongress assemblies of some northern regions. At the Turin congress, the Craxi-Signorile "axis" received more than 65 percent of the votes. Manca's once-powerful faction broke. "If I didn't watch the television news or read *La Repubblica*," Craxi quipped, "I wouldn't notice any opposition in the party."[30]

In addition to this series of astute maneuvers and political alliances, Craxi's links with the unions strengthened his position. Craxi's elevation as PSI secretary in 1976 encouraged the dispirited socialist unionists to accentuate their identity. In the CGIL, Socialists had long been subordinated to the Communists, but their leader Agostino Marianetti now pledged to "ensure that our minority status does not mean subordination."[31] Given the communist stranglehold on the CGIL, however, socialist labor fortunes revived in the UIL, the former social democratic union whose longtime secretary remained in the PSI instead of rejoining the PSDI when reunification failed in 1969.

Craxi's close friend and longtime head of UIL mechanical workers Giorgio Benvenuto chafed at De Martino's predilection for the Communists and threw his organization's influence behind Craxi at the July Midas Hotel meeting. His reasoning: "I was convinced that with him union autonomy would have made great strides, overcoming our inferiority complex toward the Communists."[32] In December 1976, Benvenuto won Craxi's consent for an alliance with the social democratic UIL unionists and became UIL secretary. As a result, Socialists gained control of a major union for the first time in many years.

Following Craxi's line, Benvenuto quickly announced that he would put workers' interests above party concerns and foster internal union democracy. He complained bitterly and loudly about the manner in which the communist-dominated CGIL had relegated Socialists to a secondary position, pledging socialist action in all three unions to end party primacy and put workers' goals first. He said: "The union [model] I propose is an uncomfortable one which elaborates original policies and encourages . . . [worker] participation in and control of the decisions which the workers make."[33]

Craxi's policy of PSI independence from the Communists thus entered union affairs, reversing a long history of socialist passiveness.

Predictably, the first months of 1977 witnessed a harsh communist reaction to Benvenuto. Hoping to enter the ruling governmental majority, the PCI supported a government austerity program designed to confront the nation's economic crisis. Directly challenging the Communists, Benvenuto objected to proposed alterations of the *scala mobile* (cost-of-living adjustments), which, he argued, would effectively eliminate it. In line with Craxi's suggestions, he made proposals that would have protected workers' rights.[34]

Surprised and angered by Benvenuto's challenge, the Communists accused the UIL secretary of courting economic ruin.[35] Instead of damaging him, however, they discovered themselves uncomfortably tarred with an antiworker brush as the workers unleashed demonstrations in favor of the *scala mobile* which targeted communist leaders. Violence erupted against Communist CGIL General Secretary Luciano Lama at the University of Rome. Benvenuto's stock soared.

Socialists and Communists

These events illustrate how the struggle between Socialists and Communists had escalated since Craxi set out to reconquer what he considered legitimate socialist space occupied by the PCI. This issue had emerged before Craxi's tenure. In January 1976, for example, an irritated Giorgio Amendola scolded the Socialists for refusing to follow PCI leadership on the EEC and NATO; the Socialists objected that the Communists had appropriated these policies from the PSI and also condemned communist rationalization of repressive Soviet actions while claiming autonomy from Moscow.[36]

In the meantime, the Communists seemed unstoppable. The enormous increase in the number and seriousness of terroristic incidents in 1977 and running battles between rival extremists created a national emergency. Furthermore, the economic crisis worsened. In order to slow inflation, the Andreotti "non-no-confidence" government froze wages— touching off a strike wave and social unrest. The six "constitutional" parties, including the PCI, discussed converting their abstention into an active majority in July 1977 but failed to agree.[37] Supported by Moro, the PCI claimed full equality in the ruling coalition as the price of their identification with Andreotti's unpopular policies. This result would have eclipsed the PSI as a viable political force.

Craxi shrewdly interpreted the July discussions as having established a privileged relationship among Berlinguer, Moro, and Andreotti. As a consequence, Craxi emphasized communist coresponsibility for Andreotti cabinet policies and disclaimed socialist responsibility for DC maladministration. In Paris for a meeting with Mitterand, Craxi told *Le Monde* that the PCI's supposed evolution away from Muscovite communism left him unconvinced and that socialist opposition to the historic compromise "constituted a threat which no one could ignore with impunity."

If Craxi fought PSI subordination to the Communists, he informed the PSI Central Committee in October 1977 that the Socialists would no longer enter center-left coalitions which sanctioned PSI inferiority to the DC. He boldly announced his intention to break the DC's near monopoly of the Quirinale in the 1978 presidential elections. Finally, amidst the grumbling of impotent socialist leftists, he denounced the historic compromise. Despite Craxi's fulminations, however, the "historic compromise" marched on.

Addressing the CPSU congress in November 1977, Berlinguer courageously reaffirmed the PCI's Eurocommunist principles: political and social pluralism, civil and religious liberty, autonomy from Moscow, the historic compromise. Later in the month, the Italian communist parliamentarians signed a statement accepting NATO.

These moves induced Republican Party Chairman Ugo La Malfa to call for establishment of a "national solidarity" government including the Communists to confront the Italian crisis. Communist-inspired labor agitation and threats of a massive general strike pressured DC recalcitrants to agree. The omnipresent Moro cautiously but firmly guided his colleagues in the operation bringing the PCI into full political partnership. The plan was that DC rightist leader Giulio Andreotti would head a one-party government as a guarantee and would obtain PCI support. Negotiations for communist entrance into the coalition continued in January and February 1978 despite an official American State Department rebuke which surprised the Communists.[38]

Within the PSI, these events produced Manca's mini-revolt and the supremacy of the Craxi-Signorile group previously discussed. Given the DC-PCI agreement, however, Craxi had little choice but to join the new coalition.

Dramatic events occurred during negotiations for the new Andreotti government. In Turin, the trial of Red Brigades founder Renato Curcio and his colleagues opened a new round of attacks upon the state by leftist guerrillas. In a textbook-perfect military operation, the Red Brigades kidnapped Aldo Moro in Rome on 16 March 1978, killing his five-man escort. The suspicious timing of this operation on the eve of the first communist entrance into the governing coalition in thirty years has fueled speculation about the real motives of the kidnappers.[39] Beyond this consideration, however, the affair had important repercussions on the socialist-communist relationship and on the PSI's image.

If the forces behind Moro's abduction aimed to prevent communist entry into the government majority, they failed; Parliament immediately confirmed the Andreotti cabinet.

While angry at the kidnapping, the Communists adamantly opposed negotiations for the DC president's release. Fearing that the DC might yield to pressure from Moro's family, the PCI declared the republic's mortal danger. As a response to the crisis, it demanded firmness, moral isolation of the Red Brigades and their sympathizers, and stepped-up police operations to find Moro.[40] Coming to blows with a leftist "Lotta

Continua" colleague who favored dealing with the Red Brigades for Moro's life, communist deputy Antonello Trombadori howled, "Jackal, I don't want the republic to die!"[41]

While the PCI headed the intransigents, the PSI led the "party favoring negotiations." Rebutting the Communists, Craxi emphasized Italy's humanitarian tradition and its civilized laws. Italian governments had negotiated in similar circumstances before and could do so again without endangering the republic. Moving from argument to decisive action, Craxi first won his party's support. Then he consulted with Giannino Guiso, Curcio's lawyer, and other persons with connections to the terrorists, put together a group of experts skilled in treating such cases, and requested the file detailing similar negotiations in Germany.

Anxious to receive political recognition, the Red Brigades offered to exchange Moro for thirteen jailed terrorists. All parties, including the PSI, refused this ultimatum. Other officials let the matter drop, but Craxi responded by suggesting the release into "exile" of one prisoner not implicated in any "incident of blood" and in particularly difficult personal circumstances, either gravely ill or the mother of a young child.

Communists, Christian Democrats, and Republicans blocked these negotiations, causing the Red Brigades to refuse socialist mediation. They demanded direct negotiations with the DC, which Craxi encouraged. Despite pressure from Moro's family, however, the Catholic party refused.[42] The Red Brigades then murdered Moro, symbolically leaving his body in the center of Rome midway between DC and PCI headquarters.

Despite the socialist secretary's failure to save Moro, Craxi's initiative had very positive effects for the PSI. Summarizing the PSI's action, Craxi said: "Our policy reflected the constitutional principle according to which the state has a duty to save the lives of its citizens when they are in danger. For us, the state is . . . not an end in itself." One informed observer has since written that "the Socialists were indeed being consistent on this point." By skillfully leading extraparliamentary leftist forces, Radicals, unionists, and prestigious intellectuals in an attempt to save Moro, the Socialists asserted their commitment to humanitarianism and limitation of state power while showing up the scarce communist sensibility toward these traditional leftist values. In the same boat with the Communists was the DC, which had violated the Christian conscience against the pope's clear wishes. Indeed, Craxi had seized the international limelight by working with the Vatican, in addition to the UN and important foreign leaders.[43]

Furthermore, by supporting the DC so adamantly and attacking the PSI's policy and Craxi personally, the PCI destroyed the basis for the "left alternative" with the Socialists, confirmed the hypothesis of a permanent catholic-communist alliance which so alarmed moderate public opinion, and demonstrated its willingness to join the corrupt DC governmental system. The PSI, on the other hand, recaptured its independent identity, demonstrated its ability to combat both DC and PCI, and left aside "its old subordination to the PCI and the DC."[44]

Confirmation arrived promptly in the local elections of May 1978. Sympathy for the Moro tragedy swelled the DC vote, but the PCI dropped 8.8 percent from its 1976 high. The *Corriere della Sera* declared Berlinguer the great loser because the PCI had lost all possibility of becoming an alternative to the DC. The surprise winner was Bettino Craxi, whose party increased it consensus by 4 percent. His challenge to the entire governing majority on the Moro case, "An initiative judged by most [leaders] a political disaster, has had the opposite consequences."[45]

Craxi's offensive continued in June 1978, when Italy voted on two referenda which would have abrogated the Reale Law and public funding for political parties. As part of the ruling coalition, the PCI swung its massive machinery in favor of keeping this legislation. The PSI, on the other hand, officially went along with its coalition partners but in fact left its members free to decide their own policy. Once again, Craxi differentiated his party from the PCI and the DC, accentuating the PSI's independent posture. Both referenda failed, but by margins embarrassingly inferior to the coalition's voting total. Craxi's political sixth sense had been correct again.

Morally defeated by the referenda results, Berlinguer attacked the PSI for dragging its feet. He set out to recoup his losses by demanding President Leone's resignation and by conditioning the choice of a new executive.[46] Leone had been under siege because of malfeasance charges leveled by *L'Espresso* writer Camilla Cederna.[47]

After Leone's resignation, Berlinguer and Craxi sparred on a replacement. Berlinguer hoped to demonstrate that the "historic compromise" coalition could determine the next president, but Craxi had announced plans for a socialist executive a year before. The socialist secretary waged an aggressive and intelligent campaign, exploiting communist hesitations attending on their recent electoral losses and catholic embarrassment at Leone's resignation.

Craxi endorsed Antonio Giolitti but failed to get him elected. During the negotiations, however, Craxi did get the parties to accept the principle of a socialist president. The choice fell on Resistance hero Sandro Pertini. Although known to have differences with the irascible Pertini, who had clear communist sympathies, Craxi agreed. Amidst great socialist jubilation, Parliament elected Pertini president of the republic with a record vote in July 1978.[48]

With this one development, Craxi won several points. He had blocked Catholics and Communists from electing "historic compromise" candidate Ugo La Malfa, he had made good his claim for the Socialist party to receive its share of national political offices on a regular basis, and he had reaffirmed PSI ability to act independently and successfully against its more powerful rivals. Despite its small numbers, the PSI could be denied no political office, not even the premiership—Craxi's "socialist alternative."

Craxi followed his political success by seizing the ideological initiative on the left. In 1977, the Socialists had proposed that the Venice Biennale theme be dissent in Eastern Europe, setting off howls of protest from the PCI and the Soviet ambassador. In 1978, Craxi's friend Ugo Finetti published a book on dissent within the PCI. After a detailed examination of PCI repression of its own members, Finetti denied that the PCI had really abandoned Leninism and concluded that Berlinguer had imposed a "monolithic and lonely revisionism" on the PCI for tactical reasons, had trailed the Spanish and French Communist parties in denouncing the dictatorship of the proletariat, had failed to support Spanish leader Santiago Carrillo's opposition to Moscow, and could not be trusted.[49]

During the summer of 1978, the PSI escalated its ideological attack by condemning the heritage of Togliatti and Lenin in the PCI. A press war resulted. *L'Unità* defended Togliatti, suggesting that the Socialists did not understand Lenin, while *Avanti!* pitilessly exposed communist contradictions and ambiguity. This debate stung Berlinguer into announcing that the Italian Communists actually sought a "third road" (*terza via*) between Eastern-style people's democracies and Western European social democracies.[50]

Berlinguer's interview whetted the press's appetite. Newspapers offered Craxi space for a reply, but the secretary carefully avoided answering the communist leader because he planned a full-scale assault against the PCI's democratic credentials. Craxi's bombshell came in July 1978, in an essay published by *L'Espresso,* the country's leading news weekly.

Ever since the beginning, Craxi argued, socialist thought combined different and even mutually exclusive elements: anarchists vs. authoritarians, collectivists vs. individualists, Stalinists vs. antistalinists. The most important struggle raged after the Russian Revolution between advocates of state power for the implementation of socialism and supporters of Western-style pluralism.

For the "pluralists," socialism surpassed liberalism and realized the individual's full potential by installing social control of the economy and strengthening society vis-à-vis the state. On the contrary, the Marxist-Leninists wished to suppress the free market and to have the state rule society. In short, these true heirs of the French revolutionary Jacobins wanted to cancel all traces of the individual.

Thus, according to Craxi, Eastern-style communism is not a deviation from Marxist-Leninist doctrine or the result of errors. It is "the concrete application of logical implications of the rigidly collectivist formulation originally adopted."

Lenin distinguished between two means of perceiving reality, "spontaneity" and "consciousness," Craxi continued. Only through the second could the goals of history be understood, but—deprived of philosophical and scientific understanding—the workers could not possess consciousness. Left to their own devices, Lenin believed, workers could only move within the limits of the capitalist system's laws, developing, at most, a "trade-union consciousness." Political consciousness could be brought to them only from the outside, by the intellectuals. It therefore became the lot of these intellectuals guided by Marxist principles to organize and direct the workers' movement.

In short, Craxi asserted, far from being the ideology of the working class, Leninism is "the philosophical justification of the historic right of the intellectuals to govern the working masses in an autocratic manner." To bolster his case, Craxi quoted the early Trotski, who criticized Lenin for confusing a dictatorship on the proletariat with the dictatorship of the proletariat and resurrecting Jacobinism. Leninist communism wishes to regenerate humanity, forcing it to seek control of all aspects of life. This aim in turn implies the bureaucratization of life and complete state ownership and control. Leninism institutionalizes a single command center and absolute centralization, through which it seeks to solve all problems of human existence. But by doing so, communism became a religion disguised as science. All of these aspects prove that communism cannot tolerate rivals or criticism and is inherently totalitarian. Thus, Antonio Gramsci theorized the totalitarian and "divine" nature of the Communist party, and Stalinism applied Leninism concretely. Consequently, "Leninism and pluralism are antithetical terms: if the first prevails, the second dies." This analysis of Marxist-Leninism revealed the "substantial incompatibility" between communism and socialism, Craxi concluded.

Unlike communism, democratic socialism seeks "socialization of the values of liberalism, diffusion of power, egalitarian distribution of wealth, equal opportunity, the strengthening and development of institutions which foster working-class participation in decision-making." Democratic socialism does not impose orthodoxy on anyone, recognizing as the most precious of human rights the right to make a mistake. Democracy—socialist *and* liberal, Craxi pointedly emphasized—presupposed many competing centers of power. This absence of monopoly impeded the imposition of totalitarianism.

Intellectuals of the revisionist left from Pierre-Joseph Proudhon to Rosa Luxemburg had warned against the evolution of Marxism-Leninism. Craxi approvingly cited Proudhon, who had foreseen communist centralization, systematic destruction of all independent thought, establishment of an inquisitorial police, controls on the family, and the organization of universal suffrage to sanction an anonymous tyranny based on mediocrity. The implications for Italy? The PCI could not be democratic because it subscribed to Leninism; for the same reason, it could not be entrusted with a role in governing Italy. This attack on the PCI's pedigree and possibilities culminated a battle which had raged in the intellectual journals for several years and should be seen as the Socialists' attempt to revitalize their own tradition and recover their rightful political space, not—in the ill-considered remark of an American observer—"a classical attack on the PCI from the right."[51]

As may be expected, Craxi's challenge touched off a furious debate between Communists and Socialists. A small contingent of left-wing Socialists headed by Michele Achilli attempted a rebellion against the secretary but failed miserably, as did a protest from De Martino. Luciano Pellicani, Craxi's ideological advisor; Paolo Flores d'Arcais, cultural league leader; Claudio Signorile; and other Socialists ably defended Craxi's position from scornful PCI attacks in newspapers and journals. The Italian press discussed Craxi's thesis as the PSI became the center of a national debate for the first time since the 1950s. The debate had repercussions abroad as well, especially in France. Caught up in the dispute, the PSI rank and file approved Craxi's initiative at the *Avanti!* fund-raising festivals during the summer and in many newspaper interviews. Signals of assent also came from the extraparliamentary press.

The quarrel spilled beyond these intellectual circles. The catholic union (CISL) denounced the PCI's "intolerant" reaction to the points raised by Craxi. UIL head Giorgio Benvenuto took umbrage at communist insults after he criticized strong PCI support for the government's economic program, which he alleged had seriously damaged worker interests. Once again, the Socialists had successfully branded the communist attitude toward workers as insensitive.[52]

The socialist-communist dispute had major repercussions in the political arena as well. Communist officials had sent signals of impatience with the current "national solidarity" governing formula, which had them with one foot inside the ruling coalition but not part of the government. Since Italian politicians first experiment with changes in national coalitions in local governments, the Communists tested the waters in the provinces.

The Socialists reacted immediately. In some cities, they favored four-party center-left coalitions, pointedly excluding the Communists; in others, they ousted procommunist Socialists from positions of power. Craxi denied communist charges of a PSI return to a privileged dialogue with the DC and countered with allegations of communist unfriendliness. But DC and other forces hostile to PCI participation in the ruling coalition blocked the communist move for greater recognition, the true PSI aim.[53]

Angry at socialist policy, communist leaders took the offensive. At the close of the summer festival for *L'Unità* in Genoa, Berlinguer adopted a hard line before a crowd of a half-million party faithful anxious to hear their leader chastise the PSI. Berlinguer reaffirmed his belief in Marx, Lenin, Gramsci, and Togliatti and vowed that the PCI would never give up its heritage.[54] By making clear his continued acceptance of Marxism-Leninism, the communist secretary confirmed Craxi's doubts about the PCI's supposed democratic evolution and lost support among influential noncommunist politicians formerly convinced that the PCI had undergone a fundamental change. Craxi's moves had clearly scuttled Berlinguer's dreaded "historic compromise."

The remainder of 1978 witnessed a series of quarrels between the Communists and the rest of the majority over Italian economic measures, EEC financial policy, and attitudes toward a number of scandals. These disputes shattered the previous trust among PCI, catholic, and lay political forces. In January 1979, the PCI Directorate announced communist withdrawal from the ruling coalition, provoking a government crisis.

The PCI had suffered a major defeat. The party had supported deflationary policies and wage restraints, causing it to lose face with the unions and the workers. In exchange, it received "the minimal formalities of participation in government." The result would be loss of electoral momentum.[55]

Craxi had been a major protagonist in achieving this result. A story making the rounds reflects the new mood. The year is 2001. God grants Berlinguer special permission to return to Earth to check on his historical reputation. Berlinguer goes straight to the Vatican library and discovers the following entry in an encyclopedia: "Enrico Berlinguer: Sardianian nobleman of Marxist tendencies. He lived in Italy during the Craxi era."[56]

Under Craxi's leadership, the PSI had finally sloughed off its inferiority complex toward the Communists, carved out its own political space, and regained its cultural identity. Paradoxically, however, the secretary now faced his most serious internal challenge.

The Last Revolt?

Craxi's frontal assault against the Communists paid handsomely but had risks. Most importantly, Craxi's actions alienated the Lombardi wing. Under Claudio Signorile, it will be recalled, Lombardi's followers had forged an alliance with Craxi which kept the secretary in power. Although the pact held fairly well at first, signs of stress had already appeared at the local level in the autumn of 1978.[57]

Italian entry into the "snake" divided the PSI. This term described the European monetary system which committed EEC currencies to fluctuate together. Since the Lombardians sided with the Communists in opposing Italian entrance, PSI parliamentarians abstained when the question came up. In December 1978, internal debate also raged over socialist deals dividing control of ENI and RAI, PSI participation in blocking an inquiry into payoffs to political parties during the center-left era, and scandals involving PSI members.

In the meantime, leftist extremists exasperated by the cultural revolution's defeat in China and a series of other international blows escalated their terror wave. Terrorists linked up with the Mafia. In April 1979, the Padua police swept down upon "Autonomia Operaia," accused of masterminding Italy's terrorist wave. The group's head, University of Padua Professor Antonio Negri, and other leaders languished in jail for years. Given the investigating judge's communist connections, Craxi criticized these developments as possibly politically motivated and emphasized the grave civil rights implications. Following the communist lead, however, PSI left-wingers attacked the secretary for his supposed softness on terrorism. Ironically, a court acquitted Negri and "Autonomia Operaia" five years later.

Economic conditions also stirred debate. While the economy seemingly picked up, much of the improvement came in the "submerged economy," which could be neither taxed nor controlled. In the legitimate economy, workers received higher increases and more benefits than those in other EEC countries. Expenses escalated, and production dropped, imperiling large private concerns and driving public industry close to ruin. Unemployment grew, especially among the young. Crime also increased dramatically, and a series of spectacular and drawn-out kidnappings drew the nation's attention to this fact.

Dispute over resolution of these problems produced definitive PCI withdrawal from the "national solidarity" coalition in January 1979. Communist criticism of the government's economic policies had support within the PSI, with Lombardi intimating that the PSI should follow suit. Despite his own reservations, Craxi opposed dropping out of the coalition.[58]

In February 1979, PCI insistence on communist ministers in any new cabinet blocked an Andreotti attempt to form a new government. President Pertini thereupon gave the mandate to venerable Republican party leader Ugo La Malfa. The Communists softened their position in homage to an old sympathizer, proposing ministers elected in their lists but not party members. DC hostility, however, sabotaged La Malfa's efforts. The result was yet another Andreotti cabinet which presided over early elections. Craxi had not welcomed La Malfa's mandate and had criticized Pertini, but he became livid at this outcome.[59]

In order to increase chances of a good PSI showing, Craxi demanded that balloting for the national elections be held on the same day as that for the European Parliament, but he failed. Consequently, the PSI turned in a poor performance in the 3 June 1979 national elections, remaining at 9.8 percent.

Luckily for the PSI secretary, the PCI vote dropped by 4 percent compared to the 1976 national elections, and the DC declined slightly. Even more fortunately, the PSI received 11 percent in the European elections a week later. Craxi subsequently argued that the party would have done substantially better if the two elections had been combined, but the 1979 elections caused the Craxi-Signorile entente to unravel.

Craxi had pitched the PSI's electoral campaign toward creation of a "socialist third force which represents at the same time the socialist pole on the left and the reference point for all the catholic and lay forces of renovation and progress." On 8 May 1979, Craxi emphasized PSI ties to European social democracy and told the Central Committee that the socialist "third force" would not brook subordination to the two major Italian parties, DC and PCI.

Craxi thus appealed to the voters to reverse the bipolar Italian political system—according to which "the DC grabs everything in the moderate area, and the PCI grabs everything on the left." This system ensured only instability, crisis, and paralysis, while a strong socialist showing could produce "five years of stability and governability."

These statements signaled Craxi's long and successful campaign to exploit PCI inability to develop into a stable government party and the steady erosion of DC prestige to play for the highest stakes: the presidency of the Council of Ministers. This aim, in fact, constituted Bettino Craxi's real "Socialist Alternative."

If the Socialists could obtain the nation's highest office and provide stability and efficiency, Craxi believed, progressive voters would reward them by supporting the PSI rather than the PCI, thus reversing the Italian anomaly of a large Communist and a small Socialist party. In order to accomplish this goal, the PSI must play an independent role, refusing to allow its small number of votes to condition it to hang on to the coattails of the large parties; hence, Craxi's emphasis on the "third force" and further PSI aggressiveness and independence. Moreover, this policy required keeping the PCI out of the government and increasing difficulties for DC-led governments.

As a result, in its appeal to the voters, the PSI Directorate decisively cut loose from the center-left experience without renouncing it. History would demonstrate that on the whole the center-left had been a success, but "Past experiences live with the conquests achieved and the errors committed, but they can never be repeated." No longer, in short, would the PSI be a passive member of ruling coalitions.[60]

The delicately balanced Italian political system provided ample space for Craxi's policy. After the June 1979 elections, President Pertini asked Andreotti to form a government. Communist opposition and Craxi's veto doomed the Christian democratic leader's efforts. For the first time, Craxi announced the principle of "alternanza," alternating control of Palazzo Chigi. Concludes Craxi's future press secretary, Antonio Ghirelli: "This meant that the veto against the Roman statesman [Andreotti] had been transformed into hostility against all Christian democratic exponents and that his own self-candidacy [as prime minister] had gained more and more prominence in Craxi's plans."[61]

The political stalemate induced Pertini to explore a "laic" solution to the crisis. In early July, he called in Craxi and Signorile and gave the PSI secretary the mandate to form a government; for this first-ever honor to a Socialist, the elegant Pertini enjoined Craxi to change from his blue jeans into more appropriate attire. The decisive socialist stand against a DC prime minister and the impossibility of a majority without PSI votes justified the president's action. In the last elections, the total vote going to the small constitutional parties had increased at the expense of the larger ones, exposing the crisis of both DC and PCI and supporting Craxi's thesis of Italian impatience with the "bipolar" political system.

The PCI had gone into the opposition but could not openly oppose a socialist prime minister after having supported a Christian democrat for three years. Irritated at being upstaged by their former junior partner, however, the Communists maneuvered against Craxi. On the other hand, remaining oriented toward the "historic compromise" and unprepared to relinquish Palazzo Chigi even after thirty-four years, Moro's heir Zaccagnini also disdained Craxi's efforts to lead a government.

Despite this powerful opposition which doomed his mission from the beginning, Craxi moved skillfully. A well-argued ten-point program pledged political, economic, and labor reforms; greater Italian international cooperation; and, above all, stability—*governabilità*. In moves which later aroused debate, Signorile secured support for a Craxi cabinet from the Italian military, police forces, bureaucracy, industry, the Bank of Italy, American Ambassador Richard Gardner—even the Vatican. As a result, "Zac" treaded gingerly in lining up the DC against the socialist secretary. Although Craxi had significant sympathies within the DC—because of either conviction or hopes of splitting the leftist parties further—Zaccagnini eliminated this support by threatening resignation if his party did not block the PSI leader. In the end, only the future vice premier in the 1983 Craxi government, Arnaldo Forlani, resisted the DC decision to sabotage the PSI secretary. An angry Craxi defined the catholic attitude as "Better Berlinguer than Craxi."[62]

The socialist assault on Palazzo Chigi proved premature, but the experience greatly increased Craxi's prestige, created euphoria within the PSI, and heartened the secretary in his new course.

Craxi's goal of creating an aggressive party which could enter into coalitions with the DC while maintaining its integrity and dropping its communist inferiority complex drew the fulminations of the left's grand old man, Riccardo Lombardi. Convinced of the "unnatural" nature of the DC-PCI alliance, the PSI left wing had expected the "national solidarity" phase of Italian politics to doom the "historic compromise," strengthen the Socialist party, and produce the "left alternative" pact between PSI and PCI. His lieutenant Signorile also believed in the "left alternative" but considered it premature and temporarily allied with Craxi.[63]

After the June 1979 elections, however, Craxi wrote off the possibility of socialist cooperation with the Communists. Hoping to patch up the PSI-PCI quarrel, Signorile sponsored a meeting between Craxi and Berlinguer on 20 September 1979. While cordial enough, Craxi made certain that the agreements reached between the two leaders remained a dead letter. Irritated, Signorile blamed the Communists only partially, complaining that his efforts encountered total indifference in his own party.[64] Furthermore, the Signorile group accused Craxi of plotting a five-party (*pentapartito*) coalition (DC-PSI-PSDI-PRI-PLI), freezing the Communists out of the government. In the meantime, Craxi's current denigrated the "left alternative." By October 1979, however, Craxi's position had weakened considerably, and Signorile secured the secretary's word to back away from the five-party-coalition idea.[65]

What had caused this erosion? In a late-September *Avanti!* editorial, Craxi focused the party's attention on major issues by lashing out against petty politics. The new legislature had begun on a bad note, he argued, and could survive only by becoming the legislature of the "Great Reform." Craxi defined his "Great Reform" vaguely as a "unitary reform in its logic, its principles, and its fundamental directions," somehow to embrace all the problems facing modern Italy. Exactly how remained unclear and unimaginative. In his 1982 book on Craxi, Antonio Ghirelli defined the "Great Reform" as "an alliance offer made equally to the PCI and the DC, a development in great style (at least in its intentions) of the 'governability' theme which Craxi had proposed to the voters in the June [electoral] campaign." Unlike his mentor Nenni, however, Craxi failed to galvanize the nation.[66]

This failed initiative got Craxi into considerable hot water. The PSI's most respected intellectuals, "Craxiani" and not, issued a manifesto attacking Craxi's formulation as disappointing, commonplace, and unbecoming a PSI leader. Signed by the flower of the socialist intelligentsia, including Norberto Bobbio, Giorgio Ruffolo, Giuliano Amato, Federico Coen, Massimo L. Salvadori, and key Craxi supporters such as Luciano Pellicani and Paolo Flores d'Arcais, the statement greatly embarrassed Craxi and provoked his ill-considered denunciation of the "intellectual caste."[67]

An elevated percentage for the PSI in several local elections and the beginnings of the ENI-Petromin petroleum scandal only temporarily relieved the pressure on Craxi. The PSI reached 14 percent in some cities, while the scandal allegedly involved payoffs to a major exponent of Signorile's group, ENI head Giorgio Mazzanti.

A subsequent debate over international affairs came close to undoing Craxi. Following deployment of Soviet SS 20 missiles, the United States requested that its NATO allies accept installation of Pershing 2 and cruise missiles. Soviet leader Leonid Breshnev appealed to the Europeans to turn the Americans down, and in Italy the PCI agreed. Craxi, however, favored redressing the missile balance and pushed PSI acquiescence. As a result, the PCI launched a full-scale attack on the secretary, and the PSI left wing followed suit. While Signorile announced the end of his alliance with Craxi, Lombardi went out for the secretary's blood.

Lombardi objected to Craxi's position on the "Euromissiles" and his entire policy. Particularly agitating Lombardi was Craxi's hostility toward the Communists and his denigration of the "left alternative" with them. When he had attempted to clarify the question, Lombardi complained, Craxi "brutally answered" that the Turin Congress had not endorsed the left alternative. Furthermore, Lombardi objected to the "third force" and "stability" themes enunciated during the recent elections. He also castigated Craxi's behavior as premier designate because of his negative attitude toward the Communists. Lombardi criticized the socialist abstention which had allowed DC leader Francesco Cossiga to form a government, stating that Craxi should have secured PCI agreement to abstention or provoked early elections. Finally, Lombardi accused Craxi of running the PSI like a dictator.[68]

Although Signorile and Craxi worked out a compromise on the American missile proposal and the weak Cossiga government substantially accepted it, about twenty socialist deputies violated party discipline by voting against the missiles in a secret ballot; others walked out of the Chamber of Deputies in protest. In the meantime, Parliament defeated the government on a series of social issues. Finally, a new wave of terrorism forced the cabinet to adopt unpopular decree laws which gave the police new powers, extended preventive detention to more than a decade, and provided for leniency to terrorists who turned state's evidence, the *pentiti*.

In an attempt to placate the left wing, Craxi took his distance from Cossiga, but in vain. On 20 December 1979, an agitated PSI Directorate meeting witnessed strong language against the secretary and the accusation that he had ruined the party. Scared Craxi followers called for an early congress to strengthen their position. The press counted Craxi out as secretary and speculated on a successor, supposedly to be elected at a Central Committee meeting scheduled for 9 January 1980.[69]

The indomitable Craxi, however, saved himself. After the Directorate meeting, he reached an agreement with the powerful Gianni De Michelis, wooing him away from Signorile. On New Year's Day, Pietro Nenni died. In his commemorative speech, Craxi bade him farewell on behalf of the nation with the "simple Italian salute" of the Spanish Civil War: "Ciao, Nenni."[70]

Nenni's death deeply moved the country and attenuated the disputes within the PSI. Party leaders rescheduled the Central Committee meeting, and the left wing agreed on a series of demands which severely limited the secretary's powers. Craxi accepted this ultimatum, which gave Lombardi Nenni's post of PSI president.[71]

The compromise gave Craxi an important respite, which he exploited to defeat the leftists and to reassert his control. The PCI had adopted a policy of overt hostility to Craxi to encourage his ouster. The left wing, therefore, could only bank on continuation of the "historic compromise" policy by the DC in order to retain its initiative. In effect, the left gambled on a Zaccagnini victory at the DC congress of February 1980. At that assembly, however, Flaminio Piccoli, Carlo Donat-Cattin, and Fanfani—the anticommunist "preambolo" faction—unseated Zaccagnini and formally undid the "historic compromise."

Meanwhile, Craxi ignored the limitations the left wing had imposed on him and pursued an independent policy. Lombardi proved unable to control him and resigned as PSI president in March 1980, officially sanctioning the left wing's defeat.[72]

After this revolt, the Socialist party has remained fairly quiescent internally, apparently achieving the unity it always craved. Even the dispute recounted above lacked the fire of the old fights, which flashed only from the seventy-nine-year-old Lombardi. In fact, for all of Craxi's reputation about never forgiving an enemy, some of his rivals subsequently achieved important positions after losing out to him. The defeated "Demartiniano" Enrico Manca, for example, strongly supported Craxi against Signorile and has become head of RAI. Signorile became a minister of transportation in the first socialist-led cabinet; Giuliano Amato, sometimes his most scathing critic, became under secretary, did the bulk of that government's practical work brilliantly, and tended to diplomatic relations among the difficult personalities both within the cabinet and in Parliament. In his efforts to utilize the best energies of former enemies, Craxi resembles Napoleon rather than Mussolini.

In October 1983, I asked Valdo Spini to explain this newfound unity. A key "Lombardian" who became vice secretary with Martelli after the 1981 Palermo congress to smooth over unfinished business between Craxi and the left, Spini answered:

> This happened also because the general situation helped him [Craxi]; especially because the action of the Communist party was not such as to give some space to the left of the Socialist party because the Communist party fought so much against Craxi. The position of the left became very difficult because if it went against Craxi it would seem as if the left were too near to the Communist party.

"If the left opposed Craxi," I said, "it would seem as if it were playing the communist game." Spini responded:

> Exactly. And . . . I think that all the party has understood that this is a historical *occasion* which the party has. If the party which has the presidency of the Council [of Ministers] and has 11.4 percent [of the votes, achieved in the 1983 elections] is divided, everything is lost. The left of the party, which has a long-term conception . . . the "alternativa"—knows very well that only a stronger Socialist party can be the protagonist of such a stretegy. So it [the left] is in favor of a situation in which the Socialist party can grow.

When I commented on the importance of this development as compared with the divisive history of the PSI, Spini laughed softly behind his cluttered desk and replied:

> This is because our generation is a younger generation, and it doesn't want if possible to fall in the fault of the [inaudible], because we had 20 percent in 1946, and I think that [the party has] many merits toward Italian democracy. Nenni was too quick to allow [splits in the party].[73]

The left appears to have concluded that Craxi's "Socialist Alternative" policy is functioning and will produce a more powerful PSI. Although criticisms of Craxi continue, the tactical positions of left and right appear to coincide. If this is true, the 1979–80 revolt will be the last—for a while.

CHAPTER 13

The Socialist-Led Government

In 1976, political theorist Norberto Bobbio argued that the PSI had condemned itself to being a permanent medium-sized party. Bobbio attributed this condition to the continual divisions, splits, reunifications, and redivisions of socialist history since 1946. By 1980, however, the PSI seemed united under Craxi's leadership. This appearance of unity had proven deceptive before, but this time the party's leader had seized the political initiative, had formulated a clear plan to increase the PSI's consensus, and had the stamina to put it into effect.

Thus, on 4 August 1983, Craxi became the first Socialist to take the oath of office as president of the Council of Ministers. This socialist-led government lasted a record time for republican Italy, until 27 June 1986. Which factors produced this extraordinary achievement?

Intellectual Revival

Upon becoming secretary in 1976, Craxi had called for socialist development of the great themes and problems which faced Italy and the PSI in the modern world. In Craxi's view, only cultural ferment could revive the party, establish a dialogue with the modernizing sectors of Italian society, and eradicate the socialist inferiority complex toward the Communists.

Characteristically, Craxi's camp linked future socialist goals to past ideals. This technique revitalized autonomous socialist tradition, the denigration of which had signaled PSI decadence in the 1950s.

A prime example was the new socialist internationalism. As mentioned earlier, in contradistinction to "Eurocommunism" Craxi emphasized "Eurosocialism," strengthened his ties to the International, and worked closely with the prestigious Willy Brandt. Inserting Italian socialist tradition into the context of the ruling European socialist parties, *Critica Sociale* traced the origins of Italian socialist internationalism to Filippo Turati. Updating that tradition and emphasizing the socialist independence so prized by Craxi, PSI foreign policy expert Umberto Giovine proposed Italian acceptance of a "noninterference" zone stretching from Italy to Hungary. In order to examine the implications, Giovine suggested direct talks between the two countries. At the same time, he reflected the posture of other European Socialists by inserting the idea within a NATO context.

Furthermore, Italian Socialists stimulated their foreign socialist colleagues to join them in a flurry of discussion and conferences on common themes. This activity peaked with the 1979 elections for the European Parliament but continued strong thereafter. In addition, Craxi pledged common European socialist planning for Europe's economic, technological, and social development and as prime minister took a leading role in European Community affairs.[1]

Another major theme was the relationship between socialism and freedom. With this issue, the Socialists embarrassed the PCI, demanded clarification of communist ideas, and gained the cultural offensive against the left's dominant party.

The debate involved interpretation of the legacy of Antonio Gramsci, the major deity of the PCI pantheon. In a series of sharp articles in the party's cultural review *Mondoperaio,* Socialists criticized the communist cultural heritage which had supposedly inspired current PCI policies. This time, the Communists went on the defensive—instead of the other way around. Published in 1976 and 1977, *Mondoperaio* gathered the socialist opinions in an influential volume suggestively entitled *Hegemony and Democracy: Gramsci and the Communist Question.*

This issue became crucial, because in seeking legitimacy as a government party, the PCI maintained that its commitment to Western democracy and pluralism originated from an independent elaboration of Gramsci's thought by way of Togliatti. This apparent contradiction allowed Socialists to question the image the PCI gave of itself.

Political philosopher Norberto Bobbio ignited the debate by flatly stating that a serious contradiction existed between pluralism and Marxism. Going one step farther, Bobbio believed that Marxists should incorporate the still vital liberal democratic tradition into their political philosophy, grafting onto liberalism socialist concepts of direct democracy and wide participation in political and economic affairs. Gramsci-citing Communists irritably claimed to have already accomplished what Bobbio suggested and dismissed the Socialists as mere Liberal Democrats—the ultimate insult.[2]

Dismissal no longer sufficed to silence the newly aggressive Socialists. The totalitarian nature of communism, Bobbio counterattacked, marked the fundamental difference between Socialists and Communists. Stimulated by this concept, other socialist writers zeroed in on all aspects of the communist heritage, especially Gramsci but also Togliatti, Lenin, and the Soviet Union. Not surprisingly, they discovered in the communist tradition the roots of totalitarianism, not pluralism.

First, Furio Diaz set the parameters of the question by examining the underpinnings of the PCI's current claim to having chosen democracy of the Western type. Closely analyzing Gramsci's writings, Diaz contended that while the communist theoretician had defended representative democracies against fascism, Gramsci "is negative and pessimistic when it comes to the whole method of 'formal' democracy." Furthermore, Diaz wrote, Gramsci had not believed in the possibility of representative systems to develop "on the democratic and pluralistic planes." By examining past communist actions and theory, Diaz discovered an "iron bond" linking Gramsci, Togliatti, the PCI, Leninism, and Soviet practice. The Communists now professed to have accepted democracy, and, understandably enough, they maintained strong ties to their tradition; but they reconciled their roots and democracy in the only way possible: through ideological mystification.[3]

The socialist historian Massimo L. Salvadori further intensified the debate. Focusing on Gramsci's much-discussed theory of hegemony—which Communists equated to consensus—Salvadori contended that the Italian philosopher consciously erected an ideological structure based on Lenin because, as Gramsci himself stated, Lenin did not have the opportunity to complete the structure himself. Salvadori forcefully identified Gramsci's hegemony theory with Leninism, writing:

> In brief, . . . Gramsci's hegemony theory is the highest and most complex expression
> of Leninism and may in no way be considered a transition from Leninism to a
> conception of political struggle . . . which conterposes . . . [this] hegemony to
> Lenin's dictatorial system and the state. Almost as if to avoid all future equivocation
> [on this point], Gramsci labeled Lenin the St. Paul of Marxism.

Salvadori acknowledged PCI evolution into a more democratic force, but he attributed this development to Italian and Western sociopolitical realities and to the sophistication of communist thinkers, not to doctrine. Communist intellectuals had selectively used parts of Gramsci's system while ignoring the core of his thought.[4]

Not surprisingly, Salvadori's argument provoked heated denials from the PCI general staff, but other socialist writers took up the cudgels. Bobbio asked the key question: "Is it possible (or proper) to exploit a revolutionary writer to justify reformist politics?"[5] Less kindly, Luciano Pellicani relentlessly exposed the totalitarian underpinnings of communism, enunciating the themes later expressed in Craxi's 1978 article on Proudhon. In fact, that essay, discussed in chapter 12 and authored by Pellicani, may be considered the political culmination of this debate.[6]

Mondoperaio editor Federico Coen summarized the intellectual value of the discussion for the Socialists: "PSI recuperation of its own, autonomous cultural-political identity, and, therefore, a relaunching of the socialist presence in our country." According to Coen, Socialists eschewed construction of rigid doctrines but rediscovered the pluralistic principles sanctioned by their long and proud tradition and vowed always to remember them in their political action.

Some of these principles include concretization and development of existing liberties, not overthrow of the system; acknowledgment that opposition at all levels is essential for democracy even in a socialist state; not centralization or bureaucratization of the economy, but worker participation in production within an economy in which the free market and planning coexist; a nontotalitarian party; greater European integration as a means of further independence from the United States and the USSR; support of freedom movements everywhere, East and West; freedom for all kinds of research from economic, political, or party control.[7]

In line with this cultural revival, the PSI secretary's office also commissioned a "Socialist Project" which would establish the guidelines of future party action. This most ambitious intellectual effort of the period primarily engaged Lombardi-Giolitti associated intellectuals such as economist Giorgio Ruffolo, economic historian Luciano Cafagna, and constitutional expert Giuliano Amato.

Already in 1975, an "Association for the Socialist Project" had been constituted and had animated important discussions on a plan which would become the basis of the transition to socialism in Italy. The year 1976 witnessed publication of an influential work summarizing the results of conventions and research on the problem. Even though this Socialist Project justified the "left alternative" with the Communists, it mobilized socialist ideological principles and hypothesized the PSI as the major force in the coming of Italian socialism. This attitude made "il progetto" acceptable to Craxi, who, indeed, craftily used the opening for a communist alliance against the PCI.

By analyzing the capitalist crisis and plotting future socialist action, the Project aimed at providing a "vaster horizon" to the Italian left while steering a middle course between humdrum political involvement, "reformism without a future," and Leninism, which led only to totalitarianism. In vain, it hoped to provide an alternative to Craxi and Berlinguer.

Interpreting the history of capitalism as a story of uneven development punctuated by long- and short-term crises, Project intellectuals dismissed Marxist predictions of capitalism's final agony. Nevertheless, they believed in the crisis of the current capitalist phase—"social capitalism." Utilizing electronics, the atom, and chemistry, the "third industrial revolution" had shifted production from human labor to technology. This development negated worker exploitation and surplus value as the origin of profit. Consequently, industrialists incorporated their profits in the pricing system. As a result, they coalesced into large concerns seeking control of the market in order to fix prices and maximize profits.

The result was constant struggle with workers, given their organization into large unions, and haphazard government intervention to stabilize the disordered system. If unions raise salaries above an "equilibrium level," inflation results; if the industrialists win, recession and unemployment. Inflationary and deflationary swings thus dominated contemporary capitalism.

Most interestingly, the Project group no longer considered socialism as inevitable. Socialism survived as an ideal with egalitarian and participatory principles incompatible with modern capitalism. Having transformed socialism from an imperative necessity into the only positive response possible to a perverse capitalism, the Project critiqued recent socialist action and set forth principles to guide future political action.

Previous socialistic experiences from Soviet to social democratic hardly corresponded to and often contradicted the socialist model of a libertarian, egalitarian, and internationalist society, Project intellectuals admitted. The reason was that both collectivists and Social Democrats "degraded" socialism by reducing its economic aspects to questions of growth and income distribution and demeaned the problem of socialist power to one of control of the state apparatus. The root cause of this attitude was the "cultural gap," the disproportion between the people's cultural level and modern society's productive forces. These "economistic" and "statalistic" degradations of socialism generated either authoritarianism or paralysis, corresponding to the Soviet and social democratic models.

For Project Socialists, cultural level signified the "autonomous capacity of society to develop culture and information and to transmit them in an ascending spiral." This capacity required the "destructuralization" of capitalism's economic and bureaucratic institutions, not their strengthening, and self-government. Before destructuralization could be achieved, socialist thinkers must produce a sophisticated scientific analysis of advanced social systems in order to acquire a thorough understanding of how they change.

The disordered growth of advanced industrial societies which characterized current capitalism "is a self-destructive process" producing ecological deterioration, military conflict, and social disaggregation. Understanding the process, socialism strives for ecological equilibrium, internationalism, and planned democracy.

Afraid of being confused with no-growth advocates, Project thinkers specified that their model aimed at a "dynamic" equilibrium based on human labor and nature and respect for the world's resources. While this ideal implied a constant *total* energy consumption, it suggested variable energy levels in different sectors of the economy, a stable population, and an exponential increase in the spread of information to the masses.

The practical consummation of these principles meant encouragement of "light technology," where possible—low energy and material requirements, increased attention to natural processes in agriculture and industry, recycling. In the consumption field, a "radical change" must encourage "sober" consumptionism instead of "opulence." Production must emphasize durable, simple, and solid goods; society should encourage flexible infrastructures and accessible services on a human scale.

The same went for the diffusion of information, social counterpart of the new economy. The Project called for a decentralized, egalitarian, and participatory social system as the basis for the free and accelerated circulation of ideas in a socialist society. Added to the human-scale concept, these principles summarize Project guidelines.

Convinced that the current capitalist crisis marked the transition to socialism, the Project called for a vast coalition of all the classes potentially sympathetic to socialism. Project researchers distinctly deemphasized the working class and made a strong pitch to the "professionalized" classes ("technicians, experts, middle management [*quadri inter-medi*]"), "culturalized" strata ("intellectuals, students"), and "neglected social groups" ("women, disadvantaged ethnic and regional groups"). In short, the Socialists appealed to all groups dissatisfied with capitalist society. These unsatisfied classes would coalesce on a concrete socialist project steeped in reality, promising compromise, and leading the transition to socialism.

These Project principles modernized Turati, the early Saragat, and the late Nenni. In discussing the practical realization of their proposed social coalition, however, Project intellectuals declared "unity of the left" indispensable—the communist alliance.[8]

This condition gave Craxi reason to be suspicious.[9] On the other hand, by offering the PCI an alliance on the basis of a PSI-animated "Progetto Socialista," the Lombardian socialist elaboration wrote finis to the PSI inferiority complex toward the Communists, allowed Craxi to make the offer, and mandated the PCI's rejection of it. In this manner, Craxi shrewdly utilized the Project against the PCI, which in effect dismissed the socialist initiative, preferring the "historic compromise." In a 1982 book, Giuliano Amato and Luciano Cafagna admitted the Project's value in strengthening PSI identity and autonomy but stated that it did not fulfill their expectations in a number of areas, especially the failure to stimulate a communist dialogue.[10]

Between 1976 and 1978, socialist intellectuals published a host of works and held conventions discussing issues raised by the Project: foreign policy, reform of state institutions, the diffusion of culture, the specifics of socialist democracy.[11] In 1978, Craxi presented a program to the Turin Socialist Congress incorporating Project principles but emphasizing its revisionary aspects and making a PCI agreement more difficult.[12] Nevertheless, this assembly sanctioned the Craxi-Signorile (Lombardi) alliance. This fusion, in turn, attracted influential intellectuals to the PSI, convincing them that the youthful new leadership had "finally understood that the two traditional alternatives of the socialist soul, the reformist and the maximalist, had finally seen the end of their days."[13]

After he defeated the Lombardi wing in 1980, Craxi had a clear field in the reformist crystallization of the Project. In his famous "theses" for the 1981 Palermo Socialist Congress, Craxi produced a draft for a governmental platform, later sharpened at a programmatic conference in 1982.

The Project shed its abstract nature during this process. Democratic aspirations took the form of proposals for constitutional reforms: greater governmental stability through importation of the German notion of "constructive no confidence"; abolition of the secret vote in Parliament; different functions for the Senate and Chamber of Deputies; rehauling civil rights legislation; a streamlined bureaucracy; a swifter, more equitable justice system; eliminating poverty. Economic principles became concretized in a combination of traditional inflation-fighting methods and utilizing public industry as a planning and investment tool to achieve full employment. Traditional educational reform, not destructuralization, would bridge the cultural gap. Craxi's theses unabashedly adopted the formerly anathema reformist label. In this way, Craxi hoped to win over the emerging "modern" intellectual and professional classes.[14]

The Project thus sowed the seeds of Craxi's program for the 1980s, even if the distance appears great. Craxi made the Project pragmatic, understandable, and subject to legislative implementation. As he put it, "There is connecting the 'Socialist Project,' . . . the reformist formulation of the 'congress theses,' and the more general action of the party, a tight nexus of continuity and consistency."

The Palermo congress unconditionally endorsed this view by accepting Craxi's theses. The PSI plan to capture the progressive levels of evolving Italian society through an updated reformism and lead the country to postindustrialism in the name of socialism has been called "a genuinely innovative formula in the context of postwar Italian politics."[15]

In the spring of 1982, the PSI Rimini "programmatic conference" completed the "difficult labor begun . . . with the 'Socialist Project.' " As had become usual in Craxi's PSI, the Rimini conference emphasized the continuity of socialist tradition and PSI renovation.[16] "1892–1982: Socialist Renovation Has a History" decked the dias, and a triangular banner surrounding the bright red socialist carnation proclaimed, "Govern the Change." The conference's major themes were institutional problems, foreign policy, the economy, cultural and social issues.

The meeting melded the Craxi right and Lombardians who had originally inspired the Project. This amalgamation and an independent leftist bent in foreign policy retained PSI credentials as a living leftist party, necessary to combat communist charges of a rightist drift. The conference, for example, emphasized PSI ties to the Revolutionary Democratic Front of El Salvador by hosting Guillermo Manuel Ungo, the front's president, despite American displeasure; at the same time, the conference hailed Afghan guerrilla fighters in picturesque robes who denounced the Soviet occupation of their country. The audience heard party experts elaborate on the electoral, governmental, and administrative reforms suggested by the Project and the theses. Key Project economist Giorgio Ruffolo discussed the limits of development and the problems of employment. Other reports closely examined public industry, labor policy, and PSI economic principles. Instead of the usual ideological disputes, the speakers quoted facts and figures and emphasized the limits of political action. "To reform well and to govern well" could have been the watchwords of the conference. Gone were the flights of fancy and ideological disputes of the past.[17]

Rimini created a new PSI:

> The debate . . . went to the core of a reformist, realistic, rational, and modern method. It dealt with problems concretely and in clear language. There was no room for abstract and inconclusive ideological disputes. . . . There appeared . . . no socialist academic distributing sermons and excommunications . . . dogmas, formulas, and preconceptions.

The Socialists had finally combined theory and practice by rediscovering the ancient adage, "philosophus purus purus asinus."[18]

In sum, by 1982, Craxi had positioned the PSI to fulfill his socialist alternative, which necessarily passed through Palazzo Chigi. The left and right wings concurred in the concrete proposals to present to the country. The nation granted the PSI center stage by recognizing the socialist formulation of critical problems. Included among these interested parties were the Communists, who, weighed down by their totalitarian tradition, traveled the reformist road only haltingly. The socialist intellectual revival had refurbished PSI prestige and placed the party at the center of national life for the first time since the 1950s.

In homage to the increased momentum and the proud socialist tradition, Craxi announced the socialist claim to a greater share of power. The PSI controlled only a small number of votes, but both major parties lacked the PSI's dynamism, and their support had been declining, while the future augured well for the Socialists. Without PSI support, the DC could not rule on the national level, and the PCI share of power in many local constituencies would greatly diminish. "I'll show you what can be done with only 10 percent of the votes," Craxi told his friends.

Finally, Craxi successfully communicated to the nation the importance of political stability. Without that factor, reforms crucial to Italian economic modernization and democratic survival could not be implemented. Could *he* provide that stability as prime minister? No one believed it. To most Italians, Craxi remained an ambitious party technician who lacked charisma and color. But the impressive performance of another Socialist, the president of the republic, bolstered the PSI's image and made the idea of a socialist premier acceptable.

The Pertini Factor

Symbol of the "old" idealistic socialism rather than Craxi's "modern" realistic socialism, President Sandro Pertini captured Italy's heart and furthered the cause of a socialist prime minister. Although the two men reputedly did not get along, Craxi intervened decisively to secure Pertini's election in 1978, after the failure of his original choice, Antonio Giolitti.

Pertini's past as an antifascist Resistance hero and his honesty, style, and outspokenness made him the country's most popular personality. Eighty-nine years of age when his term ended in 1985, Pertini played a major role in holding together a nation wracked by fifteen years of terrorism.

Elected in 1978 after the resignation of scandal-ridden Giovanni Leone, Pertini managed in an amazing tour de force to infuse new life into an office designed as the country's symbol but which had become synonymous with its ills.

The Italian Constitution awards the presidency few powers, although, given the country's complex political makeup, individual presidents have assumed important roles, usually negative. In addition to Leone, President Giovanni Gronchi sponsored Fernando Tambroni with neo-fascist support in 1960, while suspicion of Antonio Segni's plotting a coup remain alive.

Immediately after his election, Pertini altered the style and importance of the presidency, above all, but not exclusively, through the force of his personality.

Although the Italian Constitution specifies that the president may communicate with Parliament only through formal documents, thus weakening the office, Pertini and his staff argued that he may do so in other ways: interviews, action, dialogue with reporters— in other words, through popular pressure. Through frequent initiatives and tours of the country, Pertini established direct contact with the people and demonstrated himself to be a master in winning their support through his honesty and directness. This ability made prominent persons seek him out for consultation and politicians do his bidding.

The country's most prominent personalities trooped to his eighteenth-century office located in the late-Renaissance Quirinale Palace. There, among a myriad of softly chiming antique clocks, they sought the advice of the man whose age made him seem all the more a father of his country. Fiat's Gianni Agnelli consulted with Pertini in the autumn of 1984, before the industrialist's financial group bought into the *Corriere della Sera,* Italy's most prominent newspaper wracked by the P2 Masonic Lodge scandal (the renegade lodge supposedly had engaged in a vast conspiracy to capture control of the country). On an inspection tour of the Naples region devastated by a major earthquake in late 1980, the president discovered that a modern civil defense structure did not exist. Upon his return to Rome, Pertini demanded establishment of an efficient organization. Pressured by public opinion, the country's politicians complied without the lengthy delays which characterize Italy's public administration.[19] By such actions, Pertini earned the absolute trust of the politically cynical Italians.

Used to corruption on a scale which surpassed the Third French Republic, stunned Italians reacted with unanimous approval when Pertini continued to live in his apartment overlooking the Trevi Fountain instead of moving into the Presidential Palace, when he paid for his own private trips, and when his wife continued her volunteer work in a Florence hospital for drug addicts. "My wife has declared war on the Quirinale," he informed me, explaining his wife's opposition to his accepting the presidency. In his seven years as president, Pertini refused to accept cost-of-living increases to keep his salary abreast of Italy's double-digit inflation, as other public officials did. As a result, Pertini earned only about fifteen thousand dollars a year. He told me, "I have breakfast and dinner at home, and only lunch at the Quirinale. It doesn't cost [the taxpayers] much."

Besides his frugal personal habits and his rigid honesty, which contrasted so glaringly with the country's prevalent political style, Italians admired Pertini's outspokeness and clarity, a further anomaly in the subtle world of Italian politics. In 1983, the president created a furor by calling in reporters to tell them he believed that the multinational force in which Italian troops participated should be withdrawn from Beirut, thus anticipating American and French leaders. In a New Year's message to the nation, he touched off a debate by approving of the young people marching in Italy's massive antinuclear demonstrations. He would have joined them if he were young, the president said, for the future belongs to the youth. When the Soviets downed Korean Airlines Flight 007, Pertini fired off a protest telegram to Yuri Andropov without seeking the Italian Foreign Ministry's approval or even informing it, a cause for constitutional conflict under past presidents. Pertini's action caused a national debate on the implications of this action for the presidency. "I don't always go through the Foreign Ministry," the president explained with an impish smile. "With me, the Foreign Ministry trembles."

In his conversation with me, Pertini attributed his success to his efforts "to identify with the Italian people as a whole," not only with the Socialists or the left. Once he learned that a neo-fascist youth lay dying after being beaten up by leftist toughs. Pertini rushed to the hospital, where the boy's sobbing fiancée threw her arms around the grandfatherly president's neck. "It didn't matter to me that he was a Fascist," said the man who had suffered exile and prison under Mussolini. Such actions gained him the Italians' sympathy, but how did he win their trust? "I swept away the arrogance of power," the president confided to me.

Upon being elected president, Pertini called the Quirinale staff together and introduced a relaxed atmosphere into the Presidential Palace. When he learned that groups of schoolchildren regularly visited the Quirinale, Pertini instructed his staff to ask at the end of their tours if the pupils wished to meet with the president.

Playing on his name, he said, "I encouraged them to ask impertinent [*im-pertin-enti*] questions." One day, one of them timidly handed him a note listing his school building's deficiencies. The president quickly resolved the problems by personally contacting the Ministry of Education and the Vatican. "The children all call me Sandro," he said with pride. "The republic is not made up of palaces but of persons." During his presidency, he met with more than three hundred sixty thousand pupils.

Since most of Italy's population is catholic, Pertini established contact with Pope John Paul II which developed into a warm and special relationship, despite the president's atheism. The relationship fascinated catholic Italy and irritated the Christian Democrats. Musing on his friendship with the pope, the president recalled for me:

One day [in 1984], the pope calls me and says: "I would like to have lunch on the Adamello [a mountain in northern Italy]."

"Come now, Holiness, admit it. You don't want to have lunch, you want to go skiing."

"That's true. I used to ski in my youth, and I hear that there is always snow on the Adamello."

Thus originated John Paul II's world-famous ski trip with Pertini, which generated Vatican criticism. "It could have been worse," Pertini revealed. "They took a picture of the pope wearing a ski hat with a brand name on it. If I hadn't had the picture killed, they would have reproduced it in thousands of advertisements, and we would have had a real scandal!" Illustrating further his relationship with the pope, Pertini told me of a dinner he gave for John Paul. The president ascertained that his chef had been an old schoolmate of the pope's chef, then asked him to find out the pope's favorite dishes. The president became very animated and jocular as he recalled the scene:

First course. Risotto ai frutti di mare. The pope says, "This is really good."

Second course. Scaloppine al Marsala. He says, "excellent!"

Finally: dessert with whipped cream. The pope exclaims to me, "Mr. President, how did you know? This is the kind of meal I would have ordered from my own chef!"

"Your Holiness," I said, "when you have doubts, you ask the Holy Spirit, don't you?"

"Yes."

"Well, I consulted with your chef!"

In addition to the Catholics, Pertini maintained good relations with the Communists; indeed, they strongly supported him for a second term, even though he would have been ninety-seven at its end. An intransigent antifascist, Pertini spent fifteen years in Mussolini's jails with communist leaders such as Antonio Gramsci and Umberto Terracini, whom he recalls vividly. Condemned to death by the Nazis, Pertini escaped to become socialist military chief during the Resistance. A major proponent of socialist autonomy throughout his distinguished career, Pertini nevertheless advocated friendly relations with the Communists as president, frowning on Craxi's tactics of confrontation with them. As an example of his fairness, he appointed Communist party matriarch Camilla Ravera as life senator despite intense pressure against him.

When PCI Secretary Enrico Berlinguer collapsed on 7 June 1984 and died after four days in a coma, Pertini immediately flew to Padua and kept a bedside vigil closely followed on Italian television. Pertini considered Berlinguer a great leader because he loosened the PCI's dependence on the Soviet Union. After the death of his "fraternal friend," Pertini brought the body back to Rome on the presidential airplane. Berlinguer's funeral drew more than a million people to St. John's Lateran Square, the largest demonstration in Italy's history. The crowd warmly applauded Pertini and jeered Craxi, known for his feud with the dead communist leader. When in the June 1984 elections for the European Parliament PCI votes increased partly in sympathy with Berlinguer and the PSI total decreased slightly, an irritated Pertini learned that socialist leaders attributed this outcome to the president's attention to the dying communist secretary, which had received exhaustive news coverage. Pertini recounted to me:

> When I next saw Craxi, I told him that I was tired of these tales. I told him, "When you go to Verona [the next scheduled socialist congress], why don't you and [Vice Secretary] Martelli commit suicide on Romeo and Juliet's tomb? I give you my solemn word to bring back your bodies on the presidential airplane so you can increase your votes during the next elections."
>
> And then Craxi, who doesn't have a sense of humor, laughed.

Despite the often strained personal relations between the two men, Pertini asserted that he willingly gave the socialist leader the mandate to form a cabinet because conditions for the first socialist prime minister had matured. Furthermore, the exacting president readily gave Craxi high praise for doing a good job, judging him "able" and "energetic." As president, however, Pertini consciously maintained strict political neutrality and independence from the PSI, acting as stern guardian of the Constitution. As such, he did not spare the first socialist-led government his pungent criticism.

First national leader on the scene in a Christmas Eve 1984 terrorist bombing of a Naples-Milan train which killed fifteen, an angry president denounced official tendencies proclaiming the demise of Italian terrorism. At the Bologna funeral for the victims, he answered a reporter's question with the words, "I am not afraid of the people." The press widely interpreted this remark as a veiled criticism of Prime Minster Craxi, who had failed to arrive because of a snowstorm. In his 1985 New Year's message on Italian television, Pertini admonished the socialist-led government to translate its victory over inflation into a defeat for unemployment, officially at 10.3 percent but generally considered higher.

Pertini's colorful personality also allowed him to maintain good relations with foreign leaders. Despite obvious ideological differences, he exchanged frequent messages with President Ronald Reagan, whom he defined as *"simpaticissimo."* He claimed to have gotten along with President Jimmy Carter but complained that Rosalynn Carter just walked in on his conversation with her husband. Pertini exclaimed, "Nancy doesn't do that!"

Pertini recalled his American trips for me with fondness: "The State Department gave me a guide who was beautiful. I told her, 'You're Carmen.' You know, when you get to be my age, you can say certain things to beautiful women and get away with it."

Pertini accomplished the same thing with Italy. In our conversation, he attributed his success not to his age but to his honest reflection of the defects and good qualities of his people. He said, "I know that I am overly sensitive and have temper tantrums, just like the Italians."

For the first time in its postwar history, Italy found in this old and upright Socialist a president it genuinely loved. This fact helped keep the nation together during the most trying time in its recent history and made it more receptive to other socialist leaders.

"I know I am loved by the Italian people," said this gentle man, tears welling in his eyes at the thought. A clock softly chimed agreement.[20]

The 1983 Elections

Intellectual ferment, the presidency's prestige, and solid control of the PSI allowed Craxi to sustain the political momentum he had achieved against the catholic and communist "poles." During the next three years, Craxi demonstrated extraordinary leadership qualities, enabling him to attain his goal of a socialist national administration despite the PSI's low vote total. In addition, he accomplished this feat without possessing the charisma of a Nenni or a Pertini.

Immediately upon repulsing the Lombardi-Signorile challenge in the spring of 1980, Craxi revealed that his "governability" commitment implied renewed socialist participation in cabinets. Negotiations produced a second Cossiga cabinet based on DC, PSI, and PRI support. The socialist contingent was made up of nine ministers, including the key defense, transportation, health, and state industry positions. Believing in socialist regeneration only in the opposition, the PSI left wing objected to renewed PSI-DC collaboration but proved powerless to block it.

This "Cossiga II" had a brief and troubled life. In May 1980, captured terrorist leaders revealed that Marco Donat Cattin, son of the DC vice secretary, headed the terrorist organization "Prima Linea." Press reports alleged that the police had been about to arrest the young Donat Cattin, but a Cossiga warning to his father had allowed the son to flee the country. An investigation and a parliamentary debate on the issue paralyzed the government. In July, the cabinet proposed a special one-time tax of 0.50 percent on wages to confront the continuing economic emergency, but the idea encountered tremendous opposition among the workers, which the PCI focused against Cossiga. In September 1980, the government fell.

During this period, Craxi strengthened himself. Because of the controversy surrounding Cossiga, Craxi's scattered opponents in the PSI foresaw a socialist defeat in local elections scheduled for June 1980 and plotted a united front against him. In fact, however, skillful Craxi support of a Radical party referendum campaign and the abstention of that party in the elections helped boost the socialist vote to 12.7 percent. Recognizing Craxi's unassailable position, the opposition dissolved. Craxi capitalized on his newfound strength and in October 1980 induced the Central Committee to give him a new Directorate with a two-thirds majority.[21]

This greater security permitted the PSI secretary to resist a fresh onslaught by Enrico Berlinguer. The PCI had branded the Cossiga cabinet as "dangerous" and had supported a massive Fiat strike in September 1980, provoked by the Turinese company's proposed firings of twenty-four thousand workers. Finding itself in crisis because of labor's successful resistance to layoffs, Fiat maintained that inability to reduce labor costs would sink the company. As discussed above, the socialist Project had noted the declining worker role in modern society, while Craxi believed that the workers should behave more responsibly in order to overcome the economic emergency.

In addition, the PCI continued its rigid stance against the Forlani cabinet which replaced Cossiga and which the Socialists joined. Judging Craxi's governability policy negatively, the Communists suggested that the PSI had lost its character as a working-class organization.[22]

Finally, in December 1980, Communists and Socialists clashed over a fresh terrorist incident. The Red Brigades had kidnapped a judge, Giovanni D'Urso, promising to liberate him if the government agreed to close a maximum-security prison. Despite a harder stance following the earlier terrorist assassination of a friend, historian Walter Tobagi, Craxi followed the same line as he had in the Moro case and urged negotiations. The PCI assumed its usual intransigent position, but Craxi argued that the state had planned to close the facility anyway and should not reverse itself to spite the Red Brigades. After a series of intervening developments during which the Red Brigades raised their demands, D'Urso went free.

As a result, the early months of 1981 witnessed fierce polemics between PSI and PCI. The PCI accused the Socialists of being soft on terrorism; the Socialists objected to Communist "worship" of the state. In January, the outspoken Pertini charged that leftist terrorists had direct links with Moscow. "They [the terrorists] are Stalin's grandchildren," cried Craxi's *Avanti!* Craxi's position was that the Communists could not be encharged with government responsibilities because they had not cut their ideological ties with the Eastern bloc.[23]

Understanding the PSI's new capacity to hold center stage, the PCI quickly proposed a truce. In April 1981, eve of the PSI's Palermo congress, the Communists admitted that the PSI's institutional reform proposals deserved to be considered seriously by all parties.[24] Taking note of Craxi's "theses" for the congress, the authoritative communist leader Gerardo Chiaromonte examined their points of convergence with PCI policy and declared them "significant in the leftist debate."[25] The PCI finally abandoned its love affair with the "historic compromise" and suggested cooperation with the PSI to provide the nation with a different government—the "democratic alternative."

Unlike in his previous jousts with the PCI, a confident Craxi adopted a statesmanlike stance at the Palermo congress. He left himself open to discussion but, addressing Berlinguer, criticized the negative communist attitude toward the Cossiga and Forlani cabinets and accused communist leaders of actions threatening to radicalize an unstable political situation. The PCI talked about a "different" kind of government, Craxi stated, but he noted no concrete proposal constructing "a new government and a new parliamentary majority which would support it."[26] This attitude at least left the door to a PCI understanding ajar. This factor and the warm reception the socialist delegates gave Berlinguer's speech elicited a friendly communist reaction, despite initial disappointment.

Palermo marked Craxi's complete triumph. Controlling about 70 percent of the delegates, Craxi's supporters altered the rules, instituting direct election of the party secretary by the congress instead of indirectly by the Central Committee. A flash of opposition by the Lombardians proved intense but brief. The change ensured the impossibility of a "Midas revolt" against Craxi.

Finally recognizing that its PSI sympathizers had no chance of dethroning Craxi, the Communists decided to deal with him. In an editorial, communist ideological organ *Rinascita* called the Palermo assembly "a significant moment in the resumption of contact between PCI and PSI."[27] This resumption, however, failed to develop into dialogue because of socialist fears that the "democratic alternative" would once again subordinate their party to the PCI. Furthermore, the PSI remained unsatisfied with official PCI reaction to Soviet repression in Poland, even though the Communists stated that the Russian Revolution had run its course and had nothing more to teach Westerners.[28]

Poland may serve as an example of the new and energetic socialist foreign policy, destined to characterize Craxi's socialist-led cabinet. Within the context of the Western alliance, Craxi aimed at an autonomous and expanded role for Italy as an expression of the traditional international socialist support for human rights. Craxi criticized the USSR for altering the European nuclear equilibrium by installing SS 20 missiles in Eastern Europe. He called for increased Italian activity in promoting the stalled disarmament talks but confirmed the PSI's support for American "Euromissiles" on Italian soil to redress the balance if no other solution to the arms race could be found. Discussing the same issue in 1982, he carefully distinguished his position from the German, demanding dual American-Italian control of any missiles placed on Italian soil.

In another major foreign policy innovation which he would implement as prime minister, Craxi called for a greatly expanded Italian role in the Mediterranean: "We cannot accept the fact that things are done and undone in the Mediterranean without our opinion being heard or our interests being respected." Starting from this presupposition, Craxi reviewed the status of the Mediterranean states. Not surprisingly, he paid most attention to the Arab-Israeli conflict. While carefully recalling the long-standing Italian friendship for Israel and reaffirming the Jewish state's right to exist, he believed that Israel must negotiate "for everyone's rights, [including] the right of the Palestinian people to self-determination."

Finally, Craxi pledged a more active Italian role in strengthening the European Community and lined up the PSI with freedom movements everywhere, from Central America to Poland to Afghanistan. In citing the "bitterness and surprise" of the Reagan administration to the Italian socialist position on El Salvador, he noted his own "bitterness without surprise" at the administration's attitude.[29]

Corresponding to this foreign policy program, Craxi presented realistic domestic considerations which would ensure Italian political and economic recovery. First and foremost was stability to counter the Italian plague of "Yearly governments, half-yearly governments, weekly governments, governments people want to undo the day after they are formed, governments that win the Chamber's confidence and within half an hour are defeated in secret votes." Craxi's remedy was institutional reforms, the recurring theme from 1981 into his own tenure as prime minister. Craxi demanded an end to the secret vote, a holdover from prefascist Italy which in 1986 would occasion his own government's resignation. He called for reform of parliamentary procedure and the executive authority, implementation of the regions, and efficient public administration.

Craxi also addressed Italy's serious economic and financial problems. Most importantly, he cited the factors contributing to the country's over 20 percent inflation rate—private and public industry malaise, inefficient public administration, galloping welfare state costs, the burgeoning deficit, and recalcitrant unions.

While making proposals for greater public efficiency, an end to fiscal evasion, a three-year plan for the economy, and profit restraint by the production and commercial sectors, Craxi drew attention to the labor problem by courageously admonishing the unions. He singled out indexing as a major contribution to inflation and frankly stated that cost-of-living adjustment mechanisms must be altered. He also called for fewer strikes and a halt to political strikes. Workers had ample means of influencing government policies without crippling the nation, he stated. Inflation and an excessive number of strikes, he reminded the unions and their communist leaders, had ushered in fascism. He indicated that as prime minister he would not bow to unreasonable union tactics.

Craxi presented all these problems in a context which foreshadowed the PSI's 1983 campaign slogan: "The optimism of the will." Pointing out the contradiction between continual gloomy predictions and the reality of increased production and a rising standard of living for most Italians, the PSI secretary realistically defined the parameters of the Italian question. Without minimizing the country's problems, Craxi synthesized Italy's dilemma and hope as "Disordered development and unequal wealth, but development and wealth nonetheless."[30]

In short, Craxi resisted exaggerating Italy's problems and emphasized their manageability. This reasoned attitude carried over into all serious questions the nation faced, such as terrorism, which Craxi attributed primarily to the culture of "pseudo-revolutionary" violence and to the lack of democracy. More attention to civil rights and a smoother democratic machinery would cure terrorism, which, he maintained, had practically been defeated. For the first time since 1968, a political leader put the Italian situation into perspective; for the first time since the center-left, reform became the primary concern, and the Socialists set the national agenda.

In order to achieve this goal, Craxi aimed at a "laic pole"—PSI, PRI, PSDI, PLI—believing he could obtain the premiership if his party received 15 percent and this bloc as a whole 25 percent of the votes. The only reasonable response to the "imperfect bipolarism" which divided the Italian political world between Catholics and Communists, the laic pole would come as close as possible to alternating power. This concept determined socialist strategy on a number of important issues in 1981 and 1982, including opposition to repealing the abortion law by referendum. The failure of this referendum signaled a diminished church and DC influence which paralleled the PCI's slow electoral decline.[31] Now and in the future, Craxi counterposed the weight of all the smaller constitutional parties against that of DC and PCI.

Craxi's strategy received a temporary setback when the P2 scandal broke and the economy took a downturn in 1982. During a raid, the police discovered the membership list of a renegade Masonic lodge headed by Licio Gelli which had supposedly infiltrated the country's highest military and civilian ranks. In order to pressure politicians, Gelli utilized photocopies of the secret dossiers compiled by SIFAR and supposedly burned under Andreotti's orders.[32] The names of socialist leaders Enrico Manca and Silvano Labriola supposedly appeared on the list, and charges flew regarding shady financing for the PSI through banker Roberto Calvi—who later died a suspicious suicide in London—and Milan's Banco Ambrosiano.[33]

Craxi categorically denied all charges of socialist wrongdoing and attacked Andreotti as the puppet master, but the uproar damaged the PSI's image. A socialist success in limited local elections on 21 June 1981, however, led PSI leaders to downgrade the "moral question" and encouraged Craxi to renew his campaign for an "alternation" of the prime minister's position between the Christian Democrats and a "secular" party leader; "alternanza" with the DC, not "alternativa" with the Communists.[34]

In fact, the political situation took just that direction, thanks to the P2 affair, but not exactly as Craxi hoped. The Forlani government fell because the prime minister had kept the P2 membership list secret for several months. Popular revulsion proved too great for the Christian Democrats to overcome. After an unsuccessful attempt to restart the Forlani government, the mandate passed to Giovanni Spadolini, Republican party leader. In the public mind, this small party still represented economic rigor and governmental efficiency better than the Socialists.

This brilliant DC move blocked Craxi's road to the premiership. The Socialists had no choice but to show themselves pleased at this triumph of the laic pole, but they hoped either to succeed the republican leader or force early elections. Instead, the Socialists unexpectedly found in Spadolini a rival rather than a transition. A history professor steeped in the study of Giolitti, an expert on catholic politics, a former newspaper editor, a large man who devoured legendary meals in restaurants surrounding the Roman Pantheon, a person with a colorful and decisive personality, "Lo Spadolone" became Italy's most popular prime minister up to that time.

Not only that, but Spadolini combined efficiency with popularity. In his sixteen-month tenure (two governments), Spadolini coped with the P2 affair and provided hope on institutional reforms. Most importantly, in the wake of American General James Lee Dozier's kidnapping, Italian security forces freed Dozier unharmed and broke the back of the terrorist movement.[35] Even though the ground had been prepared before, the battle against terrorism took its most spectacular turns under Spadolini.

These events fueled the famous Craxi-Spadolini rivalry. The PSI cautiously withdrew its support and exploited Spadolini's legislative defeats on secret votes to weaken him. With only about 3 percent of the electorate voting for his party, Spadolini found it more difficult to justify retaining his office. Besides the PSI's opposition, the DC allowed the country to calm down after the P2 affair and then reclaimed the premiership. Indeed, the Catholics had chosen a vigorous new secretary—Ciriaco De Mita—who promised party renewal by giving the DC a new basis in society and loosening its church ties. By 11 November 1982, all of these factors forced Spadolini's resignation.

Amintore Fanfani replaced Spadolini. Fanfani's reemergence had a triple significance. First, the DC offered politics as usual, while the laic pole at least promised change. Furthermore, Fanfani had previously made overtures to the PCI; in 1982 and later, De Mita hinted at a resumption of the DC-PCI understanding to block Craxi, and the Communists flirted with the idea.[36] Finally, Fanfani's investiture signaled a shifting of the battleground to the voters—early elections. Craxi's strategy dictated increased electoral support for the lay parties, which now seemed within reach. Opinion polls indicating a PSI victory with 20 percent of the vote confirmed this tactic, which would ensure Craxi's climb to the nation's highest office. Even at the cost of unpopularity, Craxi argued that the number of government crises during the legislature's course made early elections necessary.

This strategy had so gripped Craxi's inner circle that it ignored later signs indicating

PSI faltering, apparently a response to Spadolini's resignation, socialist dealing with the DC, and PSI involvement in scandals.[37] In a luncheon conversation with me in February 1983, Giuliano Amato emphasized his conviction that the PSI would achieve the magical 20 percent in the next elections, despite my citation of opinion polls indicating that the party had scarce hope of reaching that total. Amato's response: "We think the polls are wrong."

Amato had spent the previous year in Washington and informed me that he had had a round of meetings with American Embassy and State Department officials, during which he had received expressions of support for Craxi's becoming prime minister. When I asked his opinion of why a conservative American administration might favor a Socialist as premier, Amato said that he had emphasized the usefulness to the United States of a stable Italy and had convinced the Americans that Craxi could provide that stability.

In fact, the Rome embassy boasted the presence in important positions of former State Department proponents of the center-left such as Charles Stout and Pat Garland, experienced and sophisticated analysts of the Italian situation. In a knowledgeable *Foreign Affairs* article, former cultural attaché Joseph La Palombara examined the political situation and concluded: "Taken together, these factors lead people to ask not whether the PSI will gain control of the national government, but when—and with what consequences."[38]

According to John Volpe, President Ford's ambassador to Italy, the Americans had cast an approving eye on Craxi as soon as he became PSI secretary. Volpe informed me:

> I met Craxi back in early 1976 or late 1975, when he took over from De Martino, even though he was a Socialist and some of our people didn't feel that we ought to deal closely with the Socialists. . . . But when Craxi became secretary of the party, I said, well, let's take a look at this fellow. I had him for lunch at least three or four times, usually one on one. . . . I was very impressed with the man.
>
> President Ford had already asked me to stay on as ambassador to Italy should he have won in 1976, and even before the elections I had suggested to Craxi that I hoped that he would make a visit to the United States, and I'd see to it that he got a good reception. And he had agreed to come in the spring of 1977. . . .
>
> I mentioned this invitation to my successor, mentioned my luncheons to him, and told him I thought he was a comer and would be a leader in the country, not just in the party. . . .
>
> I always had a feeling that some day that man would lead the country, and I was right in my conclusions.[39]

In the meantime, Craxi continued his march. In addition to the desired implementation of the laic pole, it made sense to force elections before De Mita embarked on an aggressive campaign to renovate the DC, transforming it into a conservative lay party less dependent on the church. Similar successful operations in Germany and Austria and the conservative trends in Great Britain and the United States made it imperative to block De Mita. As a result, the Socialists seized on the remarks of DC vice secretary Roberto Mazzotta indicating less public intervention in the economy, cutting welfare benefits, fewer union concessions, and the end of collaboration with the "socialistic parties" to denounce the "new right," to withdraw PSI support from Fanfani, and to demand new elections.[40]

DC "neo-centrism" revived discussion of the socialist-communist "alternative," but Craxi quickly countered with a renewed offer to the Christian Democrats if the voters rejected their new conservative orientation.[41]

The PSI based its electoral program on reformist revision of the socialist Project as elaborated in Craxi's theses, the Palermo congress, and the Rimini conference. In order to assure the country stability, the secretary proposed that the next cabinet should have a guaranteed three-year life span to implement a five-point program ensuring economic development, especially in the South, inflation reduction, institutional reform, and an offensive against crime and terrorism.

In economics, the Socialists pledged "rigor" and equity. While the Socialists called for reduced interest rates, as they had done traditionally, they also emphasized eliminating waste, encouraging savings, recapitalization, and reorganizing the government ministry overseeing public industry. They defended the labor pact signed by the government, the unions, and industry on 22 January 1982, which instituted guidelines on future labor policy; this agreement promised to lower inflation, reintroduce incentives in the workplace, and stimulate production.[42] Institutional reforms included eliminating laws for which no plausible justification could be discovered—probably the most revolutionary suggestion. The PSI also emphasized civil rights and called for creation of an ombudsman.

In Parliament, the socialist program advocated reduction of the number of parliamentarians, different modes of election for deputies and senators, curbing strict proportionality in elections, limiting the secret vote, preferential treatment for government legislative proposals, parliamentary investiture for the prime minister only (and not his cabinet), constructive no-confidence prohibiting Parliament from causing a government to fall without indicating its successor, and a "Cabinet Council" consisting of the most important ministers. In short, the Socialists imported concepts from other European parliamentary democracies to ensure the smooth functioning of the Italian system.

In foreign policy, the program renewed Italy's traditional alliances but called for more independence and a special role in the Mediterranean.

Threatened by this electoral activism, both DC and PCI gave Craxi's ideas a cool reception. PSI principles, however, would seize center stage during the socialist-led government's tenure.[43]

The 1983 elections gave the PSI 11.4 percent of the vote, a modest 1.6 percent gain over 1979 in the Chamber. For the first time since 1968, however, the party had advanced in national elections. The official socialist press saw the election's significance in the PSI's defeat of the DC's "neo-conservative momentum," and Craxi called the result "the signal we had asked for."[44] In fact, a major DC loss characterized the 1983 elections and made Craxi's policy possible. For the Socialists, the elections highlighted what would turn out to be the major weakness of Craxi's strategy. If he succeeded in becoming premier and in achieving genuine popularity—which he had by 1986—how would he translate these real achievements into votes for the PSI?

In fact, *Mondoperaio* editor Federico Coen offered a disturbing electoral analysis with important implications for this question. The PSI had reason for satisfaction at reversing a losing trend, Coen wrote, but when compared to recent local elections, the Socialists had slipped. This retreat had occurred in a context of declining support for both DC and PCI and of great PSI dynamism. Coen's explanation was the party's image, the difference between its words and actions. Coen charged that by exploiting to the fullest its key political role, the party had overreached itself. Given the necessity of PSI votes to form governments, Socialists sold their support to the highest bidder. By allying with the DC at the national level, with the DC or with the PCI locally, Socialists opened themselves to corruption and to charges of corruption. Socialist opportunism and the struggle for patronage had attracted to the party persons interested only in advancement and had produced scandals.

Coen objected to the PSI leadership's policy of denying blame for the low morals of many PSI members and seizing every occasion to attribute a political motivation to investigating magistrates and a critical press. Understandably, voters could not trust the Socialists to reform governmental institutions when the PSI had performed so poorly in reforming itself. More than any other, Coen concluded, this factor explained the disappointing electoral result.[45]

In fact, during the height of the campaign, a clamorous new scandal leading to the arrest of prominent Genoese socialist leaders had rocked the country. Without waiting for a thorough investigation, the gutsy Craxi reacted in his usual manner, interpreting the arrests as an attempt to sabotage the Socialists during the election.[46]

Responding to Coen, Gianni Baget Bozzo, socialist sociologist-priest, concurred in attributing the PSI's failure to take off electorally to "a loss of credibility on the moral quality plane, of the party's life-style." While Craxi concentrated on governmental affairs, Baget Bozzo warned, his substitutes managing the party would have the no less crucial task of refurbishing the PSI's image.[47]

Vice Secretary Martelli, Craxi's vicar, agreed. More flexible than Craxi, Martelli traced PSI corruption to the center-left and its patronage practices, although he blamed the nation's preferential voting system for fostering corruption in all political partics. Martelli committed himself to attracting top-quality deputies, to instituting new rules and machinery for their enforcement, and to reforming membership application procedures so as to prevent political bosses from signing up groups of yes men.[48]

The director of Milan's Sociology Institute, however, indicated that the PSI's "moral question" would not be so easily resolved. According to Guido Martinotti, the years from 1972 to 1983 had profoundly transformed the PSI's electoral base. First, the party had lost support in the advanced northern urban centers and had been progressively "southernized." In the recent elections, for example, Spadolini's Republican party had outpolled the PSI in its stronghold of Milan, indicating that the "emerging" classes had greater faith in the PRI. Electoral data suggested that the PSI drew a significant part of its strength from middle-class, middle-aged male voters with scant appeal for youth, women, and intellectuals—despite the party's great efforts to win these groups. Furthermore, according to Martinotti, the PSI appeal to the "emerging classes" had fallen flat, creating a contradiction between the socialist leadership's reformist elaboration and its social base. This contrast accounted for the PSI's opportunistic propensities.[49]

Martinotti painted a dark picture, but the malaise he identified threatened all secular parties. In this respect, Catholics and Communists had an advantage. Baget Bozzo, for example, cited DC and PCI insulation from petty thievery—Catholics by the mediating action of the clergy and its high-level corruption, Communists by their Leninist organization. In contrast, the PSI and other "normal" Italian parties suffered the usual corruptive influences.[50] On the other hand, as both Communists and Catholics have become progressively "secularized," they have also become involved in scandals.

The Socialist-Led Government

The 1983 elections resulted in a dramatic DC drop of 5.4 percent in the Chamber, variously attributed to its conservative turn, De Mita's inability to implement his plans so quickly after becoming secretary, and a desire for change. The PCI had been declining for years but kept its losses to less than 1 percent by absorbing a small leftist fringe organization and running independent leftists in its lists. If the DC had been the big loser, the PCI was the "nonwinner." In the Chamber, the laic pole commanded 23.5 percent of the seats compared to 18.5 percent in 1979. The respected commentator Alberto Ronchey suggested that further significant DC and PCI losses would occur, ending the Italian political system's "bipolarism."[51]

The unexpectedly sharp DC loss made Craxi's dream of becoming premier a reality. Immediately after the elections, Craxi's friend Rino Formica floated a trial balloon suggesting PSI implementation of the "alternative" with the Communists.[52] Promptly denying this intention, Craxi nevertheless suggested bringing the PSI into the opposition, making a cabinet impossible.[53]

This strategy produced immediate results. Interviewed on 4 July 1983, DC leader Antonio Bisaglia asked his party not to insist on the premiership but to concentrate instead on a governmental program and on De Mita's plan to renovate the party on secular lines. Bisaglia and other party leaders headed off a move to defenestrate De Mita, giving the secretary an opportunity to implement his ideas of party reform.[54] On 20 July, the DC National Council surrendered Palazzo Chigi, flashing Craxi a green light to form a government.[55] The same day, Fanfani confirmed his resignation as premier, and on 22 July 1983, President Pertini gave Craxi a mandate to form a government.[56]

His staff at the ready as befit a leader projecting a modern image, Craxi immediately began negotiations with the nation's leaders to revive the five-party coalition which had governed with Spadolini—the laic pole and the DC. On 4 August 1983, President Pertini swore in the first socialist-led cabinet.[57]

Because the Socialists held the presidency of the Council, the cabinet featured fewer socialist ministers in less important positions than had previous cabinets, although De Michelis received the crucial Labor Ministry, and Francesco Forte, Craxi's economic advisor, remained as minister without portfolio. On the other hand, the "secular" party secretaries all participated in the cabinet, including Spadolini at Defense. If this technique promised stormy cabinet sessions, at least it ensured open thrashing out of differences within the government instead of in parliamentary conflicts more likely to bring down the government. One major surprise was Andreotti as foreign minister. This appointment apparently signaled a "deal" between Craxi and the shrewd DC leader which lent stability to the government.[58]

Along with his cabinet, Craxi presented a well-articulated, broad, and specific program drafted by his staff and reinforcing the issues with which his party had gone to the polls. Beginning with economic questions, the new government aimed at lowering the inflation rate to 10 percent by 1984, from an estimated 15 percent in 1983. It hoped to accomplish this goal by reducing the deficit from 16 percent to between 14.5 and 15 percent of GNP. Two-thirds of the deficit reduction would come from less public spending; increased revenues would account from the rest. The government hoped for a further reduction in the inflation rate in 1985 and 1986 by cutting the deficit to 10 percent of GNP.

Acting on another inflation factor, the government proposed limiting salary increases to the inflation rate, slowing wage indexation, and discouraging price increases. This policy, the government hoped, would keep real wages steady while it implemented investment incentives and stimulated technological innovation. The government pledged to offer these incentives not only to large firms but also to salaried workers who set out on their own. The government would also introduce new measures regulating strikes, especially in essential services. At the same time, it would reform the country's system of unemployment benefits, which reduced work incentives. The government also pledged to increase employment by filling necessary positions in public employment, facilitating part-time employment, and launching an extraordinary plan for the establishment of three hundred thousand jobs over the next three years in the depressed South.

Connected with these objectives, Craxi proposed a sweeping reform of the Italian welfare state. He aimed at increased efficiency, reduced expenses, and guaranteeing the most needy a minimum standard of living. He also advocated gradually increasing the retirement age and tougher standards for disability pensions. At the same time, the program called for a minimum pension. The costs of Italy's socialized health insurance system would be brought under control by linking expenses to a percentage of GNP and by instituting a deductible geared to income. To combat the nation's housing shortage, the program called for increased "mobility" while protecting lower-income tenants. In fact, the housing crisis stemmed from antiquated laws which kept rents ridiculously below market and practically excluded evictions, driving landlords to keep unoccupied apartments unrented. The government promised gradual movement toward a free housing market.

In conformity with other European countries, the government's program blended a number of economic principles being implemented in the United States with domestic necessities.

With regard to institutional reforms, the Socialists insisted on their proposals strengthening the executive, speeding up the legislative process, and limiting secret voting. The program also incorporated PSI suggestions for increased local autonomy and citizen recourse against the bureaucracy.

Consistent with socialist ideals, the platform paid attention to civil rights. It called for reduction of the shamefully long period of preventive detention (more than ten years), reform of trial procedure, alternatives to jail terms for minor crimes, and institution of justices of the peace to relieve overloaded court calendars.

Finally, the program confirmed Italy's foreign policy and Italian assent to placing American cruise missiles in Sicily in 1983. At the same time, socialist emphasis on greater autonomy also found expression in a promise of an active Mediterranean policy and Italian support for both Israeli existence and Palestinian autonomy. In addition, the program pledged special Italian consideration for the economic needs of the lesser developed countries.[59]

The Socialists had hoped for comprehension from the Communists but instead discovered blind hostility. When the Socialists claimed a historical mantle for Craxi as fulfilling socialist tradition, *Unità* editor Emanuele Macaluso called them "foolish." He interpreted the new government as "the worst version of a majority which has negatively characterized the past legislature." PCI economic expert Alfredo Reichlin claimed that the program proved that only the PCI remained reformist. More moderate and perhaps recalling his own party's helplessness during the "national solidarity" coalition, Enrico Berlinguer argued that the DC had entrapped Craxi.[60]

Predictably, *Avanti!* struck an ecstatic note and lashed out at its communist comrades. It drew a parallel between the center-left and the socialist-led government. The first had opened a new era; the second promised to do so. In 1963, the center-left had established the preconditions for Italian social, economic, and cultural development; in

1983, Craxi had secured the principle of alternating power with the DC to ensure reform implementation. In both cases, communist immobility would have guaranteed Italian immobility and perpetuation of the reactionary 1950s. As the culmination of past socialist history, present PSI policy struck out against pernicious bipolarism which threatened Italian democracy. In short, the socialist-led government's constitution finally brought Italy into line with European and Mediterranean trends—France, Spain, Greece, Portugal.[61]

In addition to the PCI, the powerful guru of the Italian independent left—*La Repubblica* editor Eugenio Scalfari—piteously took apart the new government's program, writing that it could never work, and poked fun at the Craxi style.[62]

The Milan stock market, however, reacted differently. It rose.

CHAPTER 14

The New Course

An important question arose immediately upon formation of the socialist-led government. How long could a cabinet led by a party with 11.4 percent of the seats in the Chamber of Deputies survive? Would it repeat the Spadolini government's experience—a stopgap for another Christian democratic cabinet?

In October 1983, I inquired of PSI Vice Secretary Valdo Spini how the Socialists could hope to keep the presidency of the Council for long with such a small number of seats. Spini cited the strong PSI "contractual" position, the fact that now no government post could be denied to them, and the strong socialist presence in all aspects of Italian society. He also summarized the catholic and communist dilemma:

> I think that now the Communists have a special fear of electoral competition. I think that they are afraid that Craxi's success can give the Socialists an advantage from the electoral point of view. . . . The Christian Democratic party is afraid that if Craxi shows that he is more capable and can lead a government with more efficiency than the Christian Democrats, the Christian democratic electorate can go toward the Socialists.

Whether this electoral trend toward the PSI would actually occur, Spini believed, depended on how long the government lasted.[1] In fact, only the government's performance—and Craxi's in particular—could test, confirm, or derail the PSI's new course.

Economics and Labor

At the time of my conversation with Spini, Craxi had already run into predictable difficulty with the Communists and unions over his economic program. He aimed to cut the high inflation rate and increase production so the country could participate in the economic recovery then taking place in the West.

In his parliamentary remarks, the new prime minister made a gesture toward the PCI, saying that he headed a coalition open to "dialogue and collaboration." Neither "an operation of the right nor the left" dictated the economic austerity upon which his government now embarked, but simple necessity. "But Berlinguer turned up his nose" at Craxi's proffered hand.[2]

In fact, the communist-controlled union movement bristled against the government. While the catholic CISL and socialist UIL sent friendly signals, communist CGIL representatives vetoed their socialist colleagues and issued a statement which "oozed diffidence from every line." CGIL Secretary Luciano Lama initially took a softer line toward Craxi, but Berlinguer induced him to reject any tinkering with labor's wage escalator. As a consequence, the CGIL assumed a demagogic line by insisting on a special tax on the very wealthy in order to resolve the economic crisis.[3]

At the same time, the inflation rate worsened because of the strong dollar, which increased Italy's oil bill, raised the price of gasoline, and redoubled pressure on all prices. As a result, the retailer's association (Confcommercio) suggested a new round of price increases. In addition, the powerful Confindustria refused to sign a new metalworkers' contract out of fear that escalating labor costs would price Italian goods out of the international market. If Italy did not take care, Alberto Ronchey warned, it would find itself thrust back into its post-Renaissance economic depression.

The Craxi government reacted vigorously to these developments. Minister of Industry Renato Altissimo (PLI) threatened to withhold scheduled fiscal concessions and to reactivate machinery keeping tabs on unwarranted price increases. Government strategy aimed at exploiting these concessions to achieve a "pact" with commercial establishments and producers to keep prices level. It also proposed "purging" the *scala mobile* from the effects of the rising dollar.[4] The government also grappled with the bloated public industry sector, skillfully accomplishing a cut of twenty-five thousand workers without provoking union ire.[5]

The crux of Italy's economic problem, however, remained the budget deficit and public debt. The Italian debt, the prime minister declared on 28 September 1983, had "no parallel in the industrialized West" and would bankrupt the nation if it continued rising at its current pace. Economic surveys painted a bleak picture, with rising inflation and unemployment and a falling GNP in the cards. By 30 September, the government announced a plan to heal the economic situation within three years by cutting spending and increasing revenues without major tax increases.

These measures resembled others currently being adopted in the West. Significant cuts for social services were made while preserving benefits for the poorest citizens, but defense also came in for its share of reductions. The plan progressively reduced family subsidies (provided according to the number of children in a family) for families with an income below thirty-four million lire, instituted a sliding scale which increased the cost of medicines for families with earnings over five million lire, slowed or reduced cost-of-living allowances for pensioners, and cut spending for school personnel.

On the revenue side, the government planned increases or a speed-up in collection of a number of taxes, fees, and government services. Most important, it announced a pardon of the widespread construction abuses upon payment of a fee (*condono edilizio*).[6]

The storm clouds gathered immediately after Craxi's announcement of his government's plan. Union and parliamentary opposition mobilized, and the first demonstrations occurred. Noting this mounting opposition, the influential *L'Espresso* admitted that the ambitious plan had defects but commented that the economic crisis would have been nowhere as serious if previous governments had taken similar action. Finally, Italy had a prime minister with the courage to govern.[7]

In October 1983, Craxi's economic program ran into its first problems from within the government majority. Fearing that a Craxi victory would give the PSI too much prestige, the Christian Democrats called for an economic "summit." They requested "improvements" in the economic plan and demanded outright rejection of rumored taxes on treasury bills (BOT), and assurances that a special tax on total family wealth would not be imposed. At the same time, the press reported a rapprochement between some DC sectors and the PCI.[8]

On 14 October 1983, the decree law implementing the *condono edilizio* went down to defeat in a secret vote in the Chamber. There had been criticism of the decree on ecological and moral grounds, but twenty-seven coalition "snipers" cast their ballots with the PCI-led opposition. Craxi promised to represent the *condono,* but it would take three years to get through Parliament. In Greece for a meeting of Mediterranean socialist leaders, an irate Craxi denounced elements of the government majority "who, when they can, do the opposite of what they say."[9]

Soon thereafter, parliamentary confusion worsened. On 20 October, with Craxi visiting President Reagan, the government had to force a vote of confidence on a decree embodying social service cuts to get its legislation through, a technique the government found itself obliged to resort to with increasing frequency.[10] Even though open ballots characterized these tests, however, parliamentarians could call for a secret vote immediately thereafter. Only elimination of the secret ballot could alter the poisoned atmosphere, but Craxi proved unable to implement changes in this procedure.

Only two months into the new government, therefore, the Christian Democrats had demonstrated their unreliability and the Communists their indispensability for significant legislation. Craxi's majority threatened to crumble. In fact, no matter how distasteful, on certain issues public opinion forced Craxi and the Communists to cooperate, as political analyst Gianni Baget Bozzo commented in December 1983.[11]

Economic affairs produced the first example of this ephemeral de facto collaboration. In December 1983, Finance Minister Bruno Visentini (PRI) drafted legislation to close wide tax loopholes. Visentini's proposals provoked a serious tax revolt by small shop-keepers and threats by the Republicans to withdraw from the coalition. After a long fight, the legislation passed in 1984, and Craxi won high praise for his leadership. To some, it seemed that a tenuous "hypothetical working alliance of the PSI, PRI, and PCI" would emerge from the affair.[12] With consummate skill, Craxi agreed to such "working relationships" only on issues which could further his program. Otherwise, the premier took on both unions and PCI.

Craxi's handling of the crucial cost-of-living adjustments issue best illustrates this attitude. Economists had long isolated the *scala mobile* as a major contributing factor to spiraling inflation, but the unions and the PCI had proclaimed the "sacredness" of COLAs, and governments had feared to take them on. Before becoming prime minister, however, Craxi had indicated his intention to modify the wage-adjustment clauses.

At the end of 1983, Labor Minister De Michelis released statistics illustrating that labor costs had increased 16 percent, with a 1984 projected rise of 12.2 percent if no change occurred in salary structure, even if general inflation dropped to 10 percent. De Michelis suggested a series of measures balancing salary and price increases for 1984 at 10 percent. Led by the CGIL, the unions counteroffered to take less for a period of six months. On the other hand, the industrialists' association held out for a 50 percent COLA cut. Both rejected a compromise involving a combination of concessions by industry and labor and taxing treasury instruments. As the PCI sided with the CGIL, the country headed for a major confrontation.[13]

In January 1984, CGIL leader Lama threatened massive strikes to bring the government to its knees. This time, however, CISL, UIL, and the socialist CGIL contingent attacked him. The dispute threatened the highly successful labor federation which coordinated the three unions' action.[14]

On 14 February 1984, the CGIL executive council split along PCI-PSI lines, rejecting the government's proposals by a 76-to-43 vote. CISL and UIL had been prepared to accept government leadership but backed off because of the CGIL's adverse decision. Encouraged by this split, the government embodied the wage-escalator cut in a decree law. The reductions amounted to much less than had been expected—two hundred forty thousand lire for the year (one hundred fifty dollars)—and implemented a number of other fiscal measures. Attempting to mollify the workers, the government also postponed for a year rent increases due in August 1984.

As a result of this unheard-of *scala mobile* alteration, the Communists seized their opportunity to defeat Craxi. The CGIL immediately organized a general strike, opposed, however, by CISL, UIL, and the socialist CGIL representatives. *Avanti!* emphasized the consensus which this union "majority" had given Craxi, but throughout Italy the communist-controlled union organized one-day strikes and demonstrations. These massive actions proved that the Communists could still touch off mass protests, but did they really have the nation's support?

For once, the government stood its ground. The three-union federation fell apart, and the CGIL discovered itself isolated; CISL and UIL supported Craxi's action, and the government released a long list of organizations expressing favorable opinions toward its policy. Instead of resigning under union pressure, as Italian cabinets had under similar circumstances, Craxi confronted his opponents. The PCI denounced his "adventurism"; while DC representatives criticized him for heightening tensions to force through measures which would have little effect on inflation. The battle now shifted to Parliament, which would have to accept the decrees within sixty days.[15]

The real stake in this battle was Craxi's entire political strategy and the PSI's future. It was true enough that the prime minister's unprecedented action had ended the consensual strategy followed by previous governments. In the past, the CGIL and the PCI had pressured Christian democratic cabinets in order to demonstrate their capacity to deliver concessions to the workers; the governments had given in, ensuring their survival, allowing the PCI to flex its muscles, and leaving the country to foot the bill. But the Communists had prejudicially denied that "consensus" to Craxi from the beginning, despite his earnest search for compromise. In February 1984, they aimed not at winning concessions but at killing the socialist-led government and eliminating a dangerous rival. The DC had the same objective, so it allowed Craxi to proceed. The Socialists correctly perceived politics, not economics, as the conflict's real root and rallied around their secretary.[16]

In fact, on 20 February 1984, PCI Secretary Berlinguer called for the end of Craxi's government because it had become "dangerous." In addition to parliamentary opposition—including obstructionism, unused since the 1953 attempt to block the "swindle law"—Berlinguer counted on continuing street demonstrations. His hope was for a Christian democratic decision that the country would remain ungovernable without an understanding with the Communists, which would sink Craxi.

The country, however, quieted down. The government successfully argued that real wages would rise if the decree passed. The Socialists denounced the PCI for radicalizing politics, planning a return to a DC alliance, and sabotaging fellow-leftist Craxi. *Avanti!* declared: "Communist opposition to the Craxi government began even before it was formed."[17]

Despite a day of demonstrations called by the CGIL for 24 March 1984 to support PCI parliamentary opposition to the antiinflation decree, PCI and CGIL found themselves politically isolated. Not only did talks fail to reknit the three-union federation, but the press exposed the entity of the CGIL crisis. In 1983, for example, the communist-controlled union lost one hundred twenty thousand members. Not only did the greatest decline come in the activist metalworkers' sector, but the unions in general had scant appeal for workers in the emerging higher-technology area. Most dramatically, only 23 percent of the respondents favored the union position against cutting cost-of-living adjustments. Recent research has confirmed the wide-reaching trend occasioned by the electronic revolution, producing a rapid decline of the classic working class and dramatic increases in the white-collar category primarily concerned with the new technology— precisely the group to which the PSI pitched its appeal.[18]

In Parliament, the PCI exposed its real objectives by obstructing business despite government concessions on the cost-of-living decree. De Michelis agreed to DC modifications promising to restore lost wages if inflation rose above government predictions of 10 percent. Public opinion condemned communist tactics, especially since the maximum wages which could be lost now totaled only eleven thousand lire a month (less than seven dollars). In mid-March, communist obstructionism ran out of steam. In desperation, the Communists appealed to President Pertini to block the decree and sent a delegation to see him, but Pertini refused to meet with it.[19]

By the time the decree passed Parliament, its inflation-fighting capacity had long ceased to be the battle's main point. The major issue was decisive government. Italian parties had long demanded decisiveness, but the PCI could not condone its implementation by a leftist rival because if "Western socialist reformism takes root and extends itself in Italy, it will be Berlinguer who will pay." This factor explains why the PCI took to the streets as soon as Craxi demonstrated significant governing capacities, "forgetting all its soothing Eurocommunist theories." Newspaper editor Indro Montanelli arrived at similar conclusions, arguing that for the first time in a decade an Italian government had acted authoritatively.

Early in the crisis, *Il Messaggero* editor Vittorio Emiliani summarized the Socialist strategy: "The Craxi government concluded that there must be a limit to mediation, otherwise the punishment would be a slipping into the swamp of nondecision. We therefore have entered into the relatively new phase of a government which assumes the right and the duty to decide."[20]

According to the Socialists, Craxi's reformist economic policy capable of regulating income, slowing inflation, renovating production, and stimulating development marked a turning point in Italian history.

Italian governments had always followed a profoundly conservative line worthy of an old-fashioned economy, they argued. In order to maintain employment, public intervention heavily subsidized the weak and obsolete sectors of Italian industry and agriculture, leaving the strong ones to their fate. This policy put Italy at a strong disadvantage in international markets, gravely hindered its exports, and, if not reversed, would sink the country. Socialists sharply distinguished the social benefits of the system from its disadvantages. They strongly supported rationalizing benefits for workers affected by the decline of older endeavors, but future legislation must concentrate on the modern and technologically innovative sectors of the Italian economy. If Italy wished to survive in a fiercely competitive world, it must end the folly of carrying the obsolete parts of its economy for social reasons and allow the "natural death" of its unproductive firms and sectors. Even though the Socialists made special provision for agriculture and the South, they complained, "neo-liberals" and "dogmatic or purely ohstructionist sectors of the left and in the unions" pugnaciously combated this reformist modernization of Italy.[21]

The most effective of these recalcitrant forces were the PCI and CGIL. After losing the fight to implement the cost-of-living cuts, they set in motion the machinery for a referendum abrogating the *scala mobile* decree. By appealing directly to workers unschooled in economics and emphasizing only lost wages, the PCI hoped to deal the socialist-led government a death blow. Through his under secretary Giuliano Amato, Craxi negotiated to avoid this test, but to no avail.

Economics, however, came to his aid. Despite the criticism of economists that the watered-down decree would do little to slow rising prices, the annualized inflation rate dropped to 9.1 percent by October 1984, from 12.8 percent in December 1983.

The goals Craxi had adopted and which most observers had derided, the influential *Corriere della Sera* admitted, "are coming true." Not only did inflation drop for only the second time in fifteen years, but productivity increased, company earnings rose, the public debt slowed its runaway course, and economists predicted a 2.8 percent increase in GNP, the highest in Europe. International economic recovery contributed to this fresh miracle, but Craxi's decisiveness, implementation of an incomes policy, and debt reduction had been primarily responsible. Political stability, in turn, had made these policies possible, just as Craxi had predicted. What could consolidate the new Italian miracle? the *Corriere* asked. More of the same.[22]

At the end of 1984, a confident Craxi announced his 1985 inflation rate goal of 7 percent. In order to mark the victory against the country's economic crisis, he also planned introduction of the "heavy lira." Eliminating the last three zeros of the Italian currency would greatly simplify accounting procedures but above all would permanently link Craxi's name to the triumph over inflation and greatly bolster Italy's economic prestige. Fulfilling a PSI promise, the government also instituted a fund to combat world hunger and put Socialist Loris Fortuna at its head. Despite the elevated unemployment rate which continued to mar the government's record, the gloomy tide which threatened to overwhelm the Italian republic had been reversed. Craxi had given Italy, long considered the sick man of Western Europe, a new image.[23]

These developments determined the definitive failure of the communist challenge in 1985. In June 1984, Enrico Berlinguer died suddenly. Later in the month, balloting for the European Parliament awarded the PCI 33.3 percent, a higher percentage of the votes than the Christian Democrats. The *scala mobile* referendum and the local elections of 1985 thus became crucial. The coalition parties attributed the communist advance to a sympathy vote for Berlinguer, but the Communists hailed it as the long-awaited *sorpasso* (overtaking) of the DC. New PCI Secretary Alessandro Natta predicted a PCI win in both confrontations, but the Communists lost both by significant margins. The nation had rejected communist policies.

Craxi's final victory on economic policy signaled a change in the country's style. Absenteeism, strikes, low productivity, tax evasion, bloated state industry, and incredible deficits attached to social services had all become legendary in Italy. All these problems could not disappear overnight, but the nation altered its work habits and seriously discussed the more difficult issues. Between 1985 and 1986, absenteeism declined greatly, and man-hours lost to strikes diminished to among the lowest for Europe. At the same time, industrial reconversion proceeded apace, productivity increased, and industry registered higher profits.[24]

While receiving less attention than in other European countries, the government also encouraged substantial privatization. Private investors purchased a steadily increasing number of shares in IRI-owned companies, and the government set the stage for their intervention in municipally owned firms.[25]

In another amazing shift, employers seemed to be achieving their long-desired linkage of salary and productivity increases.[26] These developments combined with the drop in oil prices led Bank of Italy Chairman Carlo Ciampi to declare that the back of Italian inflation had been broken.[27] With inflation expected to fall to 5 percent by the end of 1986, Treasury Minister Giovanni Goria predicted issuance of the "heavy lira" in December of that year.[28]

This economic reflowering resulted in a sustained stock-market boom which doubled the value of stocks in four months. The boom attracted heavy international investment to Italy.[29]

Ironically enough, in 1986, Craxi won praise for his economic policy also from the communist workers who had opposed him. Once having been accused of betraying the working class, Craxi tangled with Confindustria representatives and Fiat's Gianni Agnelli. Craxi objected to scarce industrialist gratitude to the government for its direct aid in restructuring and modernizing Italian industry and warned that he would not allow industry to exploit the favorable economic situation. Craxi chose a meeting installing a new CGIL secretary to denounce reappearance of the "new right," receiving hearty applause from the unionists. The industrialists backed off.[30]

Hoping to consolidate the economic victory, Craxi's staff prepared a draft of objectives for the remaining two years of the legislature. These goals included real GNP growth of over 3 percent, with the inflation rate down to 4 percent by December. True to PSI principles, the document continued a vigorous incomes policy to protect real wages and increase both production and profit margins. At the same time, the government would favor lower interest rates, encourage an investment level of 6 percent in real terms, and ensure that the benefits of oil price declines reached the people. Major social services would be restructured to increase efficiency.

In 1985, the Italian private sector restructured itself, reduced its debt, and had its best year since 1968–69. In July 1986, prices did not rise, and the yearly rate declined to 5.9 percent for the first time in fourteen years. The balance of payments registered a strong surplus. On the thorny problem of the national debt, Craxi announced that the government could stay within the limits it had set itself without taking significant new measures. By early 1987, Craxi claimed that the Italian economy had turned in a better performance than any other European country and that it had surpassed Britain.[31]

The government's achievements and the prime minister's serious economic goals demonstrate how far the new socialist course had taken the country.

Institutional Reform

The socialist-led government's positive record on the hard-fought economic front could not be matched on the institutional reform question, nor is it likely to be. Even though public opinion supports socialist-proposed institutional reforms, history offers few examples of nations which have significantly reformed their political institutions without the stimulus of war or revolution.

Craxi set the tone for institutional reform by taking a leaf from German and English practice and instituting a cabinet "directorate" (*direttorio*) consisting of ministers representing the most important cabinet posts and all the coalition partners.

According to Craxi's under secretary and right-hand man, Giuliano Amato, the "directory" aimed at resolving "both the problem of collegiality and efficiency." Professor of constitutional law and former chairman of a commission studying reorganization of the prime minister's office, Amato specialized in analyzing the paralysis of the Italian executive which had occurred over the past twenty years. Amato favored strengthening the executive's powers with respect to the legislature by limiting the secret vote, establishing preference for government-sponsored bills, and obtaining votes on decree laws within sixty days. Here, as in economic policy, the Communists opposed the government's plans.[32]

The directorate received good press. President Pertini, for example, thought it a good idea because "The parties will become more responsible and feel themselves tied to a greater extent to the government."[33] In this respect, the directorate probably functioned well in keeping the heterogeneous *pentapartito* together so long. Efficiency is more difficult to assess, primarily because of Amato's own enormous energy in expediting the government's work, which masked the institutional results. Like its European counterparts, however, the directorate will likely remain a permanent feature in dealing with a cabinet structure of ever-greater complexity.

In contrast to areas in which the prime minister could act unilaterally, Parliament thoroughly discussed the reforms by which the Socialists hoped to improve its operations but did not implement them.

In October 1983, the government secured installation of a bicameral commission of forty deputies and senators. Its charge was to examine specific proposals for parliamentary and governmental reform and report back within a year. PSI discussion originated the most important reforms under consideration by the commission. PSI Vice Secretary Martelli called Italian parliamentary practice archaic; socialist scholar Leo Valiani maintained that parliament's antique procedures threatened the republic.[34]

The Socialists divided the institutional question into three broad categories: parliamentary and electoral reform, executive, and local autonomy.

The PSI hoped to implement the 5 percent rule—imported from Germany—which imposed a minimum for representation in Parliament. This provision would diminish the confusion which resulted from too many small parties with scant national representation taking advantage of rules to tie up business. On this subject, two major procedures cried out for change. Open voting had to take precedence over the secret ballot, and Parliament must have the right to limit debate. More legislative power also had to be turned over to the regions in order to reduce the enormous number of bills which tied up the national legislature's agenda. Furthermore, the two houses of Parliament must have different functions, dropping existing duplication. According to the Socialists, most bills should require the consent of only one house to become law (monocameral), while only some would require action by both (bicameral).

With regard to the executive power, the Socialists insisted that confidence votes be accorded to the prime minister alone, giving him greater importance than his ministers. They also reproposed the "constructive no confidence" discussed earlier. In addition, they asked for clear legal distinctions among cabinet ministries, depending on their importance. The Socialists would also have weakened the president of the republic, forbidding him to dissolve Parliament when "constructive no confidence" ended one government but had not designated a successor.[35]

Finally, the Socialists proposed the complete overhaul of local government. Their "essential" reforms consolidated small towns and made City Hall the primary deliverer of services to the people. New laws would encourage greater efficiency of existing city agencies. The province would retain important functions such as economic planning. Most importantly, property taxes would be delegated to local administrative units. The Socialists also expressed sympathy for direct election of mayors.[36]

Entrenched political forces sabotaged this ambitious program. For example, the Christian Democrats proposed an electoral premium reminiscent of the discredited "swindle law," while the Communists advocated a single chamber—a radical constitutional revision doomed from the start.[37]

In the meantime, Craxi worked to modify the secret vote. On 17 October 1983, "snipers" defeated the government's project to pardon construction abuses. An irate Craxi denounced the secret vote as a sinister means of protecting special political and economic interests. He struck out at both the PCI, which rejected eliminating the practice, and the Christian Democrats, who paid lip service to reforming the system. Craxi vowed to limit the secret vote, but parliamentary leaders dismissed his threats. "More than one demochristian leader . . . shook his shoulders and smiled," *La Repubblica* reported. In fact, any proposed rules modification could be defeated in a secret ballot.[38]

Understanding the obstacles, the Socialists hoped at least to implement open voting on fiscal affairs,[39] but communist Chamber President Nilde Jotti blocked presentation of the proposal.[40] On one memorable day, the government lost six votes. Craxi defined the "snipers" as the "sixth and illegal party of the coalition. It strikes hard and does so intending to provoke confusion and crisis."[41]

By the time Craxi's first government fell on 27 June 1986, the "snipers" had put the cabinet in the minority 163 times, an average of almost once a week. Indeed, a defeat in a secret confidence vote immediately following the granting of confidence provoked Craxi's resignation. By that time, the DC had openly demanded the premiership back, possibly encouraging Christian democratic snipers.

By 1986, however, public perception of the secret vote's pernicious effects had changed, and Craxi's resignation on the issue elicited an extremely favorable reaction. by that time, Italy had felt the benefits of stability. Commentators agreed that the secret vote gave full vent to political and personal greed and insisted that the nation rid itself of this scourge. In short, even though he failed to resolve the problem, Craxi's decisive and consistent stand opposing the secret vote increased his stature in the public's eye, made him the chief gainer in the 1986 political crisis, and contributed to his successful return as prime minister.[42]

In 1987, Craxi launched a new series of institutional reform proposals. The most important, staunchly fought by the PCI, would institute popular elections of the president of the republic. Another would adopt the German practice of automatic acceptance of decree laws if not rejected by Parliament within sixty days, instead of the Italian method which requires a favorable vote within the same period. The Socialists hope that this measure will ensure a smoothly functioning Parliament.

Besides governing institutions, the new socialist course focused the nation's attention on the real scourge for the ordinary citizen: justice. The Italian justice system suffered from leftover emergency legislation during the terrorist "years of lead" and organized-crime threats after 1974. The interlinked origins of the civil rights degradation were preventive detention and lengthy trials.

In 1983, the police could keep suspects in jail for ten years and eight months while they gathered evidence. During that year, conservative estimates put at two-thirds the proportion of the overcrowded prison population awaiting final trial. Judges issued arrest warrants on little or no evidence and kept suspects in jail while investigators marshaled evidence against them. Worse still, investigating magistrates exploited the long preventive detention period to extract confessions from suspects and to encourage them to name "accomplices." The police then arrested those so implicated and kept them in jail for years while they investigated the allegations.[43] If found innocent, the victims had no recourse against the state.

Furthermore, a law provided for mandatory arrest in cases of persons caught in the act of committing a crime of a certain entity. In addition. restrictions placed on judges in the granting of bail and a requirement mandating priority trials for those already in jail overloaded court dockets with petty thievery cases and left persons accused of more serious crimes to languish in jail while multiple jurisdictions leisurely wended their way through the cases.[44]

The socialist solution was gradual dismantling of emergency legislation, reforming trial procedure, more sensitivity to civil rights, less pretrial publicity (the Italian press regularly condemns upon arrest), limiting the power of judges, and depoliticization of the court system.[45]

In October 1983, the Craxi government drafted a series of justice reform bills. The key points included reducing the maximum preventive detention term by a quarter or, at most, limiting it to two-thirds of the maximum sentence which could be imposed for a crime (not applicable to current trials); a new code of penal procedure; increasing the number of police magistrates dealing with minor cases; greater facility for judges to grant bail (*libertà provvisoria*); reduction of mandatory arrests; institution of justices of the peace; and the right to compensation in case of false arrest. In addition, the bills also provided for the end of the demeaning procedure by which officials informed individuals of pending actions.[46] Only the minor proposals embodied in the bills passed Parliament relatively quickly.

In the meantime, a series of cases illustrating the nation's degraded justice system shook Italy. These included the Negri case, discussed earlier. As a protest, the Radical party got Negri elected to the Chamber of Deputies, where he had parliamentary immunity but where he faced the prospect that the Chamber would suspend that immunity. The PSI proposed delaying the vote until he could be brought to trial but discovered itself isolated as its coalition partners supported his immediate arrest. On the left, the PCI also favored Negri's arrest, even though protests by the communist base eventually induced the PCI to abstain in the vote which ended Negri's immunity. In January 1986, a court rejected the notion of a Negri-led terrorist organization.[47]

During the same period, two other cases illustrated the ills of Italian justice: the "Bulgarian connection" in the papal assassination attempt and the Tortora case. In the first incident, the prime defendant spent years in jail before the court released him for lack of evidence; in the second, a popular television personality accused of drug dealing by a shady Camorra character got a trial only after his embarrassing election to the European Parliament.[48]

In the Tortora case, several PSI members denounced a verdict against the accused, who subsequently won his case on appeal. In another case, they objected to a Milan court's leniency toward socialist journalist Walter Tobagi's murderer, who had turned state's evidence. Craxi intervened directly in this instance, provoking a constitutional spat when President Cossiga prohibited the magistrates' self-governing body (the CSM) from answering the prime minister.[49]

Along with institutional reform, the Craxi government's inability to alter the justice system is a major disappointment. But also in this case, Socialists have served as a catalyst for increased discussion and, eventually, change. The parties with the strongest civil rights tradition—Socialists, Liberals, and Radicals—started the machinery for three referenda on the justice system. Even though both Communists and Catholics oppose these "lib-lab" referenda, they may already have borne their first fruit. In March 1986, the Court of Accounts indicated that judges may be held accountable for errors and promised implementation of this basic right.[50]

Another important institutional issue—religion—illustrates the difficulties of change. After long negotiations, Prime Minister Craxi on 18 February 1984 signed a new Concordat with the Vatican, replacing the 1929 Lateran accords. Instead of being signed on Vatican property, as the previous document had been, the ceremony took place on Italian territory. Craxi wore his red tie under his formal clothes. "How shall I address him?" Craxi asked a political counselor, referring to the Vatican secretary of state. "One should use the title of Eminence, but you call him *signor cardinale.*"[51]

The signing ceremony's symbolic aspects suggested that republican Italy might eventually assert its prerogatives toward the church more aggressively than in the past. In fact, the Italian state no longer recognizes the catholic religion as official and will cease direct payments to the clergy in 1990. Instead of spelling out in detail the new relationship between church and state, the Concordat referred a number of important issues to joint commissions which must report to Parliament. Furthermore, the Concordat purposely left undefined other issues such as the teaching of catholicism in the public schools, to be resolved by "understandings" between the Italian state and cardinals. The press has attributed this innovation to Craxi himself.[52] The idea confers great flexibility on the agreement, perhaps eliminating the need for future concordats and possibly making it easier to reflect the further secularization of Italian society.

The first test of this concept demonstrates both the strength and the weakness of the idea. In December 1985, the demochristian minister of public instruction, Franca Falcucci, reached agreement with Cardinal Ugo Poletti on the teaching of catholicism in the public schools. She presented the "understanding" at a Cabinet meeting, after which she and the cardinal signed the understanding in front of television cameras. The reaction took the political forces by surprise. A motion by independent leftist deputy Franco Bassanini deplored the minister's action because she had not consulted Parliament. The highly favorable reaction to Bassanini's motion indicated that public opinion strongly supported his views. On 15 January 1986, at the Guatemala City airport, DC Secretary De Mita received an urgent telephone call informing him of the situation. De Mita demanded that Craxi block the motion by asking for a confidence vote on the question. Socialist representatives disagreed with Falcucci, but the parties resisted demogogically raising the anticlerical issue. At the same time, they wished to confront the matter maturely, reflecting the genuine concerns which the question raised in a secularizing society. As a result, the ruling coalition and the Communists cooperated. The cabinet quickly liberalized the Falcucci agreement, the government posed the question of confidence, and communist Chamber President Nilde Jotti blocked a vote on the Bassanini motion. Even if not completely, the new Concordat has taken a step toward recognizing the increasing secularization of Italy.[53]

As in many other fields, Italian society has outstripped its representatives on the religious issue, and this dichotomy strains an archaic political system struggling to reflect the vast changes which have occurred. With the increasing breakdown of "imperfect bipolarism" and the shock of greater stability, the creaky, complex, and confusing machinery may finally be responding to the nation's needs with greater alacrity.

Communists and the New Course

Constitution of a socialist-led government challenged Italy's two largest parties to rethink their general policies, their approach to the issues raised by the Socialists, and their attitude toward the PSI.

As has been noted, immediately upon constitution of his government, Craxi offered the Communists a dialogue. Political commentator Gianni Baget Bozzo pointed out that the new political situation challenged the PCI in addition to the DC. The Catholic party no longer offered the PCI a solid political reference point, Baget Bozzo wrote; the socialist and secular area did. If the PCI comprehended this change, it would limit its opposition to Craxi to specific measures. By not globally condemning the government, Socialists and Communists could work out differences on specific actions and eventually reach an understanding on general policy.[54]

Political analyst Giorgio Galli also emphasized the crucial question of PCI-PSI relationships on the eve of the PCI's 1983 congress. While official PCI policy mandated the "democratic alternative" with the Socialists, the Communists rendered the idea impossible by continual denunciation of the socialist-led government. It made sense for the PCI to call a truce in the PSI polemics, soften its opposition to the Craxi government, and create a friendlier atmosphere for implementation of its stated policy.[55]

As noted, however, Berlinguer immediately challenged Craxi and did his utmost to topple his government, despite socialist willingness to talk. PSI Vice Secretary Martelli accused the Communists of flatly turning down Craxi's offer to discuss mutual problems and establish a working relationship.[56] The PCI refused even to extend its unofficial collaboration as it had done so often with Christian democratic prime ministers. Furthermore, as the cabinet demonstrated its durability, PCI rhetoric escalated as the Communists accused Craxi of setting up a "regime," a euphemism for fascism.

As the PCI battled against the Craxi government, the Socialists retaliated on the local level. The fragmented national political picture replicated itself in the local governments, where socialist votes determined the majority. Consequently, the Socialists could form *giunte* with either Communists or Catholics. In the North and Center, they generally gave life to leftist administrations through alliances with the PCI. With constitution of the Craxi cabinet, De Mita insisted that local governments reflect the national situation—just as Moro had done with Nenni.

PSI official in charge of local affairs Giusi La Ganga issued a warning: continued PCI attacks on the socialist-led government jeopardized local administrations based on a PCI-PSI coalition. PCI local affairs head Renato Zangheri expressed skepticism that the Socialists would sabotage the local governments, but the Socialists caused crises in large leftist-run cities, including Florence. Turin, Milan, Naples, and Livorno.

Quick alliances with the DC, however, would prove politically costly and reduce PSI leverage, so the Socialists sought agreements with the smaller parties. They walked a tightrope, initiating lengthy discussions with PCI, DC, and other groupings as they withdrew from local coalitions. During this period, I asked Vice Secretary Spini if the Socialists planned implementation of the *pentapartito* on the local level. He denied that such a plan existed, replying that the party would decide case by case. By endangering the local administrations, however, the PSI blunted an important universally recognized PCI edge: efficiency in local government.[57]

As a consequence of these battles, clear signals of a deepening PCI crisis appeared. The Communists had lost 6 percent in the 1979 and 1983 elections, and partial voting in November 1983 confirmed the trend.

While the PCI vote declined, the Communists lost the cultural initiative. The press suffered first. The procommunist Rome daily *Paese Sera* ceased publication. Next the PCI had to restructure its flagship *L'Unità* to compensate for the newspaper's circulation decline and its increasing economic losses. Criticism and embarrassing labor agitation followed. By late 1983, a writer proclaimed the end of the communist "cultural hegemony," and press reports into 1986 reiterated this theme.

Clearly Berlinguer had blundered in his "hard" opposition to Craxi. Failure of the "historic compromise" had induced him to repropose the more traditional concept of a socialist alliance, but his hostility toward the socialist-led cabinet indicated no alteration in the haughty communist attitude toward the Socialists.

The communist view of the PSI oscillated between considering it secondary and viewing it as subordinate. Thus, the "historic compromise" relegated the PSI to inferior status, while Berlinguer's actions marked the "democratic alternative" as a gimmick for the Popular Front's reincarnation. The PCI's inability to drop its traditional mental schemes and confront the altered political situation produced a severe crisis. The PCI declared war on the Craxi government, opposed the hard economic choices made by the cabinet, and accepted NATO but opposed its policies. In short, the PCI's declining vote reflected its contradictory policies and growing isolation in the country.[58]

These warning signals prompted important PCI sectors to stage a subdued revolt in early 1984. Known as the "quadrilateral," this opposition included the communist leader in the Chamber of Deputies, Giorgio Napolitano, *L'Unità* editor Emanuele Macaluso, CGIL head Luciano Lama, and Chamber President Nilde Jotti.

Napolitano brought the problems into the open. Irritated with the relentless campaign in the Chamber against the government, Napolitano threatened resignation after the party hierarchy backed a communist deputy whom Napolitano had reprimanded for calling a surprise secret vote on a money bill. On 4 January 1984, Napolitano published an article in *L'Unità* which raised important questions. In effect, he challenged Berlinguer's hostility against the socialist-led government, suggesting that a "politically articulated" policy would be preferable to the "globally negative" one in force. Napolitano not only questioned the communist attitude toward a government led by an old ally but raised more fundamental issues. By restricting its parliamentary opposition to obstructing government proposals, a large party with governmental ambitions only discredited and isolated itself, he argued. Napolitano suggested that the parliamentary group be delegated complete responsibility for decisions regarding legislation. Even though Napolitano took care to leave the ultimate determination of policy to the PCI's central bodies, his remedy challenged the PCI's overcentralized organization by requiring radical decentralization of the PCI—a break with communist tradition.

Political commentators suggested that changes in Italian society favored Communist party "secularization"—less doctrinal rigidity, looser discipline, and a flexible bureaucracy. Since PCI power rests on the cultural isolation produced by Marxist ideology and

reinforced by a densely woven apparatus, however, communist leaders found such alterations difficult and preferred to maintain the status quo.[59]

As a result, Berlinguer clamped down hard, despite favorable press reaction and
universal encouragement for Napolitano. The PCI blamed the press for blowing the
incident out of proportion, and Napolitano dropped his challenge. On 20 February 1984,
Berlinguer reiterated his policy toward the Craxi government, struggling to conciliate his
"democratic alternative" with alienation of the PSI.[60] The new socialist course thus
produced rumblings within the PCI but no change.

After Berlinguer's unexpected death, Alessandro Natta proposed a "program government," which held forth the possibility of communist votes for government legislation. But
this "governo di programma" would have left the cabinet without a fixed majority, thereby
weakening it. Natta opposed the Craxi government, but he wanted it to "fall on the left"
and create the premise of a communist-socialist coalition. This contradictory desire further
exemplified the communist crisis. Only on Finance Minister Visentini's loophole-closing
tax bill did the PCI establish a contact point with Craxi. Even here, the PCI vacillated until
public opinion and union pressure induced the party to support it.[61]

In short, no "cultural revolution" allowed the PCI to take cognizance of changed
political conditions. In fact, since the PCI obtained a larger share of the votes than the DC
in the June 1984 European Parliament elections, Natta announced that the Communists
would demand a mandate to form a government and would probably call early national
elections should the 1985 local elections confirm the PCI's plurality status. This declaration turned out to be an enormous blunder. The 1985 elections further strengthened the
"laic pole,"[62] while the referendum loss further damaged the PCI's image. Natta pru-
dently renounced a fight on the presidency.

Ironically, foreign policy temporarily brought the two leftist parties together. In
October 1985, Palestinian terrorists hijacked the Italian cruise ship *Achille Lauro*. After
the hijacking, American fighter planes forced down an Egyptian airliner carrying the
hijackers at the NATO base of Sigonella in Sicily. Italian troops surrounded the plane.
American special forces landed and demanded custody of the hijackers. The Italians
refused. The soldiers pushed and shoved and pointed their weapons at each other. A
heated exchange between Prime Minister Craxi and President Reagan took place before
the Americans admitted Italian jurisdiction.

This incident provoked the resignation of Defense Minister Spadolini and threatened
the government. Suddenly rediscovering Craxi's leftist credentials, the Communists
strongly supported the prime minister and vowed to vote for him. This development
caused Craxi to resign without a vote for fear of completely altering his majority. An
agreement with Spadolini quickly reconstituted the cabinet.[63]

Despite speculation, the *Lauro* case did not produce a closer political relationship
between Socialists and Communists. With Mikhail Gorbachev's liberalization of USSR
policies, Natta made up with the Soviet Union on a January 1986 trip to Moscow.[64]
Despite Italian appreciation of Gorbachev's openness, the Communists had again demonstrated their continued deference to the Soviet Union. The PCI appears caught between its
hard-core membership's devotion to Moscow and a desire to resemble the SPD, openly
expressed by many of its more sophisticated leaders and reinforced by its electorate—as
distinguished from its members. In fact, at its spring 1986 Florence congress, the PCI
again called for a "program government" but failed to define its program if it should
come to power.[65]

The PCI thus seems condemned to an immobilism which the Italian voter clearly perceives. In a poll for *Corriere della Sera* released before the PCI congress, the respondents recognized communist qualities of order and efficiency, agreed that it resembled the SPD rather than a Soviet-style party, and favored PCI entrance into a coalition government. But the poll also indicated respondent awareness that the PCI remained strongly linked to Moscow, would upset relations with the Americans, and would restrict liberty. The voters requested a clear reformist program closely resembling that of the Socialists.[66]

Finally, the respondents did not believe that the PCI could make the required changes—and the responses of party members in the same poll confirmed this belief. In an interview with me in late 1984, Giorgio Ruffolo expressed the identical concept. "Obsessed with unity, the PCI is evolving," he said, "but very, very slowly; it marches like a seventeenth-century army, with all the arms, baggage, women, children, and camp followers. And the country cannot wait."[67]

In fact, polls taken in 1987 consistently indicated a 5 or 6 percent drop for the PCI in the next national election, then due in 1988.

Catholics and the New Course

The catholic reaction to the new socialist course resembled the communist in that it struggled to maintain its hegemony and had difficulty "secularizing."

The DC understood that the Communists escaped isolation by maintaining their alliances with the PSI in the provinces. Extending the national governing formula to the local level took priority for the DC upon constitution of the socialist-led cabinet. Craxi initially responded to the DC demand for "homogenization" by claiming that he had difficulty bringing the provinces into line.[68]

As noted above, however, the PSI did move on this issue, but cautiously. If the PSI abandoned the PCI completely, it risked being crushed by the DC. As a result, the PSI kept its options open, carefully maneuvering between the twin DC and PCI perils. After the PCI decline in the 1985 local elections, the ruling coalition formed *pentagiunte* in some large cities.

As a result, the DC found itself in an extremely frustrating situation. It remained the country's largest party but possessed neither the presidency of the Council nor the presidency of the republic. Furthermore, it discovered itself being eased into the opposition in the provinces while Craxi, with less than one-third of its votes, seemingly had everything. In addition, despite catholic-communist flirtation and threats to reactivate the "historic compromise," the DC could make no serious move because a significant part of its electorate still considered it an anticommunist bulwark.[69]

At the same time, the Catholics feared that a good showing by Craxi as prime minister would reduce their electorate, rather than the Communists', as Craxi argued. In order to dull his image, they criticized Craxi's economic legislation, watered it down, and spectacularly employed the secret vote to defeat government proposals.[70]

Under pressure from Secretary De Mita, the DC held a congress in early 1984. De Mita sought reconfirmation for his line after the DC's defeat in the 1983 elections. De Mita hoped to renew the party, cutting it loose from its traditional clientalistic and church foundations.

In fact, political scientists have focused on the DC link with the church as the major problem in Italian politics. Unlike other European catholic parties, the Italian DC maintained extremely close ties with the Vatican and failed to adopt an interconfessional program and philosophy. This factor cut out the secularized and intellectual elites; alienated by a force identified with the political system, these elites gravitated toward the antisystem party, the PCI, contributing to its rise as the West's largest and most powerful communist party.[71]

If the DC had "secularization" problems strikingly similar to those of the PCI, the Catholics also shared with the Communists a hegemonic mentality. In his plans for the party, De Mita accepted an alternation of power between a catholic and a communist pole, at least in theory. Thus, under De Mita's plan, the Socialists would lose their centrality, being forced to choose sides.[72]

In fact, De Mita's vision proved faulty. The Socialists had no intention of submitting to such an arrangement, and the DC's inability to challenge the prime minister directly strengthened them. Moreover, De Mita's plans for party renovation lacked specificity, and powerful elements which benefited from the party's present constitution held on to their power. Surprisingly, a little-known challenger of De Mita's won a third of the votes at the 1984 congress, while blank ballots constituted 10 percent of the ballots. Finally—as if to mock modernization plans—in the 1985 local elections, Pope John Paul II and his representatives intervened directly in what *L'Espresso* labeled a political crusade unseen in thirty years. Unhappy at this interference, De Mita nevertheless had to go along.[73]

Ironically, the congress's real winner appeared to be Bettino Craxi. Discussion revolved around the prime minister and his policies. The DC seemed unable to produce new leaders, and the delegates accepted their loss of the presidency of the Council. The country's political center of gravity had become the government and its socialist leader.[74]

By late 1985, buoyed by reconfirmation as the country's largest party in the local elections and Christian democratic reclamation of the Quirinale, and convinced that the longer the socialist-led government remained in power the more the DC stood to lose, De Mita challenged Craxi, demanding the prime minister's office for the DC. His rationale: alternating power among the coalition partners. This argument sounded strange coming from a party which had occupied the office for thirty-five years, but De Mita persisted. In the meantime, the DC multiplied its jabs at Craxi. Party leaders criticized his leadership, and secret votes against his proposals multiplied. Fabio Fabbri, PSI Senate leader, complained of DC attacks, stating that they would produce an "irreparable" political collision.[75]

By early 1986, Craxi's popularity had taken a quantum leap, especially after the *Achille Lauro* affair, making De Mita even more anxious to dislodge him from Palazzo Chigi. Commentators wrote with increasing frequency about the PSI's "centrality," its pivotal nature in the political system, and the likelihood of its seizing leadership of the left from the PCI.[76]

In January 1986, news of a possible "clarification" between Craxi and De Mita leaked out. According to reports, De Mita proffered Craxi a strengthened alliance extending beyond the current legislature if the socialist leader agreed to a Christian democratic prime minister. Craxi allegedly considered resigning at this point, before a new DC congress scheduled for the spring. Since De Mita would not likely sabotage the coalition and jeopardize his own position at the assembly, Craxi reasoned he could renovate and strengthen his government. Perhaps this public speculation produced results. When the *verifica* occurred in March 1986, it turned out to be a truce, confirming Craxi for the time being and allowing De Mita to plan his congress in peace.[77]

In April 1986, Vice Secretary Martelli announced Craxi's intention to leave Palazzo Chigi in March 1987, in conjunction with the next PSI congress.[78] Craxi had fought for the premiership in order to provide the electorate a taste of socialist government. Now he had accomplished that task and wished to devote his full energies to gearing up his party for elections due in 1988, especially in the face of disturbing news regarding the PSI's internal condition. Only by translating his popularity as prime minister into votes for the PSI could he make the PSI the strongest party on the left and reverse the Italian anomaly of a communist party larger than a socialist one.

Unplacated by Martelli's announcement, De Mita renewed his challenge to Craxi in the spring of 1986. Citing the principle of alternation once more, he demanded a DC premier. To lend credit to his threat, De Mita flirted with the Communists. He graciously praised Natta's leadership qualities and paid him other compliments. Fearing the backlash which could occur from sabotaging Craxi, both major parties opposed early elections, and this desire could spark an understanding. Speculation centered on a DC-PRI cabinet supported by PCI votes, cutting out the Socialists and teaching them a lesson.[79]

Designed to convince Craxi to relinquish Palazzo Chigi, this renewed "historic compromise" specter soon became irrelevant. In June 1986, local Sicilian elections provided the DC with a better excuse. The Socialists had expected a significant gain in those elections but remained stable at about 15 percent. PSI leaders attributed this outcome to local irritation with Craxi because of the terms of the newly adopted *condono edilizio* and entrenched DC clientelism. Expected to drop, the Catholics instead held their ground, as did the Communists. Interpreting these elections as an end to the downward spiral in DC fortunes, Christian democratic leaders may have encouraged DC "snipers" to vote against confidence in a secret ballot during Craxi's absence at a European Economic Community meeting discussing South African sanctions.

On 27 June 1986, Craxi returned to Rome and resigned. There followed a long crisis. De Mita offered a deal: he would support another Craxi term as prime minister if the socialist leader agreed to a specific resignation date and then supported a Christian democratic prime minister for an equal length of time. Unwilling to become a lame duck, Craxi refused, insisting on forming a strong government not bound by a time limit. The Christian Democrats balked, and he envisioned as an alternative a minority DC government with outside socialist support until the next elections. De Mita rejected this proposal.

Whatever the outcome, Craxi stood to gain.[80] Public opinion did not understand why a popular and effective prime minister should suddenly have to resign for no apparent reason. Furthermore, by resigning on the secret vote issue, Craxi had the country's sympathy and "fell on his feet." Craxi's approval rating soared to 67 percent in a country which normally measured such qualities in negative numbers.

Because it appeared to be interested only in power, the DC discredited itself. Leaving aside customary practice, President Cossiga aroused socialist resentment by first giving an "exploratory mandate" to Fanfani and then commissioning Andreotti to form a government. Both ran into adamant socialist vetoes, but, more importantly, the DC demonstrated its incapacity to produce a creditworthy leader capable of resolving the situation it had produced. Andreotti hinted at an agreement with the PCI, but the socialist veto stuck.

Furthermore, Craxi's stability theme seemed to have won over the country. Both labor and industry requested a cabinet which would last and decried any return to the previous governmental instability; stability, they insisted, had become the primary requisite for maintaining favorable economic conditions. The other innovation was consolidation of the "laic pole." Probably spurred by public opinion, the PRI, PSDI, and PLI secretaries agreed not to participate in or support minority governments, even as a bridge to elections.[81]

Boxed in by these developments, the DC accepted Craxi's return. On the surface, the DC seemed to have won, since Craxi agreed to resign by March 1987 and to support a Christian Democrat for prime minister. As noted, however, Martelli had previously announced Craxi's intention to resign by that date in order to prepare the PSI for the upcoming elections. In practice, the DC had won the right to Palazzo Chigi from the spring of 1987 to the next elections, due in 1988.

In presenting his second program, Craxi sounded like anything but a lame duck and looked forward to the succeeding legislature. With inflation defeated, private industry healed, and a healthy balance of payments, he aimed at decreasing unemployment, increasing public investment, and resolving the national debt problem. Taxes would not be increased, and money for a public works program had already been set aside.[82] Craxi did not refer to any agreement to resign in the spring of 1987. Any Christian democratic prime minister who follows him will have a difficult time making a good impression.

As with the PCI, the DC response to the new socialist course proved woefully inadequate. Despite De Mita's intentions and rhetoric, he failed to secularize the party, to disengage from the church, to elaborate a new program, to reduce clientalism, and to overcome the party's traditional hegemonic demands.

Foreign Policy

As the PSI had promised, the new socialist course imparted momentum to the foreign policy area. This sector had been dormant for years, as Italy followed the lead of its major ally, the United States. Immediately upon becoming prime minister, Craxi aimed at Italian prominence and independence in world affairs, within the limits of its international commitments.

The first major issue was installation of cruise missiles in Europe in 1984 as a response to the Soviet SS 20s. It will be recalled that Secretary Craxi had supported the Euromissiles and Italy had agreed to installation barring progress in talks on the issue in Geneva.

In the fall of 1983, Prime Minister Craxi visited Paris, London, and Bonn. After talks with President Mitterand, Prime Minister Thatcher, and Chancellor Kohl, Craxi informed President Reagan that while he favored the Euromissiles, he suggested suspending installation if the Russians responded positively even after the deadline of 31 December 1984—Italy was the only American ally to adopt this position. During Craxi's talks with Mitterand, the French president demonstrated willingness to discuss the missile issue at a five-power conference including the United States, the USSR, Britain, France, and China. Craxi aimed at resolving the impasse by shifting the question to this new forum and by extending the Soviet Union's time to make an acceptable proposal.[83]

Receiving no adequate Russian response, Craxi reaffirmed Italian agreement to the missile installation on a visit to Washington in October 1983. Because of Craxi's initiatives and his acceptance of the missiles while large pacifist demonstrations occurred in Europe, President Reagan lavished praise on the Italian leader. In return, Craxi requested that the Americans consult the Italians with greater frequency on matters of common concern and take their opinions into greater consideration.[84]

The first socialist president of the Council piqued the Americans' interest. For the Reagan administration, Italy had become a crucial player in the battle for Euromissile installation against a Soviet campaign to divide the European allies from the United States. This understanding and Craxi's diplomatic initiatives caused the administration to pay attention to its long-neglected ally.

Before Craxi's American trip, Reagan sent the socialist leader two personal letters and several high-level visitors, including Paul Nitze, head of the American delegation to the Geneva arms talks. For his part, Craxi aimed at refurbishing Italy's image. The American public mind long identified the Italian Socialists as communist fellow travelers, so Craxi emphasized his commitment to the West but demanded an equal voice on common themes.[85] Craxi had put the United States on notice: as a democratic and sovereign nation, Italy would exercise more frequently than in the past its right to examine common policies and, if necessary, seek their alteration.

The socialist-led government would exercise this option on a number of fronts, but the altered Italian attitude may be cited in Craxi's response to President Reagan's Strategic Defense Initiative ("Star Wars"). Because of his fear that SDI would alter the existing strategic equilibrium, Craxi qualified as the most skeptical European statesman on Star Wars. During his second trip to the United States, in March 1985, the prime minister visited the scientists at the Massachusetts Institute of Technology in order to discuss SDI technical aspects. Eventually accepting the concept, Craxi, Foreign Minister Andreotti, and Defense Minister Spadolini sought a European understanding on a common approach to the United States. He found a response from German Chancellor Kohl, with whom he united to gain American assurances that SDI technology would be shared with the European allies for its possible application to European defense systems. Responding to continuing Craxi diffidence, Reagan assured the prime minister of the availability of SDI research to the Europeans, and even the Russians, and promised not to exploit the technology for development of new offensive weapons. In the meantime, Italian firms actively participated in Star Wars research at a high level while the government sought further European consensus.[86]

As noted, Craxi's European commitment predates his election as secretary in 1976 and became a prominent part of the PSI's program. As prime minister, Craxi furthered "Eurosocialism." Italy, for example, championed Spanish and Portuguese entry into the European Community against socialist France's resistance to enlarging it. The imminent passing of the EC presidency from France to Italy foreshadowed easier entrance for Spain and Portugal, both headed by Socialists. "Eurosocialism" aided Craxi in nipping in the bud a Mitterand project for strengthening the EC by institution of a two-tier system of states within the Community. Supposedly based on the strength of the different economies, Mitterand's plan would have effectively created a Franco-German political axis. Instead, Craxi called for increasing the EC's own economic resources and continuing integration.

At a Madrid convention of EC socialist parties in April 1985, Craxi dedicated his remarks to the Community's future. Having achieved the historic decision to admit Spain and Portugal, Craxi said, the Italians would fight for the Community's "gradual transformation into a true political entity with its own institutional framework, financial autonomy, and a larger range of authority." When later in the year the European Council failed to put these principles into practice, isolating the Italians, Italy engineered the Council's spectacular reversal by the European Parliament at Strasbourg. At all turns, Italy spurred "Europeanist" solutions. This policy and its growing Mediterranean orientation enhanced the country's importance.[87]

Already in October 1983, the socialist prime ministers of five countries actually or imminently in the EC and clustered around the Mediterranean met in Athens to seek a common program. Little came of this meeting because most of these nations had different concerns. United by powerful cultural ties and by the long Craxi-Gonzalez friendship, cemented by Italy's strong support of Spanish EC membership, however, Italy and Spain developed an informal alliance.

The Italians supported Gonzalez on the NATO referendum and encouraged continued Spanish membership with promises of joint arms development. By 1986, the Mediterranean's special problems—NATO's fragility in the region, the resulting power vacuum, divergent interests of the United States and the area's native powers—encouraged an Italo-Spanish entente. In January 1986, an extraordinary high-level meeting between representatives of the Italian and Spanish governments took place in the old Greek city of Taormina, Sicily. At this first of a promised series of meetings, Spanish and Italian government heads and foreign, defense, industry, and cultural ministers discussed future industrial and scientific cooperation.

Of most immediate importance, the defense ministers discussed joint collaboration on a tank with which the Spanish army will arm itself in the 1990s. As a counter to a Franco-German offer, Oto Melara, the Italian arms concern, proposed a 50 percent Spanish interest in development and production of the tank and collaboration on foreign sales.[88]

This Latin "entente" is only one example of the more vigorous and independent Italian Mediterranean policy promised by the new socialist course.

Under a previous administration, the Italians had contributed the largest contingent to the multinational force which moved into Beirut in a vain attempt to keep the peace after the Israeli invasion. The socialist administration emphasized the "humanitarian and pacific" mission of its troops. Consequently, the Italian contingent carefully adopted a neutral stance, avoiding embroilment in local squabbles, scrupulously protecting the Shila and Shatila camps, where an Israeli-backed militia had conducted a massacre, and delivering medical services to the war-torn city. Respecting the Italian attitude, the Lebanese factions did not target Italian soldiers while attacking the Americans and the French, whose governments adopted pro-Israeli positions.[89]

By the end of 1983, the Italians reacted to escalating French and American retaliation against Shiite Moslem attacks on their troops. Following a cabinet meeting on 23 November, Craxi's press secretary stated that the government could understand isolated instances of retaliation, "But if the mission of our forces there has changed, we do not agree to stay."

In his televised New Year's message to the nation, the outspoken President Pertini denounced Israel, condemned pro-Israel American policies in Lebanon, feared the Italian contingent's involvement in a war, and suggested its withdrawal. The press reported Palazzo Chigi's embarrassment, but the Italians had already decided on a gradual disengagement from Lebanon—foreshadowing American and French withdrawal. In this case, as in others, the president perfectly represented public opinion.[90]

According to American political science professor Joseph La Palombara, Washington feared the new Italian course in foreign policy. "The Americans have become used to an Italy which has no foreign policy," La Palombara wrote, "or, more precisely, does not act in an autonomous manner in this field. It is a commonplace in Washington, for example, that Italy does not pronounce itself on great international themes before France or the German Federal Republic." Alarmed at the strange behavior of its most faithful European ally for forty years, the Americans discovered an explanation in the always-suspect PSI foreign policy, the neutralist inclinations of former PCI collaborator Andreotti, and the DC decline. La Palombara feared American sabotage of the socialist-led cabinet.[91]

Later in the year, Foreign Minister Andreotti did come under fire in Parliament, with Craxi forced to come to his rescue. According to reports in the Italian press, the Americans inspired the attack. In talks with me, however, Rome embassy officials vigorously denied the allegation.

In contradistinction to the United States, Andreotti and Craxi agreed on a more independent, pro-Arab Italian role in the Middle East, while the third component of the cabinet with responsibility in the area, Defense Minister Spadolini, vigorously dissented.

Craxi had always believed in guarantees for Israel, but he had long since committed the Socialists to Palestinian autonomy. In late 1984, Craxi made lightning trips to four influential Middle Eastern capitals and had a long conversation with PLO Chairman Yasser Arafat. Craxi believed that Arafat stood ready to renounce terrorism and formally recognize Israel in return for a Palestinian state on the West Bank federated with Jordan. Refusal to explore this interesting possibility amounted to "irresponsibility," Andreotti said in a television news interview. Craxi hoped to coordinate the negotiations with Italy's EC presidency, but the EC refused to legitimize the initiative. Furthermore, Craxi ran into resistance from Spadolini's Republicans and the Israelis, while the Americans did not relish being confronted with a difficult diplomatic choice.[92]

Craxi's novel attitude toward the Middle East—"equidistance"—differed markedly from earlier policy, characterized by American leadership and correctness toward the Arabs. Craxi also reaffirmed Italy's traditionally active policy in the Mediterranean. Convinced at the same time that justice for the Palestinian people would remove the primary cause of turmoil in the area, Craxi supported constitution of a Palestinian state combined with international guarantees for Israel. This solution reflected traditional socialist concerns for downtrodden populations as expressed in numerous PSI statements.

Italian efforts favorable to Palestinian autonomy continued into 1985, irritating both Israel and the United States. In October, Craxi issued a particularly pointed condemnation of an Israeli raid on PLO headquarters in Tunisia which killed more than sixty persons, including civilians. Later in the month, terrorists hijacked the Italian cruise liner *Achille Lauro*.

The reasons behind this hijacking remain obscure, as are those behind the Rome and Vienna airport massacres at the end of 1985. While the seemingly quick resolution of the *Achille Lauro* affair seemed to reward Italian Middle Eastern initiatives, its end suggested that selection of Italian targets may have had sabotaging the new foreign policy as its true aim. Israeli Deputy Prime Minister David Levy claimed that the hijacking would teach the Italians a lesson because they "had condemned us and praised terror." Craxi's release of reputed hijacking mastermind Mohammed Abbas because of his diplomatic immunity provoked American protests and precipitated Defense Minister Spadolini's resignation. These events caused the first cabinet crisis on a foreign policy issue in many years. Craxi had learned that balanced and independent Middle Eastern policies could get him into trouble.[93]

Spadolini discovered himself isolated in the cabinet and in the country. Polls demonstrated that while Italian public opinion did not approve of Abbas's release, it agreed with Craxi's general Middle Eastern line. Spadolini reentered the cabinet after Craxi agreed to improved consultation but won nothing on the *Achille Lauro* and the Middle East. In his speech to Parliament, the prime minister stated that armed struggle could be legitimate under certain circumstances, provoking an Israeli protest.[94]

At the end of 1985, Italy again became a target of international terrorists. As in the *Achille Lauro* case, the reasons behind the Rome airport massacre remain unclear, but suspicion is strong that extremist Libyan-led anti-Arafat terrorists selected Italian objectives to discredit the PLO chairman, divide him from European statesmen testing his intention to negotiate, and sabotage the opening of peace negotiations.

The airport killings and the terrorist escalation in late 1985 and early 1986 elicited a military response from the United States in the Gulf of Sidra and Libya. The Italians and the European allies opposed these actions, counseling the United States to take its case to the World Court. News leaked of serious disagreements between Craxi and President Reagan's ambassador charged with explaining the American position, old socialist nemesis Vernon Walters. On this occasion, Foreign Minister Andreotti mounted a spirited defense of past and present Italian foreign policy.[95]

The Italians had been patient with their former colony because of their dependence on Libyan oil, their commercial ties, and their belief in the Palestinian situation as the root cause of the area's problems. They rapidly reinforced their southern front in response to Muammar Qaddafi's military threats, however, and in the spring of 1986, the government went farther than the other European allies in banning Libyan arms sales. The Italians also took strong action against Libyan diplomats in Italy after uncovering a plot to assassinate American Ambassador Maxwell Rabb and evidence of Libyan complicity in terrorism. The Craxi government also reduced the Italian commercial presence in Libya and made Libyan investment in Italian firms more difficult.

On 15 April 1986, American forces bombed Tripoli and Benghazi. Following these raids, the Libyans launched missiles on the Italian island of Lampedusa. There followed strong action and language from Craxi, who gave directives to the armed forces and vowed retaliation should the Libyans repeat their attack. At the same news conference, however, Craxi once again strongly dissented from the American policy of military confrontation.[96]

With world attention riveted on Libya, Italian initiatives in the complicated Middle East did not achieve the desired result of greater peace and stability. The Qaddafi sideshow succeeded in temporarily taking the focus off the Palestinian question. Because of his independent policies, Craxi became the first Italian postwar leader to gain widespread international recognition. As his initiatives became more costly, however, Craxi became more prudent regarding the Middle East, but he had established himself as a force to be dealt with.

In fact, Italian prestige in the Mediterranean and the Arab world rose dramatically. Movement in these areas, combined with diplomatic activity in Eastern Europe and a greatly increased aid level to lesser developed countries in Africa and Latin America, brought Italian foreign policy to the fore of Italian politics for the first time in forty years.

This renewed momentum set off a salutary internal debate. Italian industrialists fretted lest their country become too "Mediterranean," disengaging from the northern European and "Atlantic" economies and the Western technological revolution. As might be expected, the Italians paid a price for their newfound independence in 1985 and 1986. The Western democracies excluded them from the "Club of Five" economic summit which made crucial decisions for the world economy; furthermore, increased American attention to De Mita caused continual rifts in the ruling majority.[97]

On the other hand, the new course in foreign affairs met with general approval, renewed Italian pride, contributed to Craxi's growing popularity, created a link with the opposition PCI, and increased the country's prominence in world affairs. In fact, Craxi insisted on Italy's entrance into the "Club of Five" and won his case at the Tokyo economic summit in May 1986. Combined with his domestic achievements, his foreign policy initiatives increased Craxi's attraction for communist voters, creating the possibility of a vast "Westernized" left in Italy. This development, commentators mused, would confer great stability on the country and increase the nation's capacity to influence world affairs. "Elect me secretary of the PCI," Craxi quipped to leading communist exponents, "and you will have solved all your problems." In short, Craxi has made Italy into "a new protagonist" on the international scene.[98]

A New Style

Since the end of World War II, Italian prime ministers have been colorless individuals. Political reality combined with personalities to produce a system of government which avoided hard decisions, encouraged unwarranted compromise, and let the country drift. Asked to describe the difference in style between Craxi and previous premiers, Under Secretary Giuliano Amato answered: "He is very different from the Christian Democrats who wrapped everything in velvet to the point that one could not understand . . . if under that velvet there was an intelligent person or a cretin."

Craxi, in fact, made difficult decisions after attempting compromise. Because of this style and his "decisionismo," he became the prime minister most vilified by the Italian press in recent history. In a famous interview in his early days as prime minister, he responded to these attacks by quoting Garibaldi, who had written a friend that "I am about to break my balls!" Craxi told the interviewer, "Good! I'm about to break my balls, too! Understand?" In another incident, as PSI secretary, he successfully sued *Corriere della Sera* editor Piero Ostellino for libeling his party. After reading the constant criticism of his government in Scalfari's *La Repubblica,* he said that the newspaper lacked seriousness. He saw no reason to refrain from criticizing people who criticized him, Craxi said. As prime minister, he dressed down the French ambassador about a *Le Monde* article about Italy which Craxi believed defamed the country.

Nor did he spare his cabinet colleagues. At a year-end 1984 news conference, he compared himself to the captain of a ship which had finally found the right course and stated: "If the other officers do not wish to follow orders . . . they can ask to be let off at the first port." When Defense Minister Spadolini complained about the work involved in his post, Craxi supposedly answered his rival, "In cases like these, do you know what one should do, my dear Giovanni? Get married."[99]

During the course of heading the government, the strong attacks against him by

Communists and Catholics, and the massive street demonstrations against his politics, Craxi matured. He still adopted decisive positions and reacted sharply when irritated, but he made a conscious effort to appear the statesman. He modified his strong language and gave up his leather jackets and jeans for designer clothes. Once overweight and considered a plodder with no charisma, Craxi became the most popular prime minister in the republic's history. Cartoonists used to portray him as Mussolini but now also draw him as Napoleon.

CHAPTER 15

What Remains of Socialism?

Historian H. Stuart Hughes has emphasized that nationalization of the means of production commonly associated with socialism has always been a means to an end. In fact, the socialist goal is not economic but "a moral change—a transformation in the *quality* of life from an absorption with private economic satisfactions to a concern for human personality and the well-being of the community as a whole."

Twenty-five years ago, Hughes stressed that the European socialist left struggled to adjust its aims to contemporary conditions, avoiding absorption by a consumer-oriented, politically apathetic society. European socialist leftists accordingly proposed long-range goals such as economic planning, an effective public investment policy, and elevating the population's cultural level.

Italian socialism lagged in this development, squandering its moral capital by tagging along with the Communists, engendering distrust which Hughes predicted would consume more than a decade to remedy. He wrote: "there is something amazingly innocent about Italian Socialism."[1]

Now the communist inferiority, the distrust, and the innocence are gone. As demonstrated through the "Socialist Project" and other pronouncements, the Italians have joined the European socialist mainstream by committing themselves to improving quality of life through a series of long-range programs, but they walk the same tightrope and face the same dilemma as their European brethren. Will the realities of attaining and maintaining power blur their original objective?

The Party

After 1976, the PSI leadership and intermediate cadres underwent a profound renovation, but not the membership. Even though the PSI has attained unity, major problems remain, and trends threaten serious consequences for the party's future.

Socialist membership has changed from a qualitative viewpoint, according to a study done by scholar Franco Cazzola in 1970. The traditional PSI worker component has diminished, and peasant members have increased, especially in the South. Rather than simple dissatisfaction with the PSI, however, Cazzola interpreted this development as evidence of declining political interest among workers. Cazzola noted the same phenomenon in the PCI. During ten years after 1970, the PSI's "southernization" slowed, but the worker component declined further to only 23.3 percent of the party.

Other negative long-term trends may also be noted: a decline in PSI membership as a proportion of population and decreased member participation in party activities. In percentages, the proportion of party members to eligible persons in the country dropped from 3.1 percent in 1946 to 1.8 percent in 1970. Furthermore, in 1970, Cazzola highlighted the socialist section's loss of vitality, and by 1985, the city sections appeared moribund; the provincial organizations, however, remained active.[2]

To a certain extent, these trends are common to all Italian parties although of most concern to the leftist ones. The decline in membership has also plagued the PCI, and in recent years political participation has also declined among the Communists. The problems of *L'Unità* have already been noted, while the socialist *Avanti!* has required drastic party intervention to save it. Plagued by dullness, the newspaper press of all the Italian parties is in deep crisis, read almost exclusively by a small core of the faithful and journalists who report party activities for other periodicals. Party intellectuals prefer to write for the wider-circulation national dailies such as the lively *La Repubblica*, the staid but high-quality *Corriere della Sera*, and Turin's feisty *La Stampa*.

Furthermore, the traditional electoral *comizi* have become less common and sparsely attended—replaced by television debates and advertising. Political participation in general has declined and become ''Americanized'' as Italian society has increased in complexity, become richer, and offered rival attractions.

As the level of active participation in the PSI declined, the party became further ''bureaucratized,'' while middle-class professionals increased both their numbers and control of local administration. Cazzola painted their protrait: older, possessing a university degree, belonging to the liberal professions, and holding political jobs. A 1979 survey confirmed these findings, emphasizing in addition the small number of women in the socialist hierarchy and the difficulty of attracting young people. Interestingly enough, although themselves middle class, the typical socialist *dirigente* was of worker or peasant extraction.[3]

Because of the corruption issue which has plagued the PSI, interest has focused on these local socialist administrators, the ones most involved in the scandals which have rocked the party. Because Socialists hold the balance of power and can ally in the periphery with either the DC or the PCI, they have participated in about 30 percent of the local administrations nationwide, even though they win about 14 percent of the local vote.[4] As a result, the PSI has more political positions available than personnel to fill them—the reverse of the case for Catholics and Communists. This situation attracts unqualified persons to the party because of the high probability of attaining lucrative political jobs—transforming the PSI into ''the party of the city councilors'' and fueling corruption. Given the city councilor's control of the great number of local projects, his intimate contact with local businesspeople anxious for contracts, and the ability to appropriate money, the number of tempting occasions is infinite.[5]

In the wake of scandals, the 1980s witnessed a push to renovate the PSI. Vice Secretary for Organization Valdo Spini considered the five hundred forty-one thousand membership bloated because uncommitted persons joined the party for political reasons; he aimed at reforming the membership procedure. He also emphasized prevention as a cure for corruption, rather than intervention afterward. Combined with greater powers, he believed that direct election of local PSI secretaries would reinvigorate and purify local party life. Furthermore, he insisted that the party should renew its territorial structure, either reactivating its local urban committees or encouraging imaginative policies by regional party organizations.

By resurrecting party life at the same time that a Socialist led the government, the PSI could ''filter'' the country's desires and sentiments toward the government, Spini believed. Spini thus linked internal socialist and general political reform.[6]

In order to implement these objectives, presented at a convention of local party secretaries in October 1983, Spini and Martelli proposed four basic reforms: a change in membership procedures, direct election of regional and provincial secretaries by the local congresses (reflecting the center), institution of an "internal magistrature" to prevent corruption, and replacing the Central Committee with a representative "National Council." Jokingly, Martelli said, "We want to create many Bettinos in the provinces."[7]

By the 1984 congress of Verona, the Socialists had implemented these reforms wholly or in part. Furthermore, they made a major effort to recruit new groups. For example, the PSI encouraged women to participate by instituting a minimum 15 percent representation for them on PSI directing organs and calling for further liberalization. As prime minister, Craxi demonstrated his sympathy for an increased role for women by participating in high-profile conventions on this issue. One of these initiatives, for example, involved Marisa Bellisario, dynamic head of Italtel communications.

The PSI continued to emphasize its strong worker connection, claiming a uniqueness among European Social Democrats in this regard. The party, however, declared that it would not limit itself to "organize the followers of an ideology, but intends to measure itself concretely in the reformist response to the problems of Italian society."

According to party documents, society's transformation dictated this policy. With the emergence of highly specialized professions, fresh values, views, life-styles, and expectations forcefully presented themselves. Since it wished to organize and represent these diverse new forms of being produced by modern society, the PSI no longer aimed primarily at political and educational socialization or at absolute consensus. Modern society demanded decentralization and a plurality of command centers. Reflecting this reality, the party required not "transmitters of ideological orthodoxy" but cadres capable of continually adapting ideology to reality through thorough analyses of shifting societal trends and an intimate understanding of their evolution.[8]

Although PSI pronouncements have consistently demonstrated a preoccupation with the quality of life—which remains the overriding concern of Socialists—party leaders have found it extremely difficult to institutionalize their ideals. Despite an understanding of the dilemma, Socialist party organizational forms seem suspended between the monolithic PCI model and fear of lapsing back into a squabbling, faction-ridden, politically weak organization.

Thus, the party has been accused—unjustly so far, but with a kernel of truth—of having become "the president's party." For example, political commentators observing the 1984 congress of Verona criticized the PSI for having staged an American-style political convention instead of an assembly where true debate occurred; even American embassy observers demonstrated concern at this trend. The Craxi wing responded that extensive internalization of reformist socialist principles by Italian society understandably reduced debate.[9] The principles have indeed become widely accepted, but this fact hardly explains the lack of life in the party. On the other hand, Craxi's tight control of the PSI has not prevented the left wing from speaking up. For example, it constantly requests revision of the PSI's relationship with the PCI, a position Craxi has lately encouraged.[10]

Unfortunately, Craxi seems unable to relax his tight control over the PSI, an understandable fear stemming from the PSI's past history and from his own precarious early days as secretary. This attitude has exposed him to severe criticism. During discussions for institution of the new "National Assembly" in March 1984, for example, his fiery friend Rino Formica walked out on him because the secretary-prime minister wished to nominate the one hundred "external" members of the new three-hundred-fifty-member body. Not necessarily PSI members, these persons would have some cultural connection with the socialist "area," and Craxi argued that they would infuse new life into the party. Craxi's plan, however, would have given him automatic control of the body.

Gently coaxed back into the room by Enrico Manca, Formica accepted a compromise agreement according to which the Directorate would propose the "externals," who would then be elected by the congress.[11] In October 1984, however, Craxi strengthened his domination over the party by establishing a restricted twelve-person "executive," each of whom would oversee party action in specific areas, and by parceling out seven of these positions to his loyalists. The same meeting demoted the hard-working Valdo Spini as vice secretary. A Craxi supporter of Lombardian origin, Spini owed his primary allegiance to the party. Craxi "Dauphin" Martelli became sole vice secretary ("vicar coordinator").[12]

Recognizing these problems, the PSI, in preparation for its March 1987 congress, issued a project for party reform inspired by socialist thinker Antonio Landolfi. This plan included two major innovations. The party would institute primaries of the American type which would allow it to test public opinion and permit the rank and file to express itself on socialist nominees for office. Presumably, this measure would encourage new talent to emerge and discourage corruption. In addition, the reform would create a network of clubs on the French model. Surpassing party issues, these clubs would be open to non-PSI members and discuss the great themes of modern life and society such as environmental affairs, disarmament, and the nuclear energy question. The clubs would replace the old sections, by now deserted and practically nonexistent.

It is too early to determine if the new PSI organs will resolve the party's fundamental organizational weakness, which represents the Achilles' heel of Italian socialism. This theme emerged strongly during my research, when I requested a number of important socialist observers to assess Craxi's methods, the party, and the future of socialism in Italy.

Antonio Giolitti

Spiritual leader of the PSI left wing and a major Craxi critic, Antonio Giolitti had just returned from Brussels after eight years as an EC commissioner when I spoke to him on a rainy evening in Rome, two days after Christmas 1984. Several times a contender for PSI secretary, a candidate for president of the republic in 1978, Giolitti saw danger signals in the PSI course in an October 1984 *L'Espresso* interview.[13]

Giolitti's critical perspective derives from his interpretation of objective conditions, his longtime militancy as a PSI left-winger, Lombardi's heritage, and membership in the older generation excluded from power by Craxi. Asked by me to give his opinion of Craxi's policies on the Socialist party, the coolly passionate Giolitti said:

> The Socialists . . . *do well* to be in the government, but it [the PSI] must not disappear as a party—that's all!
> The point of my criticism is above all this: there is a sort of party euthanasia. There is no more a Socialist party! I would like . . . to renew my contacts with the

Socialist party, [but] . . . either I speak with Craxi or to no one. It's useless to speak with Martelli or with Formica. . . .

What preoccupies me very much is that the Socialist party is no longer *an actor in politics*. There is an important political personality by the name of Bettino Craxi who possesses great political qualities, but there is no more Italian Socialist party; it is absent, I don't find it. I don't see it: I don't see it in Parliament; I don't see it as a transmitter of ideas, of programs; I don't see it as a party capable of selecting men . . . [or] political personnel.

The government reflects the country—only Craxi and not the party is "present" in the government, according to Giolitti. The leftist leader sees the PSI as having attained momentary prestige because its leader is prime minister, but what about the future? "This is a party which has lived in the past waiting for the conquest of this job, the presidency of the Council, and now enjoys . . . this position as the protagonist of Italian political life through Craxi's person."[14]

Giolitti argues that the lack of a well-qualified team of socialist ministers with a strong commitment to a clear program represents a major weakness of the Craxi government. This lack does not permit the nation to observe how socialist ministers undertake the task of governing—as distinguished from other parties. Giolitti wistfully recalls his own participation in cabinets during the center-left period, when socialist ministers coordinated their actions, discussed vital issues, and constantly fed their ideas back to the party, which listened and made suggestions. During that time, "there was a more intense reciprocal relationship between politics and culture." Under Craxi, one is hard put to name the PSI's ministers, so undistinguished is their action. What accounts for this state of affairs? According to Giolitti, it is "because everything pivots around Bettino Craxi." Giolitti exclaimed to me: "The *Socialists* in the government, not only Bettino Craxi in the government, the *Socialists*. That means a choice of ministers, a program, a commitment on selected issues."

"And yet," I reminded Giolitti, "the Socialist party has recently had a great intellectual thrust. I refer to the Project."

Giolitti agreed that the Socialists had made significant contributions to the debate on crucial ideological issues and governmental reforms, but he argued that the momentum had ended: "The Socialist party is no longer perceived as the carrier of these ideas. . . . the socialist party has to a certain extent committed suicide . . . dissolved . . . atrophied."

In Giolitti's view, it has become impossible to conceive of a PSI which is not in the government and does not have the presidency of the council. He cited the PSDI's unhappy precedent:

This party had its culmination with Saragat; it served to bring Saragat to the presidency of the republic, and then it ended. It became the 5 percent party; it no longer has any vitality; it is a party which can do nothing more than participate in the government. *It's clear, the Social Democratic party can do nothing other than stay in the government.* It cannot stay out of government, because outside of the government, it would disappear. It has no social basis. . . .

The Socialist party risks the same fate. It has attained the presidency of the Council with Craxi, and it ended there.

What about Craxi's plan of demonstrating how well Socialists govern, thus producing an electoral breakthrough? Giolitti compared this hope to drugging oneself. He argued:

> Yes, . . . the Socialist party lives for its expectations but does not work to create the conditions [which will determine] its political strength. Instead, the Communist party has been very successful at this. . . . The Communist party has always had this idée fixe, which, I remember well, was Togliatti's dominant idea: the essential thing is to put down roots—profound ones—in Italian society. Then you can have gains or losses in an election, but the important thing is to have roots in order to make the tree grow. Instead, the Socialist party did not make this effort to put roots where there existed a sufficiently strong trunk.

According to Giolitti, the PSI's electoral aspirations stem from a peculiarly Italian mentality:

> In Italy, there is this strange criterion of judging political relationships. It doesn't count so much whether you have 30 percent or 10 percent. What counts is if you go from 10 to 11, or from 30 to 28. Well then! [Up a point, down a point], the relationship remains one to three. The DC is three, and the PSI is one, even if the PSI increases a point in the next local elections—OK, things don't change much. But, ah! we're on the ascendant, they're dropping, so we're the winners. It's strange that the party which goes from 10 to 11 wins the elections, while the one that goes from 30 to 28 loses them. The Christian Democrats lose the elections? They're still a third of the electorate!''

But haven't social conditions changed, and will these changes eventually alter voting patterns? I asked Giolitti's opinion about the so-called disappearance of the working class. He answered without hesitation:

> I think that what the Socialist party has said and written has been hasty and superficial. Certainly, the themes of the working class and the class struggle in Marxist terms don't hold anymore, if they ever did. . . .
> Agreed, let's not talk about the working class in the sense which this term has in Marxist ideology, but . . . the condition of being a worker exists . . . the Socialist party can't say that the working class is a Marxist fantasy—we're modern, and we care about the new classes. Yes, we care *also* about the new classes and the transformations which there are in society, but—careful. Despite everything . . . there are always people who work in the factories who are called *operai*. Since there are workers, the Socialist party must also deal with this condition and with the opinions of this social category.
> This theme of ''new classes'' seems to me very fragile, very superficial, consisting of sensations, of journalistic judgments. An attentive study of what there is behind these expressions, ''new classes,'' ''emerging classes,'' it seems to me, has not been done. There is a policy of contact and linkage with these new classes, but no [theoretical discourse].[15]

Giolitti asserted that similar discussions about changing social and economic conditions occurred during the center-left, when stronger links between politicians and intellectuals gave the debate over economic planning greater force.

Giolitti grants Craxi his greatest merit in politics, where the secretary has liberated the PSI from its double inferiority complex toward Communists and Christian Democrats, but this greater autonomy, he adds, "has not become a political propellant; it has not been utilized toward great political ends. Politically, the Socialist party has not measured up to its role, to its history, or to the problems of democracy in Italy." This statement opened up once more the problem of the PSI. I inquired of Giolitti: "How do you explain the lack of opposition to Craxi within the party, and the lack of life?"

Eh! You pose a problem which I also [find] extraordinary and incomprehensible. Up to a few years ago, this was a party where every day there were [inaudible] and declarations. . . . Everybody had a different opinion on everything. It was a tower of Babel, a defect, an excess. And then instead, all of a sudden, nobody speaks anymore. *Nobody speaks anymore.* . . . No, the silence of the tomb. . . .

I explain it by the fact that in these past few years there has been a strong deterioration in party life; there has been this strong personality of the leader [in English in the conversation] which has exercised its function in a manner which is also authoritarian. It [this experience] might have been useful to renew the party's vigor and to affirm the party's autonomy, but there is the other side of the coin. Along with reaffirmation of autonomy, this political aggressivity of Craxi as a actor [*personaggio*], there has been this kind of silence which has spread in the party.

I followed this statement with a crucial question: "Do you think that a socialist 'base' still exists, that is, a base which is not interested in political favors?"

No. The Socialist party . . . has become ever more an association of political professionals at various levels—city administrations or public corporations. . . . There has been this race to participate in power. The . . . centers [*focolai*] of study, analysis, elaboration have dissolved. In effect, there no longer is a party life. . . . Members of the party who don't have political functions don't meet any more; . . . only those who exercise power at some level meet together.

Therefore, to answer your question, no, I think a base, a popular base, a base of party members—they're dead souls. They don't participate in party life. But it [a base] is there potentially . . . if a situation were created to reanimate the party's atrophied popular base. . . . There are people who want a party which is alive at all levels, not just at the governmental one. . . . [But] if the slumber lasts too long, perhaps when the alarm rings, no one will answer.

I asked about possible party reorganization, but Giolitti expressed skepticism and added ominously that the PSI's political space is in danger of being occupied:

The danger is, once the Socialist party as a reference point is lost, [its] public opinion areas, the people, the electors will put themselves on the sidelines. If the Socialist party disappears, for many this may mean abandonment of political commitment. They may not wish to go with the Communists, nor with the Christian Democrats. If one has socialist sentiments, if the Socialist party goes . . . nothing—he is left behind. I think there is a danger of "political nausea," as Benedetto Croce used to say, on the part of those for whom politics is the Socialist party.

To a certain extent, this is my case.

"But doesn't Craxi understand this danger?" I asked.

Giolitti responded, "It is a problem of character. . . . I think Craxi is driven by strong personal ambition at a high level—by a noble personal ambition. A man who wishes to become president of the Council is not driven by petty politics."

At the close of our long conversation, I asked Giolitti a final question: "What remains of socialism in Italy?"

> There remains . . . a sentiment, widespread in large strata of public opinion . . . of those social, civil, and political values which are assumed in the word *socialism:* greater liberty, more justice. greater honesty in government, the smoother . . . running of a complex modern society of the kind in which we live. I think that this widespread aspiration remains.
>
> Certainly, what I fear perhaps no longer remains . . . is the expectation that the Socialists are the suppliers, the formers, of a political personnel which is of higher quality than that produced by the other parties.
>
> The fact that the Socialists arrived in power the hard way—antifascism, the Resistance, jail—the road of a man like Sandro Pertini. . . . The people believe that if a person achieves power following the road of Sandro Pertini, they can have more trust in his honesty, in his capacity to make sacrifices.
>
> I'm afraid that this good reputation of the Socialists has to a certain extent been dissipated. Once it was expected that Socialists would be more honest than the others, more consistent, more faithful to certain ideals, that they held to certain values more tenaciously. This expectation has been deluded.

In citing Pertini as the model of the strict socialist morality, Giolitti emphasized the urgency of rebuilding this image if the Socialist party is to survive and flourish.[16]

At this point, it might be particularly instructive to illustrate a danger Giolitti cited: the disillusionment of capable persons affected by the Socialist party's "disappearance."

Paolo Flores d'Arcais

Craxi's PSI attracted many brilliant intellectuals such as Paolo Flores d'Arcais. In addition to Craxi, the "Socialist Project" drew their attention. This elaboration of socialist thought convinced them that the PSI could become a reformist party in competition with the Communist party, which they considered mediocre, corrupt, and bureaucratic. Flores d'Arcais, who never formally joined the PSI, considers the Project the high point of socialist reformism. From 1977 to 1980, he headed the cultural affairs section of *Mondoperaio* as part of the Craxi brain trust. Believing that the PSI did not live up to its reformist promise, he has become disillusioned and very pessimistic not only about the PSI's future but also about that of the nation.

Flores d'Arcais broke with the PSI in 1980, when Craxi brought the party into the government after an absence of several years. In a stormy session with Martelli, Flores d'Arcais objected to reestablishment of the center-left. No, Martelli rebutted, the Socialists had created the "left-center." Correctly so, Flores d'Arcais admitted to me, since, unlike the center-left, the Socialists had become the dominant partners of the coalition.

DC decline had made this development possible, Flores d'Arcais acknowledged, speculating that the DC may lose up to half its votes in the future and that these may indeed go to the PSI. For him, however, this consideration now matters little because he contends that the Socialists have lost their reformist charge. Nothing remains of the Project, Flores d'Arcais maintains. He takes an adamant position: intellectuals such as Amato who remain within the ruling group with Craxi have abandoned their reformism, while those such as Ruffolo who genuinely believe in reformism have little influence in the government.

In order to follow the Project road, Flores d'Arcais argues, the PSI had to stay in the opposition for a long time to establish its credentials as the true reformist party instead of the PCI. Rather than accept this difficult course, Craxi competed with the DC on its own terms. The PSI precipitated government crises and demanded the presidency of the Council, fulfilling its aim by exploiting its balance-of-power position. Given the Italian political situation—with the PCI's votes "frozen" and the DC in crisis—Craxi shrewdly seized his opportunity at occupying the country's highest office. As a result, however, Craxi became a Moro-like mediator.

Developing this comparison, Flores d'Arcais criticized Craxi's performance as prime minister. In the beginning, Craxi took hard decisions, but he soon discovered the inconveniences of "decisionismo." Mediating among the members of the coalition gained him more popularity. Consequently, Craxi dropped decisionism for old-style Italian mediation, increased his popularity, and dropped real reform. An example was the Visentini tax reform, so weak it would not be considered a reform in any other country except Italy.

Wasn't this the eternal dilemma? I asked him: if you maintain your ideological purity, you never come to power, and if you accept power, you lose your ideological purity. Understanding this dilemma and breaking the cycle had been Craxi's major merit, Flores d'Arcais agreed. For Flores d'Arcais, however, this "merit" lacked significance. He echoed the laments of other observers that the PSI had become a party of political professionals and that its base had dwindled. Radiating pessimism, completely disillusioned, refusing to believe in the PSI's capacity to reform itself or Italy, he declared that the massive inefficiency of Italian society bred plagues such as tax evasion and criminal associations. Declaring that society itself "illegal," he had completely given up hoping in change and dropped out of all political activity.[17]

Giorgio Ruffolo

Unlike Flores d'Arcais, Giorgio Ruffolo has remained active in politics. A major force behind the "Socialist Project," a disciple of Lombardi's, a friend of Giolitti's, PSI economic expert, and chairman of the Chamber of Deputies Finance Committee, Ruffolo has written influential articles that appear frequently in the daily press. A sophisticated thinker, the distinguished Ruffolo commands respect for his political achievements and as head of the Centro Europa Ricerche (CER), an economic forecasting organization. His opinions carry great weight in the Italian political and economic world.

Since Ruffolo began our conversation by noting CER's activities, I said that Italy must be particularly challenging, given the large extension of the *economia somersa* (underground economy). Ruffolo agreed, saying that while this phenomenon existed in all industrialized countries, Italy led other nations. The coexistence of advanced and backward areas and haphazard economic development characterized the Italian context. While the underground economy might have positive economic aspects, conferring great flexibility and powers of adaptation, Ruffolo maintained, it damaged Italian society because it generated an illegal labor market, exploitation of workers, and tax evasion. In this respect, the Italians had a more difficult problem than most Western countries.

This discussion brought us to the question of socialist reforms. Ruffolo maintained that the "reforming" Lombardian left—Lombardi detested the word *reformist*—and Craxi's "autonomist right" had fused. Ruffolo considered this development a positive one because these qualities marked the original aspects of socialism. Determined to create a "modern reformism," however, the PSI suddenly lost momentum. Ruffolo attributed this sudden lack of thrust to altered economic conditions in the 1970s: the oil crisis, inflation, unemployment. This situation discouraged the great structural reforms about which Socialists dreamed.

What about other reforms not dependent on these recessionary conditions—the bureaucracy, public administration? Italian society's corporate structure makes it slow and difficult to change—witness the Visentini package, where undramatic changes raised such a great fuss. Parliament is unable to put such legislation through, and the government must resort to decree laws.

How did institutional reforms fit into this picture? Political systems, Ruffolo answered, do not reform themselves drastically without great shocks. How did these factors relate to the Socialist party's inability to reform itself? Ruffolo argued that parties reform themselves and work out their programs when they are out of power. Given the Italian political situation, however, the PSI could not remain in the opposition long. Without the PSI, there could be no governing majority. Hence the PSI had to participate in governments; hence the impossibility of reforming itself.

From this situation flowed a number of problems. The PSI is a party in the government ("al governo") as distinguished from a government party ("di governo"). The PSI is thus in power with the DC at the center and elsewhere with *both* the DC and the PCI. This situation makes the PSI's political power much greater than its electoral base, favoring corruption. Furthermore, Craxi—"who also has a taste for power"—secured the premiership. To square theory with practice, the PSI argued that the country required "governability": "It made necessity a virtue."

Thus, Ruffolo said, although he is critical of the present-day PSI, he does not blame the party's condition on Craxi, although Craxi certainly savors power and is an excellent tactician.

There is nothing wrong with a political party coming to power, I responded, but one cannot mediate forever. After a phase of "decisionismo," is that what Craxi is doing? The leader of a country has to take some initiatives. What initiatives did Ruffolo believe Craxi had in mind? Craxi, Ruffolo answered, is not a man of "grand designs" but rather an excellent tactician. He probably does not have a design in mind and does not wish to be tied to one but wants to maintain his freedom of movement. He cited Craxi's action in the Visentini case—lukewarm at first, then inserting himself very well into the affair when he concluded that the nation supported the finance minister.

Reforms, Ruffolo argued, cannot come in Italy without leftist votes. But the PSI represents only 10 percent, while the other leftist votes are frozen in the PCI. The PCI is like an elephant, Ruffolo said, "majestic and impotent." These frozen votes make alternation in power impossible and make of Italy an "unfinished democracy."

But the Communists had begun debating reformism. Would they succeed in becoming a reformist party? The PCI is evolving, Ruffolo agreed, but slowly. It wants to march with all its arms, women, children, and camp followers, without losing anything. But the country cannot wait.

But in 1978, the Communists ran into international opposition—the Carter memo against them, Italy's lockout from NATO's Nuclear Planning Group. What must they do to prove that they are no longer dictatorial or tied too closely to the USSR? In Ruffolo's opinion, the PCI remains too "ambiguous." In its newspapers and its discussions, it continues to use "the pharmacist's scale" or to rely on "an adjective or a noun" in defining their position toward the Soviet Union. On the other hand, I interjected, the PCI is always clear when it condemns the United States. Ruffolo responded that no one asks the PCI to issue a manifesto renouncing Marx and Lenin but only to demonstrate greater objectivity.

As Ruffolo interprets the PCI's future, its dilemma is not whether it will march ("marciare") but whether it will rot ("marcire"). The PCI is immobilized by a recalcitrant membership blocking a progressive leadership. For example, if the PCI had not reacted harshly against the 1984 *scala mobile* decree—an essential measure—it would have faced revolt. On the other hand, the affair proved that necessary measures will be passed despite PCI opposition.

Thus, Ruffolo believes, leftist votes controlled by the Communists cannot be used to obtain reforms. Then where did the Socialist party expect to pick up the votes for reform? From groups in the DC and other parties supporting reformism, the CISL, the UIL, the socialist contingent in the CGIL, and the middle classes in Italian society, Ruffolo answered—in short, the coalition which put through the 1984 decree on the cost-of-living allowances.

Does this mean that the working class in Italy is "declining," as appears to be occurring in other Western countries? Ruffolo had no doubt. Thirty years ago, Socialists believed that the proletariat would become the "general class," but it waned instead. Alterations in PSI strategy aimed at ensuring that this development would not produce an angry, isolated workers' party, as appeared to be happening in England.

Given all these developments, what remains of socialism?

> Very little. Above all, its inspiration and its values, the hope for peace and a society based on greater justice and equality. This is a period of confusion, with the importation of neo-liberal ideas and the overthrow of New Deal principles. What is required is an amalgam of ideas—a rethinking of socialist ideals and their confrontation with the new economic reality. Everyone is attacking nationalization, public industry, and the welfare state. What is probably needed is a new version of liberal socialism.[18]

The Future of the Left

Ruffolo's call for a new amalgam of ideas has been echoed by many Socialists. While technological developments have decreased the proletariat's importance, Italian socialist intellectuals have destroyed Marx's heritage. Once uncritically wed to Marx, they have argued that turn-of-the-century revisionists have been proven correct and that the dictatorship and the terror which characterized Soviet communism represents the faithful application of Marx's revolutionary design, not a distortion.[19]

The present generation is living the end of a historical cycle, Luciano Pellicani, the dynamic editor of *Mondoperaio,* argues—the one opened by the French Revolution and characterized by the struggle of the disinherited for their full rights in modern society. As a result, at least some socialist values and traditions have been absorbed by Western institutions, becoming the common tradition of the left and the bourgeoisie, even of conservatives.

Thus, the very success of the "Social Democratic Revolution" has produced complex societies difficult to interpret and presenting a historic challenge for reformists. The decline of the great ideals which once stimulated leftist political commitment and participation has produced "the crisis of outlook in which the entire left finds itself and from which it can emerge only be redesigning its sociological map and updating its operative models and its political agenda."[20]

Exactly this concern has guided Craxi's PSI. Socialist initiatives in various fields give an excellent indication of the PSI's political agenda, while the discussion on deindustrialization, the effects on socialist theory, and the necessity of appealing to the "emerging" classes suggest a healthy confrontation with reality.

The Socialists have criticized the welfare state as not reducing social inequalities and frequently amplifying them. "It is necessary to overcome the model in which the state, and only the state, discovers all needs (present, potential, and latent) and supplies all services." This "busybody state" has proved psychologically debilitating, inefficient, and a failure in protecting society's weakest members. True to Italian socialist form, the party supports public industry and state intervention to aid the poor; but the Socialists seem determined to apply private standards of efficiency to public projects, make deprived recipients of public aid self-sufficient, and present the population with the whole gamut of options which modern society makes possible.[21]

Even if the Socialists did not have full power, the first Craxi government made a crucial beginning in this direction because, while most experts understood the terms of the Italian crisis, only the nation's first socialist prime minister took decisive action. This fact alone has had important consequences.

Traditionally, the end of August in Italy marks the restarting of the complex and cumbersome Italian political system after a well-deserved summertime hiatus, but 1986 appeared strangely different. After a long political crisis marked by a Craxi-De Mita standoff, Craxi returned to reap the fruits of his extraordinarily long and successful tenure in office. In fact, cabinet discussions which during the previous fifteen years urgently confronted fearful economic difficulties exuded optimism. The socialist-led government cut taxes and planned a 1987 deficit significantly reduced from 1985. Projections for 1987 indicated a 3.5 percent GNP increase and 4 percent inflation.

Critics argued that this scenario appeared overly optimistic. They pointed to the end of oil's precipitous price decline and Italy's continued high inflation rate when compared to other Western countries—but for once in its recent history, the nation could afford the luxury of two competing camps in economic policy.

Led by the finance and treasury ministers, the fiscal conservatives opposed letting up on the belt-tightening which, in a fresh "economic miracle," brought Italy back from an economic crisis unprecedented in contemporary Western European annals.

On the other hand, Craxi's Socialists argued that the time had come to spur further economic development through increased public investment, especially in the traditionally depressed South, and a reduction of social security levies on employers; government intervention to lighten contributions, paid entirely by employers, had halted spiraling labor costs by June 1985.[22] Rather than aiming at a neat balance sheet, the Socialists argued, the government should now concentrate on reducing the nation's high unemployment rate.[23]

Furthermore, the Socialists returned to the perennial problem of tax evasion. Attention focused on the tax system as a means of spurring equality. In line with socialist appeal to the new middle classes, Giorgio Ruffolo called for tax simplification, tax-bracket reduction, and stepped-up enforcement—an Italian version of tax reform being carried out at the same time in the United States. The major reason causing hesitation—fabled Italian administrative inefficiency—Ruffolo argued, should spur, not delay, massive financial restructuring while economic conditions permitted.[24]

With all this discussion, one special aspect strikes observers familiar with Italian affairs. Gone are the strikes, demonstrations, and political blackmail to which the opposition Communists regularly subjected weaker Christian democratic governments. Is this normalization of Italian economic dialogue a prelude to further normality in Italian political life?

During discussions which reconstituted his government, Prime Minister Craxi apparently accepted a March 1987 deadline, after which he would resign and make way for a Christian democratic premier. He was reluctant to accept such a condition on principle but forced to do so by reality, and the agreement has little practical significance. As already noted, Martelli had announced Craxi's intention to resign after the spring 1987 socialist congress to prepare the party for general elections due in 1988.

Since he became socialist secretary in 1976, Craxi aimed at liberating the Socialists from their intellectual and political subjection to the Communists, becoming prime minister, and translating the job's visibility into votes. He wished to reverse the electoral relationship between Communists and Socialists in Italy, transforming his party into a dominant political force.

While he succeeded brilliantly in the first two objectives, he is having problems with the third. While Berlinguer's Communists modified Marx, Craxi's Socialists demolished him; while the Communists remain hamstrung by the illogical thread they have woven tying Lenin and Western-style democracy, the Socialists have difficulty replacing their old gods with a commitment to Craxi's modern reformism. The result: a "crisis of outlook."

Despite Craxi's impressive performance as prime minister, this crisis has especially hit the Socialist party, essential vehicle to any electoral breakthrough. Despite its hundred-year tradition and its immense intellectual vitality in the past, the PSI not only appears adrift but perhaps confirms the old adage that sometimes "nothing fails like success." One of Craxi's closest supporters has warned him that PSI risks standing for "Partito del Silenzio Italiano."[25]

Craxi has attempted to remedy the party crisis through a rediscovery of Italian socialist roots, a linkup with Liberals and Social Democrats, and institutional changes. The liberal connection has revived the "liberal socialist" tradition and, as noted earlier, has led to cooperation on the potentially important justice referenda; collaboration with the Social Democrats has produced a closeness which may further Mauro Ferri's attempts to lead the Social Democrats into the PSI, thus strengthening it. In early 1987, the Social Democrats have become practically indistinguishable from the PSI, and Spadolini's

Republicans have made significant peace overtures.[26] These events strengthen the "laic pole."

Party alterations, however, have augmented Craxi's control, confirming critics in their charge that Craxi has transformed the once-proud PSI into a vehicle for his own personal power. The party's crisis remains grave, but no one should confuse cultural revival with resumption of the party's legendary tendency toward self-destruction. No socialist leader wants a return to the squabbling past.

The Socialists eagerly await Craxi's full-time return to party affairs to revitalize their organization. Socialists yearn for a return of the "movement" as distinguished from the "party." It is doubtful that Craxi can fulfill this desire, but he can take measures to encourage cultural revival, loosen his direct control, and make a determined and public effort to extirpate corruption in his party as a prelude to socialist mobilization for the crucial 1988 elections.

Finally, the Socialists should consider whether their conception of the party may not be based on a nineteenth-century ideal which they themselves have declared obsolete—a free association of disinterested citizens spontaneously giving themselves a superior organization and democratically ensuring changes through their possession of the key to the future. Trends in all Italian parties, including the Communist and Christian Democratic, parallel the Socialist party. With the accelerating modernization of Italian society, the parties appear subject to "Americanization"—decreasing individual participation and increasing professionalization. Furthermore, Mediterranean socialism in Spain, Portugal, France, and Greece has also been marked by the emergence of strong leaders. Italian socialism is struggling to deal with developments of this kind.

The highly structured and clientalistic world of Italian politics makes sudden electoral shifts of the American type unlikely, but Craxi has already profoundly affected the course of Italian politics. Most likely, his energy and newfound popularity will transfer to his party and increase its vote, provided he can put the corruption issue to rest.

It seems unlikely that the Italian electorate will fail to respond to the PSI's initiatives in the near future. The Socialists have demonstrated a capability of adaptation to modern conditions unknown to the Christian Democrats and Communists, former arbiters of the Italian political world. Prisoners of their respective interests and ideologies, the DC ruled Italy for thirty-five years but proved incapable of reforming the country, while the PCI dominated the left but succeeded only in frightening the nation. Challenged by a pragmatic socialist leader to aid in reform, these two forces confessed by their actions their continuing obsession with power. This realization has caused division in the PCI and heavy press criticism of DC Secretary De Mita.[27] In consequence, while the electorate has not rewarded the PSI, it has punished both DC and PCI.

Italian socialism has made an extraordinary recovery in the short decade since friends and opponents predicted its disappearance. In an even shorter time, it has challenged old political perspectives, shaken accepted norms, paced Italian politics, and set the national agenda. Once looking up to French and German models, Italian socialism has watched Mitterand's power crumble and distanced itself from the SPD after Johannes Rau's 1986 electoral defeat.[28] In the near future, Craxi may well become the leader for European Socialists to emulate.

Ideologues criticize current Italian socialism for its pragmatism and for supposedly having abandoned socialist principles. But if we recall that socialism began as a scientific

approach to improving the quality of life by adapting the conditions of modern technological society while preserving human freedom and intellectual integrity, and that this
search takes precedence over outmoded ideological considerations, we may conclude that
Italian socialist tradition continues.

While it is still precarious, the process of translating reform into reality has gained
momentum.

During the Renaissance, a noble asked his servant to plant an oak tree. "Your
lordship, the oak takes a hundred years to grow," said the servant.

"Quickly, then, don't lose an instant—run to plant it."

Epilogue

When I completed this book, a debate about the government which would follow Craxi's second cabinet raged. The PSI secretary did not renege on his agreement to support a Christian democrat as premier in March 1987, but a dispute occurred over the new government's head and its program. The person who seemed in line, Giulio Andreotti, ran into problems within his own organization and the Socialists demanded an early date for the justice and nuclear referenda which they had championed. As of March 1987, Craxi's strategy had not yielded substantial rewards in increasing his party's vote total.[1] Craxi opposed early elections because he wished to return to the PSI to gear it up for the next regularly scheduled national balloting in 1988. The other parties, notably the DC, however, feared his ability to revitalize his organization, which on the heels of a spectacularly successful tenure as prime minister might in fact translate into an electoral victory. This factor combined with a wish to delay the referenda as much as possible led the DC to favor early elections.

These elections alarmed socialist leaders who feared the party's lack of preparations and the communist comeback to center stage which the PSI-DC dispute had occasioned. If the elections produced only a slight gain for the Socialists, as recent local tests had and as critical observers never tired of emphasizing, they might have threatened Craxi's entire strategy. On the other hand, if the voters commended Craxi's performance and the Socialists made qualitative gains, the Italian political system would be on the eve of momentous changes.[2]

The 14–15 June 1987 national elections may have marked a watershed. In a country in which small vote shifts historically have had great significance, these elections suggested that the Italian electorate has become much more mobile and less ideological than in the past. The big loser: the PCI, which thus apparently paid for its failure to confront the PSI's new course adequately. Not only did the PCI do poorly among the workers, its bedrock support, but electoral analysis strongly suggested that the party's vote drop over 3 percent went to the PSI.[3]

It did the PCI leadership little good to deny this result. An unprecedented hail of rank-and-file protests demanded that the entire Directorate resign. Party secretary Natta first wavered, then secured election of Achille Occhetto as vice secretary and heir. For the first time, however, both PCI Directorate and Central Committee acrimoniously split in an open vote. This fierce "Battle of the Botteghe Oscure" sanctioned the existence of two official factions and shattered the antique Leninist principle of democratic centralism— which imposed unity by suffocating debate. Led by Giorgio Napolitano and Luciano Lama, the new minority PCI wing wishes to link up with the PSI and import reformism into the party.[4]

Despite these events, it does not appear likely that the PCI can recover easily. Unlike the PSI in 1976, the PCI did not alter its leadership after the electoral debacle, but confirmed it. If the party moves left, it will lose more votes and risk the fate of the French and Spanish Communists; if it moves right, it faces a freshly victorious and aggressive PSI led by a tough leader who has a proven record of accomplishment. In a debate with Claudio Martelli, the new communist leader Achille Occhetto demonstrated himself confused and uncertain, negating the communist crisis and claiming the Western European social democratic tradition as the PCI's own in a vain effort to avoid admitting the PSI's cultural and political momentum.[5] According to Luciano Pellicani, the PCI cannot pass from protest to positive action because all its classical theoreticians from Marx and Lenin to Gramsci have given it an ideology which "feeds on negation."[6]

The PSI emerged from the 1987 elections as the winner, increasing its vote total by about 3 percent. In addition to this numerical increase, however, several qualitative factors boosted Socialist party morale. The PSI gained a greater share of the eighteen- to twenty-four-year-old vote than the PCI (18.4 percent compared to 14 percent), making it the most attractive party to lefitst youth. The Socialists also attracted more women voters—the ratio of women to men rising to 45 percent to 55 percent as compared to 40 percent to 60 percent previously—and addressed a weakness which party leaders had universally recognized. In addition, most of the socialist electoral increase came from the center of the country northward, in the nation's postindustrial urban areas. Not only did this development create more of a regional balance in the PSI's support and halt the party's worrisome "southernization," at least for the time being, but it suggested that the modern sectors of Italian society may finally be responding to the party's appeal.[7] Furthermore, added to the smaller parties and the Greens, now apparently more receptive to socialist approaches, the "laic pole" neared 25 percent of the electorate.

Thus, according to the *Corriere della Sera,* Craxi had realized his two major objectives: breaking the bipolarism which subordinated his party to the DC or PCI and demonstrating his capacity to appeal to the communist electorate. The *Corriere* attributed the PSI's success to its proven capacity to guarantee stability while at the same time demonstrating its resolve for modernizing the political system. On the other hand, Craxi faced the dilemma of how to transfer these favorable factors to the practical political plane.[8]

After the elections, DC secretary De Mita claimed Palazzo Chigi for himself. Clearly riding the crest of the political wave and dominating the negotiations for a new cabinet, Craxi vetoed his rival.[9] At the end of July, he agreed to a cabinet headed by *demitiano* Giovanni Goria, former Treasury Minister in the socialist-led government, but would not consent to an explicit alliance. This attitude and Goria's colorless personality seemed to assure the cabinet a duration which would only allow it to conduct necessary economic business and to tread water until the DC's spring 1988 congress. As part of the negotiations, Craxi insisted on an early date for the referenda and took a number of steps which would allow the Socialists to dissociate themselves quickly from the government when the time came. By the end of the summer, the press gave the Goria cabinet low marks, and there were unflattering comparisons with the socialist-led government.[10] In September 1987, the following scenario appeared likely: After the referenda further demonstrate scant national support for DC positions, either a strong Craxi government will materialize, or more likely, new early elections will be held, probably in conjunction with the 1989 European Parliament balloting.

Furthermore, signs appeared that Craxi's DC nemesis De Mita was on his way out. The Christian democrats gained slightly in the 1987 elections, but only at the cost of heavy intervention by the Catholic church; this mobilization signaled De Mita's inability to reform his party and the DC's real failure to confront the new socialist course. Within the DC, De Mita's imposition of Goria as prime minister alienated Andreotti and other powerful notables, who expressed open dissatisfaction with the secretary during the party's national council sessions.[11]

In the meantime, Craxi dominated the political scene after the elections. He vigorously denounced both the Vatican for its interference in politics and Italian magistrates for their easy arrest propensities. Continuing his active foreign policy, he favored sending Italian warships to the Persian Gulf to join the Western allies in protecting shipping there; largely through his influence, the ships sailed in September 1987.[12]

Combined with politics, economic pressures promised to enliven the Italian scene over the short term. By late summer 1987, the boom showed signs of faltering because of political instability. Alarming signals of rekindled inflation, a growing trade deficit, a falling stock market, and increasing strikes produced demands for a return to stable government. At the same time, the man responsible for that stability, Bettino Craxi, cannot afford the perception that he is now breeding instability, nor can he allow time or events to dull the image of his remarkable administration as prime minister.

If Craxi can successfully juggle these contrasting demands and continue the task of revitalizing his party, he may well emerge as contemporary Europe's most significant socialist statesman.

Notes

Chapter 1

1. There is a moving version of Turati's escape in Vico Faggi, ed., *Sandro Pertini: Sei condanne due evasioni* (Milan: Mondadori, 1978), pp. 39–49.

2. Luigi Salvatorelli and Giovanni Mira, *Storia d'Italia nel periodo fascista* (Turin: Einaudi, 1959), p. 551.

3. Aldo Garosci, *Storia dei fuorusciti* (Bari: Laterza, 1953), pp. 32–54; Santi Fedele, *Storia della Concentrazione Antifascista 1927–1934* (Milan: Feltrinelli, 1976), pp. 22–27.

4. On Treves, see Aldo Garosci, "Claudio Treves, 40 anni dopo," *Critica Sociale*, 5 July 1973, pp. 289–93.

5. Frank Rosengarten, *The Italian anti-Fascist Press* (1919–1945) (Cleveland: Press of Case Western Reserve University, 1968), pp. 50–54.

6. On Turati's role in prefascist Italy, see Spencer Di Scala, *Dilemmas of Italian Socialism: The Politics of Filippo Turati* (Amherst: University of Massachusetts Press, 1980). On his activities in exile, see especially Alessandro Schiavi, *Esilio e morte di Filippo Turati* 1926–1932 (Rome: Opere Nuove, 1956), and the commemorative volume edited by Schiavi, *Omaggio a Turati nel centenario della nascita, 1857–1957* (Rome: Opere Nuove, 1957).

7. Salvatorelli and Mira, *Storia d'Italia*, pp. 561–65.

8. Franco Catalano, *Filippo Turati* (Milan: Avanti, 1957), pp. 305–6.

9. Filippo Turati, *Le vie maestre del socialismo*, 2nd ed. (Naples: Morano, 1966), p. 444.

10. Catalano, *Filippo Turati*, pp. 306–7.

11. The texts of Turati's speeches to the international congresses of the Socialist Workers' International in Brussels in 1928 and in Vienna in 1931 are in his *Le vie maestre*, pp. 457–67, pp. 473–81. See also Fedele, *Storia della Concentrazione*, pp. 39–45. The judgment I have quoted is Gaetano Arfé's, on p. 443.

12. Filippo Turati, "Ciò che insegna l'Italia," in Turati, *Le vie maestre*, pp. 445–56.

13. Renzo De Felice, *Le interpretazioni del fascismo*, (Bari: Laterza, 1976), pp. 201–4.

14. Giorgio Amendola, "Il tribunale speciale e l'antifascismo all'interno," in *Fascismo e antifascismo* (1918–1936) (Milan: Feltrinelli, 1963), Vol. 1, pp. 228–29.

15. Faggi, ed., *Sandro Pertini*, pp. 97–161.

16. Garosci, *Storia dei fuorusciti*, p. 60.

17. Leo Valiani, "Giustizia e Libertà," in 1945–1975, *Italia: Fascismo antifascismo resistenza rinnovamento* (Milan: Feltrinelli, 1975), pp. 153–67; Fedele, *Storia della Concentrazione*, pp. 73–116, 185–89; Salvatorelli and Mira, *Storia d'Italia*, pp. 591–92, 609; Garosci, *Storia dei fuorusciti*, pp. 55–79.

18. Gaetano Arfé, *Storia dell'Avanti!* (Milan: Avanti, 1956–58), Vol. 2, p. 14. See also Pietro Nenni's extremely positive judgment of the Concentrazione's work in "La crisi della Concentrazione Antifascista e la riclassifiazione dell'emigrazione," *Politica Socialista* 1, no. 1 (August 1934): 27–28.

19. Santi Fedele, "Gli anni del rinnovamento," in Arialdo Banfi et al., *Storia del partito*

socialista (Venice: Marsilio, 1979), Vol. 2, pp. 28–32. For a detailed discussion of Italian socialist organizations in France, see Luigi Di Lembo, "L'organizzazione dei socialisti italiani in Francia," in Istituto socialista di studi storici, *L'emigrazione socialista nella lotta contro il fascismo (1926–1939)* (Florence: Sansoni, 1982), pp. 221–61.

20. Giuseppe Tamburrano, *Pietro Nenni* (Bari: Laterza, 1986), pp. 3–6, 10–29, 40–56; Enzo Santarelli, "Nenni dal repubblicanesimo al socialismo (1908–1921)," *Studi Storici* 14, no. 4 (October–December 1973): 876–77.

21. Maria Grazia D'Angelo Bigelli, *Pietro Nenni dalle barricate a palazzo Madama* (Rome: Giorgio Giannini Editore, 1970), pp. 20–66, 72–74, 85–90, 95–99, 145–58; Tamburrano, *Pietro Nenni,* pp. 57–92.

22. Arfé, *Storia dell'Avanti!* Vol. 2, pp. 28–29.

23. Pietro Nenni, *Intervista sul socialismo italiano* (Bari: Laterza, 1977), pp. 43–48. See also D'Angelo Bigelli, *Pietro Nenni,* pp. 145–49.

24. Arfé, *Storia dell'Avanti!* Vol. 2, pp. 32–34.

25. Nenni, "La crisi della Concentrazione Antifascista," p. 28.

26. Arfé, *Storia dell'Avanti!* Vol. 2, pp. 37–47; Tamburrano, *Pietro Nenni,* pp. 107–8.

27. Ibid., pp. 48–60, for a description of Balabanoff's activities.

28. A Swiss court initially agreed with the maximalists but later reversed itself. When the newspaper was later published in Paris, the name had to be changed to *Nuovo Avanti.*

29. For the details of the Nenni group's action during this period, see Arfé, *Storia dell'Avanti!* Vol. 2, pp. 61–80. Turati's letter is reproduced in full in Turati, *Le vie maestre,* pp. 469–71.

30. Fedele, "Gli anni del rinnovamento," pp. 35–36.

31. Nenni, *Intervista sul socialismo italiano,* p. 51.

32. The texts of the Unity Charter and other relevant documents are in Franco Pedone, ed., *Il Partito Socialista Italiano nei suoi congressi* (Milan: Edizioni Avanti, 1956–63), Vol. 4, pp. 29–33. (Volume 4 was edited by Gaetano Arfé.) See also Fedele, *Storia della Concentrazione,* pp. 71–73.

33. Partito Socialista Italiano (Sezione dell'Internazionale Operaia Socialista), *Il congresso dell'unità socialista* (Paris: Imp. SFIC, 1930), pp. 4–5.

34. Ibid., pp. 10–11.

35. D'Angelo Bigelli, *Pietro Nenni,* p. 159.

36. PSI, *Il congresso dell'unità,* pp. 8–10.

37. Amendola, "Il tribunale speciale," pp. 236–37. Pertini confirmed this communist primacy in an interview with RAI television director Arrigo Petacco on 21 January 1983. (Mimeographed transcription of tape interview distributed by the Quirinale Press Office, pp. 21–24.)

38. Amendola, "Il tribunale speciale," pp. 237–38. In 1930, Italian police arrested GL's most important leaders in Italy. See Bianca Ceva, "Il processo di Giustizia e Libertà nel 1930–31," in *Fascismo e antifascismo,* Vol. 1, pp. 246–50.

39. Pedone, ed., *Il Partito Socialista Italiano,* Vol. 4, pp. 57–60.

40. Stefano Merli, ed., "La ricostruzione del movimento socialista in Italia e la lotta contro il fascismo dal 1934 alla seconda guerra mondiale," in *Annali dell'Istituto Giangiacomo Feltrinelli,* no. 5 (1962): 639–40. This is the archive of Angelo Tasca in the Giangiacomo Feltrinelli Library in Milan, with an introduction by Merli, also published separately as Istituto Giangiacomo Feltrinelli, *Documenti inediti dell'archivio Angelo Tasca* (Milan: Feltrinelli, 1963).

41. Rodolfo Morandi, *Opere di Rodolfo Morandi* (Turin: Einaudi, 1961), Vol. 1: *La democrazia del socialismo, 1923–1937,* pp. x–xiii, xvii–xxi.

42. Paolo Spriano, *Storia del Partito Comunista Italiano* (Turin: Einaudi, 1967–75), Vol. 2, pp. 374–89.

43. Pedone, ed., *Il Partito Socialista Italiano,* Vol. 4, pp. 67–69.

44. Spriano, *Storia del Partito Comunista Italiano,* Vol. 2, pp. 380–81, 391–92; and Nenni, *Intervista sul socialismo italiano,* pp. 51–52.

45. Pietro Nenni, "La lotta socialista contro il fascismo e per il potere," reprinted in Gastone Manacorda, *Il socialismo italiano nella storia dell' Italia* (Bari: Laterza, 1966), pp. 588–601.

46. For the pact's text and the accompanying socialist declaration, see Gabriele De Rosa, ed., *I partiti politici in Italia* (Rome: Minerva Italica, 1980), pp. 95–97. See also Spriano, *Storia del Partito Comunista Italiano,* Vol. 2, pp. 392–94.

47. For Modigliani's position, for example, see Partito Socialista Italiano, *23 Congresso Nazionale—3 congresso d'esilio* (Paris: Nuovo Avanti, 1937), p. 18.

48. Saragat also criticized the German Social Democrats in his "La crisi tedesca," *Politica Socialista* 1, no. 1 (August 1934): 60–62; see also Tamburrano, *Pietro Nenni,* p. 118.

49. Frank Rosengarten, *Silvio Trentin dall'interventismo alla Resistenza* (Milan: Feltrinelli, 1980), pp. 125–26.

50. Giorgio Galli, *Storia del Partito Comunista Italiano* (Milan: Il Formichiere, 1976), pp. 172–75; Arfé, *Storia dell'Avanti!* Vol. 2, pp. 101, 109–20, 138–55.

51. Carlo Vallauri, "Presenza socialista in Italia negli anni trenta," in Banfi et al., *Storia del partito socialista,* pp. 49, 53.

52. Pietro Nenni, "L'unità d'azione tra socialisti e comunisti," *Politica Socialista* 1, no. 1 (December 1934): 109.

53. Alessio, "Il fronte unico (dall'Italia)," *Politica Socialista* 1, no. 2 (December 1934): 176.

54. Merli, ed., "La ricostruzione del movimento socialista," p. 690. The protest which the CIS sent to the PCI's Political Office, dated 23 February 1936, is on pp. 718–22; Morandi's article, "Il punto di vista dei compagni d'Italia sui problemi dell'unità d'azione del Fronte popolare," signed "Valerio," appeared in the *Nuovo Avanti* on 7 March 1936 and may be found in his *La democrazia del socialismo,* pp. 156–59.

55. Merli, ed., "La ricostruzione del movimento socialista," p. 543.

56. Ibid., pp. 613–14.

57. Ibid., pp. 728–35.

58. Spriano, *Storia del Partito Comunista Italiano,* Vol. 3, pp. 18–39. For Nenni's remarks, see his "L'unità d'azione," *Politica Socialista* 2, no. 4 (August 1935): 299–305.

59. Tasca, who had become a French citizen and was influenced by a French socialist faction to which he belonged, believed that the Munich Agreement, which had brought about an Anglo-French understanding with Hitler and had isolated the Russians, must be paralleled by a socialist-inspired policy which would create antifascist majorities in the Western democracies extending from the Socialists on the left to antifascist conservative groups on the right, thus excluding the Communists, who were unacceptable to the conservatives. The Communists might, however, be allowed to support the coalitions from the outside. For the relevant developments, see Arfé, *Storia dell'Avanti!* Vol. 2, pp. 196–205, and Alexander J. De Grand, *In Stalin's Shadow: Angelo Tasca and the Crisis of the Left in Italy and France, 1910–1945* (De Kalb, Ill.: Northern Illinois University Press, 1986), pp. 138–39.

60. Merli, ed., "La ricostruzione del movimento socialista," pp. 809–10.

61. See the CIS's report, dated December 1935, in ibid., pp. 689–90.

62. *Politica Socialista* 1, no. 4 (August 1935): 35.

63. Joseph [Giuseppe Faravelli], "L'azione socialista in Italia," *Politica Socialista* 1, no. 1 (August 1934): 16–22; and Tasca's article "1914–1934" in the same issue, p. 15. Ironically, the Socialists objected to communist insistence that the pact be extended to "bourgeois" political groups considered inappropriate by the Socialists.

64. X. [Giuseppe Faravelli], "Il problema dei quadri (dall'Italia)," *Politica Socialista* 1, no. 2 (December 1934): 197–203.

65. Politica Socialista ([Angelo Tasca], "Il partito in formazione," *Politica Socialista* 2, no. 3 (March 1935): 197–203.

66. On this period in Rigola's life, see Carlo Cartiglia, *Rinaldo Rigola* (Milan: Feltrinelli, 1976), pp. 178–204.

67. Merli, ed., "La ricostruzione del movimento socialista," pp. 625–32.

68. Ibid., pp. 641–42.

69. The CIS's position on the Caldara affair can be found in *Politica Socialista* 1, no. 1 (August 1934): 37–41. Practically the entire March 1935 issue was written in Italy.

70. The CIS report is in Merli, ed., "La ricostruzione del movimento socialista," pp. 689–90. An example of the detailed questionnaires sent out by the Directorate is on pp. 638–39.

71. Arfé, *Storia dell'Avanti!* Vol. 2, pp. 130–35; and Pertini's interview with Arrigo Petacco, 21 January 1983, pp. 8–19.

72. Agostini, "I problemi della guerra (dall'Italia)," *Politica Socialista* 2, no. 4 (August 1935): 306–10. See the editorial in the same issue.

73. Antonio Pesenti, "L'avventura d'Etiopia," in *Fascismo e antifascismo,* Vol. 2, pp. 375–76.

74. Merli, ed., "La ricostruzione del movimento socialista," pp. 687–88.

75. For an example of the police's frequently successful techniques in infiltrating antifascist groups in Italy and abroad, see Domenico Zucàro, *Lettere all'OVRA di Pitigrilli* (Florence: Parenti, 1961).

76. Mario Venanzi, "Il processo Morandi," in *Fascismo e antifascismo,* Vol. 1, pp. 260–61.

77. Merli, ed., "La ricostruzione del movimento socialista," p. 767.

78. Ibid., pp. 754–57.

79. The PSI Directorate's report on clandestine activities in ibid., pp. 806–08.

Chapter 2

1. John Coverdale, *Italian Intervention in the Spanish Civil War* (Princeton: Princeton University Press, 1975), pp. 38–40.

2. Spriano, *Storia del Partito Comunista Italiano,* Vol. 3, pp. 85–89.

3. Coverdale, *Italian Intervention,* pp. 237–38.

4. Garosci, *Storia dei fuorusciti,* pp. 173–78. For events at the congress, see Pedone, *Il Partito Socialista Italiano,* Vol. 4, pp. 95–144. Tamburrano, *Pietro Nenni,* pp. 123–31, summarizes Nenni's Spanish activities.

5. Merli, ed., "La ricostruzione del movimento socialista," p. 839.

6. Arfé, *Storia dell'Avanti!* Vol. 2, pp. 212–17; Tamburrano, *Pietro Nenni,* p. 134.

7. Arfé, *Storia dell'Avanti!* Vol. 2, pp. 217–20.

8. See Denis Mack Smith, *Mussolini's Roman Empire* (New York: Viking, 1976), pp. 202–18. For a contrasting thesis, see MacGregor Knox, *Mussolini Unleashed* (New York: Cambridge University Press, 1982).

9. Garosci, *Storia dei fuorusciti,* pp. 206–7.

10. Mack Smith, *Mussolini's Roman Empire,* pp. 235–52.

11. De Rosa, ed., *I partiti politici,* p. 100.

12. *Stato Operaio* (New York) 14 (October–November 1940): 117–18. For Tasca's actions during this period, see De Grand, *In Stalin's Shadow,* pp. 155–68.

13. Spriano, *Storia del Partito Comunista Italiano,* Vol. 4, pp. 34–35.

14. Garosci, *Storia dei fuorusciti,* p. 206.

15. Rosengarten, *Silvio Trentin,* pp. 175–80; Ariane Landuyt, "Un tentativo di rinnovamento del socialismo italiano: Silone e il Centro Estero di Zurigo," in Istituto Socialisti, *L'emigrazione socialista,* pp. 78–80; Tamburrano, *Pietro Nenni,* p. 139.

16. Nenni, *Intervista sul socialismo italiano,* pp. 60–61.

17. Lelio Basso, "La ricostituzione del Partito Socialista Italiano," in *Fascismo e antifascismo,* Vol. 2, pp. 466–71. Basso would leave the PSIUP only to reenter it after receiving

programmatic clarifications and being assured of a prominent role by Pertini. See Stefano Merli, *Il "partito nuovo" di Lelio Basso* (Venice: Marsilio, 1981), pp. 16–21. For more "official" Socialist party interpretations of the causes of fascism, see Rosengarten, *The Italian anti-Fascist Press,* pp. 181–82.

18. Pietro Nenni, *Tempo di guerra fredda: Diari 1943–1956* (Milan: Sugar Co, 1981), pp. 31–33.

19. The declaration is in Carlo Vallauri, ed., *La ricostituzione dei partiti democratici* (Rome: Bulzoni, 1978), Vol. 3, pp. 1276–80.

20. The pact's text is in De Rosa, ed., *I partiti politici,* pp. 101–2.

21. Salvatorelli and Mira, *Storia d'Italia,* pp. 1050–54; and Peter Tompkins, *Italy Betrayed* (New York: Simon and Schuster, 1966), pp. 48–74.

22. The Italians continue to argue about these events with great vehemence, but good discussions may be found in Ruggero Zangrandi, *L'Italia tradita: 8 settembre 1943* (Milan: Mursia, 1971); Melton S. Davis, *Who Defends Rome? The Forty-five Days: July 25–September 8, 1943* (New York: Dial Press, 1972), pp. 403–36; Tompkins, *Italy Betrayed,* pp. 190–233. For Badoglio's version, see Pietro Badoglio, *Italy in the Second World War* (London: Oxford University Press, 1948), pp. 65–82. For an attempt at a more serene historical judgment, see Carlo Pinzani, "L'8 settembre 1943: Elementi di ipotesi per un giudizio storico," *Studi Storici* 13, no. 2 (April–June 1972): 289–337.

23. Ennio Di Nolfo and Giuseppe Muzzi, "La ricostituzione del PSI—Resistenza, Repubblica, Costituente (1943–1948)," in Giovanni Sabbatucci, ed., *Storia del socialismo italiano* (Rome: Il Poligono, 1979–81), Vol. 5, p. 80; Oreste Lizzadri, *Il regno di Badoglio e la resistenza romana* (Rome: Napoleone, 1974), pp. 153–74.

24. Roberto Finzi, *L'unità operaia contro il fascismo: Gli scioperi del marzo 1943* (Bologna: Consorzio Provinciale, 1974), pp. 66–69; and Paolo Spriano, "Gli scioperi del marzo 1943," *Studi Storici* 13, no. 4 (October–December 1972): 726–61.

25. Salvatorelli and Mira, *Storia d'Italia,* p. 1088.

26. Nenni, *Tempo di guerra fredda,* p. 50.

2. See Palmiro Togliatti, *La politica di Salerno* (Rome: Riuniti, 1969), pp. 5–41; and Aurelio Lepre, *Storia della svolta di Salerno* (Rome: Ruiniti, 1966), pp. 95–121.

28. Lawrence Gray, "From Gramsci to Togliatti: The *Partito Nuovo* and the Mass Basis of Italian Communism," in Simon Serfaty and Lawrence Gray, eds., *The Italian Communist Party Yesterday, Today, and Tomorrow* (Westport, Conn.: Greenwood Press, 1980), pp. 23–24.

29. Spriano, *Storia del Partito Comunista Italiano,* Vol. 5, pp. 332–35; and Nenni, *Tempo di guerra fredda,* pp. 62–64.

30. Lelio Basso, "Il rapporto tra rivoluzione democratica e rivoluzione socialista nella Resistenza," *Critica Marxista* 3, no. 4 (1965): 11–20; and Nenni, *Intervista sul socialismo italiano,* p. 64. On the supposed plans of the American government and their lack of basis, see Gaetano Salvemini and George La Piana, *What to Do with Italy* (New York: Buell, Sloan and Pearce, 1943), pp. 1–21; and Antonio Varsori, *Gli alleati e l'emigrazione democratica antifascista (1940–1943)* (Florence: Sansoni, 1982), pp. 262–70.

31. Nenni, *Tempo di guerra fredda,* p. 70.

32. Norman Kogan, *Italy and the Allies* (Cambridge, Mass.: Harvard University Press, 1956), pp. 56–62.

33. Nenni, *Tempo di guerra fredda,* p. 70.

34. Italo De Feo, *Diario politico 1943–1948* (Milan: Rusconi, 1973), pp. 120–21.

35. Nenni, *Tempo di guerra fredda,* pp. 84–86.

36. Giulio Andreotti, *Concerto a sei voci: Storia segreta di una crisi* (Rome: Edizioni della Bussola, 1945), pp. 15–16.

37. Guido Quazza, "The Politics of the Italian Resistance," in Stuart J. Woolf, *The Rebirth of Italy 1943–50* (London: Longman's, 1972), p. 21.

38. De Feo, *Diario politico,* pp. 153–59.

39. Nenni, *Tempo di guerra fredda,* pp. 100–107, gives a detailed account of the negotiations.

40. Arialdo Banfi, "Resistenza: Rivoluzione socialista," in Banfi et al., *Storia del partito socialista,* pp. 70–73; Stuart J. Woolf, "The Rebirth of Italy," in Woolf, *The Rebirth of Italy,* p. 216; James Edward Miller, *The United States and Italy, 1940–1950: The Politics and Diplomacy of Stabilization* (Chapel Hill: University of North Carolina Press, 1986), pp. 140–43.

41. Nenni, *Tempo di guerra fredda,* pp. 114–26; and Giulio Andreotti, *De Gasperi e il suo tempo,* 3rd ed. (Milan: Mondadori, 1964). pp. 214–15. The official Italian term for prime minister and premier is "president of the Council of Ministers." The English titles will be used to prevent confusion with "president of the republic."

42. Kogan, *Italy and the Allies,* pp. 122–26; Nenni, *Tempo di guerra fredda,* pp. 151–52; Miller, *The United States and Italy,* p. 182.

43. Franco Catalano, "The Rebirth of the Party System," in Woolf, *The Rebirth of Italy,* pp. 87–88. For a good discussion of Liberal economic policy and its implications, see John Lamberton Harper, *America and the Reconstruction of Italy, 1945–1948* (Cambridge: Cambridge University Press, 1986), pp. 137–58.

44. Arturo Carlo Jemolo, *Anni di prova* (Vicenza: N. Pozza, 1969), p. 245.

45. See *Quadro dei partiti politici d'Italia,* pp. 79–80. The Provisional Constitution's text is in Vallauri, ed., *La ricostituzione,* Vol. 3, pp. 1256–66.

46. Rodolfo Morandi, *Opere, Vol. 5: Democrazia diretta e ricostituzione capitalistica (1945– 1948),* pp. 54, 61–62.

47. Conversation with President Sandro Pertini, Quirinale Palace, 11 October 1983.

48. De Feo, *Diario politico,* pp. 276–78.

49. For the major entries in Nenni's diary dealing with the issues discussed above, see *Tempo di guerra fredda,* pp. 174, 189, 190–93, 198.

50. Giuseppe Romita, *Dalla monarchia alla repubblica* (Milan: Mursia, 1966), pp. 35–90.

51. Ibid., pp. 116–27. For an account of the buoyant effects of these local elections on Nenni, see *Tempo di guerra fredda,* pp. 205–7.

52. Romita, *Dalla monarchia,* pp. 226–36; and Nenni, *Tempo di guerra fredda,* pp. 224–30. The monarchists contended that the king had been cheated but left to save the nation from civil war. See Italicus, *Storia segreta di un mese di regno* (Rome: Sestante, 1948), pp. 12–13; Humbert's proclamation is reprinted on pp. 292–93.

53. Pietro Nenni, *Una battaglia vinta* (Rome: Edizioni Leonardo, 1946), pp. 72–77.

Chapter 3

1. Serfaty and Gray, *The Italian Communist Party,* pp. 26–27.

2. Archivio Centrale dello Stato (ACS), Ministero Interno, Direzione Pubblica Sicurezza, PSI—Affari Generali, fascicolo 175/P/93 busta 49, document dated 23 April 1945 (events refer to March 1945).

3. Giuseppe Saragat, "Programma," *Socialismo* 1, no. 1 (March 1945): 1–2.

4. Nenni, *Tempo di guerra fredda,* pp. 134–35.

5. Lelio Basso, *Il Partito Socialista Italiano* (Milan: Nuova Accademia, 1958), pp. 70–71; and Camillo De Bernardis and Raffaele De Mucci, eds., *Dalla resistenza alla alternativa socialista: I congressi del PSI dal 1946 al 1972* (Rome: IGI, 1976), pp. 6–7.

6. Pietro Nenni, "La classe lavoratrice nella battaglia per la democrazia," *Socialismo* 1, nos. 5–6 (September–December 1945): 1–3.

7. Di Nolfo and Muzzi, "La ricostituzione del PSI," pp. 92–93.

8. See Valerio Castronuovo's preface to Valdo Spini, *I socialisti e la politica di piano (1945-*

1964) (Florence: Sansoni, 1982), pp. vi–xi; and Nenni, *Intervista sul socialismo italiano*, pp. 70–71.

9. Conversation with Pertini, 11 October 1983.

10. Rodolfo Morandi, *Opere*, Vol. 3: *Lettere al fratello*, pp. 17, 63–66, 112–14.

11. [Morandi], "Presentazione della rivista 'Politica di Classe,'" in *Opere IV: Lotta di popolo*, pp. 56–57.

12. Morandi, "Difendiamo i comitati," *Avanti!* (Turinese edition), 25 July 1945, in *Opere*, Vol. 4: *Lotta di popolo*, p. 136.

13. Aldo Agosti, *Rodolfo Morandi: Il pensiero e l'azione politica* (Bari: Laterza, 1972), pp. 415–18.

14. Stefano Merli, "Dibattiti ideologici e politici nel PSIUP: Politica di Classe (1944–45)," *Rivista Storica del Socialismo* 1, no. 4 (October–December 1958): 568–69.

15. "Polo" [Morandi], "Lettera aperta ai compagni comunisti," *Opere*, Vol. 4: *Lotta di popolo*, pp. 61–64; and Agosti, *Rodolfo Morandi*, pp. 346–47, 375–80.

16. R. [Morandi], "Per un socialismo classista e collettivista," *Opere*, Vol. 4: *Lotta di popolo*, p. 54; and r. [Morandi], "Criteri organizzativi dell'economia collettiva," *Opere* Vol. 4: *Lotta di popolo*, pp. 65–69.

17. [R]ico [Morandi], "Politica realizzatrice," *Opere*, Vol. 4: *Lotta di popolo*, pp. 59–60; and Mauro [Morandi], "Idea e azione socialista," *Opere*, Vol. 4: *Lotta di popolo*, pp. 88–93.

18. Livio Maitan, "Romita e Morandi: Due testimonianze su un biennio cruciale," *Passato e Presente* 18 (November–December 1960): 2419–22; and Agosti, *Rodolfo Morandi*, pp. 417–20.

19. Morandi, ["Le vie della politica italiana e l'unità nel partito"], *Rassegna Socialista: Bollettino dell'Ufficio stampa del PSIUP*, 3 January 1946, in *Opere*, Vol. 5: *Democrazia diretta e ricostruzione capitalistica, 1945–48*, pp. 17–19.

20. Morandi, "Verso il congresso," *Socialismo* 2, no. 3, *Opere*, Vol. 5: *Democrazia diretta*, pp. 34–36.

21. Conversation with Pertini, 11 October 1983.

22. Rodolfo Morandi, "Questioni davanti al congresso," *Socialismo* 2, no. 4 (April 1946): 81–86.

23. Morandi, [Intervento al 24 congresso], *Opere*, Vol. 5: *Democrazia diretta*, pp. 70–74.

24. Rodolfo Morandi, "Dopo il congresso," *Socialismo* 2, no. 5 (May 1946): 113–15.

25. S. [Morandi], "Il partito e la classe," *Socialismo* 2, nos. 7–8, *Opere*, Vol. 5: *Democrazia diretta*, pp. 109–11.

26. Archivio Centrale dello Stato, Verbali del Consiglio dei Ministri, 21, 26, 28 March; 1, 30 April 1947. For the "Fourteen Points," see Morandi, *Opere*, Vol. 5: *Democrazia diretta*, pp. 166–67. The writers who consider them the beginning of a plan are Spini, *I socialisti e la politica di piano*, p. 17; and Agosti, *Rodolfo Morandi*, pp. 421–23.

27. Interview with Pertini, 11 October 1983.

28. [Morandi], "I consigli di gestione," *Avanti!* 17 November 1946, *Opere*, Vol. 5: *Democrazia diretta*, pp. 125–26. For the bill's text, see pp. 115–24.

29. Simona Colarizi, "Morandi e i consigli di gestione," *Mondo Operaio* 29, no. 11 (November 1976): 81–83; and Nenni, *Intervista sul socialismo italiano*, p. 71.

30. Angelo Costa, "I consigli di gestione sono di ostacolo alla produzione," in Centro Economico per la Costituente, *Convegno sui consigli di gestione: Il dibattito sui consigli di gestione* (Milan: Picardi, 1946).

31. Felice Vinci, "Piani economici e potere privato," *Avanti!* 11 May 1947.

32. Spini, *I socialisti e la politica di piano*, p. 16.

33. Morandi's speech to the First Convention of the Socialist Technical Groups in *Opere V: Democrazia diretta*, p. 188.

34. See Morandi's speech to the First Socialist Economic Conference, ["Piano economico e riforme di struttura"], in *Opere*, Vol. 5: *Democrazia diretta*, pp. 254–58.

35. Ibid., pp. 259–63.

36. *Prima conferenza economica socialista per la pacifica espansione del lavoro e delle intelligenze in una cività liberata dal bisogno. Rome: 1947–1948, Bolletino dell Istituto d'Studi Socialisti,* nos. 14–18 (1948): 25.

37. Ibid., p. 36.

38. Ibid., p. 38.

39. Agosti, *Rodolfo Morandi,* pp. 423–24.

40. Spini, *I socialisti e la politica di piano,* pp. 22–30, 40–41.

41. Agosti, *Rodolfo Morandi,* pp. 442–43.

42. Telegram no. 16475 from Prefect Antonucci, 30 June 1948, ACS, fascicolo 174/P/93 busta 49.

43. Morandi, "La politica del Fronte e il fatto elettorale," *Avanti!* 24 December 1947, *Opere,* Vol. 5: *Democrazia diretta,* p. 282.

44. Morandi, "Polemica con Riccardo Lombardi," in *Opere,* Vol. 6: *Il partito e la classe,* pp. 46–60.

Chapter 4

1. Giuseppe Saragat, "La premessa," *La Giustizia,* 25 April 1925, in Giuseppe Saragat, *Quaranta anni di lotta per la democrazia: Scritti e discorsi 1925–1965* (Milan: Mursia, 1966), pp. 5–6.

2. Giuseppe Saragat, "Massimalismo e riformismo," *Rinascita Socialista,* 15 March 1929, in Giuseppe Saragat, *Antifascismo Democrazia Socialismo: Pagine attuali degli anni dell'esilio* (Rome: Opere Nuove, 1951), pp. 106–11.

3. Saragat, "Marxismo democratico," *Rinascita Socialista,* 1 April 1929, in *Antifascismo Democrazia Socialismo,* pp. 117–24.

4. Saragat, "Democrazia e lotta di classe," in *Quaranta anni,* pp. 52–54.

5. Saragat, "L'Humanisme Marxiste," in *Quaranta anni,* pp. 119–27.

6. Saragat, "Marxismo democratico," pp. 124–26.

7. Saragat, "Noi e i comunisti," *Avanti!* 4 October 1939, in *Quaranta anni,* pp. 67–69.

8. Saragat, "Le illusioni del comunismo, *"Avanti!—L'Avvenire del Lavoratore,* 11 and 25 October 1930, in *Quaranta anni,* pp. 69–75.

9. Saragat, "Un tragico equivoco," *La Libertà,* 4 May 1933, in *Quaranta anni,* pp. 113–14.

10. Arfé, *Storia dell'Avanti!* Vol. 2, pp. 220–23.

11. See Saragat, *Quaranta anni,* pp. 216–220, 226.

12. Saragat, "La 'malattia del Secolo' del proletariato," *Avanti!—L'Avvenire del Lavoratore* 20 August 1932, in *Quaranta anni,* pp. 83–88.

13. Saragat, "Civismo," *Avanti!* 26 September 1944, in *Quaranta anni,* p. 258.

14. Antonio Landolfi, "La ricostituzione del Partito Socialista nel dopoguerra (1944–1946)," *Storia e Politica,* no. 3 (1964): 202–9; and Nenni, *Tempo di guerra fredda,* p. 152.

15. Landolfi, "La ricostituzione," pp. 214–17.

16. Di Nolfo and Muzzi, "La ricostituzione del PSI," p. 89.

17. Lelio Basso, "La crisi del Partito Socialista," *Quarto Stato* 1, no. 1 (January 1946): 2–7.

18. Maurizio Punzo, *Dalla Liberazione a Palazzo Barberini: Storia del Partito Socialista Italiano dalla ricostruzione alla scissione del 1947* (Milan: Celuc, 1973), p. 146.

19. Basso, *Il Partito Socialista Italiano,* p. 71.

20. Laura Conti, "Coscienza teorica e storica nel socialismo di Basso," *Il Filo Rosso* 8, no. 2 (January–April 1964): 43–46.

21. *Critica Sociale,* 1 January 1946.

22. [Lelio Basso], "Il convegno dei nuclei aziendiali," *Quarto Stato* 1, no. 11 (June 1946): 159–62.

23. Lelio Basso, "Per una moderna democrazia," *Critica Sociale*, 1 March 1946, pp. 71–72.

24. Merli, *Il "partito nuovo,"* pp. 54–70.

25. Merli argues against this position in ibid., pp. 70–71, unsuccessfully, in my opinion. I agree with Punzo, *Dalla Liberazione*, p. 205, who sees a substantial identity of views between Basso and Morandi.

26. Partito Socialista Italiano d'Unità Proletaria, *Progetto di statuto democratico del Partito Socialista Italiano* (Milan, 1945), pp. 1–38; and Landolfi, "La ricostituzione," pp. 220–23.

27. Punzo, *Dalla Liberazione*, pp. 202–4.

28. Nenni, *Tempo di guerra fredda*, p. 168.

29. [Lelio Basso], "Vigilia di Congresso," *Quarto Stato* 1, nos. 4–5 (March 1946): 45–47.

30. Punzo, *Dalla Liberazione*, gives a good account of these issues, pp. 133–41.

31. Nenni's report was reprinted as *Una battaglia vinta*.

32. Saragat's speech is in Partito Socialista Italiano d'Unità Proletaria, *Il 24 Congresso Nazionale* (Bologna: La Squilla, 1976), pp. 9–112.

33. Punzo, *Dalla Liberazione*, pp. 231–34.

34. Nenni, *Tempo di guerra fredda*, p. 209.

35. They are reprinted in PSIUP, *Il 24 Congresso Nazionale*, pp. 147–49.

36. The results were: "Base" (Nenni, Basso, Cacciatore—the left's motion), 46.1 percent; "Unified" (Pertini, Silone, Iniziativa Socialista—the center motion), 40.6 percent; "Critica Sociale" (center-right), 11.4 percent; "Genoese Federation" (right), 1.9 percent.

37. *L'Unità*, 18 April 1946.

38. Lelio Basso, "La scissione di Palazzo Barberini non si poteva evitare," *Almanacco Socialista*, 1978.

39. Quarto Stato, "Dopo il congresso," *Quarto Stato* 1, nos. 6–7 (April 1946): 77–78.

40. Nenni, *Tempo di guerra fredda*, p. 290.

41. The pact's text is in *Avanti!* 27 October 1946.

42. Punzo, *Dalla Liberazione*, pp. 297–300.

43. There is an excellent analysis of the results in ibid., pp. 302–6.

44. Paolo Moretti, *I due socialismi: La scissione di Palazzo Barberini e la nascita della socialdemocrazia* (Milan, Mursia, 1975), pp. 44–45, 104–6.

45. Nenni, *Tempo di guerra fredda*, p. 299.

46. Ibid., p. 302.

47. Pietro Nenni, "Perchè," *Avanti!* 22 November 1946.

48. Nenni, *Tempo di guerra fredda*, pp. 298, 299.

49. Di Scala, *Dilemmas of Italian Socialism*, p. 149.

50. See Giuseppe Averardi, *I socialisti democratici da Palazzo Barberini alla scissione del 4 luglio 1969* (Milan: SugarCo, 1977), pp. 32–34.

51. Moretti, *I due socialismi*, pp. 39–40.

52. Virgilio Dagnino, "Palazzo Barberini 27 anni dopo: Dal 'Centro Interno' alla costituzione del PSLI," *Critica Sociale*, November 1974, pp. 519–22.

53. Alberto Benzoni, *Il Partito Socialista dalla Resistenza a oggi* (Venice: Marsilio, 1980), p. 27. See also Averardi, *I socialisti democratici*, p. 28.

54. See the articles in *Avanti!* 3 April, pp. 1, 3, for examples of these charges.

55. Conversation with Pertini, 11 October 1983.

56. "Antonini inchioda Nenni: Lettera aperta sui 38,000 dollari," *L'Umanità*, 29 May 1947; and Executive Committee of the Italian-American Labor Council, "Perentorio invito a Nenni," *L'Umanità*, 13 June 1947.

57. William Colby, *Honorable Men: My Life in the CIA* (New York: Simon and Schuster, 1978), pp. 111–12.

58. "Dichiarazione per l'invalidazione del 25 Congresso del PSIUP," reprinted in Averardi, *I socialisti democratici,* pp. 38–39.

59. Letter of Giuseppe Faravelli to Vanni Montana, dated 14 December 1946, reprinted in Moretti, *I due socialismi,* pp. 204–6. See also Faravelli's letter to Antonini on pp. 207–10.

60. The "chronicle" of these meetings is in ibid., pp. 121–35.

61. Basso, "La scissione di Palazzo Barberini."

62. Sandro Pertini, "L'esistenza del partito deve essere difesa," *Avanti!* 9 January 1947.

63. Conversation with Pertini, 11 October 1983.

64. The motion is reprinted in Averardi, *I socialisti democratici,* pp. 30–32.

65. Saragat's address is reprinted in *Quaranta anni,* pp. 320–37.

66. Giuseppe Maranini, "Il partito nuovo," *Europa socialista,* 9 March 1947, reprinted in Giuseppe Maranini, *Socialismo non stalinismo* (Florence: Edizioni Alvernio, 1949), pp. 133–38. See also p. v of Saragat's preface.

67. "Composizione sociale del nostro partito," *L'Umanità* 25 August 1949.

68. See Antonio Valeri, "La crisi della libertà," *L'Umanità,* 11 April 1947.

69. For these estimates, see Averardi, *I due socialismi,* pp. 29, 42. The estimates vary according to the source.

70. Conversation with Pertini, 11 October 1983.

71. Quarto Stato, "Congresso di vittoria," *Quarto Stato* 2, no. 24 (January 1947): 2; and "R.P." [Raniero Panzieri], "Nuovo Periodo," *Socialismo* 3, nos. 1–2 (January–February 1947): 1–2.

72. Giovanni Sabbatucci, "Elettorato socialista e tradizione riformista: La scissione di Palazzo Barberini e le elezioni del 18 aprile 1948," in *Scritti storici in memoria di Enzo Piscitelli* ed. by Renzo Paci (Padua: Antenore, 1982), p. 535.

73. Nenni, *Intervista sul socialismo italiano,* pp. 83–84.

Chapter 5

1. Basso's interview is in *La Voce, Quotidiano del Mezzogiorno d'Italia* (Bari), 23 January 1947, p. 1. For his later judgment, see Basso, *Il Partito Socialista Italiano,* p. 77.

2. Pasquale Amato, "Gli anni del frontismo," in Sabbatucci, ed., *Storia del socialismo italiano* 5: 259–61.

3. Di Nolfo and Muzzi, "La ricostituzione del PSI," pp. 220–24.

4. "Parlano Saragat e Basso," *Il Nuovo Corriere,* 1 April 1947, p. 1; Santi Fedele, *Fronte popolare: La sinistra e le elezioni del 18 aprile 1948* (Milan: Bompiani, 1978), pp. 22–27, 49–50.

5. See "Le responsabilità di Basso nella scissione socialista," *Momento Sera,* 30 April 1947.

6. [Pietro Nenni], *Relazione del compagno Nenni alla riunione dei senatori e deputati del PSI, Roma, 14 ottobre 1948* (N.p.: n.d.), pp. 4–7.

7. *Avanti!* 17 October 1947; and Pietro Nenni, "La neutralità è problema di oggi," *Avanti!* 26 October 1947.

8. U.S. Department of State, *Foreign Relations of the United States, 1948, Vol. 3: Western Europe* (Washington, D.C.: Government Printing Office, 1974), p. 856.

9. Andreotti, *De Gasperi,* pp. 270–74; Miller, *The United States and Italy,* pp. 214–23. Harper finds no evidence that the Americans made the loan in return for an agreement to expel the left from the Cabinet—*America and The Reconstruction,* pp. 111–12.

10. Nenni, *Tempo di guerra fredda,* pp. 328–35.

11. Pietro Nenni, "Il governo è un posto di lotta e di responsabilità," *Avanti!* 2 February 1947.

12. Andreotti, *De Gasperi,* p. 275.

13. "I socialisti e la nuova costituzione" [Basso interview], *L'Unità,* 24 November 1946.

14. Lelio Basso, *I socialisti davanti alla costituzione* (Rome: dei Deputati Camera, 1947), pp. 8–9.

15. Paolo Vercellone, "The Italian Constitution of 1947–48," in Woolf, *The Rebirth of Italy,* pp. 121–31.

16. Giuseppe Saragat, "Storia di un tentativo per l'unità socialista," *L'Umanità,* 3 December 1947.

17. Nenni, *Tempo di guerra fredda,* pp. 363–64.

18. Ibid., pp. 357, 359–62.

19. "Un governo da rovesciare subito," *Avanti!* 31 May 1947.

20. Lelio Basso, "Logica di classe," *Socialismo* 2, no. 6 (June 1947), pp. 104–9.

21. "Filo Rosso," *Bollettino dell'Istituto di Studi Socialisti,* new series, 1, no. 4 (June 1947).

22. "Dichiarazione della Direzione del PSLI," *L'Umanità,* 1 June 1947.

23. Marcello De Cecco, "Economic Policy in the Reconstruction Period, 1945–51," in Woolf, *The Rebirth of Italy,* pp. 160–64; and Valerio Castronuovo, "La storia economica," in *Storia d'Italia: Dall'unità a oggi* 4: 376–83.

24. "Filo Rosso," *Bollettino dell'Istituto di Studi Socialisti,* new series, 1, nos. 8–9 (August 1947): 113, 115; and Pietro Nenni, "Per un governo di salute pubblica economica," *Avanti!* 24 August 1947.

25. Pietro Nenni, "Terzo tempo della nostra battaglia," *Avanti!* 15 August 1947.

26. *Avanti!* 27 July 1947.

27. Lelio Basso, "L'unità si fa a sinistra," *Avanti!* 22 June 1947; and *Il Partito Socialista Italiano,* p. 78.

28. Lelio Basso, "Il giorno più bello per la DC: Perchè io mi ero opposto all'idea del Fronte Popolare," *La Repubblica* (Rome), 15 April 1978.

29. Amato, "Gli anni," pp. 266–67.

30. Nenni, *Tempo di guerra fredda,* p. 413.

31. Ibid., p. 412.

32. Ibid.

33. For the 26th Congress, see De Bernardis and Mucci, *Dalla Resistenza alla alternativa socialista,* pp. 21–25.

34. Report to the Chief of Police, 9 April 1949, in ACS, Ministero Interni, Direzione Pubblica Sicurezza, fasc. 175/P/93, busta 49.

35. Interview with Pertini, 11 October 1983.

36. Nenni, *Tempo di guerra fredda,* pp. 354, 390.

37. Carlo Vallauri, "L'esperienza del 1948," in Banfi et al., *Storia del Partito Socialista,* pp. 90–91.

38. Giacinto Cardona, "Il Partito Socialista e il Fronte," *Avanti!* 15 April 1948.

39. Pietro Nenni, "Le elezioni dal '21 al '48," *Avanti!* 11 April 1948.

40. Pietro Nenni, "La prima vittoria del fronte," *Avanti!* 14 April 1948.

41. Pietro Nenni, "La politica estera del fronte," *Avanti!* 13 April 1948.

42. Mario Bracci, "America Amara," *Avanti!* 8 April 1948.

43. *Avanti!* 8 April 1948.

44. *Avanti!* 14 April 1948.

45. U.S. Department of State, *Foreign Relations,* Vol. 3, pp. 827–35.

46. Trevor Barnes, "The Secret Cold War: The CIA and American Foreign Policy in Europe, 1946–1956" *Historical Journal* 24, no. 2 (June 1981): 412–13.

47. Colby, *Honorable Men,* pp. 108–10, 112–14.

48. Pietro Nenni, "A una settimana dal traguardo," *Avanti!* 10 April 1948.

49. Interview with Pertini, 11 October 1983.

50. On the 1948 elections, see "Significato politico del voto del 18 Aprile," *Cronache*

Sociali, nos. 11–13 (July 1948); "Il Fronte Popolare tra USA e URSS," *Corriere della Sera,* 16 April 1978; "A trent'anni dalle elezioni del 18 aprile 1948: Intervista col Senatore Lelio Basso," *Com* [sic] *Nuovi Tempi,* 23 April 1978; Di Nolfo and Muzzi, "La ricostruzione," pp. 238–39; Giorgio Galli, *Storia del socialismo italiano,* pp. 195–96; Sabbatucci, "Elettorato socialista," pp. 530–32. The complete statistics for this election are in Italy, Istituto Centrale di Statistica, Ministero dell'Interno, *Le elezioni politiche del 1948,* 3 vols.

51. Nenni, *Tempo di guerra fredda,* pp. 426–27.

52. Pietro Nenni, "Meditazioni su una battaglia perduta," *Avanti!* 1 May 1948; Lelio Basso, "Prospettive del fronte," *Avanti!* 22 April 1948; Lucio Luzzatto, "Una politica giusta," *Avanti!* 23 April 1948; Giacinto Cardona, "Per difendere la democrazia," *Avanti!* 27 April 1948; Guido Mazzali, "Non distrarsi," *Avanti!* 28 April 1948.

53. Nenni, *Tempo di guerra fredda,* p. 426.

54. On the 27th Congress, see De Bernardis and De Mucci, *Dalla Resistenza alla alternativa socialista,* pp. 27–32; Galli, *Storia del socialismo italiano,* pp. 196–97; "Il PSI negli anni del frontismo: Interviste con Francesco De Martino, Lelio Basso, Venerio Cattani,"*Mondo Operaio,* July–August 1977, pp. 58, 62; and the report by Prefect Antonucci, in ACS, Ministero Interni, Direzione Pubblica Sicurezza, fasc. 175/P/93, busta 49, telegram no. 16475.

55. Galli, *Storia del socialismo,* p. 202.

56. Miriam Mafai, *Lombardi* (Milan: Feltrinelli, 1976), pp. 51–54.

57. Andreotti, *De Gasperi,* pp. 307–12. For socialist views of the event, see Nenni, *Tempo di guerra fredda,* pp. 444–47.

58. For an account of Directorate and Central Committee meetings during this period, see Nenni, *Tempo di guerra fredda,* pp. 447, 457, 464, 477.

59. ACS, Ministero Interni, Direzione Pubblica Sicurezza, fasc. 175/P/93, busta 49, Report from the Rome *Questore* to the Chief of Police, 9 April 1949, and report of the Naples Prefect dated 20 March 1949.

60. For the results, see De Bernardis and De Mucci, *Dalla Resistenza alla alternativa socialista,* p. 37.

61. "Il PSI negli anni del frontismo," *Mondo Operaio,* July–August 1977, pp. 59–60, 63–64.

62. Report of the Rome Police Chief, 22 May 1949, in ACS, Ministero Interni, fasc. 175/P/93, busta 49.

63. Quoted by Galli, *Storia del socialismo,* p. 207.

64. Benzoni, *Il Partito Socialista,* pp. 48–50.

65. Pietro Nenni, "I due aspetti della società sovietica," *Mondo Operaio* 5, no. 15 (August 1952).

66. Pietro Nenni, "Gli scritti di Stalin e il 19 Congresso del PC dell'URSS," *Mondo Operaio* 5, no. 21 (November 1952): 5.

67. Muriel Grinrod, *The Rebuilding of Italy: Politics and Economics* (London: Royal Institute of International Affairs, 1955), pp. 43–45.

68. "Il PSI negli anni del frontismo," *Mondo Operaio* July–August 1977, p. 62.

69. Amato, "Gli anni," pp. 309–10.

70. Antonio Landolfi, *Il socialismo italiano: Strutture comportamenti valori,* rev. ed. (Consenza: Lerici, 1977), pp. 80–90.

71. "Il PSI negli anni del frontismo," *Mondo Operaio,* July–August 1977, p. 62: and Amato, "Gli anni," p. 314.

72. Paolo Emiliani, *Dieci anni perduti: Cronache del Partito Socialista Italiano dal 1943 ad oggi* (Pisa: Nistri-Lischi, 1953), p. 29; and Galli, *Storia del socialismo italiano,* p. 207.

73. Landolfi, *Il socialismo italiano,* p. 93.

74. The relevant statistics may be found in ibid., pp. 97–100; and Amato, "Gli anni," pp. 318, 330–36.

75. "Il PSI negli anni del frontismo," *Mondo Operaio*, July–August 1977, p. 63.

76. Venerio Cattani, in ibid., p. 65.

Chapter 6

1. Conversation with Mauro Ferri, 9 January 1985.

2. Norman Kogan, *A Political History of Italy: The Postwar Years* (New York: Praeger, 1983), pp. 45–57.

3. Grinrod, *The Rebuilding of Italy*, pp. 113–14.

4. Riccardo Lombardi, quoted by Galli, *Storia del socialismo*, pp. 209–10.

5. Fernando Schiavetti, "L'attacco alla proporzionale è un attacco alla democrazia," *Mondo Operaio*, 6 January 1952, pp. 2–3.

6. Pietro Nenni, "Un problema di fondo," *Mondo Operaio* 5, no. 5 (March 1952).

7. Nenni, *Tempo di guerra fredda*, pp. 519–20; and Andreotti, *De Gasperi*, p. 421. In my conversation with Arthur M. Schlesinger, Jr., Schlesinger recalled the British Socialists as telling him in 1953 that the common view of Nenni as a "communist stooge" was mistaken.

8. Furio Diaz, "Dal frontismo all' autonomia," in Banfi, et al., *Storia del Partito Socialista, Vol. 3: Dalla Ricostruzione all' alternativa*, pp. 59–60. For Nenni's talks with the industrialists, see *Tempo di guerra fredda*, pp. 517–19.

9. Pietro Nenni, "Cause e sviluppi obbiettivi della politica di distensione," *Mondo Operaio* 5, no. 1 (January 1952).

10. Nenni, *Tempo di guerra fredda*, pp. 522–24. While the Nitti list lost, it still made a good showing by receiving 314,000 votes to the center list's 370,000.

11. Ibid., pp. 524–26.

12. Pietro Nenni, "Le elezioni del 25 maggio," *Mondo Operaio* 5, no. 7 (April 1952). In the South, the monarchist vote increased from 5.9 percent to 9.7 percent; the Neo-Fascists went from 276,000 votes in 1948 to 790,000, 11 percent of the total, in 1952. See Grinrod, *The Rebuilding of Italy*, pp. 75–78.

13. Nenni, *Tempo di guerra fredda*, pp. 527–28.

14. Conversation with Ferri, 9 January 1985.

15. Oreste Lizzadri, *Il socialismo italiano dal frontismo al centro-sinistra* (Rome: Lerici, 1969), pp. 243–44.

16. ACS, Ministero degli Interni, Direzione Pubblica Sicurezza, PSI, categoria K, Pacco 57/1, documents dated 18 June 1950, 13 June 1950, 14 December 1950; and Pacco 93, documents dated 24 November 1952 and 20 December 1952.

17. Pietro Nenni, "Validità di una politica," *Mondo Operaio* 5, no. 12 (June 1952):21.

18. Nenni, *Tempo di guerra fredda*, p. 536.

19. Pietro Nenni, "Bilancio di una polemica," *Mondo Operaio* 5, no. 12 (September 1952); and Nenni, *Tempo di guerra fredda*, pp. 546, 547–58.

20. Nenni, *Tempo di guerra fredda*, p. 548.

21. Kogan, *A Political History of Italy*, p. 64; and Grinrod, *The Rebuilding of Italy*, pp. 82–84. For Nenni's role, see *Tempo di guerra fredda*, pp. 552, 555–59, 561–63, and 569–71.

22. Giuseppe Petronio, "Alternativa Socialista," *Mondo Operaio* 6, no. 2 (January 1953).

23. Nenni, *Tempo di guerra fredda*, pp. 563–64.

24. *Il Popolo*, 9 January 1953; and *Il Messaggero*, 11 January 1953.

25. ACS, Ministero degli Interni, Direzione Pubblica Sicurezza, fasc. 175/P/93, busta 49, documents dated 9 and 12 January 1953.

26. Pietro Nenni, "La relazione del segretario del partito al CC," *Mondo Operaio* 6, no. 8 (April 1953): 4–6.

27. Conversation with Leo J. Wollemborg, Rome, 6 October 1984.

28. Leo J. Wollemborg, *Stelle, strisce, e tricolore: Trent'anni di vicende politiche fra Roma e Washington* (Milan: Mondadori, 1983), pp. 44–46.

29. Lelio Basso, "Il colpo di stato di De Gasperi," *Rinascita* 9, no. 9 (September 1952).

30. Conversation with Ferri, 9 January 1985. At the time of our conversation, Ferri was very close to Saragat and was authorized by him to represent his views to me.

31. Paolo Vittorelli, "Le elezioni politiche del 1953," *Il Ponte* 9, no. 1 (June 1953): 756–69.

32. Conversation with Ferri, 9 January 1985; and Andreotti, *De Gasperi*, pp. 457–60.

33. Nenni, *Tempo di guerra fredda*, pp. 581–83.

34. Andreotti, *De Gasperi*, pp. 470–74; and Nenni, *Tempo di guerra fredda*, pp. 584–85.

35. Pietro Nenni, "Incontro a metà strada," *Avanti!* 5 July 1953. See also the 4 and 9 July 1953 issues.

36. "La caduta di Alcide De Gasperi" [Editorial], *Mondo Operaio*, 8 August 1953.

37. [Pietro Nenni], "Promemoria per Piccioni," *Avanti!* 5 August 1953.

38. Nenni, *Tempo di guerra fredda*, pp. 588–89.

39. Pietro Nenni, "Quando la Provvidenza si chiama Togliatti," *Avanti!* 9 August 1953.

40. On the Pella government and the Trieste issue, see Kogan, *A Political History of Italy*, pp. 71–72.

41. Pietro Nenni, "Polemica cattolica sull'apertura a sinistra," *Mondo Operaio* 6, no. 19 (November 1953).

42. Conversation with Giuseppe Tamburrano, 18 December 1984.

43. Conversation with Wollemborg, 6 October 1984.

44. Conversation with Ferri, 9 January 1985.

45. Pietro Nenni, "I socialdemocratici e l'apertura a sinistra," *Mondo Operaio* 6, no. 22 (December 1953); also, Tamburrano, *Pietro Nenni*, p. 275.

46. Nenni, *Tempo di guerra fredda*, p. 606.

47. [Pietro Nenni], "Se no non vale la pena," *Avanti!* 15 January 1954.

48. Grinrod, *The Rebuilding of Italy*, pp. 104, 109–12; and [Mario Scelba], *Il programma del governo nelle dichiarazioni del Presidente del Consiglio On. Mario Scelba alla Camera e al Senato (18 e 26 febbraio—10 marzo 1954)* (Rome: Istituto Poligrafico dello Stato, 1954), pp. 32–36.

49. Nenni, *Tempo di guerra fredda*, p. 676.

50. Interview with Ferri, 9 January 1985.

51. Gaetano Arfé, "Frontismo, unificazione, alternativa," in Gaetano Arfé et al., *Trent'anni di politica socialista* (Rome: Mondo Operaio, 1977), pp. 16–17.

52. UGM, "Il compito di oggi e di domani," *Critica Sociale*, 20 November 1953.

53. Antonio Greppi, *La coscienza in pace: Cinquant'anni di socialismo* (Milan: Avanti, 1963), pp. 303–6.

54. Pietro Nenni, "Il congresso socialdemocratico," *Avanti!* 30 May 1954.

55. Averardi, *I socialisti democratici*, pp. 173–95.

56. Antonio Messineo, "Dopo le elezioni politiche del 7 giugno," *Civiltà Cattolica*, 27 June 1953.

57. Carlo Colombo, "Giudizi teologico-politici sui risultati delle elezioni," *Vita e Pensiero*, September and October 1953.

58. Nenni, "Polemica cattolica."

59. Giorgio Galli, *Storia della democrazia cristiana* (Bari: Laterza. 1978), pp. 164–68.

60. Riccardo Lombardi, "Alcune note sul piano Vanoni," *Mondo Operaio*, 5 March 1955.

61. Pietro Nenni, "Responsabilità della DC," *Avanti!* 27 June 1954.

62. Pietro Nenni, "Dopo il congresso di Napoli," *Avanti!* 4 July 1954.

63. Tullio Vecchietti, "Un congresso bifronte," *Avanti!* 1 July 1954.

64. Wollemborg, *Stelle, strisce, e tricolore*, pp. 32–33.

65. Giuseppe Tamburrano, *Storia e cronaca del centro-sinistra* (Milan: Feltrinelli, 1971), pp. 71–73; Wollemborg, *Stelle, strisce e tricolore,* p. 42.

66. Conversation with Antonio Landolfi, Rome, 18 December 1984.

67. Vittorio Foa, "L'ora del petrolio," *Avanti!* 18 June 1954; and the 6, 19, 22, 23, and 24 March 1955 issues.

68. Conversation with Professor Giuseppe Sacco, Rome, 30 October 1984. Although never proven, speculation remains rife that Mattei's death in an airplane crash was caused by sabotage.

Chapter 7

1. *Avanti!* 11 and 12 March 1955; and Nenni's editorial in the 13 March 1955 issue.

2. "Obiettivo dell' incontro coi cattolici sia la lotta contro la destra economica," *Avanti!* 29 March 1955.

3. Nenni's discourse is in *Avanti!* 1 April 1955.

4. Nenni, *Tempo di guerra fredda,* pp. 620–21.

5. Partito Socialista Italiano, *31 Congresso Nazionale del PSI* (Rome and Milan: Avanti, 1955), pp. 99–101; and Stefano Merli, ed., *Rodolfo Morandi, La politica unitaria* (Turin: Einaudi, 1975), pp. 271–73.

6. Conversation with Giovanni Pieraccini, 14 November 1984.

7. Conversation with Ferri, 9 January 1985.

8. Pietro Nenni, "Dopo il congresso," *Avanti!* 10 April 1955.

9. Tullio Vecchietti, "Significato del voto," *Avanti!* 30 April 1955; and Nenni, *Tempo di guerra fredda,* pp. 658–61.

10. Nenni, *Tempo di guerra fredda,* pp. 673–74.

11. Kogan, *A Political History of Italy,* pp. 84–85, 98.

12. Nenni, *Tempo di guerra fredda,* pp. 662–63, 665, 674–75. See also Tullio Vecchietti, "Incertezze di Fanfani," *Avanti!* 17 April 1955.

13. Nenni, *Tempo di guerra fredda,* pp. 667–68.

14. Kogan, *A Political History of Italy,* pp. 94–97; and Nenni, *Tempo di guerra fredda,* pp. 682, 713–15, 716, 720–21.

15. Amato, "Gli anni," p. 439.

16. Nenni, *Tempo di guerra fredda,* pp. 683–711; and Kogan, *A Political History of Italy,* pp. 100–103.

17. Report of the Pisa Prefect, dated 14 December 1955, in ACS, PSI, Affari Generali, fasc. 175/P/93, busta 49.

18. Pietro Nenni, *Le prospettive del socialismo dopo la destalinizzazione* 2nd ed. (Turin: Einaudi, 1962), pp. 16, 23, 31–32, 46–47; Nenni, *Tempo di guerra fredda,* p. 739; conversation with Ferri, 9 January 1985; Tamburrano, *Pietro Nenni,* pp. 281–83.

19. Roy Pryce, *The Italian Local Elections, 1956* (London: Chatto and Winders, 1957), pp. 97–102.

20. Nenni, *Tempo di guerra fredda,* p. 738; Pryce, *The Italian Local Elections,* pp. 106–10.

21. Nenni, *Tempo di guerra fredda,* pp. 736–37; and ACS, Ministero Interni, PSI, Affari Generali, Fasc. 175/P/94, busta 49, document dated Pisa, 23 June 1956.

22. Nenni, *Tempo di guerra fredda,* pp. 737, 741–45, 747–48. See also Giorgio Fenoaltea, "Il PSI e l'Internazionale," *Avanti!* 4 July 1956.

23. Valerio Evangelisti and Salvatore Sechi, "L'autonomia socialista e il centro-sinistra," in Sabbatucci, *Storia del socialismo italiano,* Vol. 6, p. 16.

24. Nenni, *Tempo di guerra fredda,* pp. 748–49.

25. "Le dichiarazioni di Nenni," *Avanti!* 28 August 1956.

26. Editorial, *Avanti!* 2 August 1956.

27. Tullio Vecchietti, "L'incontro di Pralognan," *Avanti!* 29 August 1956. In general, the left did not adopt the "conspiracy theory" put forth by Basso in his article commemorating the twentieth anniversary of Pralognan. Lelio Basso, "Il tessitore di Pralognan," *L'Unità,* 22 August 1976.

28. Lizzadri, *Il socialismo italiano,* pp. 379–80, 384, 386–88.

29. *Avanti!* 30 September 1956; Tullio Vecchietti, "Necessario chiarimento," *Avanti!* 12 September 1956; Nenni, *Tempo di guerra fredda,* pp. 751–52; Tamburrano, *Pietro Nenni,* p. 284.

30. Nenni, *Tempo di guerra fredda,* pp. 753–54; *Avanti!* 6 and 13 October 1956; and Pietro Nenni, "Su un mancato articolo," *Avanti!* 9 October 1956.

31. Nenni, *Tempo di guerra fredda,* pp. 755–56, 760–61, 763.

32. Pietro Nenni, "La corrente pura e la sporca schiuma," *Avanti!* 28 October 1956.

33. Nenni, *Tempo di guerra fredda,* pp. 754, 756, 759–63; "La Direzione del PSI sui fatti d'Ungheria," *Avanti!* 2 November 1956; "Una dichiarazione di Nenni," *Avanti!* 5 November 1956; Pietro Nenni, "Insistere e persistere," *Avanti!* 11 November 1956; and "Avanti, nella democrazia e nella libertà, per il socialismo," *Avanti!* 18 November 1956.

34. Tullio Vecchietti, "Il compito dei socialisti," *Avanti!* 30 October 1956; Tullio Vecchietti, "Quale alternativa?" *Avanti!* 24 November 1956; Tullio Vecchietti, "Polemica sul CC del PSI," *Avanti!* 20 November 1956; "Saragat ha confermato le dimissioni dal Comitato paritetico fra PSI e PSDI," *Avanti!* 14 December 1956; and "Il governo cede al ricatto dei grandi monopoli elettrici," *Avanti!* 22 December 1956.

35. Palmiro Togliatti, "La via italiana al socialismo," in Palmiro Togliatti, *Problemi del movimento operaio internazionale, 1956–1961* (Rome: Riuniti, 1962), p. 136.

36. Donald Blackmer, "The International Strategy of the Italian Communist Party," in Donald Blackmer and Annie Kriegel, *The International Role of the Communist Parties of Italy and France* (Cambridge, Mass.: Center for International Affairs, Harvard, 1975), pp. 9–12.

37. PSI, *32 Congresso Nazionale* (Rome and Milan: Avanti, 1957), pp. 90–147.

38. Landolfi, *Il socialismo italiano,* pp. 210–12.

39. Preface to Pietro Nenni, *Gli anni del centro-sinistra: Diari 1957–1966* (Milan: SugarCo, 1982), p. v.

40. Nenni, *Tempo di guerra fredda,* p. 761; Nenni, *Gli anni del centro-sinistra,* p. 56.

41. PSI, *32 Congresso Nazionale,* pp. 110–14, 116–21, 122–26.

42. Nenni, *Gli anni del centro-sinistra,* p. 10.

43. Amintore Fanfani, *Autunno 1956* (Rome: Cinque Lune, n.d.), p. 86; Tullio Vecchietti, "Sortire dal frigorifero," *Avanti!* 14 October 1956; Pietro Nenni, "La sola risposta possibile," *Avanti!* 21 October 1956; PSI, *32 Congresso Nazionale,* pp. 108, 143–44; and Nenni, *Tempo di guerra fredda,* pp. 760–61.

44. ACS, Ministero Interni, Direzione Pubblica Sicurezza, PSI, Affari Generali, Fascicolo 175/P/93, busta 49, document dated 27 March 1957 and marked "Visto dal ministro." Among those present at these meetings were: "Ravelli, agente di cambio; Mattioli, amministratore delegato della Banca Commerciale; Cominoli, commerciante in carbone; Rizzoli, editore; Marinotti, industriale." The house in Via Appiani, belonged to Dino Gentile, a major exponent of the Federazione per Gli Scambi Commerciali con la Cina; Gentile had close links with the textile industry and was very close to Nenni. At these meetings, Nenni also expressed appreciation for the politics of Fiat's Vittorio Valletta and for PSDI exponent Tremelloni's financial policies (Tremelloni participated in several cabinets). Nenni also stated that he was in close contact with Poland's Ladislaw Gomulka through Basso. (Basso had recently reentered the PSI mainstream on the left but maintained his staunch independence from the Communists and favored PSI autonomy.)

Chapter 8

1. Kogan, *A Political History of Italy,* pp. 129–46, provides an excellent analysis of the "economic miracle."

2. F. Roy Willis, *Italy Chooses Europe* (New York: Oxford University Press, 1971), pp. 158–59.

3. Nenni, *Intervista sul socialismo italiano,* p. 101.

4. Galli, *Storia della DC,* pp. 177–78; and Kogan, *A Political History of Italy,* pp. 123–24.

5. Galli, *Storia della DC,* p. 186; and Amintore Fanfani, "Italian Democracy Faces Another Test," *Foreign Affairs* 36, no. 3 (April 1958): 459.

6. For La Malfa's views, see Ugo La Malfa, "The Socialist Alternative in Italy," *Foreign Affairs* 35, no. 2 (January 1957): 311–19.

7. See Kogan, *A Political History of Italy,* pp. 120–23, 125–28. For the conservative opposition to Fanfani, see Panfilo Gentile, "Richiamo all'unità," *Corriere della Sera,* 21 January 1959.

8. Galli, *Storia della DC,* pp. 190–91.

9. Nenni, *Gli anni di centro-sinistra,* pp. 17–18; and Pietro Nenni, "Fuoco a zero," *Avanti!* 17 November 1957.

10. *Avanti!* 17 October 1958.

11. Basso, *Il Partito Socialista Italiano,* pp. 97, 141–56; and "La relazione di Basso," *Avanti!* 16 January 1959, p. 6.

12. Biagio Marzo, "Raniero Panzieri e la sinistra di classe," in Banfi et al., *Storia del Partito Socialista,* Vol. 3, pp. 77–78.

13. Partito Socialista Italiano, *Una politica socialista per il rinnovamento dell'azione di classe: Relazione del compagno Vecchietti al 33 Congresso* (Rome: SETI, 1958), pp. 10–11, 15–16, 19–22.

14. "La conclusione dei lavori del Comitato Centrale del PSI," *Avanti!* 31 October 1958. See also Nenni's report, Partito Socialista Italiano, *La relazione di Nenni al 33 Congresso del PSI: Confermare la linea politica decisa a Venezia, niente di più, niente di meno* (Rome: SETI, 1958).

15. The details are in Partito Socialista Italiano, *Libro bianco sull'illecita ingerenza dell'apparato comunista nel dibattito congressuale e nella vita del PSI* (Milan: Edit. Soc., 1959), pp. 2–24.

16. For the proceedings and related developments, see *Avanti!* 16–20 January 1959.

17. Nenni, *Gli anni del centro-sinistra,* p. 27.

18. "Il partito socialista e l'attuale momento politico," *Avanti!* 11 September 1959.

19. Giovanni Pieraccini, "Attila e le lumache," *Avanti!* 25 September 1959.

20. Pietro Nenni, "Il Congresso DC," *Avanti!* 11 October 1959.

21. Galli, *Storia della DC,* pp. 194–98.

22. Pietro Nenni, "Dopo Firenze i problemi rimangono e si aggravano," *Avanti!* 1 November 1959; and Nenni, *Gli anni di centro-sinistra,* pp. 79–80.

23. Nenni, *Gli anni del centro-sinistra,* p. 98.

24. Galli, *Storia della DC,* pp. 199–200; and Tamburrano, *Storia e cronaca del centro-sinistra,* pp. 27–34.

25. Nenni, *Gli anni del centro-sinistra,* p. 98.

26. "Michelini rivela che l'accordo DC-MSI in Sicilia è diretto ad aprire le porte al clerico-fascismo," *Avanti!* 5 February 1960. See also Tamburrano, *Storia e cronaca del centro-sinistra,* pp. 42–44.

27. Nenni, *Gli anni del centro-sinistra,* pp. 105–6.

28. "Tambroni ha deciso: Evitare alla DC ogni scelta politica," *Avanti!* 5 April 1960.

29. "Nella giusta direzione," *Avanti!* 15 April 1960; "Appuntamento con la chiarezza," *Avanti!* 16 April 1960.

30. Nenni, *Gli anni del centro-sinistra,* pp. 112–14; Galli, *Storia della DC,* pp. 200–201;

"Dietro l'ombra di un dito" and "Fin da ieri mattina la stampa di destra esortava i parlamentari dc alla ribellione," *Avanti!* 23 April 1960. Cardinal Siri was the chairman of the Bishops' Commission, and Cardinal Ottaviani belonged to the Curia.

31. Nenni, *Gli anni del centro-sinistra,* p. 114; Tamburrano, *Storia e cronaca del centro sinistra,* pp. 46–47.

32. Conversation with Wollemborg, 6 October 1984; Tamburrano. *Storia e cronaca del centro-sinistra,* pp. 48–49; Galli, *Storia della DC,* p. 464; and Giuseppe De Lutiis, *Storia dei servizi segreti in Italia* (Rome: Riuniti, 1984), pp. 57–61.

33. Pietro Nenni, "Spezzare la catena," *Avanti!* 10 July 1960; Nenni, *Gli anni del centro-sinistra,* p. 130; Giovanni Pieraccini, "Una pagina chiusa," *Avanti!* 14 July 1960; Tamburrano, *Pietro Nenni,* pp. 298–300.

34. Pietro Nenni, "Il punto aquisito," *Avanti!* 7 August 1960.

35. Pietro Nenni, "Perchè si parla di emergenza e di tregua," *Avanti!* 24 July 1960.

36. Giovanni Pieraccini, "La decisione del Comitato Centrale," *Avanti!* 4 August 1960; and "La risoluzione approvata dal Comitato Centrale del PSI," in the same issue; Nenni, *Gli anni del centro-sinistra,* pp. 135–37.

37. "La nostra battaglia," *Avanti!* 7 September 1960; and Nenni, *Gli anni del centro-sinistra,* p. 143. A description of the reforms of this period is in Kogan, *A Political History of Italy,* pp. 162–63.

38. Tamburrano, *Storia e cronaca del centro-sinistra,* pp. 53–55.

39. Clare Boothe Luce, "Italy after One Hundred Years," *Foreign Affairs* 39, no. 2 (January 1961): 235–36; telephone conversation with Robert Komer, 7 October 1985; and Wollemborg, *Stelle, strisce e tricolore,* pp. 27–29.

40. Colby, *Honorable Men,* p. 125.

41. Ibid., pp. 125–28; and telephone conversation with Komer, 7 October 1985.

42. Conversation with John Di Sciullo, Washington, 15 May 1985.

43. Alan Arthur Platt, "United States Policy toward 'The Opening to the Left' in Italy," Ph.D. dissertation, Columbia University, 1973, p. 115.

44. Conversation with Arthur M. Schlesinger, Jr., New York, 25 June 1985.

45. "Memo for JFK from Arthur Schlesinger, Jr.," 8 June 1961, John F. Kennedy Library, Box 12: Schlesinger Papers, Italy, June–December 1961.

46. "Suggested Remarks to Be Made by the Vice President at the Italy-America Dinner in New York City, June 15, 1961," JFK Library, Box 12: Schlesinger Papers, Italy, June–December 1961.

47. William Fraleigh, recorded by Joseph E. O'Connor, Rome, November 1966, p. 16, John F. Kennedy Oral History Program; and Memorandum of Conversation (Memcon), Harriman and Gronchi, Quirinale Palace, 9 March 1961, JFK Library, Box 120: NSF: CO: Italy, March 1961–December 1961; and Arthur Schlesinger, Jr., "Memorandum to Richard Goodwin," 15 November 1961, JFK Library, Box 12: Schlesinger Papers, Italy, June–December 1961.

48. Letter to Walt W. Rostow from Nando Cravieri (Italconsult), dated 3 November 1961, JFK Library, Box 12: Schlesinger Papers, Italy, June–December 1961.

49. Memcons with Saragat, Fanfani, and Gronchi, 9 and 11 March 1961, JFK Library, Box 120: NSF: CO: Italy, March 1961–December 1961. All of these memoranda are heavily "sanitized," as are other important documents obtained by the author under the Freedom of Information Act and Executive Order 12065. Government authorities denied my appeals for numerous other documents as well, and a new Executive Order issued by President Reagan has made it practically impossible for researchers to obtain declassification of documents classified more than twenty years earlier.

50. Conversation with Schlesinger, 25 June 1985.

51. Wollemborg, *Stelle, strisce e tricolore,* pp. 111–13; and Platt, "United States Policy Towards 'The Opening to the Left,'" pp. 116–21.

52. James E. King, Jr., "Notes on Italian-American Relations Based upon a Visit to Italy, April 20–28, 1961," JFK Library, Box 120: NSF: CO: Italy, March 1961–December 1961.

53. Pietro Nenni, "Where the Italian Socialists Stand," *Foreign Affairs* 40, no. 2 (January 1962): 213–23.

54. Platt, "United States Policy toward 'The Opening to the Left,'" pp. 137–42; Arthur M. Schlesinger, Jr., *A Thousand Days* (Boston: Houghton Mifflin, 1965), p. 876; and conversation with Schlesinger, 25 June 1985.

55. Mario Margiocco, *Stati Uniti e PCI* (Bari: Laterza, 1981), pp. 90–91.

56. King, "Notes on Italian-American Relations," p. 1e.

57. Conversation with Wollemborg, 6 October 1984; Wollemborg, *Stelle, strisce e tricolore*, p. 120.

58. Outerbridge Horsey, recorded by William W. Moss, John F. Kennedy Library Oral History Program, 15 April 1971, pp. 1–2.

59. Frederick G. Reinhardt, recorded by Joseph E. O'Connor, John F. Kennedy Library Oral History Program, November 1966, pp. 3–5.

60. See Platt, "United States Policy toward 'The Opening to the Left,'" pp. 147–48; Roger Hilsman, "Memorandum for Arthur M. Schlesinger, Jr., the White House," dated 23 December 1961, JFK Library, Box 120: NSF: CO: Italy, March 1961–December 1961; U.S. Department of State, Bureau of Intelligence and Research, Research Memorandum, REU-22, 19 January 1962, in JFK Library, Box 120: NSF: CO: Italy, June 1962–October 1962; see pp. 4–7 of the NIE, in the same box. See also William E. Knight's paper to the American Enterprise Institute/Hoover Foundation Conference on "Italy and Eurocommunism" (Washington, D.C., 7–9 June 1977), Kennedy Library.

61. The fragment (pp. 2, 5, and 6 of six pages) is unsigned and undated. On the basis of internal evidence, I believe it to have been written by Schlesinger, although he did not recall it when I asked him about it. On the other hand, Schlesinger believes covert aid started in 1963. The document is in Box 12: Schlesinger Papers, Italy, 1962, and was probably drafted between mid-August and September 1962. Roberto Faenza, *Il Malaffare: Dall'America di Kennedy all'Italia, a Cuba, al Vietnam* (Milan: Mondadori, 1978), pp. 346–48, intimates that the "Schlesinger group," funneled funds to the PSI through American oil companies operating in Italy," but Schlesinger himself told me that funds were not given to the PSI while he was in the government, so far as he knows. I might add that there are four boxes of secret Schlesinger papers at the JFK Library which are not open to researchers. On Knight's citation of supposed Italian-American opposition to the center-left (which was, in fact, negligible), see William E. Knight, recorded by Sheldon Stern, John F. Kennedy Library Oral History Program, 18 May 1978, p. 11.

62. Arthur Schlesinger, Jr., "Memorandum for the President," dated 3 July 1963, JFK Library, Box 12: Schlesinger Papers, Italy, January 1963–January 1964.

63. The source has asked not to be named.

64. William E. Knight, recorded by Sheldon Stern, John F. Kennedy Library Oral History Program, 18 May 1978, pp. 18–19.

65. Conversation with Schlesinger, 25 June 1985.

66. William Fraleigh, recorded by Joseph E. O'Connor, November 1966, pp. 11, 16; Nenni, *Gli anni del centro-sinistra*, pp. 288–89; Schlesinger conversation, 25 June 1985; Pertini interview, 11 October 1983.

67. Platt, "United States Policy toward 'The Opening to the Left,'" p. 168; and De Lutiis, *Storia dei servizi segreti*, pp. 69–70; Vernon A. Walters, *Silent Missions* (Garden City, N.Y.: Doubleday, 1978), p. 357. On his association with De Lorenzo, see pp. 351–54, 356. On pp. 362–63, Walters recounts that he served as an interpreter between President Segni and Schlesinger during one of the latter's trips to Rome. Schlesinger allegedly prevailed on a reluctant Segni to give him his personal views on Italian politicians for Kennedy's ears only, after which he published them. According to Walters, this incident caused a great furor in Italy, demands for Segni's

resignation, and Segni's stroke and death. According to Schlesinger, "the whole thing is total fantasy." Schlesinger informed me that he extracted a letter from Walters saying that the story was wrong and apologizing for ever having published it. (Segni did have a stroke, but not as the result of this alleged incident.) I wrote a letter and telephoned several times to set up an appointment to speak with Walters about the issues raised in this book but was unable to secure one.

68. Nenni, *Gli anni del centro sinistra,* p. 148.

69. Memcon, "Mattei and ENI," dated 17 March 1962, in the author's possession; State Department telegram no. 2668 from Secretary of State Dean Rusk, embassy telegram no. 16588 from Ambassador Reinhardt to Rusk, and Department of State telegram no. 3729 from Under Secretary McGhee to Reinhardt, in JFK Library, Box 120: NSF: CO: Italy, January 1962–October 1962. For details of the actual agreement between ENI and Stott, see the Department of State telegram dated 20 March in the same box.

70. Luce's letter, dated 5 February 1963, is in JFK Library, President's Office Files, Special Correspondence, Box 31, Folder: Luce: Henry R. and Clare Boothe, 22 January–23 August 1963, Document 2A. The replies of McGeorge Bundy and President Kennedy are located in the same folder. JFK's staff had prepared a report on the unfriendly manner in which Henry Luce's *Time* had treated the administration. See this "Content Analysis" and the memo from Theodore C. Sorensen in the same box, folder dated 14 March 1959–31 December 1962.

Chapter 9

1. "Relazione di attivtà del Comitato Centrale al 34 Congresso del PSI," *Avanti!* 10 January 1961.

2. Pietro Nenni, "Problemi e prospettive della democrazia e del socialismo: Relazione al 34 Congresso del PSI (Rome: PSI, 1961), pp. 27–40.

3. Nenni, *Gli anni del centro-sinistra,* p. 168.

4. Evangelisti and Sechi, "L'autonomia socialista e il centro sinistra," in Sabbatucci, ed., *Storia del socialismo italiano,* Vol. 6, pp. 67–68.

5. Tamburrano, *Storia e cronaca del centro-sinistra,* pp. 100–13; and the mimeographed document sent to the PSI's Program Commission, Prot. n. 8283, circ. no. 124, dated 23 June 1960 (Rome, Lelio Basso Library).

6. "Il programma del PSI per una nuova politica economica," *Avanti!* 5 January 1962; and "Il dibattito al Comitato Centrale del Partito Socialista Italiano," *Avanti!* 11 January 1962.

7. Galli, *Storia della DC,* pp. 210–11.

8. "Il CC socialista conferma: Giudizio positivo sul programma," *Avanti!* 20 February 1962, and *Avanti!* 4 March 1962; and Nenni, *Gli anni del centro-sinistra,* pp. 211, 212.

9. Reinhardt Airgram to the secretary of state, A-668, 9 March 1962, JFK Library, Box 120: NSF: CO: Italy, January 1962–October 1962.

10. Nenni, *Gli anni del centro-sinistra,* pp. 208–16; and Pietro Nenni, *La battaglia socialista per la svolta a sinistra nella terza legislatura 1958–1963* (Rome: Avanti, 1963), pp. 124–25.

11. Nenni, *Gli anni del centro-sinistra,* pp. 213–14.

12. Tamburrano, *Storia e cronaca del centro-sinistra,* pp. 148–55.

13. John C. Feuss, labor attaché, "Communists Launch Politically-Motivated Strike Wave," Foreign Service Dispatch, No. 701, 12 March 1962, in JFK Library, Box 12: Schlesinger Papers, Italy, 1962. For the positive results, see Roger Hilsman, U.S. Department of State, Bureau of Intelligence and Research, Research Memorandum RFX-2, 4 February 1963, "New Trend in Italian Collective Bargaining," JFK Library, Box 12: Schlesinger Papers, Italy, January 1963–January 1964.

14. Tamburrano, *Storia e cronaca del centro-sinistra,* pp. 240–43.

15. Alessandro Natta, ed., *Togliatti editorialista* (Rome: Riuniti, n.d.), pp. 67–68.

16. See the Amendola interview in Tamburrano, *Storia e cronaca del centro-sinistra*, p. 130.

17. Thomas L. Hughes, U.S. Department of State, Bureau of Intelligence and Research, Research Memorandum REU-12, 8 January 1964, "Italian Communists Reassert Their Independence from Moscow," JFK Library, Box 120: NSF: CO: Italy, January 1963–January 1964.

18. Galli, *Storia della DC*, pp. 210, 217–18.

19. *Avanti!* 19 October 1962.

20. Nenni, *Gli anni del centro-sinistra*, pp. 246–62.

21. Galli, *Storia della DC*, pp. 220–22.

22. Central Intelligence Agency, Report No. TDCS-3/546, 370, 7 May 1963, JFK Library, Box 120: NSF: CO: Italy, January 1963–June 1963. Another reason for the PCI increase cited at the time was the liberalization of the church under Pope John XXIII, who received Khrushchev's son-in-law and left catholic voters free to vote their consciences.

23. Nenni, *Gli anni del centro-sinistra;* and Airgram No. A-1822, 15 June 1963, JFK Library, Box 120: NSF: CO: Italy, January 1963–June 1963.

24. Edward R. Murrow, "Memorandum for the President, April 30, 1963''; U.S. Department of State, S/S 6950, "Memorandum for Mr. McGeorge Bundy, The White House, May 10, 1963''; and Thomas L. Hughes, U.S. Department of State, Bureau of Intelligence and Research, Research Memorandum REU-41, 31 May 1963, "Italian Elections Reflect Electorate's Leftward Trend," JFK Library, Box 120: NSF: CO: Italy, January 1963–June 1963.

25. *Avanti!* 18 May 1963.

26. Mafai, *Lombardi*, pp. 88–89.

27. Nenni, *Gli anni del centro-sinistra*, pp. 272–82.

28. Tamburrano, *Storia e cronoca del centro-sinistra*, p. 215; Mafai, *Lombardi*, pp. 90–91; and Nenni, *Gli anni del centro-sinistra*, pp. 282–84.

29. Airgram No. A-1847, with Neumann's memos of conversations with Lombardi and Pieraccini enclosed, Box 12: Schlesinger Papers, Italy, January 1963–January 1964. The conversations took place on 6 June 1963, and the Airgram was drafted by Fraleigh on 14 June but only sent on 24 June—a curious delay.

30. Nenni, *Gli anni del centro-sinistra*, pp. 285–87.

31. Draft of a memorandum to the president, dated 1 July 1963, and subsequently forwarded on 3 July, previously cited, JFK Library, Box 12: Schlesinger Papers, Italy, January 1963–January 1964. The reference to Schlesinger's discussions with Harriman and the name of a replacement is more strongly formulated in the draft than in the memo Schlesinger actually sent to the president.

32. [Unsigned, but probably John Di Sciullo], "Letters from Rome" (2 July and 10 July 1963), Box 12: Schlesinger Papers, Italy, January 1963–January 1964.

33. Tamburrano, *Storia e cronaca del centro-sinistra*, pp. 221–22.

34. Mafai, *Lombardi*, p. 93.

35. Nenni, *Gli anni del centro-sinistra*, p. 293; and Tamburrano, *Storia e cronaca del centro-sinistra*, p. 230.

36. Conversation with Antonio Giolitti, Rome, 27 December 1984.

37. Conversation with Wollemborg, 6 October 1984; and John Di Sciullo's Rome letters to William Tyler, 24 October and 5 November 1963, JFK Library, Box 12: Schlesinger Papers, Italy, January 1963–January 1964. See also Nenni's conversation with Neumann on the MLF issue in Nenni, *Gli anni del centro-sinistra*, pp. 296–97.

38. Central Intelligence Agency, Office of Current Intelligence, 31 May 1963, OCI No. 1925/63, "Implications of the Italian Socialist Congress," JFK Library, Box 120: NSF: CO: Italy, January 1963–June 1963.

39. Arthur Schlesinger, Jr., "Memorandum for Mr. McGeorge Bundy, November 22, 1963," JFK Library, Box 12: Schlesinger Papers, Italy, January 1963–January 1964.

40. Quoted by Mafai, *Lombardi*, pp. 98–99. See also Nenni, *Gli anni del centro-sinistra*, pp. 301–2.

Chapter 10

1. Nenni, *Gli anni del centro-sinistra*, p. 347.

2. Lelio Basso, "L'esperienza sovietica e la dittatura del proletariato," *Mondo Operaio* 10, no. 7 (July 1956): 412–22; and "Stlinismo e destalinizzazione," *I problemi dell'Ulisse* 16, nos. 48–49 (March–June 1963): 19–31.

3. Partito Socialista Italiano, *Il Partito Socialista Italiano dal congresso di Venezia al congresso di Napoli: Una cronaca necessaria, documenti per la relazione della sinistra* (Rome: SETI, 1958), pp. 28–29.

4. Vecchietti, *Una politica socialista*, pp. 10–11, 19–21.

5. Lelio Basso, "L'alternativa a de Gaulle è la politica kennediana?" *Problemi del Socialismo*, 1 (January 1963): 60–62.

6. Lelio Basso, "Crisi del governo o crisi del sistema?" *Problemi del Socialismo* 3 (March 1960): 202.

7. "La politica della maggioranza allarma i compagni per il pericolo di cedimento," *Per una politica di Alternativa Democratica: Numero unico riservato agli iscritti al Partito Socialista Italiano* (Milan), 1 December 1960, p. 2; and Lelio Basso, "La politica del PSI: Centro-sinistra e alternativa democratica," *Problemi del Socialismo* 5 (May 1960): 383–95.

8. Tullio Vecchietti, "Relazione della 'Sinistra' per il 34 Congresso del PSI." *Politica Socialista* 1 (January 1961): 24–29; Lelio Basso, "Giunte difficili o giunte impossibili?" *Problemi del Socialismo* 1 (January 1961): 74.

9. Lelio Basso, "Il nuovo governo e le prospettive future," *Problemi del Socialismo* 3 (March 1962): 137–38, 147–49; and Lelio Basso, "The Centre-Left in Italy," *New Left Review* 17 (Winter 1962): 10–11, 13–16.

10. Tullio Vecchietti, *I socialisti per la svolta a sinistra* (Rome: Arti Grafiche Privitera, 1962), pp. 6–9, 11–15.

11. Lelio Basso, "La battaglia socialista del 1963," *Problemi del Socialismo* 1 (January 1963): 3–10.

12. Lelio Basso, "E ora?" *Problemi del Socialismo* 4 (April 1963): 393–400.

13. "La relazione della sinistra al 35 Congresso del PSI," *Mondo Nuovo* 23 (September 1963): 19–22; and Partito Socialista Italiano, *35 Congresso Nazionale: Resoconto integrale* (Milan: Avanti, 1964), pp. 91–138, 592–96.

14. Lelio Basso, "Dopo il congresso," *Problemi del Socialismo* 10 (October 1963): 1093–96.

15. Partito Socialista Italiano, *Dovere dei socialisti, condannare gli accordi della Camilluccia: A cura della sinistra socialista* (Rome: Margarelli, n.d.); and *Atti parlamentari: Camera dei Deputati*, IV Legislatura—Discussioni—Seduta Pomeridiana del 17 Dicembre 1963, pp. 4317–21.

16. Lelio Basso, "A New Socialist Party," *International Socialist Journal* 2 (April 1964): 166.

17. Nenni, *Gli anni del centro-sinistra*, p. 321; and "La lettera della sinistra a Francesco De Martino," *Mondo Nuovo* 2 (January 1964): 4. For the technical details of the split, see Evangelisti and Sechi, "L'autonomia socialista e il centro-sinistra," pp. 121–25; Lelio Basso, "Ragioni e speranze della scissione socialista," *Problemi del Socialismo* 11–12 (November–December 1963): 1197–1215; and Nenni, *Gli anni del centro-sinistra*, pp. 307–10.

18. Basso, "A New Socialist Party," p. 173; and Galli, *Storia del socialismo italiano*, p. 248.

19. Lelio Basso, "Ragioni e speranze," pp. 1216–17; and Tamburrano, *Storia e cronaca del centro-sinistra*, pp. 262–63. For the PSIUP's organization, see Partito Socialista di Unità Pro-

letaria, Direzione, *Progetto del documento ideologico-politico inviato ai membri del Consiglio Nazionale il 22 aprile 1964;* and Partito di Unità Proletaria, *Bozza di Statuto per il 1 Congresso Nazionale del PSIUP, 16–19 dicembre 1965,* both mimeographed documents in the Basso Archives, Rome.

20. Enrico Mattei had perished in a suspicious airplane crash by this time.

21. Galli, *Storia del socialismo italiano,* pp. 248–49.

22. Confidential interview, Rome, 1984; and Nenni, *Gli anni del centro-sinistra,* p. 321.

23. Conversation with Landolfi, 18 December 1984.

24. Nenni, *Gli anni del centro-sinistra,* p. 310.

25. Antonio Giolitti, "Se il PSI avesse ascoltato Lombardi . . . ," *La Repubblica,* 27 September 1984.

26. Partito Socialista Italiano, Direzione, Sezione: Centr. Economica. Prot: n. 8283, 13/RL/dpa, Circ. n. 124, mimeographed document dated 23 June 1960 (author: Riccardo Lombardi), Basso Archives, Rome.

27. Valdi Spini, *I socialisti e la politica di piano,* pp. 166–67.

28. Tamburrano, *Storia e cronaca del centro-sinistra,* p. 107.

29. Conversation with Pieraccini, 14 November 1984.

30. Simona Colarizi, ed., *Riccardo Lombardi: Scritti politici* (Venice: Marsilio, 1978), Vol. 2, 29–31.

31. Giolitti, "Se il PSI avesse ascoltato Lombardi"; and Roberto Villetti, "La lezione di Lombardi," *Mondoperaio* 37, nos. 8–9 (August–September 1984): 8.

32. Kogan, *A Political History of Postwar Italy,* pp. 185–86.

33. Mafai, *Lombardi,* pp. 99–100.

34. Nenni, *Gli anni del centro-sinistra,* pp. 340–41; Tamburrano, *Pietro Nenni,* pp. 309–11.

35. Nenni, *Gli anni del centro-sinistra,* pp. 339–40, 343–44.

36. Galli, *Storia della DC,* p. 228; and Nenni, *Gli anni del centro-sinistra,* p. 348.

37. Nenni, *Gli anni del centro-sinistra,* pp. 355, 370.

38. Kogan, *A Political History of Italy,* p. 187; Nenni, *Gli anni del centro-sinistra,* pp. 358–60.

39. Galli, *Storia della DC,* pp. 228–30; and Faenza, *Il malaffare,* p. 372.

40. For the socialist account of these negotiations, see Nenni, *Gli anni del centro-sinistra,* pp. 375–79.

41. Editorials, *Avanti!* 22 and 26 July 1964.

42. This account of SIFAR is taken from Senato della Repubblica, Commissione Parlamentare d'Inchiesta sugli Eventi del Giugno-Luglio 1964, *Atti Interni, Documenti,* Volume LV. N. XXIII-1, published by the Senate in 1972, and the minority reports of the same commission, published in 1971. See also *Avanti!* 5 and 14 January and 18 February 1968.

43. Faenza, *Il malaffare,* pp. 310–21.

44. Ibid., pp. 359–73.

45. Conversation with Schlesinger, 25 June 1985. Schlesinger left government service in January 1964.

46. Tamburrano, *Storia e cronaca del centro-sinistra,* pp. 301–10, 333.

47. Conversation with Pieraccini, 14 November 1984.

48. Conversation with Giuseppe Tamburrano, 18 December 1984, and an unpublished article by Tamburrano on the twentieth anniversary of the SIFAR affair, given to me by the author. Tamburrano repeats his arguments in his biography of Nenni, pp. 324–33. See also Nenni, *Intervista sul socialismo italiano,* pp. 113–16. Despite Nenni's belief in the persistent threat of a rightist coup, he refers to *L'Espresso*'s account of SIFAR as romanticized. See Pietro Nenni, *I conti con la storia: Diari 1967–1971* (Milan: SugarCo, 1983), p. 59.

49. Conversation with Wollemborg, 6 October 1984.

50. Conversation with Giolitti, 27 December 1984.

51. Conversation with Ferri, 9 January 1985.

52. Di Scala, *Dilemmas of Italian Socialism,* pp. 7–8, 27–29, 74–75.

53. Galli, *Storia del socialismo italiano,* pp. 246, 252–56.

54. Nenni, *Intervista sul socialismo italiano,* p. 116.

55. Basso, "The Centre-Left in Italy," p. 14.

56. See De Lutiis, *Storia dei servizi segreti,* p. 75; and the treatment of the socialist leader in Faenza, *Il malaffare.*

57. Joseph La Palombara, *Italy: The Politics of Planning* (Syracuse, N.Y.: Syracuse University Press, 1966), pp. 87–102, 148–57; and Valdo Spini, "Il dibattito sulla programmazione all'inizio degli anni '60," in Arfé, et al., *Trent'anni di politica socialista,* pp. 223–25.

58. Conversation with Pieraccini, 14 November 1984.

59. Kogan, *A Political History of Italy,* pp. 201–12; and Nenni, *Intervista sul socialismo italiano,* pp. 127–30.

60. Franco Gaeta, "Bilancio del centro-sinistra," in Arfé et al., *Trent'anni di politica socialista,* pp. 131–34.

61. Nenni, *Intervista sul socialismo italiano,* pp. 125–26.

62. Conversation with Pieraccini, 14 November 1984.

63. Nenni, *Intervista sul socialismo italiano,* pp. 106–7; and Editorial, *Rinascita,* 23 July 1976.

64. Gaeta, "Bilancio del centro-sinistra," pp. 141–42.

Chapter 11

1. Ugo Indro, *La presidenza Saragat: Cronaca politica di un settennio, 1965–1971* (Milan: Mondadori, 1971), pp. 11–29; and Nenni, *Gli anni del centro-sinistra,* pp. 421, 429–33.

2. De Bernardis and De Mucci, *Dalla Resistenza alla alternativa socialista,* pp. 88–93.

3. Pietro Nenni, "Lettera ai compagni," *Avanti!* 5 September 1965; Nenni, *Intervista sul socialismo italiano,* p. 116; and Nenni, *Gli anni del centro-sinistra,* pp. 526–27.

4. Averardi, *I socialisti democratici,* pp. 285–418.

5. L'Osservatore, "Un voto per l'unificazione," *Critica Sociale,* 20 June 1966.

6. *Avanti!* 29 and 30 October 1966; Partito Socialista Italiano, *37 Congresso Nazionale del PSI,* p. 134; and Averardi, *I socialisti democratici,* pp. 419–31. Averardi conveniently groups all the relevant documents.

7. Editorial, and Gian Carlo Pajetta, "Crisi della politica estera del centro sinistra," *Rinascita,* 22 January 1966. pp. 1, 2; Aniello Coppola, "La 'kermesse' socialista," *Rinascita,* 1 October 1966, p. 8; and Kogan, *A Political History of Italy,* pp. 218–19.

8. Conversation with Ferri, 9 January 1985.

9. Nenni, *I conti con la storia,* pp. 181–82.

10. The electoral results are in Kogan, *A Political History of Italy,* pp. 220–21.

11. Nenni, *I conti con la storia,* pp. 182–88.

12. Ibid., pp. 228–32, 237–40.

13. Orazio Barrese, *Mancini* (Milan: Feltrinelli, 1976), pp. 151–59; conversation with Landolfi, 18 December 1984; and Nenni, *I conti con la storia,* p. 276.

14. Landolfi, *Il socialismo italiano,* pp. 276–83.

15. Mauro Ferri, "Intervento di Mauro Ferri," unpublished article, dated February 1982. (Manuscript provided by the author.) Conversation with Ferri, 9 January 1985; and Nenni, *I conti con la storia,* pp. 321–23, 325–29, 337–40, 344–46, 348–53.

16. Landolfi, *Il socialismo italiano,* pp. 180–89, 273–75: Walter Tobagi, "Il PSI dal centro-sinistra all'autunno caldo," in Banfi et al., *Storia del Partito Socialista Italiano,* Vol. 3, pp. 83–84; Evangelisti and Sechi, "L'autonomia socialista e il centro-sinistra," pp. 131–35.

17. Giuseppe Mammarella, *L'Italia dopo il fascismo 1943–1973* (Bologna: Il Mulino, 1974), pp. 469–70.

18. Galli, *Storia della DC*, pp. 321–34.

19. Ugo Finetti, *Libro bianco sulla crisi socialista: Tre anni, 1969–1972* (Milan: SugarCo, 1972), p. 91.

20. Barrese, *Mancini*, pp. 170–71.

21. Nenni, *I conti con la storia*, p. 530.

22. Barrese, *Mancini*, pp. 160–68.

23. Editorial, *L'Unità*, 1 May 1971.

24. Paolo Mieli, "La crisi del centro-sinistra, l'alternativa, il 'nuovo corso' socialista," in Sabbatucci, ed., *Storia del socialismo italiano*, Vol. 6, pp. 182–91; Nenni, *I conti con la storia*, pp. 670–84.

25. Finetti, *Libro bianco*, pp. 218–21, 243–47.

26. Antonio Landolfi. "Per il rinnovamento del programma e dell'azione socialista," in *Partito Socialista Italiano, Introduzione ai problemi di fondo del PSI* (N.P.: n.d.), pp. 14–20.

27. Partito Socialista Italiano, *Relazione di Giacomo Mancini al 39 Congresso Nazionale* (Rome: SETI, 1972), pp. 1–4, 6–7, 23–55.

28. Finetti, *Libro bianco*, pp. 250–52.

29. De Lutiis, *Storia dei servizi segreti*, pp. 95–141; Giorgio Bocca, *Il terrorismo italiano* (Milan: Rizzoli, 1979), pp. 53–65.

30. Michele Salvati, *Economia e politica in Italia dal dopoguerra a oggi* (Milan: Garzanti, 1984), pp. 118–33.

31. Antonio Bisaglia interview, *Corriere della Sera*, 4 November 1972; Ruggero Orfei, *L'occupazione del potere: I democristiani '45–'75* (Milan: Longanesi, 1976), pp. 260–61; and Galli, *Storia della DC*, pp. 372–78.

32. Enrico Berlinguer, "Riflessioni sull'Italia dopo i fatti del Cile," *Rinascita*, 28 September, 5 and 12 October 1973.

33. Mieli, "La crisi del centro-sinistra," pp. 217–20; and Riccardo Lombardi, "Crisi del capitalismo e alternativa," in Colarizi, ed., *Riccardo Lombardi*, Vol. 2, pp. 235–41.

34. De Martino interview, *Panorama*, 29 November 1973.

35. Galli, *Storia della DC*, pp. 379–82.

36. Mieli, "La crisi del centro-sinistra," pp. 224–36; Kogan, *A Political History of Italy*, pp. 285–86.

37. Galli, *Storia del socialismo italiano*, pp. 291–94.

38. *Corriere della Sera*, 25 July 1975; Bufalini interview, *Il Mondo*, 9 October 1975; *L'Espresso*, 26 October 1975; Spencer Di Scala, "Alliances with Italian Political Left Appear Likely," *The Christian Science Monitor*, August 15, 1975.

39. Galli, *Storia della DC*, pp. 404–13; *Corriere della Sera*, 13 September 1975.

40. Editorial, *Avanti!* 31 December 1975; *L'Espresso*, 11 January 1976.

41. Summaries of the speeches at the congress are in Claudio Martelli, *Socialisti a confronto: Saggio sul 40 Congresso del PSI, con una sintesi degli interventi principali* (Milan: SugarCo, 1976).

42. Antonio Ghirelli, *L'effetto Craxi* (Milan: Rizzoli, 1982), pp. 69–70.

43. Mieli, "La crisi del centro-sinistra," pp. 254–57.

44. Conversation with Pertini, 11 October 1983.

Chapter 12

1. Giampaolo Pansa, "E venne il giorno di Bettino," *La Repubblica*, 22 July 1983, in [Ugo Intini, ed.], *Tutti gli angoli di Craxi* (Milan: Rusconi, 1984), pp. 20–21.

2. Quoted by Ghirelli, *L'effetto Craxi*, p. 13.

3. Giancarlo Galli, *Benedetto Bettino* (Milan: Bompiani, 1982), pp. 11–19.

4. Carlo Ripa di Meana, "Virtù e debolezze di un capo," *Il Gazzettino*, in Intini, ed. *Tutti gli angoli di Craxi*, pp. 63–64.

5. For the interrelationship between Turati's local and national policies, see Spencer Di Scala, "Filippo Turati, the Milanese Schism, and the Reconquest of the Italian Socialist Party," *Il Politico* 4, no. 1 (January 1979): 153–63; and Spencer Di Scala, "Filippo Turati e la scissione del partito socialista milanese del 1901," *Rassegna di politica e di storia* 16, no. 183 (January–March 1970): 1–7.

6. Galli, *Benedetto Bettino*, pp. 34, 40–41, 46–49.

7. *La Repubblica*, 16 July 1976; *Il Manifesto*, 17 July 1976.

8. Quoted by Galli, *Benedetto Bettino*, pp. 51–52.

9. Nenni, *I conti con la storia*, pp. 461–62.

10. See Craxi's comments in "Il ruolo del PSI," *Mondo Operaio*, January 1976.

11. Ghirelli, *L'effetto Craxi*, p. 38.

12. Spencer Di Scala. "America's 'Italian Connection'—The Ties Are Frayed," *The Christian Science Monitor*, 11 December 1985.

13. Ghirelli, *L'effetto Craxi*, pp. 88, 89; Galli, *Benedetto Bettino*, pp. 25, 59–60.

14. *L'Espresso*, 25 July 1976.

15. *La Repubblica*, 21 July 1976; and *Il Tempo*, 1 August 1976.

16. Mosca's testimony is quoted by Galli, *Benedetto Bettino*, p. 68.

17. Bettino Craxi, *Costruire il futuro* (Milan: Rizzoli, 1977), pp. 130–35.

18. Ibid., pp. 141–67.

19. *Il Partito Socialista. Struttura e organizzazione: Atti della Conferenza Nazionale di Organizzazione*, pp. 17–305; and "Il PSI nelle analisi post eletorali," *Mondo Operaio*, July–August 1976.

20. Sisinio Zito, "Per il rinnovamento del PSI," *Mondo Operaio*, July–August 1976.

21. Craxi, *Costruire il futuro*, pp. 57–76.

22. Ibid., pp. 79–96.

23. Ibid., pp. 97–111, 129, 168–70.

24. *Il Messaggero*, 24 January 1977.

25. Mieli, "La crisi del centro-sinistra," p. 272.

26. Craxi's version is in *L'Espresso*. 6 March 1977.

27. *Corriere della Sera*, 14 April 1977.

28. Ghirelli, *L'effetto Craxi*, pp. 97–99.

29. *L'Espresso*, 5 June 1977; and *Paese Sera*, 30 November 1977.

30. *L'Espresso*, 29 May 1978; and Guido Gerosa, *Craxi: Il potere e la stampa* (Milan: Sperling & Kupfer, 1984), p. 298.

31. Agostino Marianetti, "Il PSI e l'area socialista," *Mondoperaio* 29, no. 9 (September 1976): 52–56.

32. Galli, *Benedetto Bettino*, p. 68. The UIL secretary was Italo Viglianesi. Under Benvenuto's leadership, membership in the mechanical workers union rose from forty thousand to one hundred forty thousand.

33. Aldo Forbice, *Austerità e democrazia operaia: Intervista a Giorgio Benvenuto* (Milan: SugarCo, 1977), pp. 67–73.

34. Giorgio Benvenuto, *Verso un nuovo sindacato: L'iniziativa della UIL per l'unità del movimento* (Venice: Marsilio, 1977), pp. 15–24.

35. Massimo Riva, "Le consequenze economiche del Signor Benvenuto," *Corriere della Sera*, 16 January 1977.

36. Luciano Vasconi, "Comunisti e Socialisti: Intervista con Giorgio Amendola," *Mondoperaio* 29, no. 1 (January 1976): 18–20.

37. Galli, *Storia della DC,* pp. 435–39.

38. Ghirelli, *L'effetto Craxi,* pp. 107–14; and Margiocco, *Stati Uniti e PCI,* pp. 280–81.

39. Giorgio Bocca, *Moro: Una tragedia italiana* (Milan: Bompiani, 1978), pp. 7–32.

40. Paolo Bufalini, *Terrorismo e democrazia: La relazione al Comitato centrale e alla Commissione centrale di controllo del PCI, 18 aprile 1978* (Rome: Riuniti, 1978), p. 17.

41. *Corriere della Sera,* 21 April 1978.

42. Bettino Craxi, "Una iniziativa costituzionale," *Avanti!* 7 November 1980.

43. The relevant documents are reproduced in Bocca, *Moro,* pp. 129–30, 140–41; Craxi's speech is in Partito Socialista Italiano, *Da Torino a Palermo: Tre anni di politica socialista* (Rome: PSI, n.d.), p. 10. The observer is Robin Erica Wagner-Pacifici, *The Moro Morality Play: Terrorism as Social Drama* (Chicago: University of Chicago Press, 1986), p. 130.

44. Giorgio Galli, *Storia del partito armato 1968–1982* (Milan: Rizzoli, 1986), pp. 168–70; Mieli, "La crisi del centro-sinistra," p. 291.

45. Gianfranco Piazzesi, "Il grande protagonista è il partito di Zaccagnini," *Corriere della Sera,* 16 May 1978.

46. Ghirelli, *L'effetto Craxi,* p. 141.

47. Camilla Cederna, *Giovanni Leone: La carriera di un presidente* (Milan: Feltrinelli, 1978).

48. *Critica Sociale,* July 1978.

49. Ugo Finetti, *Il dissenso nel PCI* (Milan: SugarCo, 1978), pp. 198–243.

50. Ernesto Galli della Loggia, "La crisi del Togliattismo," *Mondoperaio,* June 1978; *Avanti!* 21, 27 July 1978; *L'Unità,* 12, 22 July 1978. Berlinguer's interview is in *La Repubblica,* 28 July 1978. See also Pietro Ingrao, *Crisi e terza via: Intervista di Romano Ledda* (Rome: Riuniti, 1978).

51. Bettino Craxi [actually written by Luciano Pellicani], "Il vangelo socialista," *L'Espresso,* 27 August 1978. For the observer's citation, see Howard Penniman, ed., *Italy at the Polls, 1979: A Study of the Parliamentary Elections* (Washington, D.C.: American Enterprise Institute, 1981), p. 22. The debate among the intellectuals is discussed below in Chapter 13.

52. Paolo Mieli, *Litigio a sinistra* (Rome: L'Espresso, 1979), pp. 12–19, 24–32; *L'Unità, Avanti!, La Repubblica, Corriere della Sera, Paese Sera, Il Manifesto, Lotta Continua,* and *L'Espresso,* 24 August–9 September 1978; Luciano Pellicani, *Il mercato e i socialismi* (Milan: SugarCo, 1978), pp. 258–89.

53. Mieli, *Litigio a sinistra,* p. 19.

54. *L'Unità,* 18 September 1978.

55. Giuseppe Di Palma and Philip Siegelman, eds., *Italy in the 1980s: Paradoxes of a Dual Society* (San Francisco: World Affairs Council, 1983), p. 37; Peter Lange, "Crisis and Consent Change and Compromise: Dilemmas of Italian Communism in the 1970s," in Peter Lange and Sidney Tarrow, eds., *Italy in Transition: Conflict and Consensus* (London: Frank Cass, 1980), p. 125.

56. Galli, *Benedetto Bettino,* p. 134.

57. Mieli, "La crisi del centro-sinistra," p. 318.

58. Ghirelli, *L'effetto Craxi,* pp. 159–66.

59. Kogan, *A Political History of Italy,* pp. 301–2, 307–18.

60. Craxi's remarks and the Directorate's appeal are in Partito Socialista Italiano, *Da Torino a Palermo,* pp. 11–12, 20–21.

61. Ghirelli, *L'effetto Craxi,* p. 172.

62. Craxi's program is in *Partito Socialista Italiano, Da Torino a Palermo,* pp. 21–22. Signorile kept a detailed notebook of the negotiations, published in *L'Espresso,* 1 September 1979.

63. Valdo Spini, *3 congressi per un nuovo PSI: Supplemento ai Quaderni del Circolo Rosselli* (Milan: Mediolanum, 1984), p. 29.

64. *Europeo,* 28 October 1980.

65. *Panorama,* 5 November 1979.

66. "Ottava legislatura," *Avanti!* 27 September 1979; Ghirelli, *L'Effetto Craxi,* p. 184.

67. Mieli, "La crisi del contro-sinistra," pp. 332–34.

68. *L'Espresso,* 23 December 1979.

69. *La Repubblica,* 21–27 December 1979.

70. *Partito Socialista Italiano, Da Torino a Palermo,* p. 13.

71. In addition to accepting Lombardi as PSI president, Craxi agreed to enlarge the Directorate, institute a commission which would have shared power with the secretary, restructure the party so as to weaken his own current, and push for an emergency government open to the Communists.

72. Lombardi's letter of resignation is in *Avanti!* 14 March 1980.

73. Conversation with Valdo Spini, 19 October 1983.

Chapter 13

1. Umberto Giovine and Paolo Pilliteri, *Europa socialista* (Milan: Critica Sociale, 1979), pp. 5–8, 11–12, 85–87, 105–7.

2. *Egemonia e democrazia: Gramsci e la questione comunista nel dibattito di Mondoperaio* (Rome: Mondoperaio-Avanti, 1977), pp. xi–xii.

3. Furio Diaz, "Alla ricerca dei presupposti della 'scelta democratica' del PCI," reprinted in ibid., pp. 1–32.

4. Massimo L. Salvadori, "Gramsci e il PCI: Due concezioni dell'egemonia," reprinted in ibid., pp. 33–53.

5. Bobbio interview, *Egemonia e democrazia,* p. 57.

6. Luciano Pellicani, "Gramsci e il messianismo comunista," reprinted in *Egemonia e democrazia,* pp. 99–114.

7. *Egemonia e democrazia,* p. xv.

8. *Progetto socialista* (Bari: Laterza, 1976), pp. 3–59.

9. Galli, *Storia del socialismo italiano,* p. 309.

10. Giuliano Amato-Luciano Cafagna, *Duello a sinistra: Socialisti e comunisti nei lunghi anni '70* (Bologna: Il Mulino, 1982), pp. 134–35.

11. For a good sampling of this discussion, see Antonio Giolitti, et al., *Politica internazionale e progetto socialista* (Milan: Franco Angeli, 1977); Federico Coen, ed., *Quale riforma dello Stato?; I socialisti e la cultura; Organizzazione dello stato e democrazia;* and *Progetto e alternativa.*

12. Partito Socialista Italiano, *L'alternativa dei socialisti: Il progetto di programma del PSI presentato da Bettino Craxi* (Rome: Mondo Operaio, 1978), pp. xi–xii.

13. Lucio Colletti, speaking in the round table discussion "Le due anime del PSI," *Mondoperaio,* February 1980.

14. Bettino Craxi, *Le tesi per il 42 Congresso* (Milan: Arti Grafiche Fiorini, 1981), pp. 5–7, 22–26, 28–38, 40–41, 52–53. One observer correctly stated that the PSI had become an "evangelist" for basic social democratic values. See David Hine, "The Italian Socialist Party Under Craxi: Surviving But Not Reviving," in Lange and Tarrow, eds., *Italy in Transition,* p. 136.

15. Bettino Craxi, *Tre anni* (Milan: SugarCo, 1983), p. 10; John L. Harper, *Bettino Craxi and the Second Center Left Experiment* (Bologna: Johns Hopkins University, 1986), p. 13. The Palermo congress minutes have been published as PSI, *Il rinnovamento socialista per il rinnovamento dell'Italia* (Rome: PSI, n.d.).

16. Partito Socialista Italiano, *Governare il cambiamento: Conferenza programmatica del PSI, Rimini 31 marzo–4 aprile 1982* (Rome: PSI, n.d.), pp. 6–10, 268.

17. Ibid., pp. 104–60.

18. Ibid., p. 260.

19. Conversation with Michelangelo Jacobucci, head of the president's Press Service, 9 October 1984.

20. This section is based on my second conversation with Pertini during the evening of 9 October 1984.

21. Mieli, "La crisi del centro-sinistra," pp. 344–45.

22. "Comunisti e socialisti a una prova difficile," *Rinascita,* 18 July 1980; Luciano Barca, "Il surplace di Craxi," *Rinascita,* 5 September 1980; *La Repubblica,* 24 October 1980; Paolo Franchi, "Il modello di Craxi per il partito e il governo," *Rinascita,* 10 October 1980.

23. *Panorama,* 9 February 1981.

24. Pietro Barcellona, "A chi (e perchè) si deve dare o togliere potere," *Rinascita,* 10 April 1981.

25. Gerardo Chiaromonte, "Governo e governabilità: discutiamo con il PSI," *Rinascita,* 17 April 1981.

26. Craxi, *Tre anni,* p. 15.

27. Achille Occhetto, "Le sinistre dopo Palermo," *Rinascita,* 1 May 1981.

28. Spini, *3 congressi,* pp. 48–49. On Poland, Craxi called for the PCI's definitive break with Moscow, *Tre anni,* pp. 126–27. The PCI's statement on Poland is in *L'Unità,* 30 December 1981. Ghirelli, *L'effetto Craxi,* pp. 234–36, gives a good synopsis of PSI-PCI relations during this period.

29. Craxi, *Tre anni,* pp. 12–21; Partito Socialisto Italiano, *Governare il cambiamento,* pp. 261–64.

30. Craxi, *Tre anni,* pp. 22–44, 84–113, 181–82; Partito Socialista Italiano, *Governare il cambiamento,* pp. 264–65; Giorgio Benvenuto et al., *Strategia riformista e sindacato* (Milan: Arti Grafiche Fiorini, n.d.), pp. 21–22.

31. Galli, *Storia del socialismo italiano,* pp. 331–32.

32. Conversation with Pertini, 11 October 1983.

33. Silvio Bertocci, "Loggia P2: Tutti gli uomini del 'Venerabile' Procuratore," *Il Ponte* 38, no. 5 (May 1982): 431. *L'Espresso* reported in its 18 September 1983 issue that much of the Banco Ambrosiano's funds went to Solidarnosc.

34. Craxi, *Tre anni,* pp. 68–72.

35. Galli, *Storia del partito armato,* pp. 272–91.

36. *Panorama,* 9 February 1981 and 20 September 1982; *L'Espresso,* 20 July 1986.

37. *L'Espresso,* 12 December 1985.

38. Conversation with Giuliano Amato, 2 February 1983; Joseph La Palombara, "Socialist Alternatives: The Italian Variant," *Foreign Affairs* 60, no. 4 (Spring 1982): 925. See also the interview with Giorgio Ruffolo, *Europeo,* 31 January 1983.

39. Conversation with former Ambassador John Volpe, Nahant, Massachusetts, 11 June 1985.

40. *Il governo Craxi: Edizione speciale di Vita Italiana* 33, nos. 7–8 (July–August 1983): 9–26. On De Mita's intentions, see Gianni Baget Bozzo, "Che resta della DC se cade De Mita," *La Repubblica,* 1 July 1983.

41. Gianfranco Pasquino, "Il lungo rodaggio dell'alternativa," *Il Messaggero,* 10 April 1983. See the Lombardi interview in the same issue.

42. Gianni De Michelis, "Perchè difendiamo l'accordo di gennaio," *Avanti!* 19–20 June 1983.

43. Partito Socialista Italiano, Sezione Propaganda del PSI, *Rinnovare l'Italia: Governare davvero. Il programma socialista per la nona legislatura;* and *La Repubblica,* 16 June 1983.

44. *Avanti!* 28 June 1983. For an analysis of the socialist vote, see K. Robert Nilsson, "The Italian Socialist Party: An Indispensable Hostage," in Howard R. Penniman, *Italy at the Polls, 1983* (Durham: Duke University Press, 1987), pp. 78–99.

45. Federico Coen, "Una vittoria dimezzata," *Mondoperaio,* July–August 1983.

46. *La Repubblica,* 16 June 1983.

47. Gianni Baget Bozzo, "Partito socialista e questione morale," *La Repubblica,* 30 August 1983; and Coen's reply, "Tutte le carte del PSI," *La Repubblica,* 5 September 1983.

48. Martelli interview, *La Repubblica,* 11–12 September 1983.

49. Guido Martinotti, "Il PSI è cambiato ma forse non lo sa," *La Repubblica*, 14 September 1983.

50. Gianni Baget Bozzo, "Riforma del partito e legge elettorale," *La Repubblica*, 13 September 1983.

51. Alberto Ronchey, "Ricaduta o decadenza della DC?" *La Repubblica*, 27 September 1983; *Il governo Craxi*, p. 44. For interpretations and analysis of the results as they affected the DC, PCI, and the small parties, see Penniman, ed., *Italy at the Polls, 1983*, pp. 35–77, 100–19.

52. Formica interview, *La Repubblica*. 30 June 1983.

53. *La Repubblica*, 1 and 2 July 1983.

54. Bisaglia interview, *La Repubblica*, 4 July 1983; and *Il Mattino*, 14 July 1983.

55. *La Repubblica*, 20 July 1983. Speculation that Craxi was given the premiership in the hope that he would do a poor job and that Spadolini was excluded because his party had done too well in the recent elections (5.1 percent) is, in my opinion, erroneous.

56. *La Repubblica*, 23 July 1983.

57. *Il Messaggero*, 5 August 1983.

58. Eugenio Scalfari, "La volpe e il leone si misero d'accordo," *Le Repubblica*, 5 August 1983, in Eugenio Scalfari, *L'anno di Craxi (o di Berlinguer?)* (Milan: Mondadori, 1984), pp. 37–40.

59. *Il governo Craxi*, pp. 136–89.

60. Emanuele Macaluso, "Il segno politico di questa coalizione," and Alfredo Reichlin, "C'è una novità: il blocco delle retribuzioni reali," *L'Unità*, 5 August 1983; *Il governo Craxi*, p. 192.

61. Ugo Intini, "Il segno di una svolta," *Avanti!* 5 August 1983; and Claudio Martelli, " 'Pensare Paese,' " *Avanti!* 7–8 August 1983.

62. "Palazzo Chigi vale una messa?" *La Repubblica* 31 July–1 August 1983, and "Il Capo e la Nuova Frontiera," *La Repubblica*, 24–25 July 1983, in Scalfari, *L'anno di Craxi*, pp. 32–36, 26–31.

Chapter 14

1. Conversation with Spini, 19 October 1983.

2. *La Repubblica*, 10 August 1983; Antonio Padellaro, "Socialismo e rigore," *Corriere della Sera*, 10 August 1983.

3. *La Repubblica*, 11 August 1983.

4. *La Repubblica*, 21–22 August and 23 August 1983; Alberto Ronchey, "Se domani l'Italia va fuori mercato," *La Repubblica*, 30 August 1983, in *Craxi in prima pagina*, pp. 9–12.

5. *La Repubblica*, 15 September 1983 ("Economia e Sindacato" section). Ten thousand workers were pensioned at age fifty.

6. *Corriere della Sera*, 24 September 1983; *La Repubblica*, 28 and 30 September 1983; *L'Espresso*, 2 and 9 October 1983. The cuts for defense were set at fifteen hundred billion lire; the *condono edilizio* was expected to bring in six thousand billion lire. In all, the cuts amounted to forty thousand billion lire. The government hoped to keep the 1983 deficit at ninety thousand billion. The exchange rate at the time was about sixteen hundred lire to the dollar.

7. Giuseppe Turani, "Gli italiani si aspettano che . . . ," *L'Espresso*, 9 October 1983.

8. *La Repubblica*, 13 October 1983.

9. *La Repubblica*, 14 October; and Craxi interview, *Corriere della Sera*, 17 October 1983.

10. *La Repubblica*, 21 October 1983.

11. Gianni Baget Bozzo, "La politica e i fatti," *La Repubblica*, 18–19 December 1983.

12. Harper, *Bettino Craxi*, p. 20.

13. *La Repubblica*, 20 December 1983, 4, 13, and 24 January 1984; *L'Unità*, 24 January 1984; Achille Occhetto, "Questa nostra sfida," *L'Unità*, 8 January 1984; Bruno Trentin interview,

La Repubblica, 13 January 1984; and Ezio Tarantelli, "I tre tavoli dello scontro," *La Repubblica*, 28 January 1984. A pragmatic and effective advocate of compromise whom the government often heeded, Tarantelli was murdered by the Red Brigades on 27 March 1985 while trying to smooth over a referendum on the *scala mobile* question. See Spencer Di Scala, "Terrorism's 'appeal'," *The Christian Science Monitor*, 6 May 1985.

14. *La Repubblica*, 29 January 1984.

15. *La Repubblica*, 14, 15, 16, and 17 February 1984. A list of associations supporting the government's action is in *Il Messaggero*, 16 February 1984. See also Lama interview in *La Repubblica*, 18 February 1984.

16. Gino Giugni, "Sulla scala mobile una rottura politica," *La Repubblica*, 16 February 1984. On the communist intention to cause Craxi's fall, see *Il Messaggero*, 16 February 1984.

17. *La Repubblica*, 21 and 22 February 1984; *L'Espresso*, 18 February 1984; "I comunisti tornano indietro di molti anni," *Avanti!* 22 February; and Ugo Intini, "Il PCI ha rischiato grosso e ha perso," *Avanti!* 23 February 1984. Berlinguer's report to the Central Committee is in *L'Unità*, 21 February 1984.

18. "Anatomia di una crisi," *L'Espresso*, 4 March 1984; *La Repubblica*, 9 March 1984; *Avanti!* 11–12 March 1984. Paolo Sylos Labini, *Le classi sociali negli anni '80* (Bari: Laterza, 1986), pp. 25–26.

19. *La Repubblica*, 6, 7, 9, 10, 14, 18–19 March, 1984; *L'Unità*, 11 March 1984; *Corriere della Sera*, 18 March 1984: and Silvano Tosi, "Ostruzionismo: La memoria corta dei comunisti," *La Nazione*, 14 March 1984, in Intini, ed., *Craxi in prima pagina*, pp. 85–88.

20. Vittorio Emiliani, "Protesta e riformismo," *Il Messaggero*, 20 February 1984; Enzo Bettiza, "Lo scandalo è governare," *La Nazione*, 24 March 1984; Lucio Colletti, "Perchè Berlinguer esce allo scoperto," *L'Espresso*, 26 February 1984; Gianfranco Piazzesi, "Non sarà Berlinguer a decidere chi sono i buoni e i cattivi," *La Stampa*, 11 March 1984; and Indro Montanelli, "Un modo diverso di governare," *Oggi*, 28 March 1984, in Intini, ed., *Craxi in prima pagina*, pp. 59–62, 63–67, 69–72, 95–98.

21. Partito Socialista Italiano. Direzione, *Per un riformismo moderno: Tesi del PSI per il 43 Congresso, Verona 11–15 maggio 1984* (Rome: PSI, 1984), pp. 61–62, 65–73.

22. Alberto Mucci, "Un miracolo da consolidare," *Corriere della Sera*, 5 November 1984.

23. *La Repubblica*, 21 and 23–24 December 1984; *Il Messaggero*, 23 December 1984; and Spencer Di Scala, "Italy's Bettino Craxi: He Brings a New Image to His Country," *The Christian Science Monitor*, 4 March 1985.

24. *Panorama*, 2 March 1985; and *Corriere della Sera*, 18 June 1986. An observer has correctly seen the *scala mobile* referendum as the "end of an era." See Robert Leonardi and Raffaella Y. Nanetti, eds., *Italian Politics: A Review*, Vol. 1, pp. 29–46.

25. Alberto Mucci, "Il vento del privato soffia sull'impresa," *Corriere della Sera*, 11 May 1986. On Italsider, see *Corriere della Sera*, 10 July 1986; for other examples of privatization, see *Corriere della Sera*, 2 January 1985 and 17 November 1985.

26. *Corriere della Sera*, 20 and 21 May 1986.

27. Ciampi's remarks are in *Corriere della Sera*, 18 April 1986.

28. *Corriere della Sera*, 11 May 1986. As of this writing, the "heavy lira" has not been instituted.

29. *Corriere della Sera*, 20 May 1986; see also the 17 and 21 April 1986 issues.

30. *Corriere della Sera*, 4 and 5 March 1986.

31. The draft is in *Corriere della Sera*, 10 April 1986. For proposals restructuring pensons, for example, see the 10 July 1986 issue; on the economic data, see *Corriere della Sera*, 29 and 31 July and 6 August 1986. See also Craxi interview, *Panorama*. 4 January 1987; and *La Stampa*, 12 February 1987.

32. Amato interview, *La Repubblica*, 6 August 1983.

33. Pertini interview, *La Repubblica,* 7–8 August 1983.

34. *La Repubblica,* 13 October 1983; Martelli interview, *La Stampa,* 16 October 1983; Leo Valiani, " 'Piccolo costitutente,' occasione per rafforzare lo Stato," *Corriere della Sera,* 14 October 1983. For the similarity of De Mita's plans for institutional reform to socialist proposals, see *L'Espresso,* 23 October 1983. See also Giaufranco Pasquino, "The Debate on Institutional Reform," in Leonardi and Nanetti, eds., *Italian Politics,* pp. 117–33.

35. The Socialists had proposed popular election for the president before coming out for the position cited and would do so again. See Gianni Baget Bozzo, "La presidenziale," *La Repubblica,* 6 January 1984. The extremely popular Pertini came in for his share of criticism from the press for his activism; see *La Repubblica,* 10 January and 28–29 October 1984, and *L'Espresso,* 8 and 15 January 1984. For the arguments against instituting a strong president in Italy, see Antonio Lombardo, *La Grande Riforma: Governo, istituzioni, partiti* (Milan: SugarCo, 1984), pp. 124–25.

36. PSI, *Per un riformismo moderno,* pp. 33–41.

37. Bozzi interview, *La Repubblica,* 11–12 March 1984: *Il Messaggero,* 16 February 1984; Ingrao interview, *L'Espresso,* 23 February 1986.

38. *La Repubblica,* 18 and 19 October 1983.

39. Conversation with Spini, 19 October 1983.

40. *Corriere della Sera,* 26 February 1984.

41. *Corriere della Sera.* 2 February 1984; and Craxi interview, *Corriere della Sera,* 17 November 1985.

42. Alberto Ronchey, "Almeno questo," *Corriere della Sera,* 10 July 1986; Spencer Di Scala, "Italy: Stability Despite All the Turmoil," *The Christian Science Monitor,* 9 July 1986.

43. Guido Neppi Modona, "Stai in galera? Peggio per te . . . ," *La Repubblica,* 23 August 1983; Giuliano Vassalli, "Giustizia: Una macchina che gira a vuoto," *Mondoperaio,* September 1983; *L'Espresso,* 26 September 1983. There is a good discussion of the justice system in Frederic Spotts and Theodor Wieser, *Italy, A Difficult Democracy: A Survey of Italian Politics* (Cambridge: Cambridge University Press, 1986), pp. 150–69.

44. Michele Coiro, "Carcere e paleogiustizia," *Il Messaggero,* 20 September 1983.

45. PSI, *Per un riformismo moderno,* pp. 46–51; and the Luigi Covatta interview, *Avanti!* 19–30 January 1984. For the PSI view of a democratic public order, see Vincenzo Balzamo et al., *Ordine pubblico e sicurezza democratica* (Milan: La Nuova Italia, 1976).

46. *La Repubblica,* 5 October 1983.

47. *L'Espresso,* 18 September and 2 October 1983; *Corriere della Sera,* 31 January 1986.

48. Spencer Di Scala, "Italy's Troubled Justice System—Agca's 'Bulgarian Connection,' " *The Christian Science Monitor,* 1 August 1985; *The New York Times,* 30 March 1986; *Corriere della Sera,* 28 February 1986.

49. *Per un riformismo moderno,* pp. 50, 52; *Il Tempo,* 5 December 1985.

50. *Corriere della Sera,* 19 March 1986.

51. Ezio Mauro, "Concordato: Firma a Villa Madama," *La Stampa,* 19 February 1984, in Intini, ed., *Craxi in prima pagina,* pp. 215–18.

52. *La Repubblica,* 18 February 1984.

53. *Corriere della Sera,* 15 January 1986; *Il Tempo,* 16 January 1986; *L'Espresso,* 26 January 1986; Leonardi and Nanetti, eds., *Italian Politics,* pp. 134–45.

54. Gianni Baget Bozzo, "I ministri di De Mita," *La Repubblica,* 9 August 1983.

55. Giorgio Galli, "L'alternativa e il fattore Craxi," *Panorama,* 7 March 1983.

56. *La Repubblica,* 11 August and 13 September 1983.

57. La Ganga's comments are in *Corriere della Sera,* 16 September 1983; Zangheri's are in his *La Repubblica* interview, 19 October 1983. Spini gave me his views in our 19 October 1983 conversation. The high points of the local crises may be followed in *La Repubblica,* 13 September, 5 and 21 October 1983, and 29 February 1984.

58. Lucio Colletti, "Un partito senza," *L'Espresso,* 4 December 1983. On the crisis of

L'Unità and the intellectuals, see *L'Espresso*, 4 September 1983, and Paolo Franchi, "Intellettuali, stanchi del PCI," *Corriere della Sera*, 26 February 1986.

59. Alberto Jacoviello, "Napolitano, il laico," *La Repubblica*, 12 January 1984. Napolitano's article is in *L'Unità*, 4 January 1984. For the considerations on the basis of PCI power, see Giovanni Sartori, *Teoria dei partiti e caso italiano* (Milan: SugarCo, 1982), pp. 16–17.

60. On the reaction to Napolitano, see *La Repubblica*, 5 and 6 January 1984; *L'Espresso*, 15 January and 4 March 1984: Vittorio Emiliani, "Chi urla, chi parla, e chi tace," *Il Messaggero*, 8 January 1984; and Giorgio Ruffolo, "Il 'caso' Napolitano," *La Repubblica*, 18 January 1984. Berlinguer's address to the Central Committee is in *L'Unità*, 21 February 1984.

61. *L'Espresso*, 15 and 22 July and 23 December 1984; Alfredo Pieroni, "La maggioranza e l'offensiva del PCI," *Corriere della Sera*, 6 December 1984; Lama interview, *L'Espresso*, 16 December 1984.

62. Adolfo Battaglia, "New Politics Emerge in Italy," *New York Times*, 6 April 1985; Spencer Di Scala, "Some Welcome Stability in Italy's Politics," *The Christian Science Monitor*, 29 May 1985. The election results are in *La Repubblica*, 15 May 1985; there is a discussion of these elections in Leonardi and Nanetti, eds., *Italian Politics*, pp. 11–28.

63. Spencer Di Scala, "America's 'Italian Connection'—The Ties Are Frayed," *The Christian Science Monitor*, 11 December 1985.

64. *Corriere della Sera*, 28 and 31 January 1986.

65. Giuliano Urbani, "Senza voce nel PCI l'ala moderata," *Corriere della Sera*, 8 April 1986; Salvatore Veca, "Dilemmi fondamentali," *Corriere della Sera*, 10 April 1986; Alberto Ronchey, "Sull'uso del PCI," *Corriere della Sera*, 23 April 1986.

66. The results of the poll are in *Corriere della Sera*, 9 April 1986.

67. Conversation with Giorgio Ruffolo, Rome, 22 December 1984.

68. *La Repubblica*, 9 August and 20 September 1983; *Corriere della Sera* and *Il Messaggero*, 19 September 1983.

69. Conversation with DC Deputy Renato Ravasio, 4 October 1983.

70. In September 1983, for example, the Christian Democrats held a convention on the government's proposed pension reforms entitled "The Pensioners Betrayed." See *La Repubblica*, 17 September 1983.

71. Sartori, *Teoria dei partiti*, pp. 13–15.

72. For De Mita's report to the congress, see *La Repubblica*, 24 February 1984.

73. Sandro Magister, "La Crociata," *L'Espresso*, 14 April 1985; on the question of party renovation, see the De Mita interview in *La Repubblica*, 6 October 1984.

74. On the issues raised, see the Forlani interview in *La Repubblica*, 22 December 1983; Gianni Baget Bozzo, "Forse Craxi ha vinto . . . ," *La Repubblica*, 3 March 1984; and the editorial in the 1 March 1984 issue. For reports on the Congress, *La Repubblica*, 1 March 1984.

75. *Corriere della Sera*, 11 November 1985.

76. Giorgio Galli, "Bettino, primo a sinistra," *Panorama*, 9 February 1986; Gianni Statera, "Il pivot socialista," *Corriere della Sera*, 2 April 1986.

77. *La Repubblica*, 21 January 1986; *Corriere della Sera*, 7, 13, and 21 March 1986.

78. *Corriere della Sera*, 30 April 1986.

79. Chiara Valenti, "Voglio un Natta di scorta," *Panorama*, 8 June 1986.

80. Spencer Di Scala, "Italy: Stability Despite All the Turmoil," *The Christian Science Monitor*, 9 July 1986.

81. The development of the crisis may be followed in detail in the Italian press between 27 June and August 1986. On the socialist attitude, see *La Stampa*, 8, 10, 12, and 15 July 1986; *Corriere della Sera*, 18 July 1986; Craxi interview, *L'Espresso*, 6 July 1986; and *Europeo*, 12 July 1986. For the DC position, see the De Mita interview in *La Stampa*, 9 July 1986; and *Corriere della Sera*, 22 July 1986. On the Andreotti-PCI flirt, see *La Stampa*, 1 July 1986; *Stampa Sera*, 14 and 17 July 1986; *La Repubblica*, 18 July 1986; and *L'Espresso*, 20 July 1986. On the attitude of the lay

parties, see especially *Il Messaggero*, 8 July 1986, and *Corriere della Sera*, 16 July 1986. For the labor and industrialist request for stability, see *Il Messaggero*, 8 July 1986, and *La Stampa*, 8 July 1986. For a sampling of the hostility toward the DC during the crisis, see Alberto Ronchey, "I duellanti di Largo Chigi," *Corriere della Sera*, 15 July 1986; and Norberto Bobbio, "Crisi indecifrabile," *La Stampa*, 11 July 1986.

82. Craxi's program for his second government is in *Corriere della Sera*, 6 August 1986.

83. Alberto Jacoviello, "Craxi, Andreotti, Spadolini," *La Repubblica*, 28 September 1983. Craxi's talks in Paris, London, and Bonn and his correspondence with Reagan may be followed in *Corriere della Sera*, 16, 17, and 24 September 1983; and *La Repubblica*, 18–19 and 10 September 1983.

84. *La Repubblica*, 21 October 1983.

85. *L'Espresso*, 24 October 1983.

86. Pino Buongiorno, "Tutti al riparo, c'è lo scudo," *Panorama*, 2 March 1986.

87. For reports on Craxi's meetings with Kohl and Mitterand, see *La Repubblica*, 21 and 24 February 1984; on the meeting with Soares, *La Repubblica*, 26 August 1983; on the meeting of EC Socialists, *La Repubblica*, 10 April 1985; on the European Parliament's action and Italy's crucial role, *Corriere della Sera* and *Il Messaggero*, 12 December 1985; see also the Jacques Delors (European Commission president) interview in *Panorama*, 2 March 1986.

88. Spencer Di Scala, "Spain and Italy: An Informal Alliance," *The Christian Science Monitor*, 25 February 1986. See also the remarks of the Spanish prime minister to the Italian press before his 1983 visit to Craxi, in *La Repubblica*, 14 October 1983. For earlier Italian help to the Spanish nuclear industry, see Mario Silvestri, *Il costo della menzogna: Italia Nucleare 1945–1968* (Turin: Einaudi, 1968), p. 52.

89. *Avanti!* 7 September 1983.

90. *The New York Times*, 24 November 1983; *La Repubblica*, 27 December 1983 and 3 January 1984.

91. Joseph La Palombara, "Come vedono Andreotti," *La Repubblica*, 10 January 1984. For a more comprehensive view of Italo-American foreign relations, see also La Palombara's "The *Achille Lauro* Affair: A Note on Italy and the United States," *The Yale Review* 75, no. 4 (Summer 1986): 542–63.

92. Enrico Jacchia, "Middle East: Italians Busy Out Front," *International Herald Tribune*, 10 January 1985; *Corriere della Sera*, 10 December 1984; and *La Repubblica*, 10 December 1984 for Andreotti's exploitation of Italy's stance on the issue.

93. Spencer Di Scala, "Achille Lauro—and Diplomatic Ties," *The Christian Science Monitor*, 22 October 1985. See also the editorial in *L'Espresso*, 20 October 1985. The same issue has a good chronicle of the *Lauro* affair.

94. The accord's text is in *Il Tempo*, 31 October 1985. For the debate on Craxi's remarks, see *Corriere della Sera*, 1, 8, and 9 November 1985; and *Il Tempo*, 4 November 1985.

95. *Corriere della Sera*, 24 April 1986.

96. Spencer Di Scala, "Terrorism—and the Qaddafi Sideshow," *The Christian Science Monitor*, 9 April 1986; *The New York Times*, 20 April 1986; *Corriere della Sera*, 26 March, 16–23 April 1986.

97. Carlo Rossella, "Col Mediterraneo alla gola," *Panorama*, 2 March 1986.

98. *Corriere della Sera*, 6 and 8 May 1986; and Enzo Bettiza, "Questi socialisti," *Corriere della Sera*, 11 May 1986. See also Enzo Bettizza, "Una nuova protagonista sulla scena internazionale," *La Nazione*, 23 October 1983, in Intini, ed., *Craxi in prima pagina*, pp. 137–40. For communist sympathy for Craxi's actions after Sigonella and the Libyan crisis, see *Panorama*, 3 November 1985, and *Corriere della Sera*, 24 April 1986; see also Claudio Rinaldi, "Bettino il rosso," *Panorama*, 16 March 1986.

99. Amato's remarks are in *La Repubblica*, 13 October 1983. On the interview, the Spadolini anecdote, and Craxi's problems with journalists, see Gerosa, *Craxi*, pp. 16–30. David Hine makes

some good observations on Craxi's tenure in "The Craxi premiership," in Leonardi and Nanetti, eds., *Italian Politics,* pp. 105–16.

Chapter 15

1. H. Stuart Hughes, "The Socialist Dilemma in Western Europe," *Dissent* 8, no. 4 (Autumn 1961): 432–40.

2. Franco Cazzola, *Il partito come organizzazione: Studio di un caso, il PSI* (Rome: Edizioni del Tritone, 1970), pp. 69–72; Sergio Mattana, "La struttura e la base sociale del PSI," in Valdo Spini and Sergio Mattana, eds., *I quadri del PSI* (Florence: Nuova Guaraldi, 1981), pp. 64–67.

3. Cazzola, *Il partito,* p. 102; Alberto Spreafico, "Il profilo dell'amministratore locale socialista," in Spini and Mattana, eds. *I quadri,* pp. 77–81; and Mattana, "La struttura," p. 64.

4. The percentage varies according to geographical area and political jurisdiction. See Spreafico's essay, "Il profilo," pp. 76–77, for a breakdown; see also the discussion in Donald Sassoon, *Contemporary Italy: Politics, Economy and Society Since 1945* (London: Longman, 1986), pp. 218–19.

5. Conversation with Landolfi, 18 December 1984.

6. Spini, *3 congressi,* pp. 102–5; *Avanti!* 13 January 1984.

7. *La Repubblica,* 4 October 1983.

8. PSI, *Per un moderno riformismo,* pp. 128–38; PSI, *Il PSI verso il 43 Congresso,* pp. 22–35.

9. Dario Fertilio, "PSI: Il congresso della modernità," *Critica Sociale,* April–May 1984.

10. *La Repubblica,* 2 and 4 October 1984.

11. *La Repubblica,* 17 March 1984.

12. *La Repubblica,* 11 October 1984.

13. Giolitti interview, *L'Espresso,* 7 October 1984. In 1987, Giolitti was elected to Parliament on an independent leftist ticket allied to the PCI.

14. At this point and others, Giolitti made observations in confidence. I have respected his wishes.

15. This conversation took place before publication of Sylos Labini's *Le classi sociali negli anni '80,* although Giolitti is acknowledged in the preface as having read the manuscript. Sylos Labini argues, in effect, that the working class is disappearing not only in Italy but also in the most economically advanced countries.

16. Conversation with Giolitti, 27 December 1984.

17. Conversation with Paolo Flores d'Arcais, Rome, 20 December 1984. Flores d'Arcais has recently shown signs of returning to active politics.

18. Conversation with Giorgio Ruffolo, 22 December 1984. Ruffolo has since become Minister for the Environment in the Goria Cabinet.

19. This thesis is cogently argued bx Luciano Pellicani in his *Miseria del Marxismo: Da Marx al Gulag* (Milan: SugarCo, 1984).

20. Luciano Pellicani, "Il futuro della sinistra," *Mondoperaio,* August–September 1984.

21. PSI, *Il PSI verso il 43 Congresso,* pp. 21–23.

22. *Il Messaggero,* 27 August 1986.

23. *La Repubblica,* 27 August 1986.

24. Giorgio Ruffolo, "Mettete un' po' di Reagan nel motore," *La Repubblica,* 27 August 1986.

25. Gianni Baget Bozzo, "Ma adesso tutto il partito deve parlare," *La Repubblica,* 12 December 1985.

26. Conversation with Ferri, 9 January 1985; *Panorama,* 4 January 1987.

27. See the dissension of Nilde Jotti toward PCI policy on parliamentary reform in *Panorama*, 7 December 1986; the criticism of Togliatti in *Panorama*, 23 November 1986; and the story of *La Repubblica* editor Scalfari's clamorous apparent break with his old friend De Mita in *Panorama*, 7 December 1986.

28. *Panorama*, 23 November 1986.

Epilogue

1. Spencer Di Scala, "Is Andreotti Really In? Craxi Out? Hold On To Your Hats! *The Christian Science Monitor*, 19 March 1987.

2. Corbetta and Parisi, "The 1985 Local Government Elections," p. 22; Spencer Di Scala, "Italy's Eve of Momentous Change," *The Christian Science Monitor*, 15 May 1987.

3. Renato Mannheimer, "Sempre meno elettori, sempre piu' infedeli," and Dario Fertilio, "Che cosa nasconde la guerra dei numeri," *Corriere della Sera*, 22 June 1987.

4. *Corriere della Sera* 25, 27 June 1987; *La Repubblica*, 10 July 1987; *L'Espresso*, 12 July 1987.

5. The Martelli-Occhetto debate is in *L'Espresso*, 12 July 1987.

6. Luciano Pellicani, "Dimenticare Gramsci," *Avanti!* 5 July 1987.

7. Stefano Carlucci, "Voti popolari passano dal PCI al PSI," *Avanti!* 28 June 1987, and the vote analysis in *Panorama*, 12 July 1987.

8. Ugo Stille, "I dilemmi dei socialisti," *Corriere della Sera*, 12 July 1987.

9. *Panorama*, 12 July 1987, and *La Repubblica*, 11 July 1987.

10. Augusto Minzolini, "San Giovanni dimezzato," *Panorama*, 30 August 1987.

11. Interview with Flaminio Piccoli, *Panorama*, 30 August 1987; *Il Messaggero*, 16 September 1987.

12. *Europeo*, 19 September 1987, and *Il Messaggero*, 16 September 1987.

Selected Bibliography

The following is intended primarily, although not exclusively, as a bibliography on the period treated in the text. Just as in the text, there is here some extension into earlier periods and movements related to or affecting Italian socialism. To avoid making this bibliography too unwieldy, I have not included here all the articles cited in the notes. The reader will find full citations in the notes themselves. The arrangement is as follows:

1. Primary Sources
   A. Archives
   B. Documents, memoirs, diaries, collections, interviews, speeches
   C. Articles
2. Secondary Sources
   A. Books
   B. Articles
3. Periodicals
4. Newspapers
5. Unpublished Materials

Primary Sources

Archives

Archivio Centrale dello Stato (Rome)
       Verbali del Consiglio dei Ministri
       Partito Socialista Italiano—Affari Generali
       Ministero Interno, Direzione Pubblica Sicurezza
       Casellario Politico Centrale

John F. Kennedy Library (Boston)
       National Security Council, Countries File
       Arthur M. Schlesinger, Jr., Papers
       Oral Interviews
       President's Office Files

Archivio Lelio Basso (Rome)

International Institute for Social History (Amsterdam)
       Filippo Turati Papers

Documents, Memoirs, Diaries, Collections, Interviews, Speeches

Amendola, Giorgio. *Intervista sull'antifascismo*. Bari: Laterza, 1976.

Andreotti, Giulio. *Diari, 1976–1979*. Milan: Rizzoli, 1981.

Atti Parlamentari: Camera dei Deputati. Leg. 1–9.

Atti Parlamentari: Senato della Repubblica. Leg. 1–9.

Balzamo, Vincenzo, et al. *Ordine pubblico e sicurezza democratica: Atti del Convegno Nazionale del PSI, Milano 7–9 marzo 1975*. Milan: La Nuova Italia, 1976.

Basso, Lelio. *I socialisti davanti alla costituzione*. Rome: Camera dei Deputati, 1947.

Benvenuto, Giorgio, et al. *Strategia riformista e sindacato*. Milan: Arti Grafiche Fiorini, n.d.

———. *Verso un nuovo sindacato: L'iniziativa della UIL per l'unità del movimento*. Venice: Marsilio, 1977.

Bobbio, Norberto, et al. *Il marxismo e lo stato*. Rome: Quaderni di Mondo Operaio, no. 4, 1976.

Bonomi, Ivanoe, *Diario di un anno* (Milan: Garzanti, 1947).

Bufalini, Paolo. *Terrorismo e democrazia: La relazione al Comitato Centrale e alla Commissione Centrale di controllo del PCI, 18 aprile 1978*. Rome: Riuniti, 1978.

Centro Economico per la Costituente. *Convegno sui consigli di gestione: Il dibattito sui consigli di gestione*. Milan: Picardi, 1946.

Coen, Federico, ed. *Quale riforma dello Stato*. Rome: Mondo Operaio-Edizioni Avanti, 1978.

Colarizi, Simona, ed. *Riccardo Lombardi: Scritti politici*, 2 vols. Venice: Marsilio, 1978.

Colby, William. *Honorable Men: My Life in the CIA*. New York: Simon and Schuster, 1978.

Craxi, Bettino. *Costruire il futuro*. Milan: Rizzoli, 1977.

———. *Lotta politica*. Milan: SugarCo, 1978.

———. *Un passo avanti*. Milan: SugarCo, 1981.

———. *Per un polo socialista: Discorso di Bettino Craxi al 40 Congresso del PSI, 6 marzo 1976*. La Biblioteca Rossa, n.d.

———. *Prove*. Milan: SugarCo., 1980.

———. *Relazione al Comitato Centrale, Roma 15–17 novembre 1976*. Rome: SETI, 1976.

———. *Socialismo da Santiago a Praga*. Milan: SugarCo, 1976.

———. *Le tesi per il 42 Congresso, Palermo 22–26 aprile 1981: Supplemento al n. 3 della Critica Sociale di marzo 1981*. Milan: Arti Grafiche Fiorini, 1981.

———. *Tre anni*. Milan: SugarCo, 1983.

Craxi, Bettino, et al. *Marxismo, leninismo, socialismo*. Rome: Mondo Operaio, 1979.

———. *Uscire dalla crisi: Linee di un programma economico socialista*. Venice: Marsilio, 1977.

Craxi in prima pagina: L'occhio della stampa sul governo a guida socialista. La Biblioteca Rossa, [1984].

Croce, Benedetto. *Scritti e discorsi politici (1943–1947)*. Bari: Laterza, 1963.

De Feo, Italo. *Diario politico, 1943–1948*. Milan: Rusconi, 1973.

De Martino, Francesco, et al. *Il movimento operaio e socialista (1892–1963): Bilancio storiografico e problemi storici, convegno di Firenze 18–20 gennaio 1963*. Bologna: Edizioni del Gallo, 1963.

Egemonia e democrazia: Gramsci e la questione comunista nel dibattito di Mondoperaio. Supplemento al n. 718, luglio–agosto 1977 di Mondoperaio. Rome: Mondoperaio, 1977.

Faggi, Vico, ed. *Sandro Pertini: Sei condanne due evasioni*. Milan: Mondadori, 1978.

Fanfani, Amintore. *Autunno 1956: La democrazia cristiana e i problemi internazionali*. Rome: Cinque Lune, 1956.

———. *Centro-Sinistra, 1962*. Rome: Garzanti, 1963.

Fascismo e antifascismo (1918–1936): Lezioni e testimonianze, 2 vols. Milan: Feltrinelli, 1963.

Ferri, Mauro. *Cinque anni al parlamento europeo, 1979–1984*. Naples: Edizioni Scientifiche Italiane, 1984.

————. *I socialisti in parlamento: Discorsi parlamentari nella quarta legislatura.* Rome: Lerici, 1968.

Forbice, Aldo. *Austerità e democrazia operaia: Intervista a Giorgio Benvenuto.* Milan: SugarCo, 1977.

Il Governo Craxi. Edizione speciale di Vita Italiana 33, nos. 7–8 (July–August 1983).

Greppi, Antonio. *La coscienza in pace: Cinquant' anni di socialismo.* Milan: Avanti, 1963.

Gramsci, Antonio. *Opere di Antonio Gramsci.* 5 vols. Turin: Einaudi, 1966.

Ingrao, Pietro. *Crisi e terza via: Intervista di Romano Ledda.* Rome: Riuniti, 1978.

[Intini, Ugo, ed.] *Tutti gli angoli di Craxi.* Milan: Rusconi, 1984.

Istituto Centrale di Statistica, Ministero dell'Interno. *Le elezioni politiche del 1948,* 3 vols. Rome: Falilli, 1951.

Istituto Giangiacomo Feltrinelli. *Documenti inediti dell'archivio Angelo Tasca: La rinascita del socialismo italiano e la lotta contro il fascismo dal 1934 al 1939, introduzione e documenti a cura di Stefano Merli.* Milan: Feltrinelli, 1963.

La Ganga, Giuseppe. *Organizzazione dello stato e democrazia: Temi per un progetto socialista.* Milan: Franco Angeli, 1977.

Leone, Giovanni. *Cinque mesi a Palazzo Chigi.* Milan: Mondadori, 1964.

Lettere di condannati a morte della resistenza italiana, 8 settembre 1943–25 aprile 1945. Turin: Einaudi, 1955.

Libertini, Lucio, ed. *La sinistra e il controllo operaio.* Milan: Feltrinelli, 1969.

Lizzadri, Oreste. *Il regno di Badoglio e la resistenza romana.* Rome: Napoleone, 1974.

————. *Il socialismo italiano dal frontismo al centro-sinistra.* Rome: Lerici, 1969.

Lombardi, Riccardo, et al. *Crisi della DC e alternativa socialista: Per una trasformazione democratica del paese.* Venice: Marsilio, 1975.

Manacorda, Gastone, ed. *Il socialismo italiano nella storia dell'Italia.* Bari: Laterza, 1966.

Maranini, Giuseppe. *Socialismo non stalinismo.* Florence: Edizioni Alvernia, 1949.

Martelli, Claudio. *Alle radici del terrorismo: Relazione del vice segretario del PSI Claudio Martelli alla direzione del partito, Roma 15 gennaio 1982. Interventi, dati e statistiche sul terrorismo.* Rome: PSI, n.d.

Martinelli, Roberto. *SIFAR: Gli atti del processo De Lorenzo—"L'Espresso."* Milan: Mursia, 1968.

Merli, Stefano, ed. "La ricostruzione del movimento socialista in Italia e la lotta contro il fascismo dal 1943 alla seconda guerra mondiale. *Annali dell'Istituto Giangiacomo Feltrinelli,* no. 5 (1962): 541–846.

Modigliani, Vera. *Esilio.* Milan: Garzanti, 1946.

Montana, Vanni. *Amarostico: Testimonianze euro-americane.* Livorno: U. Bastogi, 1975.

Morandi, Rodolfo. *Opere di Rodolfo Morandi.* Turin: Einaudi, 1961.

————. *La politica unitaria.* Edited by Stefano Merli. Turin: Einaudi, 1975.

Natta, Alessandro, ed. *Togliatti editorialista, 1962–1964.* Rome: Riuniti, n.d.

Nenni, Pietro. *Gli anni del centro-sinistra: Diari 1957–1966.* Milan: SugarCo, 1982.

————. *La battaglia socialista per la svolta a sinistra nella terza legislatura, 1958–1963.* Rome: Avanti, 1963.

————. *I conti con la storia: Diari 1967–1971.* Milan: SugarCo, 1983.

————. *Dal patto atlantico alla politica di distensione.* Florence: Parenti, 1953.

————. *Daremo al governo la stabilità e la forza politica indispensabile per attuare il programma: Discorso alla Camera nel dibattito sulla fiducia al governo di Centro-Sinistra.* Rome: PSI, 1962.

————. *Dialogo con la sinistra cattolica.* Rome: Avanti, 1954.

————. *Discorso agli elettori: Scegli l'alternativa socialista, Milano 18 aprile 1958.* Milan: PSI, n.d. [1958].

————. *Intervista sul socialismo italiano.* Bari: Laterza, 1977.

————. *La lutte de classes en Italie*. Paris: Nouvelle Revue Socialiste, 1930.

————. *Problemi e prospettive della democrazia e del socialismo: Relazione al 34 Congresso del PSI*. Rome: PSI, 1961.

————. *Le prospettive del socialismo dopo la destalinizzazione*, 2nd ed. Turin: Einaudi, 1962.

————. *Relazione del compagno Nenni alla riunione dei senatori e deputati del PSI, Roma, 14 ottobre 1948*. N.p.: n.d.

————. *Rodolfo Morandi: Una vita, una dottrina, una politica*. Rome: P.S.I., 1955.

————. *Il socialismo nella democrazia*. Florence: Vallechi, 1966.

————. *Socialisti e comunisti*. Rome: Tip. Laziale, 1944.

————. *Lo spettro del comunismo*. Milan: Modernissima, 1921.

————. *Storia di quattro anni, 1919–1922*. Milan: SugarCo, 1976.

————. *Tempo di guerra fredda: Diari 1943–1956*. Milan: SugarCo, 1981.

————. *Una battaglia vinta*. Rome: Edizioni Leonardo, 1946.

Panzieri, Raniero. *La ripresa del marxismo in Italia*. Milan: Sapere Edizioni, 1972.

Partito Comunista Italiano. *Il comunismo italiano nella seconda guerra mondiale: Relazione e documenti presentati dalla direzione del partito al 5 Congresso del Partito Comunista Italiano*. Rome: Riuniti, 1963.

————. *Il processo ai comunisti italiani, 1923*. Rome: Libreria Editrice del PCI, 1924.

Partito Socialista Italiano (Sezione dell'Internazionale Operaia Socialista). *Il congresso dell'unità socialista*. Paris: Imp. SFIC, 1930.

Partito Socialista Italiano. *23 Congresso Nazionale—3 congresso d'esilio*. Paris: Nuovo Avanti, 1937.

————. *31 Congresso Nazionale del PSI*. Rome and Milan: Avanti, 1955.

————. *32 Congresso Nazionale*. Rome and Milan: Avanti, 1957.

————. *33 Congresso Nazionale: Resoconto stenografico*. Milan and Rome: Avanti, 1959.

————. *34 Congresso Nazionale: Resoconto stenografico*. Milan: Avanti, 1961.

————. *35 Congresso Nazionale: Resoconto integrale*. Milan: Avanti, 1964.

————. *37 Congresso e l'unificazione socialista*. Bologna: La Squilla, 1970.

————. *L'alternativa dei socialisti: Il progetto di programma del PSI presentato da Bettino Craxi*. Rome: Mondo Operaio, 1978.

————. *Da Torino a Palermo: Tre anni di politica socialista*. Rome: PSI, n.d.

————. *Dovere dei socialisti, condannare gli accordi della Camilluccia: A cura della sinistra socialista*. Rome: Manganelli, n.d.

————. *Governare il cambiamento: Conferenza programmatica del PSI, Rimini 31 marzo–4 aprile 1982*. Rome: PSI, n.d.

————. *Introduzione ai problemi di fondo del PSI*. N.p.: n.d.

————. *Libro bianco sull'illecita ingerenza dell'apparato comunista nel dibattito congressuale e nella vita del PSI*. Milan: Edit. Soc., 1959.

————. *Note illustrative dei membri autonomisti del C.C. del PSI e testo del documento*. Milan: La Stampa, n.d.

————. *Il Partito Socialista Italiano dal congresso di Venezia al congresso di Napoli: Una cronaca necessaria, documenti per la relazione della sinistra*. Rome: SETI, 1958.

————. *Il Partito Socialista: Struttura e organizzazione. Atti della conferenza nazionale di organizzazione, Firenze 6–9 febbraio 1975*. Venice: Marsilio, 1975.

————. *Il PSI verso il 43 Congresso: Sintesi dei lavori del Comitato Centrale*. Rome: PSI, 1983.

————. *Una politica socialista per il rinnovamento dell'azione di classe: Relazione di Tullio Vecchietti al 33 Congresso*. Rome: SETI, 1958.

————. *Relazione di Giacomo Mancini al 39 Congresso Nazionale*. Rome: SETI, 1972.

————. *La relazione di Nenni al 33 Congresso del PSI: Confermare la linea politica decisa a Venezia, riente di più, niente di meno*. Rome: SETI, 1958.

————. *Statuto del Partito Socialista Italiano (approvato dal 25 Congresso del Partito, Roma, gennaio 1947)*. Rome: UESISA, 1947.

————. *Tesi per il 42 Congresso del PSI, Palermo 22–26 aprile 1981*. Milan: Arti Grafiche Fiorin, 1981.

Partito Socialista Italiano, Direzione. *Per un moderno riformismo. Tesi del PSI per il 43 Congresso, Verona 11–15 maggio 1984*. Rome: PSI, 1984.

————. *Resoconto stenografico del 17 Congresso Nazionale (Livorno 15–20 gennaio 1921)*. Rome: Avanti. 1963.

Partito Socialista Italiano, Direzione, Sezione Attività Editoriali di Propaganda. *Almanacco Socialista: Le immagini del socialismo. Comunicazione politica e propaganda del PSI dalle origini agli anni ottanta*. Introduction by Bettino Craxi. N.p.: n.d.

Partito Socialista Italiano, Direzione, Sezione Problemi dello Stato. *Costituzione e organi dello Stato: Proposte per l'attuazione delle libertà civili*. Rome: Napoleone, 1977.

Partito Socialista Italiano, Direzione, Sezione Propaganda. *Il rinnovamento socialista per il rinnovamento dell'Italia: Atti del 42 Congresso del PSI, Palermo 22–26 aprile 1981*. Rome: PSI, n.d.

————. *Rinnovare l'Italia: Governare davvero. Il programma socialista per la nona legislatura*. Rome: PSI, n.d. [1983].

Partito Socialista Italiano, Federazione Giovanile Socialista Italiano. *La lunga trama nera: Otto anni di tentativi reazionari contro i lavoratori e la democrazia*. Rome: Nov. IGI, n.d.

————. *Tesi per il 27 Congresso della FGSI, Bologna 28 aprile–1 maggio 1977*. Rome: Elengraf, 1977.

Partito Socialista Italiano, Ufficio Autonomie e Poteri Locali. *Per la repubblica delle autonomie: Proposta socialista per la riforma dei poteri locali*. Milan: SugarCo, 1978.

Partito Socialista Italiano d'Unità Proletaria. *Il 24 Congresso Nazionale, Firenze 11–16 aprile 1946*. Bologna: La Squilla, 1976.

————. *Progetto di statuto democratico del Partito Socialista Italiano*. Milan, 1945.

————. *Progetto di Statuto. Numero speciale di Rassegna Socialista*, no. 12, 20–24 January 1946.

Partito Socialista Unificato, Sezione Economica. *Atti del convegno: Triangolo industriale, mezzogiorno e sviluppo economico nazionale, Torino 15–16 Iuglio 1967*. Turin: Lacaita, 1967.

Pesce, Giovanni. *Senza tregua: La guerra dei GAP*. Milan: Feltrinelli, 1976.

Prima Conferenza economica socialista per la pacifica espansione del lavoro e delle intelligenze in una civiltà liberata dal bisogno. Rome: 1947–48. Bollettino dell'Istituto di Studi Socialisti, nos. 14–18 (1948).

Progetto Socialista. Bari: Laterza, 1976.

Romita, Giuseppe. *Dalla monarchia alla Repubblica*. Milan: Mursia, 1966.

Rosselli, Carlo. *Scritti politici e autobiografici*. Naples: Polis, 1944.

————. *Socialismo Liberale*. Turin: Einaudi, 1973.

Salvemini, Gaetano. *Italian Fascist Activities in the United States*. Edited with an introduction by Philip V. Cannistraro. New York: Center for Migration Studies, 1977.

————. *Memorie di un fuoruscito*. Milan: Feltrinelli, 1965.

Saraceno, Pasquale. *Intervista sulla ricostruzione, 1943–1953*. Bari: Laterza, 1977.

Saragat, Giuseppe. *Antifascismo Democrazia Socialismo: Pagine attuali degli anni dell'esilio*. Rome: Opere Nuove, 1951.

————. *Quaranta anni di lotta per la democrazia: Scritti e discorsi 1925–1965*. Milan: Mursia, 1966.

————. *Socialismo e libertà*. Rome: Avanti, n.d.

[Scelba, Mario]. *Il programma del governo nelle dichiarazioni del Presidente del Consiglio On. Mario Scelba alla Camera e al Senato (18 e 26 febbraio–10 marzo 1954)*. Rome: Istituto Poligrafico dello Stato, 1954.

Schiavi, Alessandro, ed. *Esilio e morte di Filippo Turati, 1926–1932*. Rome: Opere Nuove, 1956.

Senato della Repubblica, Atti Interni, V Leglislatura, Documenti, Volume LV, n. XXXIII–1.

Commissione Parlamentare d'Inchiesta sugli eventi del giugno–luglio 1964. *Relazione.* Rome: Tipografia dello Stato, 1972.

Senato della Repubblica, V Legislatura, Doc. XXIII, n. 1. Commissione Parlamentare d'Inchiesta sugli eventi del giugno–luglio 1964. *Relazioni di minoranza.* Rome: Tipografia dello Stato, 1971.

Sforza, Carlo. *Cinque anni a Palazzo Chigi.* Rome: Atlante, 1952.

Sturzo, Luigi. *L'apertura a sinistra e l'unificazione socialista,* 2nd ed. Naples: Edizioni di Politica Popolare, 1956.

Tarchiani, Alberto. *America-Italia: Le dieci giornate di De Gasperi negli Stati Uniti.* Milan: Rizzoli, 1947.

Il testamento politico di Pietro Nenni. Milan: Supplemento de "L'Ordine Nuovo" di Milano, 1957.

Togliatti, Palmiro. *Lectures on Fascism.* New York: International Publishers, 1976.

———. *La politica di Salerno.* Rome: Riuniti, 1969.

Treves, Claudio. *Un socialista: Filippo Turati.* Milan: Critica Sociale, n.d.

Turati, Filippo. *Trenti'anni di Critica Sociale.* Bologna: Zanichelli, 1921.

———. *Le vie maestre del socialismo,* 2nd ed. Naples: Morano, 1966.

Turati, Filippo, and Anna Kuliscioff. *Carteggio,* 7 vols. Turin: Einaudi, 1949–1978.

U.S. Department of State. *Foreign Relations of the United States, 1948, Vol. 3: Western Europe.* Washington, D.C.: Government Printing Office, 1974.

Vallauri, Carlo, ed. *La ricostituzione dei partiti democratici,* 3 vols. Rome: Bulzoni, 1978.

Vecchietti, Tullio. *I socialisti per la svolta a sinistra.* Rome: Arti Grafiche Privitera, 1962.

———. "Relazione della 'sinistra' per il 34 Congresso del PSI." *Politica Socialista,* 1 (January 1961): 24–35.

Zucàro, Domenico, ed. *Lettere all'OVRA di Pitigrilli.* Florence: Parenti, 1961.

Zuccherini, Valentino, ed. *Progetto e alternativa socialista: Atti del seminario e del convegno dei sindacalisti socialisti della CGIL, Roma 25–27 febbraio 19785.* Rome: Mondo Operaio, 1978.

1945–1985 Italia. Fascismo antifascismo resistenza rinnovamento. Conversazioni promosse dal Consiglio regionale lombardo nel trentennale della Liberazione. Milan: Feltrinelli, 1975.

Articles

Basso, Lelio. "A New Socialist Party." *International Socialist Journal* 2 (April 1964): 161–73.

———. "L'alleanza della classe operaia con i ceti medi." *Problemi del Socialismo,* no. 12 (December 1960): 1061–71.

———. "L'alternativa a de Gaulle é la politica kennediana?" *Problemi del Socialismo* 1 (January 1963): 60–62.

———. "L'ammonimento di un voto." *Problemi del Socialismo,* no. 11 (November 1960): 945–58.

———. "Another Step Backwards." *International Socialist Journal,* no. 4 (August 1964): 407–16.

———. "L'aspetto politico dei nuclei aziendiali." *Quarto Stato,* no. 11 (30 June 1946): 159–62.

———. "La battaglia socialista del 1963." *Problemi del Socialismo* 1 (January 1963): 3–10.

———. "The Centre-Left in Italy." *New Left Review* 17 (Winter 1962): 9–16.

———. "Il colpo di stato di De Gasperi." *Rinascita* 9, no. 9 (September 1952): 467–69.

———. "Contro il patto di guerra." *Quarto Stato,* nos. 4–5 (28 February–15 March 1949): 17–22.

———. "Il convegno dei nuclei aziendiali." *Quarto Stato* 1, no. 11 (June 1946): 159–62.

———. "Crisi del governo o crisi del sistema?" *Problemi del Socialismo* 3 (March 1960): 193–213.

————. "La crisi del Partito Socialista." *Quarto Stato* 1, no. 1 (January 1946): 2–7.

————. "Dopo il congresso." *Problemi del Socialismo* 10 (October 1963): 1093–96.

————. "E ora?" *Problemi del Socialismo* 4 (April 1963): 393–401.

————. "L'esperienza sovietica e la dittatura del proletariato." *Mondo Operaio* 10, no. 7 (July 1956): 412–22.

————. "Giunte difficili o giunte impossibili?" *Problemi del Socialismo* 1 (January 1961): 74–75.

————. "Logica di classe." *Socialismo* 2, no. 6 (June 1947): 104–9.

————. "Il nuovo governo e le prospettive future." *Problemi del Socialismo* 3 (March 1962): 136–49.

————. "Per una moderna democrazia." *Critica Sociale,* 1 March 1946.

————. "La politica del PSI: Centro-sinistra e alternativa democratica." *Problemi del Socialismo* 5 (May 1960): 383–404.

————. "Ragioni e speranze della scissione socialista." *Problemi del Socialismo* 11–12 (November–December 1963): 1196–1227.

————. "Il rapporto tra rivoluzione democratica e rivoluzione socialista nella Resistenza." *Critica Marxista* 3, no. 4 (1965): 11–20.

————. "La scissione di Palazzo Barberini non si poteva evitare." *Almanacco Socialista,* 1978.

————. "Stalinismo e destalinizzazione." *I Problemi dell'Ulisse* 16, nos. 48–49 (March–June 1963): 19–31.

————. "Vigilia di Congresso." *Quarto Stato,* nos. 4–5 (March 1946): 45–47.

Basso, Lelio, et al. "La lettera della sinistra a Francesco De Martino." *Mondo Nuovo,* no. 2 (12 January 1964): 9.

"25 Congresso." *Socialismo* 2, nos. 11–12 (November–December 1946): 1–4.

Craxi, Bettino. "Il vangelo socialista." *L'Espresso,* 27 August 1978.

Dagnino, Virgilio. "Palazzo Barberini 27 anni dopo: Dal 'Centro Interno' alla costituzione del PSLI." *Critica Sociale,* November 1974, pp. 519–22.

Fallaci, Oriana. "Nenni racconta." *Europeo,* 22 April 1971.

Fanfani, Amintore. "Italian Democracy Faces Another Test." *Foreign Affairs* 36, no. 3 (April 1958): 449–59.

Garosci, Aldo. "Claudio Treves, 40 anni dopo," *Critica Sociale,* 5 July 1973, pp. 289–93.

La Malfa, Ugo. "The Socialist Alternative in Italy." *Foreign Affairs* 35, no. 2 (January 1957): 311–19.

[Mondoperaio]. "Può rinnovarsi il PSI? Intervista con Enrico Manca." *Mondoperaio* 29, no. 11 (November 1970): 20–22.

————. "Il ruolo del PSI: Intervista con Bettino Craxi, Riccardo Lombardi, Giacomo Mancini, Giovanni Mosca, Piero Boni, Ruggero Ravenna." *Mondoperaio* 29, no. 1 (January 1976): 4–17.

Morandi, Rodolfo. "Dopo il congresso." *Socialismo* 2, no. 5 (May 1946): 113–15.

————. "Questioni al congresso." *Socialismo* 2, no. 4 (April 1946): 31–36.

Mughini, Giampiero. "Palazzo Chigi vent'anni dopo: Intervista con Giuliano Amato." *Mondoperaio* 36, no. 9 (September 1983): 4–7.

Nenni, Pietro. "Bilancio di una polemica." *Mondo Operaio* 5, no. 17 (6 September 1952): 3–9.

————. "La caduta di Alcide De Gasperi." *Mondo Operaio* 6, no. 14 (8 August 1953): 1–3.

————. "Cause e sviluppi obbiettivi della politica di distensione." *Mondo Operaio* 5, no. 1 (January 1952): 1–8.

————. "La classe lavoratrice nella battaglia per la democrazia." *Socialismo* 1, nos. 5–6 (September–December 1945): 1–3.

————. "La crisi della Concentrazione Antifascista e la riclassificazione dell'emigrazion." *Politica Socialista* 1, no. 1 (August 1934): 26–31.

————. "I due aspetti della società sovietica." *Mondo Operaio* 5, no. 15 (August 1952): 1–2.

————. "Le elezioni del 25 maggio." *Mondo Operaio* 5, no. 7 (6 April 1952): 1–4.

————. "Gli scritti di Stalin e il 19 Congresso del PC dell'URSS." *Mondo Operaio* 5, no. 21 (November 1952): 3–5.

————. "Polemica cattolica sull'apertura a sinistra." *Mondo Operaio* 6, no. 19 (November 1953): 1–4.

————. "La relazione del segretario del partito al CC." *Mondo Operaio* 6, no. 8 (18 April 1953): 4–6.

————. "I socialdemocratici e l'apertura a sinistra." *Mondo Operaio* 6, no. 22 (19 December 1953): 1–4.

————. "La svolta americana." *Mondo Operaio* 6, no. 4 (21 February 1953): 1–4.

————. "Un problema di fondo." *Mondo Operaio* 5, no. 5 (1 March 1952): 1–2.

————. "Validità di una politica." *Mondo Operaio* 5, no. 12 (21 June 1952): 1–2.

————. "Where the Italian Socialists Stand." *Foreign Affairs* 40, no. 2 (January 1962): 213–23.

"Il PSI negli anni del Frontismo." *Mondo Operaio* 30, nos. 7–8 (July–August 1977): 57–65.

Petronio, Giuseppe. "Alternativa Socialista." *Mondo Operaio* 6, no. 2 (24 January 1953): 1–3.

————. "Stalin: un costruttore." *Mondo Operaio* 6, no. 6 (21 March 1953): 1–3.

Quarto Stato. "Congresso di vittoria." *Quarto Stato* 2, no. 24 (January 1947): 2.

————. "Dopo il congresso." *Quarto Stato* 1, nos. 6–7 (April 1946): 77–78.

————. "Vigilia di congresso." *Quarto Stato*, nos. 4–5 (30 March 1946): 45–47.

"La relazione della sinistra al 35 congresso del PSI." *Mondo Nuovo*, no. 23 (15 September 1963): 19–22.

R. P. [Raniero Panzieri] "Nuovo Periodo." *Socialismo* 3, nos. 1–2 (January–February 1947): 1–4.

Saragat, Giuseppe. "La crisi tedesca," *Politica Socialista*, 1, no. 1 (August 1934): 60–62.

————. "Il marxismo e lo stato." *Politica Socialista* 2, no. 3 (March 1935): 248–55.

————. "Programma." *Socialismo* 1, no. 1 (March 1945): 1–3.

————. "Socialismo e libertà." *Politica Socialista* 1, no. 1 (August 1934): 3–6.

————. "Storia di un tentativo per l'unità socialista." *L'Umanità*, 3 December 1947.

Seniga, Giulio. "Togliatti e Stalin: Testimonianza." *La Parola del Popolo*, November–December 1981.

Vasconi, Luciano. "Comunisti e Socialisti: Intervista con Giorgio Amendola." *Mondoperaio* 29, no. 1 (January 1976): 18–20.

————. "Eurosocialismo come alternativa: Intervista con Bettino Craxi." *Mondoperaio* 29, no. 10 (October 1976): 2–5.

Secondary Sources

Books

Accardi, Claudio, ed. *I socialisti: Articoli e discorsi.* Milan: SugarCo, 1978.

Acquaviva, Sabino. *Social Structure in Italy.* London: M. Robertson, 1976.

Adams, John Clarke, and Paolo Barile. *The Government of Republican Italy.* Boston: Houghton Mifflin, 1966.

Aga-Rossi, Elena. *L'Italia nella sconfitta: Politica interna e situazione internazionale durante la seconda guerra mondiale.* Naples: Edizioni Scientifiche Italiane.

Agosti, Aldo. *Rodolfo Morandi: Il pensiero e l'azione politica.* Bari: Laterza, 1972.

Alberoni, Francesco, et al. *I socialisti e la cultura: Materiale e contributi per una politica culturale alternativa.* Venice: Marsilio, 1976.

Allum, Percy A. *L'Italia tra crisi e emergenza.* Naples: Guida, 1979.

————. *Italy—Republic without Government?* New York: Norton, 1973.

Amato, Giuliano, and Luciano Cafagna. *Duello a sinistra: Socialisti e comunisti nei lunghi anni '70.* Bologna: Il Mulino, 1982.

Amato, Pasquale. *Movimenti perduti armonie ritrovate: L'associazionismo socialista tra diaspora e ripresa, 1945/1983.* Rome: Atlantide, 1983.

——. *Il PSI tra frontismo e autonomia, 1948–1954.* Cosenza: Lerici, 1978.

Andreotti, Giulio. *Concerto a sei voci: Storia segreta di una crisi.* Rome: Edizioni della Bussola, 1945.

——. *De Gasperi e il suo tempo,* 3rd ed. Milan: Mondadori, 1964.

[Anonimo]. *Ghino di Tacco: Una storia medievale.* Milan: Mondadori, 1986.

Arfé, Gaetano. *Storia dell'Avanti!* 2 vols. Milan: Avanti, 1956–58.

Arfé, Gaetano, et al. *Trent'anni di politica socialista: Atti del Convegno di Parma, gennaio 1977.* [Rome]: Mondo Operaio-Edizioni Avanti, 1977.

Averardi, Giuseppe. *I socialisti democratici da Palazzo Barberini alla scissione del 4 luglio 1969.* Milan: SugarCo, 1977.

Avolio, Giuseppe. *Agricoltura e sviluppo: La politica agraria del partito socialista dal 1973 al 1975.* Venice: Marsilio, 1975.

Badaloni, Nicola. *Marxismo come storicismo.* Milan: Feltrinelli, 1962.

Badoglio, Pietro. *Italy in the Second World War.* London: Oxford University Press, 1948.

Banfi, Arialdo, et al. *Storia del partito socialista,* 3 vols. Venice: Marsilio, 1979.

Barkan, Joanne. *Visions of Emancipation: The Italian Workers' Movement since 1945.* New York: Praeger, 1984.

Barnes, Samuel H. *Party Democracy: Politics in an Italian Socialist Federation.* New Haven: Yale University Press, 1967.

——. *Representation in Italy: Institutionalized Tradition and Electoral Choice.* Chicago: University of Chicago Press, 1977.

Barrese, Orazio. *Mancini.* Milan: Feltrinelli, 1976.

Bartoli, Domenico. *La fine della monarchia.* Milan: Mondadori, 1966.

——. *L'Italia burocratica.* Milan: Garzanti, 1965.

Barzini, Luigi. *L'antropometro italiano.* Milan: Mondadori, 1973.

Basso, Lelio. *Il Partito Socialista Italiano.* Milan: Nuova Accademia, 1958.

Battaglia, Adolfo, et al. *Dieci anni dopo, 1945–1955: Sulla vita democratica italiana.* Bari: Laterza, 1955.

Battaglia, Roberto. *Storia della resistenza.* Turin: Einaudi, 1953.

Bazzoli, Luigi, and Riccardo Renzi. *Il miracolo Mattei.* Milan: Rizzoli, 1984.

Belfiore, Antonio, and Luigi Giraldi. *L'Italia elettorale.* Rome: Civitas, 1973.

Benot, Yves. *L'autre Italie: Problems de la dictature du proletariat.* Paris: Maspero, 1977.

Benzoni, Alberto. *Il Partito Socialista dalla Resistenza a oggi.* Venice: Marsilio, 1980.

Benzoni, Alberto, and Vivo Tedesco. *Il movimento socialista nel dopoguerra.* Padua: Marsiglio, 1968.

Bisiach, Gianni. *Pertini racconta gli anni 1915–1945.* Milan: Mondadori, 1983.

Blackmer, Donald. *Unity in Diversity: Italian Communism and the Communist World.* Cambridge, Mass.: MIT Press, 1968.

Blackmer, Donald, and Annie Kriegel. *The International Role of the Communist Parties of Italy and France.* Cambridge, Mass.: Center for International Affairs, Harvard University, 1975.

Blackmer, Donald, and Sidney Tarrow. *Communism in Italy and France.* Princeton: Princeton University Press, 1975.

Bocca, Giorgio. *Moro: Una tragedia italiana.* Milan: Bompiani, 1978.

——. *La repubblica di Mussolini.* Bari: Laterza, 1977.

——. *Storia d'Italia nella guerra fascista, 1940–43.* Bari: Laterza, 1977.

——. *Il terrorismo italiano, 1970/1978.* Milan: Rizzoli, 1979.

Bryant, Andrew. *The Italians: How They Live and Work,* rev. ed. New York: Praeger, 1971.

Busino, Giovanni. *Histoire et societé en Italie.* Geneva: Droz, 1972.

Cammett, John M. *Antonio Gramsci and the Origins of Italian Communism.* Stanford: Stanford University Press, 1967.

Campbell, John C. *Successful Negotiation, Trieste, 1954: An Appraisal of the Five Participants.* Princeton: Princeton University Press, 1976.

Candeloro, Giorgio. *Storia dell'Italia Moderna,* 10 vols. Milan: Feltrinelli, 1956–84.

Cannistraro, Philip V. *La fabbrica del consenso: Fascismo e mass media.* Bari: Laterza, 1975.

Canosa, Romano. *La polizia in Italia dal 1945 a oggi.* Bologna: Il Mulino, 1976.

Carocci, Giampiero. *La Resistenza italiana.* Milan: Garzanti, 1963.

———. *Storia del fascismo.* Milan: Garzanti, 1973.

Carrillo, Elisa. *De Gasperi: The Long Apprenticeship.* Notre Dame: University of Notre Dame Press, 1965.

Cartiglia, Carlo. *Rinaldo Rigola e il sindacalismo riformista in Italia.* Milan: Feltrinelli, 1976.

Casanova, Antonio Glauco. *Perchè il 18 aprile: La lotta politica nell'Italia del dopoguerra.* Rome: Prospettive nel Mondo, 1981.

Castronovo, Valerio. "La storia economica," in *Storia d'Italia: Dall'unità a oggi,* Vol. 4, pp. 5–506. Turin: Einaudi, 1975.

Catalano, Franco. *Filippo Turati.* Milan: Avanti, 1957.

Cazzola, Franco. *Carisma e democrazia nel socialismo italiano: Struttura e funzione della direzione del PSI.* Rome: Istituto Luigi Sturzo, 1967.

———. *Governo e opposizione nel parlamento italiano: Dal centrismo al Centro-Sinistra, il sistema della crisi.* Milan: Giuffrè, 1974.

———. *Il partito come organizzazione: Studio di un caso, il PSI.* Rome: Edizioni del Tritone, 1970.

Cederna, Camilla. *Giovanni Leone: La carriera di un presidente.* Milan: Feltrinelli, 1978.

Chabod, Federico. *L'Italia contemporanea (1918–1948).* Turin: Einaudi, 1961.

Classe operaia, partiti politici e socialismo nella prospettiva italiana. Milan: Feltrinelli, 1966.

Clough, Shepard. *The Economic History of Modern Italy.* New York: Columbia University Press, 1964.

Clark, Martin. *Antonio Gramsci and the Revolution That Failed.* New Haven: Yale University Press, 1977.

———. *Modern Italy, 1871–1982.* New York: Longman, 1984.

Colapietra, Raffaele. *La lotta politica in Italia dalla liberazione di Roma alla Costituente.* Bologna: Patron, 1970.

Colarizi, Simona. *Classe operaia e ceti medi: La strategia delle alleanze nel dibattito socialista degli anni trenta.* Venice: Marsilio, 1976.

Coppa, Frank J. *Planning, Protectionism and Politics in Liberal Italy: Economics and Politics in Giolittian Italy.* Washington, D.C.: Catholic University of America Press, 1971.

Costituzione e organi dello Stato. Introduction by Bettino Craxi. Rome: Napoleone, 1977.

Coverdale, John. *Italian Intervention in the Spanish Civil War.* Princeton: Princeton University Press, 1975.

Croce, Benedetto. *Due anni di vita politica italiana, 1945–1947.* Bari: Laterza, 1948.

———. *Per la storia del comunismo in quanto realtà politica.* Bari: Laterza, 1944.

Dalla Costa, Mariarosa. *Potere femminile e sovversione sociale.* Padua: Marsiglio, 1974.

D'Angelo Bigelli, Maria Grazia. *Pietro Nenni dalle barricate a palazzo Madama.* Rome: Giorgio Giannini Editore, 1970.

Davis, Melton S. *Who Defends Rome? The Forty-five Days, July 25–September 8, 1943.* New York: Dial Press, 1972.

Deakin, Frederick William. *The Brutal Friendship.* New York: Harper & Row, 1962.

De Bernardis, Camillo, and Raffaele De Mucci, eds. *Dalla resistenza alla alternativa socialista: I congressi del PSI dal 1946 al 1972.* Rome: IGI, 1976.

De Felice, Renzo. *Le interpretazioni del fascismo.* Bari: Laterza, 1976.

———. *Intervista sul fascismo.* Bari: Laterza, 1975.

———. *Mussolini,* 4 vols. Turin: Einaudi, 1965–74.

De Grand, Alexander, J. *In Stalin's Shadow. Angelo Tasca and the Crisis of the Left in Italy and France, 1910–1945*. DeKalb, Ill.: Northern Illinois University Press, 1986.

De Lutiis, Giuseppe. *Storia dei servizi segreti in Italia*. Rome: Riuniti, 1984.

Delzell, Charles F. *Italy in the Twentieth Century*. Washington, D.C.: American Historical Association, 1980.

————. *Mussolini's Enemies: The Italian Anti-Fascist Resistance*. New York: Howard Fertig, 1974.

De Maggi, Michele. *Cronache senza regime, vicende italiane dal 1944 al 1953*. Bologna: Cappelli, 1953.

De Rosa, Gabriele. *Il partito popolare italiano*. Bari: Laterza, 1969.

————. *Sturzo*. Turin: UTET, 1977.

De Rosa, Gabriele, ed. *I partiti politici in Italia*. Rome: Minerva Italica, 1980.

Diggins, John P. *Mussolini and Fascism: The View from America*. Princeton: Princeton University Press, 1972.

Di Palma, Giuseppe. *Surviving without Governing: The Italian Parties in Parliament*. Berkeley: University of California Press, 1977.

Di Palma, Giuseppe, and Philip Siegelman, eds. *Italy in the 1980s: Paradoxes of a Dual Society*. San Francisco: World Affairs Council, 1983.

Di Scala, Spencer. *Dilemmas of Italian Socialism: The Politics of Filippo Turati*. Amherst: University of Massachusetts Press, 1980.

Di Toro, Claudio. *Prima e dopo il Centro-Sinistra*. Rome: Ideologie, 1970.

Duverger, Maurice. *Les parties politiques*. Paris: A. Colin, 1954.

Earle, John. *Italy in the 1970s*. London: David & Charles, 1975.

Einaudi, Mario, and Francois Gaguel. *Christian Democracy in Italy and France*. Notre Dame: University of Notre Dame Press, 1952.

Emiliani, Paolo. *Dieci anni perduti: Cronache del Partito Socialista Italiano dal 1943 ad oggi*. Pisa: Nistri-Lischi, 1953.

L'esperienza del centro socialista interno. Florence: CLUSF, 1977.

Faenza, Roberto. *Il malaffare: Dall'America di Kennedy all'Italia, a Cuba, al Vietnam*. Milan: Mondadori, 1978.

Faenza, Roberto, and Marco Fini. *Gli americani in Italia*. Milan: Feltrinelli, 1976.

Falconi, Carlo. *Il Pentagono vaticano*. Bari: Laterza, 1958.

Fallaci, Oriana. *Interview with History*. New York: Liveright, 1976.

Farneti, Paolo. *Diario Italiano*. Milan: Garzanti, 1983.

Fedele, Santi. *Fronte popolare: La sinistra e le elezioni del 18 aprile 1948*. Milan: Bompiani, 1978.

————. *Storia della concentrazione antifascista, 1927–1934*. Milan: Feltrinelli, 1976.

Ferrari, Pierre, and Herbert Maisl. *Le groupes communistes aux assemblees parlementaries italiennes* (1958–1963). Paris: Presses Universitaries de France, 1969.

Ferrari Aggradi, Mario. *La svolta economica della Resistenza: Primi atti della politica di programmazione*. Bologna: A. Forni, 1975.

Finetti, Ugo. *Il dissenso nel PCI*. Milan: SugarCo, 1978.

————. *Libro bianco sulla crisi socialista: Tre anni, 1969–1972*. Milan: SugarCo, 1972.

Finzi, Roberto. *L'unità operaia contro il fascismo: Gli scioperi del marzo 1943*. Bologna: Consorzio Provinciale, 1974.

Forlani, Arnaldo. *Il PSI di fronte al comunismo dal 1945 al 1956*. Rome: Cinque Lune, 1956.

Galli, Giancarlo. *Benedetto Bettino*. Milan: Bompiani, 1982.

Galli, Giorgio. *Dal bipartismo imperfetto alla possibile alternativa*. Bologna: Il Mulino, 1975.

————. *Il bipartismo imperfetto: Comunisti e democristiani in Italia*, 2nd ed. Bologna: Il Mulino, 1967.

————. *I colonelli della guerra rivoluzionaria*. Bologna: Il Mulino, 1962.

————. *La crisi italiana e la destra internazionale*. Milan: Mondadori, 1974.

————. *La sinistra italiana nel dopoguerra*. Bologna: Il Mulino, 1958.

————. *Storia del socialismo italiano*. Bari: Laterza, 1983.

————. *Storia della democrazia cristiana*. Bari: Laterza, 1978.

————. *Storia del partito armato, 1968–1982*. Milan: Rizzoli, 1986.

————. *Storia del Partito Comunista Italiano*. Milan: Il Formichiere, 1976.

————. *Storia della società italiana dall'Unità a oggi, VII: I partiti politici*. Turin: UTET, 1974.

Galli, Giorgio, and Alfonso Prandi. *Patterns of Political Participation in Italy*. New Haven: Yale University Press, 1970.

Gambino, Antonio. *Dal '68 a oggi: Come siamo e come eravamo*. Bari: Laterza, 1979.

Garosci, Aldo. *Storia dei fuorusciti*. Bari: Laterza, 1953.

Germino, Dante, and Stefano Passigli. *The Government and Politics of Contemporary Italy*. New York: Harper & Row, 1968.

Gerosa, Guido. *Craxi: Il potere e la stampa*. Milan: Sperling & Kupfer, 1984.

————. *Nenni*. Milan: Longanesi, 1972.

Ghirelli, Antonio. *L'effetto Craxi*. Milan: Rizzoli, 1982.

Giolitti, Antonio, et al. *Politica internazionale e progetto socialista in Italia*. Milan: Franco Angeli, 1977.

Giovine, Umberto, ed. *Disugualianze nel mondo*. Milan: SugarCo, 1977.

Giovine, Umberto, and Paolo Pilliteri. *Europa socialista*. Introduction by Bettino Craxi. Milan: Critica Sociale, 1979.

Gorresio, Vittorio. *Berlinguer*. Milan: Feltrinelli, 1976.

Graziano, Luigi. *La politica estera della repubblica italiana*. Padua: Marsiglio, 1968.

Grinrod, Muriel. *The Rebuilding of Italy: Politics and Economics*. London: Royal Institute of International Affairs, 1955.

Guiducci, Roberto. *Socialismo e verità: Pamphlets di politica e cultura*. Turin: Einaudi, 1956.

Harper, John Lamberton. *America and the Reconstruction of Italy, 1945–1948*. Cambridge: Cambridge University Press, 1986.

————. *Bettino Craxi and the Second Center Left Experiment*. Occasional paper no. 52, April 1986. Bologna: Research Institute, Johns Hopkins University, Bologna Center, 1986.

Haupt, Werner. *Kriegsschauplatz Italien, 1943–1945*. Stuttgart: Motorbuchvertag, 1977.

Hayward, Jack, and Michael Watson, eds. *Planning, Politics and Public Policy: The British, French and Italian Experience*. London: Cambridge University Press, 1975.

Horowitz, Daniel L. *The Italian Labor Movement*. Cambridge, Mass.: Harvard University Press, 1963.

Hughes, H. Stuart. *The United States and Italy*, rev. ed. New York: Norton, 1965.

Indro, Ugo. *La presidenza Sarogat: Cronaca politica di un settennio, 1965–1971*. Milan: Mondadori, 1971.

Istituto socialista di studi storici. *L'emigrazione socialista nella lotta contro il fascismo (1926–1939)*. Florence: Sansoni, 1982.

Italicus. *Storia segreta di un mese di regno*. Rome: Sestante: 1948.

1945–1975 Italia: Fascismo antifascismo resistenza rinnovamento. Milan: Feltrinelli, 1975.

Jemolo, Arturo Carlo. *Anni di prova*. Vicenza: N. Pozza, 1969.

————. *Chiesa e stato in Italia: Dalla unificazione a Giovanni XXIII*. Turin: Einaudi, 1965.

————. *La politica dei partiti nel 1953*. Parma: Guanda, 1953.

Katz, Robert. *The Fall of the House of Savoy*. New York: Macmillan, 1971.

Kiros, Teodros. *Toward the Construction of a Theory of Political Action: Antonio Gramsci*. London: University Press of America, 1985.

Knox, MacGregor. *Mussolini Unleashed*. New York: Cambridge University Press, 1982.

Kogan, Norman. *Italy and the Allies*. Cambridge, Mass.: Harvard University Press, 1956.

————. *A Political History of Italy: The Postwar Years*. New York: Praeger, 1983.

————. *The Politics of Italian Foreign Policy*. New York: Praeger, 1963.

Krippendorff, Ekkehart, ed. *The Role of the United States in the Reconstruction of Italy and West Germany.* Berlin: John F. Kennedy-Institut fur Nordamerikastudien, 1981.

Landolfi, Antonio. *Il socialismo italiano: Strutture comportamenti valori,* rev. ed. Cosenza: Lerici, 1977.

————. *Lo stato, la cassa, il mezzogiorno: La crisi dell'intervento pubblico nel sud.* Rome: Savelli, 1974.

Lange, Peter. *Studies on Italy: 1943–1975.* Turin: Fondazione Giovanni Agnelli, 1977.

Lange, Peter, and Sidney Tarrow, eds. *Italy in Transition: Conflict and Consensus.* London: Frank Cass, 1980.

Lange, Peter, George Ross, and Maurizio Vannicelli. *Unions, Change and Crisis: French and Italian Union Strategy and the Political Economy, 1945–1980.* London: Allen and Unwin, 1982.

La Palombara, Joseph. *Democracy Italian Style.* New Haven: Yale University Press, 1987.

————. *Interest Groups in Italian Politics.* Princeton: Princeton University Press, 1964.

————. *The Italian Labor Movement: Problems and Prospects.* Ithaca: Cornell University Press, 1957.

————. *Italy: The Politics of Planning.* Syracuse, N.Y.: Syracuse University Press, 1966.

Leonardi, Robert, and Raffaella Y. Nanetti. *Italian Politics: A Review,* Volume 1. London: Pinter, 1986.

Lepre, Aurelio. *Storia della svolta di Salerno.* Rome: Riuniti, 1966.

Levine, Irving R. *Main Street, Italy.* Garden City, N.Y.: Doubleday, 1963.

Lindemann, Albert S. *The "Red Years."* Berkeley: University of California Press, 1974.

Lo Bianco, Francesco. *Un tentativo di fronte popolare in Italia.* Rome: Edizioni Roma, 1939.

Lombardo, Antonio. *La Grande Riforma: Governo, istituzioni, partiti.* Milan: SugarCo, 1984.

Lutz, Vera. *Italy: A Study in Economic Development.* London: Oxford University Press, 1962.

Lyttelton, Adrian. *The Seizure of Power: Fascism in Italy, 1919–1929.* New York: Scribner's, 1973.

Mack Smith, Denis. *Italy,* rev. ed. Ann Arbor: University of Michigan Press, 1969.

————. *Mussolini.* New York: Vintage Books, 1982.

————. *Mussolini's Roman Empire.* New York: Viking, 1976.

Mafai, Miriam. *Lombardi.* Milan: Feltrinelli, 1976.

Maier, Charles S. *Recasting Bourgeois Europe.* Princeton: Princeton University Press, 1975.

Malvestiti, Piero. *La lotta politica in Italia dal 25 luglio 1943 alla nuova costituzione.* Milan: Bernabò, 1968.

Mammarella, Giuseppe. *L'Italia dopo il fascismo, 1943–1973.* Bologna: Il Mulino, 1974.

Marchetti, Victor, and John D. Marks. *The CIA and the Cult of Intelligence.* New York: Alfred A. Knopf, 1974.

Martelli, Claudio. *Socialisti a confronto: Saggio sul 40 Congresso del PSI, con una sintesi degli interventi principali.* Milan: SugarCo, 1976.

Margiocco, Mario. *Stati Uniti e PCI.* Bari: Laterza, 1981.

Merli, Stefano. *Il "partito nuovo" di Lelio Basso.* Venice: Marsilio, 1981.

Mieli, Paolo. *Litigio a sinistra.* Rome: L'Espresso, 1979.

Mieli, Renato, ed. *Il PCI allo specchio.* Milan: CESES-Rizzoli, 1983.

Miller, James Edward. *The United States and Italy, 1940–1950: The Politics and Diplomacy of Stabilization.* Chapel Hill: University of North Carolina Press, 1986.

Milza, Pierre. *L'Italie fasciste devant l'opinion francaise, 1920–1940.* Paris: A. Colin, 1967.

Molaioli, Angelo. *Ciao, Nenni.* [Rome]: Almanacco Socialista, 1980.

Monetary Policy in Italy. Paris: OECD, 1973.

Moretti, Paolo. *I due socialismi: La scissione di Palazzo Barberini e la nascita della social-democrazia.* Milan: Mursia, 1975.

Napolitano, Giorgio, and Eric Hobsawm. *The Italian Road to Socialism.* Westport, Conn.: Lawrence Hill, 1977.

Negri, Guglielmo. *Il quadro costituzionale: Tempi e istituti della libertà.* Milan: Giuffrè, 1984.

Negri, Guglielmo, and C. Pappagallo. *L'Italia negli anni settanta: Diario di una crisi politica.* Rome: Armando Armando, 1981.

Neufeld, Maurice. *Italy: School for Awakening Countries.* Ithaca: Cornell University Press, 1961.

Nichols, Peter. *The Politics of the Vatican.* New York: Praeger, 1968.

Orfei, Ruggero. *L'occupazione del potere: I democristiani, '45–'75.* Milan: Longanesi, 1976.

Organizzazione dello stato e democrazia. Milan: Franco Angeli, 1977.

Peaslee, Amos J. *Constitutions of Nations,* 3rd ed., Vol. 3. The Hague: Martinus Nijhoff, 1968.

Pedone, Franco, ed. *Il Partito Socialista Italiano nei suoi congressi,* 4 vols. Milan: Edizioni Avanti, 1959–63.

———. *Il socialismo italiano di questo dopoguerra.* Milan: Edizioni del Gallo, 1968.

Peggio, Eugenio. *La crisi economica italiana.* Milan: Rizzoli, 1976.

Pellicani, Luciano. *Gramsci e la questione comunista.* Florence: Vallecchi, 1976.

———. *Il mercato e i socialismi.* Milan: SugarCo, 1978.

———. *Miseria del Marxismo: Da Marx al Gulag.* Milan: SugarCo, 1984.

———. *I rivoluzionari di professione.* Florence: Vallechi, 1975.

Penniman, Howard R., ed. *Italy at the Polls: The Parliamentary Elections of 1976.* Washington, D.C.: American Enterprise Institute, 1977.

———. *Italy at the Polls, 1979: A Study of the Parliamentary Elections.* Washington, D.C.: American Enterprise Institute, 1981.

———. *Italy at the Polls, 1983. A Study of the National Elections.* Durham: Duke University Press, 1987.

Pietra, Italo. *Moro: Fu vera gloria?* Milan: Garzanti, 1983.

Podbielski, Giselle. *Italy: Development and Crisis in the Post-War Economy.* Oxford: Clarendon Press, 1974.

Preti, Luigi. *Italia malata,* 3rd ed. Milan: Mursia, 1973.

Pryce, Roy. *The Italian Local Elections, 1956.* London: Chatto and Windus, 1957.

Punzo, Maurizio. *Dalla Liberazione a Palazzo Barberini: Storia del Partito Socialista Italiano dalla ricostruzione alla scissione del 1947.* Milan: Celuc, 1973.

Putnam, Robert D. *Beliefs of Politicians: Conflict and Democracy in Britain and Italy.* New Haven: Yale University Press, 1973.

Quadro dei partiti politici d'Italia. Rome: De Luigi, 1944.

Quazza, Guido. *Resistenza e storia d'Italia.* Milan: Feltrinelli, 1976.

Rosengarten, Frank. *The Italian anti-Fascist Press (1919–1945).* Cleveland: Press of Case Western Reserve University, 1968.

———. *Silvio Trentin Dall'interventismo alla Resistenza.* Milan: Feltrinelli, 1980.

Sabbatucci, Giovanni, ed. *Storia del socialismo italiano,* 6 vols. Rome: Il Poligono, 1979–81.

Saladino, Salvatore. *Italy from Unification to 1919: Growth and Decay of a Liberal Regime.* New York: Thomas Y. Crowell, 1970.

Salomone, A. William. *Italy in the Giolitian Era: Italian Democracy in the Making, 1900–1914.* Philadelphia: University of Pennsylvania Press, 1960.

Salomone, A. William, ed. *Italy from the Risorgimento to Fascism: An Inquiry into the Origins of the Totalitarian State.* New York: Anchor Books, 1970.

Salvadori, Massimo L. *Egemonia e pluralismo: Il dibattito sul rapporto fra socialismo e democrazia.* Venice: Marsilio, 1977.

———. *Gaetano Salvemini.* Turin: Einaudi, 1963.

Salvati, Michele. *Economia e politica in Italia dal dopoguerra a oggi.* Milan: Garzanti, 1984.

Salvatorelli, Luigi, and Giovanni Mira. *Storia d'Italia nel periodo fascista.* Turin: Einaudi, 1959.

Salvemini, Gaetano. *Le origini del fascismo italiano.* Milan: Feltrinelli, 1966.

Salvemini, Gaetano, and George La Piana. *What to Do with Italy*. New York: Buell, Sloan and Pearce, 1943.

Santarelli, Enzo. *La revisione del marxismo in Italia*. Milan: Feltrinelli, 1964.

Sarti, Roland. *Fascism and the Industrial Leadership in Italy*. Berkeley: University of California Press, 1971.

——. *Long Live the Strong: A History of Rural Society in the Apennine Mountains*. Amherst: University of Massachusetts Press, 1985.

Sartori, Giovanni. *Teoria dei partiti e caso italiano*. Milan: SugarCo, 1982.

Sassoon, Donald. *Contemporary Italy: Politics, Economy and Society since 1945*. London: Longman, 1986.

Scalfari, Eugenio. *L'anno di Craxi (o di Berlinguer?)*. Milan: Mondadori, 1984.

Schiavi, Alessandro. *Filippo Turati*. Rome: Opere Nuove, 1955.

Schiavi, Alessandro, ed. *Omaggio a Turati nel centenario della nascita, 1857–1957*. Rome: Opere Nuove, 1957.

Schlesinger, Arthur M., Jr. *A Thousand Days*. Boston: Houghton Mifflin, 1965.

Serfaty, Simon, and Lawrence Gray, eds. *The Italian Communist Party Yesterday, Today, and Tomorrow*. Westport, Conn.: Greenwood Press, 1980.

Settembrini, Domenico. *Socialismo al bivio*. Milan: SugarCo, 1978.

——. *Socialismo e rivoluzione dopo Marx*. Naples: Guida, 1975.

Schacter, Gustav. *The Italian South: Economic Development in Mediterranean Europe*. New York: Random House, 1965.

Silj, Alessandro. *Never Again without a Rifle: The Origins of Italian Terrorism*. New York: Karz Publishers, 1979.

Silvestri, Mario. *Il costo della menzogna: Italia nucleare 1945–1968*. Turin: Einaudi, 1968.

Socialismo, nazionalità, autonomie. Florence: La Nuova Italia, 1983.

I socialisti e la cultura. Venice: Marsilio, n.d.

Sommaruga, Rodolfo. *Che cosa vogliono i parititi?* Rome: Editoriale Romana, 1944.

Spadolini, Giovanni. *Diario del dramma Moro (marzo–maggio 1978): I cinquantaquattro giorni che hanno cambiato l'Italia*. Florence: Le Monnier, 1978.

——. *Italia di minoranza: Lotta politica e cultura dal 1915 a oggi*. Florence: Le Monnier, 1983.

Spadolini, Giovanni, et al. *L'antifascismo italiano negli Stati Uniti durante la seconda guerra mondiale*. Introduction by A. William Salomone. Rome: Archivio Trimestrale, 1984.

Spini, Valdo. *I socialisti e la politica di piano (1945–1964)*. Florence: Sansoni, 1982.

——. *3 congressi per un nuovo PSI: Supplemento ai Quaderni del Circolo Rosselli*. Milan: Mediolanum, 1984.

Spini, Valdo, and Sergio Mattana, eds. *I quadri del PSI*. Florence: Nuova Guaraldi, 1981.

Spotts, Frederic, and Theodor Wieser. *Italy, A Difficult Democracy: A Survey of Italian Politics*. Cambridge: Cambridge University Press, 1986.

Spriano, Paolo. *Storia del Partito Comunista Italiano*, 5 vols. Turin: Einaudi, 1967–75.

Sterling, Claire. *The Terror Network*. New York: Holt, Rinehart & Winston, 1981.

Stern, Robert. *Foreign Trade and Economic Growth in Italy*. New York: Praeger, 1967.

Sylos Labini, Paolo. *Le classi sociali negli anni '80*. Bari: Laterza, 1986.

——. *Saggio sulle classi sociali*. Bari: Laterza, 1974.

Taddei, Francesca, and Marco Talluri. *Guida alla storia del PSI: La ripresa del pensiero socialista tra eresia e tradizione*. Florence: Nuova Guaraldi, 1981.

Tamburrano, Giuseppe. *Pietro Nenni*. Bari: Laterza, 1986.

——. *Storia e cronaca del centro-sinistra*. Milan: Feltrinelli, 1971.

Tannenbaum, Edward R., and Emiliana P. Noether. *Modern Italy: A Topical History since 1861*. New York: New York University Press, 1974.

Tarrow, Sidney. *Between Center and Periphery: Grassroots Politicians in Italy and France*. New Haven: Yale University Press, 1977.

————. *Peasant Communism in Southern Italy*. New Haven: Yale University Press, 1967.

Tasca, Angelo. *Nascita e avvento del fascismo*. 2 vols. Bari: Laterza, 1965.

Togliatti, Palmiro. *Problemi del movimento operaio internazionale, 1956–1961*. Rome: Riuniti, 1962.

Tompkins, Peter. *Italy Betrayed*. New York: Simon and Schuster, 1966.

Tortoreto, E. *La politica di Riccardo Lombardi dal 1944 al 1949*. Genoa: Edizioni di Movimento Operaio e Socialista, 1972.

Toscano, Mario. *Alto Adige, South Tyrol: Italy's Frontier with the German World*. Baltimore: John Hopkins University Press, 1975.

Vannicelli, Primo. *Italy, NATO, and the European Community: The Interplay of Foreign Policy and Domestic Politics*. Cambridge, Mass.: Center for International Affairs, Harvard University, 1974.

Varsori, Antonio. *Gli alleati e l'emigrazione democratica antifascista (1940–1943)*. Florence: Sansoni, 1982.

Vigorelli, Ezio. *L'italiano è socialista e non lo sa*. Milan: Mondadori, 1952.

Villari, Rosario, ed. *Il Sud nella storia d'Italia: Antologia della questione meridionale*. Bari: Laterza, 1966.

Wagner-Pacifici, Robin Erica. *The Moro Morality Play: Terrorism as Social Drama*. Chicago: University of Chicago Press, 1986.

Walters, Vernon A. *Silent Missions*. Garden City, N.Y.: Doubleday, 1978.

Webster, Richard. *Christian Democracy in Italy, 1860–1960*. London: Hollis & Carter, 1961.

West, Morris. *The Salamander*. New York: Pocket Books, 1974.

Willis, F. Roy. *Italy Chooses Europe*. New York: Oxford University Press, 1971.

Wollemborg, Leo J. *Stelle, strisce, e tricolore: Trent'anni di vicende politiche fra Roma e Washington*. Milan: Mondadori, 1983.

Woolf, Stuart J. *The Rebirth of Italy, 1943–50*. London: Longman's, 1972.

Zangrandi, Ruggero. *L'Italia tradita: 8 settembre 1943*. Milan: Mursia, 1971.

————. *Il lungo viaggio attraverso il fascismo*. Milan: Feltrinelli, 1962.

————. *1943: 25 luglio–8 settembre*. Milan: Feltrinelli, 1964.

Zariski, Raphael. *Italy: The Politics of Uneven Development*. Hinsdale, Ill.: Dryden Press, 1972.

Articles

Alasco, Antonio. "Alle origini dei gruppi extraparlamentari in Italia: Il Partito Socialista Rivoluzionario Italiano." *Storia Contemporanea* 13, no. 3 (June 1982): 489–506.

[Almirante, Giorgio]. "TVI Forum: Italy. Interview with Giorgio Almirante." *Terrorism, Violence, Insurgency Journal* 1, no. 8 (May 1980): 2–4.

Amato, Giuliano. "Riforma dello stato e alternativa della sinistra." *Mondoperaio* 30, nos. 7–8 (July–August 1977): 45–46.

Amato, Giuliano, and Luciano Cafagna. "Nenni e il socialismo italiano." *Mondoperaio* 33, no. 2 (February 1980): 89–102.

Amendola, Giorgio. "Situazione italiana e movimento socialista italiano in Togliatti." *Annali dell'Istituto Giangiacomo Feltrinelli* 15 (1973): 1371–91.

Amendola, Giorgio, et al. "6 domande su riforme e riformismo." *Critica Marxista* 3, nos. 5–6 (September–December 1965): 3–162.

Andreasi, Annamaria. "Bruno Buozzi e il movimento sindacale italiano." *Annali dell'Istituto Giangiacomo Feltrinelli* 14 (1972): 382–421.

Artoni, Roberto, et al. "Il 'Rapporto Spaventa' sul debito pubblico." *Mondoperaio* 38, nos. 1–2 (January–February 1985): 102–10.

Baccianini, Mario. "Contrattare è bello: Intervista a Pierre Carniti." *Mondoperaio* 36, no. 9 (September 1983): 21–27.

———. "L'evasione fiscale autorizzata: Intervista con Paolo Sylos-Labini." *Mondoperaio* 37, no. 12 (December 1984): 9–11.

Barbagallo, Francesco. "Il PCI, i ceti medi e la democrazia nel Mezzogiorno (1943–1947)." *Studi Storici* 26, no. 3 (July–September 1985): 523–44.

Barcellona, Pietro. "La crisi delle politiche di programmazione." *Critica Marxista* 20, no. 4 (December 1982): 5–28.

Barnes, Trevor. "The Secret Cold War: The CIA and American Foreign Policy in Europe, 1946–1956." *Historical Journal* 24, no. 2 (June 1981): 399–415.

Barzini, Luigi. "Italy: The Fragile State." *Foreign Affairs* 46, no. 3 (April 1968): 562–74.

Bayne, E. A. "Non-Crisis in Italy." *Foreign Affairs* 45, no. 2 (January 1967): 353–62.

Bertocci, Silvio. "Loggia P2: Tutti gli uomini del 'Venerabile' Procuratore." *Il Ponte* 38, no. 5 (May 1982): 429–33.

Bobbio, Norberto. "Questione socialista questione comunista." *Mondoperaio* 29, no. 9 (September 1976): 41–51.

———. "Un partito tra due fuochi." *Mondoperaio* 33, no. 2 (February 1980): 11–14.

Bottiglieri, Bruno. "Tra Pella e Vanoni: La politica economica degli ultimi governi De Gasperi." *Storia Contemporanea* 15, no. 4 (August 1984): 781–839.

Buozzi, Bruno. "Le condizioni della classe lavoratrice in Italia, 1922–1943." *Annali dell'Istituto Giangiacomo Feltrinelli* 14 (1972): 423–76.

Cannistraro, Philip V. "Il fascismo italiano visto dagli Stati Uniti: cinquant'anni di studi e di interpretazioni." *Storia Contemporanea* 3, no. 2 (September 1971): 599–624.

———. "Luigi Antonini and the Italian Anti-Fascist Movement in the United States, 1940–1943." *Journal of American Ethnic History* (Fall 1985): 21–40.

Cannistraro, Philip V., and Elena Aga Rossi. "La politica etnica e il dilemma dell'antifascismo italiano negli Stati Uniti: Il caso di Generoso Pope." *Storia Contemporanea* 17, no. 2 (April 1986): 217–43.

Chiarante, Giuseppe. "Dopo il voto del 21 giugno: Crisi democristiana e alternativa." *Critica Marxista* 19, no. 4 (July–August 1981): 75–87.

Coen, Federico. "Una politica estera per l'Italia e per l'Europa." *Mondoperaio* 36, no. 9 (September 1983): 2–3.

Colarizi, Simona. "Morandi e i consigli di gestione." *Mondoperaio* 29, no. 11 (November 1976): 80–83.

———. "Il PSI in esilio (1926–1933)." *Storia Contemporanea* 6, no. 1 (March 1974): 47–91.

Conti, Laura. "Coscienza teorica e storica nel socialismo di Basso." *Il Filo Rosso* 8, no. 2 (January–April 1964): 34–47.

Cravieri, Piero. "Chi ha paura della riforma del salario?" *Mondoperaio* 37, no. 10 (October 1984): 15–17.

De Leonardis, Massimo. "La Gran Bretagna e la monarchia italiana (1943–1946)." *Storia Contemporanea* 12, no. 1 (February 1981): 57–134.

Delzell, Charles. "The Italian Anti-Fascist Resistance in Retrospect: Three Decades of Historiography." *Journal of Modern History* 47, no. 1 (March 1975): 66–96.

Di Nolfo, Ennio. "The United States and Italian Communism 1942–1946: World War II to the Cold War." *Journal of Italian History* 1, no. 1 (Spring 1978): 74–94.

Di Scala, Spencer. "Filippo Turati, the Milanese Schism, and the Reconquest of the Italian Socialist Party." *Il Politico* 44, no. 1 (January 1979): 153–63.

———. "Parliamentary Socialists, the *Statuto* and the Giolittian System." *Austrialian Journal of Politics and History* 25, no. 2 (August 1979): 155–68.

Drake, Richard. "The Red and the Black: Terrorism in Contemporary Italy." *International Political Science Review* 5, no. 3 (1984): 279–98.

"Le due anime del PSI: Tavola rotonda." *Mondoperaio* 33, no. 2 (February 1980): 5–10.

Durand, Jean-Dominique. "Alcide De Gasperi ovvero la politica ispirata." *Storia Contemporanea* 15, no. 4 (August 1984): 545–91.

Forte, Francesco. "Il pubblico, il privato e il caso Mediobanca." *Mondoperaio* 37, no. 12 (December 1984): 2–4.

Forte, Francesco, and Stefano Da Venezia. "La politica industriale in Italia: Spunti per una riflessione." *Mondoperaio* 37, no. 10 (October 1984): 4–8.

Gelibter, Giulio. "Fra intesa ed Eurocomunismo: Nuovi schemi di equilibrio." *L'Est,* nos. 1–2 (June 1976): 163–71.

Hughes, H. Stuart. "The Socialist Dilemma in Western Europe." *Dissent* 8, no. 4 (Autumn 1961): 432–40.

Joseph [Giuseppe Faravelli]. "L'azione socialista in Italia." *Politica Socialista* 1, no. 1 (August 1934): 16–22.

Landolfi, Antonio. "La ricostituzione del Partito Socialista nel dopoguerra (1944–1946)." *Storia e Politica,* no. 3 (1964): 198–241.

La Palombara, Joseph. "The *Achille Lauro* Affair: A Note on Italy and the United States." *Yale Review* 75, no. 4 (Summer 1986): 542–63.

———. "Socialist Alternatives: The Italian Variant." *Foreign Affairs* 60, no. 4 (Spring 1982): 924–42.

Leonardi, Robert, and Alan A. Platt. "La politica estera americana nei confronti della sinistra italiana, 1945–1976." *Il Mulino* 26, no. 2 (July–August 1977): 546–73.

Lepre, Aurelio. "Togliatti e l'antifascismo." *Studi Storici* 26, no. 3 (July–September 1985): 507–21.

Levi, Arrigo. "Italy: The Crisis of Governing." *Foreign Affairs* 49, nos. 1–4 (October 1970–July 1971): 148–60.

Levi, Fabio. "Organizzazione del lavoro e classe operaia alla FIAT, 1945–1948." *Rivista di Storia Contemporanea,* no. 3 (July 1977): 314–40.

Lombardo, Antonio. "La competizione Est-Ovest e le forze politiche anti-sistema nelle democrazie occidentali." *L'Est,* nos. 1–2 (June 1976): 107–38.

Luce, Clare Boothe. "Italy after One Hundred Years." *Foreign Affairs* 39, no. 2 (January 1961): 221–39.

Luzzato, Lucio. "Appunti per una biografia di R. Morandi." *Mondo Operaio* 8, no. 15–16 (1955).

Maitan, Livio. "Romita e Morandi: Due testimonianze su un biennio cruciale." *Passato e Presente* 18 (November–December 1969): 2410–30.

Marianetti, Agostino. "Il PSI e l'area socialista." *Mondoperaio* 29, no. 9 (September 1976): 52–56.

Merli, Stefano. "Dibattiti ideologici e politici nel PSIUP: Politica di Classe (1944–45)." *Rivista Storica del Socialismo* 1, no. 1 (October–December 1958): 563–76.

Miller, James E. "Carlo Sforza e l'evoluzione della politica americana verso l'Italia, 1940–1943." *Storia Contemporanea* 7, no. 4 (August 1976): 825–53.

———. "La politica dei 'prominenti'' italo-americani nei rapporti dell'Oss." *Italia Contemporanea,* no. 139 (June 1980): 51–70.

———. "Strategie della stabilizzazione: Gli Stati Uniti e l'Italia, 1917–1950." *Storia Contemporanea* 15, no. 4 (August 1984): 745–79.

Noether, Emiliana. "Italy Reviews Its Fascist Past: A Bibliographical Essay." *American Historical Review* 61, no. 4 (July 1956): 877–99.

Noiret, Serge. "Nitti e Bombacci: Aspetti di un dialogo impossibile. I bolshevicki contro la rivoluzione italiana. Novembre 1919–febbraio 1920." *Storia Contemporanea* 17, no. 3 (June 1986): 397–441.

Pastorelli, Pietro. "L'adesione dell'Italia al Patto atlantico." *Storia Contemporanea* 14, no. 6 (December 1983): 1015–30.

Pellicani, Luciano. "Considerazioni sul messianismo marxista." *L'Est,* nos. 1–2 (June 1976): 9–47.

———. "Il futuro della sinistra." *Mondoperaio* 37, nos. 8–9 (August–September 1984): 2–3.

Pinzani, Carlo. "L'8 settembre 1943: Elementi di ipotesi per un giudizio storico." *Studi Storici* 13, no. 2 (April–June 1972): 289–337.

Pizzorno, Alessandro. "Scambio politico e identità collettiva nel conflitto di classe." *Rivista Italiana di Scienza Politica* 7, no. 2 (August 1977): 165–98.

Politica Socialista [Angelo Tasca]. "Il partito in formazione." *Politica Socialista* 2, no. 3 (March 1935): 195–203.

Preti, Domenico. "La politica agraria del fascismo." *Studi Storici* 14, no. 4 (October–December 1973): 802–69.

Quartara, Rosaria. "L'Italia e il piano Marshall (1947–52)." *Storia Contemporanea* 15, no. 4 (August 1984): 647–722.

Sabbatucci, Giovanni. "Elettorato socialista e tradizione riformista: La scissione di Palazzo Barberini e le elezioni del 18 aprile 1948." In *Scritti storici in memoria di Enzo Piscitelli*, ed. by Renzo Paci. Padua: Antenore, 1982, pp. 525–35.

Santacroce, Alberto. "Il PSI nelle analisi post-elettorale." *Mondoperaio* 29, nos. 7–8 (July–August 1976): 27–29.

Santarelli, Enzo. "Nenni dal repubblicanesimo al socialismo (1908–1921): Contributo ad una biografia." *Studi Storici* 14, no. 4 (October–December 1973): 870–905.

Settembrini, Domenico. "Tra rivoluzione e controrivoluzione: Considerazioni impolitiche." *L'Est*, nos. 1–2 (June 1976): 49–106.

Spini, Valdo. "Il discorso sull'economia e le scelte politiche (1945–1975)." *Il Ponte* 31, nos. 11–12 (November–December 1975): 1279–1373.

———. "Saraceno, Morandi e la ricostruzione." *Mondoperaio* 30, nos. 7–8 (July–August 1977): 66–70.

Spriano, Paolo. "L'esperienza di Tasca a Mosca e il 'socialfascismo.'" *Studi Storici* 10, no. 1 (January–March 1969): 83–113.

———. "La mancata fusione Pci-Psi nel 1923." *Studi Storici* 7, no. 4 (October–December 1966): 709–46.

———. "Le riflessioni dei comunisti italiani sulle società dell'Est e il 'socialismo reale.'" *Studi Storici* 23, no. 1 (January–March 1982): 51–74.

———. "Gli scioperi del marzo 1943." *Studi Storici* 13, no. 4 (October–December 1972): 726–61.

Sylos-Labini, Paolo. "Rivoluzione tecnologica e occupazione: Intervista a Wassily Leontief." *Mondoperaio* 38, nos. 1–2 (January–February 1985): 111–14.

Tempestini, Attilio. "Le correnti democristiane: Struttura e ideologia dal 1943 al 1980." *Il Ponte* 38, no. 5 (May 1982): 457–75.

Vaccarino, Giorgio. "Die Wiederhestellung der Democratie in Italien (1943–1945)." *Vierteljahrshepte fur Zeitgeschichte*, no. 21 (July 1973): 284–324.

Valiani, Leo. "Il liberalsocialismo." *Rivista Storica Italiana* 81, no. 1 (March 1969): 74–84.

Varsori, Antonio. "La Gran Bretagna e le elezioni politiche italiane del 18 aprile 1948." *Storia Contemporanea* 13, no. 1 (February 1982): 5–70.

Vassali, Giuliano. "Giustizia: Come riattivare una macchina inceppata." *Mondoperaio* 36, no. 9 (September 1983): 9–16.

Vigezzi, Brunello. "De Gasperi, Sforza, la diplomazia italiana e la percezione della politica di potenza dal trattato di pace al Patto Atlantico." *Storia Contemporanea* 16, no. 4 (August 1965): 661–85.

Villetti, Roberto. "La Lezione di Lombardi." *Mondoperaio* 37, nos. 8–9 (August–September 1984): 2–3.

Vittorelli, Paolo. "Le elezioni politiche del 1953." *Il Ponte* 9, no. 1 (June 1953): 756–69.

Williams, Raymond. "Towards Many Socialisms." *Socialist Review*, no. 85 (January–February 1986): 45–65.

Zariski, Raphael. "Italian Socialist Party: A Case Study in Factional Conflict." *American Political Science Review*, no. 56 (June 1962): 372–90.

Zito, Sisinio. "Per il rinnovamento del PSI." *Mondoperaio* 29, nos. 7–8 (July–August 1976): 20–23.

Periodicals

American Historical Review
Annali dell'Istituto Giangiacomo Feltrinnelli
Bollettino dell'Istituto di Studi Socialisti
Critica Marxista
Critica Sociale
L'Espresso
L'Est
Europeo
Foreign Affairs
Historical Journal
Italian Quarterly
Journal of Italian History
Journal of Modern History
Mondo Nuovo
Mondo Operaio, now *Mondoperaio*
Il Mulino
Panorama
La Parola del Popolo
Per una Politica di Alternativa Democratica. Numero unico riservato agli iscritti al Partito Socialista Italiano. Milan, 1 dicembre 1960.
Politica Socialista
Il Ponte
Problemi del Socialismo
Quaderni del Circolo Rosselli
Quarto Stato
Rinascita
Rivista Italiana di Scienza Politica
Rivista di Storia Contemporanea
Rivista Storica Italiana
Stato Operaio
Socialismo
Storia Contemporanea
Studi Storici
Terrorism, Violence, Insurgency Journal

Newspapers

Avanti! (Rome)
The Christian Science Monitor (Boston)
Corriere della Sera (Milan and Rome)
Il Messaggero (Rome)
Il Mattino (Naples)
The New York Times

Paese Sera (Rome)
La Repubblica (Rome)
La Stampa (Turin)
L'Umanità (Milan)
L'Unità (Rome)

Unpublished Materials

Dalton, Richard Joseph. "Church-State Relations in Italy: L'apertura a Sinistra, 1958–1963."
    Ph.D. diss., University of Connecticut, 1972.

Ferri, Mauro. "Intervento dell'On. Mauro Ferri." Typescript of an article on PSI-PSDI unification,
    dated February 1982.

Ferri, Mauro. Untitled typescript article on the Socialists in the European parliament, dated 31
    October 1984.

Gilsdorf, Robert Raymond. "Factionalism in the Italian Christian Democratic Party, 1958–1963."
    Ph.D. diss., Yale University, 1970.

Joes, Anthony James. "Italy Moves to the Left: Cleavage and Integration in a Multi-Party Sys-
    tem." Ph.D. diss., University of Pennsylvania, 1970.

Nenni, Pietro. "La relazione del segretario del partito al Comitato Centrale, Roma, 8 febbraio
    1960." Mimeographed. Archivio Basso.

Nillson, Karl R. "Italy's 'Opening to the Right': the Tambroni Experiment of 1960." Ph.D. diss.,
    Columbia University, 1964.

Partito Socialista Italiano, Direzione, Sezione: Centr. Economica. Prot: N. 8283, circ. N.
    124/13/RL/dpa "L'economia italiana nel quadro internazionale dalla guerra fredda alla
    distensione." Mimeographed, with covering letter dated 23 June 1960. [author: Riccardo
    Lombardi]. Archivio Basso.

Partito Socialista di Unità Proletaria. "Bozza di Statuto per il 1 Congresso Nazionale del PSIUP."
    Mimeographed, with covering letter dated 16–19 December 1965. Archivio Basso.

Partito Socialista di Unità Proletaria, Direzione. "Progetto del documento ideologico-politico invia-
    to ai membri del Consiglio Nazionale il 22 aprile 1964." Mimeographed. Archivio Basso.

Petacco, Arrigo. Typescript of an interview with President Sandro Pertini, dated 21 January 1983.
    Provided by the head of the president's Press Service.

Platt, Alan Arthur. "United States Policy Toward 'The Opening to the Left' in Italy." Ph.D. diss.,
    Columbia University, 1973.

Tamburrano, Giuseppe. Typescript of an untitled article on the twentieth anniversary of the SIFAR
    affair.

Tables

TABLE 1. PSI Membership, 1945–1980
(in thousands)

1945	700	1963	491
1946	860	1964	446
1947	822	1965	437
1948	351	1966	697
1949	430	1967	633
1950	700	1968	n.a.
1951	720	1969	n.a.
1952	750	1970	506
1953	780	1971	592
1954	754	1972	560
1955	770	1973	465
1956	710	1974	511
1957	477	1975	539
1958	486	1976	498
1959	484	1977	482
1960	489	1978	472
1961	465	1979	484
1962	491	1980	510

TABLE 2. PSI Vote Tally, 1946–1983
(Chamber of Deputies)

Year	Votes	Percent
1946	4,758,129	20.7
1948*	8,137,047	31.0
1953	3,441,306	12.7
1958	4,208,111	14.2
1963	4,257,300	13.8

(continued)

The tables in this section are from Sergio Mattana, "La struttura e la base sociale del PSI," *I Quadri del PSI: Quaderni del Circolo Rosselli* 1, no. 1 (January–March 1981), pp. 55–75.

TABLE 2.   (*Continued*)

Year	Votes	Percent
1968†	4,605,832	14.5
1972	3,208,497	9.6
1976	3,540,309	9.6
1979	3,591,579	9.8
1983‡	4,221,785	11.4

*Popular Democratic Front.
†PSU.
‡Howard Penniman, ed. *Italy at the Polls, 1983*, p. 202.

TABLE 3.   Geographical Distribution
of PSI Members from 1946 to 1971
(in percentages)

Area	1946	1961	1971
North	50.0	43.7	34.9
Center	20.0	25.2	17.0
South	30.0	31.1	48.1

TABLE 4.   Geographical Distribution
of PSI Voters from 1946 to 1972
(in percentages)

Area	1946	1963	1972
North	67.5	55.3	53.7
Center	16.4	19.4	17.4
South	16.1	25.3	28.9

TABLE 5.   PSI Membership by Sex
and Geographical Area in 1979,
in Percentages

Area	Male	Female
North	83.6	16.4
Center	86.3	13.7
South	86.7	13.3

TABLE 6. White-Collar and Professional
PSI Membership in 1979
(in Percentages)

Area	White-collar and professionals
North	17.9
Center	13.9
South	12.2
National average	15.1

Chronology

1926

Mussolini establishes a dictatorship; political parties dissolved; PSI and PSULI reestablish themselves in exile.

1927

April: Foundation of the Concentrazione Antifascista.

1928

August: Turati highlights fascist danger for Europe at the 3rd Congress of the Workers' International in Brussels.

1929

Lateran Accords between Italy and the church; Pertini sentenced to eleven years' imprisonment; foundation of GL.

1930

July: Reunification of PSI and PSULI.

1931

November: Agreement between PSI and GL; GL enters the Concentrazione Antifascista.

1932

March: Death in exile of PSI founder Filippo Turati.

1933

January: Adolf Hitler takes power in Germany.

September: Trial run of underground review *Politica Socialista*.

1934

Establishment of the CIS.

May: Self-dissolution of the Concentrazione Antifascista.

August: Unity-of-action pact between PSI and PCI.

1935

July–August: Third International's 7th Congress announces Popular Front tactics.

October: Italy invades Ethiopia; League of Nations institutes sanctions.

1936

July–October: Spanish Civil War begins; Italian exiles fight Mussolini's troops.

1937

March: Rodolfo Morandi and other CIS exponents arrested.

July: Renewal of unity-of-action pact.

1938

Reestablishment of CIS.

1939

August: Non-Aggression Pact between Hitler and Stalin.

September: Socialists denounce unity-of-action pact; World War II begins.

1940

June: Italy enters World War II.

1941

October: Toulouse Agreement among PSI, PCI, and GL; beginning of Resistance.

1943

July: Mussolini removed from power.

August: Agreement between PSI and socialist groups in Italy; foundation of PSIUP; renewal of unity-of-action pact.

September: Italian armistice.

1944

March: Industrial strikes in northern Italy.

June: Togliatti announces communist collaboration with Badoglio government; liberation of Rome.

1945

April: Liberation of northern Italy.

July–August: PSIUP calls for constitution of a single party with the PCI.

November: Parri government falls.

December: De Gasperi prime minister.

1946

May: Abdication of King Victor Emmanuel III in favor of his son.

June: Referendum abolishes monarchy.

1947

January: De Gasperi visit to the United States; Saragat splits from PSIUP and forms PSLI.

May: PSI and PCI excluded from national government.

June: Communists win majority in CGIL.

December: Formal constitution of Popular Democratic Front between PCI and PSI.

1948

January: Italian Republican Constitution enters into force; 26th Socialist Congress adopts single electoral slate with Communists.

April: Popular Democratic Front defeated by DC in national elections.

1949

March: Italy joins NATO; PSI expelled from COMISCO.

May: 28th PSI Congress gives majority to left wing; Nenni named secretary, Morandi vice secretary.

1950

September: Basso resigns from PSI Directorate; "democratic centralism" imported into PSI.

1951

April: PSDI formed from Saragat's PSLI and other social democratic groups.

June–July: Reconstitution of International in Frankfurt (social democratic).

1952

May: Local elections confirm decline of DC observed the previous year.

1953

January: Parliament approves "electoral bonus" law.

March: Stalin dies.

June: Defeat of centrist coalition signals end of De Gasperi's power.

October: "Opening to the left" debate begins.

November–December: Italo-Yugoslav tension over Trieste.

1954

June: Fanfani ends De Gasperi control at DC Naples congress.

1955

March–April: PSI Turin congress opens dialogue with DC.

April: Supported by Nenni, leftist DC exponent Giovanni Gronchi elected president of republic.

July: Death of Rodolfo Morandi.

December: Italy enters United Nations.

1956

February: Khrushchev reveals Stalin's crimes.

April: Nenni brands Stalinism an inherent part of communism.

June: Riots in Poland.

August: Nenni and Saragat meet at

Pralognan and discuss socialist reunification.

October: Unity-of-action pact between PCI and PSI replaced with loose "consultation pact."

November: Soviet troops invade Hungary after revolution.

1957

February: 32nd PSI Congress at Venice adopts Nenni policy but elects his opponents to party offices.

March: Treaty of Rome establishing EEC and Euratom signed.

1958

October: Election of Pope John XXIII.

December: Charles De Gaulle elected president of French republic.

1959

January: Nenni opening to the left wins at 33rd PSI Congress at Naples; Moro becomes DC secretary.

October: Leftist DC currents favorable to opening to the left win 42 percent of votes at party's Florence congress.

1960

April: Tambroni cabinet receives confidence vote with MSI support.

June–July: Rioters protesting against Tambroni clash with police throughout Italy.

August: Socialists concede abstention in vote on Fanfani "parallel convergences" government.

1961

January–February: Center-left local administrations constituted in Milan and other important cities.

June: President John F. Kennedy indicates benevolent attitude toward center-left government during Fanfani trip to Washington, D.C.

July: Publication of Encyclical *Mater et magister,* interpreted as favorable to socially progressive governments.

September: DC San Pelligrino Convention enunciates economic principles favorable to center-left.

1962

January: Socialist economic program for center-left approved by Central Committee.

March: Socialist agreement on new Fanfani government leads to PSI abstention in vote of confidence.

May: Segni elected president of republic.

June: Fanfani government approves bill for nationalization of electric industry.

1963

April: New elections witness fall in PSI and DC votes and increase in PCI percentage.

May: Fanfani resigns; Moro receives mandate to form center-left government.

June: "Camilluccia Accords" reached on center-left government program; Lombardi withdraws support from Nenni, causing failure of agreement.

July: Kennedy visits Rome.

November: Assassination of Kennedy.

December: "Organic" center-left Moro government with socialist participation.

1964

January: PSI left wing splits and forms PSIUP; Moro government resigns.

July: Possible SIFAR preparations for coup d'etat; Moro center-left government reconstituted as result of lessened socialist demands.

December: Saragat elected president of republic.

1965

November: 36th PSI Congress puts reunification with PSDI once more on the table.

1966

October: Unification of PSI and PSDI to form PSU.

1967

April: SIFAR scandal made public.

1968

February–March: Student revolt begins in Italy.

August: Soviet troops invade Czechoslovakia and end "Prague Spring."

1969

April: Riots in Battipaglia usher in troubled decade.

July: PSU splits.

October: Beginning of "Hot Autumn" of labor unrest.

November: Riots in Milan kill policeman; divorce law passed by Chamber of Deputies.

December: Bomb in Milan's Banca dell'Agricoltura kills thirteen; beginning of "strategy of tension."

1970

January: Approval of financial structure for regions.

May: Legislation embodying workers' rights approved.

June: First regional elections.

July: Reggio Emilia "revolt" begins.

November: De Martino proposes closer socialist relations with PCI ("more advanced equilibria").

December: Attempted coup d'etat by Junio Valerio Borghese fails.

1971

April: Parliamentary approval of legislation on agricultural rents alarms conservatives.

1972

March: Enrico Berlinguer elected PCI secretary.

May: PSI drops to 9.6 percent in early national elections.

June: Andreotti establishes center-right cabinet in which PLI replaces PSI.

July: PSIUP dissolves itself and enters PCI; CGIL, CISL, and UIL establish labor federation.

November: De Martino replaces Mancini as PSI secretary.

1973

July: Socialists reenter government; new edition of center-left.

September: Military coup in Chile overthrows Allende.

October: Berlinguer proposes "historic compromise."

November: Arab oil boycott following Yom Kippur War; energy crisis begins.

December: Lombardi proposes "left alternative" with Communists as rebuttal to "historic compromise."

1974

March: Red Brigades kidnap Judge Mario Sossi in Genoa.

May: Prodivorce advocates win referendum; bomb in Brescia attributed to Fascists kills eight.

August: Bomb on Bologna-bound train kills twelve.

1975

May: Parliament votes the "Reale Law" giving police wide powers against terrorism and crime.

September: Moro announces "third phase" indicating DC opening to Communists.

1976

February: Lockheed scandal involving high government officials explodes.

June: Early elections; PSI remains at 9.6 percent.

July: PSI Central Committee replaces Secretary De Martino with Craxi; Andreotti forms government based on abstention of "constitutional" parties.

September: Socialist Giorgio Benvenuto becomes secretary of UIL.

1977

May: Revolt of Manca current against Craxi.

October: Elaboration of "Socialist Project."

1978

March: Red Brigades kidnap Aldo Moro; Craxi urges negotiations; Andreotti heads government based on national solidarity coalition, including PCI.

April: Craxi wins PSI's 41st Congress.

May: Moro assassinated.

July: Socialist Sandro Pertini elected president of republic.

August: Craxi publishes polemical article against Communists.

1979

June: Early elections leave PSI stationary at 9.8 percent, but receive 11 percent in elections for European parliament.

July: Craxi asked to form government but fails.

September: Craxi duels with Signorile.

December: Death of Pietro Nenni; Italy agrees to "Euromissiles."

1980

January–March: Craxi recovers power in PSI.

November: Berlinguer announces end of "historic compromise."

1981

January: Fierce polemics between Socialists and Communists continue.

February: Craxi renames current "reformist" and publishes "theses" for upcoming PSI congress.

April: Craxi dominates PSI's 42nd Congress.

June: PRI Secretary Spadolini becomes first non-DC prime minister in thirty-five years.

1982

January: Italian security forces liberate General James Lee Dozier; defeat of Italian terrorism follows.

April: PSI Rimini Programmatic Conference concretizes "Socialist Project."

1983

June: General elections witness drop in DC tally, setting stage for Craxi government.

August: First socialist-led government sworn in; record Craxi stay in power begins.

October: Prime Minister Craxi visits United States.

1984

February: Decree law trimming automatic wage escalator sets off communist-inspired labor agitation aimed at unseating Craxi; new concordat signed with church.

June: PCI Secretary Berlinguer dies suddenly.

1985

January: Italian Middle East initiatives signal more active and independent foreign policy.

May: Communist tally drops in local elections.

June: Communist-inspired referendum to abrogate cost of living decree defeated.

October: *Achille Lauro* hijacking and aftermath hurt ties with United States.

December: International terrorists massacre passengers at Rome and Vienna airports.

1986

April: United States bombs Libya, which attempts retaliation against Italian island of Lampedusa.

May: Craxi secures enlarging of economic "Club of Five" to include Italy.

June: End of first Craxi government.

August: Second Craxi government; economic boom continues.

1987

June: Early elections produce significant increases for PSI across the entire country; PCI decreases, with its lost vote apparently going to the Socialists.

Index